CONSUMER BEHAVIOUR
A European Perspective

SECOND EDITION

CONSUMER BEHAVIOUR
A European Perspective

Michael Solomon

Gary Bamossy

Søren Askegaard

FT Prentice Hall
FINANCIAL TIMES

An imprint of **Pearson Education**
Harlow, England • London • New York • Boston • San Francisco • Toronto • Sydney • Singapore • Hong Kong
Tokyo • Seoul • Taipei • New Delhi • Cape Town • Madrid • Mexico City • Amsterdam • Munich • Paris • Milan

Pearson Education Limited
Edinburgh Gate
Harlow
Essex CM20 2JE
England

and Associated Companies throughout the world

Visit us on the World Wide Web at:
www.pearsoned.co.uk

———————————————

First published by Prentice Hall Europe 1999
Second edition published 2002

ISBN-10: 0-273-65182-X
ISBN 13: 976-0-273-65182-6
British Library Cataloguing-in-Publication Data
A catalogue record for this book is available from the British Library

10 9 8 7 6 5
07 06 05

Typeset in 10pt Garamond Book by 3
Printed and bound by Mateu-Cromo, Madrid, Spain

Brief contents

Contents

Part D A PORTRAIT OF EUROPEAN CONSUMERS

Preface

We wrote this book because we're fascinated by the everyday activities of people. The field of consumer behaviour is, to us, the study of how the world is influenced by the action of marketers. We're fortunate enough to be teachers and researchers whose work allows us to study consumers. Given that we're also consumers, we can find both professional and personal interest in learning more about how this process works. As consumers and future managers, we hope you find this study fascinating as well. Whether you're a student, manager, or professor, we're sure you can relate to the trials and tribulations associated with last-minute shopping, preparing for a big night out, agonizing over a purchase decision, fantasizing about a week in the Caribbean, celebrating a holiday, or commemorating a landmark event, such as graduating from university, getting a driver's licence, or (dreaming about) winning the lottery.

Buying, having and being

Our understanding of this field goes beyond looking at the act of *buying* only, by examining the activities relating to *having* and *being* as well. Consumer behaviour is much more than buying things: it also embraces the study of how having (or not having) things affects our lives, and how our possessions influence the way we feel about ourselves and about each other – our state of being. In addition to understanding why people buy things, we also try to appreciate how products, services and consumption activities contribute to the broader social world we experience. Whether shopping, cooking, cleaning, playing football, lying on the beach, or even looking at ourselves in the mirror, our lives are touched by the marketing system.

The field of consumer behaviour is young, dynamic and in flux. It is constantly being cross-fertilized by perspectives from many different disciplines. We have tried to express the field's staggering diversity in this text. Consumer researchers represent virtually every social science discipline, plus a few represent the physical sciences and the arts for good measure. From this melting pot has come a healthy debate among research perspectives, viewpoints regarding appropriate research methods, and even deeply held beliefs about what are and what are not appropriate issues for consumer researchers to study in the first place.

A European perspective on consumers and marketing strategy

The main objective for this adaptation has been to increase significantly its relevance for European students and scholars, while retaining the accessibility, contemporary approach, and the level of excellence in the discussions of consumer behaviour theory and applications established over the last five editions of Michael Solomon's *Consumer Behavior*. Based on the 5th American edition, we have tried to satisfy the need for a comprehensive consumer behaviour textbook with a significant

European content. Hence, we have added illustrative examples and cases which are analysed and discussed in a European consumer context, as well as numerous European scholarly references. The text also includes a number of advertisements of European origin to visualize various elements in the marketing applications of consumer behaviour theory. These changes, which focus on European consumers and research, have been made throughout the book. However, the most substantial changes have been made in the chapters dealing with demographic groups, subcultures and lifestyles, where the American perspective provided in earlier editions of Solomon's text has been replaced with a European one.

The internationalization of market structures makes it increasingly necessary for business people to acquire a clear perspective and understanding of cultural differences and similarities among consumers from various countries. One of the challenges of writing this book has been to develop materials which illustrate *local* as well as *pan-European* and *global* aspects of consumer behaviour. In this spirit, we have kept a number of American and other non-European examples to illustrate various similarities and differences on the global consumer scene. The book also emphasizes the importance of understanding consumers in formulating marketing strategy. Many (if not most) of the fundamental concepts of marketing are based on the practitioner's ability to know people. To illustrate the potential of consumer research to inform marketing strategy, the text contains numerous examples of specific applications of consumer behaviour concepts by marketing practitioners.

Pedagogical features

Throughout the text there are numerous boxed illustrative examples which highlight particular aspects of the impact and informing role that consumer behaviour has on marketing activities. These colour-coded boxes are labelled 'Multicultural dimensions', 'Marketing opportunity', or 'Marketing pitfall', and feature examples from several European and global markets. Other features within each chapter are there to assist you in learning and reviewing this text, and to check and critically review your understanding of topics; these include: an opening illustrative vignette, highlighted Key Terms, a Chapter Summary, and Consumer Behaviour Challenge questions. To familiarize yourself with these features and how they will benefit your study of this text, they are reproduced and described in the 'Guided Tour' (pages xv–xvii).

Case study problems

At the end of each major section in the text there are a number of case study problems. The case material covers various companies, industries and countries, and integrates the topics covered in the preceding chapters. The questions at the end of each case study are designed to allow you to apply your understanding to real-life events and consumer behaviour activities, and to develop your analytical skills.

Guided tour of the book

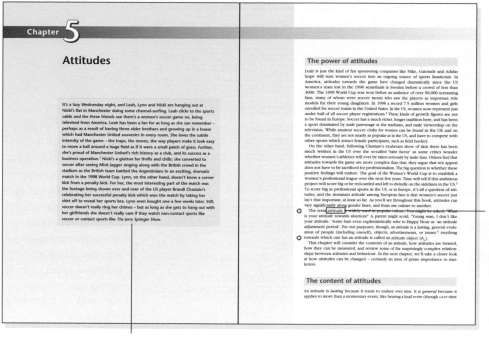

Key terms
Colour-highlighted within the text where they first appear, and with an icon ⊳ in the margin to assist rapid navigation and revision of the core material.

Opening vignette
Each chapter opens with a short, country-specific illustrative scenario, setting the scene for the chapter material and highlighting the interrelationships between the individual and his or her social realities.

Multicultural dimensions
These illustrative boxes appear within every chapter, highlighting cultural differences in consumer behaviour across countries and continents.

Colour photographs
Over 80 colour photographs and company advertisements are integrated throughout the text, bringing consumer behaviour topics to life.

Guided tour of the book

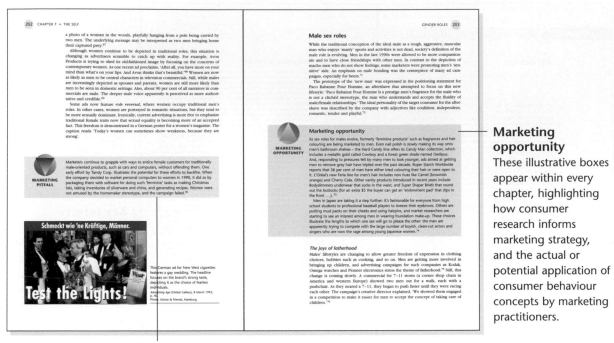

Marketing opportunity
These illustrative boxes appear within every chapter, highlighting how consumer research informs marketing strategy, and the actual or potential application of consumer behaviour concepts by marketing practitioners.

Marketing pitfall
These illustrative boxes appear within every chapter, highlighting the mistakes or ethically suspect marketing activities of companies that have generated controversy.

Chapter summary
The end-of-chapter bullet points summarize the key concepts and issues, providing a concise checklist of the topics and issues covered.

Consumer behaviour challenge
Each chapter ends with about 10 short, discursive-style questions, encouraging you to review and critically examine topics and issues individually or as part of a group discussion.

Notes
Updated notes at the end of each chapter.

Key terms list
An alphabetical collation of all the key terms in the chapter including a page reference where each term was first introduced, providing a convenient basis for revision.

Case study problems

At the end of each major section in the text there are a number of case study problems. The case material covers various companies, industries and countries, and integrates the topics covered in preceding chapters. The questions at the end of each case study are designed to allow you to apply your understanding to real-life events and consumer behaviour activities, and to develop your analytical skills.

Companion website

A companion website accompanies the book at *www.booksites.net/solomon_euro*.

Structure of the text

The structure of this textbook is simple: it goes from micro to macro. Think of the book as a sort of photograph album of consumer behaviour: each chapter provides a 'snapshot' of consumers, but the lens used to take each picture gets successively wider. The book begins with issues related to the individual consumer and expands its focus until it eventually considers the behaviours of large groups of people in their social settings. The topics to be covered correspond to the Wheel of Consumer Behaviour presented in the following figure.

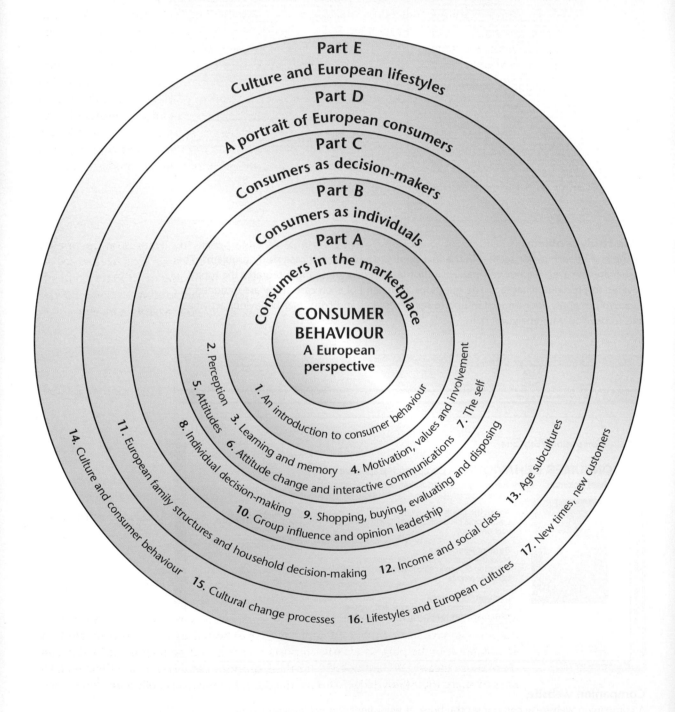

Following the Introductory chapter, Part B, 'Consumers as individuals', considers the consumer at the most micro level. It examines how the individual receives information from his or her immediate environment and how this material is learned, stored in memory, and used to form and modify individual attitudes – both about products and about oneself. Part C, 'Consumers as decision-makers', explores the ways in which consumers use the information they have acquired to make decisions about consumption activities, both as individuals and as group members. Part D, 'A portrait of European consumers', further expands the focus by considering how the consumer functions as a part of a larger social structure. This structure includes the influence of different social groups with which the consumer belongs and/or identifies, featuring social class and age groups. Finally, Part E, 'Culture and European lifestyles', completes the picture as it examines the relationship between consumption, marketing, and mass culture. This discussion focuses on the relationship of marketing to the expression of cultural values and lifestyles, how products and services are related to rituals and cultural myths, and the interface between marketing efforts and the creation of art, music, and other forms of popular culture that are so much a part of our daily lives. It also includes chapters on major cultural change processes such as fashion and diffusion of innovations, and on new cultural forces shaping consumer behaviour as we move further into the twenty-first century, such as environmentalism, political consumption, globalization and postmodernism.

Website support

A companion website features additional thought-provoking features on the impact of the internet. The Tangled Web describes website offerings that have failed to deliver in terms of consumer satisfaction, positioning pricing or product concept. Net Opportunities describe innovative web offerings which seem to have 'hit the mark' in their target markets. Take a look at *www.booksites.net/solomon_euro.*

Lecturer supplementary material

For lecturers the companion website features a downloadable Instructor's Manual, which will include:

● Chapter-based teaching notes and outlines

● Answers to the end-of-chapter Consumer Behaviour Challenges

● Student projects and assignments

● Debriefs to the Case Study problems

● PowerPoint presentations which go well beyond materials presented in the text.

Take a look at *www.booksites.net/solomon_euro.*

Acknowledgements

Many of our colleagues from the business world as well as from universities throughout Europe have made significant contributions to both the first and second editions of this book by helping us identify important issues, and helping us think through them more clearly. We are grateful for their support, enthusiasm, and their willingness to share their knowledge with us. In addition, numerous colleagues developed

European case materials and chapter-opening vignettes for this text, or provided valuable comments and feedback in the market research process and reviewing of manuscript drafts. To them, our special thanks:

Christian Alsted, *Alsted Marketing Research, Copenhagen, Denmark*

Suzanne C. Beckmann, *Copenhagen Business School and Saatchi & Saatchi, Denmark*

Anders Bengtsson, *Lund University, Sweden*

Peter Bjork, *Swedish School of Economics and Business Administration, Finland*

Josee Bloemer, *Limburgs Universitair Centrum, Belgium*

Janeen Arnold Costa, *University of Utah, USA*

Geoff Crowther, *Huddersfield University, UK*

Fabian F. Csaba, *Bilkent University, Ankara, Turkey*

Anitta Desgaard, *Copenhagen Business School, Denmark*

Karin Ekström, *Göteborg University, Sweden*

Basil Englis, *Berry College, Georgia, USA*

A. Fuat Firat, *Arizona State University West, Phoenix, USA*

James Fitchett, *University of Exeter, UK*

Güliz Ger, *Bilkent University, Ankara, Turkey*

David Harvey, *Huddersfield University, UK*

Susan Hayward, *RISC International, Paris, France*

Johann de Heer, *Tilburg University, Netherlands*

Benoît Heilbrunn, *Ecole de Management de Lyon, France*

Patrick Hetzel, *Université Paris II Panthéon-Assas, France*

Margaret Hogg, *UMIST, Manchester, UK*

Carina Holmberg, *Stockholm School of Economics, Sweden*

Howard Jackson, *Huddersfield University, UK*

Anna Lund Jepsen, *University of Southern Denmark, Denmark*

Ignaas van Kooten, *Vrije Universiteit, Amsterdam*

Gaynor Lea-Greenwood, *Manchester Metropolitan University, UK*

Eoin Lonergan, *University of North London, UK*

Damien McLoughlin, *University College, Dublin, Ireland*

Raj Minhas, *Sheffield University, UK*

Gabriele Morello, *ISIDA, Palermo, Italy*

Israel D. Nebenzahl, *Ben-Ilan University, Ramat-Gan, Israel*

Caroline Oates, *University of Sheffield, UK*

Anna Olofsson, *Gazoline Advertising, Umeå, Sweden*

Jacob Östberg, *Lund University, Sweden*

Per Østergaard, *SDU Odense University, Denmark*

Anne Marie Parlevliet, *Amsterdam, Netherlands*

Lara Pearce, *The Henley Centre, London, UK*

Maria Piacentini, *Strathclyde University, UK*

Toygun Ozdem, *Bilkent University, Ankara, Turkey*

Henry S. J. Robben, *Technische Universiteit Delft, Netherlands*

Diana Storm, *SDU Odense University, Denmark*

Carolyn Strong, *University of Wales, Cardiff, UK*

Finn Thomassen, *University of Aalborg, Denmark*

Alladi Venkatesh, *University of California, Irvine, USA*

Joop de Vries, *RISC International, Paris, France*

Gill Wright, *University of Bradford, UK*

Tuire Ylikoski, *Helsinki School of Business, Finland*

We'd also like to express our sincere thanks to our students in Denmark and the Netherlands who gave us suggestions on earlier drafts of this work. In particular, our Student Assistants: Nanine Plaatje, Trinske Antonides (Amsterdam), and Sofie Kristensen and Karen Malene Andreasen (Odense) were excellent help in collecting material for the book and in reviewing our work-in-progress. Thanks also to our friends and colleagues at Syddansk Universitet, Odense Universitet, the Vrije Universiteit, Amsterdam, and the University of Utah for their support and inspiration throughout this project.

Gary and Søren want to offer a special and personal word of thanks to Mike Solomon. While we were busy getting together the materials for this second European edition, Mike was already working hard on the manuscript for the 5th edition of *Consumer Behavior*. He shared materials with us as soon as they were ready, providing us with a pace and structure which kept us focused and on schedule (!). Mike was the perfect senior author – there when we needed something from him, and otherwise a positive source of energy and enthusiasm, coming from a comfortable distance. Ultimately, a great deal of synergy developed in our work together. We ended up sharing new materials, sources of research, and ideas in a mutual process of give and take. Thanks for giving us this opportunity to work with you, Mike.

Finally, Gary Bamossy would like to thank Janeen, Joost, Lieke and Jason. There are many time demands in taking on a book project, and as it develops, you recognize that you get an extra amount of support from the people you love. Søren Askegaard would like to thank Caroline, Steen and Niels, his favourite fellow consumers, who perpetually tempted him to engage in a variety of leisurely consumption activities instead of revising this book.

Permissions acknowledgements

The publishers are grateful to the following for permission to reproduce copyright material:

Figure 2.4 from Fischler, C., (1990) *L'Homnivore*, Paris: Editions Odile Jacob, used with permission; Figure 2.5 from Heilbrunn, B., (2001) 'Les Facteurs d'attachement à la marque', PhD dissertation, University of Paris Dauphine, used with permission; Table 4.3 from Kahle, L. *et al*, 'Implications of Social Values for Consumer Communications' in B. English, ed, *Global and Multinational Advertising*, Lawrence Erlbaum Associates, used with permission; Elsevier Science for Figure 4.4 from Nielsen, N.A., Bech-Larsen, T. and Grunert, K.G. (1998) 'Consumer Purchase Motives and Product Perceptions: A Laddering Study on Vegetable Oil in Three Countries', *Food Quality and Preference* 9(6) 455–66 and Figure 15.1 from Solomon, M. (1988) 'Building Up and Breaking Down: The Impact of Cultural Sorting on Symbolic Consumption' in J. Sheth and E.C. Hirschman, eds, *Research in Consumer Behaviour* 325–51; Routledge for Figure 4.5 adapted from Ratneshwar, S., Mick, D.G. and Huffman, C. (2000) 'Introduction', *The Why of Consumption*: 1–8; The University of Chicago Press for Figure 6.3 from Mitchell, A.A. (1986) 'The Effect of Verbal & Visual Components', *Journal of Consumer Research* 13 (June): 21, Figure 10.2 from Bearden, W.O. and Etzel, M.J. (1982) 'Reference Group Influence on Product and Brand Purchase Decisions', *Journal of Consumer Research* (September): 185, Figure 14.1 from McCracken, G. (1986) 'Culture and Consumption: A Theoretical Account of the Structure and Movement of the Cultural

Meaning of Consumer Goods', *Journal of Consumer Research* 13 (June): 72, Figure 16.11 adapted from Peñalosa, L. (1994) *Atravesando Fronteras*/Border Crossings: A Critical Ethnographic Exploration of the Consumer Acculturation of Mexican Immigrants, *Journal of Consumer Research* 21 (June): 32–54, Table 4.5 from Richens, M.L. and Dawson, S. (1992) 'A Consumer Values Orientation for Materialism and its Measurement', *Journal of Consumer Research* 20 (December), Table 6.2 from McQuarrie, E.F. and Mick, D.G. (1992) 'On Resonance: A Critical Pluralistic Inquiry', *Journal of Consumer Research* 19 (September): 182, Table 8.2 from Bloch, P.H., Sherell, D.L. and Ridgway, N. (1986) 'Consumer Search: An Extended Framework', *Journal of Consumer Research* 13 (June): 120, Table 10.1 adapted from Whan Park, C. and Parker Lessig, V. (1977) 'Students and Housewives: Differences in Susceptibility to Reference Group Influence' *Journal of Consumer Research* 4 (September): 102, Table 14.1 from Rook, D.W. (1985) 'The Ritual Dimension of Consumer Behaviour', *Journal of Consumer Research* 12 (December): 251–64 and Table 14.2 from Ruth, J.A., Otnes, C.C. and Brunel, F.F. (1999) 'Gift Receipt and the reformulation of interpersonal relationships' *Journal of Consumer Research* 25 (March): 385–402; The American Marketing Association for Figure 6.4 adapted from Rathans, A.J., Swasy, J.L. and Marks, L. (1986) 'Effects of Television Commercial Repetition: Receiver Knowledge', *Journal of Marketing Research* 23 (February): 50–61, Figure 9.6 adapted from Jacoby, J., Berning, C.K. and Dietvorst, T.F. (1977) 'What about disposition?', *Journal of Marketing* 41 (April): 23, Figure 10.4 adapted from Feick, L. and Price, L. (1987) 'The Market Maven: A Diffuser of Marketplace Information', *Journal of Marketing* 51 (January): 83–7, Table 4.2 from Laurent, G. and Kapferer, J-N. (1985) 'Measuring Consumer Involvement Profiles', *Journal of Marketing Research* 22 (February): 45 and Table 13.1 from Holbrook, M.B. and Schindler, R.M. (1994) 'Age, Sex and Attitude Toward the Past as Predicters of Consumers' Aesthetic Tastes for Cultural Products', *Journal of Marketing Research* 31 (August): 416; Figure 7.1 from the *Salt Lake City Tribune*, 11 March 1997, used with permission; Figure 9.2 from *Journal of Personality and Social Psychology*, 1980, 38, 311–22. Copyright © 1980 by the American Pyschological Association. Adapted with permission; The University of Miami for Figure 9.3 from Page-Wood, E.S., Kaufman, C.J. and Lane, P.M. (1990) 'The Art of Time', *Proceedings of the Academy of Marketing Science* © Academy of Marketing Science; Figure 9.4 from Venkatesh, A. (1998) 'Cybermarketscapes and Consumer Freedoms and Identities', *European Journal of Marketing* 32(7/8): 664–76, used with permission; Figure 9.5 from Rook, D. (1990) 'Is Impulse Buying (Yet) a Useful Marketing Concept?' unpublished manuscript, University of Southern California, used with permission; Cambridge University Press for Figure 10.3 from Gergen, K.J. and Gergen, M., *Social Psychology* (NewYork: Harcourt Brace Jovanovich, 1981), adapted from F.C. Barlett (1932) *Remembering*; Figure 11.5 adapted from McNeal, J. and Chyon-Hwa Yeh, 'Born to Shop', *American Demographics*, June 1993, 36 and Table 13.4 from Mischis, G.P., 'Life Stages of the Mature Market', *American Demographics*, September 1996, used with permission from Media Central; The Henley Centre, Strategic Marketing Consultancy for Figures 12.5, 2.7 and 13.1 from *Frontiers: Planning for Consumer Change in Europe (1996/97)*; Figure 14.2 from Venkatesh, A., 'Ethnoconsumerism: A New Pardigm to Study Cultural and Cross-Cultural Consumer Behavior', in J.A. Costa and G. Bamossy, eds, *Marketing in a Multicultural World*, copyright © 1995 by Sage Publications. Reprinted by permission of Sage Publications; The University of Florida for Figure 14.4 based on Mick, D.G., DeMoss, M. and Faber, R.J. (1990) *Latent Motivations and Meanings of Self-Gifts*, research report, Centre of Retailing

Education and Research; Figure 16.7 © 2001 by SRI Consulting Business Intelligence. All rights reserved; The Association for Consumer Research for Table 7.1 adapted from Debevec, K. and Iyer, E. (1986) 'Sex Roles and Consumer Perceptions of Promotions, Products, and Self: What Do We Know and Where Should We Be Headed', *Advances in Consumer Research* 13, Table 8.3 adapted from Duncan, C.P. (1990) 'Consumer Market Beliefs: A Review of the Literature and an Agenda for Future Research', *Advances in Consumer Research* 17: 729–735, Table 11.1 adapted from Gilly, M.C. and Enis, B.M. (1982) 'Recycling the Family Life Cycle: A Proposal for Redefinition' in A.A. Mitchell, (ed.) *Advances in Consumer Research* 9: 274 and Table 16.3 adapted from Smith, D. and Skalnik, J. (1995) 'Changing Patterns in the Consumption of Alcoholic Beverages in Europe and the United States' in Flemming Hansen, (ed), *European Advances in Consumer Research* 2; Sheffield Publishing Company for Table 15.3 from Berger, A.A. (1984) *Signs in Contemporary Culture: An Introduction to Semiotics,* © 1984, 1999 Sheffield Publishing Company, reprinted with permission of the publisher; MCB UP Ltd. for Table 15.4 from Foxall, G.R. and Bhate, S. (1993) 'Cognitive Style and Personal Involvement as Explicators of Innovative Purchasing of Health Food Brands', *European Journal of Marketing,* 27(2): 5–16; Table 16.2 adapted from Brunø, K., *et al*, 'An Analysis of National and Cross-National Consumer Segments Using the Food-Related Lifestyle Instrument in Denmark, France, Germany and Great Britain', MAPP Working Paper no.35, Aarhus School of Business, January 1996. Used with permission; GfK AG Germany for Table 16.4 from Davison, J.A. and Grab, E. (1993) 'The Contributions of Advertising Testing to the Development of Effective International Adverising: The KitKat Case Study' *Marketing and Research Today* (February): 15–24.

Plates
Chapter 1: The Procter & Gamble Company; Levi Strauss & Co.; American Association of Advertising Agencies; Chapter 2: Lexus, a Division of Toyota Motor Sales, USA Inc.; The Procter & Gamble Company; Sunkist Growers, Inc.; William Grant & Sons, Inc.; Campbell Soup Company; Tuborg; Marketing Denmark; GRW Advertising; Toyota Singapore and Saatchi & Saatchi Ltd.; Chapter 4: TAGHeuer USA; Leo-Burnett-Paris; Smith & Wollensky Steakhouse; Chapter 6: Linda Evangelista photograph © Stephen Wayda; Paradiset DDB; PepsiCo, Inc. Heineken Brouwerijen B.V.; John Wiley & Sons, Inc.; Chapter 7: Nutrio.com Inc.; Haggar; Goldsmith/Jeffrey and Bodyslimmers; Soloflex, Inc.; Chapter 8: Bernard Wolf La Guillotine Beer; Minolta Corporation; Chris Wimpey Photography, TeamOne Advertising; Chapter 9: Volkswagen of South Africa; Karen Malene Andreasen; Chapter 10: Brogan & Partners Convergence Marketing; Case Study 6: Ogilvy & Mather; Chapter 12: Tim Barnwell/Stock Boston; Chapter 13: SAGA Magazine; Chapter 14: Bianco Danmark A/S; Publishers Custom Reprints; Chapter 15: Robson-Brown Ad Agency; Maidenform, Inc; Jim Beam Brand, Inc.; Archive Photos; Chapter 16: Nordfalks AB; Chapter 17: BDH, Manchester; Volkswagen and DDB Needham Worldwide BV; Leo Burnett; Adbusters Media Foundation; Fabiana; Jeffrey Aaronson/Aspen Network; Hans Brinker Budget Hotel.

Whilst every effort has been made to trace the owners of copyright material, in a few cases this has proved impossible and we take this opportunity to offer our apologies to any copyright holders whose rights we may have unwittingly infringed.

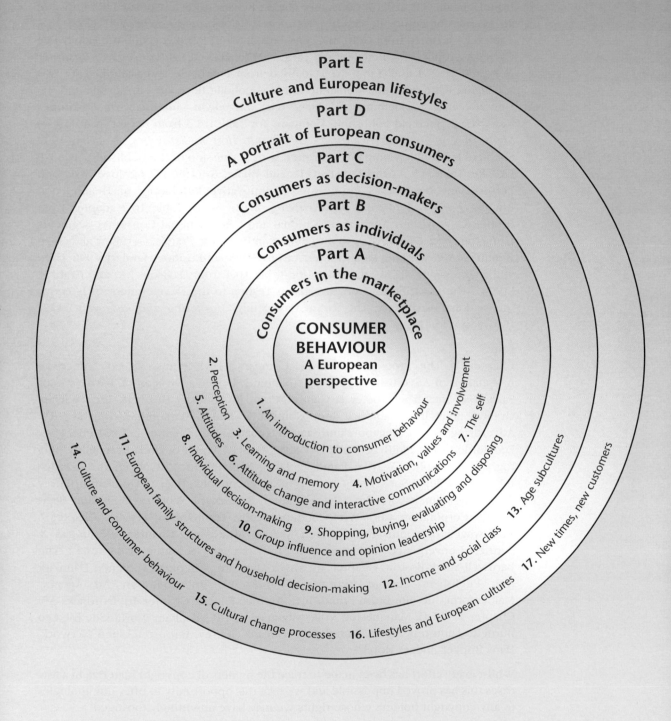

Part E
Culture and European lifestyles

Part D
A portrait of European consumers

Part C
Consumers as decision-makers

Part B
Consumers as individuals

Part A
Consumers in the marketplace

CONSUMER
BEHAVIOUR
A European
perspective

1. An introduction to consumer behaviour

2. Perception
3. Learning and memory
4. Motivation, values and involvement
5. Attitudes
6. Attitude change and interactive communications
7. The self

8. Individual decision-making
9. Shopping, buying, evaluating and disposing
10. Group influence and opinion leadership

11. European family structures and household decision-making
12. Income and social class
13. Age subcultures

14. Culture and consumer behaviour
15. Cultural change processes
16. Lifestyles and European cultures
17. New times, new customers

Part A

CONSUMERS IN THE MARKETPLACE

This introductory part comprises one chapter which previews much of what this book is about, and gives an overview of the field of consumer behaviour. The chapter examines how the field of marketing is influenced by the actions of consumers, and also how we as consumers are influenced by marketers. It also overviews consumer behaviour as a discipline of enquiry, and describes some of the different approaches that researchers use in order better to understand what makes consumers behave as they do.

Chapter 1

An introduction to consumer behaviour

Nathalie is working at her computer. It is early autumn and the beginning of a new term at her Danish university. Time for getting new books and study materials. As a second-year student, she's not surprised to find that several of the required books are still unavailable at the campus bookshop.

She goes online to check if she can get her books from one of the internet bookshops. She uses her favourite portal (*www.jubii.dk*) to check out the Scandinavian bookshops, which she figures might be able to deliver the books faster than their international competitors. None of them have all of the books in stock that she needs, and she really feels that she should get all of the books from the same store. On an impulse, Nathalie visits a student shop which sells used books and provides search facilities for Barnes & Noble. She searches for a couple of the titles she is looking for, but the search facility does not seem to work. For a moment, she considers putting some of her used books up for sale, then decides not to let herself be distracted, and moves on to the UK version of *Amazon.com*. She has heard from friends that prices are a little steeper here (relative to the other internet bookshops), but she knows this site well by now. Besides, the books she wants are in stock and can be delivered in about a week, maybe less. Considering that the chances that the books she needs will appear in the campus bookshop on time seem pretty slim, Nathalie decides to go ahead and buy them now online.

While she fills out the order form, she tries to plan where to go next. She and her friend are looking for an interesting topic for a course project and she wants to look in the social science section of *www.yahoo.com* for some inspiration. Also, she wants to visit a few of her favourite sites for news, music, and travel. 'A little information update before meeting the girls this afternoon for coffee,' she thinks to herself. She clicks 'OK' to her order confirmation, and is glad to have that out of the way. She navigates her way to yahoo.com and starts her search. All the while, she is thinking to herself that it would be nice also to spend a little time checking out the latest in fashion and beauty tips; a little treat to herself while she still has some time on her hands. Suddenly Nathalie remembers that there were also a couple of study plans to print out from the university website – and a few emails to answer. She checks her email account and is a little surprised to see that she received so much mail today – seems like everybody just realized that summer is over and wants to get started on new projects. It makes her feel joyful, even sort of invigorated . . .

Diana Storm, University of Southern Denmark, Odense University

Consumption in Europe? The European consumer?

This is a book about consumer behaviour, written from a European perspective. But what does that mean exactly? Obviously, to write about a 'European' consumer or a 'European's consumer behaviour' is problematic. Some of the general theory about the psychological or sociological influences on consumer behaviour may be common to all Western cultures. On the one hand, some theories may be culturally specific. Certain groups of consumers do show similar kinds of behaviour across national borders. On the other hand, the ways in which people live their consumption life vary greatly from one European country to another, and sometimes even within different regions of the same country. As a student of consumer behaviour, you might want to ask yourself: 'In which consumption situations do I seem to have a great deal in common with fellow students from other European countries? And in what ways do I seem to resemble more closely my compatriots? In what ways do subcultures in my country exert a strong influence on my consumption patterns, and how international are these subcultures?'

This book is about consumer behaviour theory in general, and we will illustrate our points with examples from various European markets as well as from the United States (US) and other countries. Each chapter features 'Multicultural dimensions' boxes which spotlight international aspects of consumer behaviour. From both a global and a Pan-European perspective, these issues will be explored in depth in Chapters 15 and 16.

Consumer behaviour: people in the marketplace

You can probably relate to at least some general aspects of Nathalie's behaviour. This book is about people like Nathalie. It concerns the products and services they buy and use, and the ways these fit into their lives. This introductory chapter briefly describes some important aspects of the field of consumer behaviour, including the topics studied, who studies them, and some of the ways these issues are approached by consumer researchers.

But first, let's return to Nathalie: the sketch which started the chapter allows us to highlight some aspects of consumer behaviour that will be covered in the rest of the book.

● As a consumer, Nathalie can be described and compared to other individuals in a number of ways. For some purposes, marketers might find it useful to categorize Nathalie in terms of her age, sex, income or occupation. These are some examples of descriptive characteristics of a population, or *demographics*. In other cases, marketers would rather know something about Nathalie's interests in fashion or music, or the way she spends her leisure time. This sort of information often comes under the category *psychographics*, which refers to aspects of a person's lifestyle and personality. Knowledge of consumer characteristics plays an extremely important role in many marketing applications, such as defining the market for a product or deciding on the appropriate techniques to employ when targeting a certain group of consumers.

● Nathalie's purchase decisions are heavily influenced by the opinions and behaviours of her friends. A lot of product information, as well as recommendations to use or avoid particular brands, is picked up in conversations among real people, rather than by way of television commercials, magazines or advertising messages. The bonds among Nathalie's group of friends are in part cemented by the products they all use. There is also pressure on each group member to buy things that will meet with the group's approval, and often a price to pay in the form of group rejection or embarrassment when one does not conform to others' conceptions of what is good or bad, 'in' or 'out'.

● As a member of a large society, people share certain cultural values or strongly held beliefs about the way the world should be structured. Other values are shared by members of *subcultures*, or smaller groups within the culture, such as ethnic groups, teens, people from certain parts of the country, or even 'Hell's Angels'. The people who matter to Nathalie – her *reference group* – value the idea that women in their early twenties should be innovative, style-conscious, independent and up-front (at least a little). While many marketers focus on either very young targets or the thirty-somethings, some are recognizing that another segment which ought to be attracting marketers' interest is the rapidly growing segment of older (50+) people.[1]

● When browsing through the websites, Nathalie is exposed to many competing 'brands'. Many offerings did not grab her attention at all; others were noticed but rejected because they did not fit the 'image' with which she identified or to which she aspired. The use of *market segmentation strategies* means targeting a brand only to specific groups of consumers rather than to everybody – even if that means that other consumers will not be interested or may choose to avoid that brand.

● Brands often have clearly defined *images* or 'personalities' created by product advertising, packaging, branding and other marketing strategies that focus on positioning a product a certain way or by certain groups of consumers adopting the product. One's leisure activities in particular are very much lifestyle statements: it says a lot about what a person is interested in, as well as something about the type of person she would like to be. People often choose a product offering, a service or a place, or subscribe to a particular idea, because they like its image, or because they feel its 'personality' somehow corresponds to their own. Moreover, a consumer may believe that by buying and using the product, its desirable qualities will somehow magically 'rub off'.

● When a product succeeds in satisfying a consumer's specific needs or desires, as *http://www.amazon.co.uk* did for Nathalie, it may be rewarded with many years of *brand* or *store loyalty*, a bond between product or outlet and consumer that may be very difficult for competitors to break. Often a change in one's life situation or self-concept is required to weaken this bond and thus create opportunities for competitors.

● Consumers' evaluations of products are affected by their appearance, taste, texture or smell. We may be influenced by the shape and colour of a package, as well as by more subtle factors, such as the symbolism used in a brand name, in an advertisement, or even in the choice of a cover model for a magazine. These judgements are affected by – and often reflect – how a society feels that people should define themselves at that point in time. Nathalie's choice of a new hairstyle, for example, says something about the type of image women like her want to project. If asked, Nathalie might not be able to say exactly why she considered some websites and rejected others. Many product meanings are hidden below the surface of the packaging, the design and advertising, and this book will discuss some of the methods used by marketers and social scientists to discover or apply these meanings.

● *Amazon.co.uk* has a combined American and international image that appeals to Nathalie. A product's image is often influenced by its *country of origin*, which helps to determine its 'brand personality'. In addition, our opinions and desires are increasingly shaped by input from around the world, thanks to rapid advancements in communications and transportation systems, (witness the internet!). In today's global culture, consumers often prize products and services that 'transport' them to different locations and allow them to experience the diversity of other cultures.

What is consumer behaviour?

The field of **consumer behaviour** covers a lot of ground: it is the study of the processes involved when individuals or groups select, purchase, use or dispose of products, services, ideas or experiences to satisfy needs and desires. Consumers take many forms, ranging from a six-year-old child pleading with her mother for wine gums to an executive in a large corporation deciding on an extremely expensive computer system. The items that are consumed can include anything from tinned beans to a massage, democracy, rap music, and even other people (the images of rock stars, for example). Needs and desires to be satisfied range from hunger and thirst to love, status or even spiritual fulfilment. There is a growing interest in consumer behaviour, not only in the field of marketing but from the social sciences in general. This follows a growing awareness of the increasing importance of consumption in our daily lives, in our organization of daily activities, in our identity formation, in politics and economic development, and in the flows of global culture, where consumer culture seems to spread, albeit in new forms, from North America and Europe to other parts of the world.[2] Indeed, consumption can be regarded as playing such an important role in our social, psychological, economical, political and cultural lives that today it has become the 'vanguard of history'.[3]

Consumers are actors on the marketplace stage

The perspective of **role theory**, which this book emphasizes, takes the view that much of consumer behaviour resembles actions in a play,[4] where each consumer has lines, props and costumes that are necessary to a good performance. Since people act out many different roles, they may modify their consumption decisions according to the particular 'play' they are in at the time. The criteria that they use to evaluate products and services in one of their roles may be quite different from those used in another role.

Another way of thinking about consumer roles is to consider the various 'plays' that the consumer may engage in. One classical role here is the consumer as a 'chooser' – somebody who, as we have seen with Nathalie, can choose between different alternatives and explores various criteria for making this choice. But the consumer can have many other things at stake than just 'making the right choice'. We are all involved in a communication system through our consumption activities, whereby we communicate our roles and statuses. We are also sometimes searching to construct our identity, our 'real selves', through various consumption activities. Or the main purpose of our consumption might be an exploration of a few of the many possibilities the market has to offer us, maybe in search of a 'real kick of pleasure'. On the more serious side, we might feel victimized by fraudulent or harmful offerings, and we may decide to take action against such risks from the marketplace by becoming active in consumer movements. Or we may react against the authority of the producers by co-opting their products, and turning them into something else, as when military boots all of a sudden became 'normal' footwear for peaceful girls. We may decide to take action as 'political consumers' and boycott products from companies or countries whose behaviour does not meet our ethical or environmental standards. Hence, as consumers we can be choosers, communicators, identity-seekers, pleasure-seekers, victims, rebels and activists – sometimes simultaneously.[5]

Consumer behaviour is a process

In its early stages of development, the field was often referred to as *buyer behaviour*, reflecting an emphasis on the interaction between consumers and producers at the time of purchase. Marketers now recognize that consumer behaviour is an ongoing *process*, not merely what happens at the moment a consumer hands over money or a credit card and in turn receives some good or service.

The **exchange**, in which two or more organizations or people give and receive something of value, is an integral part of marketing.[6] While exchange remains an important part of consumer behaviour, the expanded view emphasizes the entire consumption process, which includes the issues that influence the consumer before, during and after a purchase. Figure 1.1 illustrates some of the issues that are addressed during each stage of the consumption process.

Figure 1.1 Some issues that arise during stages in the consumption process

	Consumer's perspective	**Marketer's perspective**
Pre-purchase issues	How does a consumer decide that he/she needs a product? What are the best sources of information to learn more about alternative choices?	How are consumer attitudes towards products formed and/or changed? What cues do consumers use to infer which products are superior to others?
Purchase issues	Is acquiring a product a stressful or pleasant experience? What does the purchase say about the consumer?	How do situational factors, such as time pressure or store displays, affect the consumer's purchase decision?
Post-purchase issues	Does the product provide pleasure or perform its intended function? How is the product eventually disposed of, and what are the environmental consequences of this act?	What determines whether a consumer will be satisfied with a product and whether he/she will buy it again? Does this person tell others about his/her experiences with the product and affect their purchase decisions?

Consumer behaviour involves many different actors

A consumer is generally thought of as a person who identifies a need or desire, makes a purchase and then disposes of the product during the three stages in the consumption process. In many cases, however, different people may be involved in the process. The *purchaser* and *user* of a product may not be the same person, as when a parent chooses clothes for a teenager (and makes selections that can result in 'fashion suicide' from the teenager's point of view). In other cases, another person may act as an *influencer*, providing recommendations for (or against) certain products without actually buying or using them. For example, a friend, rather than a parent, accompanying a teenager on a shopping trip may pick out the clothes that he or she decides to purchase.

Finally, consumers may be organizations or groups in which one person may make the decisions involved in purchasing products that will be used by many, as when a purchasing agent orders the company's office supplies. In other organizational situations, purchase decisions may be made by a large group of people – for example, company accountants, designers, engineers, sales personnel and others – all of whom will have a say in the various stages of the consumption process. As we'll see in a later chapter, one important organization is the family, where different family members play pivotal roles in decision-making regarding products and services used by all.

Consumers' impact on marketing strategy

Surfing websites or discussing products and brands can be a lot of fun – almost as much fun as actually making the purchases! But, on the more serious side, why should managers, advertisers and other marketing professionals bother to learn about this field?

The answer is simple: understanding consumer behaviour is good business. A basic marketing concept states that firms exist to satisfy consumers' needs. These needs can only be satisfied to the extent that marketers understand the people or organizations that will use the products and services they offer, and that they do so *better* than their competitors.

Consumer response may often be the ultimate test of whether or not a marketing strategy will succeed. Thus, knowledge about consumers is incorporated into virtually every facet of a successful marketing plan. Data about consumers help marketers to define the market and to identify threats and opportunities in their own and other countries that will affect how consumers receive the product. In every chapter, we'll see how developments in consumer behaviour can be used as input to marketing strategies. Boxes headed 'Marketing opportunity' will highlight some of these possibilities. Sony's introduction of the Walkman is one good example of how consumers initially turned down the product when the concept was tested in the market.[7] The product was launched anyway and the Walkman was an immense success – Sony revolutionized the mobile music experience and sold almost 300 million Walkmans in the process. This does not mean that Sony now eschews consumer research, as is demonstrated by these few examples of marketing actions that resulted from studies focused on understanding consumers:

● Recent research found that today's teens see portable cassette players as dinosaurs. Sony's advertising agency followed 125 teens to see how they use products in their day-to-day lives. Now the product has been relaunched with a removable 'Memory Stick' instead of a cassette player so it can work with MP3 files. The Walkman also needed a fresh message, so Sony's agency decided to use an alien named Plato to appeal to teens. This character was chosen to appeal to today's culturally ethnically diverse marketplace. As the account director explained, 'An alien is no one, so an alien is everyone'.[8]

- A woman in a consumer group which was discussing dental hygiene commented that tartar felt 'like a wall' on her teeth. This imagery was used in ads for Colgate Tartar Control, in which room-sized teeth were shown covered by walls of tartar.[9]

- Researchers for a manufacturer of Swiss chocolate found that many chocolate lovers hide secret 'stashes' around their houses. One respondent confessed to hiding chocolate bars inside her lingerie drawer. The result was an ad campaign theme of 'The True Confessions of Chocaholics'.[10]

Market segmentation: to whom are we marketing?

Whether within or across national boundaries, effective **market segmentation** delineates segments whose members are similar to one another in one or more characteristics and different from members of other segments. Depending on its goals and resources, a company may choose to focus on just one segment or several, or it may ignore differences among segments by pursuing a mass market strategy. On the internet-based market, *Amazon.com* tries to reach multiple segments at the same time, while *eToys.com* focuses on gifts for kids.[11]

In many cases, it makes a lot of sense to target a number of market segments. The likelihood is that no one will fit any given segment description exactly, and the issue is whether or not consumers differ from our profile in ways that will affect the chances of their adopting the products we are offering.

Many segmentation variables form the basis for slicing up a larger market, and a great deal of this book is devoted to exploring the ways marketers describe and characterize different segments. The segmentation variables listed in Table 1.1 are grouped into four categories, which also indicate where in the book these categories are considered in more depth.

Table 1.1 Variables for market segmentation

Category	Variables	Location of discussion
Demographics	Age	Chapter 13
	Gender	Chapter 7
	Social class, occupation, income	Chapter 12
	Ethnic group, religion	Chapter 16
	Stage in life	Chapter 11
	Purchaser vs. user	Chapter 11
Geographic	Region	Chapter 16
	Country differences	Chapter 16
Psychographic	Self-concept, personality	Chapter 7
	Lifestyle	Chapter 16
Behavioural	Brand loyalty, extent of usage	Chapter 8
	Usage situation	Chapter 9
	Benefits desired	Chapter 4

While consumers can be described in many ways, the segmentation process is valid only when the following criteria are met:

- Consumers within the segment are similar to one another in terms of product needs, and these needs are different from consumers in other segments.
- Important differences among segments can be identified.
- The segment is large enough to be profitable.
- Consumers in the segment can be reached by an appropriate marketing mix.
- The consumers in the segment will respond in the desired way to the marketing mix designed for them.

Demographics are statistics that measure observable aspects of a population, such as birth rate, age distribution or income. The national statistical agencies of European countries and pan-European agencies such as EuroStat are major sources of demographic data on families, but many private firms gather additional data on specific population groups. The changes and trends revealed in demographic studies are of great interest to marketers, because the data can be used to locate and predict the size of markets for many products, ranging from mortgages to baby food.

In this book, we'll explore many of the important demographic variables that make consumers the same as, or different from, others. We'll also consider other important characteristics that are not so easy to measure, such as **psychographics** – differences in consumers' personalities and tastes which can't be measured objectively. For now, let's summarize a few of the most important demographic dimensions, each of which will be developed in more detail in later chapters. However, a word of caution is needed here. The last couple of decades have witnessed the growth of new consumer segments that are less dependent on demographics and more likely to borrow behavioural patterns and fashions across what were formerly more significant borders or barriers. It is now not so uncommon to see men and women, or grandmothers and granddaughters, having similar tastes. Hence, useful as they might be, marketers should beware of using only demographic variables to predict consumer tastes.

Age

Consumers in different age groups have very different needs and wants. While people who belong to the same age group differ in many other ways, they do tend to share a set of values and common cultural experiences that they carry throughout life.[12] Levi Strauss, for example, has been trying to develop the idea that it is a 'brand for life' by introducing products such as Dockers to meet the needs of their consumers as they grow older. As a Levi's marketing executive explained, 'In the 1960s, growth [in the jeans market] was due to adoption of jeans by 15- to 18-year-olds ... Now these people are 25–49 and Dockers meshes perfectly with what the Levi brand image is about for them.'[13]

Gender

Many products, from fragrances to footwear, are targeted at men or women. Differentiating by sex starts at a very early age – even nappies are sold in pink-trimmed versions for girls and blue for boys. As proof that consumers take these differences seriously, market research has revealed that many parents refuse to put baby boys in pink nappies![14]

One dimension that makes segmenting by gender so interesting is that the behaviours and tastes of men and women are constantly evolving. In the past most marketers assumed that men were the primary decision-makers for car purchases, but this perspective is changing with the times.

Sometimes, the gender segmentation can be an unintended product of an advertising strategy. Wranglers launched a European campaign featuring macho Wild West values such as rodeo riding, after an earlier campaign, featuring a supermodel, had made their sales of jeans to women grow 400 per cent but put men off their brand.[15]

MARKETING OPPORTUNITY

Websites for women

Segmenting by gender is alive and well in cyberspace.[16] In France, for example, a group of women started the country's first women's electronic magazine and web portal called *Newsfam.com.* These entrepreneurs are hoping to reproduce the success of American sites like *iVillage.com* and *Women.com.*[17] To underscore the idea that men and women differ in their tastes and preferences (the French would say *vive la difference!*), a website for high-tech products called *Hifi.com* opened a sister site just for women called *herhifi.com.* It avoids jargon, offers friendly advice and finds ways to make home entertainment systems relevant to women.[18] Probably a sound strategy, considering that six out of every ten new internet users are female.[19]

Family structure

A person's family and marital status is yet another important demographic variable, since this has such a big effect on consumers' spending priorities. Young bachelors and newlyweds are the most likely to take exercise, go to wine bars and pubs, concerts and the cinema, and to consume alcohol. Families with young children are big purchasers of health foods and fruit juices, while single-parent households and those with older children buy more junk food. Home maintenance services are most likely to be used by older couples and bachelors.[20]

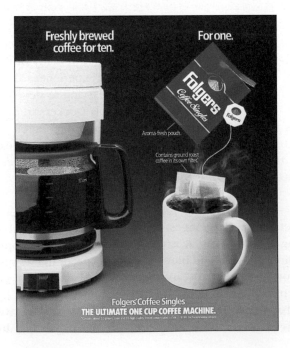

Marketers are paying increasing attention to demographic changes in European households.

© The Procter & Gamble Company. Reprinted by permission.

Social class and income

People in the same social class are approximately equal in terms of their incomes and social status. They work in roughly similar occupations and tend to have similar tastes in music, clothing, and so on. They also tend to socialize with one another, and share many ideas and values.[21] The distribution of wealth is of great interest to marketers, since it determines which groups have the greatest buying power and market potential.

Race and ethnicity

Immigrants from various countries in Africa and Asia are among the fastest-growing ethnic groups in Europe. As our societies grow increasingly multicultural, new opportunities develop to deliver specialized products to racial and ethnic groups, and to introduce other groups to these offerings.

Sometimes, this adaptation is a matter of putting an existing product or service into a different context. For example, in Great Britain there is a motorway service station and cafeteria targeted at the Muslim population. It has prayer facilities, no pork menus and serves *halal* meat.[22] And now, Turks in Berlin do not have to rely solely on the small immigrants' greengroceries and kiosks known from so many other European cities. A Turkish chain has opened the first department store in Berlin, carrying Turkish and Middle Eastern goods only, catering to both the large Turkish population as well as to other immigrant groups and Germans longing for culinary holiday memories.[23]

Multicultural dimensions

As we will discuss shortly, people can express their self and their cultural and religious belonging through consumption patterns. At times, this has led to cultural clashes, as in an example involving France or Denmark, where young Muslim women's wearing of headscarves either in the school or at work caused some debate. Wearing a headscarf is criticized for being a religious statement, which should not be allowed in the explicitly secular French public schools, as a sign of oppression of women or as incompatible with the 'modern' image of the employing company. However, a headscarf is not just a headscarf. There are at least four culturally bound ways of displaying this controversial textile: the 'Italian way', known from stars of the 1950s and 1960s such as Sophia Loren, Claudia Cardinale or Gina Lollobrigida on the back seats of scooters and revived by nostalgia movements, the 'women's lib' way with the knot in the back as displayed by many Scandinavian women in the 1970s, the 'German Hausfrau' version with a bow in the front, and the much-disputed Muslim version. In Turkey, one may see a lot of women wearing headscarves, but one can tell from the way they are tied whether this is a religious expression from a religious woman or rather an expression of a cultural tradition, and as such more a rural than a religious reference.[24]

Geography

In Europe, most of the evidence points to the fact that cultural differences persist in playing a decisive role in forming our consumption patterns and our unique expressions of consumption. At the same time, global competition tends to have a homogenizing effect in some markets such as music, sports, clothing and entertainment, and multinational companies such as Sony, Pepsi, Nintendo, Nike and Levi Strauss continue to dominate or play important roles in shaping markets.[25] With the creation of the single European market, many companies have begun to consider even more the possibilities of standardized marketing across national boundaries in

Europe. The increasing similarity of the brands and products available in Europe does not mean that the consumers are the same, however! Variables such as personal motivation, cultural context, family relation patterns and rhythms of everyday life, all vary substantially from country to country and from region to region. And consumption of various product categories is still very different: in 1995 the per capita consumption of cheese per annum was 16.9 kg in France and 6.1 kg in Ireland; consumption of potatoes was 13.8 kg in Italy and 59.9 kg in Finland.[26] In marketing research, the possibility of operating with standard criteria for something as 'simple' as demographics for market segmentation is constantly under discussion. But to date the results have not always been encouraging.[27]

To sum up, a European segmentation must be able to take into consideration:

- Consumption which is common across cultures (the global or regional, trends, lifestyles and cultural patterns that cross borders); and

- Consumption which is specific between different cultural groups (differences in values, lifestyles, behavioural patterns, etc. among different cultures and subcultures).

Even then, the problem of specifying the relevant borders arises. Cultural borders do not always follow national borders. Although national borders are still very important for distinguishing between cultures, there may be important regional differences within a country, as well as cultural overlap between two countries.[28] Add to this immigration and the import of foreign (often American) cultural phenomena, and you begin to understand why it is very difficult to talk about European countries as being culturally homogeneous. For example, it is important to distinguish between, say, Dutch *society* with all its multicultural traits and Dutch *culture*, which may be one, albeit dominant, cultural element in Dutch society. Furthermore, Dutch culture (as is the case with all cultures) is not a *static* but a *dynamic* phenomenon, which changes over time and from contact, interaction and integration with other cultures.

MARKETING OPPORTUNITY

New segments

Marketers have come up with so many ways to segment consumers – from the overweight to overachievers – that you might think they had run out of segments. Hardly. Changes in lifestyle and other characteristics of the population are constantly creating new opportunities. The following are some 'hot' market segments.

The gay community: In more and more societies, the gay minority is becoming increasingly visible. New media featuring homosexual lifestyles and the consumption patterns attached to them flourish and marketers claim that the gay community is as attractive a marketing niche as many other subcultures and that this group forms a 'hungry target'.[29] For example, in the marketing of Copenhagen as a tourist destination, the gay community has been explicitly chosen as one of the target markets. The gay segment tends to be economically upmarket and is frequently involved in travelling and short holidays to metropolitan areas. So the tourist board has tried to reach it through specific marketing activities targeted at gay environments in Europe.[30]

Single females: A worldwide study by Young and Rubicam has discovered a new and interesting market segment, that of well-educated, intelligent women who choose to stay single and pursue their life and career goals without husband or children. Furthermore, they represent heavy-spending consumers. They are reportedly brand-loyal and highly influenced by their friends in terms of consumption choices. The way to reach this attractive consumer group is to speak to their feelings of independence and self-respect.[31]

Disabled people: In the wake of legislation on the rights of disabled people, some marketers are starting to take notice of the estimated 10–15 per cent of the population who have some kind of disability. Initiatives include special phone numbers for hearing-impaired customers and assistance services for disabled people. IBM and Nissan have also used disabled actors in their advertising campaigns.[32] Mattel Inc., which produces Barbie, launched a sister-doll, Becky, in a wheelchair – a reflection of the growing awareness of the disabled population in society.

Relationship marketing: building bonds with consumers

Marketers are carefully defining customer segments and listening to people as never before. Many of them have realized that the key to success is building lifetime relationships between brands and customers. Marketers who believe in this philosophy – so-called **relationship marketing** – are making an effort to keep in touch with their customers on a regular basis, and are giving them reasons to maintain a bond with the company over time. Various types of membership of retail outlets, petrol companies and co-operative movements illustrate this. One co-operative chain offers reductions to its members on such diverse goods as travelling, clothing, home appliances, electronics and garden furniture.[33] A new trend is to form consortia of diverse companies from different sectors, such as supermarkets, banks, petrol retailers, telecommunications and the entertainment and leisure industry. The consortium then issues a loyalty card to help secure a stable clientele.[34]

Some companies establish these ties by offering services that are appreciated by their customers. Many companies donate a small percentage of the purchase price to a charity such as the Red Cross or the World Wildlife Fund, or for the care of the poor and marginalized in society. This cements the relationship by giving customers an additional reason to continue buying the company's products year after year.

Another revolution in relationship building is being brought to us by courtesy of **database marketing**. This involves tracking consumers' buying habits by computer and crafting products and information tailored precisely to people's wants and needs.

Keeping close tabs on their customers allows database marketers to monitor their preferences and communicate with those who show an interest in their products or services. Information is passed to the appropriate division for follow-up. Blockbuster Entertainment Corp. is testing a system that makes recommendations based on a consumer's prior video rentals and offers special promotions based on these choices.[35] However, some consumers feel threatened by this kind of surveillance and resist such marketing efforts. Hence, attempts have been made to ensure that database marketing conforms to the requirements of respondent confidentiality.[36]

Marketing's impact on consumers

For better or worse, we live in a world that is significantly influenced by marketers. We are surrounded by marketing stimuli in the form of advertisements, shops and products competing for our attention and our cash. Much of what we learn about the world is filtered by marketers, whether through conspicuous consumption depicted in glamorous magazine advertising or via the roles played by family members in TV commercials. Ads show us how we ought to act with regard to recycling, alcohol consumption and even the types of house or car we aspire to. In many ways we are 'at the mercy' of marketers, since we rely on them to sell us products that are safe and perform as promised, to tell us the truth about what they are selling, and to price and distribute these products fairly.

Popular culture

▶ **Popular culture**, the music, films, sports, books and other forms of entertainment consumed by the mass market, is both a product of and an inspiration for marketers. Our lives are also affected in more fundamental ways, ranging from how we acknowledge social events such as marriages, deaths or holidays to how we view societal issues such as air pollution, gambling and addiction. The football World Cup, Christmas shopping, tourism, newspaper recycling, cigarette smoking and Barbie dolls are all examples of products and activities that touch many of us in our lives.

Marketing's role in the creation and communication of popular culture is especially emphasized in this book. This cultural influence is hard to ignore, although many people fail to appreciate the extent to which their view of the world – their film and music icons, the latest fashions in clothing, food and interior design, and even the physical features that they find attractive or not in sexual partners – are influenced by the marketing system. Product placement, whereby products and brands are exposed in popular movies or TV series, or sponsorships of various mediated or live events such as concerts or quizzes, are examples of companies' new ways to command our attention. How about sleeping with corporations? Holiday Inn Family Suites Resort in Lake Buena Vista, Florida, offers rooms decorated in corporate themes including the Orange Minute Maid suite and the Edy's Ice Cream suite. A Coca-Cola executive (there is a polar bear motif in the Coca-Cola suite) comments, 'Families ... feel like they can actually interact with our brands within a room.'[37] Now there's a happening vacation for you ...

Consider the product characters that marketers use to create a personality for their products. From the Michelin Man to Ronald McDonald, popular culture is peopled with fictional heroes. In fact, it is likely that more consumers will recognize characters such as these than can identify former prime ministers, captains of industry or artists. They may not exist, but many of us feel that we 'know' them, and they certainly are effective *spokes-characters* for the products they promote. If you don't believe it, visit ***www.toymuseum.com***.

The meaning of consumption

One of the fundamental premises of consumer behaviour is that people often buy products not for what they do, but for what they *mean*.[38] This principle does not imply that a product's primary function is unimportant, but rather that the roles ▶ products play and the **meaning** that they have in our lives go well beyond the tasks they perform. The deeper meanings of a product may help it to stand out from other, similar goods and services – all things being equal, a person will choose the brand that has an image (or even a personality!) consistent with his or her underlying ideas.

For example, although most people probably can't run faster or jump higher if they are wearing Nikes versus Reeboks, many die-hard loyalists swear by their favourite brand. These arch-rivals are marketed in terms of their image – meanings

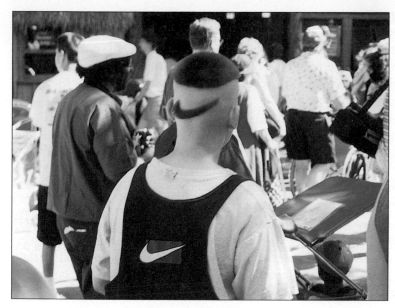

People use brands to express their identities to various degrees. The relationship between consumption and self is the topic of Chapter 7.

Photo by Søren Askegaard.

that have been carefully crafted with the help of legions of rock stars, athletes, slickly produced commercials – and many millions of dollars. So, when you buy a Nike 'swoosh' you may be doing more than choosing footwear – you may also be making a lifestyle statement about the type of person you are, or want to be. For a relatively simple item made of leather and laces, that's quite a feat!

As we have already seen, the hallmark of marketing strategies at the beginning of the twenty-first century is an emphasis on building relationships with customers. The nature of these relationships can vary, and these bonds help us to understand some of the possible meanings products have for us. Here are some of the types of relationship a person may have with a product:[39]

- *Self-concept attachment* – the product helps to establish the user's identity.
- *Nostalgic attachment* – the product serves as a link with a past self.
- *Interdependence* – the product is a part of the user's daily routine.
- *Love* – the product elicits bonds of warmth, passion or other strong emotion.

One American consumer researcher has developed a classification scheme in an attempt to explore the different ways that products and experiences can provide meaning to people.[40] This consumption typology was derived from a two-year analysis of supporters of a baseball team, but it is easily transferable to the European context.

This perspective views consumption as a type of action in which people make use of consumption objects in a variety of ways. Focusing on an event such as a football match is a useful reminder that when we refer to consumption, we are talking about intangible experiences, ideas and services (the thrill of a goal or the antics of a team mascot) in addition to tangible objects (like the food and drink consumed at the stadium). This analysis identified four distinct types of consumption activities:

1 *Consuming as experience* – when the consumption is a personal emotional or aesthetic goal in itself. This would include activities like the pleasure derived from learning how to interpret the off-side rule, or appreciating the athletic ability of a favourite player.

2 *Consuming as integration* – using and manipulating consumption objects to express aspects of the self. For example, some fans express their solidarity with the team by identifying with, say, the mascot and adopting some of its characteristic traits. Attending matches in person rather than watching them on TV allows the fan to integrate his or her experience more completely with his/her self – the feeling of 'having been there'.

3 *Consuming as classification* – the activities that consumers engage in to communicate their association with objects, both to self and to others. For example, spectators might dress up in the team's colours and buy souvenirs to demonstrate to others that they are die-hard fans. Unfortunately, the more hard-core express their contempt for opponents' supporters violently. There is a profound 'us' and 'them' dichotomy present here.

4 *Consuming as play* – consumers use objects to participate in a mutual experience and merge their identities with that of a group. For example, happy fans might scream in unison and engage in an orgy of jumping and hugging when their team scores a goal – this is a different dimension of shared experience compared with watching the game at home.

The global consumer

One highly visible – and controversial – by-product of sophisticated marketing strategies is the movement towards a **global consumer culture**, in which people are united by their common devotion to brand-name consumer goods, film stars and rock stars.[41] Some products in particular have become so associated with an American lifestyle that they are prized possessions around the world. In Chapters 16 and 17 we will pay special attention to the good and bad aspects of this cultural homogenization.[42]

On the other hand, popular culture continues to evolve as products and styles from different cultures mix and merge in new and interesting ways. For example, although superstars from the USA and the UK dominate the worldwide music industry, there is a movement afoot to include more diverse styles and performers. In Europe local music acts are grabbing a larger share of the market and pushing

Levi's jeans have become a worldwide status symbol and an icon for American consumer culture.
Courtesy of Levi Strauss & Co.

international (that is, English-speaking) acts down the charts. Revenue from Spanish-language music has quadrupled in five years. In Asia, new songs are being written to accompany promotions for American movies. For example, in Hong Kong the movie *Lethal Weapon 4* was promoted with a song by a local heavy metal band called Beyond. Shots from the movie were mixed with clips of band members even though they don't appear in the film and the song is not included in the soundtrack.[43]

A 'cousin' of the global consumer is the much debated Euro-consumer. Marketing researchers are heavily involved in a debate about the possibilities of finding market segments that are European rather than national in character. In a study on the consumption of luxury goods, it was concluded that one could draw a demographic portrait of the average European consumer of luxury goods. However, important differences between the countries were also detected. Consumers who expressed more positive attitudes towards cultural change were also more likely to consume luxury goods, independent of their demographics and social class.[44] Given these findings, it is questionable how much is gained from working with the concept of the Euro-consumer in terms of segment description. For a product such as cars, which intuitively and in terms of functionality would seem relatively easy to market as a European-wide product, the models still appear in a variety of versions to suit particular national needs and wants. The Euro-consumer will be discussed in detail in Chapter 16.

Marketing ethics

In business, conflicts often arise between the goal to succeed in the marketplace and the desire to conduct business honestly and maximize the well-being of consumers by providing them with safe and effective products and services. Some people argue that by the time people reach university, secondary school or are actually employed by companies, it is a little late to start teaching them ethics! Still, many universities and corporations are now focusing very intently on teaching and reinforcing ethical behaviour.

Prescribing ethical standards of conduct

Professional organizations often devise a code of ethics for their members. For example, European or national consumer protection laws or various national marketing associations' codes of ethics provide guidelines for conduct in many areas of marketing practice. These include:

- Disclosure of all substantial risks associated with a product or service.
- Identification of added features that will increase the cost.
- Avoidance of false or misleading advertising.
- Rejection of high-pressure or misleading sales tactics.
- Prohibition of selling or fund-raising under the guise of conducting market research.

Socially responsible behaviour

Whether intentionally or not, some marketers do violate their bond of trust with consumers. In some cases these actions are illegal, as when a manufacturer deliberately mislabels the contents of a package or a retailer adopts a 'bait-and-switch' selling strategy, whereby consumers are lured into the store with promises of inexpensive products with the sole intent of getting them to switch to higher-priced goods. A similar problematic issue of the luring of consumers is the case of misleading claims, for instance on food products' labels.[45] For example, what about a label such as '100% fat-free strawberry jam'?

In other cases, marketing practices have detrimental effects on society even though they are not explicitly illegal. The introduction of so-called alcopops, a mix of alcohol and soda or lemonade, targeted more or less explicitly at the teen market, has caused considerable debate in various European countries. Following negative press coverage, sales have gone down in Sweden and the UK, and the two largest retail chains in Denmark withdrew these drinks from their product range.[46] Others have run into difficulties by sponsoring commercials depicting groups of people in an unfavourable light to get the attention of a target market. One may recall the heated debate as to whether Benetton's advertising campaigns are attempts to sensitize consumers to the world's real problems, as the company contends, or to exploit unfortunate people – as in the ads depicting an AIDS victim, a dead Croat soldier or a ship packed with Albanian refugees – in order to sell more Benetton clothing.[47]

A crucial barometer of ethical behaviour is what actions a marketer takes once a company is made aware of a problem with its advertising or products. In 1996 a Danish hypermarket chain which for years had run a campaign guaranteeing the lowest prices compared to competitors was involved in a scandal when it was discovered that employees were under instruction to change price tags just before a newspaper journalist checked them.[48]

In contrast, Procter & Gamble voluntarily withdrew its 'Rely' tampons following reports of women who had suffered toxic shock syndrome (TSS) after using them. Although scientists did not claim a causal link between Rely and the onset of TSS, the company agreed to undertake extensive advertising notifying women of the symptoms of TSS and asking them to return their boxes of 'Rely' for a refund. The company took a $75 million loss and sacrificed an unusually successful new product which had already captured about 25 per cent of the huge sanitary product market.[49]

Faced with the rising phenomenon of the 'political consumer' – a consumer who expresses his or her political and ethical viewpoints by selecting and avoiding products from companies which are antithetical to these viewpoints – the industry is increasingly coming to realize that ethical behaviour is also good business in the long run, since the trust and satisfaction of consumers translates into years of loyalty from customers. However, many problems remain. Throughout this book, ethical issues related to the practice of marketing are highlighted. Special boxes headed 'Marketing pitfall' feature dubious marketing practices or the possible adverse effects on consumers of certain marketing strategies.

MARKETING PITFALL

Women for s@le! The charge against abuse of marketing techniques has taken on new dimensions with the rise of the internet. Would you like to buy a Latvian girl for escort service? Or a Russian bride by mail order? The trade in women from eastern Europe, Asia or Latin America has reached new heights with the easier contact made possible by the internet. Obvious problems are created by the difficulty of distinguishing between serious marriage bureaus or au pair agencies on the one side and organized traders of women for various kinds of prostitution services on the other. According to human rights organizations, many women who believe that they are going to marry the prince of their lives end up as 'sexual services workers', sometimes under slavery-like conditions.[50]

Public policy and consumerism

Public concern for the welfare of consumers has been an issue since at least the beginning of the twentieth century. This is normally referred to as **consumer policy**. Partly as a result of consumers' efforts, many national and international agencies have been established to oversee consumer-related activities. Consumers themselves continue to have a lively interest in consumer-related issues, ranging from environmental concerns, such as pollution caused by oil spills or toxic waste, the use of additives and genetically manipulated material in food and so on, to excessive violence and sex on television.

Consumer research and consumer welfare

The field of consumer behaviour can play an important role in improving our lives as consumers.[51] Many researchers play a role in formulating or evaluating public policies, such as ensuring that products are labelled accurately, that people can comprehend important information presented in advertising, or that children are not exploited by programme-length toy commercials masquerading as television shows.

Of course, to a large degree consumers are dependent on their governments to regulate and police safety and environmental standards. The extent of supervision may depend on such factors as the national political and cultural climate. Debates within the EU concerning regulation of the use of pesticides and food additives are examples here. In addition, a country's traditions and beliefs may make it more sympathetic to one or the other point of view expressed by consumers or producers. For example, the cross-Atlantic debate concerning market acceptance of genetically modified food products has also given rise to research about consumers' attitudes toward the acceptability and labelling of such products.[52]

There is also a growing movement to develop knowledge about **social marketing**, which attempts to encourage such positive behaviours as increased literacy and to discourage negative activities such as drunk driving.[53] A project in Sweden aimed at curbing adolescent drinking illustrates social marketing at work. The Swedish Brewers' Association is investing 10 million Skr (about $7.5 million) in a cooperative effort with the Swedish Non-Violence Project to change teens' attitudes to alcohol consumption.

Table 1.2 EU priorities for consumer policy

Ten major priorities for the future development of consumer policy have been defined by the European Commission:

- Major improvement in the education and information of consumers
- Completion, review and updating of the legislative framework to protect consumer interests in the internal market
- Review of the consumer aspects of financial services
- Review of the protection of consumer interests in the supply of essential public utility services
- Helping consumers to benefit from the information society
- Improving consumer confidence in foodstuffs
- Practical encouragement of sustainable consumption
- Strengthening and increasing consumer representation
- Helping the development of consumer policies in central and eastern Europe
- Review of consumer policy in developing countries.

Source: European Commission web page **www.cec.org.uk**.

'Smokers are more sociable than others . . . while it lasts.'

This Norwegian ad represents the many anti-smoking campaigns running in European markets.

Source: Lurzer's vol. 3, 1997.

Consumer researchers working on the project discovered that Swedish adolescents freely admit that they 'drink in order to get drunk' and enjoy the feeling of being intoxicated, so persuading them to give up alcohol is a formidable task. However, the teens reported they are also afraid of losing control over their own behaviour, especially if there is a risk of their being exposed to violence. And while worries about the long-term health effects of drinking don't concern this group (after all, at this age many believe they will live forever), female adolescents reported a fear of becoming less attractive as a result of prolonged alcohol consumption.

Based on these findings, the group commissioned to execute this project decided to stress a more realistic message of 'drink if you want to, but within a safe limit. Don't lose control, because if you do, you might get yourself into violent situations.' They made up the motto 'Alco-hole in your head' to stress the importance of knowing one's limits. This message is being emphasized along with strong visual images that appear on billboards, in video spots that depict situations involving young drinkers getting out of control, and in school presentations given by young people who will be credible role models for teens.[54]

Do marketers manipulate consumers?

One of the most common and stinging criticisms of marketing is that marketing techniques (especially advertising) are responsible for convincing consumers that they 'need' many material goods and that they will be unhappy and somehow inferior if they do not have these 'necessities'. The issue is complex, and one that is certainly worth considering: do marketers give people what they want, or do they tell people what they ought to want?

Philosophers have approached this issue when considering the concept of free will. It has been argued that in order to claim that consumers are acting autonomously in response to ads, the capacity for free will and free action must be present. That is, the consumer must be capable of deciding *independently* what to do, and not be prevented from carrying out that decision. This, it has been argued, is probably true for purely informative advertising, where only the product or store information required to make a rational decision is provided, whereas the case·for advertising where imagery or underlying motivations are tapped is not as clear.[55] Such a view presupposes that informative advertising is somehow more objective than imagery-based advertising. But functionality and utility are also important images of a specific cultural context that uses references to our reason to seduce us.[56] Three issues related to the complex relationship between marketing practices and consumers' needs are considered here.

Do marketers create artificial needs?

The marketing system has come under fire from both ends of the political spectrum. On the one hand, some conservative traditionalists believe that advertising contributes to the moral breakdown of society by presenting images of hedonistic pleasure. On the other hand, some leftists argue that the same misleading promises of material pleasure function to buy off people who would otherwise be revolutionaries working to change the system.[57] Through advertising, then, the system creates demand that only its products can satisfy.

One possible response to such criticism is that a need is a basic biological motive, while a want represents one way that society has taught us that the need can be satisfied. For example, while thirst is biologically based, we are taught to want Coca-Cola to satisfy that thirst rather than, say, goat's milk. Thus, the need is already there: marketers simply recommend ways to satisfy it. A basic objective of advertising is to create awareness that these needs exist, rather than to create them.

However, marketers are important engineers of our environment. And beyond the level of banality, needs are always formed by the social environment. Thus, in a sense, needs are always 'artificial' because we are interested in needs only in their social form. Alternatively, needs are never artificial because they are always 'real' to the people who feel them. 'Needs' are something we are socialized to have. In the case of the Coca-Cola vs. goat's milk example, it should be remembered that we do not eat and drink solely to satisfy a biological need. We eat and drink for a number of reasons, all of them embedded in our cultural context. What is the need of a sofa? A TV? A car? A textbook on consumer behaviour? Thus a better response would be that marketers do not create artificial needs, but they do contribute heavily to the

This ad was created by the American Association of Advertising Agencies to counter charges that ads create artifical needs. Compare this message with the Marketing opportunity on page 22. What is your conclusion?

Used with permission of American Association of Advertising Agencies.

socialization of people in contemporary society and thus to the establishment of the *social* system of needs. Consequently, marketers must take a share of responsibility for the development of society.

Is advertising necessary?

As the social commentator Vance Packard wrote over 30 years ago, 'Large-scale efforts are being made, often with impressive success, to channel our unthinking habits, our purchasing decisions, and our thought processes by the use of insights gleaned from psychiatry and the social sciences.' [58] The economist John Kenneth Galbraith believed that radio and television are important tools to accomplish this manipulation of the masses. Since virtually no literacy is required to use these media, they allow repetitive and compelling communications to reach almost everyone.

Goods are arbitrarily linked to desirable social attributes. One influential critic even argued that the problem is that we are not materialistic enough – that is, we do not sufficiently value goods for the utilitarian functions they deliver, but instead focus on the irrational value of goods for what they symbolize. According to this view, 'Beer would be enough for us, without the additional promise that in drinking it we show ourselves to be manly, young at heart, or neighbourly. A washing machine would be a useful machine to wash clothes, rather than an indication that we are forward-looking or an object of envy to our neighbours.'[59]

Such arguments seem somewhat outdated at the beginning of the twenty-first century, when advertising has been embraced as an art form in itself. Today, children are brought up to be both consumers and readers of advertising. A predominantly functional approach to consumption, as in the former planned economies of eastern Europe, did not make people happier, nor did it prevent them from establishing mythologies about other goods, such as the scarce and expensive ones from the West. Advertisers, just like marketers, are important communicators. Their importance must be accompanied by a sense of responsibility concerning the social and individual effect of their messages.

MARKETING OPPORTUNITY

As eastern European countries turn into market economies, some fear that consumers are being exploited as Western advertisements bombard them with products they didn't know they needed. In Poland, for example, previously taboo items like women's sanitary towels are being advertised for the first time, and new markets are being created for products such as pet food. The actions of one Polish entrepreneur illustrate how a consumer's search for social approval can be channelled into a want for a product.

Beginning with an ad campaign featuring Miss Poland, he single-handedly created a market for electronic hair removers (Polish women usually did not shave their legs). He also persuaded a leading Polish fashion designer to announce that hairy legs were out of fashion in Europe, and he organized local beauty contests to find the best legs. At the last report, he was selling 30,000 hair removers a month.[60]

Do marketers promise miracles?

Consumers are led to believe via advertising that products have magical properties; they will do special and mysterious things for them that will transform their lives. They will be beautiful, have power over others' feelings, be successful, be relieved of all ills, and so on. In this respect, advertising functions as mythology does in primitive societies: it provides simple, anxiety-reducing answers to complex problems. Is this a problem in itself?

Yes and no. The consumer is not an automaton that will react in a predefined way to certain stimuli. On the other hand, we are all partly socialized by the market and its messages. So, whereas the manipulative effectiveness of advertising is often overstated, there is little doubt that advertising creates and changes patterns of consumption. This is especially so in the new market economies, where the population does not maintain the same distance from and critical attitude to advertising messages and imagery.

But the effect is in general more subtle than simple manipulative persuasion. In most cases, advertisers simply do not know enough about people to manipulate them directly. Consider that the failure rate for new products ranges from 40 to 80 per cent. The main effect of advertising may often be found on the more general level, in the promotion of the idea that your self and your personal relationships, your success and your image all depend on your consumer choices.

Consumer behaviour as a field of study

Although people have been consumers for a very long time, it is only recently that consumption *per se* has been the focus of formal study. In fact, while many business schools now require that marketing students take a consumer behaviour course, most universities and business schools did not even offer such a course until the 1970s. Much of the impetus for the attention now being given to consumer behaviour was the realization by many business people that the consumer really *is* the boss.

Interdisciplinary influences on the study of consumer behaviour

Consumer behaviour is a very new field and, as it grows, it is being influenced by many different perspectives. Indeed, it is hard to think of a field that is more interdisciplinary. People with a background in a very wide range of fields – from psychophysiology to literature – can now be found doing consumer research. Consumer researchers are employed by universities, manufacturers, museums, advertising agencies and governments. Professional groups, such as the Association for Consumer Research, have been formed since the mid-1970s.

Researchers approach consumer issues from different perspectives. You might remember a fable about blind men and an elephant. The gist of the story is that each man touched a different part of the animal, and, as a result, the descriptions each gave of the elephant were quite different. This analogy applies to consumer research as well. A similar consumer phenomenon can be studied in different ways and at different levels depending on the training and interests of the researchers studying it.

Figure 1.2 covers some of the disciplines in the field and the level at which each approaches research issues. These disciplines can be loosely characterized in terms of their focus on micro vs. macro consumer behaviour topics. The fields closer to the top of the pyramid concentrate on the individual consumer (micro issues), while those towards the base are more interested in the aggregate activities that occur among larger groups of people, such as consumption patterns shared by members of a culture or subculture (macro issues).

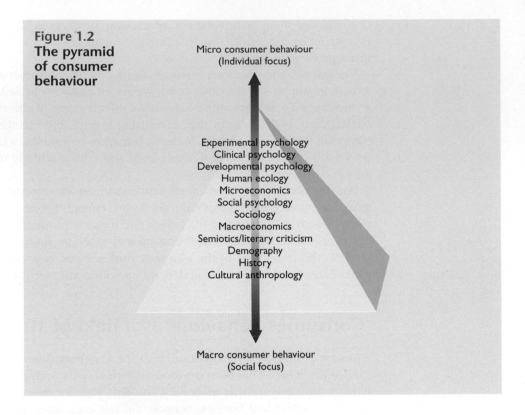

**Figure 1.2
The pyramid
of consumer
behaviour**

Micro consumer behaviour
(Individual focus)

Experimental psychology
Clinical psychology
Developmental psychology
Human ecology
Microeconomics
Social psychology
Sociology
Macroeconomics
Semiotics/literary criticism
Demography
History
Cultural anthropology

Macro consumer behaviour
(Social focus)

The issue of strategic focus

Many people regard the field of consumer behaviour as an applied social science. Accordingly, the value of the knowledge generated has traditionally been measured in terms of its ability to improve the effectiveness of marketing practice. Recently, though, some researchers have argued that consumer behaviour should not have a strategic focus at all; the field should not be a 'handmaiden to business'. It should instead focus on understanding consumption for its own sake, rather than because the knowledge can be applied by marketers.[61] This view is probably not held by most consumer researchers, but it has encouraged many to expand the scope of their work beyond the field's traditional focus on the purchase of consumer goods. And it has certainly led to some fierce debates among people working in the field! In fact, it can also be argued that business gets better research from non-strategic research projects because they are unbiased by strategic goals. Take a relatively simple and common consumer object like the women's magazine, found in every culture in a variety of versions. How much is there to say about the 'simple' act of buying such a magazine? Well, quite a lot. Table 1.3 lists some potential issues relevant for the marketing of or advertising in women's magazines which can be researched based on the variety of disciplines influencing consumer research.

This more critical view of consumer research has led to the recognition that not all consumer behaviour and/or marketing activity is necessarily beneficial to individuals or to society. As a result, current consumer research is likely to include attention to the 'dark side' of consumer behaviour, such as addiction, prostitution, homelessness, shoplifting or environmental waste. This activity builds upon the earlier work of researchers who, as we have seen, have studied consumer issues related to public policy, ethics and consumerism.

Table 1.3 Interdisciplinary research issues in consumer behaviour

Disciplinary focus	Magazine usage sample research issues
Experimental Psychology: product role in perception, learning and memory processes	How specific aspects of magazines, such as their design or layout, are recognized and interpreted; which parts of a magazine are most likely to be read
Clinical Psychology: product role in psychological adjustment	How magazines affect readers' body images (e.g. do thin models make the average woman feel overweight?)
Microeconomics/Human Ecology: product role in allocation of individual or family resources	Factors influencing the amount of money spent on magazines in a household
Social Psychology: product role in the behaviours of individuals as members of social groups	Ways that ads in a magazine affect readers' attitudes towards the products depicted; how peer pressure influences a person's readership decisions
Sociology: product role in social institutions and group relationships	Pattern by which magazine preferences spread through a social group
Macroeconomics: product role in consumers' relations with the marketplace	Effects of the price of fashion magazines and expense of items advertised during periods of high unemployment
Semiotics/Literary Criticism: product role in the verbal and visual communication of meaning	Ways in which underlying messages communicated by models and ads in a magazine are interpreted
Demography: product role in the measurable characteristics of a population	Effects of age, income and marital status of a magazine's readers
History: product role in societal changes over time	Ways in which our culture's depictions of 'femininity' in magazines have changed over time
Cultural Anthropology: product role in a society's beliefs and practices	Ways in which fashions and models in a magazine affect readers' definitions of masculine vs. feminine behaviour (e.g. the role of working women, sexual taboos)

The issue of two perspectives on consumer research

One general way to classify consumer research is in terms of the fundamental assumptions the researchers make about what they are studying and how to study it. This set of beliefs is known as a **paradigm**. Like other fields of study, consumer behaviour is dominated by a paradigm, but some believe it is in the middle of a *paradigm shift*, which occurs when a competing paradigm challenges the dominant set of assumptions.

The basic set of assumptions underlying the dominant paradigm at this point in time is called **positivism**. This perspective has significantly influenced Western art and science since the late sixteenth century. It emphasizes that human reason is supreme and that there is a single, objective truth that can be discovered by science.

Positivism encourages us to stress the function of objects, to celebrate technology and to regard the world as a rational, ordered place with a clearly defined past, present and future.

The newer paradigm of **interpretivism** questions these assumptions. Proponents of this perspective argue that our society places too much emphasis on science and technology, and that this ordered, rational view of consumers denies the complexity of the social and cultural world in which we live. Others feel that positivism puts too much emphasis on material well-being, and that its logical outlook is dominated by an ideology that stresses the homogeneous views of a predominantly Western and male culture.

Interpretivists on the other hand stress the importance of symbolic, subjective experience, and the idea that meaning is in the mind – that is, we each construct our own meanings based on our unique and shared cultural experiences, so there are no single right or wrong references. To the value we place on products, because they help us to create order in our lives, is added an appreciation of consumption as a set of diverse experiences.

The major differences between these two perspectives are summarized in Table 1.4.

In addition to the cross-cultural differences in consumer behaviour discussed earlier, it is also clear that research styles differ significantly between Europe and North America and also within European countries. For example, studies have shown that European researchers tend to consider the cultural dimension much more than their American counterparts.[62] Further, two special sessions at a recent European consumer research conference revealed that there seem to be important differences between the way consumer behaviour is conceived in Germany and Great Britain, for example.[63]

Consumer research is still moving on. From its original emphasis on buying behaviour and the factors influencing the decision-making process, the field gradually widened to become a study of consumer behaviour in a more general sense, also taking into consideration what happened before and after the purchase. After the introduction of the interpretivist approach, a broader research perspective has

Table 1.4 Positivist vs. interpretivist approaches to consumer behaviour

Assumptions	Positivist approach	Interpretivist approach
Nature of reality	Objective, tangible Single	Socially constructed Multiple
Goal	Prediction	Understanding
Knowledge generated	Time-free Context-independent	Time-bound Context-dependent
View of causality	Existence of real causes	Multiple, simultaneous shaping events
Research relationship	Separation between researcher and subject	Interactive, co-operative, with researcher being part of phenomenon under study

Source: Adapted from Laurel A. Hudson and Julie L. Ozanne, 'Alternative Ways of Seeking Knowledge in Consumer Research', *Journal of Consumer Research* 14 (March 1988): 508–21. Reprinted with the permission of The University of Chicago Press.

included many new and non-psychological facets in the increasingly complex portraits of consumers. And it can be argued that the field increasingly looks beyond the single individual and his or her social background and environment to describe and analyse the complex relationships that have led us to start characterizing our present society as a **consumer society**.[64] The facts of living in a consumer society and being surrounded by consumer culture permeate this book but will be dealt with in more detail in Chapter 14.

Chapter summary

- Consumer behaviour is the study of the processes involved when individuals or groups select, purchase, use or dispose of products, services, ideas or experiences to satisfy needs and desires.

- A consumer may purchase, use and/or dispose of a product, but these functions may be performed by different people. In addition, consumers may be thought of as role players who need different products to help them play their various parts.

- Market segmentation is an important aspect of consumer behaviour. Consumers can be segmented along many dimensions, including product usage, demographics (the objective aspects of a population, such as age and sex) and psychographics (psychological and lifestyle characteristics). Emerging developments, such as the new emphasis on relationship marketing and the practice of database marketing, mean that marketers are much more attuned to the wants and needs of different consumer groups.

- Marketing activities exert an enormous impact on individuals. Consumer behaviour is relevant to our understanding of both public policy issues (e.g. ethical marketing practices) and of the dynamics of popular culture.

- It is often said that marketers create artificial needs. Although this criticism is oversimplified, it is true that marketers must accept their share of the responsibility for how society develops and what is considered necessary to have and what is acceptable, nice and fun to do within society.

- The field of consumer behaviour is interdisciplinary: it is composed of researchers from many different fields who share an interest in how people interact with the marketplace. These disciplines can be categorized by the degree to which their focus is micro (the individual consumer) or macro (the consumer as a member of groups or of the larger society).

- There are many perspectives on consumer behaviour, but research orientations can roughly be divided into two approaches. The positivist perspective, which currently dominates the field, emphasizes the objectivity of science and the consumer as a rational decision-maker. The interpretivist perspective, in contrast, stresses the subjective meaning of the consumer's individual experience and the idea that any behaviour is subject to multiple interpretations rather than one single explanation.

KEY TERMS

Consumer behaviour (*p. 5*)
Consumer policy (*p. 19*)
Consumer society (*p. 27*)
Database marketing (*p. 13*)
Demographics (*p. 9*)
Exchange (*p. 6*)
Global consumer culture (*p. 16*)
Interpretivism (*p. 26*)
Market segmentation (*p. 8*)

Meaning (*p. 14*)
Paradigm (*p. 25*)
Popular culture (*p. 14*)
Positivism (*p. 25*)
Psychographics (*p. 9*)
Relationship marketing (*p. 13*)
Role theory (*p. 5*)
Social marketing (*p. 19*)

For additional material see the companion website at:
www.booksites.net/solomon_euro

Consumer behaviour challenge

1. This chapter states that people play different roles and that their consumption behaviours may differ depending on the particular role they are playing. State whether you agree or disagree with this perspective, giving examples from your own life.

2. Some researchers believe that the field of consumer behaviour should be a pure, rather than an applied, science. That is, research issues should be framed in terms of their scientific interest rather than their applicability to immediate marketing problems. Do you agree?

3. In recent years, there has been a large debate about the influence that internet shopping will have on our consumer lives. Try listing the changes that you personally have made in your buying and consumption patterns due to e-commerce. Compare these changes with changes experienced by other people from various social groups, e.g. somebody from your parents' generation, an IT freak, or somebody with a lower educational background.

4. Name some products or services that are widely used by your social group. State whether you agree or disagree with the notion that these products help to form bonds within the group, and support your argument with examples from your list of products used by the group.

5. Although demographic information on large numbers of consumers is used in many marketing contexts, some people believe that the sale of data on customers' incomes, buying habits, and so on constitutes an invasion of privacy and should be banned. Comment on this issue from both a consumer's and a marketer's point of view.

6. List the three stages in the consumption process. Describe the issues that you considered in each of these stages when you made a recent important purchase.

7. State the differences between the positivist and interpretivist approaches to consumer research. For each type of inquiry, give examples of product dimensions that would be more usefully explored using that type of research over the other.

8. What aspects of consumer behaviour are likely to be of interest to a financial planner? To a university administrator? To a graphic arts designer? To a social worker in a government agency? To a nursing instructor?

9 Select a product and brand that you use frequently and list what you consider to be the brand's determinant attributes. Without revealing your list, ask a friend who is approximately the same age but of the opposite sex to make a similar list for the same product (the brand may be different). Compare and contrast the identified attributes and report your findings.

10 Collect ads for five different brands of the same product. Report on the segmentation variables, target markets and emphasized product attributes in each ad.

Notes

1. Christian Alsted, 'De unge, smukke og rige – oldies', *Markedsføring* 11 (1992): 30.
2. Mike Featherstone, ed., *Global Culture. Nationalism, Globalization, and Modernity* (London: Sage, 1990).
3. Daniel Miller, 'Consumption as the Vanguard of History', in D. Miller, ed., *Acknowledging Consumption* (London: Routledge, 1995): 1-57.
4. Erving Goffman, *The Presentation of Self in Everyday Life* (Garden City, NY: Doubleday, 1959); George H. Mead, *Mind, Self, and Society* (Chicago: University of Chicago Press, 1934); Michael R. Solomon, 'The Role of Products as Social Stimuli: A Symbolic Interactionism Perspective', *Journal of Consumer Research* 10 (December 1983): 319-29.
5. Yiannis Gabriel and Tim Lang, *The Unmanageable Consumer* (London: Sage Publications, 1995).
6. Frank Bradley, *Marketing Management: Providing, Communicating and Delivering Value* (London: Prentice-Hall, 1995).
7. Cf. the extremely interesting account for the history of the Sony Walkman in Paul du Gay *et al.*, *Doing Cultural Studies: The Story of the Sony Walkman* (London: Sage/Open University, 1997).
8. Quoted in Evan Ramstad, 'Walkman's Plan for Reeling in the Ears of Wired Youths', *Wall Street Journal Interactive Edition* (18 May 2000).
9. Jeffrey F. Durgee, 'On Cézanne, Hot Buttons, and Interpreting Consumer Storytelling', *Journal of Consumer Marketing* 5 (Fall 1988): 47-51.
10. Annetta Miller, 'You Are What You Buy', *Newsweek* (4 June 1990) 2: 59.
11. George Anders, 'Web Giants Amazon, eToys Bet on Opposing Market Strategies', *Wall Street Journal Interactive Edition* (2 November 1999).
12. Natalie Perkins, 'Zeroing in on Consumer Values', *Ad Age* (22 March 1993): 23.
13. Quoted in March Magiera, 'Levi's Broadens Appeal', *Ad Age* (17 July 1989): 1(2).
14. Jennifer Lawrence, 'Gender-specific Works for Diapers – Almost Too Well', *Ad Age* (8 February 1993): S-10 (2).
15. 'Wrangler Ad Ropes in Men', *Marketing* (27 March 1997).
16. 'Tech Brands Face a Gender Divide', *American Demographics* (February 2000): 16.
17. Amy Barrett, 'Site Blends Frivolous, Serious to Draw French Women Online', *Wall Street Journal Interactive Edition* (11 April 2000).
18. Erika Check, Walaika Haskins, and Jennifer Tanaka, 'Different Appeals', *Newsweek* (13 March 2000): 15.
19. Casey Greenfield, 'Hits & Mrs.', *Yahoo! Internet Life* (March 2000): 132-5.
20. Charles M. Schaninger and William D. Danko, 'A Conceptual and Empirical Comparison of Alternative Household Life Cycle Models', *Journal of Consumer Research* 19 (March 1993): 580-94; Robert E. Wilkes, 'Household Life-Cycle Stages, Transitions, and Product Expenditures', *Journal of Consumer Research* 22, 1 (June 1995): 27-42.
21. Richard P. Coleman, 'The Continuing Significance of Social Class to Marketing', *Journal of Consumer Research* 10 (December 1983): 265-80.
22. BBS Radio (4 January 1997).
23. *Information* (26 September 2000): 11.
24. Özlem Sandikci and Güliz Ger, 'Fundamental Fashions: The Cultural Politics of the Turban and the Levi's', paper presented at the 2000 Association for Consumer Research Conference, Salt Lake City (19-22 October 2000).
25. Jean-Claude Usunier, *Marketing Across Cultures*, 3rd edn (London: Prentice-Hall, 2000).
26. Euromonitor, *European Marketing Data and Statistics*, 32nd edn (1997).
27. Rena Bartos, 'International Demographic Data? Incomparable!', *Marketing and Research Today* (November 1989): 205-12.
28. Søren Askegaard and Tage Koed Madsen, 'The Local and the Global: Homogeneity and Heterogeneity in Food Consumption in European Regions', *International Business Review* 7(6) (1998): 549-68.
29. *Information* (4 February 1997).
30. *Markedsføring* 18 (7 September 2000): 16.
31. *Markedsføring* 17 (25 August 2000): 8.
32. Richard Vezina, Alain d'Astous and Sophie Deschamps, 'The Physically Disabled Consumer: Some Preliminary Findings and an Agenda for Future

Research', in F. Hansen, ed., *European Advances in Consumer Research* 2 (Provo, UT: Association for Consumer Research, 1995): 277–81.

33. *Samvirke* 3 (March 1997).

34. 'Play Your Cards Right', *Marketing* (17 April 1997): 32–3.

35. Jonathan Berry, 'Database Marketing', *Business Week* (5 September 1994): 56 (7).

36. Barry Leventhal, 'An Approach to Fusing Market Research with Database Marketing', *Journal of the Market Research Society* 39(4) (1997): 545–58.

37. Rafer Guzman, 'Hotel Offers Kids a Room with a Logo', *Wall Street Journal Interactive Edition* (6 October 1999).

38. Sidney J. Levy, 'Symbols for Sale', *Harvard Business Review* 37 (July–August 1959): 117–24.

39. Susan Fournier, 'Consumers and Their Brands. Developing Relationship Theory in Consumer Research', *Journal of Consumer Research* 24 (March 1998): 343–73.

40. Douglas B. Holt, 'How Consumers Consume: A Typology of Consumption Practices', *Journal of Consumer Research* 22(1) (June 1995): 1–16.

41. For a discussion of this trend, see Russell W. Belk, 'Hyperreality and Globalization: Culture in the Age of Ronald McDonald', *Journal of International Consumer Marketing* 8 (3/4) (1995): 23–37.

42. For a fully fledged study of this process, see Tom O'Dell, *Culture Unbound. Americanization and Everyday Life in Sweden* (Lund: Nordic Academic Press, 1997).

43. Louise Lee, (no headline), *Wall Street Journal Interactive Edition* (22 September 1998).

44. Bernard Dubois and Gilles Laurent, 'Is there a Euro Consumer for Luxury Goods?', in W.F. van Raaij and G. Bamossy, eds, *European Advances in Consumer Research* 1 (Provo, UT: Association for Consumer Research, 1993): 58–69.

45. R. Pearce, 'Social Responsibility in the Marketplace: Assymetric Information in Food Labelling', *Business Ethics: A European Review* 8(1) (1999): 26–36.

46. *Politiken* (14 November 1997): 13.

47. Pasi Falk, 'The Advertising Genealogy', in P. Sulkunen, J. Holmwood, H. Radner and G. Schulze, eds, *Constructing the New Consumer Society* (London: Macmillan, 1997): 81–107.

48. *Morgenavisen Jyllands-Posten* (22 November 1996): 1, 6, 7.

49. Larry Edwards, 'The Decision Was Easy', *Advertising Age* 2 (26 August 1987): 106.

50. *Information* (2–3 September 2000): 11.

51. For scientific consumer research and discussions related to public policy issues, there is a special European journal, the *Journal of Consumer Policy*.

52. G. K. Hadfield and D. Thompson, 'An Information-based Approach to Labeling Bio-technology Consumer Products', *Journal of Consumer Policy* 21 (1998): 551–78; H. Sheehy, M. Legault and D. Ireland

'Consumers and Biotechnology: A Synopsis of Survey and Focus Group Research', *Journal of Consumer Policy* 21 (1998): 359–86.

53. Cf. Philip Kotler and Alan R. Andreasen, *Strategic Marketing for Nonprofit Organizations*, 4th edn (Englewood Cliffs, NJ: Prentice Hall, 1991); Jeff B. Murray and Julie L. Ozanne, 'The Critical Imagination: Emancipatory Interests in Consumer Research', *Journal of Consumer Research* 18 (September 1991): 192–44; William D. Wells, 'Discovery-Oriented Consumer Research', *Journal of Consumer Research* 19 (March 1993): 489–504.

54. Bertil Swartz, '"Keep Control": The Swedish Brewers' Association Campaign to Foster Responsible Alcohol Consumption Among Adolescents', paper presented at the ACR Europe Conference, Stockholm, June 1997; Anna Oloffson, Ordpolen Informations AB, Sweden, personal communication, August 1997.

55. Roger Crisp, 'Persuasive Advertising, Autonomy, and the Creation of Desire', *Journal of Business Ethics* 6 (1987): 413–18.

56. Søren Askegaard and A. Fuat Firat, 'Towards a Critique of Material Culture, Consumption and Markets' in S. Pearce, ed., *Experiencing Material Culture in the Western World* (London: Leicester University Press, 1997): 114–39.

57. William Leiss, Stephen Kline and Sut Jhally, *Social Communication in Advertising: Persons, Products, & Images of Well-Being* (Toronto: Methuen, 1986); Jerry Mander, *Four Arguments for the Elimination of Television* (New York: William Morrow, 1977).

58. Vance Packard, *The Hidden Persuaders* (London: Longmans Green, 1957).

59. Raymond Williams, 'Advertising: The Magic System', in *Problems in Materialism and Culture* (London: New Left Books, 1962).

60. Steven Engelberg, 'Advertising Pervades Poland, Turning Propaganda to Glitz', *New York Times* (26 May 1992) 2: A1.

61. Morris B. Holbrook, 'The Consumer Researcher Visits Radio City: Dancing in the Dark', in E. C. Hirschman and M.B. Holbrook, eds., *Advances in Consumer Research* 12 (Provo, UT: Association for Consumer Research, 1985): 28–31.

62. Jean-Claude Usunier, 'Integrating the Cultural Dimension into International Marketing', Proceedings of the Second Conference on the Cultural Dimension of International Marketing (Odense: Odense University, 1995): 1–23.

63. Flemming Hansen, ed., *European Advances in Consumer Research* 2 (Provo, UT: Association for Consumer Research, 1995).

64. Per Østergaard and Christian Jantzen, 'Shifting Perspectives in Consumer Research: From Buyer Behaviour to Consumption Studies' in S. C. Beckmann and R. Elliott, eds., *Interpretive Consumer Research* (Copenhagen: Copenhagen Business School Press, 2000): 9–23.

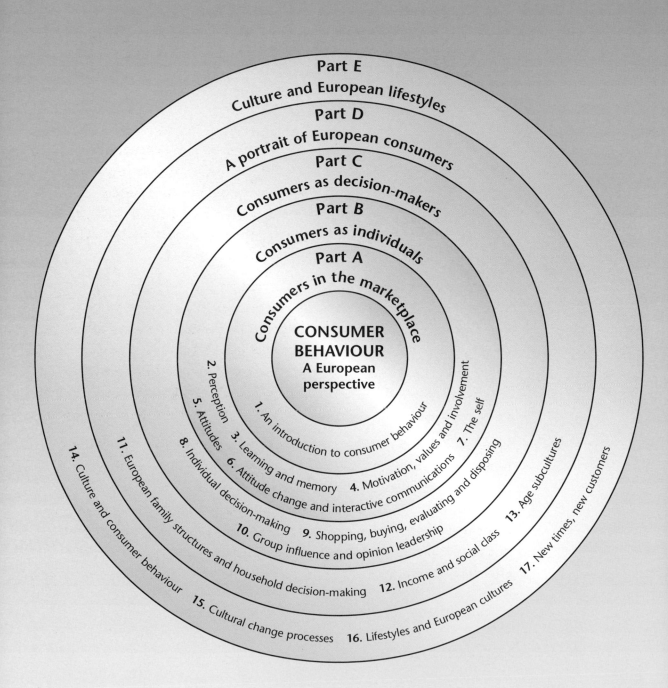

Part E
Culture and European lifestyles

Part D
A portrait of European consumers

Part C
Consumers as decision-makers

Part B
Consumers as individuals

Part A
Consumers in the marketplace

CONSUMER
BEHAVIOUR
A European
perspective

1. An introduction to consumer behaviour
2. Perception
3. Learning and memory
4. Motivation, values and involvement
5. Attitudes
6. Attitude change and interactive communications
7. The self
8. Individual decision-making
9. Shopping, buying, evaluating and disposing
10. Group influence and opinion leadership
11. European family structures and household decision-making
12. Income and social class
13. Age subcultures
14. Culture and consumer behaviour
15. Cultural change processes
16. Lifestyles and European cultures
17. New times, new customers

Part B

CONSUMERS AS INDIVIDUALS

In this part, we focus on the internal dynamics of consumers. While 'no man is an island', each of us is to some degree a self-contained receptor for information from the outside world. We are constantly confronted with advertising messages, products, other people persuading us to buy, and reflections of ourselves. Each chapter in this part will consider a different aspect of the consumer – sensations, memories and attitudes – that is invisible to others.

Chapter 2 describes the issues of perception and meaning; how information about products and other people is perceived and interpreted by the individual. Chapter 3 focuses on the ways this information is stored mentally and how it adds to our existing knowledge about the world as it is learned. Chapter 4 discusses our reasons or motivations for absorbing this information and how particular needs and wants influence the way we think about products.

Chapters 5 and 6 discuss how attitudes – our evaluations of all these products, ad messages, and so on – are formed and (sometimes) changed by marketers. When all of these 'internal' parts are put together, the unique role of each individual consumer as a self-contained agent in the marketplace will be clear. The last chapter in this part, Chapter 7, further explores how our views about ourselves affect what we do, want and buy.

Chapter 2

Perception and interpretation

Fabienne is a 35-year-old mother of two and works at the French National Railway Company's headquarters in Lyon Part Dieu. Twice a week she uses her two-hour lunch break to go to the nearby shopping centre, the biggest in Lyon. Today she had just two things in mind: a quick bite to eat and a present for her son, Georges-Hubert. As she enters the shopping centre she is immediately drawn to the appetizing aroma of pizza coming from a nearby fast-food restaurant. She decides to stop and buy a slice and a small bottle of mineral water. Next she decides to go to a shop called Nature et Découvertes, the French version of the Californian Nature Company. She has never been there before, but Catherine, her 14-year-old daughter, says that all her friends are talking about it. It seems to be the perfect place to buy a small microscope for Georges-Hubert's birthday.

On entering the shop she is very surprised. As in all shops her eyes are immediately and highly stimulated, but what makes this shop different is that there is more to it than that: all five of her senses are appealed to. The background music lets Fabienne discover birdsong, the sound of the forest, nature itself. As she is able to handle the products, Fabienne can familiarize herself with new shapes, new materials. An appeal is also made to her sense of taste when she is offered a cup of herbal tea. Finally, the natural aromas from the woods and plants combined with synthetic aromatics recreate the delicious atmosphere of the undergrowth to appeal to her sense of smell.

Fabienne likes the shop very much and for half an hour loses all sense of time. She wanders round as if in a trance. When she finally goes to the cash desk she realizes that not only does she have the little microscope in her hands, but a candle as well, and a book on trees.

Patrick Hetzel, University of Paris II, Panthéon-Assas

Introduction

We live in a world overflowing with sensations. Wherever we turn, we are bombarded by a symphony of colours, sounds and odours. Some of the 'notes' in this symphony occur naturally, such as the barking of a dog, the shadows of the evening sky or the heady smell of a rosebush. Others come from people: the person sitting next to you might have dyed blonde hair, bright pink jeans, and be wearing enough perfume to make your eyes water.

Marketers certainly contribute to this commotion. Consumers are never far from advertisements, product packages, radio and television commercials, and advertising hoardings that clamour for their attention. Each of us copes with this bombardment by paying attention to some stimuli and screening out others. When we do make a decision to purchase, we are responding not only to these influences but to our interpretations of them. The aim of Nature et Découvertes is to open the doors to the emotions, to a sense of wonder, to get in touch with one's capacity for pleasure. Unlike many other sales outlets there is an overdetermined motivation to create sensory effects to the utmost, to play on all five senses simultaneously. In a situation like this, the appeal is not so much to Fabienne's mind as to her perceptions, her emotions.

This chapter focuses first on the process of perception, in which sensations are absorbed by the consumer and used to interpret the surrounding world. After discussing the stages of this process, the chapter examines how the five senses (sight, smell, sound, touch and taste) affect consumers. It also highlights some of the ways in which marketers develop products and communications that appeal to the senses. Perception is especially interesting from an information-processing approach to the consumer, since it is the crucial threshold through which the information that will be processed will have to pass.

From an interpretive perspective, the issue of meaning becomes the more relevant one, since the crucial question here is how meanings are created, organized and used to make sense of the world and act in it according to a variety of social and personal schemes. Here, focus is shifted from the more objective existence of perceivable stimuli to the subjective processes of interpreting and understanding whatever phenomena appear relevant for the consumer.

The perceptual process

As you sit in a lecture hall, you may find your attention shifting. One minute you are concentrating on the lecture, the next you catch yourself daydreaming about the weekend ahead before you realize that you are missing some important points and tune back into the lecture.

People undergo stages of information processing in which stimuli are input and stored. However, we do not passively process whatever information happens to be present. Only a very small number of the stimuli in our environment are ever noticed. Of these, an even smaller number are attended to. And the stimuli that do

Figure 2.1 An overview of the perceptual process

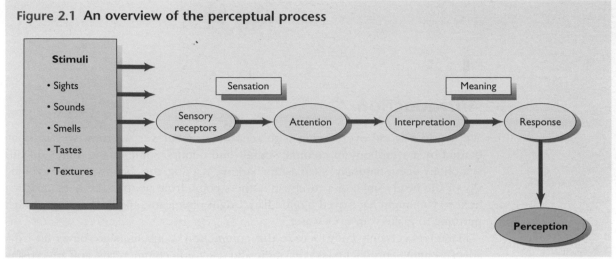

enter our consciousness are not processed objectively. The meaning of a stimulus is interpreted by the individual, who is influenced by his or her unique biases, needs and experiences. These three stages of *exposure (or sensation)*, *attention* and *interpretation* make up the process of perception. The stages involved in selecting and interpreting stimuli are illustrated in Figure 2.1, which provides an overview of the perceptual process.

From sensation to perception

Sensation refers to the immediate response of our sensory receptors (e.g. eyes, ears, nose, mouth, fingers) to such basic stimuli as light, colour and sound. **Perception** is the process by which these stimuli are selected, organized and interpreted. We process raw data (sensation); however, the study of perception focuses on what we add to or take away from these sensations as we assign meaning to them.

The subjective nature of perception is demonstrated by a controversial advertisement developed for Benetton. Because a black man and a white man were shown handcuffed together, the ad was the target of many complaints about racism after it appeared in magazines and on hoardings, even though the company has a reputation for promoting racial tolerance. People interpreted it to mean that the black man had been arrested by a white man.[1] Even though both men are dressed identically, people's prior assumptions shaped the ad's meaning. Of course, the company's goal was exactly that: to expose us to our own perceptual prejudice through the ambiguity of the photo.

Such interpretations or assumptions stem from our **schemas**, or organized collections of beliefs and feelings. That is, we tend to group the objects we see as having similar characteristics, and the schema to which an object is assigned is a crucial determinant of how we choose to evaluate this object at a later time.

Sensory systems

External stimuli, or sensory inputs, can be received on a number of channels. We may see an advertising hoarding, hear a jingle, feel the softness of a cashmere sweater, taste a new flavour of ice cream or smell a leather jacket.

UNITED COLORS
OF BENETTON.

One in a series of controversial ads from Benetton, trying to expose our prejudice to ourselves.

The inputs picked up by our five senses constitute the raw data that generate many types of responses. For example, sensory data emanating from the external environment (e.g. hearing a song on the radio) can generate internal sensory experiences: the song on the radio triggers a young man's memory of his first dance and brings to mind the smell of his date's perfume or the feel of her hair on his cheek.

Sensory inputs evoke historical imagery, in which events that actually occurred are recalled. Fantasy imagery results when an entirely new, imaginary experience is the response to sensory data. These responses are an important part of **hedonic consumption**, or the multi-sensory, fantasy and emotional aspects of consumers' interactions with products.[2] The data that we receive from our sensory systems determine how we respond to products.

Although we usually trust our sensory receptors to give us an accurate account of the external environment, new technology is making the linkage between our

This ad for a luxury car emphasizes the contribution of all our senses to the evaluation of a driving experience. Lexus use a lot of sensory imagery in their campaigns. In a recent British campaign, Lexus used the slogan 'The loudest sound you will hear inside the Lexus is yourself thinking', thereby alluding to a classic campaign for Rolls-Royce, which in the 1950s stated: 'At sixty miles an hour, the loudest sound you'll hear is the electric clock.'
©1993 by Lexus, a division of Toyota Motor Sales, USA, Inc. Used by permission.

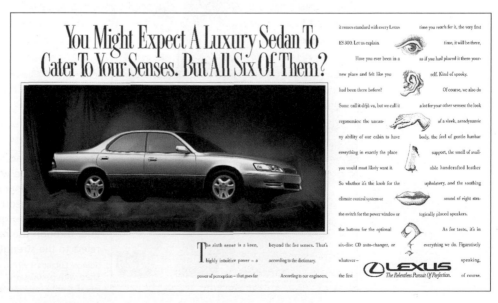

You Might Expect A Luxury Sedan To Cater To Your Senses. But All Six Of Them?

senses and reality more questionable. Computer-simulated environments, or *virtual reality*, allow surgeons to 'cut into' a person without drawing blood or an architect to see a building design from different perspectives. This technology, which creates a three-dimensional perceptual environment which the viewer experiences as being virtually real, is already being adapted to everyday pursuits, such as virtual reality games.

Enterprising business people will no doubt continue to find new ways to adapt this technology for consumers' entertainment – perhaps by developing 'virtual catalogues' which allow a person to browse through a shop without leaving his or her armchair. Until that time, though, we are mostly affected by marketers' ability to manipulate real sensory inputs along five distinct channels. In this section, we'll take a brief look at some of the processes involved in the business applications of sensory stimuli.

Vision

Marketers rely heavily on visual elements in advertising, store design and packaging. Meanings are communicated on the visual channel through a product's size, styling, brightness and distinctiveness compared with competitors.

Colour in the marketplace

Colours are rich in symbolic value and cultural meanings. For example, the display of red, white and blue evokes feelings of patriotism for both British and French people. Such powerful cultural meanings make colour a central aspect of many marketing strategies. Colour choices are made with regard to packaging, advertising and even shop fittings. Indeed, there is evidence to suggest that some colours (particularly red) are arousing while others (such as blue) are relaxing. The power of colours to evoke positive and negative feelings makes this an important consideration in advertising design. The popularity of different colours varies greatly across cultures. For example, in the mid-1980s while the British seemed to prefer avocado bathrooms, the French tended to opt for blue.[3] Thus, sometimes cultural differences in

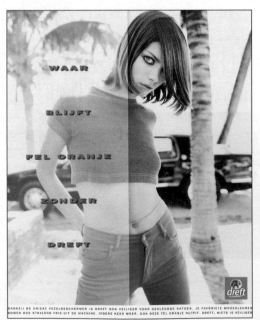

The text in the ad reads: 'Where would the bright orange be without Dreft?' Orange is the national colour of the Netherlands, so the ad simultaneously underlines the colour-protecting qualities of the product and, through the national colour code, refers to the strength of the Dutch nation.
Source: Lurzer's 1997.
Used with permission.

colour preferences create the need for marketing strategies tailored to different countries. These variations affect products made for kids as well as adults. In Italy, bambini ride in wild yellow and orange pushchairs. German infants are wheeled about in chartreuse. But in the USA, blue is the only colour pushchair that sells.[4]

The ability of colours to 'colour' our expectations is frequently exploited by marketers. Recently, marketers of products from beer and soft drinks to deodorant and petrol have launched new 'clear' products, which are intended to convey such qualities as purity and simplicity as a counter to over-elaborate product claims.[5] Green too has been gaining in popularity as consumers' ecological consciousness has grown.

Multicultural dimensions

Cultural differences in colour preferences create the need for marketing strategies tailored to different countries. While many northern European women now believe that heavy make-up is unprofessional and not very flattering, traditional femininity is still valued by Latin Americans. Mexican women, for example, are passionate in their love for vibrant lipsticks and nail varnish. Mexican girls are taught to be attentive to their appearance from early childhood. Baby girls have pierced ears, and housewives typically get dressed up in brightly coloured high heels to go to the supermarket. For these women, the 'natural look' is out. As one legal secretary in Mexico City explained, 'When you don't wear make-up, men look at you like you are sick or something.'[6]

Today colour is a key issue in package design. But the choice used to be made casually. The familiar Campbell's soup can was produced in red and white because a company executive liked the football kit at a particular university! Now colour is a serious business, and companies frequently employ consultants to assist in these decisions. In Switzerland an instant coffee container was redesigned with diagonal strips of mauve. The package won a design award, but sales dropped off significantly. Consumers did not associate the colour mauve with coffee.[7]

Colour also plays a dominant role in web page design: it directs a viewer's eye across the page, ties together design ideas, separates visual areas, organizes contextual relationships, creates mood and captures attention. Saturated colours such as green, yellow, cyan and orange are considered the best hues to capture attention, but don't overdo it: extensive use of these hues can overwhelm people and cause visual fatigue.[8]

Some colour combinations come to be so strongly associated with a particular corporation that they become known as the company's trade dress, and the company may even be granted exclusive use of the colours. Eastman Kodak is one such company and has successfully protected its yellow, black and red in court. As a rule, however, this protection is granted only if there is the possibility that consumers might be confused about what they are buying if a competitor uses the same colour combination.[9]

Since the number of competing brands for many types of products has proliferated, colour can be a critical spur to sales. When introducing a white cheese as a 'sister product' to an existing blue 'Castello' cheese, a Danish company launched it in a red package and under the name of Castello Bianco. The red package was chosen for maximum visibility and signal effect. Although taste tests were very positive, sales were disappointing. A semiotic analysis of consumer interpretations showed that the red packaging and the name gave the consumers the wrong association about the product type and its degree of sweetness (due to associations with

As the old saying goes, 'A picture is worth a thousand words'. The visual elements of a marketing message often speak volumes about a product's attributes. In this case, the message about roominess conveyed by this Singaporean ad for Mitsubishi is clear.

Euro RSCG Ball Partnership, Singapore.

the vermouth 'Martini Bianco'). It was relaunched in a white packaging and with the name 'white Castello', and almost immediately sales figures more than doubled.[10]

In a given year, certain colours appear to be 'hot' and show up over and over again in clothing, home furnishings, cars, and so on. But favourite colours disappear as fast as they come, to be replaced by another set of 'hot' colours the next year or season.

Consumers' colour choices may be affected by these trends. One simple reason is that consumers' choices are largely limited by the colours available in the stores. Few people, however, realize the extent to which these 'hot' colours result from choices made by industry insiders, in a process known as colour forecasting. Colour experts in various consulting groups meet periodically to predict what colours will best reflect a season in one year's, five years' and sometimes even ten years' time. Members make colour predictions based on cultural and social trends, and these recommendations are then used by manufacturers in production forecasting.

Smell

Odours can stir the emotions or have a calming effect. They can invoke memories or relieve stress. Some of our responses to scents result from early associations that call up good or bad feelings, and that explains why businesses are exploring connections between smell, memory and mood.[11] As one marketer noted, an example 'is a baby-powder scent that is frequently used in fragrances because the smell connotes comfort, warmth, and gratification'.[12] Another study found that consumers who viewed ads for either flowers or chocolate and who also were exposed to flowery or chocolatey odours spent more time processing the product information and were more likely to try different alternatives within each product category.[13]

Consumers' love of fragrances has contributed to a very large industry. Because this market is extremely competitive (30–40 new scents are introduced each year) and expensive (it costs an average of £30 million to introduce a new fragrance), manufacturers are scrambling to find new ways to expand the use of scents and odours in our daily lives. While traditional floral scents, such as rose and jasmine, are still widely used, newer fragrances feature such scents as melon peach (Elizabeth Arden's Sunflowers) and a blend of peach, mandarin orange, waterlily and white cloud rose (Sun Moon Stars by Karl Lagerfeld).[14] In addition to the perfume market, home fragrance products, consisting primarily of pot-pourri, room sprays and atomizers, drawer liners, sachets and scented candles, represent important markets. But the use of smell goes further than that. For example, plastic may give off an unpleasant 'artificial' smell, that most people would not like to associate with food. Therefore, it is an important task for the producers of the many kinds of plastic bowls and containers that we use in our kitchens to develop a nice and neutral odour for their products.[15] A new wrinkle in the use of scents is fragranced clothes. The textile industry is developing New Age fabrics with 'scentual' properties by embedding fragrances in microcapsules that are sewn to clothing. A French lingerie company is selling lingerie that emits scents when touched. Korean men are even buying lavender-scented suits to cover up liquor and cigarette odours.[16] The capsules 'pop' when jostled, so the more the man moves the better he smells – until the capsules wear out, at least.

Sound

Music and sound are also important to marketers. Consumers spend vast amounts of money each year on compact discs and cassettes, advertising jingles maintain brand awareness and background music creates desired moods.[17] Many aspects of sound affect people's feelings and behaviours. One British company stresses the importance of the sound a packaging gives when opened, after having watched consumers

MARKETING OPPORTUNITY

Step into British Airways' first class and business class lounge at London's Heathrow Airport, and one of the first things you'll notice is the smell. It is a fragrance called Meadow Grass, which the airline sprays into the air to enhance its brand image among its most valued customers. Upmarket British shirt retailer Thomas Pink also makes the effort to convey a 'signature smell', by introducing sensors in stores which emit the smell of freshly laundered cotton whenever customers pass by. 'The fragrance is air-dried linen, which is very evocative. Some customers like the smell so much they want to buy it' (it isn't for sale). Now, more than ever, there's more to advertising than meets the eye. Highly specialized sensory marketers are busy devising ways for marketers to tap the other four senses. Apart from smell, the sensation of touch is also making its way into the retail environment in new ways. Britain's Asda grocery chain (a unit of Wal-Mart Stores) removed the wrapping from several brands of toilet tissue in its stores so that shoppers could feel and compare textures. The result, the retailer says, was soaring sales for its own in-store brand, resulting in a 50 per cent increase in shelf space for the line. Even audio messages are taking on new approaches – instead of the in-store broadcast of 'Attention Shoppers', the sensory design research lab at the UK's Central St Martin's College has developed a very narrowcast wavelength, so that a customer feels like he or she is being personally spoken to regarding a product on a particular aisle. Finally, proponents of sensory marketing believe that computers and the internet are the next steps in bringing a rich set of stimuli to consumers. DigiScents, Inc. is a California-based developer of hardware and software which equips computers to emit scents, which will be loaded into cartridges of printers. DigiScents has already signed a strategic alliance with Procter & Gamble, and is working with the candy manufacturer eCandy (*eCandy.com*).[18]

open, close and reopen it several times during a test, clearly also listening to the right sound of the opening procedure.[19]

Another area of research that has widespread applications in consumer contexts is the effect of background music on mood. *Muzak* is heard by millions of people every day. This so-called 'functional music' is played in stores, shopping centres and offices either to relax or stimulate consumers. There is general agreement that muzak contributes to the well-being and buying activities of customers, though no scientific proof of this exists.

Touch

Although relatively little research has been done on the effects of tactile stimulation on consumer behaviour, common observation tells us that this sensory channel is important. Moods are stimulated or relaxed on the basis of sensations of the skin, whether from a luxurious massage or the bite of a winter wind.

Touch has even been shown to be a factor in sales interactions. There are considerable cultural differences in the world as well as within Europe concerning the appropriate amount and kind of touching in interpersonal interactions. In general, northern Europeans touch less than their southern European counterparts. Many British think the French shake hands excessively.[20]

Tactile cues have symbolic meaning. People associate the textures of fabrics and other products with underlying product qualities. The perceived richness or quality of the material in clothing, bedding or upholstery is linked to its 'feel', whether it is rough or smooth, soft or stiff. A smooth fabric such as silk is equated with luxury, while denim is considered practical and durable. Some of these tactile/quality associations are summarized in Table 2.1. Fabrics that are composed of rare materials or that require a high degree of processing to achieve their smoothness or fineness tend to be more expensive and thus are seen as being classier. Similarly, lighter, more delicate textures are assumed to be feminine. Roughness is often positively valued for men, while smoothness is sought by women.

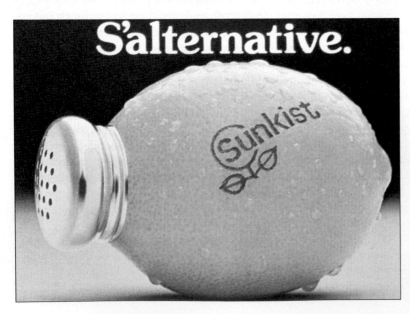

This ad metaphorically illustrates the natural quality and taste sensation of a lemon as a substitute for salt.
Used with permission.

COULD GLENFIDDICH EVER BE ANY SMOOTHER?
PERHAPS IF SERVED OVER A LITTLE ICE.

Just as fabrics are prized for their textures, some types of alcohol are rated according to their 'feel'. The British Lexus ad mentioned on page 37 quotes a car magazine saying that the engine is 'as velvety as the finest malt whisky'. This ad for a Scotch malt whisky emphasizes the product's smoothness metaphorically by equating its taste with the experience of gliding over ice.

William Grant & Sons, Inc.

Table 2.1 Tactile oppositions to fabrics

Perception	Male	Female	
High-class	Wool	Silk	Fine
Low-class	Denim	Cotton	↑↓
	Heavy	Light	Coarse

Taste

Our taste receptors contribute to our experience of many products. Sensory analysis is used to study the perception of the sensory qualities of various products. One study used sensory analysis to assess butter biscuits: the crispness, buttery taste, rate of melt, density, 'molar packing' (the amount of cookie that sticks to the teeth) and the 'notes' of the biscuit, such as sweetness, saltiness or bitterness.[21]

Food companies go to great lengths to ensure that their products taste as they should. Companies may use a group of 'sensory panellists' as tasters. These consumers are recruited because they have superior sensory abilities, and are then given six months' training. Or they rely on lay people, that is, ordinary consumers. In a blind taste test, panellists rate the products of a company and its competitors on a number of points. The results of such studies are important both to discover different consumer preferences and, thus, different consumer segments, and for the positioning of a company or a brand in terms of the most important sensory qualities of the product.[22]

Are blind taste tests worth their salt? While taste tests often provide valuable information, their results can be misleading when it is forgotten that objective taste is only one component of product evaluation. The most famous example of this mistake concerns New Coke, Coca-Cola's answer to the Pepsi Challenge.[23] The new formulation was preferred to Pepsi in blind taste tests (in which the products were not identified) by an average of 55 per cent to 45 per cent in 17 markets, yet New Coke ran into problems when it replaced the older version. Consumers' impassioned protests and letter-writing campaigns eventually forced the company to bring back 'Classic Coke'. People do not buy a cola for taste alone; they are buying intangibles such as brand image as well. Coca-Cola's unique position as part of an American, fun-loving lifestyle is based on years of marketing efforts that involve a lot more than taste alone. In 2000 Pepsi revived its Pepsi Challenge; the original promotion was widely believed to have been a driving force behind Coke's disastrous introduction of its sweeter New Coke.[24] This market blunder illustrates that taste is not solely a physiological process but depends on a variety of other factors as well, including aesthetics of the tasted product, situational contexts and a variety of cultural factors.[25]

Sometimes taste test failures can be overcome by repositioning the product. For example, Vernor's ginger ale did poorly in a taste test against leading ginger ales. When the research team introduced it as a new type of soft drink with a more tangy taste, it won easily. As an executive noted, 'People hated it because it didn't meet the preconceived expectations of what a ginger ale should be.'[26]

Exposure

▶ **Exposure** is the degree to which people notice a stimulus that is within range of their sensory receptors. Consumers concentrate on certain stimuli, are unaware of others, and even go out of their way to ignore some messages. An experiment by a bank illustrates consumers' tendencies to miss or ignore information in which they are not interested. After a law was passed in America requiring banks to explain details about money transfer in electronic banking, the Northwestern National Bank distributed a pamphlet to 120,000 of its customers at considerable cost to provide the required information – hardly exciting bedtime reading. In 100 of the leaflets, a phrase in the middle of the pamphlet offered the reader $10.00 just for finding that paragraph. Not a single person claimed it.[27]

Sensory thresholds

If you have ever blown a dog whistle and watched pets respond to a sound you cannot hear, you know that there are some stimuli that people simply are not capable of perceiving. And, of course, some people are better able to pick up sensory information than others.

▶ When we define the lowest intensity of a stimulus that can be registered on a sensory channel, we speak of a threshold for that receptor. The **absolute threshold** refers to the minimum amount of stimulation that can be detected on a sensory channel. The absolute threshold is an important consideration in designing marketing stimuli. A hoarding might have the most entertaining story ever written, but this genius is wasted if the print is too small for passing motorists to read it.

▶ The **differential threshold** refers to the ability of a sensory system to detect changes or differences between two stimuli. The issue of when and if a change will be noticed is relevant to many marketing situations. Sometimes a marketer may want to ensure that a change is noticed, such as when merchandise is offered at a discount. In other situations, the fact that a change has been made is downplayed, as in the case of price increases or when the size of the product is decreased (e.g. a chocolate bar).

The minimum change in a stimulus that can be detected is also known as the JND, which stands for 'just noticeable difference'. Many companies choose to update

The slight changes in the design of Campbell's canned soups illustrate the company's efforts to keep the central, traditional features of the brand packaging while making sure that the product does not begin to look dated.
Courtesy of Campbell Soup Company.

their packages periodically, making small changes that will not necessarily be noticed at the time. When a product icon is updated, the manufacturer does not want people to lose their identification with a familiar symbol.

Selective exposure

Experience, which is the result of acquiring stimulation, is one factor that determines how much exposure to a particular stimulus a person accepts. Perceptual filters based on consumers' past experiences influence what we decide to process.

Perceptual vigilance is a factor in selective exposure. Consumers are more likely to be aware of stimuli that relate to their current needs. These needs may be conscious or unconscious. A consumer who rarely notices car ads will become very much conscious of them when he or she is in the market for a new car. A newspaper ad for a fast-food restaurant that would otherwise go unnoticed becomes significant when one glances at the paper during a 5 o'clock class.

The advent of the video recorder has allowed consumers armed with remote control fast-forward buttons to be much more selective about which TV messages they are exposed to. By 'zipping', viewers can fast-forward through commercials when watching their favourite programmes. A video recorder marketed by Mitsubishi can remove the need for zipping. It distinguishes between the different types of TV signals used to broadcast programmes and commercials and automatically pauses during ads.[28]

Zipping has enhanced the need for advertising creativity. Interesting commercials do not get zipped as frequently. Evidence indicates that viewers are willing to stop fast-forwarding to watch an appealing or novel commercial. In addition, longer commercials and those that keep a static figure on the screen (such as a brand name or a logo) appear to counteract the effects of zipping; they are unaffected by a speed increase, since the figure remains in place.[29]

Perceptual selection

Although we live in an 'information society', we can have too much of a good thing. Consumers are often in a state of sensory overload, exposed to far more information than they are able or willing to process. People in a noisy, crowded bar or party for several hours may feel the need to step outside periodically to take a break. A consumer can experience a similar feeling of being overwhelmed after being forced to sift through the claims made by hundreds of competing brands. Further, the competition for our attention is increasing steadily with the increasing number of exposures to television commercials and other types of advertising.

Because the brain's capacity to process information is limited, consumers are very selective about what they pay attention to. **Perceptual selectivity** means that people attend to only a small portion of the stimuli to which they are exposed. Consumers practise a form of psychic economy, picking and choosing among stimuli, to avoid being overwhelmed by *advertising clutter*. The most advertising-ridden society is the USA, where the average adult is exposed to about 3000 pieces of advertising information every single day.[30] Television networks are jamming a record number of commercials into their shows – an average of 16 minutes and 43 seconds per programming hour.[31] And to make matters worse, this onslaught is growing as we now are bombarded by *banner ads* when we surf the Web as well. These online ads can in fact increase brand awareness after only one exposure, but only if they motivate surfers to click through and see what information is awaiting them.[32]

MARKETING PITFALL

Consumers and marketers are increasingly annoyed by advertising clutter. Advertising professionals feel that the proliferation of ads in both traditional media as well as non-traditional locations, such as in cinemas and on TV monitors in doctors' waiting rooms, is threatening the quality of their work. They fear that consumers will be so bombarded by competing stimuli that they won't be in a receptive frame of mind when their messages are transmitted. Consumers are also fed up. More and more surveys reveal that it takes a very good ad to avoid consumer boredom and hold the attention: either a good joke, nice aesthetics or some real information – whatever these may be.

Stimulus organization

People do not perceive a single stimulus in isolation. Our brains tend to relate incoming sensations to imagery of other events or sensations already in our memories based on some fundamental organizational principles. A number of perceptual principles describe how stimuli are perceived and organized.

The gestalt

These principles are based on work in **gestalt psychology**, a school of thought which maintains that people derive meaning from the totality of a set of stimuli, rather than from any one individual stimulus. The German word *Gestalt* roughly means whole, pattern or configuration, and this perspective is best summarized by the saying 'the whole is greater than the sum of its parts'. A piecemeal perspective that analyses each component of the stimulus separately will be unable to capture the total effect. The gestalt perspective provides several principles relating to the way stimuli are organized. Three of these principles, or perceptual tendencies, are illustrated in Figure 2.2.

Figure 2.2 Principles of stimulus organization derived from gestalt psychology

Principle of closure   Principle of similarity   Principle of figure-ground

The gestalt **principle of closure** implies that consumers tend to perceive an incomplete picture as complete. That is, we tend to fill in the blanks based on our prior experience. This principle explains why most of us have no trouble reading a neon sign, even if one or two of its letters are burned out, or filling in the blanks in an incomplete message, as illustrated by the J&B ad shown below. The principle of closure is also at work when we hear only part of a jingle or theme. Utilization of the principle of closure in marketing strategies encourages audience participation, which increases the chance that people will attend to the message.

The **principle of similarity** tells us that consumers tend to group together objects that share similar physical characteristics. That is, they group like items into sets to form an integrated whole. This principle is used by companies who have extended product lines, but wish to keep certain features similar, such as the shape of a bottle, so that it is easy for the consumer to recognize that he or she is in fact buying a shampoo of brand X.

Another important gestalt concept is the **figure-ground principle**, in which one part of a stimulus (the figure) will dominate while other parts recede into the background. This concept is easy to understand if one thinks of a photograph with a clear and sharply focused object (the figure) in the centre. The figure is dominant, and the

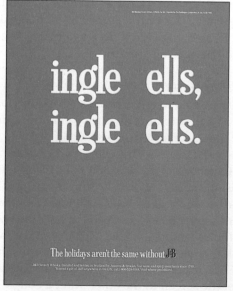

This J&B ad illustrates the use of the principle of closure, in which people participate in the ad by mentally filling in the gaps.
The Paddington Corporation.

eye goes straight to it. The parts of the configuration that will be perceived as figure or ground can vary depending on the individual consumer as well as other factors. Similarly, in marketing messages that use the figure-ground principle, a stimulus can be made the focal point of the message or merely the context that surrounds the focus.

Attention

▶ **Attention** is the degree to which consumers focus on stimuli within their range of exposure. Because consumers are exposed to so many advertising stimuli, marketers are becoming increasingly creative in their attempts to gain attention for their products.

A dynamic package is one way to gain this attention. Some consulting firms have established elaborate procedures to measure package effectiveness, using such instruments as an angle meter, which measures package visibility as a shopper moves down the aisle and views the package from different angles. Also, data from eye-tracking tests, in which consumers' eye movements as they look at packages and ads are followed and measured, can result in subtle but powerful changes that enhance their impact. Eye-tracking tests are also used to evaluate in-store displays.[33]

Some marketing analysts suggest that the internet has transformed the way business is done – they claim we are now operating in an *attention economy*. This means that the primary goal is to attract eyeballs, not dollars, to a website. The idea is that the amount of information companies can provide to consumers online is infinite – but there's only so much time people can devote to accessing it. So, a goal of interactive media is to buy and sell attention, as when a firm is paid to divert the traffic on one website to another site.[34] For example, many web companies, including *Amazon.com*, feature *affiliate programmes*, where people are paid to drive shoppers via links on their home pages to merchants. They get a cut of between 5 and 25 per cent of any transaction that results from their lead.[35]

Adaptation

▶ One factor affecting attention is **adaptation**, or the degree to which consumers continue to notice a stimulus over time. The process of adaptation occurs when consumers no longer pay attention to a stimulus because it is so familiar. Almost like drug addiction, a consumer can become 'habituated' and require increasingly stronger 'doses' of a stimulus for it to continue to be noticed. For example, a consumer on the way to work might read a new advertising hoarding, but after a few days it becomes part of the passing scenery.

Countering advertising clutter

Many marketers are attempting to counter the sensory overload caused by advertising clutter in order to call attention to their products. One expensive strategy involves buying large blocks of advertising space in order to dominate consumers' attention. IBM has experimented with buying two or three consecutive full-page newspaper ads. And Coca-Cola once bought a full five-minute block of commercial time on Danish television shortly before Christmas.

Other companies are using 'bookend ads', where a commercial for one product is split into parts that are separated by commercials for other products. The first part creates conflict, and the second resolves it. This technique motivates the viewer to keep watching in order to get the rest of the story. For example, a TV commercial for Tuborg's special Christmas brew beer showed a cartoon Santa Claus in his sleigh going from one side of the screen to the other. After a couple of other commercials, he reappears, this time meeting a Tuborg delivery van going in the opposite direction. He quickly turns his sleigh round and follows the van as Tuborg wishes everybody a merry Christmas and a happy new year.

Some advertisers have taken to printing part of their ads upside down to get the reader's attention. Perhaps reflecting differences in level of cultural involvement in advertising, the editor of a professional advertising newsletter noted, 'I find people don't like to work at reading their ads! Americans don't like it. There's a disorienting aspect they find uncomfortable. The English, on the other hand, like it.'[36]

Another solution has been to put ads in unconventional places, where there will be less competition for attention. These include the backs of supermarket shopping trolleys, underground pedestrian passes, floors of sports stadiums and even films, as the growing interest in product placement has shown.[37] More obscure places where advertisements can be found are public toilets,[38] petrol pump handles and on the steps in the London Underground.[39] And, of course, runner Linford Christie's specially designed contact lenses with the Puma logo created a lot of publicity.[40] An executive at Campbell's Soup, commenting on the company's decision to place ads in church bulletins, noted, 'We have to shake consumers up these days in order to make them take notice . . . Television alone won't do that. Now we have to hit them with our ads where they shop and play and on their way to work.'[41] Of course, such a policy may backfire if people are getting more and more weary of the difficulty of finding advertising-free moments in their lives.

Creating contrast

When many stimuli are competing to be noticed, one will receive attention to the extent that it differs from those around it. Stimuli that fall into unpredictable patterns often command a lot of attention. Size and colour differences are also powerful ways to achieve contrast. A black-and-white object in a colour ad is quite noticeable, as is a block of printed type surrounded by large amounts of white space. The size of the stimulus itself in contrast to the competition is also important. Similarly, a commercial that is intentionally produced in black and white may generate specific attention in a series of coloured TV commercials

MARKETING OPPORTUNITY

The music industry is trying new formats to reach potential buyers. MCA Records paid a major cinema chain to screen a music video by Tom Petty and the Heartbreakers prior to showing its scheduled films, while Mercury Records launched a bus placard campaign in 18 cities to promote a new John Mellencamp album. As the senior vice-president of marketing for MCA noted, 'There is a real strong corollary between people who see films and buy music. And one thing you know for sure is that when they are in a movie house, you've got them. They are all looking at the screen.'[42]

Self-referential advertising

In general, advertisements where sympathy and credibility are created by mocking advertising or other cultural stereotypes are becoming more and more common.[43] The pink Energizer Bunny™, who began life in regular Eveready Battery commercials, now goes gaily marching through fake commercials for such totally unrelated products as Alarm bath and shower soap – where the Bunny is appropriately dressed in raingear. As illustrated by the film stills shown on page 54, the Bunny's antics take the actors in these simulated commercials by surprise and usually the viewers as well. A mortgage company used the cliché of a homecoming soldier and the young waiting wife to advertise new restoration loans. After we have seen the woman

'What makes life a little greener . . . ?' This ad (part of a long-running and very successful campaign) for one of the Tuborg beer brands (Tuborg Green Label) uses a colour coding referring to both green as part of the brand name and the positive associations with the colour green: Spring, Freshness, Nature . . . At the same time, it uses the figure-ground principle to invite people to recognize the well-known shapes of a beer bottle and the unique 8-like shape of the Green Tuborg label in the ad.

Courtesy of Tuborg Marketing Denmark.

gazing out of the window and the soldier in the troop transport, he finally arrives home – only to hit his head hard on a low-hanging tie beam.[44]

Consequently, one of the hallmarks of modern advertising is that it creates a condition where advertising is becoming self-referential. An increasing number of ads and commercials are referring, often ironically or tongue-in-cheek, to other advertisements, and thus create a universe of their own, which in many ways is independent from the goods actually advertised. For example, Tasters' Choice coffee perfected the concept of an ongoing series of 'soap opera' commercials where a romantic relationship was slowly cultivated between two actors, a commercial form later adopted by other coffee brands such as Nestlé's Gold Blend.

Advertising thus becomes an art in itself and is appreciated as such rather than as deceptive information about products.[45] To a large extent, over time the relationship between the symbol and reality is increasingly difficult to discern, and the 'artificial' associations between advertisement symbols, product symbols and the real world may take on a life of their own. These developments towards a still more complex advertising universe have led to an increasing interest in the way consumer objects get meaning, both in advertisements and in our daily consumer lives. Marketers and consumers simply cannot take for granted any more that deciding what things mean is a straightforward process. If it ever was . . .

Interpretation: the meaning of things

▶ **Interpretation** refers to the meaning that people assign to phenomena, whether these come from stimuli from the outside world or the ideas and concepts coming from the person's own mind. Just as people differ in terms of the stimuli that they perceive, so the eventual assignment of meanings to these stimuli varies as well. Two people can see or hear the same event, but their interpretation of it may be completely different.

Consumers assign meaning to stimuli based on the *schema*, or set of beliefs, to which the stimulus is assigned. During a process known as **priming**, certain properties of a stimulus are more likely to evoke a schema than others. As evidenced by the case of Castello cheese quoted earlier, a brand name can communicate expectations about product attributes and colour consumers' perceptions of product performance by activating a schema.

A related field of study is *symbolic consumption*,[46] which focuses not so much on the good as stimulus *per se*, but rather on the meanings attached to the act of consuming the good. Here, in many cases, the good becomes a sign for some attributes that characterize the consumer, such as trendiness, wealth, femininity or other attributes that place the consumer in some subcultural context.

Polysemy is the word used to indicate that each sign, a product or an advertisement, conveys a number of meanings.[47] Consumers tend to project their own experiences and aspirations to assign meaning. Although ambiguity in product advertisements used to be seen as undesirable to marketers, polysemy is used creatively more and more frequently to generate contrast, paradox, controversy or interest. For example, a popular ad for Benson & Hedges cigarettes featured a group of people sitting around a dinner table, while a man wearing only pyjama bottoms stood in the background. This ambiguous character yielded valuable publicity for the company as people competed to explain the meaning of the mysterious 'pyjama man'.

The role of symbolism in interpretation

When we try to make sense of a marketing phenomenon, whether a distinctive package, an elaborately staged television commercial or perhaps a model on the cover of a magazine, we do so by interpreting its meaning in the light of associations we have with these images. For this reason much of the meaning we take away is influenced

An illustration of how to read an advertisement semiotically. Note again the reference to smoothness, also found in some of the other alcohol ads in this chapter.
Schieffelin & Somerset Co.

by what we make of the symbolism we perceive. After all, on the surface many marketing images have virtually no literal connection to actual products. What does a cowboy have to do with a bit of tobacco rolled into a paper tube? How can celebrities such as the female band All Saints enhance the image of a pre-pay phone service?[48]

For assistance in understanding how consumers interpret the meanings of symbols, some marketers are turning to a field of study known as **semiotics**, which examines the correspondence between signs and symbols and their role in the assignment of meaning.[49] Semiotics is important to the understanding of consumer behaviour, since consumers use products to express their social identities. Products are given meanings by their producers and we rely on advertising to work out what those meanings are. As one set of researchers put it, 'advertising serves as a kind of culture/consumption dictionary; its entries are products, and their definitions are cultural meanings'.[50] However, as we shall see, the meanings of products in use may vary a lot from those intended by the marketer.

According to the semiotician Charles Sanders Peirce, every message has three basic components: an object, a sign and an interpretant. A marketing message such as a Marlboro ad can be read on different levels. On the lowest level of reading, the **object** would be the product that is the focus of the message (e.g. Marlboro cigarettes). The **sign** is the sensory imagery that represents the intended meanings of the object (the contents of the ad, in this case the cowboy). The **interpretant** is the meaning derived (e.g. this man smokes these cigarettes). But this man is not any man. He is a cowboy – and not just any cowboy. The interpretant 'man (cowboy) smoking these cigarettes' in itself becomes a sign, especially since we have already seen many examples of these ads from this company. So, on the second, connotative level, this sign refers to the fictive personality of 'the Marlboro Man', and its interpretant consists of all the connotations attached to the Marlboro Man, for example his being a 'rugged, individualistic American'. On the third level, called the ideological level, the interpretant of the 'rugged, individualistic American' becomes a sign for what is stereotypically American. So its object is 'America', and the interpretant all the ideas and characteristics that we might consider as typically and quintessentially American. This semiotic relationship is shown in Figure 2.3. By means of such a chain of meanings, the Marlboro ad both borrows from and contributes to the reinforcement of a fundamental 'myth of America'. We will return to the discussion of myths and consumption in Chapter 14.

From the semiotic perspective of Peirce, signs are related to objects in one of three ways. They can resemble objects, be connected to them with some kind of causal or other relation, or be conventionally tied to them.[51] An *icon* is a sign that resembles the product in some way (e.g. Apple Computers uses the image of an apple to represent itself). An *index* is a sign that is connected to a product because they share some property (e.g. the pine tree on certain cleaning products conveys the shared property of fresh, natural scent). A **symbol** is a sign that is related to a product through purely conventional associations (e.g. the Mercedes star which in addition to the Mercedes-Benz company provides associations with German industrial quality and ingenuity).

The Cognac Hennessy ad illustrates some of the subtle semiotic processes that convey meaning in advertising. The product, cognac, is a luxury alcoholic beverage associated with a soft, smooth taste, luxurious surroundings, and a large price tag. The label is an icon – it literally represents the product. Silk is used as an index that shares properties with the cognac – it is smooth and also associated with luxury. The woman wrapped in a silk gown is a symbol – she stands for sex appeal, smoothness

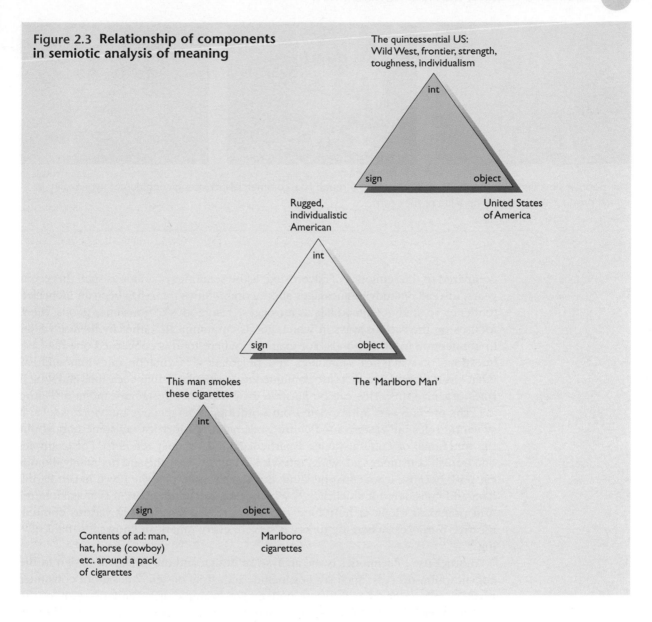

Figure 2.3 **Relationship of components in semiotic analysis of meaning**

and luxury. The creators of the ad hope that these properties will transfer to people's perceptions of the product.

Our symbolic world provides a powerful 'playground' for marketers to convey product attributes to consumers. For example, expensive cars, designer fashions and diamond jewellery – all widely recognized symbols of success – frequently appear in ads to associate products with affluence or sophistication. The rhetoric of advertising is an additional field of analysis which has been useful for the discussion of how advertising communicates its messages.[52] Semiotic analysis of ads has been connected to product and brand life cycles in order to establish some guidelines about when to use the most complex advertising forms.[53] However, one problem with a semiotic analysis of ads is the difference between the meanings generated by a concentrated analytical reader and a consumer in a real-life situation – how many will actually capture the finer nuances in a quick glance at an ad in a magazine?[54]

With the possible exception of fashion, which we shall return to in a later chapter, one aspect of the semiotics of consumption, which used to be relatively neglected

The popular pink Energizer Bunny™, gaily marching through fake commercials, creates a condition of hyperreality in which product symbols take on a life of their own.
The Eveready Battery Company Inc.

compared to the semiotics of advertising, is the semiotics of goods as such. In recent years, instead of studying messages about commodities there has been an increased tendency to study commodities as messages.[55] Semiotics of consumer goods, then, focuses on the various ways in which goods communicate either by themselves or in connection to other goods. For example, where food is concerned one may ask questions of syntactics, semantics and pragmatics.[56] Syntactic questions address what kinds of food products are combined for particular eating occasions and which rules organize this. This can be illustrated by the mock restaurant menu in Figure 2.4. The menu is very appropriate from a nutritional perspective but violates several syntactic rules in Western food cultures. Semantic properties say something about the functional or cultural values a particular food product refers to. For example, one Danish consumer said, when interviewed on TV, that she and her family did not eat pork because it was unappetizing. But she also said that she loved Italian Parma ham and considered it a delicacy.[57] Which semantic differentiation is at stake here? And pragmatics look at how food products are used for serving various communicative purposes. When the turkey is served, every American knows it's thanksgiving.[58]

Another use of semiotics is the analysis of design and the effects of design in the consumption process. Such studies include industrial design,[59] design of consumer goods[60] and design of distribution outlets. For example, in a semiotic study of the meanings and expectations consumers would attach to a new hypermarket, four different value profiles among potential customers were generated using a semiotic technique known as the **semiotic square**. Its point of departure is that all meanings are based on an opposition. Thus, night is only meaningful in relation to day, man in relation to woman, etc. But in addition to this first opposition comes a second one consisting of the negation of the first one. Thus, not only can we conceive of male and female but also of 'non-male' (e.g. a sissy!) and 'non-female' (e.g. a tomboy). In this context, utilitarian values were opposed to existential values, the former referring to practical and economical aspects of shopping in the hypermarket and the latter to the hypermarket's relation to life values and personal experiences. Furthermore, non-utilitarian (or ludic, referring to customers' search for playfulness at the shopping centre) and non-existential (or critical, referring to a customer's careful analysis of features such as quality/price ratios) values were generated. These four value profiles were linked to preferences for different designs of the hypermarket and its interior, thus helping the planners to conceive a type of hypermarket that was pleasing to most consumers.[61] This included the organization of walkways

Figure 2.4 This menu from the restaurant 'Au Gourmet Sans Entraves' (which translates as something like 'The Gourmet Without Rules') illustrates how culture shapes our expectations, i.e. our meanings, about what to eat when, and with what. How many broken rules can you find? This is probably also culture-dependent. Remember that it was constructed by a Frenchman, who obviously had a certain set of inappropriate constellations and timings in mind.

AU GOURMET SANS ENTRAVES

Restaurant
***

MENU

Breakfast	Dinner
(10.30 – 13.30)	(15.00 – 19.30)
Salad of Exotic	Season's Salad
Fruits	Wild Salmon Escalope with
Spaghetti alla Carbonara	Beef Marrow
Onion Soup with	Soup Du Barry
Toast	Sorbets
Ice Tea	Capuccino
	Butter Croissants
	Liqueur or Kir
	Royal

Source: Claude Fischler, *L'homnivore* (Paris: Editions Odile Jacob, 1990). Used with permission.

and aisles, plazas, the placement of various product categories, and so on. No wonder, in such staged environments, that other researchers have studied the relationship between reality and fiction in a shopping centre environment using a semiotic square.[62]

An obvious but surprisingly underrepresented field of usage for semiotics is the study of brand meanings. The communication of logos[63] or the differences between various brands may be studied through the various meanings the brands evoke among consumers. An innovative use of semiotics is the suggestion that brands may play roles in our daily lives that can be compared to roles played by different personalities in traditional stories or narratives such as folk tales or fairytales. It is thus possible to speak of a *hero* brand, the brand positioned as the benevolent solver of problems. While this may seem pretty obvious, one might also think of a *villain* brand, which could be the aggressive competitor challenging the virtues of the market leaders, or brands targeting various counter-cultural segments.[64] For example, the cola war between Pepsi and Coca-Cola has been seen as the villain

Figure 2.5 Main functions of a brand in a semiotic square perspective

Source: Benoit Heilbrunn, 'Les facteurs d'attachement à la marque', PhD dissertation, University of Paris-Dauphine, 2001. Used with permission.

brand of the youthful 'new generation' brand sneering at the 'nicer' but also more boring and 'politically and morally correct' market leader. This positioning game, in turn, sets the stage for the marketing opportunities of eventual local brands.[65]

More recently, the above-mentioned approach to studying hypermarkets has been extended to include the benefits consumers get from brands. Hence, it is suggested that brands may generally specialize in appealing to either practical, experiential, critical, or ludic values. Figure 2.5 shows the semiotic square used in both the hypermarket and the brand study, and exemplifies the main functions of a brand, i.e. what a brand may provide its consumers, in relation to the four valorizations.

There are of course other ways of analysing brand meanings than the purely semiotic one. The important thing, which is also demonstrated by the cola story referred to above, is that the meaning of a brand must be seen not only in light of the design and appearance of the product and brand logo itself and the individual interpreting it and using it but also in the context of the marketing environment with its multitude of messages and profilings and the general social environment with its dominant values and symbols.[66]

Brand positioning

Thus, characteristics of a product must be interpreted in a specific context: in light of what we already know about a product category and the characteristics of existing brands. Perceptions of a brand comprise both its functional attributes (its features, its price, and so on) and its symbolic attributes (its image, and what we think it says about us when we use it). We'll look more closely at issues such as brand image in later chapters, but for now it's important to keep in mind that our evaluation of a product typically is the result of what it means rather than what it does. This meaning – as perceived by consumers – constitutes the product's market position, and it may have more to do with our expectations of product performance as communicated by its colour, packaging or styling than with the product itself.

How does a marketer determine where a product actually stands in the minds of consumers? One technique is to ask them what attributes are important to them, and how they feel competitors rate on these attributes. This information can be used to construct a perceptual map, a vivid way to paint a picture of where products or

Figure 2.6 HMV perceptual map

brands are 'located' in consumers' minds. GRW Advertising created the perceptual map shown in Figure 2.6 for HMV, a chain of British music shops. The agency wanted to know more about how its target market, frequent buyers of CDs, perceived the different stores they might patronize. GRW plotted perceptions of such attributes of competitors as selection, price, service and 'hipness' on an imaginary street map. Based on this research, the firm determined that HMV's strengths were service, selection, and the stores' abilities to cater to local taste because store managers can order their own stock. This map was used in the strategic decision to specialize in music products as opposed to competing by offering other items sold by the competition, such as video games, fragrances and computer CD-ROMs.[67]

Positioning strategy

A **positioning strategy** is a fundamental part of a company's marketing efforts as it uses elements of the marketing mix (i.e. product design, price, distribution and marketing communications) to influence the consumer's interpretation of its meaning. There are many dimensions that can be used to establish a brand's position in the marketplace. These include:[68]

- *Lifestyle*: Grey Poupon mustard is a 'higher class' condiment.
- *Price leadership*: L'Oréal's Noisôme face cream is sold in upmarket beauty shops

in the United States, while its Plenitude brand is available for one-sixth of the price in discount stores – even though both are based on the same chemical formula.[69]

● *Attributes*: Bounty paper towels are 'the quicker picker upper'.

● *Product class*: the Mazda Miata is a sporty convertible.

● *Competitors*: Northwestern Insurance is 'the quiet company'.

● *Occasions*: Wrigley's gum is an alternative at times when smoking is not permitted.

● *Users*: Levi's Dockers are targeted primarily at men in their twenties to forties.

● *Quality*: at Ford, 'quality is job 1'.

New meanings?

The increased focus on the meaning of various consumption processes plays a central role in much of the recent challenging consumer behaviour theory. Due to the fact that consumers have become increasingly aware of how they communicate through their consumption as well as what they communicate has led to the designation of the present world as a 'semiotic world'.[70] Furthermore, it has been argued that we feel more confident in creating our own messages rather than just following what is proposed by marketing or fashion statements. This tendency to eclecticism means that we are more and more likely to match things, such as articles of clothing, furniture or even lifestyles, that traditionally have not been perceived as fitting together. In some of the final chapters of this book where we are dealing with issues such as consumer culture and postmodernism, we will elaborate on some of these new ways of generating meanings through consumption.

Chapter summary

● Perception is the process by which physical sensations such as sights, sounds and smells are selected, organized and interpreted. The eventual interpretation of a stimulus allows it to be assigned meaning. A perceptual map is a widely used marketing tool which evaluates the relative standing of competing brands along relevant dimensions.

● Marketing stimuli have important sensory qualities. We rely on colours, odours, sounds, tastes and even the 'feel' of products when forming evaluations of them.

● Not all sensations successfully make their way through the perceptual process. Many stimuli compete for our attention, and the majority are not noticed or comprehended.

● People have different thresholds of perception. A stimulus must be presented at a certain level of intensity before it can be detected by sensory receptors.

● Some of the factors that determine which stimuli (above the threshold level) do get perceived are the amount of exposure to the stimulus, how much attention it generates and how it is interpreted. In an increasingly crowded stimulus environment, advertising clutter occurs when too many marketing-related messages compete for attention.

● A stimulus that is attended to is not perceived in isolation. It is classified and organized according to principles of perceptual organization. These principles are guided by a gestalt, or overall, pattern. Specific grouping principles include closure, similarity and figure-ground relationships.

- But beyond perception, interpretation is the decisive factor in getting meaning from our surroundings. We make sense of the world through the interpretation of signs. This interpretation is often shared by others, thus forming common languages and cultures. The degree to which the symbolism is consistent with our previous experience affects the meaning we assign to related objects. Every marketing message contains a relationship between the product, the sign or symbol, and the interpretation of meaning. A semiotic analysis involves the correspondence between message elements and the meaning of signs.

- Signs provide meaning in various ways and may be typified as icons, indexes and symbols. The intended meaning may be literal (e.g. an icon like a street sign with a picture of children playing). The meaning may be indexical: it relies on shared characteristics (e.g. the horizontal stripe in a stop sign means do not pass beyond this). Finally, meaning can be conveyed by a symbol, where an image is given meaning by convention or by agreement by members of a society (e.g. 'Stop' signs are octagonal, while 'Give Way' signs are triangular).

- Semiotic analysis is becoming increasingly popular in our attempts to understand meanings attached to products or brands and their positioning, but also in understanding shopping environments, for example.

KEY TERMS

Absolute threshold *(p. 44)*	**Perceptual selectivity** *(p. 46)*
Adaptation *(p. 48)*	**Polysemy** *(p. 51)*
Attention *(p. 48)*	**Positioning strategy** *(p. 57)*
Differential threshold *(p. 44)*	**Priming** *(p. 51)*
Exposure *(p. 44)*	**Principle of closure** *(p. 47)*
Figure-ground principle *(p. 47)*	**Principle of similarity** *(p. 47)*
Gestalt psychology *(p. 46)*	**Schema** *(p. 36)*
Hedonic consumption *(p. 37)*	**Semiotic square** *(p. 54)*
Interpretant *(p. 52)*	**Semiotics** *(p. 52)*
Interpretation *(p. 50)*	**Sensation** *(p. 36)*
Object *(p. 52)*	**Sign** *(p. 52)*
Perception *(p. 36)*	**Symbol** *(p. 52)*

For additional material see the companion website at:
www.booksites.net/solomon_euro

Consumer behaviour challenge

1 Many studies have shown that our sensory detection abilities decline as we grow older. Discuss the implications of the absolute threshold for marketers attempting to appeal to the elderly.

2 Interview 3–5 male and 3–5 female friends regarding their perceptions of both men's and women's fragrances. Construct a perceptual map for each set of products. Based on your map of perfumes, do you see any areas that are not adequately served by current offerings? What (if any) gender differences did you obtain regarding both the relevant dimensions used by raters and the placement of specific brands along these dimensions?

3 Assume that you are a consultant for a marketer who wants to design a package for a new premium chocolate bar targeted at an affluent market. What recommendations would you provide in terms of such package elements as colour, symbolism and graphic design? Give the reasons for your suggestions.

4 Do you believe that marketers have the right to use any or all public spaces to deliver product messages? Where would you draw the line in terms of places and products that should be restricted?

5 Find one ad that is rich in symbolism and perform a semiotic analysis of it. Identify each type of sign used in the ad and the product qualities being communicated by each. Comment on the effectiveness of the signs that are used to communicate the intended message.

6 Collect a set of current ads for one type of product (e.g. personal computers, perfumes, laundry detergents or trainers) from magazines, and analyse the colours employed. Describe the images conveyed by different colours, and try to identify any consistency across brands in terms of the colours used in product packaging or other aspects of the ads.

7 Look through a current magazine and select one ad that captures your attention over the others. Give the reasons why.

8 Find ads that utilize the techniques of contrast and novelty. Give your opinion of the effectiveness of each ad and whether the technique is likely to be appropriate for the consumers targeted by the ad.

9 Try to construct new and alternative chains of meaning to Figure 2.5 after it has become known that the actor who 'played' the Marlboro Man for many years died of lung cancer.

Notes

1. Kim Foltz, 'Campaign on Harmony Backfires for Benetton', *New York Times* (20 November 1989): D8.
2. Elizabeth C. Hirschman and Morris B. Holbrook, 'Hedonic Consumption: Emerging Concepts, Methods, and Propositions', *Journal of Marketing* 46 (Summer 1982): 92–101.
3. Maryon Tysoe, 'What's Wrong with Blue Potatoes?', *Psychology Today* (December 1985) 2: 6.
4. Barbara Carlton, 'Pink, Yellow or Green Just Won't Cut It; American Parents Choose Navy Strollers', *Wall Street Journal Interactive Edition* (25 March 1998).
5. 'Crystal Clear Persuasion', *Tufts University Diet & Nutrition Letter* (January 1993): 1.
6. Dianne Solis, 'Cost No Object for Mexico's Makeup Junkies', *Wall Street Journal* (7 June 1994): B1.
7. Tysoe, 'What's Wrong with Blue Potatoes?'
8. Mike Golding and Julie White, *Pantone Color Resource Kit* (New York: Hayden Publishing, 1997); Caroline Lego, *Effective Web Site Design: A Marketing Strategy for Small Liberal Arts Colleges,* Coe College, unpublished honours thesis, 1998; T. Long, 'Human Factors Principles for the Design of Computer Colour Graphics Display', *British Telecom Technology Journal* 2(3) (July 1994): 5–14; Morton Walker, *The Power of Color* (Garden City, NY: Avery Publishing Group, 1991).
9. Meg Rosen and Frank Alpert, 'Protecting Your Business Image: The Supreme Court Rules on Trade Dress', *Journal of Consumer Marketing* 11(1) (1994): 50–5.

10. 'Ny emballage og nyt navn fordoblede salget', *Markedsføring* 12 (1992): 24.

11. Pam Scholder Ellen and Paula Fitzgerald Bone, 'Does it Matter if it Smells? Olfactory Stimuli as Advertising Executional Cues', *Journal of Advertising* 27(4) (Winter 1998): 29–40.

12. Quoted in Cynthia Morris, 'The Mystery of Fragrance', *Essence* 71 (May 1988) 3: 71.

13. Deborah J. Mitchell, Barbara E. Kahn and Susan C. Knasko, 'There's Something in the Air: Effects of Congruent or Incongruent Ambient Odor on Consumer Decision Making', *Journal of Consumer Research* 22 (September 1995): 229–38; for a review of olfactory cues in store environments, see also Eric R. Spangenberg, Ayn E. Crowley and Pamela W. Henderson, 'Improving the Store Environment: Do Olfactory Cues Affect Evaluations and Behaviors?', *Journal of Marketing* 60 (April 1996): 67–80.

14. Suein L. Hwang, 'Seeking Scents that No One Has Smelled', *Wall Street Journal* (10 August 1994): B1 2.

15. Joel Leonard, Fragrance Consultant, 'The Smell in Marketing', guest lecture at Odense University, 12 September 1994.

16. Hae Won Choi, 'Korean Men Seek Fashion Scents and Lavender Suits Them Just Fine', *Wall Street Journal Interactive Edition* (15 February 1999).

17. Gail Tom, 'Marketing with Music', *Journal of Consumer Marketing* 7 (Spring 1990): 49–53; J. Vail, 'Music as a Marketing Tool', *Advertising Age* (4 November 1985): 24.

18. Sarah Ellison and E. White, 'When There's More to an Ad Than Meets the Eye', *Wall Street Journal* (24 November 2000): A11.

19. *Marketing* (3 April 1997).

20. Jean-Claude Usunier, *Marketing Across Cultures*, 3rd edn (London: Prentice-Hall, 2000).

21. Anne C. Bech, Erling Engelund, Hans Jørn Juhl, Kai Kristensen and Carsten Stig Poulsen, 'QFood. Optimal Design of Food Products', *MAPP Working Paper* 19 (Aarhus: The Aarhus School of Business, 1994); Hans Jørn Juhl, 'A Sensory Analysis of Butter Cookies – An Application of Generalized Procrustes Analysis', *MAPP Working Paper* 20 (Aarhus: The Aarhus School of Business, 1994).

22. Andreas Scharf, 'Positionierung neuer bzw. modifizierter Nahrungs- und Genußmittel durch integrierte Markt- und Sensorik-forschung', *Marketing ZFP* 1 (1st quarter 1995): 5–17.

23. See Tim Davis, 'Taste Tests: Are the Blind Leading the Blind?', *Beverage World* 3 (April 1987): 43.

24. Betsy McKay, 'Pepsi to Revive a Cola-War Barb: The Decades-Old Blind Taste Test', *Wall Street Journal Interactive Edition* (21 March 2000).

25. Jean-Jacques Boutaud, 'Sensory Analysis: Towards the Semiotics of Taste', in E. Arnould and L. Scott, eds, *Advances in Consumer Research* 26 (Provo, UT: Association for Consumer Research, 1999): 337–40.

26. Quoted in Davis, 'Taste Tests': 44.

27. '$10 Sure Thing', *Time* (4 August 1980): 51.

28. David Kilburn, 'Japanese VCR Edits Out the Ads', *Advertising Age* (20 August 1990): 16.

29. Craig Reiss, 'Fast-Forward Ads Deliver', *Advertising Age* (27 October 1986) 2: 3; Steve Sternberg, 'VCRs: Impact and Implications', *Marketing and Media Decisions* 22 (December 1987) 5: 100.

30. James B. Twitchell, *Adcult USA: The Triumph of Advertising in American Culture* (New York: Columbia University Press, 1996).

31. Joe Flint, 'TV Networks are "Cluttering" Shows with a Record Number of Commercials', *Wall Street Journal Interactive Edition* (2 March 2000).

32. Gene Koprowsky, 'Eyeball to Eyeball', *Critical Mass* (Fall 1999): 32 (5).

33. 'It's All in the Mind', *Marketing* (27 March 1997): 31–4.

34. John Browning and Spencer Reiss, 'Encyclopedia of the New Economy, Part I', *Wired* (March 1998): 105 (8).

35. 'Raking It In On the Web', *Trend Letter* (2 March 2000): 6.

36. Quoted in Stuart Elliott, 'When Up Is Down, Does It Sell?', *New York Times* (21 February 1992) 2: D1.

37. 'Reklamer i det skjulte', *Markedsføring* 7 (1996): 28.

38. 'Toilet Ads', *Marketing* (5 December 1996): 11.

39. 'Rare Media Well Done', *Marketing* (16 January 1997): 31.

40. Christian Alsted and Hanne Hartvig Larsen, 'Toward a Semiotic Typology of Advertising Forms', *Marketing and Semiotics. Selected Papers from the Copenhagen Symposium*, ed. Hanne Hartvig Larsen, David Glen Mick and Christian Alsted (Copenhagen: Handelshøjskolens forlag, 1991): 75–103.

41. Kim Foltz, *New York Times* (23 October 1989): D11.

42. Michael Lev, 'Music Industry Broadens Its Campaigns', *New York Times* (17 January 1992): D15.

43. Stephen Brown, *Postmodern Marketing* (London: Routledge, 1995).

44. 'Realkredit for mennesker', *Markedsføring* 4 (1996): 10.

45. Chantal Cinquin, 'Homo Coca-Colens: From Marketing to Semiotics and Politics', in Jean Umiker-Sebeok, ed., *Marketing and Semiotics. New Directions in the Study of Signs for Sale* (Berlin: Mouton de Gruyter, 1987): 485–95.

46. Cf. the early introduction of the field: Elisabeth C. Hirschman and Morris B. Holbrook, eds, *Symbolic Consumer Behavior* (Ann Arbor, MI: Association for Consumer Research, 1981).

47. Mark Gottdiener, *Postmodern Semiotics* (Oxford: Blackwell, 1995).

48. 'BT Cellnet Free Lifetime Offer to Boost Pre-Pay', *Marketing* (17 June 1999): 4.

49. See David Mick, 'Consumer Research and Semiotics: Exploring the Morphology of Signs, Symbols, and Significance', *Journal of Consumer Research* 13 (September 1986): 196–213. See also Martial

Pasquier, *Marketing et semiotique* (Fribourg: Editions Universitaires Fribourg, 1999).

50. Teresa J. Domzal and Jerome B. Kernan, 'Reading Advertising: The What and How of Product Meaning', *Journal of Consumer Marketing* 9 (Summer 1992): 48-64, at 49.

51. Winfried Nöth, *Handbook of Semiotics* (London: Sage, 1994); Mick, 'Consumer Research and Semiotics'; Charles Sanders Peirce, in Charles Hartshorne, Paul Weiss and Arthur W. Burks, eds, *Collected Papers* (Cambridge, MA: Harvard University Press, 1931-58).

52. Jacques Durand, 'Rhetorical Figures in the Advertising Image', in Jean Umiker-Sebeok, ed., *Marketing and Semiotics. New Directions in the Study of Signs for Sale* (Berlin: Mouton de Gruyter, 1987): 295-318.

53. Christian Alsted and Hanne Hartvig Larsen, 'Toward a Semiotic Typology of Advertising Forms', *Marketing and Semiotics. Selected Papers from the Copenhagen Symposium*, ed. Hanne Hartvig Larsen, David Glen Mick and Christian Alsted (Copenhagen: Handelshøjskolens forlag, 1991): 75-103.

54. David Glen Mick, James E. Burroughs, Patrick Hetzel and Mary Yoko Brannen, 'A Global Review of Semiotic Consumer Research: Progress, Problems and Prospects', Working Paper (Madison: University of Wisconsin, 1999).

55. Winfried Nöth, 'The Language of Commodities. Groundwork for a Semiotics of Consumer Goods', *International Journal of Research in Marketing* 4 (1988): 173-86.

56. Benoît Heilbrunn, School of Management, Lyon, personal communication.

57. DR2 TV, 14 October 2000.

58. Melanie Wallendorf and Eric Arnould, '"We Gather Together": Consumption Rituals on Thanksgiving Day', *Journal of Consumer Research* 18 (June 1992): 13-31.

59. Odile Solomon, 'Semiotics and Marketing. New Directions in Industrial Design Applications', *International Journal of Research in Marketing* 4 (1988): 201-15.

60. Benoît Heilbrunn, 'In Search of the Lost Aura. The Object in the Age of Marketing Romanticism', in S. Brown, A.M. Doherty and B. Clarke, eds, *Romancing the Market* (London: Routledge, 1998): 187-201.

61. Solomon, 'Semiotics and Marketing'.

62. Patrick Hetzel, 'When Hyperreality, Reality, Fiction and Non-Reality are Brought Together: A Fragmented Vision of the Mall of America Through Personal Interpretation', in B. Englis and A. Olofsson, eds, *European Advances in Consumer Research* 3 (Provo, UT: Association for Consumer Research, 1998): 261-6.

63. Benoît Heilbrunn, 'Representation and Legitimacy: A Semiotic Approach to the Logo', in W. Nöth, ed., *Semiotics of the Media* (Berlin: Mouton de Gruyter, 1997): 175-89.

64. Benoît Heilbrunn, 'My Brand the Hero: A Semiotic Analysis of the Consumer Brand Relationship', in M. Lambkin *et al.*, F. van Raaij and B. Heilbrunn, eds, *European Perspectives on Consumer Research* (London: Prentice-Hall, 1998): 370-401.

65. Søren Askegaard and Fabian Csaba, 'The Good, the Bad, and the Jolly: Taste, Image and the Symbolic Resistance to the Coca-colonization of Denmark', in S. Brown and A. Patterson, eds, *Imagining Marketing* (London: Routledge, 2001): 124-40.

66. Mark Ligas and June Cotte, 'The Process of Negotiating Brand Meaning: A Symbolic Interactionist Perspective', in E. Arnould and L. Scott, eds, *Advances in Consumer Research* 26 (Provo, UT: Association for Consumer Research, 1999): 609-14.

67. Stuart Elliott, 'Advertising: A Music Retailer Whistles A New Marketing Tune To Get Heard Above The Cacophony Of Competitors', *New York Times* (2 July 1996): D7; personal communication, GRW Advertising (April 1997).

68. Adapted from Michael R. Solomon and Elnora W. Stuart, *Marketing: Real People, Real Choices* (Upper Saddle River, NJ: Prentice Hall, 1997).

69. William Echikson, 'Aiming at High and Low Markets', *Fortune* (22 March 1993): 89.

70. James Ogilvy, 'This Postmodern Business', *Marketing and Research Today* (February 1990): 4-22.

Chapter 3

Learning and memory

Mario Rossi is a 60-year-old Italian insurance man, and still very active in his field. He is a pleasant, sociable and easy-going fellow, and has made a very good career for himself. Together with his wife and four children, he lives in a comfortable flat in the suburbs of Rome. Although Rome is full of historical sites to visit, Mario is a staunch nature-lover, and he prefers to 'get back to nature' in his free time.

Mario's dog, Raphael, recognizes the sound of his master's old Fiat drawing up outside as he arrives home late after work. Mario's 'first love' was a Fiat 126, and in spite of his good income he keeps the old car running. Relaxing and sipping a glass of Chianti is just what he needs after a hard day's work. The furniture in his sitting room, and even his television set, are not the latest models, but he likes it that way – the old objects give him a sense of security. Slowly winding down, he looks forward to spending the weekend with his family and friends at his house in the countryside. He grew up there, and is very attached to the old villa and everything in it.

He often imagines what it will be like when he retires, when he will be able to live there permanently, surrounded by his family. It will be like the good old days, when he was a boy and life was uncomplicated, less chaotic. He pictures them all sitting around the table enjoying a leisurely meal (with pasta, of course!) made from home-grown produce, and afterwards sitting together.

This peaceful fantasy is in stark contrast to the reality of last weekend! His two eldest sons had gone off to a football match. The youngest ones restlessly complained about the fact that there was still no internet connection in the house, and then went into another room to settle down in front of the television for what they called an afternoon's entertainment!

Gabriele Morello, ISIDA, Palermo, Italy

▶ **Learning** refers to a relatively permanent change in behaviour which comes with experience. This experience does not have to affect the learner directly: we can learn vicariously by observing events that affect others.[1] We also learn even when we are not trying to do so. Consumers, for example, recognize many brand names and can hum many product jingles, even for those product categories they themselves do not use. This casual, unintentional acquisition of knowledge is known as *incidental learning*. Like the concept of perception discussed in the last chapter, learning is an ongoing process. Our knowledge about the world is constantly being revised as we are exposed to new stimuli and receive feedback that allows us to modify behaviour in other, similar situations. The concept of learning covers a lot of ground, ranging from a consumer's simple association between a stimulus such as a product logo (e.g. Coca-Cola) and a response (e.g. 'refreshing soft drink') to a complex series of cognitive activities (e.g. writing an essay on learning for a consumer behaviour exam). Psychologists who study learning have advanced several theories to explain the learning process. These range from those focusing on simple stimulus–response associations to perspectives that regard consumers as complex problem-solvers who learn abstract rules and concepts by observing others. Understanding these theories is important to marketers as well, because basic learning principles are at the heart of many consumer purchase decisions. In this chapter, we'll explore how learned associations among feelings, events and products – and the memories they evoke – are an important aspect of consumer behaviour.

Behavioural learning theories

▶ **Behavioural learning theories** assume that learning takes place as the result of responses to external events. Psychologists who subscribe to this viewpoint do not focus on internal thought processes. Instead, they approach the mind as a 'black box' and emphasize the observable aspects of behaviour, as depicted in Figure 3.1. The observable aspects consist of things that go into the box (the stimuli, or events perceived from the outside world) and things that come out of the box (the responses, or reactions to these stimuli).

This view is represented by two major approaches to learning: classical conditioning and instrumental conditioning. People's experiences are shaped by the feedback they receive as they go through life. Similarly, consumers respond to brand names, scents, jingles and other marketing stimuli based on the learned connections they have formed over time. People also learn that actions they take result in rewards and punishments, and this feedback influences the way they respond in similar situations in the future. Consumers who are complimented on a product choice will be more likely to buy that brand again, while those who get food poisoning at a new restaurant will not be likely to patronize it in the future.

Classical conditioning

▶ **Classical conditioning** occurs when a stimulus that elicits a response is paired with another stimulus that initially does not elicit a response on its own. Over time, this

Figure 3.1 The consumer as a 'black box': a behaviourist perspective on learning

second stimulus causes a similar response because it is associated with the first stimulus. This phenomenon was first demonstrated in dogs by Ivan Pavlov, a Russian physiologist doing research on digestion in animals.

Pavlov induced classically conditioned learning by pairing a neutral stimulus (a bell) with a stimulus known to cause a salivation response in dogs (he squirted dried meat powder into their mouths). The powder was an unconditioned stimulus (UCS) because it was naturally capable of causing the response. Over time, the bell became a conditioned stimulus (CS): it did not initially cause salivation, but the dogs learned to associate the bell with the meat powder and began to salivate at the sound of the bell only. The drooling of these canine consumers over a sound, now linked to feeding time, was a conditioned response (CR).

This basic form of classical conditioning primarily applies to responses controlled by the autonomic (e.g. salivation) and nervous (e.g. eye blink) systems. That is, it focuses on visual and olfactory cues that induce hunger, thirst or sexual arousal. When these cues are consistently paired with conditioned stimuli, such as brand names, consumers may learn to feel hungry, thirsty or aroused when later exposed to the brand cues.

Classical conditioning can have similar effects for more complex reactions, too. Even a credit card becomes a conditioned cue that triggers greater spending, especially since it is a stimulus that is present only in situations where consumers are spending money. People learn that they can make larger purchases when using credit cards, and they also have been found to leave larger tips than they do when using cash.[2] Small wonder that American Express® reminds us, 'Don't leave home without it.' Conditioning effects are more likely to occur after the conditioned and unconditioned stimuli have been paired a number of times.[3] Repeated exposures increase the strength of stimulus–response associations and prevent the decay of these associations in memory.

Conditioning will not occur or will take longer if the CS is only occasionally presented with the UCS. One result of this lack of association may be **extinction**, which occurs when the effects of prior conditioning are reduced and finally disappear. This can occur, for example, when a product is overexposed in the marketplace so that its original allure is lost. The Lacoste polo shirt, with its distinctive crocodile logo, is a good example of this effect. When the once-exclusive crocodile started to appear on baby clothes and many other items, it lost its cachet and was soon replaced by other contenders, such as the Lauren polo player.[4]

Stimulus generalization refers to the tendency of stimuli similar to a CS to evoke similar, conditioned responses.[5] Pavlov noticed in subsequent studies that his dogs would sometimes salivate when they heard noises that only resembled a bell (e.g. keys jangling). People react to other, similar stimuli in much the same way that they responded to an original stimulus. A chemist shop's bottle of own-brand mouthwash deliberately packaged to resemble Listerine mouthwash may evoke a similar response among consumers who assume that this 'me-too' product shares other characteristics of the original.

▶ **Stimulus discrimination** occurs when a stimulus similar to a CS is not followed by a UCS. In these situations, reactions are weakened and will soon disappear. Part of the learning process involves making a response to some stimuli but not to other, similar stimuli. Manufacturers of well-established brands commonly urge consumers not to buy 'cheap imitations' because the results will not be what they expect.

Operant conditioning

▶ **Operant conditioning**, also known as instrumental conditioning, occurs as the individual learns to perform behaviours that produce positive outcomes and to avoid those that yield negative outcomes. This learning process is most closely associated with the psychologist B. F. Skinner, who demonstrated the effects of instrumental conditioning by teaching animals to dance, pigeons to play ping-pong, and so on, by systematically rewarding them for desired behaviours.[6]

While responses in classical conditioning are involuntary and fairly simple, those in instrumental conditioning are made deliberately to obtain a goal and may be more complex. The desired behaviour may be learned over a period of time, as intermediate actions are rewarded in a process called *shaping*. For example, the owner of a new shop may award prizes to shoppers just for coming in, hoping that over time they will continue to drop in and eventually buy something.

Also, classical conditioning involves the close pairing of two stimuli. Instrumental learning occurs as a result of a reward received following the desired behaviour and takes place over a period in which a variety of other behaviours are attempted and abandoned because they are not reinforced. A good way to remember the difference is to keep in mind that in instrumental learning the response is performed because it is instrumental to gaining a reward or avoiding a punishment. Consumers over time come to associate with people who reward them and to choose products that make them feel good or satisfy some need.

Operant conditioning (instrumental learning) occurs in one of three ways. When
▶ the environment provides **positive reinforcement** in the form of a reward, the response is strengthened, and appropriate behaviour is learned. For example, a woman who is complimented after wearing Obsession perfume will learn that using this product has the desired effect, and she will be more likely to keep buying the
▶ product. **Negative reinforcement** also strengthens responses so that appropriate behaviour is learned. A perfume company, for example, might run an ad showing a woman sitting alone on a Saturday night because she did not use its fragrance. The message to be conveyed is that she could have avoided this negative outcome if only she had used the perfume. In contrast to situations wherein we learn to do certain
▶ things in order to avoid unpleasantness, **punishment** occurs when a response is followed by unpleasant events (such as being ridiculed by friends for wearing an offensive-smelling perfume). We learn not to repeat these behaviours.

When trying to understand the differences between these mechanisms, keep in mind that reactions from a person's environment to behaviour can be either positive or negative and that these outcomes or anticipated outcomes can be applied or removed. That is, under conditions of both positive reinforcement and punishment, the person receives a reaction after doing something. In contrast, negative reinforcement occurs when a negative outcome is avoided: the removal of something negative is pleasurable and hence is rewarding. Finally, when a positive outcome is no longer received, extinction is likely to occur, and the learned stimulus–response connection will not be maintained (as when a woman no longer receives compliments on her perfume). Thus, positive and negative reinforcement strengthen the future linkage between a response and an outcome because of the pleasant experience. This tie is weakened under conditions of both punishment and extinction because of the unpleasant experience. The relationships among these four conditions are easier to understand by referring to Figure 3.2.

An important factor in operant conditioning is the set of rules by which appropriate reinforcements are given for a behaviour. The issue of what is the most effective reinforcement schedule to use is important to marketers, because it relates to the amount of effort and resources they must devote to rewarding consumers in order to condition desired behaviours.

- *Fixed-interval reinforcement.* After a specified period has passed, the first response that is made brings the reward. Under such conditions, people tend to respond slowly immediately after being reinforced, but their responses speed up as the time for the next reinforcement approaches. For example, consumers may crowd into a store for the last day of its seasonal sale and not reappear again until the next one.

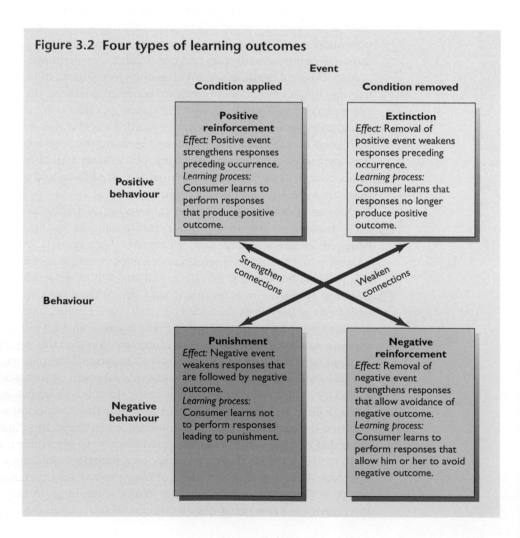

Figure 3.2 Four types of learning outcomes

Event

	Condition applied	**Condition removed**
Positive behaviour	**Positive reinforcement** *Effect:* Positive event strengthens responses preceding occurrence. *Learning process:* Consumer learns to perform responses that produce positive outcome.	**Extinction** *Effect:* Removal of positive event weakens responses preceding occurrence. *Learning process:* Consumer learns that responses no longer produce positive outcome.
Negative behaviour	**Punishment** *Effect:* Negative event weakens responses that are followed by negative outcome. *Learning process:* Consumer learns not to perform responses leading to punishment.	**Negative reinforcement** *Effect:* Removal of negative event strengthens responses that allow avoidance of negative outcome. *Learning process:* Consumer learns to perform responses that allow him or her to avoid negative outcome.

Behaviour

Strengthen connections / Weaken connections

- *Variable-interval reinforcement*. The time that must pass before reinforcement is delivered varies around some average. Since the person does not know exactly when to expect the reinforcement, responses must be performed at a consistent rate. This logic is behind retailers' use of so-called secret shoppers – people who periodically test for service quality by posing as customers at unannounced times. Since store employees never know exactly when to expect a visit, high quality must be constantly maintained.

- *Fixed-ratio reinforcement*. Reinforcement occurs only after a fixed number of responses. This schedule motivates people to continue performing the same behaviour over and over again. For example, a consumer might keep buying groceries at the same store in order to earn a gift after collecting 50 books of trading stamps.

- *Variable-ratio reinforcement*. The person is reinforced after a certain number of responses, but he or she does not know how many responses are required. People in such situations tend to respond at very high and steady rates, and this type of behaviour is very difficult to extinguish. This reinforcement schedule is responsible for consumers' attraction to slot machines. They learn that if they keep feeding money into the machine, they will eventually win something (if they don't go broke first).

Cognitive learning theory

▶ **Cognitive learning** occurs as a result of mental processes. In contrast to behavioural theories of learning, cognitive learning theory stresses the importance of internal mental processes. This perspective views people as problem-solvers who actively use information from the world around them to master their environment. Supporters of this viewpoint also stress the role of creativity and insight during the learning process.

The issue of consciousness

A lot of controversy surrounds the issue of whether or when people are aware of their learning processes. While behavioural learning theorists emphasize the routine, automatic nature of conditioning, proponents of cognitive learning argue that even these simple effects are based on cognitive factors: that is, expectations are created that a stimulus will be followed by a response (the formation of expectations requires mental activity). According to this school of thought, conditioning occurs because subjects develop conscious hypotheses and then act on them.

On the one hand, there is some evidence for the existence of nonconscious procedural knowledge. People apparently do process at least some information in an automatic, passive way, which is a condition that has been termed mindlessness.[7] When we meet someone new or encounter a new product, for example, we have a tendency to respond to the stimulus in terms of existing categories, rather than taking the trouble to formulate different ones. Our reactions are activated by a trigger feature, some stimulus that cues us towards a particular pattern. For example, men in one study rated a car in an ad as superior on a variety of characteristics if a seductive woman (the trigger feature) was present in the ad, despite the fact that the men did not believe the woman's presence actually had an influence.[8]

None the less, many modern theorists are beginning to regard some instances of conditioning as cognitive processes, especially where expectations are formed about the linkages between stimuli and responses. Indeed, studies using masking effects, wherein it is difficult for subjects to learn CS/UCS associations, show sub-

Figure 3.3 Components of observational learning

stantial reductions in conditioning.[9] For example, an adolescent girl may observe that women on television and in real life seem to be rewarded with compliments and attention when they smell nice and wear alluring clothing. She works out that the probability of these rewards occurring is greater when she wears perfume and deliberately wears a popular scent to obtain the pay-off of social acceptance.

Observational learning

▶ **Observational learning** occurs when people watch the actions of others and note the reinforcements they receive for their behaviours. This type of learning is a complex process: people store these observations in memory as they accumulate knowledge, perhaps using this information at a later point to guide their own behaviours. This process of imitating the behaviour of others is called modelling. For example, a woman shopping for a new kind of perfume may remember the reactions a friend received when wearing a certain brand several months earlier, and she will base her behaviour on her friend's actions. In order for observational learning in the form of modelling to occur, four conditions must be met.[10] These factors are summarized in Figure 3.3.

1 The consumer's attention must be directed to the appropriate model whom, for reasons of attractiveness, competence, status or similarity, it is desirable to emulate.

2 The consumer must remember what is said or done by the model.

3 The consumer must convert this information into actions.

4 The consumer must be motivated to perform these actions.

Marketing applications of learning principles

Understanding how consumers learn is very important to marketers. After all, many strategic decisions are based on the assumption that consumers are continually accumulating information about products and that people can be 'taught' to prefer some alternatives over others.

Behavioural learning applications

Many marketing strategies focus on the establishment of associations between stimuli and responses. Behavioural learning principles apply to many consumer phenomena, ranging from the creation of a distinctive brand image to the perceived linkage between a product and an underlying need.

How marketers take advantage of classical conditioning principles

The transfer of meaning from an unconditioned stimulus to a conditioned stimulus explains why 'made-up' brand names like Marlboro, Coca-Cola or IBM can exert such powerful effects on consumers. The association between the Marlboro Man and the cigarette is so strong that in some cases the company no longer even includes the brand name in its ad. When nonsense syllables (meaningless sets of letters) are paired with such evaluative words as beauty or success, the meaning is transferred to the nonsense syllables. This change in the symbolic significance of initially meaningless words shows that complex meanings can be conditioned. Recent studies have shown that attitudes formed through classical conditioning are enduring.[11]

These conditioned associations are crucial to many marketing strategies that rely on the creation and perpetuation of positive **brand equity**, in which a brand has strong positive associations in a consumer's memory and commands a lot of loyalty as a result.[12] As we will see in the next chapter, a product with brand equity holds a tremendous advantage in the marketplace.

Repetition One advertising researcher argues that more than three exposures are wasted. The first creates awareness of the product, the second demonstrates its relevance to the consumer, and the third serves as a reminder of the product's benefits.[13] However, even this bare-bones approach implies that repetition is needed to ensure that the consumer is actually exposed to (and processes) the ad at least three times. Marketers attempting to condition an association must ensure that the consumers they have targeted will be exposed to the stimulus a sufficient number of times.

Les histoires de Mario.

Le poisson de Provigo.

One innovative way to employ repetition without causing wearout is illustrated by these related advertising hoarding images.

Cossette Communications Marketing for Provigo Supermarkets, 1986.

On the other hand, it is possible to have too much of a good thing. Consumers can become so used to hearing or seeing a marketing stimulus that they cease to pay attention to it (see Chapter 2). This problem, known as advertising wear-out, can be reduced by varying the way in which the basic message is presented.

Conditioning product associations Advertisements often pair a product with a positive stimulus to create a desirable association. Various aspects of a marketing message, such as music, humour or imagery, can affect conditioning. In one study, subjects who viewed a slide of pens paired with either pleasant or unpleasant music were more likely later to select the pen that appeared with pleasant music.[14]

The order in which the conditioned stimulus and the unconditioned stimulus is presented can affect the likelihood that learning will occur. Generally speaking, the unconditioned stimulus should be presented prior to the conditioned stimulus. The technique of backward conditioning, such as showing a soft drink (the CS) and then playing a jingle (the UCS), is generally not effective.[15] Because sequential presentation is desirable for conditioning to occur, classical conditioning is not very effective in static situations, such as in magazine ads, where (in contrast to TV or radio) the marketer cannot control the order in which the CS and the UCS are perceived.

Just as product associations can be formed, so they can be extinguished. Because of the danger of extinction, a classical conditioning strategy may not be as effective for products that are frequently encountered, since there is no guarantee they will be accompanied by the CS. A bottle of Pepsi paired with the refreshing sound of a carbonated beverage being poured over ice may seem like a good example of conditioning. Unfortunately, the product would also be seen in many other contexts where this sound was absent, reducing the effectiveness of the conditioning.

By the same reasoning, a novel tune should be chosen over a popular one to pair with a product, since the popular song might also be heard in many situations in which the product is not present.[16] Music videos in particular may serve as effective UCSs because they often have an emotional impact on viewers and this effect may transfer to ads accompanying the video.[17]

Applications of stimulus generalization The process of stimulus generalization is often central to branding and packaging decisions that attempt to capitalize on consumers' positive associations with an existing brand or company name, as exemplified by a hairdressing establishment called United Hairlines.[18] In one 20-month period, Procter & Gamble introduced almost 90 new products. Not a single product carried a new brand name. In fact, roughly 80 per cent of all new products are actually extensions of existing brands or product lines.[19] Strategies based on stimulus generalization include the following:

- *Family branding*, in which a variety of products capitalize on the reputation of a company name. Companies such as Campbell's, Heinz, Philips and Sony rely on their positive corporate images to sell different product lines.
- *Product line extensions*, in which related products are added to an established brand. Dole, which is associated with fruit, was able to introduce refrigerated juices and juice bars, while Sun Maid went from raisins to raisin bread. Other recent extensions include Woolite rug cleaner, and the various models of Nike Air shoes.[20]
- *Licensing*, in which well-known names are 'rented' by others. This strategy is

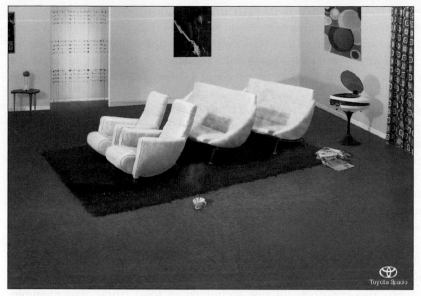

Many marketing strategies focus on the establishment of associations between stimuli and responses. Associating products with the imagery of riding in a Toyota with one's comfortable, modern living room is one example of this stimulus–reponse application.

Used with permisson of Toyota Singapore and Saatchi & Saatchi Ltd.

increasing in popularity as marketers try to link their products and services with well-established figures. Companies as diverse as McDonald's and Harley-Davidson have authorized the use of their names on products. Japan Airlines recently licensed the rights to use Disney characters, and, in addition to painting Mickey Mouse and Donald Duck on several of its planes, the carrier is requiring its flight attendants to wear mouse ears on some domestic flights![21]

● Marketers are increasingly capitalizing on the public's enthusiasm for films and popular TV programmes by developing numerous product tie-ins.

● *Look-alike packaging*, in which distinctive packaging designs create strong associations with a particular brand. This linkage is often exploited by makers of generic or private-label brands who wish to communicate a quality image by putting their products in very similar packages. As one chemist chain store executive commented, 'You want to tell the consumer that it's close to the national brand. You've got to make it look like, within the law, close to the national brand. They're at least attracted to the package.'[22]

Applications of stimulus discrimination An emphasis on communicating a product's distinctive attributes *vis-à-vis* its competitors is an important aspect of positioning, in which consumers learn to differentiate a brand from its competitors (see Chapter 2). This is not always an easy task, especially in product categories where the brand names of many of the alternatives look and sound alike. For example, a recent survey showed that many consumers have a great deal of trouble distinguishing between products sold by the top computer manufacturers. With a blur of names like OmniPlex, OptiPlex, Premmia, Premium, ProLinea, ProLiant, etc., this confusion is not surprising.[23]

Companies with a well-established brand image try to encourage stimulus discrimination by promoting the unique attributes of their brands: thus the constant reminders for American Express® traveller's cheques: 'Ask for them by name . . .' . On the other hand, a brand name that is used so widely that it is no longer distinctive becomes part of the public domain and can be used by competitors, as has been the case for such products as aspirin, cellophane, yo-yos and escalators.

How marketers take advantage of instrumental conditioning principles

Principles of instrumental conditioning are at work when a consumer is rewarded or punished for a purchase decision. Businesspeople shape behaviour by gradually reinforcing consumers for taking appropriate actions. For example, a car dealer might encourage a reluctant buyer to try sitting in a showroom model, then suggest a test drive, and so on.

Marketers have many ways of reinforcing consumers, ranging from a simple thank you after a purchase to substantial rebates and follow-up phone calls. For example, a life insurance company obtained a much higher rate of policy renewal among a group of new customers who received a thank you letter after each payment compared to a control group that did not receive any reinforcement [24]

A popular technique known as **frequency marketing** reinforces regular purchasers by giving them prizes with values that increase along with the amount purchased. This operant learning strategy was pioneered by the airline industry, which introduced 'frequent-flyer' programmes in the early 1980s to reward loyal customers. Well over 20 per cent of food stores now offer trading stamps or some other frequent-buyer promotion. Manufacturers in the fast-moving consumer goods (FMCG) category also make use of this technique in food stores. For example, Douwe Egberts, the coffee manufacturer owned by Sara Lee, offers stamps which can be saved and redeemed for a whole range of coffee-related products such as espresso makers, service sets and coffee grinders, including their classic (and nostalgic) hand coffee grinder.

In some industries, these reinforcers take the form of clubs, including a Hilton Hotel Club. Club members usually earn bonus points to set against future purchases, and some get such privileges as magazines and free telephone numbers and sometimes even invitations to exclusive outings.

How marketers take advantage of cognitive learning principles

Consumers' ability to learn vicariously by observing how the behaviour of others is reinforced makes the lives of marketers much easier. Because people do not have to be directly reinforced for their actions, marketers do not necessarily have to reward or punish them for purchase behaviours. Instead, they can show what happens to desirable models who use or do not use their products and know that consumers will often be motivated to imitate these actions at a later time. For example, a perfume commercial may depict a woman surrounded by a throng of admirers who are providing her with positive reinforcement for using the product. Needless to say, this learning process is more practical than providing the same personal attention to each woman who actually buys the perfume!

Consumers' evaluations of models go beyond simple stimulus–response connections. For example, a celebrity's image is often more than a simple reflexive response of good or bad: it is a complex combination of many attributes.[25] In general, the degree to which a model will be emulated depends upon his or her social attractiveness. Attractiveness can be based upon several components, including physical appearance, expertise or similarity to the evaluator.

These factors will be addressed further in Chapter 6, which discusses personal characteristics that make a communication's source more or less effective in changing consumers' attitudes. In addition, many applications of consumer problem-solving are related to ways information is represented in memory and recalled at a later date. This aspect of cognitive learning is the focus of the next section.

This cosmetics ad illustrates the principle of vicarious reinforcement. The model uses the product and is shown reaping the reward – the approval of her boyfriend.
Maybelline, Inc.

The role of learning in memory

Memory involves a process of acquiring information and storing it over time so that it will be available when needed. Contemporary approaches to the study of memory employ an information-processing approach. They assume that the mind is in some ways like a computer: data are input, processed and output for later use in revised form. In the **encoding** stage, information is entered in a way the system will recognize. In the **storage** stage, this knowledge is integrated with what is already in memory and 'warehoused' until needed. During **retrieval**, the person accesses the desired information.[26] The memory process is summarized in Figure 3.4.

As suggested by Mario's memories and musings at the beginning of the chapter, many of our experiences are locked inside our heads, and we maintain those memories and recall those experiences if prompted by the right cues. Marketers rely on consumers to retain information they have learned about products and services, trusting that it will later be applied in situations where purchase decisions must be made. During the consumer decision-making process, this internal memory is combined with external memory – which includes all the product details on packages in shopping lists, and through other marketing stimuli – to permit brand alternatives to be identified and evaluated.[27] Research supports the idea that marketers can distort a consumer's recall of a product experience. What we think we 'know' about products can be influenced by advertising messages to which we are exposed after using them. This *post-experience advertising* is more likely to alter actual memories when it is very similar or activates memories about the actual experience. For example,

Figure 3.4 The memory process

| External inputs | → | **Encoding** Information is placed in memory. | → | **Storage** Information is retained in memory. | → | **Retrieval** Information stored in memory is found as needed. |

advertising can make a remembered product experience more favourable than it actually was.[28]

Encoding of information for later retrieval

The way information is encoded or mentally programmed helps to determine how it will be represented in memory. In general, incoming data that are associated with other information already in memory stand a better chance of being retained. For example, brand names that are linked to physical characteristics of a product category (e.g. Coffee Mate creamer or Sani-Flush toilet bowl cleaner) or that are easy to visualize (e.g. Tide detergent) tend to be more easily retained in memory than more abstract brand names.[29]

Types of memory

A consumer may process a stimulus simply in terms of its sensory meaning, such as its colour or shape. When this occurs, the meaning may be activated when the person sees a picture of the stimulus. We may experience a sense of familiarity on seeing an ad for a new snack food we recently tasted, for example.

In many cases, though, meanings are encoded at a more abstract level. *Semantic meaning* refers to symbolic associations, such as the idea that rich people drink champagne or that fashionable men wear an earring.

Episodic memories are those that relate to events that are personally relevant, such as Mario's.[30] As a result, a person's motivation to retain these memories will be strong. Couples often have 'their song' that reminds them of their first date or wedding. The memories that might be triggered upon hearing this song would be quite different and unique for them.

Commercials sometimes attempt to activate episodic memories by focusing on experiences shared by many people. Recall of the past may have an effect on future behaviour. A university fund-raising campaign can get higher donations by evoking pleasant memories. Some especially vivid associations are called *flashbulb* memories. These are usually related to some highly significant event. One method of conveying product information is through a *narrative* or a story. Much of the social information that an individual acquires is represented in memory this way. Therefore, utilizing this method in product advertising can be an effective marketing technique. Narratives persuade people to construct a mental representation of the information they are viewing. Pictures aid in this construction and allow for a more developed and detailed mental representation.[31]

Memory systems

According to the information-processing perspective, there are three distinct memory systems: sensory memory, short-term memory (STM) and long-term memory (LTM). Each plays a role in processing brand-related information. The interrelationships of these memory systems are summarized in Figure 3.5.

Sensory memory permits storage of the information we receive from our senses. This storage is very temporary: it lasts a couple of seconds at most. For example, a person might be walking past a bakery and get a brief, but enticing, whiff of bread baking inside. While this sensation would only last for a few seconds, it would be sufficient to allow the person to determine if he or she should investigate further. If the information is retained for further processing, it passes through an attentional gate and is transferred to short-term memory.

Short-term memory also stores information for a limited period of time, and its

Figure 3.5 Relationships among memory systems

capacity is limited. Similar to a computer, this system can be regarded as working memory: it holds the information we are currently processing. Verbal input may be stored acoustically (in terms of how it sounds) or semantically (in terms of its meaning).[32]

The information is stored by combining small pieces into larger ones in a process known as 'chunking'. A chunk is a configuration that is familiar to the person and can be manipulated as a unit. For example, a brand name can be a chunk that summarizes a great deal of detailed information about the brand.

Initially, it was believed that STM was capable of processing 5–9 chunks of information at a time, and for this reason phone numbers were designed to have seven digits.[33] It now appears that 3–4 chunks is the optimum size for efficient retrieval (seven-digit phone numbers can be remembered because the individual digits are chunked, so we may remember a three-digit exchange as one piece of information).[34]

Long-term memory is the system that allows us to retain information for a long period of time. In order for information to enter into long-term memory from short-term memory, elaborative rehearsal is required. This process involves thinking about the meaning of a stimulus and relating it to other information already in memory. Marketers sometimes assist in the process by devising catchy slogans or jingles that consumers repeat on their own.

Storing of information in memory

Relationships among the types of memory are a source of some controversy. The traditional perspective, known as multiple-store, assumes that STM and LTM are separate systems. More recent research has moved away from the distinction between the two types of memory, instead emphasizing the interdependence of the systems. This work argues that, depending upon the nature of the processing task, different levels of processing occur that activate some aspects of memory rather than others. These approaches are called **activation models of memory**.[35] The more effort it takes to process information (so-called deep processing), the more likely it is that information will be placed in long-term memory.

Activation models propose that an incoming piece of information is stored in an associative network containing many bits of related information organized according to some set of relationships. The consumer has organized systems of concepts relating to brands, stores, and so on.

Knowledge structures

These storage units, known as **knowledge structures**, can be thought of as complex spiders' webs filled with pieces of data. This information is placed into nodes, which are connected by associative links within these structures. Pieces of information that are seen as similar in some way are chunked together under some more abstract category. New, incoming information is interpreted to be consistent with the structure already in place.[36] According to the hierarchical processing model, a message is processed in a bottom-up fashion: processing begins at a very basic level and is subject to increasingly complex processing operations that require greater cognitive capacity. If processing at one level fails to evoke the next level, processing of the ad is terminated, and capacity is allocated to other tasks.[37]

Links form between nodes as an associative network is developed. For example, a consumer might have a network for 'perfumes'. Each node represents a concept related to the category. This node can be an attribute, a specific brand, a celebrity identified with a perfume, or even a related product. A network for perfumes might include concepts like the names Chanel, Obsession and Charlie, as well as attributes like sexy and elegant.

When asked to list perfumes, the consumer would recall only those brands contained in the appropriate category. This group constitutes that person's **evoked set**. The task of a new entrant that wants to position itself as a category member (e.g. a new luxury perfume) is to provide cues that facilitate its placement in the appropriate category. A sample network for perfumes is shown in Figure 3.6.

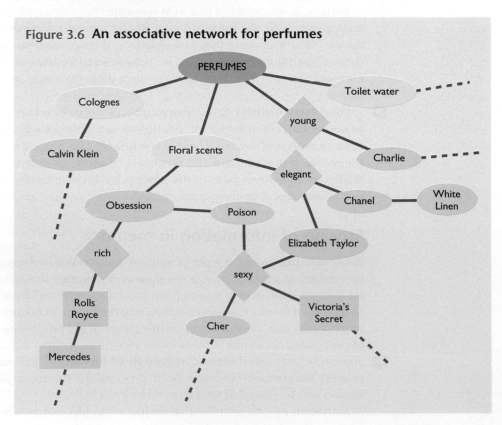

Figure 3.6 An associative network for perfumes

Spreading activation

A meaning can be activated indirectly: energy spreads across nodes of varying levels of abstraction. As one node is activated, other nodes associated with it also begin to be triggered. Meaning thus spreads across the network, bringing up concepts including competing brands and relevant attributes that are used to form attitudes towards the brand.

This process of spreading activation allows consumers to shift back and forth between levels of meaning. The way a piece of information is stored in memory depends upon the type of meaning assigned to it. This meaning type will, in turn, determine how and when the meaning is activated. For example, the memory trace for an ad could be stored in one or more of the following ways:

- *Brand-specific* – in terms of claims made for the brand.
- *Ad-specific* – in terms of the medium or content of the ad itself.
- *Brand identification* – in terms of the brand name.
- *Product category* – in terms of how the product works, where it should be used, or experiences with the product.
- *Evaluative reactions* – in terms of whether 'that looks like fun'.[38]

Levels of knowledge

Knowledge is coded at different levels of abstraction and complexity. Meaning concepts are individual nodes (e.g. elegant). These may be combined into a larger unit, called a *proposition* (also known as a belief). A proposition links two nodes together to form a more complex meaning, which can serve as a single chunk of information. For example, a proposition might be that 'Chanel is a perfume for elegant women'.

Propositions are, in turn, integrated to produce a complex unit known as a **schema**. As was noted at the beginning of the chapter, a schema is a cognitive framework that is developed through experience. Information that is consistent with an existing schema is encoded more readily.[39] The ability to move up and down between levels of abstraction greatly increases processing flexibility and efficiency. For this reason, young children, who do not yet have well-developed schemas, are not able to make efficient use of purchase information compared to older children.[40]

One type of schema that is relevant to consumer behaviour is a script, a sequence of procedures that is expected by an individual. For example, consumers learn service scripts that guide expectations and purchasing behaviour in business settings. Consumers learn to expect a certain sequence of events, and they may become uncomfortable if the service departs from the script. A service script for your visit to the dentist might include such events as (1) driving to the dentist, (2) reading old magazines in the waiting room, (3) hearing your name called and sitting in the dentist's chair, (4) having the dentist probe your teeth, (5) having the dentist scale and polish your teeth, and so on. This desire to follow a script helps to explain why such service innovations as automatic bank machines and self-service petrol stations have met with resistance by some consumers, who have trouble adapting to a new sequence of events.[41]

Retrieving of information for purchase decisions

Retrieval is the process whereby information is accessed from long-term memory. As evidenced by the popularity of the board game Trivial Pursuit, or the television programme *Who Wants to be a Millionaire?* people have a vast quantity of information stored in their heads that is not necessarily available on demand. Although most of the information entered in long-term memory does not go away, it may be difficult or impossible to retrieve unless the appropriate cues are present.

Factors influencing retrieval

Some differences in retrieval ability are physiological. Older adults consistently display inferior recall ability for current items, such as prescription information, though events that happened to them when they were younger may be recalled with great clarity.[42]

Other factors are situational, relating to the environment in which the message is delivered. Not surprisingly, recall is enhanced when the consumer pays more attention to the message in the first place. Some evidence indicates that information about a pioneering brand (the first brand to enter a market) is more easily retrieved from memory than follower brands because the product's introduction is likely to be distinctive and, in the short term, no competitors divert the consumer's attention.[43] In addition, descriptive brand names are more likely to be recalled than are those that do not provide adequate cues as to what the product is.[44]

The viewing environment of a marketing message can also affect recall. For example, commercials shown during baseball games yield the lowest recall scores among sports programmes because the activity is stop-and-go rather than continuous. Unlike football or basketball, the pacing of baseball gives many opportunities for attention to wander even during play. Similarly, General Electric found that its commercials do better in television programmes with continuous activity, such as stories or dramas, compared to variety or talk shows, which are punctuated by a series of acts.[45] Finally, a large-scale analysis of TV commercials found that commercials shown first in a series of ads are recalled better than those shown last.[46]

State-dependent retrieval In a process termed state-dependent retrieval, people are better able to access information if their internal state is the same at the time of recall as it was when the information was learned.

This phenomenon, called the *mood congruence effect*, underscores the desirability of matching a consumer's mood at the time of purchase when planning exposure to marketing communications. A consumer is more likely to recall an ad, for example, if his or her mood or level of arousal at the time of exposure is similar to that in the purchase environment. By recreating the cues that were present when the information was first presented, recall can be enhanced.[47]

Familiarity and recall As a general rule, prior familiarity with an item enhances its recall. Indeed, this is one of the basic goals of marketers who are trying to create and maintain awareness of their products. The more experience a consumer has with a product, the better use that person is able to make of product information.[48]

However, there is a possible fly in the ointment: as noted earlier in the chapter, some evidence indicates that over-familiarity can result in inferior learning and/or recall. When consumers are highly familiar with a brand or an advertisement, they may attend to fewer attributes because they do not believe that any additional effort will yield a gain in knowledge.[49] For example, when consumers are exposed to the technique of radio replay, where the audio track from a television ad is replayed on the radio, they do very little critical, evaluative processing and instead mentally replay the video portion of the ad.[50]

Salience and recall The salience of a brand refers to its prominence or level of activation in memory. As noted in Chapter 2, stimuli that stand out in contrast to their environment are more likely to command attention, which, in turn, increases the likelihood they will be recalled. Almost any technique that increases the novelty of a stimulus also improves recall (a result known as the von Restorff effect).[51] This effect explains why unusual advertising or distinctive packaging tends to facilitate brand recall.[52]

As we saw in Chapter 2, introducing a surprise element in an ad (e.g. the Energizer Bunny™ who unexpectedly marches through a commercial) can be particularly effective. This strategy aids recall even if the stimulus is not relevant to the factual information being presented.[53] In addition, so-called mystery ads, where the brand is not identified until the end, are more effective at building associations in memory between the product category and that brand – especially in the case of novel brands.[54]

Pictorial vs. verbal cues There is some evidence for the superiority of visual memory over verbal memory, but this advantage is unclear because it is more difficult to measure recall of pictures.[55] However, the available data indicate that information presented in pictorial form is more likely to be recognized later.[56] Certainly, visual aspects of an ad are more likely to grab a consumer's attention. In fact, eye-movement studies indicate that about 90 per cent of viewers look at the dominant picture in an ad before they bother to view the copy.[57]

While pictorial ads may enhance recall, however, they do not necessarily improve comprehension. One study found that television news items presented with illustrations (still pictures) as a backdrop result in improved recall for details of the news story, even though understanding of the story's content docs not improve.[58] Visual imagery can be especially effective when it includes verbal cues that relate to the consumer's existing knowledge.

Factors influencing forgetting

Marketers obviously hope that consumers will not forget their products. However, in a poll of more than 13,000 adults, over half were unable to remember any specific ad they had seen, heard or read in the previous 30 days.[59] Forgetting is obviously a problem for marketers.

Early memory theorists assumed that memories fade due to the simple passage of time. In a process of decay, the structural changes in the brain produced by learning simply go away. Forgetting also occurs due to **interference**: as additional information is learned, it displaces the earlier information.

Stimulus–response associations will be forgotten if the consumers subsequently learn new responses to the same or similar stimuli in a process known as *retroactive interference*. Or prior learning can interfere with new learning, a process termed *proactive interference*. Since pieces of information are stored in memory as nodes that are connected to one another by links, a meaning concept that is connected by a larger number of links is more likely to be retrieved. But, as new responses are learned, a stimulus loses its effectiveness in retrieving the old response.[60]

These interference effects help to explain problems in remembering brand information. Consumers tend to organize attribute information by brand.[61] Additional attribute information regarding a brand or similar brands may limit the person's ability to recall old brand information. Recall may also be inhibited if the brand name is composed of frequently used words. These words cue competing associations and result in less retention of brand information.[62]

In one study, brand evaluations deteriorated more rapidly when ads for the brand appeared with messages for 12 other brands in the same category than when the ad was shown with ads for 12 dissimilar products.[63] By increasing the salience of a brand, the recall of other brands can be impaired.[64] On the other hand, calling a competitor by name can result in poorer recall for one's own brand.[65]

Finally, a phenomenon known as the *part-list cueing effect* allows marketers to utilize the interference process strategically. When only a portion of the items in a category are presented to consumers, the omitted items are not as easily recalled. For example, comparative advertising that mentions only a subset of competitors (preferably those that the marketer is not very worried about) may inhibit recall of the unmentioned brands with which the product does not compare favourably.[66]

Products as memory markers

Products and ads can themselves serve as powerful retrieval cues. Indeed, the three types of possessions most valued by consumers are furniture, visual art and photos. The most common explanation for this attachment is the ability of these things to summon memories of the past.[67] Products are particularly important as markers when our sense of past is threatened, as when a consumer's current identity is challenged due to some change in role caused by divorce, moving, graduation, and so on.[68] Products have mnemonic qualities that serve as a form of external memory by prompting consumers to retrieve episodic memories. For example, family photography allows consumers to create their own retrieval cues, with the 11 billion amateur photos taken annually forming a kind of external memory bank for our culture.

Researchers are just beginning to probe the effects of autobiographical memories on buying behaviour. These memories appear to be one way that advertisements create emotional responses: ads that succeed in getting us to think about our own past also appear to get us to like these ads more – especially if the linkage between the nostalgia experience and the brand is strong.[69]

The power of nostalgia

Nostalgia has been described as a bitter-sweet emotion, where the past is viewed with both sadness and longing. References to 'the good old days' are increasingly common, as advertisers call up memories of distant youth – feelings they hope will translate to what they're selling today. A stimulus is at times able to evoke a weakened response much later, an effect known as spontaneous recovery, and this reestablished connection may explain consumers' powerful nostalgic reactions to songs or pictures they have not been exposed to in many years.

Many European companies are making use of nostalgic appeals, some of which are not based on the too distant past! Berlin's Humboldt University and City Museum have staged a fashion show of the1960s, displaying clothes, appliances and posters from the communist era. The show, entitled *Ostalgie*, which is a play on words for 'East Nostalgia' in the German language, gave a nostalgic view of a time when goods might have been shoddy, but when there was no unemployment or homelessness. There's growing interest in the Trabant (the joke used to be that you could double the value of a Trabant by filling it with sand) which has resulted in the Son of Trabant, built in the same factory where they used to build the original. Likewise, western European multinationals are relaunching local brands of east European origin in response to a backlash against the incursion of foreign products. From cigarettes to yogurt, multinationals are trying to lure consumers by combining yesteryear's product names with today's quality. Local brands like Nestlé's Chokito or Unilever's Flora margarine brands are now among the companies' best-selling products in eastern European markets. Considerable care goes into the production values

Classic American TV shows are popular around the world, but few are as admired as *Dallas* is in Romania. In that eastern European country, the show's star, J. R. Ewing, is revered. Although many US viewers saw J. R. as a greedy, unprincipled villain they 'loved to hate', in Romania J. R. has become the symbol of American enterprise and a role model for the new capitalists who are trying to transform the country's economy. So, it's only fitting that J. R. was selected to endorse Lukoil, a brand of Russian motor oil. Advertisements in the Romanian market claim that the oil is 'the choice of a true Texan'![70] (Does Texan George W. Bush know where Romania is on the map?)

of campaigns which are intended to evoke nostalgia. Mulino Bianco, the Italian producer of cakes, biscuits and cereals, carefully developed a campaign depicting the quiet aspects of rural life to increase sales of cakes, which are typically served only on special occasions. The campaign showed a white farmhouse on a green hill, next to a water-mill. Parents, children and friends are shown in a slow, relaxed, informal atmosphere, far from the hectic urban commitments of work. The object was to evoke a relationship between 'the good old days' and cakes, and to present cakes as genuine food to be eaten every day during normal meals. In Italy, where the tension to escape from the hectic urban life is high, the campaign was quite successful. In France, where eating habits are different, and the appeal to rural life is weaker, the same campaign was not successful.[71]

The rebirth of the Beetle

Hoping to win back former buyers – and to lure new ones – Volkswagen has in the past few years unveiled an updated version of the small, round-shouldered car that became a generational icon in the US in the 1960s and 1970s. Back in those days, the 'Bug' was cramped and noisy, but it was a hit because it was relatively cheap, fuel-efficient, and had symbolic value as a protest against Detroit's 'big boats'. In contrast to the Bug of old, the new one caters to consumers craving for space, with more headroom and legroom in front. Jens Neumann, the VW executive in charge of North America, feels 'The Beetle is the core of the VW soul. If we put it back in people's minds, they will think of our other products more.' The revised Beetle's resemblance to the old one is literally skin deep. Unlike the original, which had an air-cooled engine in the rear, the new Beetle is packed with the latest German technology, including an optional fuel-efficient turbo-diesel direct-injection motor. Otherwise the car is essentially a Golf with a number of Beetle-type characteristics to evoke nostalgia: curvy body panels; round dashboard dials and controls; circular sideview mirrors; side running boards; and indented door handles you grip to open. In the US, VW has deliberately priced the Bug above cars that appeal to most first-time buyers because it intends to attract far more than the college-age market. 'It is a classless car, and the Beetle will target a broad swathe of people who simply *love* the car, and aren't just looking for a utilitarian commuting box.' So far, the car boasts the youngest demographics in the US automobile industry. However, while the reintroduction of the Beetle has been successful in the US, its nostalgic appeal has not extended to Europe, where VW's Golf model is far more popular.[72]

Memory and aesthetic preferences

In addition to liking ads and products that remind us of our past, our prior experiences also help to determine what we like now. Some recent research indicates that

With an eye on the future, and nostalgia for the past: the Mercedes and the Trabant represent different aspects of learning, memory and aesthetics for consumers in the eastern part of Germany.
Photo by Julia Helmsley.

people's tastes in such products as films and clothing are influenced by what was popular during certain critical periods of their youth. For example, liking for specific songs appears to be related to how old a person was when those songs were popular: on average, songs that were popular when an individual was 23–24 years old are the most likely to be favoured.[73] In the United States, the Nickelodeon cable network programmes its Nick at Nite segment, which features repeats, by selecting the shows that were highly rated when its major audience was 12 years old.[74] Similar programming strategies are followed by several satellite stations throughout Europe. In addition, it seems that men form preferences for women's clothing styles that were in vogue when these men were in their early twenties.[75]

More generally, many marketers understand that life-long brand loyalties are formed at a fairly early age: they view the battle for the hearts (and wallets) of students and young adults as a long-term investment. These age-related preferences will be further addressed in Chapter 13.

Measuring memory for advertising

Because advertisers pay so much money to place their messages in front of consumers, they are naturally concerned that people will actually remember these messages at a later point. It seems that they have good reason to be concerned. In one study, less than 40 per cent of television viewers made positive links between commercial messages and the corresponding products; only 65 per cent noticed the brand name in a commercial; and only 38 per cent recognized a connection to an important point.[76]

More worryingly, only 7 per cent of television viewers can recall the product or company featured in the most recent television commercial they watched. This figure represents less than half the recall rate recorded in 1965 and may be attributed to such factors as the increase of 30- and 15-second commercials and the practice of airing television commercials in clusters rather than in connection with single-sponsor programmes.[77]

Recognition vs. recall
One indicator of good advertising is, of course, the impression it makes on consumers. But how can this impact be defined and measured? Two basic measures of

impact are recognition and recall. In the typical recognition test, subjects are shown ads one at a time and asked if they have seen them before. In contrast, free recall tests ask consumers to produce independently previously acquired information and then perform a recognition test on it.

Under some conditions, these two memory measures tend to yield the same results, especially when the researchers try to keep the viewers' interest in the ads constant.[78] Generally, though, recognition scores tend to be more reliable and do not decay over time in the way recall scores do.[79] Recognition scores are almost always better than recall scores because recognition is a simpler process and more retrieval cues are available to the consumer.

Both types of retrieval play important roles in purchase decisions. Recall tends to be more important in situations where consumers do not have product data at their disposal, and so they must rely upon memory to generate this information.[80] On the other hand, recognition is more likely to be an important factor in a store, where consumers are confronted with thousands of product options and information (i.e. where external memory is abundantly available) and where the task may simply be to recognize a familiar package. Unfortunately, package recognition and familiarity can have a negative consequence in that warning labels may be ignored, since their existence is taken for granted and not really noticed.[81]

The Starch Test

A widely used commercial measure of advertising recall for magazines is called the Starch Test, a syndicated service founded in 1932. This service provides scores on a number of aspects of consumers' familiarity with an ad, including such categories as 'noted', 'associated' and 'read most'. It also scores the impact of the component parts of an overall ad, giving such information as 'seen' for major illustrations and 'read some' for a major block of copy.[82] Such factors as the size of the ad, whether it appears towards the front or the back of the magazine, if it is on the right or left page, and the size of illustrations play an important role in affecting the amount of attention given to an ad as determined by Starch scores.

Problems with memory measures

While the measurement of an ad's memorability is important, the ability of existing measures to assess these dimensions accurately has been criticized for several reasons.

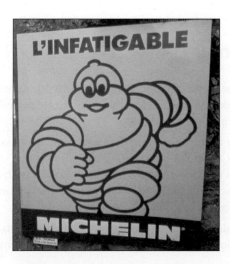

A picture is worth a thousand words. Product icons – like the Michelin Man who has appeared in ads and on packaging for more than 30 years – are a significant factor in product recognition.

Response biases Results obtained from a measuring instrument are not necessarily due to what is being measured, but rather to something else about the instrument or the respondent. This form of contamination is called a **response bias**. For example, people tend to give 'yes' responses to questions regardless of what is asked. In addition, consumers are often eager to be 'good subjects' by pleasing the experimenter. They will try to give the responses they think he or she is looking for. In some studies, the claimed recognition of bogus ads (ads that have not been seen before) is almost as high as the recognition rate of real ads.[83]

Memory lapses People are also prone to forgetting information unintentionally. Typical problems include omitting (the leaving out of facts), averaging (the tendency to 'normalize' things and not report extreme cases), and telescoping (the inaccurate recall of time).[84] These distortions call into question the accuracy of various product usage databases that rely upon consumers to recall their purchase and consumption of food and household items. In one study, for example, people were asked to describe what portion of various foods – small, medium or large – they ate in a normal meal; however, different definitions of 'medium' were used (e.g. 185 ml versus 375 ml). Regardless of the measurement specified, about the same number of people claimed they normally ate medium portions.[85]

Memory for facts vs. feelings Although techniques are being developed to increase the accuracy of memory scores, these improvements do not address the more fundamental issue of whether recall is necessary for advertising to have an effect. In particular, some critics argue that these measures do not adequately tap the impact of 'feeling' ads where the objective is to arouse strong emotions rather than to convey concrete product benefits. Many ad campaigns, including those for Hallmark cards, Chevrolet and Pepsi, use this approach.[86] An effective strategy relies on a long-term build-up of feeling rather than on a one-shot attempt to convince consumers to buy the product.

Also, it is not clear that recall translates into preference. We may recall the benefits touted in an ad but not believe them. Or the ad may be memorable because it is so obnoxious, and the product becomes one we 'love to hate'. The bottom line is that while recall is important, especially for creating brand awareness, it is not necessarily sufficient to alter consumer preferences. To accomplish this, marketers need more sophisticated attitude-change strategies. These issues will be discussed in Chapters 5 and 6.

Chapter summary

- Learning is a change in behaviour that is caused by experience. Learning can occur through simple associations between a stimulus and a response or via a complex series of cognitive activities.

- Behavioural learning theories assume that learning occurs as a result of responses to external events. Classical conditioning occurs when a stimulus that naturally elicits a response (an unconditioned stimulus) is paired with another stimulus that does not initially elicit this response. Over time, the second stimulus (the conditioned stimulus) comes to elicit the response as well.

- This response can also extend to other, similar, stimuli in a process known as stimulus generalization. This process is the basis for such marketing strategies as licensing and family branding, in which a consumer's positive associations with a product are transferred to other contexts.

- Operant or instrumental conditioning occurs as the person learns to perform behaviours that produce positive outcomes and avoid those that result in negative outcomes. While classical conditioning involves the pairing of two stimuli, instrumental learning occurs when reinforcement is delivered following a response to a stimulus. Reinforcement is positive if a reward is delivered following a response. It is negative if a negative outcome is avoided by not performing a response. Punishment occurs when a response is followed by unpleasant events. Extinction of the behaviour will occur if reinforcement is no longer received.

- Cognitive learning occurs as the result of mental processes. For example, observational learning takes place when the consumer performs a behaviour as a result of seeing someone else performing it and being rewarded for it.

- Memory refers to the storage of learned information. The way information is encoded when it is perceived determines how it will be stored in memory. The memory systems known as sensory memory, short-term memory and long-term memory each play a role in retaining and processing information from the outside world.

- Information is not stored in isolation, it is incorporated into knowledge structures, where it is associated with other related data. The location of product information in associative networks and the level of abstraction at which it is coded help to determine when and how this information will be activated at a later time. Some factors that influence the likelihood of retrieval include the level of familiarity with an item, its salience (or prominence) in memory and whether the information was presented in pictorial or written form.

- Products also play a role as memory markers: they are used by consumers to retrieve memories about past experiences (autobiographical memories) and are often valued for their ability to do this. This function also contributes to the use of nostalgia in marketing strategies.

- Memory for product information can be measured through either recognition or recall techniques. Consumers are more likely to recognize an advertisement if it is presented to them than to recall one without being given any cues.

KEY TERMS

Activation models of memory (p. 77)
Behavioural learning theories (p. 65)
Brand equity (p. 71)
Classical conditioning (p. 65)
Cognitive learning (p. 69)
Encoding (p. 75)
Evoked set (p. 78)
Extinction (p. 66)
Frequency marketing (p. 74)
Interference (p. 81)
Knowledge structures (p. 78)
Learning (p. 65)
Long-term memory (p. 77)
Memory (p. 75)

Negative reinforcement (p. 67)
Nostalgia (p. 82)
Observational learning (p. 70)
Operant conditioning (p. 67)
Positive reinforcement (p. 67)
Punishment (p. 67)
Response bias (p. 86)
Retrieval (p. 75)
Schema (p. 79)
Sensory memory (p. 76)
Short-term memory (p. 76)
Stimulus discrimination (p. 67)
Stimulus generalization (p. 66)
Storage (p. 75)

For additional material see the companion website at:
www.booksites.net/solomon_euro

Consumer behaviour challenge

1 Identify three patterns of reinforcement and provide an example of how each is used in a marketing context.

2 Describe the functions of short-term and long-term memory. What is the apparent relationship between the two?

3 Devise a 'product jingle memory test'. Compile a list of brands that are or have been associated with memorable jingles, such as Opal Fruits or Heinz Baked Beans. Read this list to friends, and see how many jingles are remembered. You may be surprised at the level of recall.

4 Identify some important characteristics for a product with a well-known brand name. Based on these attributes, generate a list of possible brand extension or licensing opportunities, as well as some others that would most likely not be accepted by consumers.

5 Collect some pictures of 'classic' products that have high nostalgia value. Show these pictures to consumers and allow them to free associate. Analyse the types of memories that are evoked, and think about how these associations might be employed in a product's promotional strategy.

Notes

1. Robert A. Baron, *Psychology: The Essential Science* (Boston: Allyn & Bacon, 1989).
2. Richard A. Feinberg, 'Credit Cards as Spending Facilitating Stimuli: A Conditioning Interpretation', *Journal of Consumer Research* 13 (December 1986): 348–56.
3. R. A. Rescorla, 'Pavlovian Conditioning: It's Not What You Think It Is', *American Psychologist* 43 (1988): 151–60; Elnora W. Stuart, Terence A. Shimp and Randall W. Engle, 'Classical Conditioning of Consumer Attitudes: Four Experiments in an Advertising Context', *Journal of Consumer Research* 14 (December 1987): 334–9; Terence A. Shimp, Elnora W. Stuart and Randall W. Engle, 'A Program of Classical Conditioning Experiments Testing Variations in the Conditioned Stimulus and Context', *Journal of Consumer Research* 18(1) (June 1991): 1–12.
4. 'Anemic Crocodile', *Forbes* (15 August 1994): 116.
5. Baron, *Psychology*.
6. For a comprehensive approach to consumer behaviour based on operant conditioning principles, see Gordon R. Foxall, 'Behavior Analysis and Consumer Psychology', *Journal of Economic Psychology* 15 (March 1994): 5–91. Foxall also sets out some consumer behaviour based on a neo-behaviourist perspective. By identifying environmental determinants, he develops four classes of consumer behaviour: *accomplishment, pleasure, accumulation* and *maintenance*. For an extensive discussion on this approach, see the entire special issue of Gordon R. Foxall, 'Science and Interpretation in Consumer Behavior: A Radical Behaviourist Perspective', *European Journal of Marketing* 29(9) (1995): 3–99.
7. Ellen J. Langer, *The Psychology of Control* (Beverly Hills, CA: Sage, 1983); Klaus G. Grunert, 'Automatic and Strategic Processes in Advertising Effects', *Journal of Marketing* 60 (1996): 88–91.
8. Robert B. Cialdini, *Influence: Science and Practice*, 2nd edn (New York: William Morrow, 1984).
9. Chris T. Allen and Thomas J. Madden, 'A Closer Look at Classical Conditioning', *Journal of Consumer Research* 12 (December 1985): 301–15.
10. Albert Bandura, *Social Foundations of Thought and Action: A Social Cognitive View* (Englewood Cliffs, NJ: Prentice Hall, 1986); Baron, *Psychology*.
11. Allen and Madden, 'A Closer Look at Classical Conditioning'; Chester A. Insko and William F. Oakes, 'Awareness and the Conditioning of Attitudes', *Journal of Personality and Social Psychology* 4 (November 1966): 487–96; Carolyn K. Staats and Arthur W. Staats, 'Meaning Established by Classical Conditioning', *Journal of Experimental Psychology* 54 (July 1957): 74–80; Randi Priluck Grossman and Brian D. Till, 'The Persistence of Classically

Conditioned Brand Attitudes', *Journal of Advertising* 21(1) (Spring 1998): 23–31.

12. Stijn M. J. van Osselaer and Hjoseph W. Alba, 'Consumer Learning and Brand Equity', *Journal of Consumer Research* 27(1) (June 2000): 1–16; Kevin Lane Keller, 'Conceptualizing, Measuring, and Managing Customer-Based Brand Equity', *Journal of Marketing* 57 (January 1993): 1–22; Patrick Bawise, 'Brand Equity: Snark or Boojum?', *International Journal of Research in Marketing* 10 (1993) 93–104; W. Fred van Raaij and Wim Schoonderbeer, 'Meaning Structure of Brand Names and Extensions', in W. Fred van Raaij and Gary J. Bamossy, eds, *European Advances in Consumer Research* (Provo, UT: Association for Consumer Research, 1993): 479–84; Gil McWilliam, 'The Effect of Brand Typology on Brand Extension Fit: Commercial and Academic Research Findings', in *European Advances in Association for Consumer Research*: 485–91; Elyette Roux and Frederic Lorange, 'Brand Extension Research: A Review', in *European Advances in Consumer Research*: 492–500; 'The Art of Perception', *Marketing* (28 November 1996): 25–9.

13. Herbert Krugman, 'Low Recall and High Recognition of Advertising', *Journal of Advertising Research* (February/March 1986): 79–86.

14. Gerald J. Gorn, 'The Effects of Music in Advertising on Choice Behavior: A Classical Conditioning Approach', *Journal of Marketing* 46 (Winter 1982): 94–101.

15. Calvin Bierley, Frances K. McSweeney and Renee Vannieuwkerk, 'Classical Conditioning of Preferences for Stimuli', *Journal of Consumer Research* 12 (December 1985): 316–23; James J. Kellaris and Anthony D. Cox, 'The Effects of Background Music in Advertising: A Reassessment', *Journal of Consumer Research* 16 (June 1989): 113–18.

16. Frances K. McSweeney and Calvin Bierley, 'Recent Developments in Classical Conditioning', *Journal of Consumer Research* 11 (September 1984): 619–31.

17. Basil G. Englis, 'The Reinforcement Properties of Music Videos: "I Want My . . . I Want My . . . I Want My . . . MTV"' (paper presented at the meetings of the Association for Consumer Research, New Orleans, 1989).

18. 'Giving Bad Puns the Business', *Newsweek* (11 December 1989): 71.

19. Bernice Kanner, 'Growing Pains – and Gains: Brand Names Branch Out', *New York* (13 March 1989): 22.

20. Peter H. Farquhar, 'Brand Equity', *Marketing Insights* (Summer 1989): 59.

21. John Marchese, 'Forever Harley', *New York Times* (17 October 1993): 10; 'Spamming the Globe', *Newsweek* (29 August 1994): 8.

22. Quoted in 'Look-Alikes Mimic Familiar Packages', *New York Times* (9 August 1986): D1; 'Action Fails to Match Spirit of Lookalike Law', *Marketing* (27 March 1997): 19.

23. Laurie Hays, 'Too Many Computer Names Confuse Too Many Buyers', *Wall Street Journal* (29 June 1994): B1 (2 pp.).

24. Blaise J. Bergiel and Christine Trosclair, 'Instrumental Learning: Its Application to Customer Satisfaction', *Journal of Consumer Marketing* 2 (Fall 1985): 23–8.

25. Terence A. Shimp, 'Neo-Pavlovian Conditioning and Its Implications for Consumer Theory and Research', in Thomas S. Robertson and Harold H. Kassarjian, eds, *Handbook of Consumer Behavior* (Englewood Cliffs, NJ: Prentice Hall, 1991).

26. K. K. Desai and Wayne Hoyer, 'Descriptive Characteristics of Memory-Based Consideration Sets: Influence of Usage Occasion Frequency and Usage Location Familiarity, *Journal of Consumer Research* 27, (3), (December 2000): 309–23; R. C. Atkinson and R. M. Shiffrin, 'Human Memory: A Proposed System and Its Control Processes', in K. W. Spence and J. T. Spence, eds, *The Psychology of Learning and Motivation: Advances in Research and Theory* (New York: Academic Press, 1968): 89–195.

27. James R. Bettman, 'Memory Factors in Consumer Choice: A Review', *Journal of Marketing* (Spring 1979): 37–53. For a study that explored the relative impact of internal versus external memory on brand choice, cf. Joseph W. Alba, Howard Marmorstein and Amitava Chattopadhyay, 'Transitions in Preference Over Time: The Effects of Memory on Message Persuasiveness', *Journal of Marketing Research* 29 (November 1992): 406–17. For other research on memory and advertising, see H. Shanker Krishnan and Dipankar Chakravarti, 'Varieties of Brand Memory Induced by Advertising: Determinants, Measures, and Relationships', in David A. Aaker and Alexander L. Biel, eds, *Brand Equity & Advertising: Advertising's Role in Building Strong Brands* (Hillsdale, NJ: Lawrence Erlbaum Associates, 1993): 213–31; Bernd H. Schmitt, Nader T. Tavassoli and Robert T. Millard, 'Memory for Print Ads: Understanding Relations Among Brand Name, Copy, and Picture', *Journal of Consumer Psychology* 2(1) (1993): 55–81; Marian Friestad and Esther Thorson, 'Remembering Ads: The Effects of Encoding Strategies, Retrieval Cues, and Emotional Response', *Journal of Consumer Psychology* 2(1) (1993): 1–23; Surendra N. Singh, Sanjay Mishra, Neeli Bendapudi and Denise Linville, 'Enhancing Memory of Television Commercials Through Message Spacing', *Journal of Marketing Research* 31 (August 1994): 384–92.

28. Kathryn R Braun, 'Postexperience Advertising Effects on Consumer Memory', *Journal of Consumer Research* 25 (March 1999): 319–34.

29. Kim Robertson, 'Recall and Recognition Effects of Brand Name Imagery', *Psychology & Marketing* 4 (Spring 1987): 3–15.

30. Endel Tulving, 'Remembering and Knowing the Past', *American Scientist* 77 (July/August 1989): 361.

31. Rashmi Adaval and Robert S. Wyer, Jr., 'The Role of Narratives in Consumer Information Processing',

Journal of Consumer Psychology 7(3) (1998), 207–246.

32. Baron, *Psychology*.

33. George A. Miller, 'The Magical Number Seven, Plus or Minus Two: Some Limits on Our Capacity for Processing Information', *Psychological Review* 63 (1956): 81–97.

34. James N. MacGregor, 'Short-Term Memory Capacity: Limitation or Optimization?', *Psychological Review* 94 (1987): 107–8.

35. See Catherine A. Cole and Michael J. Houston, 'Encoding and Media Effects on Consumer Learning Deficiencies in the Elderly', *Journal of Marketing Research* 24 (February 1987): 55–64; A. M. Collins and E. F. Loftus, 'A Spreading Activation Theory of Semantic Processing', *Psychological Review* 82 (1975): 407–28; Fergus I. M. Craik and Robert S. Lockhart, 'Levels of Processing: A Framework for Memory Research', *Journal of Verbal Learning and Verbal Behavior* 11 (1972): 671–84.

36. Walter A. Henry, 'The Effect of Information-Processing Ability on Processing Accuracy', *Journal of Consumer Research* 7 (June 1980): 42–8.

37. Anthony G. Greenwald and Clark Leavitt, 'Audience Involvement in Advertising: Four Levels', *Journal of Consumer Research* 11 (June 1984): 581–92.

38. Kevin Lane Keller, 'Memory Factors in Advertising: The Effect of Advertising Retrieval Cues on Brand Evaluations', *Journal of Consumer Research* 14 (December 1987): 316–33. For a discussion of processing operations that occur during brand choice, see Gabriel Biehal and Dipankar Chakravarti, 'Consumers' Use of Memory and External Information in Choice: Macro and Micro Perspectives', *Journal of Consumer Research* 12 (March 1986): 382–405.

39. Susan T. Fiske and Shelley E. Taylor, *Social Cognition* (Reading, MA: Addison-Wesley, 1984).

40. Deborah Roedder John and John C. Whitney, Jr, 'The Development of Consumer Knowledge in Children: A Cognitive Structure Approach', *Journal of Consumer Research* 12 (March 1986): 406–17.

41. Michael R. Solomon, Carol Surprenant, John A. Czepiel and Evelyn G. Gutman, 'A Role Theory Perspective on Dyadic Interactions: The Service Encounter', *Journal of Marketing* 49 (winter 1985): 99–111.

42. Roger W. Morrell, Denise C. Park and Leonard W. Poon, 'Quality of Instructions on Prescription Drug Labels: Effects on Memory and Comprehension in Young and Old Adults', *The Gerontologist* 29 (1989): 345–54.

43. Frank R. Kardes, Gurumurthy Kalyanaram, Murali Chandrashekaran and Ronald J. Dornoff, 'Brand Retrieval, Consideration Set Composition, Consumer Choice, and the Pioneering Advantage' (unpublished manuscript, University of Cincinnati, OH, 1992).

44. Nijar Dawar and Philip Parket, 'Marketing Universals: Consumers' Use of Brand Name, Price, Physical Appearance, and Retailer Reputation as Signals of Product Quality', *Journal of Marketing* 58 (1994) 81–95; Judith Lynne Zaichkowsky and Padma Vipat, 'Inferences from Brand Names', in van Raaij and Bamossy, eds, *European Advances in Consumer Research*: 534–40.

45. Krugman, 'Low Recall and High Recognition of Advertising'.

46. Rik G. M. Pieters and Tammo H. A. Bijmolt, 'Consumer Memory for Television Advertising: A Field Study of Duration, Serial Position, and Competition Effects', *Journal of Consumer Research* 23 (March 1997): 362–72.

47. Margaret G. Meloy, 'Mood-Driven Distortion of Product Information', *Journal of Consumer Research* 27(3) (December 2000): 345–59.

48. Eric J. Johnson and J. Edward Russo, 'Product Familiarity and Learning New Information', *Journal of Consumer Research* 11 (June 1984): 542–50.

49. Eric J. Johnson and J. Edward Russo, 'Product Familiarity and Learning New Information', in Kent Monoe, ed., *Advances in Consumer Research* 8 (Ann Arbor, MI: Association for Consumer Research, 1981): 151–5; John G. Lynch and Thomas K. Srull, 'Memory and Attentional Factors in Consumer Choice: Concepts and Research Methods', *Journal of Consumer Research* 9 (June 1982): 18–37.

50. Julie A. Edell and Kevin Lane Keller, 'The Information Processing of Coordinated Media Campaigns', *Journal of Marketing Research* 26 (May 1989): 149–64.

51. Lynch and Srull, 'Memory and Attentional Factors in Consumer Choice'.

52. Joseph W. Alba and Amitava Chattopadhyay, 'Salience Effects in Brand Recall', *Journal of Marketing Research* 23 (November 1986): 363–70; Elizabeth C. Hirschman and Michael R. Solomon, 'Utilitarian, Aesthetic, and Familiarity Responses to Verbal Versus Visual Advertisements', in *Advances in Consumer Research* 11, ed. Thomas C. Kinnear (Provo, UT: Association for Consumer Research, 1984): 426–31.

53. Susan E. Heckler and Terry L. Childers, 'The Role of Expectancy and Relevancy in Memory for Verbal and Visual Information: What is Incongruency?', *Journal of Consumer Research* 18 (March 1992): 475–92.

54. Russell H. Fazio, Paul M. Herr and Martha C. Powell, 'On the Development and Strength of Category-Brand Associations in Memory: The Case of Mystery Ads', *Journal of Consumer Psychology* 1(1) (1992): 1–13.

55. Hirschman and Solomon, 'Utilitarian, Aesthetic, and Familiarity Responses to Verbal Versus Visual Advertisements'.

56. Terry Childers and Michael Houston, 'Conditions for a Picture-Superiority Effect on Consumer Memory', *Journal of Consumer Research* 11 (September 1984): 643–54; Terry Childers, Susan Heckler and Michael Houston, 'Memory for the Visual and Verbal Components of Print Advertisements', *Psychology & Marketing* 3 (Fall 1986): 147–50.

57. Werner Krober-Riel, 'Effects of Emotional Pictorial

Elements in Ads Analyzed by Means of Eye Movement Monitoring', in Thomas C. Kinnear, ed., *Advances in Consumer Research* 11 (Provo, UT: Association for Consumer Research, 1984): 591–6.

58. Hans-Bernd Brosius, 'Influence of Presentation Features and News Context on Learning .rom Television News', *Journal of Broadcasting & Electronic Media* 33 (Winter 1989): 1–14.

59. Raymond R. Burke and Thomas K. Srull, 'Competitive Interference and Consumer Memory for Advertising', *Journal of Consumer Research* 15 (June 1988): 55–68.

60. Ibid.

61. Johnson and Russo, 'Product Familiarity and Learning New Information'.

62. Joan Meyers-Levy, 'The Influence of Brand Names Association Set Size and Word Frequency on Brand Memory', *Journal of Consumer Research* 16 (September 1989): 197–208.

63. Michael H. Baumgardner, Michael R. Leippe, David L. Ronis and Anthony G. Greenwald, 'In Search of Reliable Persuasion Effects: II. Associative Interference and Persistence of Persuasion in a Message-Dense Environment', *Journal of Personality and Social Psychology* 45 (September 1983): 524–37.

64. Alba and Chattopadhyay, 'Salience Effects in Brand Recall'.

65. Margaret Henderson Blair, Allan R. Kuse, David H. Furse and David W. Stewart, 'Advertising in a New and Competitive Environment: Persuading Consumers to Buy', *Business Horizons* 30 (November/December 1987): 20.

66. Lynch and Srull, 'Memory and Attentional Factors in Consumer Choice'.

67. Russell W. Belk, 'Possessions and the Extended Self', *Journal of Consumer Research* 15 (September 1988): 139–68.

68. Russell W. Belk, 'The Role of Possessions in Constructing and Maintaining a Sense of Past', in Marvin E. Goldberg, Gerald Gorn and Richard W. Pollay, eds, *Advances in Consumer Research* 16 (Provo, UT: Association for Consumer Research, 1989): 669–78.

69. Hans Baumgartner, Mita Sujan and James R. Bettman, 'Autobiographical Memories, Affect and Consumer Information Processing', *Journal of Consumer Psychology* 1 (January 1992): 53–82; Mita Sujan, James R. Bettman and Hans Baumgartner, 'Influencing Consumer Judgments Using Autobiographical Memories: A Self-Referencing Perspective', *Journal of Marketing Research* 30 (November 1993): 422–36.

70. Roger Thurow, 'Bucharest is Plastered with J.R. Ewing in an Ad Push by Russian Oil Company', *Wall Street Journal Interactive Edition* (21 December 1999).

71. Gabriella Stern, 'VW Hopes Nostalgia will Spur Sales of Retooled Beetle, Fuel US Comback', *Wall Street Journal, Europe* (7 May 1997): 4; 'Ostalgie for the Day When They'd Never Had it so Good', *The*

Independent (10 February 1997); Almar Latour, 'Shelf Wars', *Central European Economic Review* 4 (Dow Jones, May 1997); G. Morello, *The Hidden Dimensions of Marketing* (Amsterdam: Vrije Universiteit, 1993): 13.

72. Kevin Goldman, 'New Campaigns Tip the Hat to Nostalgia', *Wall Street Journal* (9 August 1994): B4. Jean Halliday, 'VW Beetle: Liz Vanzura', *Advertising Age* 70 (1999): 4; Daniel Howes, 'VW Beetle is A Bust In Europe, Where Golf is Car Of Choice', *Detroit News* (13 April 1999): B1.

73. Morris B. Holbrook and Robert M. Schindler, 'Some Exploratory Findings on the Development of Musical Tastes', *Journal of Consumer Research* 16 (June 1989): 119–24.

74. Randall Rothenberg, 'The Past is Now the Latest Craze', *New York Times* (29 November 1989): D1.

75. Cf. Morris B. Holbrook, 'Nostalgia and Consumption Preferences: Some Emerging Patterns of Consumer Tastes', *Journal of Consumer Research* 20 (September 1993): 245–56; Robert M. Schindler and Morris B. Holbrook, 'Critical Periods in the Development of Men's and Women's Tastes in Personal Appearance', *Psychology & Marketing* 10(6) (November/December 1993): 549–64; Morris B. Holbrook and Robert M. Schindler, 'Age, Sex, and Attitude Toward the Past as Predictors of Consumers' Aesthetic Tastes for Cultural Products', *Journal of Marketing Research* 31 (August 1994): 412–22.

76. 'Only 38% of T.V. Audience Links Brands with Ads', *Marketing News* (6 January 1984): 10.

77. 'Terminal Television', *American Demographics* (January 1987): 15.

78. Richard P. Bagozzi and Alvin J. Silk, 'Recall, Recognition, and the Measurement of Memory for Print Advertisements', *Marketing Science* (1983): 95–134.

79. Adam Finn, 'Print Ad Recognition Readership Scores: An Information Processing Perspective', *Journal of Marketing Research* 25 (May 1988): 168–77.

80. Bettman, 'Memory Factors in Consumer Choice'.

81. Mark A. deTurck and Gerald M. Goldhaber, 'Effectiveness of Product Warning Labels: Effects of Consumers' Information Processing Objectives', *Journal of Consumer Affairs* 23(1) (1989): 111–25.

82. Finn, 'Print Ad Recognition Readership Scores'.

83. Surendra N. Singh and Gilbert A. Churchill, Jr, 'Response-Bias-Free Recognition Tests to Measure Advertising Effects', *Journal of Advertising Research* 29 (June/July 1987): 23–36.

84. William A. Cook, 'Telescoping and Memory's Other Tricks', *Journal of Advertising Research* 27 (February/March 1987): 5–8.

85. 'On a Diet? Don't Trust Your Memory', *Psychology Today* (October 1989): 12.

86. Hubert A. Zielske and Walter A. Henry, 'Remembering and Forgetting Television Ads', *Journal of Advertising Research* 20 (April 1980): 7–13.

Chapter 4

Motivation, values and involvement

It's been two years since Peter gave up smoking, drinking and junk food. He now devotes the same enthusiasm to working out that he used to bring to partying. Peter has become a dedicated triathlete. Participating in this sport, which involves running, swimming and cycling, has become so important to Peter that he now structures his entire life around his training regime. He even decided to forgo an important class he would have liked to have taken because it was on at the same time as he did his daily run.

Peter has become so engrossed in the sport that his friends hardly see him – he spends most of his free time (when not in training) reading magazines dedicated to the sport, shopping for special equipment such as running shoes and Lycra tights for winter training, or travelling to triathlon events all over Europe. His girlfriend complains that lately he likes looking at himself in the mirror more than he likes looking at her.

Peter remains committed – he's nothing if not dedicated to the cause . . .

Introduction

Some people are so involved in an activity that they can be termed *fanatic consumers*. Whether they are training for a triathlon, watching television or playing music, these people tend to become totally engrossed in an activity to the point where such involvement has been called a 'positive addiction'. One survey of triathletes (like Peter) found that intense commitment to the sport resulted in a highly modified daily schedule, unwillingness to stop training even if injured, major dietary changes and – most relevant to marketers – a substantial financial commitment to travel to races, specialized clothing and health club membership.[1]

The forces that drive people to buy and use products can sometimes seem quite straightforward, as when a person purchases a box of cornflakes after consuming the previous one. But some questions remain unanswered, such as why do we eat cornflakes rather than other things? And why do we buy one brand rather than another? As hard-core triathletes like Peter demonstrate, the consumption of an everyday product such as running shoes may be related to deep-seated experiences. In some cases, these emotional responses create a deep commitment to the product. Sometimes, people are not even fully aware of the forces that drive them towards some products and away from others. Often these choices are influenced by the person's *values* – his or her priorities and beliefs about the world.

To understand motivation is to understand *why* consumers do what they do. Why do people choose to bungy jump from a bridge or go white-water rafting, while others spend their leisure time playing chess or gardening? Everything that we do is rooted in a number of reasons, whether to quench a thirst, kill boredom or attain a deep spiritual experience. Marketing students are taught from day one that the goal of marketing is to satisfy consumers' needs. However, this insight is useless unless we can discover *what* those needs are and *why* they exist.

The motivation process: a psychological perspective

Motivation refers to the processes that cause people to behave as they do. From a *psychological perspective*, motivation occurs when a **need** is aroused that the consumer wishes to satisfy. Once a need has been activated, a state of tension exists that drives the consumer to attempt to reduce or eliminate the need. This need may be predominantly utilitarian (i.e. a desire to achieve some functional or practical benefit, as when a person requires a pair of durable sneakers, or sports shoes) or it may be predominantly hedonic (i.e. an experiential need, involving emotional responses or fantasies, as when Peter buys special running shoes for a triathlon event). The distinction between the two is, however, a matter of degree. The desired end-state is the consumer's **goal**. Marketers try to create products and services that will provide the desired benefits and permit the consumer to reduce this tension.

Whether the need is utilitarian or hedonic, a discrepancy exists between the

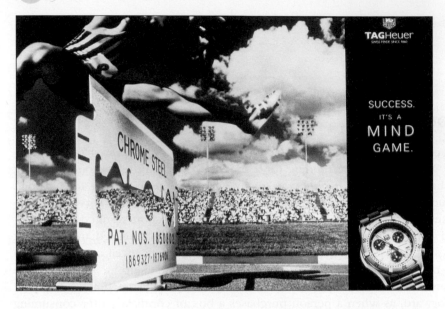

The Swiss watchmaker TAGHeuer uses the sport metaphor of world-class competition to emphasize motivation, and top performance.
Used with permission of TAGHeuer.

consumer's present state and some ideal state. This gulf creates a state of tension. The magnitude of this tension determines the urgency the consumer feels to reduce the tension, and this degree of arousal is called a drive. A basic need can be satisfied in any number of ways, and the specific path a person chooses is influenced by his or her unique set of experiences, cultural background and so on.

These personal and cultural factors combine to create a **want**, which is one manifestation of a need. For example, hunger is a basic need that must be satisfied by all: the lack of food creates a state of tension that can be reduced by the intake of such products as pizzas, chocolate biscuits, raw fish or bean sprouts. Throughout the world, the consumer's specific route to hunger reduction is culturally determined.

Once the goal is attained, tension is reduced and the motivation recedes (temporarily). Motivation can be described in terms of its strength, or the pull it exerts on the consumer, and its direction, or the particular way the consumer attempts to reduce motivational tension.

Motivational strength

The degree to which a person is willing to expend energy to reach one goal as opposed to another reflects his or her underlying motivation to attain that goal. Many theories have been advanced to explain why people behave the way they do. Most share the basic idea that people have some finite amount of energy that must be directed towards certain goals.

Biological vs. learned needs

Early work on motivation ascribed behaviour to instinct, the innate patterns of behaviour that are universal in a species. This view is now largely discredited. For one thing, the existence of an instinct is difficult to prove or disprove. The instinct is inferred from the behaviour it is supposed to explain (this type of circular explanation is called a *tautology*).[2] It is like saying that a consumer buys products that are status symbols because he or she is motivated to attain status, which is hardly a satisfying explanation.

Drive theory

▶ **Drive theory** focuses on biological needs that produce unpleasant states of arousal (e.g. your stomach rumbles during a morning class). We are motivated to reduce the tension caused by this arousal. Tension reduction has been proposed as a basic mechanism governing human behaviour.

In marketing, tension refers to the unpleasant state that exists if a person's consumption needs are not fulfilled. A person may be irritable if he hasn't eaten, or he may be dejected or angry if he cannot afford the new car he wants. This state activates goal-oriented behaviour, which attempts to reduce or eliminate this unpleasant state and return to a balanced one, known as *homeostasis*.

Those behaviours that are successful in reducing the drive by eliminating the underlying need are strengthened and tend to be repeated. (This aspect of the learning process was discussed in Chapter 3.) Your motivation to leave class early in order to grab a snack would be greater if you hadn't eaten in 24 hours than if you had eaten only two hours earlier. If you did sneak out and got indigestion after, say, wolfing down a packet of crisps, this behaviour would be less likely to be repeated the next time you wanted a snack. One's degree of motivation, then, depends upon the distance between one's present state and the goal.

Drive theory, however, runs into difficulties when it tries to explain some facets of human behaviour that run counter to its predictions. People often do things that *increase* a drive state rather than decrease it. For example, people may delay gratification. If you know you are going out for a five-course dinner, you might decide to forgo a snack earlier in the day even though you are hungry at that time. And, as we shall see in the discussion of desire, the most rewarding thing may often be the tension of the drive state itself rather than its satisfaction. It's not the kill, it's the thrill of the chase.

Expectancy theory

Most current explanations of motivation focus on cognitive factors rather than bio-
▶ logical ones to understand what drives behaviour. **Expectancy theory** suggests that behaviour is largely pulled by expectations of achieving desirable outcomes – *positive incentives* – rather than pushed from within. We choose one product over another because we expect this choice to have more positive consequences for us. Thus the term *drive* is used here more loosely to refer to both physical and cognitive, i.e. learned, processes.

Motivational direction

Motives have direction as well as strength. They are goal-oriented in that specific objectives are desired to satisfy a need. Most goals can be reached by a number of routes, and the objective of marketers is to convince consumers that the alternative they offer provides the best chance to attain the goal. For example, a consumer who decides that he needs a pair of jeans to help him reach his goal of being accepted by others or of projecting an appropriate image can choose between Levi's, Diesel, Wranglers, FUBU, Calvin Klein, and many other alternatives, each of which promises to deliver certain benefits.

Needs vs. wants

The specific way a need is satisfied depends on the individual's unique history, learning experiences and his or her cultural environment. The particular form of consumption used to satisfy a need is termed a want. For example, two classmates may feel their stomachs rumbling during a lunchtime lecture. If neither has eaten since the night before, the strength of their respective needs (hunger) might be about the same. However, the way each person goes about satisfying this need might be quite different. The first person may be a health fanatic who fantasizes about a big bowl of salad, while the second person may be equally aroused by the prospect of a greasy slice of pizza.

A start to the discussion of needs and wants can best be illustrated by considering two basic types of need. People are born with a need for certain elements necessary to maintain life, such as food, water, air and shelter. These needs can be viewed as *biogenic needs*. People have many other needs, however, that are not innate. *Psychogenic needs* are acquired in the process of becoming a member of a culture. These include the need for status, power, affiliation, and so on. Psychogenic needs reflect the priorities of a culture, and their effect on behaviour will vary in different environments. For example, a French consumer may be driven to devote a good chunk of his income to products that permit him to display his wealth and status, while his Scandinavian counterpart may work equally hard to ensure that he does not stand out from his group. These cultural differences in the expression of consumer values will be discussed more fully in Chapter 16.

This distinction is revealing because it shows how difficult it is to distinguish needs from wants. How can we tell what part of the motivation is a psychogenic need and what part is a want? Both are profoundly formed by culture, so the distinction is problematic at best. As for the biogenic needs, we know from anthropology that satisfaction of these needs leads to some of the most symbolically rich and culturally based activities of humankind. The ways we want to eat, dress, drink and provide shelter are far more interesting to marketers than our need to do so. And, in fact, human beings need very little in the strict sense of the word. Charles Darwin was astonished to see the native Americans of Tierra del Fuego sleep naked in the snow. Hence, the idea of satisfaction of biogenic needs is more or less a given thing for marketing and consumer research because it is on the most basic level nothing more than a simple prerequisite for us to be here. Beyond that level, and of much greater interest (and challenge!) to marketers, is a concept embedded in culture such as wants.[3]

As we have seen, another traditional distinction is between the motivation to satisfy either utilitarian or hedonic needs. The satisfaction of utilitarian needs implies that consumers will emphasize the objective, tangible attributes of products, such as fuel economy in a car, the amount of fat, calories and protein in a cheeseburger, and the durability of a pair of blue jeans. Hedonic needs are subjective and experiential. Here, consumers may rely on a product to meet their needs for excitement, self-confidence, fantasy, and so on. Of course, consumers may be motivated to purchase a product because it provides *both* types of benefit. For example, a mink coat may be bought because it feels soft and luxurious against the skin and because it keeps one warm on a snowy day. But again the distinction tends to hide more than it reveals, because functionality can bring great pleasure to people and is an important value in the modern world.[4]

Motivational conflicts

A goal has *valence*, which means that it can be positive or negative. A positively valued goal is one towards which consumers direct their behaviour: they are motivated to *approach* the goal and will seek out products that will be instrumental in attaining it. Peter used his athletic equipment to help him improve his triathlon performance, his goal. However, not all behaviour is motivated by the desire to approach a goal. Sometimes, consumers are motivated to *avoid* a negative outcome. They will structure their purchases or consumption activities to reduce the chances of attaining this end result. For example, many consumers work hard to avoid rejection, a negative goal. They will stay away from products that they associate with social disapproval. Products such as deodorants and mouthwashes frequently rely upon consumers' negative motivation by depicting the onerous social consequences of underarm odour or bad breath. Peter would most likely be especially vigilant about avoiding junk food as he prepared for a forthcoming meeting.

Because a purchase decision may involve more than one source of motivation, consumers often find themselves in situations where different motives, both positive and negative, conflict with one another. Since marketers are attempting to satisfy consumers' needs, they can also be helpful by providing possible solutions to these dilemmas. As shown in Figure 4.1, three general types of conflicts can occur: approach–approach, approach–avoidance and avoidance–avoidance.

Approach–approach conflict

In an approach–approach conflict, a person must choose between two desirable alternatives. A student might be torn between going home for the holidays or going on a skiing trip with friends. Or he or she might have to choose between two CDs.

The **theory of cognitive dissonance** is based on the premise that people have a need for order and consistency in their lives and that a state of tension is created when beliefs or behaviours conflict with one another. The conflict that arises when choosing between two alternatives may be resolved through a process of cognitive dissonance reduction, in which people are motivated to reduce this inconsistency (or dissonance) and thus eliminate unpleasant tension.[5]

A state of dissonance occurs when there is a psychological inconsistency between two or more beliefs or behaviours. It often occurs when a consumer must make a

Figure 4.1 **Three types of motivational conflict**

choice between two products, where both alternatives usually possess both good and bad qualities. By choosing one product and not the other, the person gets the bad qualities of the chosen product and loses out on the good qualities of the one not chosen. This loss creates an unpleasant, dissonant state that the person is motivated to reduce. People tend to convince themselves after the fact that the choice they made was the right one by finding additional reasons to support the alternative they chose, or perhaps by 'discovering' flaws with the option they did not choose. A marketer can try to resolve an approach–approach conflict by bundling several benefits together. For example, many low-calorie products claim that they have 'all the taste' *and* 'half the calories', allowing the consumer to avoid having to choose between better taste or fewer calories.

Approach–avoidance conflict

Many of the products and services we desire have negative consequences attached to them as well. We may feel guilty or ostentatious when buying a high-status product or feel like a glutton when contemplating a box of chocolates. When we desire a goal but wish to avoid it at the same time, an approach–avoidance conflict exists. Some solutions to these conflicts include the proliferation of fake furs, which eliminate guilt about killing animals to make a fashion statement, and the above-mentioned low-calorie foods that promise good food without the calories. Some marketers counter consumer resistance to overconsumption and spending by promising more (benefits) from less, as in a recent (2000) Audi advertisement, whereas other marketers try to overcome guilt by convincing consumers that they deserve luxuries (e.g. when the model for L'Oréal cosmetics claims 'Because I'm worth it!').

Avoidance–avoidance conflict

Sometimes consumers find themselves caught 'between a rock and a hard place'. They may face a choice with two undesirable alternatives. A person may be faced with the option of either throwing more money into an old car or buying a new one. Marketers frequently address this conflict by messages that stress the unforeseen benefits of choosing one option (e.g. by emphasizing special credit plans to ease the pain of new car payments).

Classifying consumer needs

Much research has been done on classifying human needs. On the one hand, some psychologists have tried to define a universal inventory of needs that could be traced systematically to explain virtually all behaviour. Others have focused on specific needs (which often are included in general models) and their ramifications for behaviour. For example, one study of working women found that those who were high in achievement motivation were more likely to choose clothing they considered businesslike, and less likely to be interested in apparel that accentuated their femininity.[6]

Maslow's hierarchy of needs

One influential approach to motivation was proposed by the psychologist Abraham Maslow. Maslow's approach is a general one originally developed to understand personal growth and the attainment of 'peak experiences'.[7] Maslow formulated a hierarchy of needs, in which levels of motives are specified. A hierarchical approach implies that the order of development is fixed - that is, a certain level must be attained before the next, higher, one is activated. This universal approach to motivation has been adapted by marketers because it (indirectly) specifies certain types of product benefits people might be looking for, depending upon the different stages in their development and/or their environmental conditions. However, as we shall see it contains many problems, and we shall devote space to it here because it is a 'standard' in marketing knowledge rather than because we believe in its theoretical and practical value.

Maslow's levels are summarized in Figure 4.2. At each level, different priorities exist in terms of the product benefits a consumer is looking for. Ideally, an individual progresses up the hierarchy until his or her dominant motivation is a focus on 'ultimate' goals, such as justice and beauty. Unfortunately, this state is difficult to achieve (at least on a regular basis); most of us have to be satisfied with occasional glimpses or peak experiences.

The implication of Maslow's hierarchy is that one must first satisfy basic needs before progressing up the ladder (i.e. a starving man is not interested in status symbols, friendship or self-fulfilment). This hierarchy is not set in stone. Its use in marketing has been somewhat simplistic, especially since the same product or activity can satisfy a number of different needs.

Sex, for example, is characterized as a basic biological drive. While this observation is true throughout most of the animal kingdom, it is obviously a more complicated phenomenon for humans. Indeed, this activity could conceivably fit into every level of Maslow's hierarchy. A sociobiologist, who approaches human behaviour in terms of its biological origins, might argue that reproductive behaviour provides security because it ensures continuation of a person's gene pool and the provision of children to care for the person in old age. Sex can also express love and affiliation at the belongingness level. In addition, sex is often used as a vehicle to

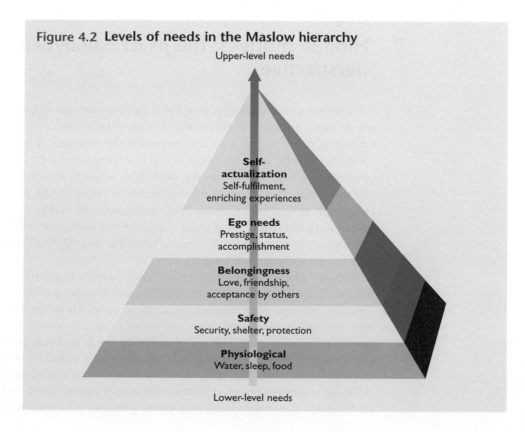

Figure 4.2 **Levels of needs in the Maslow hierarchy**

Upper-level needs

Self-actualization
Self-fulfilment, enriching experiences

Ego needs
Prestige, status, accomplishment

Belongingness
Love, friendship, acceptance by others

Safety
Security, shelter, protection

Physiological
Water, sleep, food

Lower-level needs

attain status, domination over another and to satisfy ego needs; it can be a significant determinant of self-respect. Finally, a sexual experience can be self-actualizing in that it may provide an ecstatic, transcendental experience. The same thing could be said for almost any kind of consumer experience. While eating certainly is necessary for our survival, it also is very much a social act (belongingness), a status act as in the consumption of champagne or other expensive wines, and an act through which the gourmet or the caring, cooking mother or father can obtain self-actualization. The house gives us shelter, but is also a security device, a home for the family, a status object and a field for actualizing our personal aspirations.

Another problem with taking Maslow's hierarchy too literally is that it is culture-bound. The assumptions of the hierarchy may be restricted to a highly rational, materialistic and individualistic Western culture, and people in other cultures may question the order of the levels as specified. A religious person who has taken a vow of celibacy would not necessarily agree that physiological needs must be satisfied for self-fulfilment to occur. Neither do all people in Western cultures seem to live according to Maslow's hierarchy. In fact, research based on visual rather than verbal data has indicated that spiritual survival is a stronger motivator than physical survival, as can be seen from patriots giving their life for the idea of nation, religious fanatics for their God, or suicidal people drawing the consequence of a 'spiritual death' by ending their physical lives.[8]

Similarly, many Asian cultures operate on the premise that the welfare of the group (belongingness needs) is more highly valued than the needs of the individual (esteem needs). The point is that this hierarchy, while widely applied in marketing, does not include the cultural formation of needs. It provides a picture of a jungle law society, an economy of survival, where the culture-(re)producing and self-actualizing aspects of human activities are not taken into account.

Hidden motives: the psychoanalytical perspective

A motive is an underlying reason for behaviour and not something researchers can see or easily measure. Furthermore, the same behaviour can be caused by a configuration of different motives. To compound the problem of identifying motives, the consumer may be unaware of the actual need/want he or she is attempting to satisfy, or alternatively he or she may not be willing to admit that this need exists. Because of these difficulties, motives must often be *inferred* by the analyst. Although some consumer needs undoubtedly are utilitarian and fairly straightforward, some researchers feel that a great many purchase decisions are not the result of deliberate, logical decisions. On the contrary, people may do things to satisfy motives of which they are not even aware.

Sigmund Freud had a profound, if controversial, impact on many basic assumptions of human behaviour. His work changed the way we view such topics as adult sexuality, dreams and psychological adjustment. **Freudian theory** developed the idea that much of human behaviour stems from a fundamental conflict between a person's desire to gratify his or her physical needs and the necessity to function as a responsible member of society. This struggle is carried out in the mind among three systems. (Note that these systems do not refer to physical parts of the brain.)

The *id* is entirely oriented towards immediate gratification – it is the 'party animal' of the mind. It operates according to the pleasure principle: behaviour is guided by the primary desire to maximize pleasure and avoid pain. The id is selfish and illogical. It directs a person's psychic energy towards pleasurable acts without regard for the consequences.

The *superego* is the counterweight to the id. This system is essentially the person's conscience. It internalizes society's rules (especially as communicated by parents) and works to prevent the id from seeking selfish gratification.

Finally, the *ego* is the system that mediates between the id and the superego. It is in a way a referee in the fight between temptation and virtue. The ego tries to balance these two opposing forces according to the reality principle. It finds ways to gratify the id that will be acceptable to the outside world. These conflicts occur on an unconscious level, so the person is not necessarily aware of the underlying reasons for his or her behaviour.

Some of Freud's ideas have also been adapted by consumer researchers. In particular, his work highlights the potential importance of unconscious motives underlying purchases. The implication is that consumers cannot necessarily tell us their true motivation for choosing a product, even if we can devise a sensitive way to ask them directly.

Motivational research

The first attempts to apply Freudian ideas to understand the deeper meanings of products and advertisements were made in the 1950s as a perspective known as **motivational research** was developed. This approach was largely based on psychoanalytic (Freudian) interpretations, with a heavy emphasis on unconscious motives. A basic assumption is that socially unacceptable needs are channelled into acceptable outlets. Product use or avoidance is motivated by unconscious forces which are often determined in childhood.

This form of research relies on *depth interviews* probing deeply into each person's purchase motivations. These can be derived only after questioning and interpretation on the part of a carefully trained interviewer. This work was pioneered by Ernest Dichter, a psychoanalyst who was trained in Vienna in the early part of the twentieth century. Dichter conducted in-depth interview studies on over 230 different products, and many of his findings have been incorporated in marketing campaigns.[9] For example, Esso (or Exxon) for many years reminded consumers to 'Put a Tiger in Your Tank' after Dichter found that people responded well to this powerful animal symbolism containing vaguely suggestive overtones.

Criticisms of motivational research

Motivational research has been attacked for two quite opposite reasons. Some feel it does not work, while others feel it works *too* well. On the one hand, social critics attacked this school of thought for giving advertisers the power to manipulate consumers.[10] On the other hand, many consumer researchers felt the research lacked sufficient rigour and validity, since interpretations were subjective and indirect.[11] Because conclusions are based on the analyst's own judgement and are derived from discussions with a small number of people, some researchers are doubtful about the degree to which these results can be generalized to a large market. In addition, because the original motivational researchers were heavily influenced by orthodox Freudian theory, their interpretations usually carried strong sexual overtones. This emphasis tends to overlook other plausible causes for behaviour. It is worth noting that it has been argued that such over-interpretations and disregard of the more mundane and obvious were more common in the American market than in the

British, for example, leading to a greater discrediting in the USA than in Europe of qualitative research in general and motivational research in particular.[12]

The positive side of motivational research

Motivational research had great appeal at least to some marketers for several reasons, some of which are detailed here. Motivational research tends to be less expensive than large-scale, quantitative survey data because interviewing and data processing costs are relatively small.

The knowledge derived from motivational research may help in the development of marketing communications that appeal to deep-seated needs and thus provide a more powerful hook to relate a product to consumers. Even if they are not necessarily valid for all consumers in a target market, these insights can be valuable when used in an exploratory way. For example, the rich imagery that may be associated with a product can be used creatively when developing advertising copy.

Some of the findings seem intuitively plausible after the fact. For example, motivational studies concluded that coffee is associated with companionship, that people avoid prunes because they remind them of old age, and that men fondly equate the first car they owned as a young man with the onset of their sexual freedom.

Other interpretations were hard for some people to accept, such as the observation that to a woman baking a cake symbolizes giving birth, or that men are reluctant to give blood because they feel that their vital fluids are being drained. On the other hand, some people do refer to a pregnant woman as 'having a bun in the oven'.[13] Motivational research for the Red Cross did find that men (but not women) tend to overestimate drastically the amount of blood that is taken during a donation. This group counteracted the fear of loss of virility by symbolically equating the act of giving blood with fertilization: 'Give the gift of life'. Despite its drawbacks, motivational research continues to be employed as a useful diagnostic tool. Its validity is enhanced, however, when it is used in conjunction with the other research techniques available to the consumer researcher.

Consumer desire

▶ Most recently, researchers have begun to discuss the importance of the concept of **desire** for understanding consumer behaviour. Desire as a motivational construct is quite revolutionary, since it turns the attention away from satisfaction and over to the thrills of the process of desiring.[14] This is opening up a better understanding of consumer insatiability than can be provided by needs and wants. Desire, furthermore, better captures the seductive spirit of the positioning of many contemporary brands and the deep feelings involved in consumer goods' contribution to the formation of consumers' self-images. Because emotions, unruly passions and bodily cravings and pleasures are so central to the experience of desiring, desire reintroduces the bodily aspect of motivation without reducing it to biogenic needs.[15] On the contrary, the concept of desire also emphasizes that, even though desires, needs and wants are felt psychologically, the concept of society (often called 'the Other' in the literature on desire) is very central to the understanding of desire. Thus, desire would refer to the *sociogenic* nature of needs.[16]

One study of consumer desires in Denmark, Turkey and the United States concluded that desires were much more profound than wants, that desire is cyclical and basically insatiable, and that what is desired is more often various kinds of social relationship mediated by consumption experiences than consumption in itself.

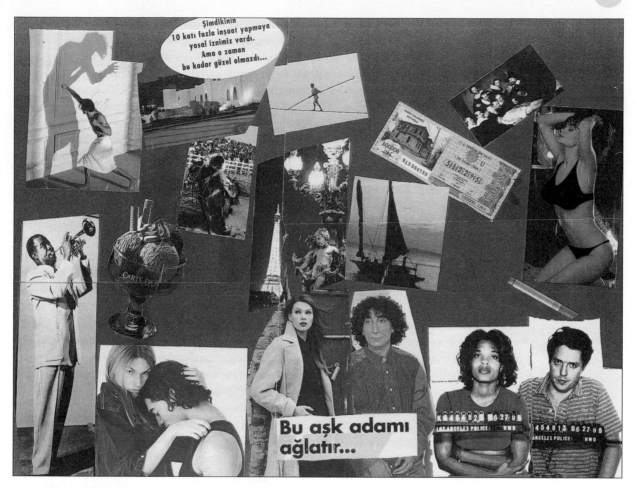

An example of a collage used to explore consumer desire.

Finally, desire has an interesting relationship with control. On the one hand, control kills desire, as expressed in many consumers' antonyms to desire being an overly routinized lifestyle with the same repetitive patterns day in and day out – what the French call 'metro-boulot-dodo' (the cyclus of metro-work-sleep). On the other hand, it is potentially harmful because it contains an important element of excess and lack of control over oneself.[17] The study used collages among other techniques to explore consumer desire, and the collage shown here illustrates some of the featured findings: that desire is positive but potentially harmful if out of control (the balance, the fight with one's own shadow) and can lead to impossible dreams (the ugly man and the model) or to excess and violation of norms (Hugh Grant and the prostitute).

Desire is one way of dealing with very passionate consumers, stressing the very emotional and sometimes irrational side of consumer behaviour. If consumer desire is investigated from a more rationalizing and cognitive psychological perspective, it tends to be dealt with under the term consumer *involvement*.

Consumer involvement

As we have seen, a consumer's motivation to attain a goal influences his or her desire to expend the effort necessary to attain the products or services believed to be instrumental in satisfying that objective. However, not everyone is motivated to the same extent – one person might be convinced that he or she can't live without the latest style or modern convenience, while another is not interested in this item at all. For example, a consumer in Brighton, England, loved a local restaurant called the All In One so much that he had its name and phone number tattooed on his forehead. The owner remarked, 'I'm not going to give him free pizza, because he did it of his own free will. But whenever he comes in, he'll go straight to the front of the queue.'[18] **Involvement** refers to 'a person's perceived relevance of the object based on their inherent needs, values, and interests'.[19] This definition implies that aspects of the person, the product and the situation combine to determine the consumer's motivation to process product-related information at a given point in time. When consumers are intent on doing what they can to satisfy a need, they will be motivated to pay attention and process any information felt to be relevant to achieving their goals.

On the other hand, a person may not bother to pay any attention to the same information if it is not seen as relevant to satisfying some need. One person who prides himself on his knowledge of exercise equipment may read anything he can find about the subject, spend his spare time in sports shops, and so on, while another person may skip over this information without giving it a second thought.

Involvement can be viewed as the motivation to process information.[20] To the degree that there is a perceived linkage between a consumer's needs, goals or values and product knowledge, the consumer will be motivated to pay attention to product information. When relevant knowledge is activated in memory, a motivational state is created that drives behaviour (e.g. shopping). This subjective feeling of personal relevance is termed felt involvement. As felt involvement with a product increases, people devote more attention to ads related to the product, exert more cognitive effort to understand these ads, and focus their attention on the product-related information in them.[21] However, this kind of 'rational' involvement may be the exception rather than the rule, even for such products as stereos, TVs and VCRs, as a company executive from Philips once argued.[22]

Levels of involvement: from inertia to passion

The type of information processing that will occur thus depends upon the consumer's level of involvement. It can range from *simple processing*, where only the basic features of a message are considered, all the way to *elaboration*, where the incoming information is linked to one's pre-existing knowledge systems.[23]

A person's degree of involvement can be conceived as a continuum, ranging from absolute lack of interest in a marketing stimulus at one end, to obsession at the other. Consumption at the low end of involvement is characterized by **inertia**, where decisions are made out of habit because the consumer lacks the motivation to consider alternatives. At the high end of involvement, we can expect to find the type of passionate intensity reserved for people and objects that carry great meaning to the individual. The passion of some consumers for famous people demonstrates the high end of the involvement continuum. Celebrity worship is evident in activities ranging from autograph collections to the sky-high prices that possessions that used to belong to stars such as John Lennon, Elton John or Jimi Hendrix can fetch at auctions. For the most part, however, a consumer's involvement level with products falls somewhere in the middle, and the marketing strategist must determine the relative level of importance to understand how much elaboration of product information will occur.

The many faces of involvement

As previously defined, involvement can take many forms. Involvement can be cognitive, as when a 'webhead' is motivated to learn all she can about the latest spec of a new multimedia PC, or emotional, as when the thought of a new Armani suit gives

Multicultural dimensions

Presumably, a person who has had all of his or her needs satisfied lives in 'paradise'. Conceptualizations of paradise have implications for the marketing and consumption of any products, such as vacation travel, that seek to invoke an ideal state. However, the definition of just what constitutes paradise appears to differ across cultures. To pursue this idea further, the concept of paradise was compared between groups of American and Dutch college students. Informants in both cultures constructed a collage of images to illustrate their overall concept of paradise, and they wrote an essay to accompany and explain this collage. Some similarities were evident in the two societies: both Americans and Dutch emphasized the personal, experiential aspects of paradise, saying 'paradise is different for everyone . . . a feeling . . . a state of being'. In addition, individuals in both societies said that paradise must include family, friends, and significant others.

However, the Dutch and Americans differed in important and interesting ways. The Americans consistently emphasized hedonism, materialism, individuality, creativity, and issues of time and space consistent with a society in which time is segmented and viewed almost as a commodity (more on this in Chapter 10). Conversely, the Dutch respondents showed a concern for social and environmental responsibility, collective societal order and equality, and a balance between work and play as part of paradise. For instance, one Dutch student said that 'Respect for animals, flowers, and plants . . . regenerating energy sources, such as wind, water, and sun' are all important parts of paradise. Marketers should expect that, because concepts of paradise differ somewhat, different images and behaviours may be evoked when Americans and Dutch are confronted with marketing messages such as 'Hawaii is Paradise', or 'you can experience paradise when you drive this car'.[24]

A Dutch respondent's collage emphasizes this person's conception of paradise as a place where there is interpersonal harmony and concern for the environment.

a clotheshorse goosebumps.[25] Further, the very act of buying the Armani may be very involving for people who are passionately devoted to shopping. To complicate matters further, advertisements, such as those produced for Nike or Adidas, may themselves be involving for some reason (e.g. because they make us laugh, cry or inspire us to work harder).

It seems that involvement is a fuzzy concept, because it overlaps with other things and means different things to different people. Indeed, the consensus is that there are actually several broad types of involvement.[26]

Product involvement is related to a consumer's level of interest in making a particular purchase. Many sales promotions are designed to increase this type of involvement.

Message-response involvement (also known as advertising involvement) refers to the consumer's interest in processing marketing communications.[27] Television is considered a low-involvement medium because it requires a passive viewer who exerts relatively little control (remote control 'zipping' notwithstanding) over content. In contrast, print is often seen as a higher-involvement medium. The reader is actively involved in processing the information and may choose to fixate on particular aspects of the text and/or picture as a sign of involvement in what he or she has read before moving on.[28] The role of message characteristics in changing attitudes is further discussed in Chapter 6.

MARKETING OPPORTUNITY

Quick Burger, France's second largest fast-food chain, discovered a route to increasing customers' involvement. The company became a partner in a marketing programme called Multipoints, an interactive service which allowed consumers to collect points that could then be redeemed for discounts and prizes. More than 70,000 French consumers signed up for the service. Using a device that resembled a calculator, participants entered codes they found in print ads and advertising hoardings or heard on radio programmes. They could even hold the device against their TV screens during programming that was specially encoded to dispense credits. People could win points for playing along with certain game shows and answering questions correctly. They could then redeem their points for merchandise at Quick Burger restaurants and other locations (including selected travel agencies and news-stands) by plugging their device into a computer terminal. The hamburger chain awarded consumers 500 free points per week just for visiting, which gave them additional motivation to patronize Quick Burger instead of its arch-rival, McDonald's.[29]

Ego involvement (sometimes termed *enduring involvement*) refers to the importance of a product to a consumer's self-concept. This concept implies a high level of social risk: the prospect of the product not performing its desired function may result in embarrassment or damage to the consumer's self-concept (Chapter 7 is devoted to the importance of the self-concept for consumer behaviour issues). For example, Peter's running shoes are clearly an important part of his self-identity (they are said to have high sign value). This type of involvement is independent of particular purchase situations. It is an ongoing concern related to the self and hedonic experiences (e.g. the emotions felt as a result of using the product).[30]

Measuring involvement

The measurement of involvement is important for many marketing applications. For example, research evidence indicates that a viewer who is more involved with a tele-

Table 4.1 A scale to measure product involvement

To me (object to be judged) is

1	important	_:_:_:_:_:_:_	unimportant*
2	boring	_:_:_:_:_:_:_	interesting
3	relevant	_:_:_:_:_:_:_	irrelevant*
4	exciting	_:_:_:_:_:_:_	unexciting*
5	means nothing	_:_:_:_:_:_:_	means a lot to me
6	appealing	_:_:_:_:_:_:_	unappealing*
7	fascinating	_:_:_:_:_:_:_	mundane*
8	worthless	_:_:_:_:_:_:_	valuable
9	involving	_:_:_:_:_:_:_	uninvolving*
10	not needed	_:_:_:_:_:_:_	needed

Note: Totalling the ten items gives a score from a low of 10 to a high of 70.
*Indicates item is reverse scored. For example, a score of 7 for item no. 1 (important/unimportant) would actually be scored as 1.

Source: Judith Lynne Zaichkowsky, 'The Personal Involvement Inventory: Reduction, Revision, and Application to Advertising', *Journal of Advertising* 23(4) (December 1994): 59–70.

vision show will also respond more positively to commercials contained in that show, and that these slots will have a greater chance of influencing his or her purchase intentions.[31] The many conceptualizations of involvement have led to some confusion about the best way to measure the concept. The scale shown in Table 4.1 is one widely used method.[32]

A pair of French researchers have argued that no single component of involvement is predominant. Recognizing that consumers can be involved with a product because it is a risky purchase and/or its use reflects upon or affects the self, they advocate the development of an *involvement profile* containing five components:[33]

- The perceived importance of the potential negative consequences of a bad purchase.
- The probability of making a bad purchase.
- The pleasure value of the product category.
- The sign value of the product category.

These researchers asked a sample of housewives to rate a set of 14 product categories on each of the above facets of involvement. The results are shown in Table 4.2. These data indicate that no single component captures consumer involvement, since this quality can occur for different reasons. For example, the purchase of a durable product such as a vacuum cleaner is seen as risky, because one is stuck with a bad choice for many years. However, the vacuum cleaner does not provide pleasure (hedonic value), nor is it high in sign value (i.e. its use is not related to the person's self-concept). In contrast, chocolate is high in pleasure value but is not seen as risky or closely related to the self. Dresses and bras, on the other hand, appear to be involving for a combination of reasons.

Table 4.2 Involvement profiles for a set of French consumer products

	Importance of negative consequences	Subjective probability of mispurchase	Pleasure value	Sign value
Dresses	121	112	147	181
Bras	117	115	106	130
Washing machines	118	109	106	111
TV sets	112	100	122	95
Vacuum cleaners	110	112	70	78
Irons	103	95	72	76
Champagne	109	120	125	125
Oil	89	97	65	92
Yoghurt	86	83	106	78
Chocolate	80	89	123	75
Shampoo	96	103	90	81
Toothpaste	95	95	94	105
Toilet soap	82	90	114	118
Detergents	79	82	56	63

Average product score = 100.
Source: Gilles Laurent and Jean-Noël Kapferer, 'Measuring Consumer Involvement Profiles', *Journal of Marketing Research* 22 (February 1985): 45, Table 3.

Segmenting by involvement levels

A measurement approach of this nature allows consumer researchers to capture the diversity of the involvement construct, and it also provides the potential to use involvement as a basis for market segmentation. For example, a yoghurt manufacturer might find that even though its product is low in sign value for one group of consumers, it might be highly related to the self-concept of another market segment, such as health food enthusiasts or avid dieters. The company could adapt its strategy to account for the motivation of different segments to process information about the product. These variations are discussed in Chapter 6. Note also that involvement with a product class may vary across cultures. While this sample of French consumers rated champagne high in both sign value and personal value, the ability of champagne to provide pleasure or be central to self-definition might not transfer to other countries. For example, whereas a typical French family would find champagne an absolutely essential part of the celebration of a marriage, a Danish family, especially from a rural area, might find consumption of champagne an excessive luxury and perhaps also to some extent a sign of decadence.[34]

Strategies to increase involvement

Although consumers differ in their levels of involvement with respect to a product message, marketers do not have to sit back and hope for the best. By being aware of some basic factors that increase or decrease attention, they can take steps to increase the likelihood that product information will get through. A consumer's motivation to process relevant information can be enhanced fairly easily by the marketer who uses one or more of the following techniques:[35]

● Appeal to the consumer's hedonic needs. For example, ads using sensory appeals generate higher levels of attention.[36]

- Use novel stimuli such as unusual cinematography, sudden silences or unexpected movements in commercials.

- Use prominent stimuli such as loud music and fast action to capture attention in commercials. In print formats, larger ads increase attention. Also, viewers look longer at coloured pictures as opposed to black-and-white.

- Include celebrity endorsers to generate higher interest in commercials. This strategy will be discussed in Chapter 6.

- Build a bond with consumers by maintaining an ongoing relationship with them. The routes to cultivating brand loyalty will be discussed further in Chapter 8.

- The internet has provided companies with new possibilities for creating loyalty bonds with customers. For example, girls can now customize their own doll at Mattel's My Design website, located at **www.barbie.com/mydesign**. They can specify her skin tone, hair and eye colour and outfits. They can also name the doll, and she comes with a personality profile they can tailor from choices on the website.[37]

Values

Generally speaking, a **value** can be defined as a belief about some desirable end-state that transcends specific situations and guides selection of behaviour.[38] Thus, values are general and different from attitudes in that they do not apply to specific situations only. A person's set of values plays a very important role in his or her consumption activities, since many products and services are purchased because (it is believed) they will help us to attain a value-related goal. Two people can believe in the same behaviours (e.g. vegetarianism) but their underlying belief systems may be quite different (e.g. animal activism vs. health concerns). The extent to which people share a belief system is a function of individual, social and cultural forces. Advocates of a belief system often seek out others with similar beliefs, so that social networks overlap and as a result believers tend to be exposed to information that supports their beliefs (e.g. environmentalists rarely hang out with large-scale farmers).[39]

As we'll see in Chapters 16 and 17, the specific values that motivate people vary across cultures, yet within each culture there is usually a set of underlying goals that most members of that culture agree are important. One comparison of management practices concerning industrial buying behaviour in Europe and North America concluded that in Europe, development of relationships is seen as more important, whereas in North America, rigour and competitiveness are the key issues.[40] Such differences may be interpreted as pointing to fundamental differences in values in the business worlds of the two continents. But large differences can also be detected within Europe, for example between the Anglo-Saxon approach, which is closer to the American model described above, and the Germanic–Alpine (including Scandinavia) model, which is more oriented towards the relationship approach.[41]

Core values

Every culture has a set of values that it imparts to its members.[42] For example, people in one culture might feel that being a unique individual is preferable to subordinating one's identity to the group, while another group may emphasize the virtues of group membership. In many cases, values are universal. Who does not desire health, wisdom or world peace? But on the other hand, values do change over time. Right now in Japan young people are working hard to adopt Western values and behaviours – which explains why the current fashion for young people is bleached, blond hair, chalky make-up and a deep tan. But as the government has encouraged this pattern of spending and personal liberation, it has also challenged values of the past and, for instance, increased the school drop-out rate by 20 per cent.[43] Similar concerns about the consequences of what is often called a value crisis are also discussed in European societies. Likewise, one may wonder what happened to the traditional Scandinavian modesty – in both Denmark and Sweden people are now showing more willingness to share their private lives with thousands of others in either talk shows or docu-soaps of the *Big Brother* variety.

Sometimes, one must be careful of interpreting social events in terms of values. For example, a hugely successful advertisement in Japan promoted breast cancer awareness by showing an attractive woman in a sundress drawing stares from men on the street as a voice-over said, 'If only women paid as much attention to their breasts as men do.' The same ad flopped in France – according to the *Wall Street Journal* because the use of humour to talk about a serious disease offended the French.[44] Does this seem like a plausible explanation to you?

Value systems

One perspective on the study of values stresses that what sets cultures apart is the *relative importance*, or ranking, of these universal values. This set of rankings constitutes a culture's **value system**.[45] To illustrate the difference in value systems, consider the results of a comparison between the adherence to a set of values in a variety of countries (see Table 4.3).[46] What can one draw from such a table? In one of the studies that constituted this table, Norway, Germany and the USA were compared.[47] The value of sense of belonging is very important in Germany and Norway, but much less so in the US, which is coherent with many other studies underlining the individualistic character of the American culture. Likewise, the value of security is very important in Germany and the US but much less so in Norway. The results seem to indicate that the value of security in the US is understood in terms of social security, whereas in Germany it is understood more in terms of social relationships.

Table 4.3 Distribution of LOV (List of Values) values in different countries (% rating as most important value)

	Germany	USA	Norway	France	Denmark	USSR	Japan
Self-fulfilment	4.8	9.6	7.7	30,9	7.1	8.8	36.7
Sense of belonging	28.6	7.9	33.4	1.7	13.0	23.9	2.3
Security	24.1	20.6	10.0	6.3	6.3	5.7	10.9
Self-respect	12.9	21.1	16.6	7.4	29.7	10.1	4.7
Warm relationships with others	7.9	16.2	13.4	17.7	11.3	23.3	27.6
Fun and enjoyment in life/Excitement*	10.1	4.5	3.6	16.6	16.8	9.7	7.5
Being well respected	6.1	8.8	8.4	4.0	5.0	8.5	2.1
Sense of accomplishment	5.4	11.4	6.8	15.4	10.9	10.1	8.3

* The value 'excitement' was collapsed into 'fun and enjoyment' because just a negligible percentage in certain samples selected this as the most important value.
Source: Reprinted from Lynn Kahle, Sharon Beatty and John Mager, 'Implications of Social Values for Consumer Communications: The Case of the European Community', in B. Englis, ed., *Global and Multinational Advertising* (Hillsdale, NJ: Lawrence Erlbaum Ass.): 47–64.

Many advertisements appeal to people's values to persuade them to change or modify their behaviours. This ad, sponsored by the City of Paris, says to dog owners: 'You are quite right not to clean up after your dog. After all, he'll take care of that for you.' Used with permission of Leo-Burnett-Paris.

In Norway it is interpreted much as in the US, but it does not represent the same importance due to the elaborate social security of the Norwegian welfare state: they are simply inclined to take security for granted. Thus, it is obvious that unless one understands the context, one may draw very erroneous conclusions from this kind of research, for instance that security is not very important.

Every culture is characterized by its members' endorsement of a value system. These end-states may not be equally endorsed by everyone, and in some cases, values may even seem to contradict one another (e.g. Westerners in general appear to value both conformity and individuality and seek to find some accommodation between the two). None the less, it is usually possible to identify a general set of *core values* which uniquely define a culture. These beliefs are taught to us by *socialization agents*, including parents, friends and teachers. The process of learning the beliefs and behaviours endorsed by one's own culture is termed **enculturation**. In contrast, the process of learning the value system and behaviours of another culture (often a priority for those who wish to understand consumers and markets in foreign countries) is called **acculturation**.

As we saw in the example above, such core values must be understood in the local context – that is, the meaning of the values changes when the cultural context shifts. 'Security' is *not* the same for English, Scandinavian, German and Italian consumers. This is a serious challenge to the idea that it is possible to compare value systems by studying the rankings of universal sets of values across countries.

Applications of values to consumer behaviour

Despite their importance, values have not been widely applied to direct examinations of consumer behaviour. One reason is that such broad-based concepts as freedom, security or inner harmony are more likely to affect general purchasing patterns than to differentiate between brands within a product category. For this reason, some researchers have found it convenient to make distinctions among such broad-based *cultural values* as security or happiness, *consumption-specific values* such as convenient shopping or prompt service, and *product-specific values* such as ease of use or durability.[48] However, such a distinction may border on abusing the value concept, since it is normally taken to represent the most general and profound level in the social psychological hierarchy.

Since values drive much of consumer behaviour (at least in a very general sense), it could be said that virtually all types of consumer research ultimately are related to the identification and measurement of values. This process can take many forms, ranging from qualitative research techniques such as ethnography to quantitative techniques such as laboratory experiments and large-scale surveys. This section describes some attempts by researchers to measure cultural values and apply this knowledge to marketing strategy. A number of companies track changes in values through large-scale surveys. The results of these studies are then sold to marketers, who pay a fee to receive regular updates on changes and trends. One Young and Rubicam study recently tracked the new segment of single, professional career women without any ambitions of creating a family. They are among the highest consuming segments and are characterized by central values such as freedom and independence.[49] Some of these services are discussed in Chapter 15. Many companies use value inventories in order to adapt their strategies. SAS, the airline, which for a long time addressed 'hard values' of their key segment, business travellers, realized that this segment had started to express more informal and 'softer' values, and they changed their communication profile accordingly.[50]

Such ideas are reflected in a recent theory of consumer value. According to this theory, value for a consumer is the consumer's evaluation of a consumer object in terms of which general benefit the consumer might get from consuming it.[51] As such, the value at stake in consumption is tied much more to the consumption experience than to general existential values of the person. Thus, it is suggested that the consumer experience may generate eight distinct types of consumer value:

- *Efficiency* – referring to all products aimed at providing various kinds of convenience for the consumer.

- *Excellence* – addressing situations where the experience of quality is the prime motivation.

- *Status* – when the consumer pursues success and engages in impression management and conspicuous consumption.

- *(Self-)Esteem* – situations where the satisfaction of possessing is in focus, as is the case with materialism.

- *Play* – the value of having fun in consuming.

- *Aesthetics* – searching for beauty in one's consumption of, e.g., designer products, fashion or art.

- *Ethics* – referring to motivations behind, e.g., morally or politically correct consumption choices.

- *Spirituality* – experiencing magical transformations or sacredness in the consumption, as known from devoted collectors.[52]

Sometimes companies may overestimate the change in values. This could be the case for the discussion about the 'rudest poster advertisement of the summer' in 2000, an ad for Organics Colour Active Shampoo featuring a young woman on the beach peering down her own bikini bottoms juxtaposed with the declaration 'keeps hair colour so long, you'll forget your natural one'. However, maybe the provocation was deliberate – at least, no plans were announced to withdraw the campaign voluntarily.[53]

The Rokeach Value Survey

The psychologist Milton Rokeach identified a set of **terminal values**, or desired end-states, that apply (to various degrees) to many different cultures. *The Rokeach Value Survey*, a scale used to measure these values, also includes a set of **instrumental values**, which are composed of actions needed to achieve these terminal values.[54] These two sets of values appear in Table 4.4. This set of values has been used in many studies, for example to investigate the changes in the value system of post-Soviet Russia.[55]

The List of Values (LOV)

Although some evidence indicates that differences in these global values do translate into product-specific preferences and differences in media usage, the Rokeach Value Survey has not been widely applied to consumer behaviour issues.[56] As an alternative, the List of Values (LOV) scale was developed to isolate values with more direct marketing applications.[57]

This instrument identifies nine consumer values which can be related to differences in consumption behaviours. The instrument includes the following values: sense of belonging, fun and enjoyment in life, warm relationships with others, self-fulfilment, being well respected, excitement, sense of accomplishment, security and

Table 4.4 Two types of values in the Rokeach Value Survey

Instrumental values	Terminal values
Ambitious	A comfortable life
Broadminded	An exciting life
Capable	A sense of accomplishment
Cheerful	A world at peace
Clean	A world of beauty
Courageous	Equality
Forgiving	Family security
Helpful	Freedom
Honest	Happiness
Imaginative	Inner harmony
Independent	Mature love
Intellectual	National security
Logical	Pleasure
Loving	Salvation
Obedient	Self-respect
Polite	Social recognition
Responsible	True friendship
Self-controlled	Wisdom

Source: Richard W. Pollay, 'Measuring the Cultural Values Manifest in Advertising', *Current Issues and Research in Advertising* (1983): 71–92.

self-respect. This was the instrument used in the studies summarized in Table 4.3 above. Likewise, in a comparative study of French and German consumers, the values of sense of belonging and self-respect were much more popular in Germany, whereas the values of fun and enjoyment in life, self-fulfilment and self-accomplishment were chosen as the most important values in France significantly more often.[58]

However, it should be noticed that the cross-cultural validity of such value instruments is, at best, difficult to obtain since, as we have already said, the meaning of values may differ significantly in different cultural contexts.[59] For example, the LOV did not do very well in a test of its cross-cultural validity.[60]

Schwartz value survey

This very elaborate set of values, containing 56 different values organized in ten so-called motivational domains, has been demonstrated to be among the more cross-culturally valid instruments.[61] The structuring of values in interrelated motivational domains provides a theoretical framework for this approach to values which many researchers find satisfactory compared to other value inventories. More specifically, it has been demonstrated to better distinguish between cultures[62] and types of media consumption behaviour[63] than the traditional dichotomy of individualism and collectivism. The values are located in a space demarcated by the poles 'openness to change' vs. 'conservation' and 'self-transcendence' vs. 'self-enhancement'. These dimensions seem relatively universal for a lot of syndicated lifestyle and value surveys (see also Chapter 16). A mapping of the motivational domains can be seen in Figure 4.3 The Schwartz value survey was used to profile Danish consumers with environmentally friendly attitudes and behaviour, where it turned out that such values as 'protecting the environment' and 'unity with nature' but also 'mature love', 'broadminded' and 'social justice' characterized the 'green' segment, whereas values such as 'authority', 'social power', 'national security' and 'politeness' were the most characteristic of the non-green segment.[64] (See also Chapter 9.)

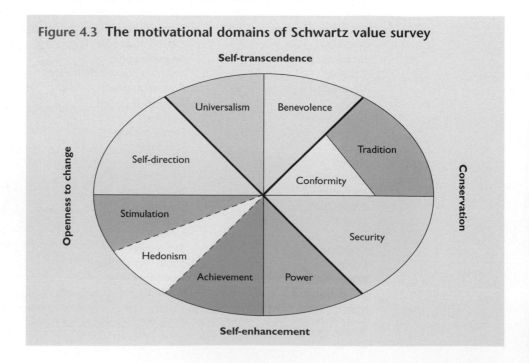

Figure 4.3 The motivational domains of Schwartz value survey

The means–end chain model

Another research approach that incorporates values is termed a **means–end chain** model. This approach assumes that very specific product attributes are linked at levels of increasing abstraction to terminal values. The person has valued end-states, and he or she chooses between alternative means to attain these goals. Products are thus valued as the means to an end. Through a technique called **laddering**, consumers' associations between specific attributes and general consequences are uncovered. Consumers are helped to climb up the 'ladder' of abstraction that connects functional product attributes with desired end-states.[65]

To understand how laddering works, consider somebody who expresses a liking for a light beer. Probing might reveal that this attribute is linked to the consequence of not getting drunk. A consequence of not getting drunk is that he or she will be able to enjoy more interesting conversations, which in turn means that he or she will be more sociable. Finally, a better sociability results in better friendship, a terminal value for this person.[66]

Laddering is not without problems, however, since the laddering technique might generate invalid answers if the respondent is pushed up the ladder by too strong an emphasis on the sequence in the means–end chain. Consumers should be allowed to jump back and forth, to make loops and forks and blind alleys, which requires more skill of the interviewer but is also a more accurate representation of the respondent's thought processes.[67] Furthermore, it has been argued that in researching the demand for status goods, using laddering techniques can be problematic since motivations for conspicuous consumption are difficult for consumers to express or reveal.[68]

MECCAs

The notion that products are consumed because they are instrumental to attaining more abstract values is central to one application of this technique, called the Means–End Conceptualization of the Components of Advertising Strategy (MECCAs). In this approach, researchers first generate a map depicting relationships between functional product or service attributes and terminal values. This information is then used to develop advertising strategy by identifying such elements as:[69]

- *Message elements* – the specific attributes or product features to be depicted.
- *Consumer benefit* – the positive consequences of using the product or service.
- *Executional framework* – the overall style and tone of the advertisement.
- *Leverage point* – the way the message will activate the terminal value by linking it with specific product features.
- *Driving force* – the end-value upon which the advertising will focus.

This technique was used to develop an advertising strategy for the Danish fish trade organization. In spite of the country's huge fishing industry and the supply of fresh fish, the Danish per capita consumption of fish was considerably lower than in several other European countries. A study was carried out using a means–end approach to investigate Danish consumers' attitudes to eating fish. It was concluded that some of the main problems were found in the lack of ideas for preparation and variation of fish-based meals among Danish housewives. This was in sharp contrast to the traditional driving force used by the organization, stressing that fish is healthy.[70]

Based on these results, an advertising campaign was created. Its message elements emphasized fish as a convenient and delicious food. The consumer benefit was the quick and easy preparation, which made dinner or lunch an easy task to accomplish. The executional framework was a humorous one. Two middle-aged, traditional-looking people were portrayed in various situations, where the male was sceptical about the idea of eating fish for lunch or dinner. In one of the TV spots, the wife was seen talking to somebody else over the telephone. Her remarks led the TV viewers (and the husband listening in the background) to think that they were talking about the other family's sex life ('You do it TWICE a week!', 'It takes FIFTEEN minutes!!!', 'so HE likes that'). In fact, a friend was telling her about how she prepared fish for dinner. The leverage point was that these recipes would allow the wife to prepare delicious meals very quickly, which in turn would make for a happy family life, the driving force (terminal value). Almost immediately after the campaign, the trade organization registered an increase in the interest and the consumption of fresh fish.[71]

Figure 4.4 shows three different hierarchical value maps, or sets of ladders, from a study of consumers' perceptions and motivations with regard to cooking oils. The three ladders demonstrate some important differences between the three markets. Health is the most often referred to central concept for the Danes and is linked to several personal values. The British also focus on health but the links to personal values are fewer and less differentiated, indicating a lower product involvement. Saving money and avoiding waste is more important to the British than to the other samples. The French focus a lot on previous knowledge of the product, indicating more routine with buying oils. Theirs is also the only culture that links oil (especially olive oil) with cultural identity and fundamental food culture.[72] These ladders illustrate the central importance of cultural and contextual differences for consumers' motivation structures.

Materialism: the ultimate 'why' of consumption?

Materialism may be considered a more general value underlying other consumer values, thus reassuring that an obvious way of realizing one's values is through consumption.

Consumption as a goal

Members of 'cargo cults' in the South Pacific literally worshipped cargo that was salvaged from crashed aircraft or washed ashore from ships. These people believed that the ships and planes passing near their islands were piloted by their ancestors, and they tried to attract them to their villages. During the Second World War, they went so far as to construct fake planes from straw in the hope of luring real ones.[73]

While not everyone literally worships material goods in this way, things do play a central role in many people's lives. **Materialism** refers to the importance people attach to worldly possessions. Westerners in general (and Americans in particular) are often stereotyped as being members of a highly materialistic society where people often gauge their worth and that of others in terms of how much they own.

In Europe, we often take the existence of an abundance of products and services for granted, until we remember how recent many of these developments are. The

**Figure 4.4
Hierarchical
value maps
for vegetable
oil in three
countries**

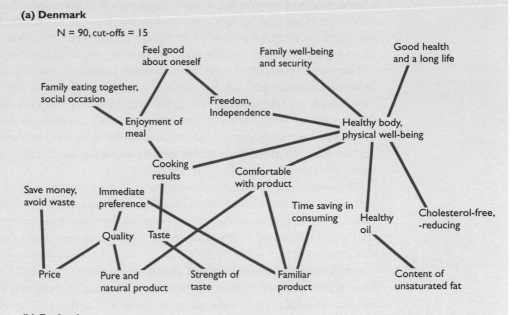

(a) Denmark

N = 90, cut-offs = 15

(b) England

N = 50, cut-offs = 9

(c) France

N = 50, cut-offs = 9

Source: N. A. Nielsen,
T. Bech-Larsen and
K. G. Grunert,
'Consumer Purchase
Motives and Product
Perceptions: A
Laddering Study on
Vegetable Oil in Three
Countries', *Food
Quality and Preference*
9(6) (1998): 455–66.

commonness of ownership of cars, freezers, telephones and televisions is all a post-1950s phenomenon. In fact, one way to think about marketing is as a system that provides a certain standard of living to consumers. To some extent, then, our lifestyles are influenced by the standard of living we have come to expect and desire.

The living standard of consumers in many countries, particularly in Asia, has also increased considerably in recent years. And new products are steadily becoming 'necessities'. A Gallup study of 22,500 adults in 17 European countries found that ownership of such items as microwave ovens, VCRs and cellular phones has 'exploded' in recent years.[74] Advertising encourages this emphasis on consumption and increasingly portrays consumption as an end in itself, rather than as a means to attain well-being.[75]

Of course, not everyone stresses the value of materialism to the same degree. Individual differences have been found among consumers in terms of this emphasis. One approach partitions the value of materialism into three categories: success, centrality and happiness.[76] The scale items used to measure these categories are shown in Table 4.5.

Cross-cultural differences have also been analysed. One study including 12 countries resulted in the following ranking in degree of materialism from highest to lowest: Romania, USA, New Zealand, Ukraine, Germany, Turkey, Israel, Thailand,

---

Table 4.5 A scale to measure categories of materialism

Category	Scale items
Success	• 'I admire people who own expensive homes, cars and clothes.' • 'Some of the most important achievements in life include acquiring material possessions.' • 'I don't put much emphasis on the amount of material objects people own as a sign of success.'* • 'The things I own say a lot about how well I'm doing in life.' • 'I like to own things that impress people.' • 'I don't pay much attention to the material objects other people own.'* • 'I usually buy only the things I need.'*
Centrality	• 'I try to keep my life simple, as far as possessions are concerned.'* • 'The things I own aren't all that important to me.'* • 'I enjoy spending money on things that aren't practical.' • 'Buying things gives me a lot of pleasure.' • 'I like a lot of luxury in my life.' • 'I put less emphasis on material things than most people I know.'* • 'I have all the things I really need to enjoy life.'*
Happiness	• 'My life would be better if I owned certain things I don't have.' • 'I wouldn't be any happier if I owned nicer things.'* • 'I'd be happier if I could afford to buy more things.' • 'It sometimes bothers me quite a bit that I can't afford to buy all the things I'd like.'

Note: Respondents indicate whether they agree or disagree with each item on a five-point scale.
*Items with an asterisk are reverse scored.

Source: Adapted from Marsha L. Richins and Scott Dawson, 'A Consumer Values Orientation for Materialism and Its Measurement: Scale Development and Validation', *Journal of Consumer Research* 20 (December 1992), Table 3. Reprinted with permission of The University of Chicago Press.

India, UK, France and Sweden.[77] From these results, several conclusions can be drawn. First of all, materialism is not directly linked to affluence, as has often been proposed. On the contrary, some of the most materialistic cultures are the ones where most consumers (feel that they) lack a lot of things. But this obviously is not the only explanation, since the US, New Zealand and Germany score relatively high as well, and India scores low. Since neither wealth, 'Westernness' nor any other single variable can explain these differences, it must be concluded that materialism is a consequence of several factors, including such things as social stability, access to information, reference models, as well as historical developments and cultural values.

This study was followed up by another one based on qualitative depth interviews, adding more insight into consumers' different ways of coping with their own materialism which was generally perceived as something negative. Basically, two ways of dealing with materialism were found: either you condemn materialism and provide an explanation why your personal materialism is a particularly good one, or you admit to being a 'bad' materialist but provide an excuse for being so. The different kinds of attitudes towards materialism are listed below:

- *Justifying materialism (my materialism is a good materialism)*

  - 'I am a passionate connoisseur, not a vulgar materialist – I have passion for and knowledge about the things I collect, it is not just a matter of having as much as possible.'

  - 'Terminal materialism is bad, but instrumental materialism is good, for instance to provide security for my family.'

  - 'I spend my money so that I can share my goods with others and give them pleasure.'

- *Excusing (materialism is bad, but . . .)*

  - 'Society (or the media, or the environment) made me do it.'

  - 'It's just the way of the modern world – everybody is like that.'

  - 'I deserve it since I have been deprived of opportunities for so long (e.g. people in newly marketized economies).'[78]

The 'why' of consumption

As we have seen in this chapter, there are many reasons why we want to engage in consumption activities. One of the main lessons to retain is probably that the 'why?' question cannot stand alone, but must be asked with reference to a number of other questions such as 'who?', indicating personal, group and cultural differences; 'when?' and 'where?', indicating situational and contextual differences; 'how?', pointing to the reflexive and emotional processes involved; and finally 'what?' kind of consumption item and consumer behaviour are we talking about. These dimensions, which are all to some extent addressed later in this book, are illustrated in Figure 4.5.

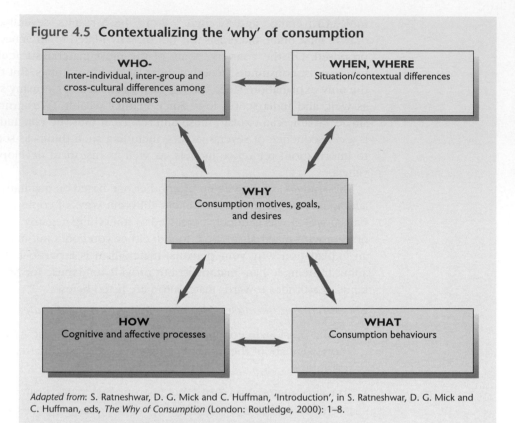

Figure 4.5 Contextualizing the 'why' of consumption

Adapted from: S. Ratneshwar, D. G. Mick and C. Huffman, 'Introduction', in S. Ratneshwar, D. G. Mick and C. Huffman, eds, *The Why of Consumption* (London: Routledge, 2000): 1–8.

Chapter summary

● Marketers have claimed that they try to satisfy consumer needs, but the reason why any product is purchased can vary widely. The identification of consumer motives is an important step in ensuring that the appropriate needs and wants will be met by a product.

● Traditional approaches to consumer behaviour have focused on the abilities of products to satisfy rational needs (utilitarian motives), but hedonic motives (e.g. the need for exploration or for fun) play an increasing and decisive role in many purchase decisions. Hence there has been a shift away from talking about needs and towards talking about goals, wants and desires.

● The same product can satisfy different goals, wants and desires, depending upon the consumer's state at the time. In addition, the consumer's degree of involvement with the product must be considered.

● Since consumers are not necessarily able or willing to communicate their underlying desires to marketers, various techniques such as projective tests can be employed to assess desires indirectly.

● Consumer motivations are often driven by underlying values. In this context, products take on meaning because they are seen as being instrumental in helping the person to achieve some goal that is linked to a value, such as individuality or freedom.

- Values are basic, general principles used to judge the desirability of end-states. All cultures form a value system which sets them apart from other cultures. Some researchers have developed lists to account for such value systems and used them in cross-cultural comparisons.

- One approach to the study of values is the means–end chain, which tries to link product attributes to consumer values via the consequences that usage of the product will have for the consumer.

- Materialism may be considered a more general value underlying other consumer values, thus reassuring that an obvious way of realizing one's values is through consumption.

KEY TERMS

Acculturation (*p. 111*)
Desire (*p. 102*)
Drive theory (*p. 95*)
Enculturation (*p. 111*)
Expectancy theory (*p. 95*)
Freudian theory (*p. 100*)
Goal (*p. 93*)
Inertia (*p. 104*)
Instrumental values (*p. 113*)
Involvement (*p. 104*)
Laddering (*p. 115*)

Materialism (*p. 116*)
Means–end chain (*p. 115*)
MECCAs (*p. 115*)
Motivation (*p. 93*)
Motivational research (*p. 101*)
Need (*p. 93*)
Terminal values (*p. 113*)
Theory of cognitive dissonance (*p. 97*)
Value (*p. 109*)
Value system (*p. 110*)
Want (*p. 94*)

For additional material see the companion website at:
www.booksites.net/solomon_euro

Consumer behaviour challenge

1 Describe three types of motivational conflicts, citing an example of each from current marketing campaigns.

2 Should consumer researchers have the right to probe into the consumer's unconscious? Is this a violation of privacy, or just another way to gather deep knowledge of purchase motivations?

3 What is the difference between a want and a desire? Think about your own feelings and try to describe the differences.

4 Describe how a man's level of involvement with his car would affect how he is influenced by different marketing stimuli. How might you design a strategy for a line of car batteries for a segment of low-involvement consumers, and how would this strategy differ from your attempts to reach a segment of men who are very involved in working on their cars?

5   Interview members of a celebrity fan club. Describe their level of involvement with the 'product', and devise some marketing opportunities to reach this group.

6   'High involvement is just a fancy term for expensive'. Do you agree?

7   Collect a sample of ads that appear to appeal to consumers' values. What value is being communicated in each, and how is this done? Is this an effective approach to designing a marketing communication?

8   Construct a hypothetical means–end chain model for the purchase of a bouquet of roses. How might a florist use this approach to construct a promotional strategy?

9   Think about some of the excuses or explanations you have used towards yourself or towards others for materialistic wants. How do they correspond to the explanations and excuses accounted for here?

Notes

1. Ronald Paul Hill and Harold Robinson, 'Fanatic Consumer Behavior: Athletics as a Consumption Experience', *Psychology & Marketing* 8 (Summer 1991): 79–100.

2. Robert A. Baron, *Psychology: The Essential Science* (Needham, MA: Allyn & Bacon, 1989).

3. Jean Baudrillard, 'La genèse idéologique des besoins', *Cahiers internationaux de sociologie* 47 (1969): 45–68.

4. Søren Askegaard and A. Fuat Firat, 'Towards a Critique of Material Culture, Consumption, and Markets', in S. Pearce, ed., *Experiencing Material Culture in the Western World* (London: Leicester University Press): 114–39.

5. Leon Festinger, *A Theory of Cognitive Dissonance* (Stanford, CA: Stanford University Press, 1957).

6. Mary Kay Ericksen and M. Joseph Sirgy, 'Achievement Motivation and Clothing Preferences of White-Collar Working Women', in Michael R. Solomon, ed., *The Psychology of Fashion* (Lexington, MA: Lexington Books, 1985): 357–69.

7. Abraham H. Maslow, *Motivation and Personality*, 2nd edn (New York: Harper & Row, 1970).

8. Richard Maddock, 'A Theoretical and Empirical Substructure of Consumer Motivation and Behaviour', in Flemming Hansen, ed., *European Advances in Consumer Research* 2 (Provo, UT: Association for Consumer Research, 1995): 29–37.

9. Ernest Dichter, *A Strategy of Desire* (Garden City, NY: Doubleday, 1960); Ernest Dichter, *The Handbook of Consumer Motivations* (New York: McGraw-Hill, 1964); Jeffrey J. Durgee, 'Interpreting Dichter's Interpretations: An Analysis of Consumption Symbolism in The Handbook of Consumer Motivations', *Marketing and Semiotics. Selected Papers from the Copenhagen Symposium*, ed. Hanne Hartvig Larsen, David G. Mick and Christian Alsted (Copenhagen: Handelshøjskolens forlag 1991): 52–74; Pierre Martineau, *Motivation in Advertising* (New York: McGraw-Hill, 1957).

10. Vance Packard, *The Hidden Persuaders* (New York: D. McKay, 1957).

11. Harold Kassarjian, 'Personality and Consumer Behavior: A Review', *Journal of Marketing Research* 8 (November 1971): 409–18.

12. Bill Schlackman, 'An Historical Perspective', in Sue Robson and Angela Foster, *Qualitative Research in Action* (London: Edward Arnold, 1988): 15–23.

13. Cf. also Russell W. Belk, Güliz Ger and Søren Askegaard, 'Metaphors of Consumer Desire', in Kim P. Corfman and John Lynch, Jr, eds, *Advances in Consumer Research* 23 (Provo, UT: Association for Consumer Research, 1996): 368–73.

14. Richard Elliott, 'Existential Consumption and Irrational Desire', *European Journal of Marketing*, 31(3/4), (1997): 285–96.

15. Russell W. Belk, Güliz Ger and Søren Askegaard, 'The Missing Streetcar Named Desire', in S. Ratneshwar, D. G. Mick & C. Huffman, eds, *The Why of Consumption* (London: Routledge, 2000): 98–119.

16. Robert Bocock, *Consumption* (London: Routledge 1993).

17. Russell W. Belk, Güliz Ger and Søren Askegaard, 'Consumer Desire in Three Cultures', in D. MacInnis and M. Brucks, eds, *Advances in Consumer Research*, 14 (Provo, UT: Association for Consumer Research, 1997): 24–8.

18. Quoted in 'Forehead Advertisement Pays Off', *Montgomery Advertiser* (4 May 2000): 7A.

19. Judith Lynne Zaichkowsky, 'Measuring the Involvement Construct in Marketing', *Journal of Consumer Research* 12 (December 1985): 341–52.

20. Andrew Mitchell, 'Involvement: A Potentially Important Mediator of Consumer Behavior', in

William L. Wilkie, ed., *Advances in Consumer Research* 6 (Provo, UT: Association for Consumer Research, 1979): 191-6.

21. Richard L. Celsi and Jerry C. Olson, 'The Role of Involvement in Attention and Comprehension Processes', *Journal of Consumer Research* 15 (September 1988): 210-24.

22. Ton Otker, 'The Highly Involved Consumer: A Marketing Myth?', *Marketing and Research Today* (February 1990): 30-6.

23. Anthony G. Greenwald and Clark Leavitt, 'Audience Involvement in Advertising: Four Levels', *Journal of Consumer Research* 11 (June 1984): 581-92.

24. Gary J. Bamossy and Janeen Costa, 'Consuming Paradise: A Cultural Construction' (paper presented at the Association for Consumer Research Conference, June 1997, Stockholm).

25. Judith Lynne Zaichkowsky, 'The Emotional Side of Product Involvement', in Paul Anderson and Melanie Wallendorf, eds, *Advances in Consumer Research* 14 (Provo, UT: Association for Consumer Research, 1987): 32-5.

26. For a discussion of interrelationships between situational and enduring involvement, see Marsha L. Richins, Peter H. Bloch and Edward F. McQuarrie, 'How Enduring and Situational Involvement Combine to Create Involvement Responses', *Journal of Consumer Psychology* 1 (1992) 2: 143-53.

27. Rajeev Batra and Michael L. Ray, 'Operationalizing Involvement as Depth and Quality of Cognitive Responses', in Alice Tybout and Richard Bagozzi, eds, *Advances in Consumer Research* 10 (Ann Arbor, MI: Association for Consumer Research, 1983): 309-13.

28. Carmen Garcia, Vicente Ponsoda and Herminia Estebaranz, 'Scanning Ads: Effects of Involvement and of Position of the Illustration in Printed Advertisements', in S. Hoch and R. Meyer, eds, *Advances in Consumer Research*, 27 (Provo, UT: Association for Consumer Research, 2000): 104-9.

29. Bruce Crumley, 'Multipoints Add Up for Quick Burger', *Advertising Age* (29 November 1993): 14.

30. Marsha L. Richins and Peter H. Bloch, 'After the New Wears Off: The Temporal Context of Product Involvement', *Journal of Consumer Research* 13 (September 1986): 280-5.

31. Kevin J. Clancy, 'CPMs Must Bow to "Involvement" Measurement', *Advertising Age* (20 January 1992): 26.

32. For a newer, modified version of this scale, see Edward F. McQuarrie and J. Michael Munson, 'A Revised Product Involvement Inventory: Improved Usability and Validity', in John F. Sherry, Jr and Brian Sternthal, eds, *Advances in Consumer Research* 19 (Provo, UT: Association for Consumer Research, 1992): 108-15.

33. Gilles Laurent and Jean-Noel Kapferer, 'Measuring Consumer Involvement Profiles', *Journal of Marketing Research* 22 (February 1985): 41-53; this scale was later validated on an American sample as well, cf. William C. Rodgers and Kenneth C. Schneider, 'An Empirical Evaluation of the Kapferer-Laurent Consumer Involvement Profile Scale', *Psychology & Marketing* 10 (July/August 1993) 4: 333-45.

34. Culture clash experienced by one of the authors.

35. Morris B. Holbrook and Elizabeth C. Hirschman, 'The Experiential Aspects of Consumption: Consumer Fantasies, Feelings, and Fun', *Journal of Consumer Research* 9 (September 1982): 132-40.

36. Deborah J. MacInnis, Christine Moorman and Bernard J. Jaworski, 'Enhancing and Measuring Consumers' Motivation, Opportunity, and Ability to Process Brand Information from Ads', *Journal of Marketing* 55 (October 1991): 332-53.

37. K. Oanh Ha, 'Have it Your Way', *Montgomery Advertiser* (9 November 1998): 2D.

38. Shalom H. Schwartz and Warren Bilsky, 'Toward a Universal Psychological Structure of Human Values', *Journal of Personality and Social Psychology* 53 (1987): 550-62.

39. Ajay K. Sirsi, James C. Ward and Peter H. Reingen, 'Microcultural Analysis of Variation in Sharing of Causal Reasoning about Behavior', *Journal of Consumer Research* 22 (March 1996): 345-72.

40. Bernard Cova and Robert Salle, 'Buying Behaviour in European and American Industry: Contrasts', *European Management Journal* 9(4) (1991): 433-6.

41. Christian Dussart, 'Capitalism against Capitalism: Political and Economic Implications of Marketing Practice in Europe', in M. J. Baker, ed, *Perspectives on Marketing Management*, 4 (London: John Wiley & Sons, 1994): 119-34.

42. Richard W. Pollay, 'Measuring the Cultural Values Manifest in Advertising', *Current Issues and Research in Advertising* (1983): 71-92.

43. Howard W. French, 'Vocation for Dropouts is Painting Tokyo Red', *New York Times on the Web* (5 March 2000).

44. Sarah Ellison, 'Sexy-Ad Reel Shows What Tickles in Tokyo Can Fade Fast in France', *Wall Street Journal Interactive Edition* (31 March 2000).

45. Milton Rokeach, *The Nature of Human Values* (New York: Free Press, 1973).

46. Lynn Kahle, Sharon Beatty and John Mager, 'Implications of Social Values for Consumer Communications: The Case of the European Community', in B. Englis, ed., *Global and Multinational Advertising* (Hillsdale, NJ: Lawrence Erlbaum Ass.): 47-64.

47. Suzanne C. Grunert and Gerhard Scherhorn, 'Consumer Values in West Germany: Underlying Dimensions and Cross Cultural Comparison with North America', *Journal of Business Research* 20 (1990): 97-107.

48. Donald E. Vinson, Jerome E. Scott and Lawrence R. Lamont, 'The Role of Personal Values in Marketing and Consumer Behavior', *Journal of Marketing* 41 (April 1977): 44-50.

49. *Markedsføring* (25 August 2000): 8.

50. *Markedsføring* (12 November 1999): 2.

51. Morris B. Holbrook, *Consumer Value* (London: Routledge, 1999).

52. Ibid. This book contains a chapter by various consumer researchers on each of the value types.

53. *Marketing* (24 August 2000): 2.

54. Milton Rokeach, *Understanding Human Values* (New York: The Free Press, 1979); see also J. Michael Munson and Edward McQuarrie, 'Shortening the Rokeach Value Survey for Use in Consumer Research', in Michael J. Houston, ed., *Advances in Consumer Research* 15 (Provo, UT: Association for Consumer Research, 1988): 381–6.

55. Jacques-Marie Aurifeille, 'Value Changes and Their Marketing Implications: A Russian Survey', in W. F. van Raaij and G. Bamossy, eds, *European Advances in Consumer Research* 1 (Provo, UT: Association for Consumer Research, 1993): 249–61.

56. B. W. Becker and P. E. Conner, 'Personal Values of the Heavy User of Mass Media', *Journal of Advertising Research* 21 (1981): 37–43; Vinson, Scott and Lamont, 'The Role of Personal Values in Marketing and Consumer Behavior'.

57. Sharon E. Beatty, Lynn R. Kahle, Pamela Homer and Shekhar Misra, 'Alternative Measurement Approaches to Consumer Values: The List of Values and the Rokeach Value Survey', *Psychology & Marketing* 2 (1985): 181–200.

58. Pierre Valette-Florence, Suzanne C. Grunert, Klaus G. Grunert and Sharon Beatty, 'Une comparaison franco-allemande de l'adhésion aux valeurs personnelles', *Recherche et Applications en Marketing* 6(3) (1991): 5–20.

59. Klaus G. Grunert, Suzanne C. Grunert and Sharon Beatty, 'Cross-cultural Research on Consumer Values', *Marketing and Research Today* 17 (1989): 30–9.

60. Suzanne C. Grunert, Klaus G. Grunert and Kai Kristensen, 'Une méthode d'estimation de la validité interculturelle des instruments de mesure: Le cas de la mesure des valeurs des consommateurs par la liste des valeurs LOV', *Recherche et Applications en Marketing* 8(4) (1993): 5–28.

61. Shalom H. Schwartz and Warren Bilsky, 'Toward a Theory of Universal Content and Structure of Values: Extensions and Cross Cultural Replications', *Journal of Personality and Social Psychology* 58 (1990): 878–91; Shalom H. Schwartz, 'Universals in the Content and Structure of Values: Theoretical Advance and Empirical Test in 20 Countries', in M. Zanna, ed., *Advances in Experimental Social Psychology*, 25 (San Diego, CA: Academic Press, 1992): 1–65.

62. Shalom H. Schwartz, 'Beyond Individualism/ Collectivism. New Cultural Dimensions of Values' in U. Kim *et al.*, eds, *Individualism and Collectivism* (Thousand Oaks, CA: Sage, 1994): 85–119.

63. Sarah Todd, Rob Lawson and Haydn Northover, 'Value Orientation and Media Consumption Behavior', in B. Englis and A. Olofsson, eds, *European Advances in Consumer Behaviour* 3 (Provo, UT: Association for Consumer Research): 328–32.

64. Suzanne C. Grunert and Hans Jørn Juhl, 'Values, Environmental Attitudes, and Buying of Organic Foods', *Journal of Economic Psychology* 16 (1995): 39–62.

65. Thomas J. Reynolds and Jonathan Gutman, 'Laddering Theory, Method, Analysis, and Interpretation', *Journal of Advertising Research* 28 (February/March 1988): 11–34; Beth Walker, Richard Celsi and Jerry Olson, 'Exploring the Structural Characteristics of Consumers' Knowledge', in Melanie Wallendorf and Paul Anderson, eds, *Advances in Consumer Research* 14 (Provo, UT: Association for Consumer Research, 1986): 17–21.

66. Andreas Hermann, 'Wertorientierte Produkt- und Werbegestaltung', *Marketing ZFP* 3 (3rd quarter 1996): 153–63.

67. Klaus G. Grunert and Suzanne C. Grunert, 'Measuring Subjective Meaning Structures by the Laddering Method: Theoretical Considerations and Methodological Problems', *International Journal of Research in Marketing* 12(3) (1995): 209–25. This volume of *IJRM* is a special issue on means–end chains and the laddering technique.

68. Roger Mason, 'Measuring the Demand for Status Goods: An Evaluation of Means–End Chains and Laddering', in Flemming Hansen, ed., *European Advances in Consumer Research* 2 (Provo, UT: Association for Consumer Research, 1995): 78–82.

69. Thomas J. Reynolds and Alyce Byrd Craddock, 'The Application of the MECCAs Model to the Development and Assessment of Advertising Strategy: A Case Study', *Journal of Advertising Research* (April/May 1988): 43–54.

70. Elin Sørensen, Klaus G. Grunert and Niels Asger Nielsen, 'The Impact of Product Experience, Product Involvement and Verbal Processing Style on Consumers' Cognitive Structures with Regard to Fresh Fish', *MAPP Working Paper* 42 (Aarhus: The Aarhus School of Business, October 1996).

71. Reported on the 3rd MAPP research centre conference (October 1996).

72. N. A. Nielsen, T. Bech-Larsen and K. G. Grunert, 'Consumer Purchase Motives and Product Perceptions: A Laddering Study on Vegetable Oil in Three Countries', *Food Quality and Preference* 9(6) (1998): 455–66.

73. Russell W. Belk, 'Possessions and the Extended Self', *Journal of Consumer Research* 15 (September 1988): 139–68; Melanie Wallendorf and Eric J. Arnould, '"My Favourite Things": A Cross-Cultural Inquiry into Object Attachment, Possessiveness, and Social Linkage', *Journal of Consumer Research* 14 (March 1988): 531–47.

74. 'Europeans More Active as Consumers', *Marketing News* (10 June 1994): 17.

75. Russell W. Belk and Richard W. Pollay, 'Images of Ourselves: The Good Life in Twentieth Century Advertising', *Journal of Consumer Research* 11 (March 1985): 887–97.

76. Marsha L. Richins and Scott Dawson, 'A Consumer Values Orientation for Materialism and Its Measurement: Scale Development and Validation', *Journal of Consumer Research* 20 (December 1992).

77. Güliz Ger and Russell Belk, 'Cross-Cultural Differences in Materialism', *Journal of Economic Psychology* 17 (1996): 55–77.

78. Güliz Ger and Russell Belk, 'Accounting for Materialism in Four Cultures', *Journal of Material Culture* 4(2) (1999): 183–204.

Chapter 5

Attitudes

It's a lazy Wednesday night, and Leah, Lynn and Nicki are hanging out at Nicki's flat in Manchester doing some channel-surfing. Leah clicks to the sports cable and the three friends see there's a women's soccer game on, being televised from America. Leah has been a fan for as long as she can remember – perhaps as a result of having three older brothers and growing up in a house which had Manchester United souvenirs in every room. She loves the subtle intensity of the game – the traps, the moves, the way players make it look easy to move a ball around a huge field as if it were a small patch of grass. Further, she's proud of Manchester United's rich history as a club, and its success as a business operation.[1] Nicki's a glutton for thrills and chills: she converted to soccer after seeing Mick Jagger singing along with the British crowd in the stadium as the British team battled the Argentinians in an exciting, dramatic match in the 1998 World Cup. Lynn, on the other hand, doesn't know a corner kick from a penalty kick. For her, the most interesting part of the match was the footage being shown over and over of the US player Brandi Chastain's celebrating her successful penalty kick which won the match by taking her shirt off to reveal her sports bra. Lynn even bought one a few weeks later. Still, soccer doesn't really ring her chimes – but as long as she gets to hang out with her girlfriends she doesn't really care if they watch non-contact sports like soccer or contact sports like *The Jerry Springer Show*.

The power of attitudes

Leah is just the kind of fan sponsoring companies like Nike, Gatorade and Adidas hope will turn women's soccer into an ongoing source of sports fanaticism. In America, attitudes towards the game have changed dramatically since the US women's team lost in the 1996 semi-finals in Sweden before a crowd of less than 3000. The 1999 World Cup was won before an audience of over 90,000 screaming fans, many of whom were soccer moms who saw the players as important role models for their young daughters. In 1998 a record 7.5 million women and girls enrolled for soccer teams in the United States. In the US, women now represent just under half of all soccer player registrations.[2] These kinds of growth figures are not to be found in Europe. Soccer has a much richer, longer tradition here, and has been a sport dominated by male patronage at the stadiums, and male viewership on the television. While amateur soccer clubs for women can be found in the UK and on the continent, they are not nearly as popular as in the US, and have to compete with other sports which attract female participants, such as field hockey.

On the other hand, following Chastain's exuberant show of skin there has been much written in the US over the so-called 'babe factor' as some critics wonder whether women's athletics will ever be taken seriously by male fans. Others feel that attitudes towards the game are more complex than that; they argue that sex appeal does not have to be sacrificed for professionalism. The big question is whether these positive feelings will endure. The goal of the Women's World Cup is to establish a women's professional league over the next few years. Time will tell if this ambitious project will score big or be red-carded and left to dwindle on the sidelines in the US.[3] To score big in professional sports in the US, or in Europe, it's all a question of attitudes, and the dominant attitude among European fans is that women's soccer just isn't that important, at least so far. As you'll see throughout this book, attitudes can vary significantly along gender lines, and from one culture to another.

The term **attitude** is widely used in popular culture. You might be asked, 'What is your attitude towards abortion?' A parent might scold, 'Young man, I don't like your attitude.' Some bars even euphemistically refer to Happy Hour as 'an attitude adjustment period'. For our purposes, though, an attitude is a lasting, general evaluation of people (including oneself), objects, advertisements, or issues.[4] Anything towards which one has an attitude is called an **attitude object (A$_o$)**.

This chapter will consider the contents of an attitude, how attitudes are formed, how they can be measured, and review some of the surprisingly complex relationships between attitudes and behaviour. In the next chapter, we'll take a closer look at how attitudes can be changed – certainly an issue of prime importance to marketers.

The content of attitudes

An attitude is *lasting* because it tends to endure over time. It is *general* because it applies to more than a momentary event, like hearing a loud noise (though over time you might develop a negative attitude towards all loud noises). Consumers have attitudes towards very product-specific behaviours (e.g. using Mentodent rather than Colgate toothpaste), as well as towards more general consumption-related behaviours (e.g. how often you should brush your teeth). Attitudes help to determine who a person goes out with, what music he or she listens to, whether he or she will recycle or discard cans, or whether he or she chooses to become a consumer researcher for a living.

The functions of attitudes

The **functional theory of attitudes** was initially developed by the psychologist Daniel Katz to explain how attitudes facilitate social behaviour.[5] According to this pragmatic approach, attitudes exist because they serve a function for the person. That is, they are determined by a person's motives. Consumers who expect that they will need to deal with similar information at a future time will be more likely to start forming attitudes in anticipation of this event.[6]

Two people can each have the same attitude towards an object for very different reasons. As a result, it can be helpful for a marketer to know why an attitude is held before attempting to change it. The following are attitude functions as identified by Katz:

- *Utilitarian function*. The utilitarian function is related to the basic principles of reward and punishment. We develop some of our attitudes towards products simply on the basis of whether these products provide pleasure or pain. If a person likes the taste of a cheeseburger, that person will develop a positive attitude towards cheeseburgers. Ads that stress straightforward product benefits (e.g. you should drink Diet Coke 'just for the taste of it') appeal to the utilitarian function.

- *Value-expressive function*. Attitudes that perform a value-expressive function express the consumer's central values or self-concept. A person forms a product attitude not because of its objective benefits, but because of what the product says about him or her as a person (e.g. 'What sort of woman reads *Elle*?'). Value-expressive attitudes are highly relevant to lifestyle analyses, where consumers cultivate a cluster of activities, interests and opinions to express a particular social identity.

- *Ego-defensive function*. Attitudes that are formed to protect the person, from either external threats or internal feelings, perform an ego-defensive function. An early marketing study indicated that housewives in the 1950s resisted the use of instant coffee because it threatened their conception of themselves as capable homemakers.[7] Products that promise to help a man project a 'macho' image (e.g. Marlboro cigarettes) may be appealing to his insecurities about his masculinity. Another example of this function is deodorant campaigns that stress the dire, embarrassing consequences of underarm odour.

- *Knowledge function*. Some attitudes are formed as the result of a need for order, structure or meaning. This need is often present when a person is in an ambiguous situation or is confronted with a new product (e.g. 'Bayer wants you to know about pain relievers').

An attitude can serve more than one function, but in many cases a particular one will be dominant. By identifying the dominant function a product serves for consumers (i.e. what benefits it provides), marketers can emphasize these benefits in their communications and packaging. Ads relevant to the function prompt more favourable thoughts about what is being marketed and can result in a heightened preference for both the ad and the product.

One American study determined that for most people coffee serves more of a utilitarian function than a value-expressive function. As a consequence, subjects responded more positively to copy for a fictitious brand of coffee that read, 'The delicious, hearty flavour and aroma of Sterling Blend coffee comes from a blend of the freshest coffee beans' (i.e. a utilitarian appeal) than they did to copy that read, 'The coffee you drink says something about the type of person you are. It can reveal your rare, discriminating taste' (i.e. the value-expressive function). In European countries with a strong 'coffee culture', such as Germany, the Benelux and Scandinavian countries, ads are more likely to stress the value-expressive function, wherein the more social and ritualistic aspects of coffee consumption are expressed.[8]

As we saw in the experiences of the three Manchester women watching a soccer game, the importance of an attitude object may differ quite a bit for different people. Understanding the attitude's centrality to an individual and to others who share similar characteristics can be useful to marketers who are trying to devise strategies that will appeal to different customer segments. A study of football game attendance illustrates that varying levels of commitment result in different fan 'profiles'.[9] The study identified three distinct clusters of fans:[10]

- One cluster consisted of the real die-hard fans like Leah who were highly committed to their team and who displayed an enduring love of the game. To reach these fans, the researchers recommended that sports marketers should focus on providing them with greater sports knowledge and relate their attendance to their personal goals and values.

- A second cluster was like Nicki – their attitudes were based on the unique, self-expressive experience provided by the game. They enjoyed the stimulation of cheering for a team and the drama of the competition itself. These people are more likely to be 'brand switchers', fair-weather fans who shift allegiances when the home team no longer provides the thrills they need. This segment can be appealed to by publicizing aspects of the visiting teams, such as advertising the appearance of stars who are likely to give the fans a game they will remember.

- A third cluster was like Lynn – they were looking for camaraderie above all. These consumers attend games primarily to take part in small-group activities such as a pre- or post-game party which may accompany the event. Marketers could appeal to this cluster by providing improved peripheral benefits, such as making it easier for groups to meet at the stadium, improving parking, and offering multiple-unit pricing.

The ABC model of attitudes and hierarchies of effects

Most researchers agree that an attitude has three components: affect, behaviour and cognition. **Affect** refers to the way a consumer feels about an attitude object. **Behaviour** involves the person's intentions to do something with regard to an attitude object (but, as will be discussed later, an intention does not always result in an actual behaviour). **Cognition** refers to the beliefs a consumer has about an attitude object. These three components of an attitude can be remembered as the ABC model of attitudes.

This model emphasizes the interrelationships between knowing, feeling and

Figure 5.1 Three hierarchies of effects

Beliefs → Affect → Behaviour → **Attitude** Based on cognitive information processing

Beliefs → Behaviour → Affect → **Attitude** Based on behavioural learning processes

Affect → Behaviour → Beliefs → **Attitude** Based on hedonic consumption

doing. Consumers' attitudes towards a product cannot be determined simply by identifying their beliefs about it. For example, a researcher may find that shoppers 'know' a particular camcorder has an 8:1 power zoom lens, auto-focus and a flying erase head, but such findings do not indicate whether they feel these attributes are good, bad or irrelevant, or whether they would actually buy the camcorder.

While all three components of an attitude are important, their relative importance will vary depending upon a consumer's level of motivation with regard to the attitude object. Attitude researchers have developed the concept of a **hierarchy of effects** to explain the relative impact of the three components. Each hierarchy specifies that a fixed sequence of steps occurs en route to an attitude. Three different hierarchies are summarized in Figure 5.1.

The standard learning hierarchy

Leah's positive attitude towards soccer closely resembles the process by which most attitudes have been assumed to be constructed. A consumer approaches a product decision as a problem-solving process. First, he or she forms beliefs about a product by accumulating knowledge (beliefs) regarding relevant attributes. Next, the consumer evaluates these beliefs and forms a feeling about the product (affect).[11] Over time, Leah assembled information about the sport, began to recognize the players, and learned which teams were superior to others. Finally, based on this evaluation, the consumer engages in a relevant behaviour, such as buying the product or supporting a particular team by wearing its shirt. This careful choice process often results in the type of loyalty displayed by Leah: the consumer 'bonds' with the product over time and is not easily persuaded to experiment with other brands. The standard learning hierarchy assumes that a consumer is highly involved in making a purchase decision.[12] The person is motivated to seek out a lot of information, carefully weigh alternatives, and come to a thoughtful decision. As we saw in Chapter 4, this process is likely to occur if the decision is important to the consumer or in some way central to the consumer's self-concept. If you understand the level of fan support for Manchester United, then you'll appreciate just how central Leah's attitudes about soccer (or, in this case, Manchester United) are for her.

The low-involvement hierarchy

In contrast to Leah, Nicki's interest in the attitude object (soccer) is at best luke-warm. She is not particularly knowledgeable about the sport, and she may have an emotional response to an exciting game but not to a specific team. Nicki is typical of a consumer who forms an attitude via the *low-involvement hierarchy of effects.* In this sequence, the consumer does not initially have a strong preference for one brand over another, but instead acts on the basis of limited knowledge and then forms an evaluation only after the product has been purchased or used.[13] The attitude is likely to come about through behavioural learning, in which the consumer's choice is reinforced by good or bad experiences with the product after purchase. Nicki will probably be more likely to tune in to future games if they continue to have the same level of drama and excitement as the UK–Argentina match.

The possibility that consumers simply don't care enough about many decisions to assemble a set of product beliefs carefully and then evaluate them is important, because it implies that all of the concern about influencing beliefs and carefully com-municating information about product attributes may be largely wasted. Consumers aren't necessarily going to pay attention anyway; they are more likely to respond to simple stimulus–response connections when making purchase decisions. For example, a consumer choosing between paper towels might remember that 'Brand X absorbs more quickly than Brand Y', rather than bothering to compare systemati-cally all of the brands on the shelf.

The notion of low involvement on the part of consumers is a bitter pill for some marketers to swallow. Who wants to admit that what they market is not very import-ant or involving? A brand manager for, say, a brand of chewing gum or cat food may find it hard to believe that consumers don't put that much thought into purchasing her product because she herself spends many of her waking (and perhaps sleeping) hours thinking about it.

Steak is our life.
All we ask is that you make it your lunch.

Smith & Wollensky.
The quintessential New York City steakhouse.
49th St. & 3rd Ave. (212)753-1530.

Winner of The *Wine Spectator's* 1987 Grand Award.

This ad for New York's famous Smith and Wollensky restaurant emphasizes that marketers and others associated with a product or service are often more involved with it than are their customers.

For marketers, the ironic silver lining to this low-involvement cloud is that under these conditions, consumers are not motivated to process a lot of complex brand-related information. Instead, they will be swayed by principles of behavioural learning, such as the simple responses caused by conditioned brand names, point-of-purchase displays, and so on. This results in what we might call the *involvement paradox:* the less important the product is to consumers, the more important are many of the marketing stimuli (e.g. packages, jingles) that must be devised to sell it.

The experiential hierarchy

In recent years researchers have begun to stress the significance of emotional response as a central aspect of an attitude. According to the experiential hierarchy of effects, consumers act on the basis of their emotional reactions (just as Lynn enjoys watching the telly with her friends, regardless of what is on). Although the factors of beliefs and behaviour are recognized as playing a part, a consumer's overall evaluation of an attitude object is considered by many to be the core of an attitude.

This perspective highlights the idea that attitudes can be strongly influenced by intangible product attributes such as package design, and by consumers' reactions to accompanying stimuli such as advertising and even the brand name. As discussed in Chapter 4, resulting attitudes will be affected by consumers' hedonic motivations, such as how the product makes them feel or the fun its use will provide. Numerous studies indicate that the mood a person is in when exposed to a marketing message influences how the ad is processed, the likelihood that the information presented will be remembered, and how the person will feel about the advertised item and related products in the future.[14]

One important debate about the experiential hierarchy concerns the independence of cognition and affect. On the one hand, the *cognitive-affective model* argues that an affective judgement is the last step in a series of cognitive processes. Earlier steps include the sensory registration of stimuli and the retrieval of meaningful information from memory to categorize these stimuli.[15]

On the other hand, the *independence hypothesis* takes the position that affect and cognition involve two separate, partially independent systems; affective responses do not always require prior cognitions.[16] The number one song in the 'Top Ten' hit parade may possess the same attributes as many other songs (dominant bass guitar, raspy vocals, persistent downbeat), but beliefs about these attributes cannot explain why one song becomes a classic while another sharing the same characteristics ends up in the bargain bin at the local record shop. The independence hypothesis does not eliminate the role of cognition in experience. It simply balances this traditional, rational emphasis on calculated decision-making by paying more attention to the impact of aesthetic, subjective experience. This type of holistic processing is more likely to occur when the product is perceived as primarily expressive or delivers sensory pleasure rather than utilitarian benefits.[17]

There's more to marketing than product attitudes

Marketers who are concerned with understanding consumers' attitudes have to contend with an even more complex issue: in decision-making situations, people form attitudes towards objects other than the product itself that can influence their ultimate selections. One additional factor to consider is attitudes towards the act of buying in general. As we'll see later in the chapter, sometimes people are reluctant, embarrassed or just too lazy to expend the effort to obtain a desired product or service.

In addition, consumers' reactions to a product, over and above their feelings about the product itself, are influenced by their evaluations of its advertising. Our evaluation of a product can be determined solely by our appraisal of how it is depicted in marketing communications – that is, we don't hesitate to form attitudes about products we've never even seen in person, much less used.

▶ The **attitude towards the advertisement (A$_{ad}$)** is defined as a predisposition to respond in a favourable or unfavourable manner to a particular advertising stimulus during a particular exposure occasion. Determinants of A$_{ad}$ include the viewer's attitude towards the advertiser, evaluations of the ad execution itself, the mood evoked by the ad and the degree to which the ad affects viewers' arousal levels.[18] A viewer's feelings about the context in which an ad appears can also influence brand attitudes. For example, attitudes about an ad and the brand depicted will be influenced if the consumer sees the ad while watching a favourite TV programme.[19] The effects demonstrated by A$_{ad}$ emphasize the importance of an ad's entertainment value in the purchase process.[20]

The feelings generated by advertising can have a direct impact on brand attitudes. Commercials can evoke a wide range of emotional responses, from disgust to happiness. Further, there is evidence that emotional responses will vary from one group of consumers to another. In an empirical study of students and housewives in Belgium and Holland, the results showed that the Belgians were more positive towards the hedonic and socio-cultural aspects of advertising than their Dutch counterparts. In the UK, Ford's ad campaign research on the Ford Ka, which is targeting an image-oriented market, showed it annoyed 41 per cent of 55–64-year-olds, compared with only 18 per cent of 25–34-year-olds. These feelings can be influenced both by the way the ad is done (i.e. the specific advertising execution) and by the consumer's reactions to the advertiser's motives. For example, many advertisers who are trying to craft messages for adolescents and young adults are encountering problems because this age group, having grown up in a 'marketing society', tends to be sceptical about attempts to persuade them to buy things.[21] These reactions can, in turn, influence memory for advertising content.[22] At least three emotional dimensions have been identified in commercials: pleasure, arousal and intimidation.[23] Specific types of feelings that can be generated by an ad include the following:[24]

● *Upbeat feelings* – amused, delighted, playful
● *Warm feelings* – affectionate, contemplative, hopeful
● *Negative feelings* – critical, defiant, offended.

Forming attitudes

We all have lots of attitudes, and we don't usually question how we got them. No one is born with the conviction that, say, Pepsi is better than Coke or that heavy metal music liberates the soul. Where do these attitudes come from?

An attitude can form in several different ways, depending on the particular hierarchy of effects in operation. It can occur because of classical conditioning, wherein an attitude object, such as the name Pepsi, is repeatedly paired with a catchy jingle ('You're in the Pepsi Generation . . .'). Or it can be formed through instrumental conditioning, in which consumption of the attitude object is reinforced (e.g. Pepsi quenches the thirst). Alternatively, the learning of an attitude can be the outcome of a very complex cognitive process. For example, a teenager may come to model the behaviour of friends and media figures who drink Pepsi because she believes that this act will enable her to fit in with the desirable images of the Pepsi Generation.

It is thus important to distinguish between types of attitudes, since not all are formed the same way.[25] A highly brand-loyal consumer like Leah, the Manchester United fan, has an enduring, deeply held positive attitude towards an attitude object, and this involvement will be difficult to weaken. On the other hand, another consumer like Nicki, who likes the drama and excitement more than the subtle aspects of soccer, may have a mildly positive attitude towards a product but be quite willing to abandon it when something better comes along. This section will consider the differences between strongly and weakly held attitudes and briefly review some of the major theoretical perspectives that have been developed to explain how attitudes form and relate to one another in the minds of consumers.

Levels of commitment to an attitude

Consumers vary in their commitment to an attitude; the degree of commitment is related to their level of involvement with the attitude object, as follows:[26]

- *Compliance*. At the lowest level of involvement, compliance, an attitude is formed because it helps in gaining rewards or avoiding punishments from others. This attitude is very superficial: it is likely to change when the person's behaviour is no longer monitored by others or when another option becomes available. A person may drink Pepsi because that is the brand the café sells and it is too much trouble to go elsewhere for a Coca-Cola.

- *Identification*. A process of identification occurs when attitudes are formed in order for the consumer to be similar to another person or group. Advertising that depicts the social consequences of choosing some products over others is relying on the tendency of consumers to imitate the behaviour of desirable models.

- *Internalization*. At a high level of involvement, deep-seated attitudes are internalized and become part of the person's value system. These attitudes are very difficult to change because they are so important to the individual. For example, many consumers had strong attitudes towards Coca-Cola and reacted quite negatively when the company attempted to switch to the New Coke formula. This allegiance to Coke was obviously more than a minor preference for these people: the brand had become intertwined with their social identities, taking on patriotic and nostalgic properties.

The consistency principle

Have you ever heard someone say, 'Pepsi is my favourite soft drink. It tastes terrible', or 'I love my husband. He's the biggest idiot I've ever met'? Perhaps not very often, because these beliefs or evaluations are not consistent with one another. According to the **principle of cognitive consistency**, consumers value harmony among their thoughts, feelings and behaviours, and they are motivated to maintain uniformity among these elements. This desire means that, if necessary, consumers will change their thoughts, feelings or behaviours to make them consistent with their other experiences. The consistency principle is an important reminder that attitudes are not formed in a vacuum. A significant determinant of the way an attitude object will be evaluated is how it fits with other, related attitudes already held by the consumer.

This public service advertisement hopes to form young people's attitudes towards drinking. Of course, individuals will vary in their level of commitment to drinking. Does this ad strike you primarily at a cognitive, or an emotional, level? What is your attitude towards the ad?

Cognitive dissonance theory revisited

In the last chapter, we discussed the role played by cognitive dissonance when consumers are trying to choose between two desired products. Cognitive dissonance theory has other important ramifications for attitudes, since people are often confronted with situations in which there is some conflict between their attitudes and behaviours.[27]

The theory proposes that, much like hunger or thirst, people are motivated to reduce this negative state by making things fit with one another. The theory focuses on situations where two cognitive elements are inconsistent with one another.

A cognitive element can be something a person believes about himself, a behaviour he performs or an observation about his surroundings. For example, the two cognitive elements 'I know smoking cigarettes causes cancer' and 'I smoke cigarettes' are dissonant. This psychological inconsistency creates a feeling of discomfort that the smoker is motivated to reduce. The magnitude of dissonance depends upon both the importance and the number of dissonant elements.[28] In other words, the pressure to reduce dissonance is more likely to be observed in high-involvement situations in which the elements are more important to the individual.

Dissonance reduction can occur by either eliminating, adding or changing elements. For example, the person could stop smoking (eliminating) or remember Great-Aunt Sophia, who smoked until the day she died at age 90 (adding). Alternatively, he might question the research that links cancer and smoking (changing), perhaps by believing industry-sponsored studies that try to refute this connection.

Dissonance theory can help to explain why evaluations of a product tend to increase after it has been purchased, i.e. post-purchase dissonance. The cognitive element 'I made a stupid decision' is dissonant with the element 'I am not a stupid person', so people tend to find even more reasons to like something after buying it.

A field study performed at a horse race demonstrates post-purchase dissonance. Gamblers evaluated their chosen horses more highly and were more confident of

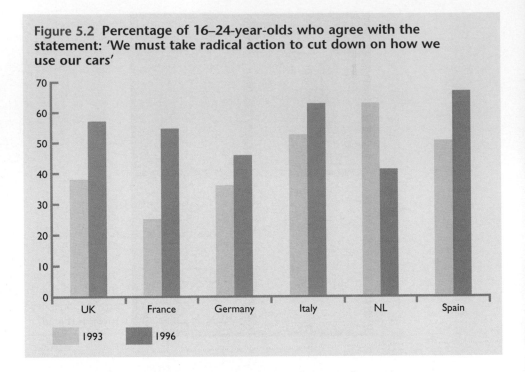

Figure 5.2 Percentage of 16–24-year-olds who agree with the statement: 'We must take radical action to cut down on how we use our cars'

their success after they had placed a bet than before. Since the gambler is financially committed to the choice, he or she reduces dissonance by increasing the attractiveness of the chosen alternative relative to the unchosen ones.[29] One implication of this phenomenon is that consumers actively seek support for their purchase decisions, so marketers should supply them with additional reinforcement to build positive brand attitudes.

While the consistency principle works well in explaining our desire for harmony among thoughts, feelings and behaviours, and subsequently in helping marketers understand their target markets, it isn't a perfect predictor of the way in which we hold seemingly *related* attitudes. Consider the results of a large European study of young adults, wherein attitudes towards the environment were being analysed. Figure 5.2 shows the percentage of 16–24-year-olds who agree with the statement: 'We must take radical action to cut down on how we use our cars'. A few preliminary conclusions can be made from this graph. First, European youth's attitude towards addressing cutting down on the use of cars seems generally positive. Not only is it positive, but the attitude seems to be gaining in support over time (from 1993 to 1996), with the exception of the sample from the Netherlands. Now compare the results of attitudes towards car usage with the results of paying more for environmentally friendly products, shown in Figure 5.3 (both results are from the same samples). Here, the attitude of *not* having to pay more for environmentally friendly products is strong, stable over time, and across countries, with the Dutch sample reporting a somewhat greater willingness to pay more for environmental products. So, while congruity theory would predict that seemingly related attitudes are positively correlated, consumers can and do hold attitudes that are not always consistent, at least on the surface!

Self-perception theory

Do attitudes necessarily change following behaviour because people are motivated to feel good about their decisions? **Self-perception theory** provides an alternative

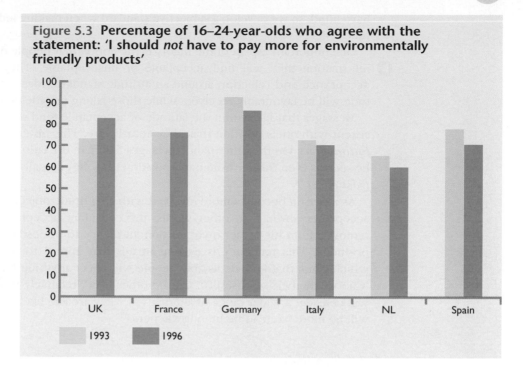

Figure 5.3 Percentage of 16–24-year-olds who agree with the statement: 'I should *not* have to pay more for environmentally friendly products'

explanation of dissonance effects.[30] It assumes that people use observations of their own behaviour to determine what their attitudes are, just as we assume that we know the attitudes of others by watching what they do. The theory states that we maintain consistency by inferring that we must have a positive attitude towards an object if we have bought or consumed it (assuming that we freely made this choice).

Self-perception theory is relevant to the low-involvement hierarchy, since it involves situations in which behaviours are initially performed in the absence of a strong internal attitude. After the fact, the cognitive and affective components of attitude fall into line. Thus, buying a product out of habit may result in a positive attitude towards it after the fact – namely, why would I buy it if I didn't like it?

Self-perception theory helps to explain the effectiveness of a sales strategy called the **foot-in-the-door technique**, which is based on the observation that a consumer is more likely to comply with a request if he or she has first agreed to comply with a smaller request.[31] The name of this technique comes from the practice of door-to-door selling, when the salesperson was taught to plant his or her foot in a door so the prospect could not slam it shut. A good salesperson knows that he or she is more likely to get an order if the customer can be persuaded to open the door and talk. By agreeing to do so, the customer has established that she or he is willing to listen. Placing an order is consistent with this self-perception. This technique is especially useful for inducing consumers to answer surveys or to donate money to charity. Such factors as the time-lag between the first and second requests, the similarity between the two requests, and whether the same person makes both requests have been found to influence their effectiveness.[32]

Social judgement theory

Social judgement theory assumes that people assimilate new information about attitude objects in the light of what they already know or feel.[33] The initial attitude acts as a frame of reference, and new information is categorized in terms of this existing standard. Just as our decision that a box is heavy depends in part on other boxes we have lifted, so we develop a subjective standard when making judgements about attitude objects.

One important aspect of the theory is the notion that people differ in terms of the information they will find acceptable or unacceptable. They form **latitudes of acceptance and rejection** around an attitude standard. Ideas that fall within a latitude will be favourably received, while those falling outside this zone will not.

Messages that fall within the latitude of acceptance tend to be seen as more consistent with one's position than they actually are. This process is called an *assimilation effect*. On the other hand, messages falling in the latitude of rejection tend to be seen as even further from one's position than they actually are, resulting in a *contrast effect*.[34]

As a person becomes more involved with an attitude object, his or her latitude of acceptance shrinks. In other words, the consumer accepts fewer ideas that are removed from his or her own position and tends to oppose even mildly divergent positions. This tendency is evident in ads that appeal to discriminating buyers, which claim that knowledgeable people will reject anything but the very best (e.g. 'Choosy mothers choose Jif'). On the other hand, relatively uninvolved consumers will consider a wider range of alternatives. They are less likely to be brand-loyal and will be more likely to be brand-switchers.[35]

Balance theory

Balance theory considers relations among elements a person might perceive as belonging together.[36] This perspective involves relations (always from the perceiver's subjective point of view) among three elements, so the resulting attitude structures are called *triads*. Each triad contains (1) a person and his or her perceptions of (2) an attitude object and (3) some other person or object.

These perceptions can be positive or negative. More importantly, people *alter* these perceptions in order to make relations among them consistent. The theory specifies that people desire relations among elements in a triad to be harmonious, or balanced. If they are not, a state of tension will result until perceptions are changed and balance is restored.

Elements can be perceived as going together in one of two ways. They can have a *unit relation*, where one element is seen as belonging to or being a part of the other (something like a belief), or a *sentiment relation*, where the two elements are linked because one has expressed a preference (or dislike) for the other. A couple might be seen as having a positive sentiment relation. If they marry, they will have a positive unit relation. The process of divorce is an attempt to sever a unit relation.

To see how balance theory might work, consider the following scenario:

● Monica would like to go out with Anthony, who is in her consumer behaviour class. In balance theory terms, Monica has a positive sentiment relation with Anthony.

● One day, Anthony attends class wearing clothing that allows his fellow students to see his tattoo. Anthony has a positive unit relation with the tattoo. It belongs to him and is literally a part of him.

● Monica does not like tattooed men. She has a negative sentiment relation with tattoos.

According to balance theory, Monica faces an unbalanced triad, and she will experience pressure to restore balance by altering some aspect of the triad, as shown in Figure 5.4. She could, for example, decide that she does not like Anthony

Figure 5.4 Alternative routes to restoring balance in a triad

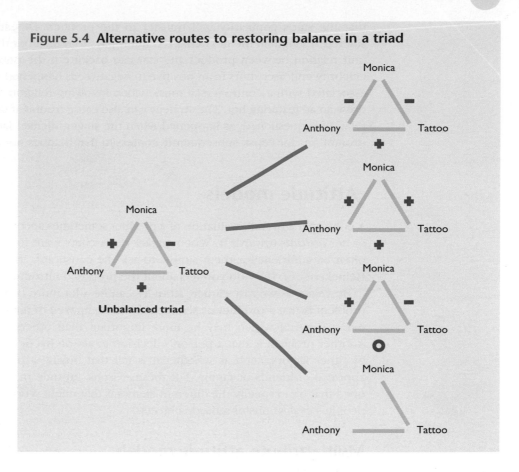

after all. Or her liking for Anthony could prompt a change in her attitude towards tattoos. Finally, she could choose to 'leave the field' by thinking no more about Anthony and his controversial tattoo. Note that while the theory does not specify which of these routes will be taken, it does predict that one or more of Monica's perceptions will have to change in order to achieve balance. While this distortion is an oversimplified representation of most attitude processes, it helps to explain a number of consumer behaviour phenomena.

Balance theory reminds us that when perceptions are balanced, attitudes are likely to be stable. On the other hand, when inconsistencies are observed, we are more likely to observe changes in attitudes. Balance theory also helps to explain why consumers like to be associated with positively valued objects. Forming a unit relation with a popular product (e.g. buying and wearing fashionable clothing or driving a high-performance car) may improve one's chances of being included as a positive sentiment relation in other people's triads.

Finally, balance theory is useful in accounting for the widespread use of celebrities to endorse products. In cases where a triad is not fully formed (e.g. one involving perceptions about a new product or one about which the consumer does not yet have a well-defined attitude), the marketer can create a positive sentiment relation between the consumer and the product by depicting a positive unit relation between the product and a well-known personality. In other cases, behaviours are discouraged when admired people argue against them, as is the goal when athletes feature in government-sponsored anti-drug campaigns.

This 'balancing act' is at the heart of celebrity endorsements, in which it is hoped that the star's popularity will transfer to the product. This strategy will be considered at length in the next chapter. But it pays to remember that this creation of a unit relation between product and star can backfire if the public's opinion of the celebrity endorser shifts from positive to negative, as happened when Madonna was associated with a controversial music video involving religion and sex. Pepsi withdrew an ad featuring her. The strategy can also cause trouble if the star–product unit relation is questioned, as happened when the singer Michael Jackson, who also did promotions for Pepsi, subsequently confessed that he does not drink the brand.

Attitude models

A consumer's overall evaluation of a product sometimes accounts for the bulk of his or her *attitude* towards it. When market researchers want to assess attitudes, it can often be sufficient for them simply to ask the consumer, 'How do you feel about Heineken?', or 'How do you feel about the proposed introduction of the euro?'

However, as we saw earlier, attitudes can be a lot more complex than that. One problem is that a product or service may be composed of many attributes, or qualities – some of which may be more important than others to particular people. Another problem is that a person's decision to act on his or her attitude is affected by other factors, such as whether it is felt that buying a product will meet with approval of friends or family. For these reasons, attitude models have been developed that try to specify the different elements that might work together to influence people's evaluations of attitude objects.

Multiattribute attitude models

A simple response does not always tell us everything we need to know about why the consumer has certain feelings towards a product or about what marketers can do to change the consumer's attitude. For this reason, **multiattribute attitude models** have been extremely popular among marketing researchers. This type of model assumes that a consumer's attitude (evaluation) of an attitude object (A_o) will depend on the beliefs he or she has about several or many attributes of the object. The use of a multiattribute model implies that an attitude towards a product or brand can be predicted by identifying these specific beliefs and combining them to derive a measure of the consumer's overall attitude. We'll describe how these work, using the example of a consumer evaluating a complex attitude object that should be very familiar: a university.

Basic multiattribute models specify three elements:[37]

- *Attributes* are characteristics of the A_o. Most models assume that the relevant characteristics can be identified. That is, the researcher can include those attributes that consumers take into consideration when evaluating the A_o. For example, scholarly reputation is an attribute of a university.
- *Beliefs* are cognitions about the specific A_o (usually relative to others like it). A belief measure assesses the extent to which the consumer perceives that a brand possesses a particular attribute. For example, a student might have a belief that Oxford colleges have a strong academic standing.
- *Importance weights* reflect the relative priority of an attribute to the consumer. Although an A_o can be considered on a number of attributes, some will be more important than others (i.e. they will be given greater weight), and these weights

are likely to differ across consumers. In the case of universities, for example, one student might stress the school's library resources, while another might assign greater weight to the social environment in which the university is located.

Measuring attitude elements

Suppose a supermarket chain wanted to measure shoppers' attitudes towards its retail outlets. The firm might administer one of the following types of attitude scales to consumers by mail, phone or in person.[38]

Single-item scales One simple way to assess consumers' attitudes towards a store or product is to ask them for their general feelings about it. Such a global assessment does not provide much information about specific attributes, but it does give managers some sense of consumers' overall attitudes. This single-item approach often uses a Likert scale, which measures respondents' overall level of agreement or feelings about an attitude statement.

How satisfied are you with your grocery store?
Very satisfied   Somewhat satisfied   Satisfied   Not at all satisfied

Multiple-item batteries Attitude models go beyond such a simple measure, since they acknowledge that an overall attitude may often be composed of consumers' perceptions about multiple elements. For this reason, many attitude measures assess a set of beliefs about an issue and combine these reactions into an overall score. For example, the supermarket might ask customers to respond to a set of Likert scales and combine their responses into an overall measure of store satisfaction:

1 My supermarket has a good selection of produce.
2 My supermarket maintains sanitary conditions.
3 I never have trouble finding exotic foods at my supermarket.

Agree   Agree   Neither agree   Disagree   Disagree
strongly   somewhat   nor disagree   somewhat   strongly

The *semantic-differential scale* is useful for describing a person's set of beliefs about a company or brand, and it is also used to compare the images of competing brands. Respondents rate each attribute on a series of rating scales, where each end is anchored by adjectives or phrases, such as this one:

My supermarket is
Dirty 1—2—3—4—5—6—7 Clean

Semantic-differential scales can be used to construct a profile analysis of the competition, where the images of several stores or products can be compared visually by plotting the mean ratings for each object on several attributes of interest. This simple technique can help to pinpoint areas where the product or store diverges sharply from the competitors (in either a positive or a negative way). The fictitious profiles of three different types of cinemas are shown in Figure 5.5. Based on these findings, the management of a multi-screen cinema might want to emphasize its wide selection of films and/or try to improve its image as a modern cinema, or improve its cleanliness.

The Fishbein model

The most influential multiattribute model is the Fishbein model, named after its primary developer.[39] The model measures three components of attitude.

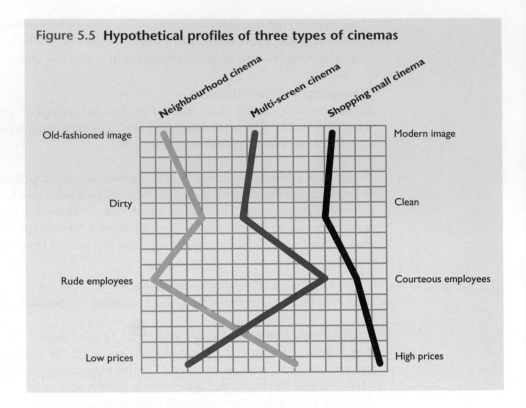

Figure 5.5 Hypothetical profiles of three types of cinemas

1 *Salient beliefs* people have about an A_o (i.e. those beliefs about the object that are considered during evaluation).

2 *Object-attribute linkages*, or the probability that a particular object has an important attribute.

3 *Evaluation* of each of the important attributes.

Note, however, that the model makes some assumptions that may not always be warranted. It assumes that we have been able to specify adequately all the relevant attributes that, for example, a student will use in evaluating his or her choice about which college to attend. The model also assumes that he or she will go through the process (formally or informally) of identifying a set of relevant attributes, weighing them and summing them. Although this particular decision is likely to be highly involving, it is still possible that his or her attitude will be formed by an overall affective response (a process known as *affect-referral*).

By combining these three elements, a consumer's overall attitude towards an object can be computed. (We'll see later how this basic equation has been modified to increase its accuracy.) The basic formula is

$$A_{ijk} = \Sigma B_{ijk} I_{ik}$$

where i = attribute; j = brand; k = consumer; I = the importance weight given attribute i by consumer k; B = consumer k's belief regarding the extent to which brand j possesses attribute i; and A = a particular consumer k's attitude score for brand j.

The overall attitude score (A) is obtained by multiplying a consumer's rating of each attribute for all the brands considered by the importance rating for that attribute.

Table 5.1 The basic multiattribute model: Sandra's college decision

Attribute (i)	Importance (I)	Beliefs (b)			
		Smith	Princeton	Rutgers	Northland
Academic reputation	6	8	9	6	3
All women	7	9	3	3	3
Cost	4	2	2	6	9
Proximity to home	3	2	2	6	9
Athletics	1	1	2	5	1
Party atmosphere	2	1	3	7	9
Library facilities	5	7	9	7	2
Attitude score		163	142	153	131

Note: These hypothetical ratings are scored from 1 to 10, and higher numbers indicate 'better' standing on an attribute. For a negative attribute (e.g. cost), higher scores indicate that the school is believed to have 'less' of that attribute (i.e. to be cheaper).

To see how this basic multiattribute model might work, let's suppose we want to predict which college a middle-school graduate is likely to attend. After months of waiting, Sandra has been accepted at four colleges. Since she must now decide between these, we would first like to know which attributes Sandra will consider in forming an attitude towards each college. We can then ask Sandra to assign a rating regarding how well each college performs on each attribute and also determine the relative importance of the attributes to her. An overall attitude score for each college can then be computed by summing scores on each attribute (after weighing each by its relative importance). These hypothetical ratings are shown in Table 5.1. Based on this analysis, it seems that Sandra has the most favourable attitude towards Smith. She is clearly someone who would like to attend an all-women's college with a solid academic reputation rather than a college that offers a strong athletics programme or a party atmosphere.

Strategic applications of the multiattribute model

Imagine you are the director of marketing for Northland University, another institution Sandra is considering. How might you use the data from this analysis to improve your image?

Capitalize on relative advantage If one's brand is viewed as being superior on a particular attribute, consumers like Sandra need to be convinced that this particular attribute is an important one. For example, while Sandra rates Northland's social atmosphere highly, she does not believe this attribute is a valued aspect for a college. As Northland's marketing director, you might emphasize the importance of an active social life, varied experiences or even the development of future business contacts forged through strong school friendships.

Strengthen perceived product/attribute linkages A marketer may discover that consumers do not equate his or her brand with a certain attribute. This problem is commonly addressed by campaigns that stress the product's qualities to consumers (e.g. 'new and improved'). Sandra apparently does not think much of Northland's academic quality, sports facilities or library. You might develop an informational campaign to improve these perceptions (e.g. 'Little-known facts about Northland').

Add a new attribute Product marketers frequently try to create a distinctive position from their competitors by adding a product feature. Northland might try to emphasize some unique aspect, such as a supervised work-experience programme for business graduates, which takes advantage of links with the local community.

Influence competitors' ratings Finally, you might try to decrease the positive rating of competitors. This type of action is the rationale for a strategy of comparative advertising. One tactic might be to publish an ad that lists the tuition fees of a number of local colleges, as well as their attributes with which Northland can be favourably compared, as the basis for emphasizing the value for money obtained at Northland.

Using attitudes to predict behaviour

Although multiattribute models have been used by consumer researchers for many years, they have been plagued by a major problem: in many cases, knowledge of a person's attitude is not a very good predictor of behaviour. In a classic demonstration of 'do as I say, not as I do', many studies have obtained a very low correlation between a person's reported attitude towards something and his or her actual behaviour towards it. Some researchers have been so discouraged that they have questioned whether attitudes are of any use at all in understanding behaviour.[40] This questionable linkage can be a big headache for advertisers when consumers love a commercial yet fail to buy the product. A Norwegian charity won an award for a popular advertising campaign on which it spent 3 million Nkr (£300,000), only to find that it resulted in just 1.7 million Nkr in donations.[41]

The extended Fishbein model

The original Fishbein model, which focused on measuring a consumer's attitude towards a product, has been extended in a number of ways to improve its predictive ability. The revised version is called the **theory of reasoned action**.[42] The model is still not perfect, but its ability to predict relevant behaviour has been improved.[43] Some of the modifications to this model are considered here.

Intentions vs. behaviour
Many factors might interfere with actual behaviour, even if the consumer's intentions are sincere. He or she might save up with the intention of buying a stereo system. In the interim, though, any number of things – being made redundant or finding that the desired model is out of stock – could happen. It is not surprising, then, that in some instances past purchase behaviour has been found to be a better predictor of future behaviour than is a consumer's behavioural intention.[44] The theory of reasoned action aims to measure behavioural intentions, recognizing that certain uncontrollable factors inhibit prediction of actual behaviour.

Social pressure
The theory acknowledges the power of other people in influencing behaviour. Many of our behaviours are not determined in isolation. Much as we may hate to admit it, what we think others would like us to do may be more relevant than our own individual preferences.

In the case of Sandra's college choice, note that she is very positive about going to an all-female institution. However, if she feels that this choice would be unpopular (perhaps her friends will think she is mad), she might ignore or downgrade this preference when making her final decision. A new element, the subjective norm (SN), was thus added to include the effects of what we believe other people think we should do. The value of SN is arrived at by including two other factors: (1) the intensity of a normative belief (NB) that others believe an action should be taken or not taken, and (2) the motivation to comply (MC) with that belief (i.e. the degree to which the consumer takes others' anticipated reactions into account when evaluating a course of action or a purchase).

Attitude towards buying

The model now measures **attitude towards the act of buying (A_{act})**, rather than only the attitude towards the product itself. In other words, it focuses on the perceived consequences of a purchase. Knowing how someone feels about buying or using an object proves to be more valid than merely knowing the consumer's evaluation of the object itself.[45]

To understand this distinction, consider a problem that might arise when measuring attitudes towards condoms. Although a group of college students might have a positive attitude towards condom use, does this necessarily predict that they will buy and use them? A better prediction would be obtained by asking the students how likely they are to buy condoms. While a person might have a positive A_o towards condoms, A_{act} might be negative due to the embarrassment or the trouble involved.

Obstacles to predicting behaviour

Despite improvements to the Fishbein model, problems arise when it is misapplied. In many cases the model is used in ways for which it was not intended or where certain assumptions about human behaviour may not be warranted.[46] Other obstacles to predicting behaviour are as follows:

- The model was developed to deal with actual behaviour (e.g. taking a slimming pill), not with the outcomes of behaviour (e.g. losing weight) which are assessed in some studies.

- Some outcomes are beyond the consumer's control, such as when the purchase requires the co-operation of other people. For instance, a woman might seek a mortgage, but this intention will be worthless if she cannot find a banker to give her one.

- The basic assumption that behaviour is intentional may be invalid in a variety of cases, including those involving impulsive acts, sudden changes in one's situation, novelty-seeking or even simple repeat-buying. One study found that such unexpected events as having guests, changes in the weather or reading articles about the health qualities of certain foods exerted a significant effect on actual behaviours.[47]

- Measures of attitude often do not really correspond to the behaviour they are supposed to predict, either in terms of the A_o or when the act will occur. One common problem is a difference in the level of abstraction employed. For example, knowing a person's attitude towards sports cars may not predict whether he or she will purchase a Porsche 911. It is very important to match the level of specificity between the attitude and the behavioural intention.

- A similar problem relates to the time-frame of the attitude measure. In general, the longer the time between the attitude measurement and the behaviour it is supposed to assess, the weaker the relationship will be. For example, predictability would improve markedly by asking consumers the likelihood that they would buy a house in the next week as opposed to within the next five years.

● Attitudes formed by direct, personal experience with an A_o are stronger and more predictive of behaviour than those formed indirectly, such as through advertising.[48] According to the attitude accessibility perspective, behaviour is a function of the person's immediate perceptions of the A_o in the context of the situation in which it is encountered. An attitude will guide the evaluation of the object, but only if it is activated from memory when the object is observed. These findings underscore the importance of strategies that induce trial (e.g. by widespread product sampling to encourage the consumer to try the product at home, by taste tests, test drives, etc.) as well as those that maximize exposure to marketing communications.

MARKETING PITFALL

Free the carp?

For Joseph Vladsky, the insight came one December evening in Warsaw at a supermarket packed with Christmas shoppers. While walking past the fish department, he saw something that stopped him in his tracks. There, in white plastic tubs, were carp – more carp, it seemed, than water. Some were floating belly up. A group of shoppers peered eagerly into the tubs, selecting the main course for their holiday supper. Shop assistants in stained aprons fished out the chosen carp, tossed them onto scales, then dropped them, still flopping, into plastic bags. If asked, the shop assistants would kill the carp with a quick blow to the head from a thick wooden stick or metal pipe. 'Christmas is supposed to be a joyful time', Mr Vladsky recalls thinking. 'But then you go to the market, and there's a tank of fish, dying, being killed. How terrible.'

   Carp have graced east European holiday tables since the seventeenth century, when Christian monks first recognized the Asian import as a substitute for meatless feasts. Hundreds of years later, having carp for Christmas came to symbolize defiance of Communist rule. Today, Polish consumers still buy their carp live, and deliver the fatal blow at home, letting the fish swim out their final days in the family bathtub. Lately, however, sales have been stagnant, even though the price has fallen more than 30 per cent over the past three years. Newly affluent Poles seem to prefer salmon or mahi-mahi. Others simply hate waiting for the carp to get out of the bathtub and into the oven (there is a lingering smell in the tub!), and then there are those like Mr Vladsky who object to the seasonal slaughter. Recent media coverage by the Animal Protection Society regarding the inhumane and insanitary conditions surrounding 'Christmas Carp' have slowed the consumption of carp. In Mr Vladsky's case, his children became so attached to the carp in their friend's bathtub that they gave them names, and started treating them as pets. Slowly, attitudes towards killing live carp for Christmas are changing . . .[49]

Question: How would you apply Fishbein's (no pun intended) multiattribute model to predict future behaviour of Polish consumption of carp, given the changing attitudes described above?

Multicultural dimensions

The theory of reasoned action has primarily been applied in the West. Certain assumptions inherent in the model may not necessarily apply to consumers from other cultures. Several of the following diminish the universality of the theory of reasoned action:

● The model was developed to predict the performance of any voluntary act. Across cultures, however, many consumer activities, ranging from taking exams and entering military service to receiving an inoculation or even choosing a marriage partner, are not necessarily voluntary.

● The relative impact of subjective norms may vary across cultures. For example, Asian cultures tend to value conformity and face-saving, so it is possible that subjective norms involving the anticipated reactions of others to the choice will have an even greater impact on behaviour for many Asian consumers.

● The model measures behavioural intentions and thus presupposes that consumers are actively anticipating and planning future behaviours. The intention concept assumes that consumers have a linear time sense, i.e. they think in terms of past, present and future. As will be discussed in a later chapter, this time perspective is not held by all cultures.

● A consumer who forms an intention is (implicitly) claiming that he or she is in control of his or her actions. Some cultures tend to be fatalistic and do not necessarily believe in the concept of free will. Indeed, one study comparing students from the United States, Jordan and Thailand found evidence for cultural differences in assumptions about fatalism and control over the future.[50]

Tracking attitudes over time

An attitude survey is like a snapshot taken at a single point in time. It may tell us a lot about the position of a person, issue or object at that moment, but it does not permit many inferences about progress made over time or any predictions about possible future changes in consumer attitudes. To accomplish these tasks, it is necessary to develop an attitude-tracking programme. This activity helps to increase the predictability of behaviour by allowing researchers to analyse attitude trends over an extended period of time. It is more like a film than a snapshot. For example, a longitudinal survey conducted by the Henley Centre, of Europeans' attitudes regarding the process of moving towards European union, shows how attitudes can shift over time, and how the shift can be different for different age cohorts. Figure 5.6 shows the results of a large-scale study carried out in six countries. The percentage of respondents reporting that they 'feel as much European as they do a citizen of their own country' is not particularly strong (especially in the UK), and the percentage of the population supporting the sentiment seems to be declining over time (1991–6).

These results would suggest that as Europe moves towards a more integrated union with a common currency, consumers from individual countries are holding more closely to their own national identity. Now compare these findings from the general population with the results of the same question put to European young adults (16–24 years) (Figure 5.7). The margin of sampling error would account for the generally small differences across time and countries, with the exception of the UK, where there has been a significant increase over the five-year period in the percentage of young adults who support the statement (albeit at a much lower level than the other countries in the survey).

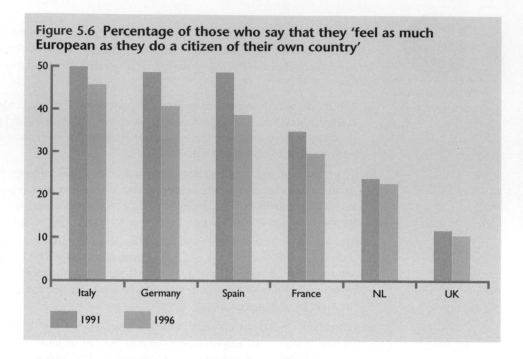

Figure 5.6 Percentage of those who say that they 'feel as much European as they do a citizen of their own country'

Tracking studies

Attitude tracking involves the administration of an attitude survey at regular intervals. Preferably, the same methodology will be used each time so that results can be reliably compared. Several services, such as Gallup, the Henley Centre or the Yankelovich Monitor, track consumer attitudes over time.

This activity can be extremely valuable for strategic decision-making. For example, one financial services firm monitored changes in consumer attitudes towards one-stop banking centres. Although a large number of consumers were enthusiastic about the idea when it was first introduced, the number of people who liked the concept did not increase over time despite the millions of dollars invested in advertising to promote the centres. This finding indicated some problems with the way the concept was being presented, and the company decided to 'go back to the drawing board', and eventually came up with a new way to communicate the advantages of this service.

Changes to look for over time

Some of the dimensions that can be included in attitude tracking include the following:

● *A focus on changes in different age groups.* Attitudes tend to change as people age (a life-cycle effect). In addition, cohort effects occur, that is, members of a particular generation (e.g. teens, generation X, or the elderly) tend to share certain outlooks. Also, historical effects can be observed as large groups of people are affected by profound cultural changes (e.g. the democratization of eastern Europe).

● *Scenarios about the future.* Consumers are frequently tracked in terms of their future plans, confidence in the economy, and so on. These measures can provide valuable data about future behaviour and yield insights for public policy. For example, Americans tend to overestimate how much they will earn after retirement, which is potentially a dangerous miscalculation.

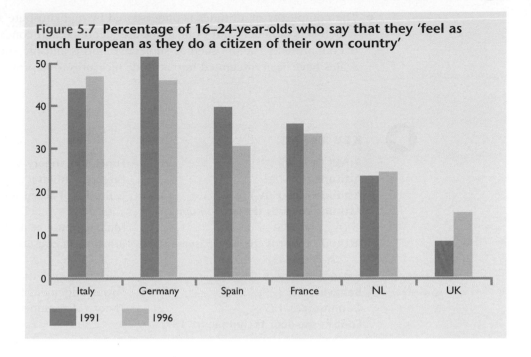

Figure 5.7 Percentage of 16–24-year-olds who say that they 'feel as much European as they do a citizen of their own country'

- *Identification of change agents*. Social phenomena can change people's attitudes towards basic consumption activities over time, as when consumers' willingness to buy fur products shifts. Or people's likelihood to seek divorce may be affected by such facilitators as changes in the legal system that make this easier, or by inhibitors, such as the prevalence of AIDS and the value of two salaries in today's economy.[51]

Chapter summary

- An attitude is a predisposition to evaluate an object or product positively or negatively.

- Social marketing refers to attempts to change consumers' attitudes and behaviours in ways that are beneficial to the society as a whole.

- Attitudes are made up of three components: beliefs, affect and behavioural intentions.

- Attitude researchers traditionally assumed that attitudes were learned in a predetermined sequence, consisting first of the formation of beliefs (cognitions) regarding an attitude object, followed by an evaluation of that object (affect) and then some action (behaviour). Depending on the consumer's level of involvement and the circumstances, though, attitudes can result from other hierarchies of effects.

- A key to attitude formation is the function the attitude plays for the consumer (e.g. is it utilitarian or ego-defensive?).

- One organizing principle of attitude formation is the importance of consistency among attitudinal components – that is, some parts of an attitude may be altered to conform with others. Such theoretical approaches to attitudes as cognitive dissonance theory, balance theory and congruity theory stress the vital role of consistency.

● The complexity of attitudes is underscored by multiattribute attitude models, in which sets of beliefs and evaluations are identified and combined to predict an overall attitude. Factors such as subjective norms and the specificity of attitude scales have been integrated into attitude measures to improve predictability.

KEY TERMS

Affect (*p. 129*)
Attitude (*p. 127*)
Attitude object (A$_o$) (*p. 127*)
Attitude towards the act of buying
  (A$_{act}$) (*p. 145*)
Attitude towards the advertisement
  (A$_{ad}$) (*p. 133*)
Balance theory (*p. 138*)
Behaviour (*p. 129*)
Cognition (*p. 129*)
Foot-in-the-door technique (*p. 137*)

Functional theory of attitudes (*p. 128*)
Hierarchy of effects (*p. 130*)
Latitudes of acceptance and rejection
  (*p. 138*)
Multiattribute attitude models (*p. 140*)
Principle of cognitive consistency
  (*p. 134*)
Self-perception theory (*p. 136*)
Social judgement theory (*p. 137*)
Theory of reasoned action (*p. 144*)

For additional material see the companion website at:
www.booksites.net/solomon_euro

Consumer behaviour challenge

1 Contrast the hierarchies of effects outlined in the chapter. How will strategic decisions related to the marketing mix be influenced by which hierarchy is operative among target consumers?

2 List three functions played by attitudes, giving an example of how each function is employed in a marketing situation. To examine European countries' attitudes towards a wide variety of issues, go to the website: *http://europa.eu.int/en/comm/dg10/infcom/epo/eo.html*. Which sorts of attitudes expressed in different countries seem utilitarian, value-expressive or ego-defensive? Why?

3 Think of a behaviour exhibited by an individual that is inconsistent with his or her attitudes (e.g. attitudes towards cholesterol, drug use or even buying things to attain status or be noticed). Ask the person to elaborate on why he or she does the behaviour, and try to identify the way the person has resolved dissonant elements.

4 Using a series of semantic-differential scales, devise an attitude survey for a set of competing automobiles. Identify areas of competitive advantage or disadvantage for each model you incorporate.

5 Construct a multiattribute model for a set of local restaurants. Based on your findings, suggest how restaurant managers can improve their establishments' image using the strategies described in the chapter.

Notes

1. 'It's a Funny Old Game', *The Economist* (10 February 2001): 57–8.

2. Bill Saporito, 'Crazy for the Cup: With a 3–0 Start, the US Aims for Another World Soccer Title', *Time* (28 June 1999): 62–4.

3. Bill Saporito, 'Flat-Out Fantastic', *Time* (19 July 1999): 58 (2); Mark Hyman, 'The "Babe Factor" in Women's Soccer', *Business Week* (26 July 1999): 118.

4. Robert A. Baron and Donn Byrne, *Social Psychology: Understanding Human Interaction*, 5th edn (Boston: Allyn & Bacon, 1987).

5. Daniel Katz, 'The Functional Approach to the Study of Attitudes', *Public Opinion Quarterly* 24 (Summer 1960): 163–204; Richard J. Lutz, 'Changing Brand Attitudes through Modification of Cognitive Structure', *Journal of Consumer Research* 1 (March 1975): 49–59.

6. Russell H. Fazio, T. M. Lenn and E. A. Effrein, 'Spontaneous Attitude Formation', *Social Cognition* 2 (1984): 214–34.

7. Mason Haire, 'Projective Techniques in Marketing Research', *Journal of Marketing* 14 (April 1950): 649–56.

8. Sharon Shavitt, 'The Role of Attitude Objects in Attitude Functions', *Journal of Experimental Social Psychology* 26 (1990): 124–48; see also J. S. Johar and M. Joseph Sirgy, 'Value-Expressive versus Utilitarian Advertising Appeals: When and Why to Use Which Appeal', *Journal of Advertising* 20 (September 1991): 23–34.

9. For the original work that focused on the issue of levels of attitudinal commitment, see H. C. Kelman, 'Compliance, Identification, and Internalization: Three Processes of Attitude Change', *Journal of Conflict Resolution* 2 (1958): 51–60.

10. Lynn R. Kahle, Kenneth M. Kambara and Gregory M. Rose, 'A Functional Model of Fan Attendance Motivations for College Football', *Sports Marketing Quarterly* 5(4) (1996): 51–60.

11. For a study that found evidence of simultaneous causation of beliefs and attitudes, see Gary M. Erickson, Johny K. Johansson and Paul Chao, 'Image Variables in Multi-Attribute Product Evaluations: Country-of-Origin Effects', *Journal of Consumer Research* 11 (September 1984): 694–9.

12. Michael Ray, 'Marketing Communications and the Hierarchy-of-Effects', in P. Clarke, ed., *New Models for Mass Communications* (Beverly Hills, CA: Sage, 1973): 147–76.

13. Herbert Krugman, 'The Impact of Television Advertising: Learning without Involvement', *Public Opinion Quarterly* 29 (Fall 1965): 349–56; Robert Lavidge and Gary Steiner, 'A Model for Predictive Measurements of Advertising Effectiveness', *Journal of Marketing* 25 (October 1961): 59–62.

14. For some recent studies see Andrew B. Aylesworth and Scott B. MacKenzie, 'Context is Key: The Effect of Program-Induced Mood on Thoughts about the Ad', *Journal of Advertising*, 27(2) (Summer 1998): 17 (at 15); Angela Y. Lee and Brian Sternthal, 'The Effects of Positive Mood on Memory', *Journal of Consumer Research* 26 (September 1999): 115–28; Michael J. Barone, Paul W. Miniard and Jean B. Romeo, 'The Influence of Positive Mood on Brand Extension Evaluations', *Journal of Consumer Research* 26 (March 2000): 386–401. For a study that compared the effectiveness of emotional appeals across cultures, see Jennifer L. Aaker and Patti Williams, 'Empathy Versus Pride: The Influence of Emotional Appeals Across Cultures', *Journal of Consumer Research* 25 (December 1998): 241–61.

15. Punam Anand, Morris B. Holbrook and Debra Stephens, 'The Formation of Affective Judgments: The Cognitive–Affective Model Versus the Independence Hypothesis', *Journal of Consumer Research* 15 (December 1988): 386–91; Richard S. Lazarus, 'Thoughts on the Relations Between Emotion and Cognition', *American Psychologist* 37(9) (1982): 1019–24.

16. Robert B. Zajonc, 'Feeling and Thinking: Preferences Need No Inferences', *American Psychologist* 35(2) (1980): 151–75.

17. Banwari Mittal, 'The Role of Affective Choice Mode in the Consumer Purchase of Expressive Products', *Journal of Economic Psychology* 4(9) (1988): 499–524.

18. Scot Burton and Donald R. Lichtenstein, 'The Effect of Ad Claims and Ad Context on Attitude Toward the Advertisement', *Journal of Advertising* 17(1) (1988): 3–11; Karen A. Machleit and R. Dale Wilson, 'Emotional Feelings and Attitude Toward the Advertisement: The Roles of Brand Familiarity and Repetition', *Journal of Advertising* 17(3) (1988): 27–35; Scott B. Mackenzie and Richard J. Lutz, 'An Empirical Examination of the Structural Antecedents of Attitude toward the Ad in an Advertising Pretesting Context', *Journal of Marketing* 53 (April 1989): 48–65; Scott B. Mackenzie, Richard J. Lutz and George E. Belch, 'The Role of Attitude Toward the Ad as a Mediator of Advertising Effectiveness: A Test of Competing Explanations', *Journal of Marketing Research* 23 (May 1986): 130–43; Darrel D. Muehling and Russell N. Laczniak, 'Advertising's Immediate and Delayed Influence on Brand Attitudes: Considerations Across Message-Involvement Levels', *Journal of Advertising* 17(4) (1988): 23–34; Mark A. Pavelchak, Meryl P. Gardner and V. Carter Broach, 'Effect of Ad Pacing and Optimal Level of Arousal on Attitude Toward the Ad', in Rebecca H. Holman and Michael R. Solomon, eds, *Advances in Consumer Research* 18

(Provo, UT: Association for Consumer Research, 1991): 94–9. Some research evidence indicates that a separate attitude is also formed regarding the brand name itself: see George M. Zinkhan and Claude R. Martin, Jr, 'New Brand Names and Inferential Beliefs: Some Insights on Naming New Products', *Journal of Business Research* 15 (1987): 157–72.

19. John P. Murry, Jr, John L. Lastovicka and Surendra N. Singh, 'Feeling and Liking Responses to Television Programs: An Examination of Two Explanations for Media-Context Effects', *Journal of Consumer Research* 18 (March 1992): 441–51.

20. Barbara Stern and Judith Lynne Zaichkowsky, 'The Impact of Entertaining Advertising on Consumer Responses', *Australian Marketing Researcher* 14 (August 1991): 68–80.

21. For a recent study that examined the impact of scepticism on advertising issues, see David M. Boush, Marian Friestad and Gregory M. Rose, 'Adolescent Skepticism Toward TV Advertising and Knowledge of Advertiser Tactics', *Journal of Consumer Research* 21 (June 1994): 165–75; see also Lawrence Feick and Heribert Gierl, 'Skepticism about Advertising: A Comparison of East and West German Consumers', *International Journal of Research in Marketing* 13 (1996): 227–35; Rik Pieters and Hans Baumgartner, 'The Attitude Toward Advertising of Advertising Practitioners, Homemakers and Students in The Netherlands and Belgium', in W. Fred van Raaij and Gary J. Bamossy, eds, *European Advances in Consumer Research* (Provo, UT: Association for Consumer Research, 1993): 39–45.

22. Basil G. Englis, 'Consumer Emotional Reactions to Television Advertising and Their Effects on Message Recall', in S. Agres, J. A. Edell and T. M. Dubitsky, eds, *Emotion in Advertising: Theoretical and Practical Explorations* (Westport, CT: Quorum Books, 1990): 231–54.

23. Morris B. Holbrook and Rajeev Batra, 'Assessing the Role of Emotions as Mediators of Consumer Responses to Advertising', *Journal of Consumer Research* 14 (December 1987): 404–20.

24. Marian Burke and Julie Edell, 'Ad Reactions over Time: Capturing Changes in the Real World', *Journal of Consumer Research* 13 (June 1986): 114–18.

25. Kelman, 'Compliance, Identification, and Internalization': 51–60.

26. See Sharon E. Beatty and Lynn R. Kahle, 'Alternative Hierarchies of the Attitude–Behaviour Relationship: The Impact of Brand Commitment and Habit', *Journal of the Academy of Marketing Science* 16 (Summer 1988): 1–10.

27. Leon Festinger, *A Theory of Cognitive Dissonance* (Stanford, CA: Stanford University Press, 1957).

28. Chester A. Insko and John Schopler, *Experimental Social Psychology* (New York: Academic Press, 1972).

29. Robert E. Knox and James A. Inkster, 'Postdecision Dissonance at Post Time', *Journal of Personality and Social Psychology* 8(4) (1968): 319–23.

30. Daryl J. Bem, 'Self-Perception Theory', in Leonard Berkowitz, ed., *Advances in Experimental Social Psychology* (New York: Academic Press, 1972): 1–62.

31. Jonathan L. Freedman and Scott C. Fraser, 'Compliance without Pressure: The Foot-in-the-Door Technique', *Journal of Personality and Social Psychology* 4 (August 1966): 195–202; for further consideration of possible explanations for this effect, see William DeJong, 'An Examination of Self-Perception Mediation of the Foot-in-the-Door Effect', *Journal of Personality and Social Psychology* 37 (December 1979): 221–31; Alice M. Tybout, Brian Sternthal and Bobby J. Calder, 'Information Availability as a Determinant of Multiple-Request Effectiveness', *Journal of Marketing Research* 20 (August 1988): 280–90.

32. David H. Furse, David W. Stewart and David L. Rados, 'Effects of Foot-in-the-Door, Cash Incentives and Follow-ups on Survey Response', *Journal of Marketing Research* 18 (November 1981): 473–8; Carol A. Scott, 'The Effects of Trial and Incentives on Repeat Purchase Behavior', *Journal of Marketing Research* 13 (August 1976): 263–9.

33. Muzafer Sherif and Carl I. Hovland, *Social Judgment: Assimilation and Contrast Effects in Communication and Attitude Change* (New Haven, CT: Yale University Press, 1961).

34. For a recent treatment, see Joan Meyers-Levy and Brian Sternthal, 'A Two-Factor Explanation of Assimilation and Contrast Effects', *Journal of Marketing Research* 30 (August 1993): 359–68.

35. Mark B. Traylor, 'Product Involvement and Brand Commitment', *Journal of Advertising Research* (December 1981): 51–6.

36. Fritz Heider, *The Psychology of Interpersonal Relations* (New York: Wiley, 1958).

37. William L. Wilkie, *Consumer Behavior* (New York: Wiley, 1986).

38. A number of criteria beyond the scope of this book are important in evaluating methods of attitude measurement, including such issues as reliability, validity and sensitivity. For an excellent treatment of attitude-scaling techniques, see David S. Aaker and George S. Day, *Marketing Research*, 4th edn (New York: Wiley, 1990).

39. Martin Fishbein, 'An Investigation of the Relationships Between Beliefs About an Object and the Attitude Toward that Object', *Human Relations* 16 (1983): 233–40.

40. Allan Wicker, 'Attitudes Versus Actions: The Relationship of Verbal and Overt Behavioral Responses to Attitude Objects', *Journal of Social Issues* 25 (Autumn 1969): 65.

41. Laura Bird, 'Loved the Ad. May (or May Not) Buy the Product', *Wall Street Journal* (7 April 1994): B1 (2 pp.); 'Which Half?', *The Economist* (8 June 1996): 80.

42. Icek Ajzen and Martin Fishbein, 'Attitude–Behavior Relations: A Theoretical Analysis and Review of Empirical Research', *Psychological Bulletin* 84 (September 1977): 888–918.

43. Morris B. Holbrook and William J. Havlena, 'Assessing the Real-to-Artificial Generalizability of Multi-Attribute Attitude Models in Tests of New Product Designs', *Journal of Marketing Research* 25 (February 1988): 25–35; Terence A. Shimp and Alican Kavas, 'The Theory of Reasoned Action Applied to Coupon Usage', *Journal of Consumer Research* 11 (December 1984): 795–809.

44. Richard P. Bagozzi, Hans Baumgartner and Youjae Yi, 'Coupon Usage and the Theory of Reasoned Action', in Rebecca H. Holman and Michael R. Solomon, eds, *Advances in Consumer Research* 18 (Provo, UT: Association for Consumer Research, 1991): 24–7; Edward F. McQuarrie, 'An Alternative to Purchase Intentions: The Role of Prior Behavior in Consumer Expenditure on Computers', *Journal of the Market Research Society* 30 (October 1988): 407–37; Arch G. Woodside and William O. Bearden, 'Longitudinal Analysis of Consumer Attitude, Intention, and Behavior Toward Beer Brand Choice', in William D. Perrault, Jr, ed., *Advances in Consumer Research* 4 (Ann Arbor, MI: Association for Consumer Research, 1977): 349–56.

45. Michael J. Ryan and Edward H. Bonfield, 'The Fishbein Extended Model and Consumer Behavior', *Journal of Consumer Research* 2 (1975): 118–36.

46. Blair H. Sheppard, Jon Hartwick and Paul R. Warshaw, 'The Theory of Reasoned Action: A Meta-Analysis of Past Research with Recommendations for Modifications and Future Research', *Journal of Consumer Research* 15 (December 1988): 325–43.

47. Joseph A. Cote, James McCullough and Michael Reilly, 'Effects of Unexpected Situations on Behavior-Intention Differences: A Garbology Analysis', *Journal of Consumer Research* 12 (September 1985): 188–94.

48. Russell H. Fazio, Martha C. Powell and Carol J. Williams, 'The Role of Attitude Accessibility in the Attitude-to-Behavior Process', *Journal of Consumer Research* 16 (December 1989): 280–8; Robert E. Smith and William R. Swinyard, 'Attitude–Behavior Consistency: The Impact of Product Trial Versus Advertising', *Journal of Marketing Research* 20 (August 1983): 257–67.

49. Elizabeth Williamson, 'Free the Carp? That's One Way to Get Them Out of the Bathtub', *Wall Street Journal* (22 December 2000): A1.

50. Joseph A. Cote and Patriya S. Tansuhaj, 'Culture Bound Assumptions in Behavior Intention Models', in Thom Srull, ed., *Advances in Consumer Research* 16 (Provo, UT: Association for Consumer Research, 1989): 105–9.

51. Matthew Greenwald and John P. Katosh, 'How to Track Changes in Attitudes', *American Demographics* (August 1987): 46.

Chapter 6

Attitude change and interactive communications

For Margaret, the unthinkable was about to happen. Here she was with a big cigar in her mouth. A few short months ago, Margaret had believed that cigars were smoked by large, foul-smelling, older men. Lately, though, her attitudes had started to change. First, her friend Mary Ann, returning from business trips to Stockholm and New York, reported that cigar-smoking among women was definitely more commonplace there than in Manchester. Then, she seemed to be reading more and more news stories about famous women lighting up. The clincher was coming across her heroine, supermodel Linda Evangelista, on the cover of *Cigar Aficionado*. Somehow, knowing that an elegant woman like Linda was a cigar fan put to rest any anxieties Margaret had about sacrificing her femininity if she took a puff now and then. Now, the signs were everywhere – women were shedding their disdain for smoke-filled rooms and flocking to cigar bars. The Consolidated Cigar Corporation picked up early on this trend and introduced its Cleopatra Collection, featuring versions of its cigars tapered at both ends to make it easier for women to light and hold in their mouths.[1]

Apparently, many women have taken up cigar smoking as a way to navigate the 'old boy network', and as a form of rebellion. That didn't worry Margaret, but she did find that she actually liked to relax after a good meal and savour the taste. Seemingly overnight, her beliefs about the unsavoury characteristics of cigar smokers had changed – and several of her friends admired her pluck for lighting up in public. She even went so far as to surf the net for more information about cigar products. She particularly liked the cigarwoman.com website, where she could access several cigar retailers, read about women's experiences, ideas and opinions regarding cigars, and even participate in a message board about attitudes of women who smoke cigars.

Changing attitudes through communication

Prominent women from Marlene Dietrich to Madonna have sported cigars for their shock value and as a way to communicate the notion of rebellion and political incorrectness. More recently, though, the cigar industry itself has climbed on the bandwagon as some canny marketers realized the potential to nurture a new market by persuading 'everyday' women like Margaret to light up. Of course, inspiring such a radical change in behaviour first required an equally drastic change in the way women felt about the product and their beliefs about who used it and what this usage said about the type of people they were.

As consumers we are constantly bombarded by messages inducing us to change our attitudes. These attempts can range from logical arguments to graphic pictures, and from intimidation by peers to exhortations by celebrities. To make things even more complicated, communications flow both ways – the consumer may choose to access information in order to learn more about these options, as Margaret did by surfing the net.

This chapter will review some of the factors that help to determine the effectiveness of such communication devices. Our focus will be on some basic aspects of communication that specifically help to determine how and if attitudes will be created or modified. This objective relates to **persuasion**, which refers to an active attempt to change attitudes. Persuasion is, of course, the central goal of many marketing communications.

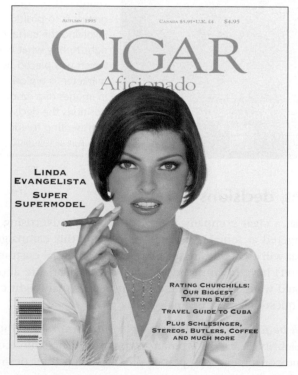

Supermodel Linda Evangelista posing as *Cigar Aficionado*'s cover girl.
Used with permission.

This anti-fur ad ran in Hong Kong. It relies on a graphic description of fur industry practices to discourage consumers from considering the purchase of a fur coat.
RSPCA Hong Kong

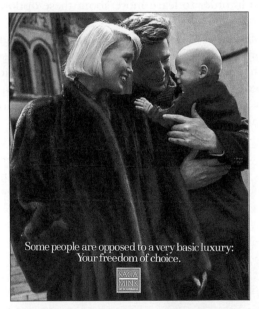

One way that the fur industry is trying to counteract the graphic messages of anti-fur groups is to position the debate as one involving the curtailment of the personal right to buy what one chooses. This ad, which was placed by a Scandinavian fur marketer, is typical: it wraps the fur wearer in images of a wholesome family scene and positions the decision to buy a fur as representing freedom of choice.
Saga Furs of Scandinavia.

Decisions, decisions

Suppose that a cigar company wants to create an advertising campaign for a new product targeted at female smokers. As it plans this campaign, it must develop a message that will create desire for the cigar by potential customers – many of whom (like Margaret) have been raised to believe that cigars are about the last thing any woman would want. To craft persuasive messages that might change this attitude, a number of questions must be answered:

● *Who will be featured smoking a cigar in an ad?* Should it be linked to a glamorous celebrity? A career woman? A rock star? The source of a message helps to determine consumers' acceptance of it as well as their desire to try the product.

- *How should the message be constructed?* Should it emphasize the negative consequences of being left out while others are enjoying themselves in the cigar bar? Should it directly compare the cigar with others already on the market, or perhaps present a fantasy where a tough-minded female executive meets a dashing stranger while ducking out of a board meeting for a smoke? Product benefits can be expressed in many ways.

- *What media should be used to transmit the message?* Should it be depicted in a print ad? On television? Sold door-to-door? If a print ad is produced, should it be run in the pages of *Vogue*? *Good Housekeeping*? *Cigar Aficionado*? Sometimes *where* something is said can be as important as *what* is said. Ideally, the attributes of the product should be matched to those of the medium. For example, magazines with high prestige are more effective at communicating messages about overall product image and quality, while specialized, expert magazines do a better job at conveying factual information.[2]

- *What characteristics of the target market might influence the ad's acceptance?* If targeted users are frustrated in their daily lives, these women might be more receptive to a fantasy appeal. If they don't smoke cigars or know anyone who does, they may not pay any attention to a traditional cigar ad at all.

The elements of communication

Marketers and advertisers have traditionally tried to understand how marketing messages can change consumers' attitudes by thinking in terms of the **communications model**, which specifies that a number of elements are necessary for communication to be achieved. In this model, a *source* must choose and encode a message (i.e. initiate the transfer of meaning by choosing appropriate symbolic images which represent that meaning). For example, the publishers of *Cigar Aficionado* magazine attempted to send the message that it's 'cool' for women to light up by highlighting famous females who are cigar fans. This meaning must be put in the form of a *message*. There are many ways to say something, and the structure of the message has a major effect on how it is perceived. In the example shown at the beginning of this chapter a visual image of a well-known supermodel holding a cigar spoke volumes about the sexiness and trendiness of cigars. The message must be transmitted via a *medium*, which could be television, radio, magazines, advertising hoardings, personal contact, and so on. In this case, the message appeared in a specialized magazine targeted to current – and prospective – cigar smokers. The message is then decoded by one or more *receivers*, like Margaret, who interpret the symbols in the light of their own experiences. Finally, *feedback* must be received by the source, which uses the reactions of receivers to modify aspects of the message. Favourable reactions by readers led *Cigar Aficionado* to continue to feature prominent women in its pages. The traditional communications process is depicted in Figure 6.1.

An updated view: interactive communications

While the traditional communications model is not entirely wrong, it doesn't tell the whole story – especially in today's dynamic world of interactivity.[3] The traditional model was developed to understand mass communications, where information is transferred from a producer (source) to many consumers (receivers) at one time – typically via newspaper, television or radio. This perspective essentially views advertising as the process of transferring information to the buyer before a sale. A mess-

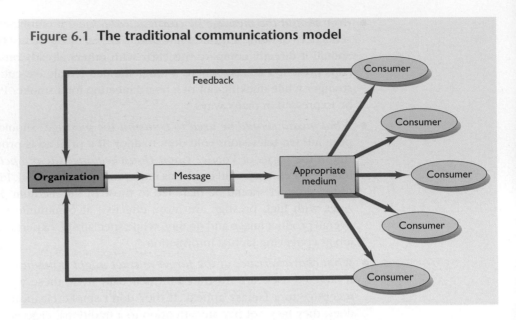

Figure 6.1 **The traditional communications model**

age is perishable – it is repeated (perhaps frequently) for a fairly short period of time and then 'vanishes' as a new 'campaign' is substituted.

This traditional communications model was strongly influenced by a group of theorists known as the Frankfurt School, which dominated mass communications research for most of the twentieth century. In this view, the media exert direct and powerful effects on individuals, and are often used by those in power to brainwash and exploit them. The receiver is basically passive and is simply the receptacle for many messages, and may often be duped or persuaded to act based on what he or she hears or sees.

Uses and gratifications

Is this an accurate picture of the way we relate to marketing communications? Proponents of **uses and gratifications theory** argue that consumers are an active, goal-directed audience who draw on mass media as a resource to satisfy needs. Instead of asking what media do for or to people, they ask what people do *with* their media.[4]

The uses and gratifications approach emphasizes that media compete with other sources to satisfy needs, and that these needs include diversion and entertainment as well as information. This means that the line between marketing information and entertainment is continuing to blur – especially as companies are being forced to design more attractive retail outlets, catalogues and websites in order to induce consumers to stop at them. Toyota's site (*www.toyota.com*) provides a lot more than the latest specifications about available car options: it includes interests like gardening, travel and sports.

Indeed, research with young people in Great Britain finds that they rely on advertising for many gratifications including entertainment (some report that the 'adverts' are better than the programmes), escapism, play (some report singing along with jingles, others make posters out of magazine ads) and self-affirmation (ads can reinforce their own values or provide role models). It's important to note that this perspective is not arguing that media play a uniformly positive role in our lives, only that recipients are making use of the information in a number of ways. For example, marketing messages have the potential to undermine self-esteem. A comment by one study participant illustrates this negative impact. She observes that when she's watching TV with her boyfriend '... really, it makes you think "Oh no, what must I be like?" I mean you're sitting with your boyfriend and he's saying "Oh, look at her. What a body!" '[5]

An interactionist perspective on communication

The **interactionist** perspective on communication does not describe human communication as 'mechanistically' as does the classic communications model. Briefly, interactionism relies on three basic premises about communication, which focus on the meaning of objects, ideas and actions:[6]

1 Human beings act towards objects on the basis of the meanings that objects have for them.

2 The meaning of objects is derived from the social interaction that they provide.

3 These meanings are processed and modified through an interpretive process which a person uses in dealing with the object encountered.

The interactionist perspective tones down the importance of the external stimuli, and views consumers as 'interpreters', wherein meaning does not arise from the objects themselves, nor from the psyche, but from interaction patterns. This view argues that meanings are not given 'once and for all' and are readily retrievable from memory. Rather, they are recreated and interpreted anew in each communicative action. Hence, the central role of the 'communicating self' must be taken into consideration. The self is seen as an active participant in the creation of meaning from the various signs in the marketplace rather than as a passive decoder of meanings which may be inherent in the message. Thus, from an interactionist perspective, there is no sender and receiver as such, only *communicators* who are always engaged in mutual sending and receiving of messages. Here, the self is both an object (a 'me') and a subject ('I') of action. The 'me' contains the consciousness of the acting self seen in relation to past experiences of the self and of others. There is thus a constant interpretation of both the self and the other as objects, as well as the object of the communication (the 'message' in the traditional communication model) going on. Figure 6.2 provides an overview of this interactionist communication model.

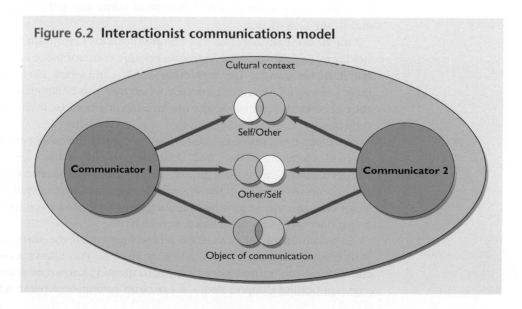

Figure 6.2 Interactionist communications model

The model is comprised of several components.[7] The first component is that of *role and role taking*. Here, the communicator performs a role, following some scripts of past experiences, interpreting the situation and acting accordingly. These are efforts of seeing the 'other' from the perspective of 'self'. But the role-playing also involves taking the role of the 'other' to see oneself or seeing the self from the perspective of the other (imagining the image that the other may have).

The second component is *orientation*, which suggests that these roles we carry out are oriented towards an object. This object might be one of the communicators but also any other idea, thing or person. To the extent that the interpretive orientations of the communicators are similar, we can say that there is agreement, or congruence, between them, and that the communicators share the meanings pertaining to themselves and the object. Congruence is typically a matter of degree, and neither total congruence nor total incongruence are possible. Finally, there is the component of *cultural embeddedness*, which suggests that the symbols and other communicative devices used in the communicative process occur in a cultural context.

As an example, consider a company and its advertising agency. As part of the creative process, the ways in which the ad agency see themselves, the selected target market, the product and campaign in question and the cultural context of the country will play a role in how they interpret the message they are about to create and send out. Likewise, the consumer's past experiences with this company's products, the meanings that the consumer attaches, based on cultural background and present context (e.g. present aspirations), coupled with the campaign seen in relation to former campaigns, are all important to the interpretation of the campaign's elements and the subsequent interpretation of the whole message (see Question 4 at the end of this chapter to assess a recent global print and web campaign for encouraging young men to purchase a particular brand of cognac).

Who's in charge of the remote?

Technological and social developments are making it increasingly obvious to everybody that people are playing an interactive role in communications. In other words, consumers are to a greater extent becoming active partners, not only in interpreting but also in forming messages in the communications process; their input is helping to shape the messages they and others like them receive, and furthermore they may seek out these messages rather than sit at home and wait to see them on television and in the newspaper.

One of the early signs of this communications revolution was the humble handheld remote control device. As VCRs became commonplace in the home, consumers had more say in what they wanted to watch – and when. No longer were they at the mercy of the TV networks to decide when to see their favourite programme; nor did they necessarily have to forsake one programme because it conflicted with another's time slot.

Since that time, of course, our ability to control our media environment has mushroomed. Caller ID devices and answering machines allow us to decide if we will accept a phone call during dinner, and to know the source of the message before picking up the phone. A bit of surfing allows us to identify kindred spirits around the globe, to request information about products, and even to provide suggestions to product designers and market researchers.

As a final example, consider a technology called the *radio data system* (RDS), which has been adopted by the BBC in the UK. This allows a radio station to transmit data on the unused portion of its frequency, known as a subcarrier. RDS is the concept behind Coupon Radio, a car radio system now being tested that allows lis-

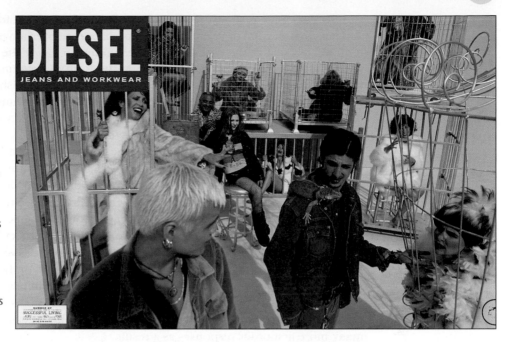

The traditional communications model takes the view that information is transferred from a source (manufacturer) to a receiver (consumer), in a relatively one-way, passive fashion. A more dynamic view of how consumers relate to marketing communication comes from uses and gratification theory, which sees consumers as an active, goal-directed audience. This perspective would suggest that some consumers would simply ignore the advert on the right. Others may reject it, develop counter-arguments about the message, or elaborate on the message in terms of what it means to them. Whether ignored, rejected, accepted, or elaborated on, messages serve as a dynamic link between senders and receivers. Used with permission.

teners to 'capture' information and give stations and advertisers feedback about their choices. A driver who hears a new song he or she likes could request more information about the musicians, or get the names and addresses of retailers that sell an advertised product.[8]

Levels of interactive response

The key to understanding the dynamics of interactive marketing communications is to consider exactly what is meant by a response.[9] The early perspective on communications primarily regarded feedback in terms of behaviour – did the recipient go out and buy the soap powder after being exposed to an ad for it?

However, a variety of other responses are possible as well, including building awareness of the brand, informing us about product features, reminding us to buy a new package when we've run out and – perhaps most importantly – building a long-term relationship. Therefore a transaction is *one* type of response, but forward-thinking marketers realize that customers can interact with them in other valuable ways as well. For this reason it is helpful to distinguish between two basic types of feedback.

First-order response Direct marketing vehicles such as catalogues and television infomercials are interactive – if successful, they result in an order which is most definitely a response! So, let's think of a product offer that directly yields a transaction as a *first-order response*. In addition to providing revenue, sales data are a valuable source of feedback which allow marketers to gauge the effectiveness of their communications efforts.

Second-order response However, a marketing communication does not have to result in an immediate purchase to be an important component of interactive marketing. Messages can prompt useful responses from customers, even though these recipients do not necessarily place an order immediately after being exposed to the communication. Customer feedback in response to a marketing message that is not in the form of a transaction is a *second-order response*.

A second-order response may take the form of a request for more information about a good, service or organization, or perhaps receipt of a 'wish list' from the customer that specifies the types of product information he or she would like to get in the future. This response may even be in the form of recommendations for other potential customers. The two telephone giants MCI and British Telecom offer a 20 per cent discount to customers who give them the phone numbers of people they call regularly. The phone company then targets these people with promotion messages to get *them* to switch companies as well.

A second-order response programme, the Pepperidge Farm No Fuss Pastry Club, illustrates how a firm communicates directly with users without trying to make an immediate sale. The club boasts more than 30,000 members who have been generated through a combination of promotion efforts, including a magazine mail-in offer, an offer on packages of Pepperidge Farm products, publicity created by news reports about the club and a sign-up form available in grocery stores. Pepperidge Farm uses surveys to determine members' attitudes towards issues related to its business, and the company also collects valuable information on how these people use frozen puff pastry products.[10] Though the company's immediate goal is not to generate the first-order response of selling frozen pastry, it knows that the second-order responses received from club members will result in loyal customers over time – and many more first-order responses as a result.

The source

Regardless of whether a message is received by 'snail mail' or email, common sense tells us that the same words uttered or written by different people can have very different effects. Research on *source effects* has been carried out for over 30 years. By attributing the same message to different sources and measuring the degree of attitude change that occurs after listeners hear it, it is possible to determine what aspects of a communicator will induce attitude change.[11]

Under most conditions, the source of a message can have a big impact on the likelihood the message will be accepted. The choice of a source to maximize attitude change can tap into several dimensions. The source can be chosen because he or she is an expert, attractive, famous, or even a 'typical' consumer who is both likable and trustworthy. Two important source characteristics are *credibility* and *attractiveness*.[12]

How do marketing specialists decide which dimension to stress? There should be a match between the needs of the recipient and the potential rewards offered by the source. When this match occurs, the recipient is more motivated to process the message. People who tend to be sensitive about social acceptance and the opinions of others, for example, are more persuaded by an attractive source, while those who are more internally oriented are swayed by a credible, expert source.[13]

The choice may also depend on the type of product. While a positive source can help to reduce risk and increase message acceptance, particular types of sources are more effective at reducing different kinds of risk. Experts are effective at changing attitudes towards utilitarian products that have high *performance risk*, such as vacuum cleaners (i.e. they may be complex and not work as expected). Celebrities are more effective when they focus on products such as jewellery and furniture that have high *social risk*, where the user of such products is aware of their effect on the impression others have of him or her. Finally, 'typical' consumers, who are appealing sources because of their similarity to the recipient, tend to be most effective when endorsing everyday products that are low-risk, such as biscuits.[14]

Source credibility

▶ **Source credibility** refers to a source's perceived expertise, objectivity or trustworthiness. This characteristic relates to consumers' beliefs that a communicator is competent and willing to provide the necessary information to evaluate competing products adequately. A credible source can be particularly persuasive when the consumer has not yet learned much about a product or formed an opinion of it.[15]

Building credibility

Credibility can be enhanced if the source's qualifications are perceived as relevant to the product being endorsed For example, the footballer Gary Lineker is popularly known in the UK as 'Mr Nice' – a personality type which was a natural for the crisp manufacturer Walker to tie into their advertising campaign that Walker's crisps are 'so nice that the nicest people would nick [steal] them'. Before the campaign unprompted awareness of Walker's ads was around 40 per cent. Following Lineker's antics of stealing packets of crisps from little boys, awareness never fell below 60 per cent, and sales have soared.[16] Similarly, Ronald Biggs, whose claim to fame was his role in the British 'Great Train Robbery' in 1963, successfully served as a spokesman in Brazil, where he lived in exile until 2001, for a company that makes door locks – a topic about which he was presumably knowledgeable![17] Tommy Hilfiger cultivated a rebellious, street-smart image by using rapper Snoop Doggy Dogg (who was acquitted of murder charges) to help launch his line and Coolio, a former crack addict and thief, as a runway model.[18] Parents may not be thrilled by these message sources – but isn't that the point?

Source biases

A consumer's beliefs about a product's attributes can be weakened if the source is perceived to be the victim of bias in presenting information.[19] *Knowledge bias* implies that a source's knowledge about a topic is not accurate. *Reporting bias* occurs when a source has the required knowledge, but his or her willingness to convey it accurately is compromised – for example, when an expert endorses a product. While his or her credentials might be appropriate, the fact that the expert is perceived as a 'hired gun' compromises credibility.

Source attractiveness

▶ **Source attractiveness** refers to the source's perceived social value. This quality can emanate from the person's physical appearance, personality, social status or his or her similarity to the receiver (we like to listen to people who are like us). A compelling source has great value and endorsement deals are constantly in the works. Even dead sources can be attractive: the great-grandson of the artist Renoir is putting his famous ancestor's name on bottled water, and the Picasso family licensed their name to the French car maker Citroën.[20]

Star power: celebrities as communications sources

The sight of a supermodel holding a cigar had a big impact on Margaret's attitudes towards cigar smoking. The use of celebrity endorsers is an expensive but commonly used strategy. While a celebrity endorsement strategy is expensive, it can pay off handsomely.[21] Oasis soft drinks is a case in point. Oasis had a very successful soft drink launch in 1995 and is market leader in the adult soft drinks sector of the UK. The drink capitalized on the vibrant nature of the TV personality and transvestite Lily Savage, who provided the voice-over for the ads. Ms Savage was seen as ideal for launching the Oasis brand because of her 'larger than life persona, memorable personality and appeal to young people. She is seen as very down-to-earth, very British and with a witty sense of humour – exactly the kind of attitude the brand wanted to own'.[22]

When used properly, famous or expert spokespeople can be of great value in improving the fortunes of a product. Celebrities increase awareness of a firm's advertising and enhance both company image and brand attitudes.[23] One reason for this effectiveness is that consumers are better able to identify products that are associated with a spokesperson.[24]

More generally, star power works because celebrities represent *cultural meanings* – they symbolize important categories such as status and social class (e.g. a 'working-class heroine' like Roseanne), gender (e.g. a 'manly man' like Sylvester Stallone or Paul Hogan, or a strong feminine character, such as Reebok's new endorser, Venus Williams[25]), age (e.g. the boyish Michael J. Fox) and even personality types (e.g. the eccentric Kramer from *Seinfeld*). Ideally, the advertiser decides what meanings the product should convey (that is, how it should be positioned in the marketplace), and then chooses a celebrity who has come to evoke that meaning. The product's meaning thus moves from the manufacturer to the consumer, using the star as a vehicle.[26]

Famous people can be effective because they are credible, attractive, or both, depending on the reasons for their fame. The computer guru Bill Gates is unlikely to be a 'fashion symbol' to most Europeans, but he may be quite effective at influencing people's attitudes towards unrestricted access to the internet (and he's apparently a fashion symbol to the Koreans – see the 'Multicultural dimension'!). On the other hand, Elizabeth Hurley may not be perceived as an expert in cosmetics, but Estée Lauder is expecting her to be a persuasive source for a message about perfumes and cosmetics.

The effectiveness of celebrities as communications sources often depends upon their perceived credibility. Consumers may not trust a celebrity's motives for endorsing a product, or they may question the star's competence to evaluate the product's claims. This 'credibility gap' appears to be widening. In a recent one-year period, for example, the number of consumers who found celebrity advertising 'less than credible' jumped to 52 per cent. The greatest erosion of confidence was found in younger consumers, 64 per cent of whom thought that celebrities appeared in ads just for the money.[27] The lack of credibility is aggravated by incidences where celebrities endorse products that they do not really believe in, or in some cases do not use. After Pepsi paid over $5 million to singer Michael Jackson in an endorsement deal, the company was not pleased by his later confession that he doesn't drink cola – and cola fans weren't too impressed either.[28]

In spite of this 'credibility gap', there are some celebrities who endorse so many products that they can be seen as 'serial advertisers'. John Cleese, for example, endorses nine different organizations, promoting everything from soft drinks to telecommunications to anti-smoking campaigns (Schweppes, Sainsbury's, Talking Pages, American Express, Sony, Compaq, Cellnet, Norwich Union Direct and anti-smoking!). Here, the concept of interactive communications discussed earlier in the chapter comes into play: 'There is a complicity between the audience and someone like Cleese. He knows that we know that he knows he is selling something, but if he entertains, engages, or surprises us, then we'll forgive him'.[29]

Multicultural dimensions

Does this work for you?

Park Jin Sung combs through a rack of button-down shirts at a clothes shop in Seoul. After close examination, he picks out one in light blue that has a stiff, narrow collar and buttons spaced just right, so that the top two can be left open without exposing too much chest. 'Bill would wear this. The collar on this other one is too floppy. Definitely not Bill's style,' Mr Park says. William H. Gates, Chairman of Microsoft Corp., may not be considered the epitome of chic in Europe, but in Seoul, Korea, he is a serious style icon. Young South Koreans believe that 'dressing for success' means copying Mr Gates's wardrobe, down to his round, tortoise-shell glasses, unpolished shoes and wrinkle-free trousers.[30] While Bill Gates doesn't even try to be an endorser of style in Korea, or elsewhere, some celebrities choose to maintain their credibility by endorsing products only in other countries. Many celebrities who do not do many American advertisements appear frequently in Japan. Mel Gibson endorses Asahi beer, Sly Stallone appears for Kirin beer, Sean Connery plugs Ito hams and the singer Sheena was featured in ads for Shochu liquor – dressed in a kimono and wig. Even the normally reclusive comedian and film director Woody Allen featured in a campaign for a large Tokyo department store.[31]

MARKETING PITFALL

For celebrity campaigns to be effective, the endorser must have a clear and popular image. In addition, the celebrity's image and that of the product he or she endorses should be similar – this effect is known as the **match-up hypothesis**.[32] Many promotional strategies employing stars fail because the endorser has not been selected very carefully – some marketers just assume that because a person is 'famous' he or she will serve as a successful spokesperson.

The images of celebrities can, however, be pre-tested to increase the probability of consumer acceptance. One widely used technique is the so-called '*Q' rating* (Q stands for quality) developed by a market research company. This rating considers two factors in surveys: consumers' level of familiarity with a name and the number of respondents who indicate that a person, programme or character is a favourite. While not the most sophisticated research technique, the Q rating acknowledges that familiarity with a celebrity's name in itself is not sufficient to gauge popularity since some widely known people are also widely disliked. Celebrities with a low Q rating include Michael Jackson, Madonna and Cyndi Lauper. Those with high ratings include Stevie Wonder, Billy Joel, Phil Collins, Whitney Houston, Cher and Dolly Parton.[33] However, even a high Q rating does not guarantee success if the celebrity's specific image doesn't match up with the featured product.

Another potential problem is what to do about celebrity endorsers who 'misbehave'. Pepsi had to abandon its sponsorship of Michael Jackson after the singer was accused of child abuse. Madonna met a similar fate following the release of her controversial *Like a Prayer* music video. Then, of course, there's always O. J. Simpson . . . To avoid some of these problems, most endorsement contracts now contain a morality clause which allows the company to release the celebrity if so warranted.[34] Other advertisers are looking a lot more favourably at characters like Bugs Bunny, who tend to stay out of trouble!

'What is beautiful is good'

Almost everywhere we turn, beautiful people are trying to persuade us to buy or do something. Our society places a very high premium on physical attractiveness, and we tend to assume that people who are good-looking are cleverer, more fashionable, and so on. Such an assumption is called a *halo effect*, which occurs when persons who rank high on one dimension are assumed to excel on others as well. The effect can be explained in terms of the consistency principle discussed in Chapter 5, which states that people are more comfortable when all of their judgements about a person go together. This notion has been termed the 'what is beautiful is good' stereotype.[35]

MARKETING OPPORTUNITY

'The best a man can get' each morning is a clean, close shave with a razor, shaving cream and same-brand toiletries, according to the global ad campaign of Gillette Co., the Boston-based shaving industry giant. But is a wet shave with a razor the best a European woman can get, too? That's the question facing Gillette and other companies as they pitch their new generation of designed-for-women shaving systems in Europe, hoping to entice women to wet shave. Currently, the world's biggest markets are the US, India and Russia. In eastern Europe, razor blades were in short supply during the Communist era. Today, sales of premium shaving systems are exploding in countries such as Russia and Poland.

The market potential in western Europe is huge. Only 30 per cent of European women wet shave, compared to 75 per cent in the United States. What's more, there is still a large number of European women who don't remove hair from their underarms and legs at all. If the percentage of women wet shaving in Europe were to reach American levels, the total sales of blades would increase by 500 million annually.

Unlike in the US, where women have been removing body hair for decades, attitudes differ in Europe, and are often deeply rooted in cultural traditions, economic conditions and varying perceptions of beauty. Many of these behaviours are learned from the family or from female role models, and changing culturally linked behaviour is difficult. In France and the UK, for example, most women share behaviours of their American counterparts and wet shave. Spanish women also remove body hair – a habit which can be traced back to the Moorish influence – but they usually go to waxing salons, or they wax at home. In Germany, shaving has more of a generational influence, with wet shaving being more common among younger women who have been influenced by the media, cinema, foreign travel and supermodels with sleek legs and underarms.

Due to the complex market structure, shaving companies confront two challenges: one is to convince women who wet shave (but usually grab a simple disposable razor for use in the shower) to switch to new shaving systems which include ergonomically designed razors, pastel colours, built-in lubricants and special blade design elements to avoid nicks and cuts. The other major goal is to introduce women to hair removal – and wet shaving as the preferred method.[36]

A physically attractive source tends to facilitate attitude change. His or her degree of attractiveness exerts at least modest effects on consumers' purchase intentions or product evaluation.[37] How does this happen?

One explanation is that physical attractiveness functions as a cue that facilitates or modifies information-processing by directing consumers' attention to relevant marketing stimuli. Some evidence indicates that consumers pay more attention to ads that feature attractive models, though not necessarily to the ad copy.[38] In other words, an ad with a beautiful person may stand a better chance of getting noticed, but is not necessarily read. While we may enjoy looking at a beautiful or handsome person, these positive feelings do not necessarily affect product attitudes or purchase intentions.[39]

Beverages: Non-Alcoholic

Nunca
mais vá
à praia de
camiseta.

You'll never have to go to the beach in a T-shirt again.

The logic behind the celebrity match-up hypothesis can be applied to the selection of models who are physically attractive, even if they are not (yet) famous. Certain beauty 'types' are distinguishable, and are believed to match up with specific brand images. This Brazilian ad for Diet Pepsi portrays a 'wholesome' beauty type whose figure becomes associated with the Diet soft drink Pepsi.
Used with permission.

Beauty can also function as a source of information. The effectiveness of highly attractive spokespeople in ads appears to be largely limited to those situations where the advertised product is overtly related to attractiveness or sexuality.[40] The *social adaptation perspective* assumes that information seen to be instrumental in forming an attitude will be more heavily weighted by the perceiver. We filter out irrelevant information to minimize cognitive effort.

Under the right circumstances, an endorser's level of attractiveness constitutes a source of information instrumental to the attitude-change process and thus functions as a central, task-relevant cue.[41] An attractive spokesperson, for this reason, is more likely to be an effective source when the product is relevant to attractiveness. For example, attractiveness affects attitudes towards ads for perfume or aftershave (where attractiveness is relevant) but not for coffee ads, where attractiveness is not. Finally, in the global marketplace the notions of what comprises 'beauty' and 'attractiveness' are certainly culturally based (see the 'Marketing opportunity' for Gillette opposite).

The sleeper effect

While in general more positive sources tend to increase attitude change, exceptions can occur. Sometimes a source can be obnoxious or disliked and still manage to be effective at getting the product's message across. In some instances the differences in attitude change between positive sources and less positive sources seem to get erased over time. After a while people appear to 'forget' about the negative source and change their attitudes anyway. This process is known as the **sleeper effect**.[42]

The explanation for the sleeper effect is the subject of debate, as is the more basic question regarding whether and when it really exists. Initially, the *dissociative cue hypothesis* proposed that over time the message and the source become dissociated in the consumer's mind. The message remains on its own in memory, causing the delayed attitude change termed the sleeper effect.[43] A more recent explanation is the *availability-valence hypothesis*, which emphasizes the selectivity of memory owing to limited capacity.[44] If the associations linked to the negative source are less available than those linked to the message information, the residual impact of the message enhances persuasion. Consistent with this view is the fact that the sleeper effect has been obtained only when the message was encoded deeply: it had stronger associations in memory than did the source.[45]

Countries as product endorsers?

Do you take care to distinguish between Australian and Chilean wines, take pride in eating original Greek feta cheese, or go to some lengths to convince guests that they will like authentic Italian grappa? If so, then you're like most consumers, who *sometimes* pay real attention to the influence that country-of-origin information has on the process of evaluating and choosing products. The crucial word here is *sometimes*, since the effects of country-of-origin information can range from strong to weak to non-existent. At the cognitive level, there are many products for which the additional information of country of origin plays little or no role in our decision process. For example, most consumers would have no doubts about buying a pocket calculator made in China or the Philippines, because we believe that this 'simple' technology has diffused across borders, and that these less industrialized countries can make calculators as well as any other country.

Fashion and clothing manufacturing technology has also diffused around the world, but would you prefer to buy an Armani suit made in Italy or in the Philippines? Research has shown that a strong brand name can compensate for a product manufactured in a country with an unknown or weak image. Sony consumer electronics may be assembled in less industrialized countries, but as consumers we have beliefs about the quality that underlies Sony's name. A shirt with the soundalike name Ralph Loren or LaCost may be made in the Maldives or Sri Lanka, but consumers believe that the fashion designing and quality controls will be consistent with their image of the brand name. Honda has even shipped cars produced in the US back to Japan, as a statement of their belief in the quality of the 'American-made' Hondas!

Like brand names, country-of-origin information provides consumers with cognitive-based information, as well as prompting affective-based reactions. Although the research results on country-of-origin effects are mixed, it is clear that the 'made in' label can be important to us, depending on the consumption situation (Russian caviar might make a good impression on your boss, but how about picking her up in a Russian car?) and the level of involvement we feel towards the product or service. With the rise in patriotism, regionalism and ethnic identity around the world, multinational and regional countries, as well as country-sponsored export agencies, will continue to promote their country, and its positive associations.[46]

The message

A major study of over 1000 commercials identified factors that appear to determine whether or not a commercial message will be persuasive. The single most important feature was whether the communications contained a brand-differentiating message. In other words, did the communication stress a unique attribute or benefit of the product? Other good and bad elements are depicted in Table 6.1.[47]

Characteristics of the message itself help to determine its impact on attitudes. These variables include how the message is said as well as what is said. Some of the issues facing marketers include the following:

● Should the message be conveyed in words or pictures?

● How often should the message be repeated?

● Should a conclusion be drawn, or should this be left up to the listener?

● Should both sides of an argument be presented?

● Is it effective to make an explicit comparison with competitors' products?

● Should blatant sexual appeal be used?

● Should negative emotions, such as fear, ever be aroused?

● How concrete or vivid should the arguments and imagery be?

● Should the ad be funny?

Sending the message

The saying 'one picture is worth a thousand words' captures the idea that visual stimuli can deliver a big impact economically, especially when the communicator wants to influence receivers' emotional responses. For this reason, advertisers often place great emphasis on vivid and creative illustrations or photography.[48]

But a picture may not be as effective at communicating factual information. Ads that contain the same information, presented in either visual or verbal form, have been found to elicit different reactions. The verbal version affects ratings on the utilitarian aspects of a product, while the visual version affects aesthetic evaluations.[49] Verbal elements are more effective when reinforced by an accompanying picture, especially if the illustration is *framed* (the message in the picture is strongly related to the copy).[50]

Because it requires more effort to process, a verbal message is most appropriate for high-involvement situations, such as in print contexts where the reader is motivated to pay close attention to the advertising. Because verbal material decays more

---

Table 6.1 Positive and negative effects of elements in television commercials

Positive effects	Negative effects
Showing convenience of use	Extensive information on components, ingredients or nutrition
Showing new product or improved features	
Casting background (i.e. people are incidental to message)	Outdoor setting (message gets lost)
	Large number of on-screen characters
Indirect comparison to other products	Graphic displays
Demonstration of the product in use	
Demonstration of tangible results (e.g. bouncy hair)	
An actor playing the role of an ordinary person	
No principal character (i.e. more time is devoted to the product)	

Source: Adapted from David W. Stewart and David H. Furse, 'The Effects of Television Advertising Execution on Recall, Comprehension, and Persuasion', *Psychology & Marketing* 2 (Fall 1985): 135–60. Copyright © 1985, John Wiley & Sons, Inc.

This ad pokes fun at the typical elements one would expect to see in a persuasive communication targeted at beer drinkers.

Courtesy of Heineken Brouwerijen B.V., Amsterdam, The Netherlands.

rapidly in memory, more frequent exposures are needed to obtain the desired effect. Visual images, in contrast, allow the receiver to 'chunk' information at the time of encoding (see Chapter 3). Chunking results in a stronger memory trace which aids retrieval over time.[51]

Visual elements may affect brand attitudes in one of two ways. First, the consumer may form inferences about the brand and change his or her beliefs because of an illustration's imagery. For example, people who saw an ad for a box of tissues accompanied by a photo of a sunset were more likely to believe that the brand came in attractive colours. Second, brand attitudes may be affected more directly; for example, a strong positive or negative reaction elicited by the visual elements will influence the consumer's attitude towards the ad (A_{ad}), which will then affect brand attitudes (A_b). This *dual component model* of brand attitudes is illustrated in Figure 6.3.[52]

Vividness

Pictures and words may both differ in *vividness*. Powerful descriptions or graphics command attention and are more strongly embedded in memory. The reason may be because they tend to activate mental imagery, while abstract stimuli inhibit this process.[53] Of course, this effect can cut both ways: negative information presented in a vivid manner may result in more negative evaluations at a later time.[54]

Figure 6.3 Effects of visual and verbal components of advertisements on brand attitude

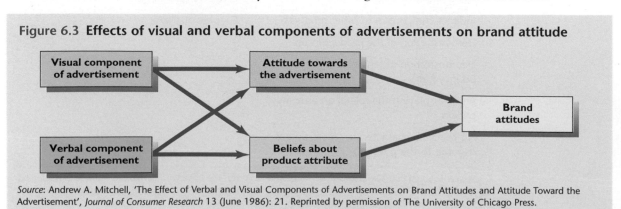

Source: Andrew A. Mitchell, 'The Effect of Verbal and Visual Components of Advertisements on Brand Attitudes and Attitude Toward the Advertisement', *Journal of Consumer Research* 13 (June 1986): 21. Reprinted by permission of The University of Chicago Press.

The concrete discussion of a product attribute in ad copy also influences the importance of that attribute, because more attention is drawn to it. For example, the copy for a watch that read 'According to industry sources, three out of every four watch breakdowns are due to water getting into the case' was more effective than this version: 'According to industry sources, many watch breakdowns are due to water getting into the case'.[55]

Repetition

Repetition can be a two-edged sword for marketers. As noted in Chapter 3, multiple exposures to a stimulus are usually required for learning (especially conditioning) to occur. Contrary to the saying 'familiarity breeds contempt', people tend to like things that are familiar to them, even if they were not keen on them initially.[56] This is known as the *mere exposure* phenomenon. On the other hand, as we saw in Chapter 2, too much repetition creates *habituation*, so that the consumer no longer pays attention to the stimulus out of fatigue or boredom. Excessive exposure can cause *advertising wear-out*, which can result in negative reactions to an ad after seeing it too much.[57]

The fine line between familiarity and boredom has been explained by the **two-factor theory**, which proposes that two separate psychological processes are operating when a person is repeatedly exposed to an ad. The positive side of repetition is that it increases familiarity and thus reduces uncertainty about the product. The negative side is that, over time, boredom increases with each exposure. At some point the amount of boredom incurred begins to exceed the amount of uncertainty reduced, resulting in wear-out. This pattern is depicted in Figure 6.4. Its effect is

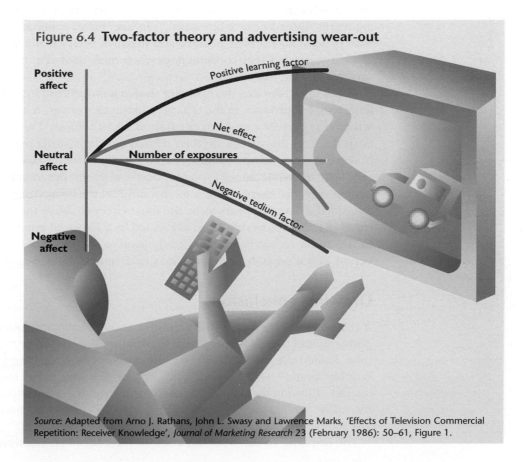

Figure 6.4 Two-factor theory and advertising wear-out

Positive affect

Positive learning factor

Net effect

Neutral affect — Number of exposures

Negative tedium factor

Negative affect

Source: Adapted from Arno J. Rathans, John L. Swasy and Lawrence Marks, 'Effects of Television Commercial Repetition: Receiver Knowledge', *Journal of Marketing Research* 23 (February 1986): 50–61, Figure 1.

especially pronounced in cases where each exposure is of a fairly long duration (such as a 60-second commercial).[58]

The theory implies that advertisers can overcome this problem by limiting the amount of exposure per repetition (such as using 15-second spots). They can also maintain familiarity but alleviate boredom by slightly varying the content of ads over time through campaigns that revolve around a common theme, although each spot may be different.

Constructing the argument

Many marketing messages are similar to debates or trials, where someone presents arguments and tries to convince the receiver to shift his or her opinion accordingly. The way the argument is presented can thus be very important.

One vs. two-sided arguments

Most messages merely present one or more positive attributes about the product or reasons to buy it. These are known as *supportive arguments*. An alternative is to use a *two-sided message*, where both positive and negative information is presented. Research has indicated that two-sided ads can be quite effective, yet they are not widely used.[59]

Why would a marketer want to devote advertising space to publicizing a product's negative attributes? Under the right circumstances, the use of *refutational arguments*, where a negative issue is raised and then dismissed, can be quite effective. This approach can increase source credibility by reducing reporting bias. Also, people who are sceptical about the product may be more receptive to a balanced argument instead of a 'whitewash'.[60] In one novel application, a Château Potelle winery ad included both positive and negative reviews of a wine by two experts. The ad suggested that consumers develop their own taste rather than relying on reviews in wine magazines.[61]

This is not to say that the marketer should go overboard in presenting major problems with the product. In the typical refutational strategy, relatively minor attributes which may present a problem or fall short when compared with competitors are discussed. These drawbacks are then refuted by emphasizing positive, important attributes. For example, the car-hire firm Avis got a lot of mileage out of claiming to be only 'No. 2', while an ad for Volkswagen woefully described one of its cars as a 'lemon' because there was a scratch on the glove compartment chrome strip.[62] A two-sided strategy appears to be the most effective when the audience is well educated (and is presumably more impressed by a balanced argument).[63] It is also best to use when receivers are not already loyal to the product: 'preaching to the converted' about possible drawbacks may raise doubts unnecessarily.

Drawing conclusions

A related factor is whether the argument should draw conclusions, or whether the points should merely be presented, permitting the consumer to arrive at his or her own. Should the message say 'Our brand is superior', or should it add 'You should buy our brand'? On the one hand, consumers who make their own inferences instead of having them spoon-fed will form stronger, more accessible attitudes. On the other, leaving the conclusion ambiguous increases the chance that the desired attitude will not be formed.

The response to this issue depends on the consumers' motivation to process the ad and the complexity of the arguments. If the message is personally relevant, people will pay attention to it and spontaneously form inferences. However, if the arguments are hard to follow or consumers' motivation to follow them is absent, it is safer for the ad to draw conclusions.[64]

Types of message appeals

Emotional vs. rational appeals

A few years ago, both Toyota and Nissan introduced a large luxury car that sold for over £30,000. The two companies chose very different ways to communicate their products' attributes, as can be seen in the ads shown here. Toyota's advertising for its Lexus model used a rational appeal, with ads concentrating on the large number of technical advancements incorporated in the car's design. Print ads were dominated by copy describing these engineering features.

In sharp contrast, Nissan's controversial campaign for its Infiniti used an emotional appeal, with a series of print and television ads that did not discuss the car at all. Instead the ads focused on the Zen-like experience of driving and featured long shots of serene landscapes. As one executive involved with the campaign explained, 'We're not selling the skin of the car; we're selling the spirit.'[65] While these ads were innovative, most American consumers had trouble grasping the Japanese conception of luxury. Later ads for the Infiniti emphasized functional features of the car to compensate for this initial confusion.

The goal of an emotional appeal is to establish a connection between the product and the consumer, a strategy known as *bonding*.[66] Emotional appeals have the potential to increase the chance that the message will be perceived, they may be more likely to be retained in memory and they can also increase the consumer's involvement with the product. Although Nissan's gamble on emphasizing the aesthetic aspects of its product did not pay off in this case, other emotional appeals are quite effective. Many companies turned to this strategy after realizing that con-

These ads demonstrate rational vs. emotional message appeals. At the time of the initial ad campaign for the new Infiniti models, the ads for rival Lexus (top) emphasized design and engineering, while the ads for Infiniti (bottom) did not even show the car.

Image © 1989; Bo Hylan Photography. Created by TeamOne Advertising.

sumers do not find many differences between brands, especially those in well-estab-lished, mature categories. Ads for products ranging from cars (Lincoln Mercury) to cards (Hallmark) focus instead on emotional aspects. Mercury's capitalization on emotional attachments to old rock songs succeeded in lowering the median age of their consumers for some models by ten years.[67]

The precise effects of rational vs. emotional appeals are hard to gauge. Though recall of ad contents tends to be better for 'thinking' ads than for 'feeling' ads, con-ventional measures of advertising effectiveness (e.g. day-after recall) may not be adequate to assess cumulative effects of emotional ads. These open-ended measures are oriented towards cognitive responses, and feeling ads may be penalized because the reactions are not as easy to articulate.[68]

**MARKETING
PITFALL**

As the foot soldiers of Nike Inc. first set out to conquer foreign lands and win World War Shoe, they marched forth under this doctrine: *Speak loudly and carry a big shtick*. 'Europe, Asia, and Latin America: Barricade your stadiums. Hide your trophies. Invest in some deodorant', blared a Nike ad in *Soccer America* magazine. At least on Europe's hallowed football (or 'soccer') fields, the early results are not nearly as victorious as Nike would have liked. Their television ads throughout Europe have inspired controversy, frenzy and outrage – just the way that Nike typically likes it. But Nike is discovering that its iconoclastic culture is not as universal as it thought. With annual sales approaching $9 billion, Nike is pinning its future on the international sneaker (trainers) and sportswear markets. The company believes its domestic sales in America, which average an astounding $20 per person, may be peaking. By contrast, per capita Nike sales in Japan are $4, in Germany $3, and in China just over 2 cents. The trick will be for Nike to keep the cool edge that has appealed to America's sneaker-buying culture while recognizing that sometimes subtlety is better than shock tactics, and homage better than outrage, when dealing with tradition-bound European and Asian cultures.[69]

While they can make a strong impression, emotional appeals also run the risk of not getting across an adequate amount of product-related information. This poten-tial problem is reminding some advertisers that the arousal of emotions is functional only to the extent that it sells the product. Procter & Gamble's original ads for Bounce fabric softener showed a happy young couple dancing to the song 'Jump', with the message that Bounce is for clothes 'you can't wait to jump into'. In more recent spots, a woman discusses why the product makes her clothes feel and smell better. It is still somewhat emotional and experiential, but the main selling point of 'softness without static cling' is driven home.[70]

Sex appeals

Under the assumption that 'sex sells', many marketing communication campaigns – for everything from cognac to cars – feature erotic suggestions that range from subtle hints to blatant displays of flesh. Of course, the prevalence of sex appeals varies from country to country. Bare flesh is so much a part of French advertising that a minor backlash is brewing as some critics complain that the advertising industry is making sex boring![71] Perhaps not surprisingly, female nudity in print ads generates negative feelings and tension among female consumers, while men's reac-tions are more positive.[72]

Does sex work? Although the use of sex does appear to draw attention to an ad, its use may actually be counterproductive to the marketer. Ironically, a provocative picture can be too effective: it attracts so much attention that it hinders processing and recall of the ad's contents. Sexual appeals appear to be ineffective when used merely as an attention-grabber. They do, however, appear to work when the product is *itself* sexually related (see Question 4 at the end of this chapter).

Humorous appeals

The use of humour can be problematic, particularly since what is funny to one person may be offensive or incomprehensible to another. Different cultures may have different senses of humour and use funny material in diverse ways. For example, commercials in the UK are more likely to use puns and satire than those in the US.[73]

Does humour work? Overall, humorous advertisements do get attention. One study found that recognition scores for humorous alcohol ads were better than average. However, the verdict is mixed as to whether humour affects recall or product attitudes in a significant way.[74] One function it may play is to provide a source of *distraction*. A funny ad inhibits the consumer from counterarguing, thereby increasing the likelihood of message acceptance.[75]

Humour is more likely to be effective when the brand is clearly identified and the funny material does not 'swamp' the message. This danger is similar to that of beautiful models diverting attention from copy points. Subtle humour is usually better, as is humour that does not make fun of the potential consumer. Finally, humour should be appropriate to the product's image. An undertaker or a bank might want to avoid humour, while other products adapt to it quite well. Sales of Sunsweet pitted prunes improved dramatically based on the claim 'Today the pits, tomorrow the wrinkles'.[76]

This humorous ad for Dristan cold medicine, which ran in Hong Kong, reads: 'Is this the only way to get rid of a stuffed-up runny nose and the headaches a cold can bring?' Visual humour is often an effective way to get attention and cut through advertising clutter.
Bates Hong Kong, Ltd.

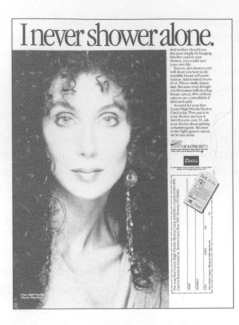

I never shower alone.

Fear appeals have a greater chance of being effective if they also provide consumers with a possible solution to the problem. Here, celebrity Cher gives concrete advice about breast self-examinations.

Coors Brewing Company and AMC Cancer Research Center.

Fear appeals

▶ **Fear appeals** highlight the negative consequences that can occur unless the consumer changes a behaviour or an attitude. This strategy is widespread: fear appeals are used in over 15 per cent of all television ads.[77] The arousal of fear is a common tactic for social policy issues, such as convincing consumers to stop smoking or to drive safely (i.e. to reduce physical risk). It can also be applied to social risk issues by threatening one's success with the opposite sex, career, and so on. This tactic has been half-jokingly called 'slice of death'.

Does fear work? Fear appeals are usually most effective when only a moderate amount of fear is induced.[78] As shown in Figure 6.5, increasing levels of fear do not result in increased change: the relationship instead resembles an inverted U-shaped curve. If the threat is too great, the audience tends to deny that it exists as a way to rationalize the danger.

A study that manipulated subjects' degree of anxiety about AIDS, for example, found that condom ads were evaluated positively when a moderate amount of fear was induced. In this context, copy that promoted the use of the condom because

Figure 6.5 The relationship between fear and attitude change

Attitude change

Degree of fear

'sex is a risky business' (moderate fear) resulted in more attitude change than either a low fear appeal that emphasized the product's sensitivity or a high fear appeal that discussed the certainty of death from AIDS.[79] Similarly, scare tactics have not been as effective as hoped in getting teenagers to cut down on their consumption of alcohol or drugs. Teenagers simply tune out the message or deny its relevance to them.[80]

Fear appeals appear to be most effective when the consumer is already afraid of the problem discussed in the ad. The threats should not be excessive and a solution to the problem should be presented (otherwise, consumers will tune out the ad since they can do nothing to solve the problem).[81] Appeals also work better when source credibility is high.[82]

Multicultural dimensions

American gun manufacturers are capitalizing on women's fears regarding self- and home defence. According to the National Rifle Association, 15–20 million American women own guns. At least three manufacturers have introduced guns for women. One company makes a .32 magnum model called a 'Bonnie', to go with a .38 'Clyde' for his-and-hers shooting. Smith & Wesson introduced the LadySmith, a revolver with a slimmed-down grip.[83] The company's ads have been criticized for preying on the fears of women. They include such copy as 'The world is different today than when you grew up' and 'Personal security is a very real issue'. A magazine called *Women & Guns* now has a readership of over 25,000.[84] In addition to gun safety, it features articles on firearm fashions. The cover of a recent issue featured an attractive woman wearing a pistol holder strapped above her knee with the caption 'Self-Defense Goes Thigh High'.

The message as artform: metaphors be with you

Marketers may be thought of as storytellers who supply visions of reality similar to those provided by authors, poets and artists. These communications take the form of stories because the product benefits they describe are intangible and must be given tangible meaning by expressing them in a form that is concrete and visible. Advertising creatives rely (consciously or not) on various literary devices to com-

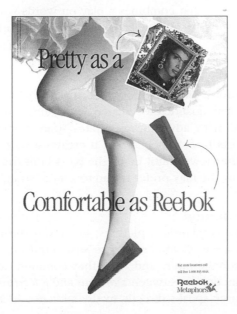

Reebok uses the metaphor 'pretty as a picture' to promote its line of Metaphors shoes.
Reebok International Ltd.

Table 6.2 Some examples of advertising resonance

Product/headline	Visual
Embassy Suites: 'This Year, We're Unwrapping Suites by the Dozen'	Chocolate kisses with hotel names underneath each
Toyota auto parts: 'Our Lifetime Guarantee May Come as a Shock'	Man holding a shock absorber
Bucks filter cigarettes: 'Herd of These?'	Cigarette pack with a picture of a stag
Bounce fabric softener: 'Is There Something Creeping Up Behind You?'	Woman's dress bunched up at the back of her due to static
Pepsi: 'This Year, Hit the Beach Topless'	Pepsi bottle cap lying on the sand
ASICS athletic shoes: 'We Believe Women Should Be Running the Country'	Woman jogging in a rural setting

Source: Adapted from Edward F. McQuarrie and David Glen Mick, 'On Resonance: A Critical Pluralistic Inquiry into Advertising Rhetoric', *Journal of Consumer Research* 19 (September 1992): 182, Table 1. Reprinted with permission of The University of Chicago Press.

municate these meanings. For example, a product or service might be personified by a character such as the Jolly Green Giant or the California Raisins. Many ads take the form of an allegory, where a story is told about an abstract trait or concept that has been personified as a person, animal, vegetable, and so on.

A **metaphor** involves the use of an explicit comparison, such as 'A is B' (e.g. 'United Airlines is your friend in faraway places'). The device was used literally by Reebok to equate its Metaphors line of shoes with comfort, as seen in the ad shown on the previous page. Metaphors allow the marketer to activate meaningful images and apply them to everyday events. In the stock market, 'white knights' battle 'hostile raiders' using 'poison pills', while Tony the Tiger allows us to equate Frosties cereal with strength, and Merrill Lynch's bull sends the message that the company is 'a breed apart'.[85]

Resonance is another type of literary device that is frequently used in advertising. It is a form of presentation that combines a play on words with a relevant picture. Table 6.2 gives some examples of actual ads that rely on the principle of resonance. While metaphor substitutes one meaning for another, resonance uses an element that has a double meaning, such as a pun, where there is a similarity in the sound of a word but a difference in meaning.

For example, an ad for a diet strawberry shortcake dessert might bear the copy 'berried treasure' so that qualities associated with buried treasure – being rich, hidden and associated with adventurous pirates – are conveyed for the brand. Because the text departs from expectations, it creates a state of tension or uncertainty on the part of the viewer until he or she works out the wordplay. Once the consumer 'gets it', he or she may prefer the ad to a more straightforward message.[86]

Forms of story presentation

Just as a story can be told in words or pictures, so the way the audience is addressed can also make a difference. Commercials are structured like other artforms, borrowing conventions from literature and art as they communicate their messages.[87]

One important distinction is between a *drama* and a *lecture*.[88] A lecture is like a speech where the source speaks directly to the audience in an attempt to inform them about a product or persuade them to buy it. Because a lecture clearly implies an attempt at persuasion, the audience will regard it as such. Assuming listeners are motivated to do so, the merits of the message will be weighed, along with the credibility of the source. Cognitive responses, such as counter-arguments, will occur. The appeal will be accepted to the extent that it overcomes objections and is congruent with a person's beliefs.

In contrast, a drama is similar to a play or film. While an argument holds the viewer at arm's length, a drama draws the viewer into the action. The characters only address the audience indirectly; they interact with each other about a product or service in an imaginary setting. Dramas attempt to be experiential – to involve the audience emotionally. In *transformational advertising*, the consumer associates the experience of product usage with some subjective sensation. Thus, ads for the Infiniti attempted to transform the 'driving experience' into a mystical, spiritual event.

The source vs. the message: sell the steak or the sizzle?

Two major components of the communications model, the source and the message, have been reviewed. Which aspect has more impact on persuading consumers to change their attitudes? Should marketers worry about *what* is said, or *how* it's said and *who* says it?

The answer is, it depends. Variations in a consumer's level of involvement, as discussed in Chapter 4, result in the activation of very different cognitive processes when a message is received. Research indicates that this level of involvement will determine which aspects of a communication are processed. The situation appears to resemble a traveller who comes to a fork in the road: one or the other path is chosen, and this path has a big impact on the factors that will make a difference in persuasion attempts.

The elaboration likelihood model

The **elaboration likelihood model (ELM)** assumes that once a consumer receives a message he or she begins to process it.[89] Depending on the personal relevance of this information, one of two routes to persuasion will be followed. Under conditions of high involvement, the consumer takes the *central route to persuasion*. Under conditions of low involvement, a *peripheral route* is taken instead. This model is shown in Figure 6.6.

The central route to persuasion

When the consumer finds the information in a persuasive message to be relevant or somehow interesting, he or she will attend carefully to the message content. The person is likely to think actively about the arguments presented and generate *cognitive responses*. On hearing a radio message warning about drinking alcohol while pregnant, an expectant mother might say to herself, 'She's right. I really should stop drinking alcohol now that I'm pregnant.' Or, she might offer *counter-arguments*, such as, 'That's a load of nonsense. My mother had a cocktail every night when she was pregnant with me, and I turned out OK.' If a person generates counter-arguments in response to a message, it is less likely that he or she will yield to the

Figure 6.6 The elaboration likelihood model of persuasion

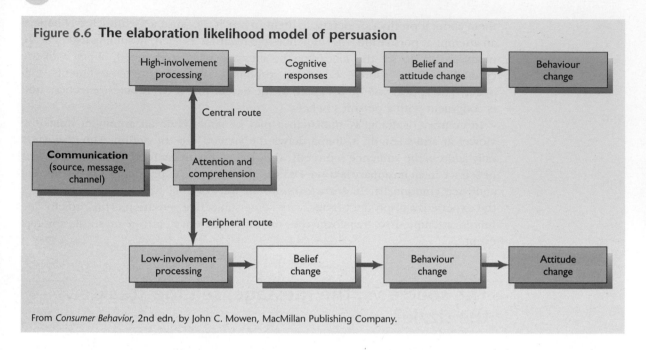

From *Consumer Behavior*, 2nd edn, by John C. Mowen, MacMillan Publishing Company.

message, while the generation of further supporting arguments increases the probability of compliance.[90]

The central route to persuasion is likely to involve the traditional hierarchy of effects, as discussed in Chapter 5. Beliefs are carefully formed and evaluated, and the resulting strong attitudes will be likely to guide behaviour. The implication is that message factors, such as the quality of arguments presented, will be important in determining attitude change. Prior knowledge about a topic results in more thoughts about the message and also increases the number of counter-arguments.[91]

The peripheral route to persuasion

In contrast, the peripheral route is taken when the person is not motivated to think deeply about the arguments presented. Instead, the consumer is likely to use other cues in deciding on the suitability of the message. These cues may include the product's package, the attractiveness of the source or the context in which the message is presented. Sources of information extraneous to the actual message content are called *peripheral cues* because they surround the actual message.

The peripheral route to persuasion highlights the paradox of low involvement discussed in Chapter 4: when consumers do not care about a product, the stimuli associated with it increase in importance. The implication here is that low-involvement products may be purchased chiefly because the marketer has done a good job in designing a 'sexy' package, choosing a popular spokesperson or perhaps just creating a pleasant shopping environment.

Support for the ELM model

The ELM model has received a lot of research support.[92] In one study, undergraduates were exposed to one of several mock advertisements for Break, a new brand of low-alcohol beer. Using the technique of *thought-listing*, they were asked to provide their thoughts about the ads, which were later analysed. Two versions of the ads are shown opposite.[93] Three independent variables crucial to the ELM model were manipulated:

- *Message processing involvement.* Some subjects were motivated to be highly involved with the ads. They were promised a gift of low-alcohol beer for participating in the study and were told that the brand would soon be available in their area. Low-involvement subjects were not promised a gift and were told that the brand would be introduced in a distant area.

- *Argument strength.* One version of the ad used strong, compelling arguments to drink Break (e.g. 'Break contains one-half of the amount of alcohol of regular beers and, therefore, has less calories than regular beer …'), while the other listed only weak arguments (e.g. 'Break is just as good as any other regular beer').

- *Source characteristics.* While both ads contained a photo of a couple drinking the beer, their relative social attractiveness was varied by their dress, their posture and non-verbal expressions, and the background information given about their educational achievements and occupations.

Consistent with the ELM model, high-involvement subjects had more thoughts related to the ad messages than did low-involvement subjects, who devoted more cognitive activity to the sources used in the ad. The attitudes of high-involvement subjects were more likely to be swayed by powerful arguments, while the attitudes of low-involvement subjects were more likely to be influenced by the ad version using attractive sources. The results of this study, paired with others, indicate that the relative effectiveness of a strong message and a favourable source depends on consumers' level of involvement with the product being advertised.[94]

These results underscore the basic idea that highly involved consumers look for the 'steak' (e.g. strong, rational arguments). Those who are less involved are more affected by the 'sizzle' (e.g. the colours and images used in packaging or endorsements by famous people). It is important to remember, however, that the *same* communications variable can be both a central and a peripheral cue, depending on its relation to the attitude object. The physical attractiveness of a model might serve as a peripheral cue in a car commercial, but her beauty might be a central cue for a product such as shampoo, where the product's benefits are directly tied to enhancing attractiveness.[95]

Source: J. Craig Andrews and Terence A. Shimp, 'Effects of Involvement, Argument, Strength, and Source Characteristics on Central and Peripheral Processing in Advertising', *Psychology & Marketing 7* (Fall 1990): 195–214. © 1990 John Wiley & Sons, Inc. Reprinted by permission of John Wiley & Sons, Inc.

Introducing the new breakthrough in beer.

There are times when you want the taste and refreshment that only beer can provide, without the alcohol content of regular beer-- now you have that choice with **BREAK** beer.

- Break contains one-half the amount of alcohol of regular beers, and therefore, has less calories than regular beer-- both important in today's health conscious world.
- Unlike regular beer, Break's lower alcohol and lower calorie content allow you to have a great tasting beer while keeping physically and mentally fit.
- Break is a smart choice for those times when you want to relax without becoming intoxicated.
- If you're thinking about switching from regular beer, Break is the one to try.
- So enjoy yourself with Break, a great tasting beer that won't slow you down.

John and Becky Fitzgerald enjoying the great taste of Break.
EDUCATION: *recent graduates of a major university.*
PROFESSION:
John, orthopedic surgeon.
Becky, corporate lawyer.
HOBBIES: *running, raquetball, photography, and travel.*

For the good times, without the bad times.

Introducing the new breakthrough in beer.

There are times when you want the taste and refreshment that only beer can provide, without the alcohol content of regular beer-- now you have that choice with **BREAK** beer.

- Break is just as good as any other regular beer.
- You really can't tell the difference between Break and regular beer.
- Break has been designed with the beer drinker in mind.
- If desired, one can obtain the full strength effect of a regular beer by drinking a few more Break beers than one would normally drink.
- So enjoy yourself with Break, the beer of the future.

John and Becky Fitzgerald enjoying the great taste of Break.
EDUCATION: *high school graduates.*
PROFESSION:
John, sales clerk for a department store.
Becky, toll booth operator.
HOBBIES: *bowling, TV, movies, and stock-car races.*

For the good times, without the bad times.

Chapter summary

- *Persuasion* refers to an attempt to change consumers' attitudes.

- The *communications model* specifies the elements needed to transmit meaning. These include a source, message, medium, receiver and feedback.

- Two important characteristics that determine the effectiveness of a source are its *attractiveness* and *credibility*. While celebrities often serve this purpose, their credibility is not always as strong as marketers hope.

- Some elements of a message that help to determine its effectiveness are whether it is conveyed in words or pictures, whether an emotional or a rational appeal is employed, the frequency with which it is repeated, whether a conclusion is drawn, whether both sides of the argument are presented, and whether the message includes fear, humour or sexual references.

- Advertising messages often incorporate elements from art or literature such as dramas, lectures, metaphors, allegories and resonance.

- The relative influence of the source vs. the message depends upon the receiver's level of involvement with the communication. The *elaboration likelihood model* specifies that a less involved consumer is more likely to be swayed by source effects, while a more involved consumer is more likely to attend to and process components of the actual message.

KEY TERMS

Communications model (*p. 157*)
Elaboration likelihood model (ELM)
  (*p. 179*)
Fear appeals (*p. 176*)
Interactionist (*p.159*)
Match-up hypothesis (*p. 165*)
Metaphor (*p. 178*)

Persuasion (*p. 155*)
Resonance (*p. 178*)
Sleeper effect (*p.167*)
Source attractiveness (*p. 163*)
Source credibility (*p. 163*)
Two-factor theory (*p.171*)
Uses and gratifications theory (*p. 158*)

For additional material see the companion website at:
www.booksites.net/solomon_euro

Consumer behaviour challenge

1. The chapter's opening vignette discusses the theoretical and managerial issues in changing attitudes through communications. Identify and discuss the ethical issues of using marketing techniques which promote the use of tobacco. Are these issues similar to the ethical issues in promoting 'wet shaving' among European women? Why or why not?

2 Create a list of celebrities who match up with products in your country. What are the elements of the celebrities and products that make for a 'good match'? Why? Which celebrities have a global or European-wide appeal, and why?

3 A government agency wants to encourage the use of designated drivers by people who have been drinking. What advice would you give the organization about constructing persuasive communications? Discuss factors that might be important, including the structure of the communications, where they should appear and who should deliver them. Should fear appeals be used, and if so, how?

4 Go to the Martell cognac website at *www.martell.com* and review the company's site. To attract more young men to the lagging spirits brand, the 'I am Martell' ad campaign and website aim to build a cult following around a French woman, synonymous with the brand. Martell's new global campaign relies heavily on sex appeal. How does this campaign seem to match up with your country's cultural values? Does the campaign seem persuasive to you? Why, or why not?

5 Why would a marketer consider saying negative things about his or her product? When is this strategy feasible? Can you find examples of it?

6 A marketer must decide whether to incorporate rational or emotional appeals in a communications strategy. Describe conditions that are more favourable to using one or the other.

7 Collect ads that rely on sex appeal to sell products. How often are benefits of the actual product communicated to the reader?

8 To observe the process of counter-argumentation, ask a friend to talk through a commercial. Ask him or her to respond to each point in the ad or to write down reactions to the claims made. How much scepticism regarding the claims can you detect?

9 Make a log of all the commercials shown on one television channel over a six-hour period. Categorize each according to product category, and whether they are presented as drama or argument. Describe the types of messages used (e.g. two-sided arguments), and keep track of the types of spokespeople (e.g. television actors, famous people, animated characters). What can you conclude about the dominant forms of persuasive tactics currently employed by marketers?

10 Collect examples of ads that rely on the use of metaphors or resonance. Do you feel these ads are effective? If you were working with the products, would you feel more comfortable with ads that use a more straightforward, 'hard-sell' approach? Why, or why not?

Notes

1. Tim Triplett, 'Women and Cigars: Puffery or Promise?', *Marketing News* (4 December 1995): 1 (3). See also *www.cigarwoman.com* and *www.cigar.com* for articles, online newsletters and interactive features on women and cigars.

2. Gert Assmus, 'An Empirical Investigation into the Perception of Vehicle Source Effects', *Journal of Advertising* 7 (Winter 1978): 4–10; for a more thorough discussion of the pros and cons of different media, see Stephen Baker, *Systematic Approach to Advertising Creativity* (New York: McGraw Hill, 1979).

3. Alladi Venkatesh, Ruby Roy Dholakia and Nikhilesh Dholakia, 'New Visions of Information Technology and Postmodernism: Implications for Advertising and Marketing Communications', in Walter Brenner and Lutz Kolbe, eds, *The Information Superhighway and Private Households: Case Studies of Business Impacts* (Heidelberg: Physical-Verlag, 1996): 319–37; Donna L. Hoffman and Thomas P. Novak, 'Marketing in Hypermedia Computer-Mediated Environments: Conceptual Foundations', *Journal of Marketing* 60(3) (July 1996): 50–68; for an early theoretical discussion of interactivity in communications paradigms, cf. R. Aubrey Fisher, *Perspectives on Human Communication* (New York: Macmillan, 1978).

4. First proposed by Elihu Katz, 'Mass Communication Research and the Study of Popular Culture: An Editorial

Note on a Possible Future for this Journal', *Studies in Public Communication* 2 (1959): 1-6. For a recent discussion of this approach, cf. Stephanie O'Donohoe, 'Advertising Uses and Gratifications', *European Journal of Marketing* 28(8/9) (1994): 52-75.

5. Quoted in Stephanie O'Donohoe, 'Advertising Uses and Gratifications', *European Journal of Marketing* 28(8/9) (1994): 52-75, at 66.

6. Herbert Blumer, *Symbolic Interactionism: Perspective and Method* (Berkeley: University of California Press, 1969): 2.

7. Fischer, *Perspectives on Human Communication*: 174-8.

8. Michael Wilke, 'A Radio Entrepreneur Reaches for the Interactive Age', *New York Times* (4 September 1994): F7.

9. This section is adapted from a discussion in Michael R. Solomon and Elnora W. Stuart, *Marketing: Real People, Real Choices* (Upper Saddle River, NJ: Prentice Hall, 1997).

10. Thomas L. Harris, 'PR Gets Personal', *Direct Marketing* (April 1994): 29-32.

11. Carl I. Hovland and W. Weiss, 'The Influence of Source Credibility on Communication Effectiveness', *Public Opinion Quarterly* 15 (1952): 635-50.

12. Herbert Kelman, 'Processes of Opinion Change', *Public Opinion Quarterly* 25 (Spring 1961): 57-78; Susan M. Petroshuis and Kenneth E. Crocker, 'An Empirical Analysis of Spokesperson Characteristics on Advertisement and Product Evaluations', *Journal of the Academy of Marketing Science* 17 (Summer 1989): 217-26.

13. Kenneth G. DeBono and Richard J. Harnish, 'Source Expertise, Source Attractiveness, and the Processing of Persuasive Information: A Functional Approach', *Journal of Personality and Social Psychology* 55(4) (1988): 541-6.

14. Hershey H. Friedman and Linda Friedman, 'Endorser Effectiveness by Product Type', *Journal of Advertising Research* 19(5) (1979): 63-71.

15. S. Ratneshwar and Shelly Chaiken, 'Comprehension's Role in Persuasion: The Case of its Moderating Effect on the Persuasive Impact of Source Cues', *Journal of Consumer Research* 18 (June 1991): 52-62.

16. 'Reach for the Stars', *Marketing Today* (September 1996): 104-5.

17. 'Robber Makes it Biggs in Ad', *Advertising Age* (29 May 1989): 26.

18. Robert LaFranco, 'MTV Conquers Madison Avenue', *Forbes* (3 June 1996): 138.

19. Alice H. Eagly, Andy Wood and Shelly Chaiken, 'Causal Inferences About Communicators and Their Effect in Opinion Change', *Journal of Personality and Social Psychology* 36(4) (1978): 424-35.

20. Kruti Trivedi, 'Great-Grandson of Artist Renoir Uses His Name for Marketing Blitz', *Wall Street Journal Interactive Edition* (2 September 1999).

21. Judith Graham, 'Sponsors Line Up for Rockin' Role', *Advertising Age* (11 December 1989): 50.

22. Nicole Dickenson, 'Can Celebrities Ruin a Launch?', *Campaign* (3 May 1996): 34.

23. Michael A. Kamins, 'Celebrity and Noncelebrity Advertising in a Two Sided Context', *Journal of Advertising Research* 29 (June-July 1989): 34; Joseph M. Kamen, A. C. Azhari and J. R. Kragh, 'What a Spokesman Does for a Sponsor', *Journal of Advertising Research* 15(2) (1975): 17-24; Lynn Langmeyer and Mary Walker, 'A First Step to Identify the Meaning in Celebrity Endorsers', in Rebecca H. Holman and Michael R. Solomon, eds, *Advances in Consumer Research* 18 (Provo, UT: Association for Consumer Research, 1991): 364-71.

24. Jeffrey Burroughs and Richard A. Feinberg, 'Using Response Latency to Assess Spokesperson Effectiveness', *Journal of Consumer Research* 14 (September 1987): 295-9.

25. Joseph Pereira, 'Reebok Serves Up Tennis Star in New Ads', *Wall Street Journal* (18 January 2001): B2.

26. Grant McCracken, 'Who is the Celebrity Endorser? Cultural Foundations of the Endorsement Process', *Journal of Consumer Research* 16(3) (December 1989): 310-21.

27. Thomas R. King, 'Credibility Gap: More Consumers Find Celebrity Ads Unpersuasive', *Wall Street Journal* (5 July 1989): B5; Bruce Haring, 'Company Totes up Popularity Quotients', *Billboard Magazine* 101 (1989): 12.

28. Pamela G. Hollie, 'A Rush for Singers to Promote Goods', *New York Times* (14 May 1984): D1.

29. Dominique Midgely, 'Variety Performers Avoid Over-Exposure', *Marketing* (February 1996): 9.

30. Choi Hae Won, 'Bill Gates, Style Icon? Oh Yes – In Korea, Where Geek is Chic', *Wall Street Journal* (4 January 2001): A1.

31. Marie Okabe, 'Fading Yen for Foreign Stars in Ads', *Singapore Straits-Times* (1986).

32. Michael A. Kamins, 'An Investigation into the "Match-Up" Hypothesis in Celebrity Advertising: When Beauty May Be Only Skin Deep', *Journal of Advertising* 19(1) (1990): 4-13; Lynn R. Kahle and Pamela M. Homer, 'Physical Attractiveness of the Celebrity Endorser: A Social Adaptation Perspective', *Journal of Consumer Research* 11 (March 1985): 954-61.

33. Haring, 'Company Totes Up Popularity Quotients': 12.

34. Larry Armstrong, 'Still Starstruck', *Business Week* (4 July 1994): 38; Jeff Giles, 'The Risks of Wishing Upon a Star', *Newsweek* (6 September 1993): 38.

35. Karen K. Dion, 'What is Beautiful is Good', *Journal of Personality and Social Psychology* 24 (December 1972): 285-90. See also Christian Derbaix and Lennart Sjöberg, 'Movie Stars in Space: A Comparison of Preference and Similarity Judgments', *International Journal of Research in Marketing* 11 (1994): 261-74.

36. Ernest Beck, 'Shaving Industry Targets European Women', *Wall Street Journal Europe* (6 May 1977): 4.

37. Michael J. Baker and Gilbert A. Churchill, Jr, 'The

Impact of Physically Attractive Models on Advertising Evaluations', *Journal of Marketing Research* 14 (November 1977): 538–55; Marjorie J. Caballero and William M. Pride, 'Selected Effects of Sales-person Sex and Attractiveness in Direct Mail Advertisements', *Journal of Marketing* 48 (January 1984): 94–100; W. Benoy Joseph, 'The Credibility of Physically Attractive Communicators: A Review', *Journal of Advertising* 11(3) (1982): 15–24; Kahle and Homer, 'Physical Attractiveness of the Celebrity Endorser': 954–61; Judson Mills and Eliot Aronson, 'Opinion Change as a Function of Communicator's Attractiveness and Desire to Influence', *Journal of Personality and Social Psychology* 1 (1965): 173–7.

38. Leonard N. Reid and Lawrence C. Soley, 'Decorative Models and the Readership of Magazine Ads', *Journal of Advertising Research* 23(2) (1983): 27–32.

39. Marjorie J. Caballero, James R. Lumpkin and Charles S. Madden, 'Using Physical Attractiveness as an Advertising Tool: An Empirical Test of the Attraction Phenomenon', *Journal of Advertising Research* 23 (August/September 1989): 16–22.

40. Baker and Churchill, Jr, 'The Impact of Physically Attractive Models on Advertising Evaluations'; George E. Belch, Michael A. Belch and Angelina Villareal, 'Effects of Advertising Communications: Review of Research', in *Research in Marketing* (Greenwich, CT: JAI Press, 1987): 9, 59–117; A. E. Courtney and T. W. Whipple, *Sex Stereotyping in Advertising* (Lexington, MA: Lexington Books, 1983).

41. Kahle and Homer, 'Physical Attractiveness of the Celebrity Endorser'.

42. Anthony R. Pratkanis, Anthony G. Greenwald, Michael R. Leippe and Michael H. Baumgardner, 'In Search of Reliable Persuasion Effects: III. The Sleeper Effect is Dead, Long Live the Sleeper Effect', *Journal of Personality and Social Psychology* 54 (1988): 203–18.

43. Herbert C. Kelman and Carl I. Hovland, 'Reinstatement of the Communication in Delayed Measurement of Opinion Change', *Journal of Abnormal Psychology* 4(48) (1953) 3: 327–35.

44. Darlene Hannah and Brian Sternthal, 'Detecting and Explaining the Sleeper Effect', *Journal of Consumer Research* 11 (September 1984): 632–42.

45. David Mazursky and Yaacov Schul, 'The Effects of Advertisement Encoding on the Failure to Discount Information: Implications for the Sleeper Effect', *Journal of Consumer Research* 15 (June 1988): 24–36.

46. For an excellent review of the country-of-origin literature, see Nicholas Papadopoulos and Louise Heslop, *Product and Country Images: Research and Strategy* (New York: The Haworth Press, 1993). See also Zeynep Gürhan-Canli and Durairaj Maheswaran, 'Determinants of Country-of-Origin Evaluations', *Journal of Consumer Research* 27 (1) (June 2000): 96–108; Israel D. Nebenzahl, Eugene D. Jaffe and Shlomo I. Lampert, 'Towards a Theory of Country

Image Effect on Product Evaluation', *Management International Review* 37 (1997): 27–49; Johny K. Johansson, 'Why Country of Origin Effects are Stronger than Ever', in Basil Englis and Anna Olofsson, eds, *Association for Consumer Research*, European Conference, Stockholm (June 1997); Allan Jaeger, 'Crafting the Image of the Netherlands Abroad', *The Netherlander* (31 May 1997): 13.

47. David W. Stewart and David H. Furse, 'The Effects of Television Advertising Execution on Recall, Comprehension, and Persuasion', *Psychology & Marketing* 2 (Fall 1985): 135–60.

48. R. C. Grass and W. H. Wallace, 'Advertising Communication: Print vs. TV', *Journal of Advertising Research* 14 (1974): 19–23.

49. Elizabeth C. Hirschman and Michael R. Solomon, 'Utilitarian, Aesthetic, and Familiarity Responses to Verbal versus Visual Advertisements', in Thomas C. Kinnear, ed., *Advances in Consumer Research* 11 (Provo, UT: Association for Consumer Research, 1984): 426–31.

50. Andrew A. Mitchell and Jerry C. Olson, 'Are Product Attribute Beliefs the Only Mediator of Advertising Effects on Brand Attitude?', *Journal of Marketing Research* 18 (1981) 3: 318–32.

51. Terry L. Childers and Michael J. Houston, 'Conditions for a Picture-Superiority Effect on Consumer Memory', *Journal of Consumer Research* 11 (September 1984): 643–54.

52. Andrew A. Mitchell, 'The Effect of Verbal and Visual Components of Advertisements on Brand Attitudes and Attitude Toward the Advertisement', *Journal of Consumer Research* 13 (June 1986): 12–24.

53. John R. Rossiter and Larry Percy, 'Attitude Change through Visual Imagery in Advertising', *Journal of Advertising Research* 9 (1980) 2: 10–16.

54. Jolita Kiselius and Brian Sternthal, 'Examining the Vividness Controversy: An Availability-Valence Interpretation', *Journal of Consumer Research* 12 (March 1986): 418–31.

55. Scott B. Mackenzie, 'The Role of Attention in Mediating the Effect of Advertising on Attribute Importance', *Journal of Consumer Research* 13 (September 1986): 174–95.

56. Robert B. Zajonc, 'Attitudinal Effects of Mere Exposure', Monograph, *Journal of Personality and Social Psychology* 8 (1968): 1–29.

57. George E. Belch, 'The Effects of Television Commercial Repetition on Cognitive Response and Message Acceptance', *Journal of Consumer Research* 9 (June 1982): 56–65; Marian Burke and Julie Edell, 'Ad Reactions Over Time: Capturing Changes in the Real World', *Journal of Consumer Research* 13 (June 1986): 114–18; Herbert Krugman, 'Why Three Exposures May Be Enough', *Journal of Advertising Research* 12 (December 1972): 11–14.

58. Robert F. Bornstein, 'Exposure and Affect: Overview and Meta-Analysis of Research, 1968–1987', *Psychological Bulletin* 106 (1989) 2: 265–89; Arno

Rethans, John Swasy and Lawrence Marks, 'Effects of Television Commercial Repetition, Receiver Knowledge, and Commercial Length: A Test of the Two-Factor Model', *Journal of Marketing Research* 23 (February 1986): 50–61.

59. Linda L. Golden and Mark I. Alpert, 'Comparative Analysis of the Relative Effectiveness of One- and Two-Sided Communication for Contrasting Products', *Journal of Advertising* 16 (1987); Kamins, 'Celebrity and Noncelebrity Advertising in a Two-Sided Context'; Robert B. Settle and Linda L. Golden, 'Attribution Theory and Advertiser Credibility', *Journal of Marketing Research* 11 (May 1974): 181–5.

60. See Alan G. Sawyer, 'The Effects of Repetition of Refutational and Supportive Advertising Appeals', *Journal of Marketing Research* 10 (February 1973): 23–33; George J. Szybillo and Richard Heslin, 'Resistance to Persuasion: Inoculation Theory in a Marketing Context', *Journal of Marketing Research* 10 (November 1973): 396–403.

61. Lawrence M. Fisher, 'Winery's Answer to Critics: Print Good and Bad Reviews', *New York Times* (9 January 1991): D5.

62. Golden and Alpert, 'Comparative Analysis of the Relative Effectiveness of One- and Two-Sided Communication for Contrasting Products'.

63. Belch *et al.,* 'Effects of Advertising Communications'.

64. Frank R. Kardes, 'Spontaneous Inference Processes in Advertising: The Effects of Conclusion Omission and Involvement on Persuasion', *Journal of Consumer Research* 15 (September 1988): 225–33.

65. Michael Lev, 'For Car Buyers, Technology or Zen', *New York Times* (22 May 1989): D1.

66. 'Connecting Consumer and Product', *New York Times* (18 January 1990): D19.

67. Edward F. Cone, 'Image and Reality', *Forbes* (14 December 1987): 226.

68. H. Zielske, 'Does Day-After Recall Penalize 'Feeling' Ads?', *Journal of Advertising Research* 22 (1982): 19–22.

69. Roger Thurow, 'In Global Push, Nike Finds its Brash Ways Don't Always Pay Off', *Wall Street Journal Europe* (6 May 1997): A1.

70. Cone, 'Image and Reality'.

71. John Lichfield, 'French Get Bored with Sex', *The Independent*, London (accessed via **ssnewslink.com**, 30 July 1997).

72. Belch *et al.,* 'Effects of Advertising Communications'; Courtney and Whipple, 'Sex Stereotyping in Advertising'; Michael S. LaTour, 'Female Nudity in Print Advertising: An Analysis of Gender Differences in Arousal and Ad Response', *Psychology & Marketing* 7 (1990) 1: 65–81; B. G. Yovovich, 'Sex in Advertising – The Power and the Perils', *Advertising Age* (2 May 1983): M4–M5.

73. Marc G. Weinberger and Harlan E. Spotts, 'Humor in US versus U.K. TV Commercials: A Comparison', *Journal of Advertising* 18 (1989) 2: 39–44.

74. Thomas J. Madden, 'Humor in Advertising: An Experimental Analysis', working paper no. 83-27 (University of Massachusetts, 1984); Thomas J. Madden and Marc G. Weinberger, 'The Effects of Humor on Attention in Magazine Advertising', *Journal of Advertising* 11 (1982) 3: 8–14; Weinberger and Spotts, 'Humor in US versus U.K. TV Commercials'.

75. David Gardner, 'The Distraction Hypothesis in Marketing', *Journal of Advertising Research* 10 (1970): 25–30.

76. 'Funny Ads Provide Welcome Relief During These Gloom and Doom Days', *Marketing News* (17 April 1981): 3.

77. Lynette S. Unger and James M. Stearns, 'The Use of Fear and Guilt Messages in Television Advertising: Issues and Evidence', in *1983 AMA Educators' Proceedings*, ed. Patrick E. Murphy *et al.* (Chicago: American Marketing Association, 1983): 16–20.

78. Michael L. Ray and William L. Wilkie, 'Fear: The Potential of an Appeal Neglected by Marketing', *Journal of Marketing* 34 (1970) 1: 54–62.

79. Ronald Paul Hill, 'An Exploration of the Relationship Between AIDS Related Anxiety and the Evaluation of Condom Advertisements', *Journal of Advertising* 17 (1988) 4: 35–42.

80. Randall Rothenberg, 'Talking Too Tough on Life's Risks?', *New York Times* (16 February 1990): D1.

81. Judith Waldrop, 'They're Coming to Take You Away (Fear as a Form of Persuasion)', *American Demographics* (15 June 1988): 2; John F. Tanner, Jr, James B. Hunt and David R. Eppright, 'The Protection Motivation Model: A Normative Model of Fear Appeals', *Journal of Marketing* 55 (July 1991): 36–45.

82. Brian Sternthal and C. Samuel Craig, 'Fear Appeals: Revisited and Revised', *Journal of Consumer Research* 1 (December 1974): 22–34.

83. 'A Drive to Woo Women – And Invigorate Sales', *New York Times* (2 April 1989).

84. Carrie Goerne, 'Gun Companies Target Women: Foes Call it "Marketing to Fear"', *Marketing News* (31 August 1992) 2: 1.

85. Barbara Stern, 'Literary Criticism and Consumer Research: Overview and Illustrative Analysis', *Journal of Consumer Research* 16 (1989): 322–34; see also Cynthia Crossen, 'A is to B as C is to . . .' *Wall Street Journal* (22 August 2000): A1; Mark Stefik, *Internet Dreams: Archetypes, Myths, and Metaphors* (Cambridge, MA: MIT Press, 1996).

86. Edward F. McQuarrie and David Glen Mick, 'On Resonance: A Critical Pluralistic Inquiry into Advertising Rhetoric', *Journal of Consumer Research* 19 (September 1992): 180–97.

87. See Linda M. Scott, 'The Troupe: Celebrities as Dramatis Personae in Advertisements', in Rebecca H.

Holman and Michael R. Solomon, eds, *Advances in Consumer Research* 18 (Provo, UT: Association for Consumer Research, 1991): 355–63; Stern, 'Literary Criticism and Consumer Research', 322–34; Judith Williamson, *Decoding Advertisements* (Boston: Marion Boyars, 1978).

88. John Deighton, Daniel Romer and Josh McQueen, 'Using Drama to Persuade', *Journal of Consumer Research* 16 (December 1989): 335–43.

89. Richard E. Petty, John T. Cacioppo and David Schumann, 'Central and Peripheral Routes to Advertising Effectiveness: The Moderating Role of Involvement', *Journal of Consumer Research* 10 (1983) 2: 135–46.

90. Jerry C. Olson, Daniel R. Toy and Philip A. Dover, 'Do Cognitive Responses Mediate the Effects of Advertising Content on Cognitive Structure?', *Journal of Consumer Research* 9 (1982) 3: 245–62.

91. Julie A. Edell and Andrew A. Mitchell, 'An Information Processing Approach to Cognitive Responses', in S. C. Jain, ed., *Research Frontiers in Marketing: Dialogues and Directions* (Chicago: American Marketing Association, 1978).

92. See Mary Jo Bitner and Carl Obermiller, 'The Elaboration Likelihood Model: Limitations and Extensions in Marketing', in Elizabeth C. Hirschman and Morris B. Holbrook, eds, *Advances in Consumer Research* 12 (Provo, UT: Association for Consumer Research, 1985): 420–5; Meryl P. Gardner, 'Does Attitude Toward the Ad Affect Brand Attitude under a Brand Evaluation Set?', *Journal of Marketing Research* 22 (1985): 192–8; C. W. Park and S. M. Young, 'Consumer Response to Television Commercials: The Impact of Involvement and Background Music on Brand Attitude Formation', *Journal of Marketing Research* 23 (1986): 11–24; Petty, Cacioppo and Schumann, 'Central and Peripheral Routes to Advertising Effectiveness'; for a discussion of how different kinds of involvement interact with the ELM, see Robin A. Higie, Lawrence F. Feick and Linda L. Price, 'The Importance of Peripheral Cues in Attitude Formation for Enduring and Task-Involved Individuals', in Holman and Solomon, eds, *Advances in Consumer Research* 18: 187–93.

93. J. Craig Andrews and Terence A. Shimp, 'Effects of Involvement, Argument Strength, and Source Characteristics on Central and Peripheral Processing in Advertising', *Psychology & Marketing* 7 (Fall 1990): 195–214.

94. Richard E. Petty, John T. Cacioppo, Constantine Sedikides and Alan J. Strathman, 'Affect and Persuasion: A Contemporary Perspective', *American Behavioral Scientist* 31 (1988) 3: 355–71.

95. Richard D. Ashmore, Michael R. Solomon and Laura Longo, 'Thinking about Female Fashion Models' Looks: A Multidimensional Approach to the Structure of Perceived Physical Attractiveness', *Personality and Psychology Bulletin* 22(11) (November 1996): 1083–104; Basil G. English, Michael R. Solomon and Richard D. Ashmore, 'Beauty Before the Eyes of Beholders: The Cultural Encoding of Beauty Types in Magazine Advertising and Music Television', *Journal of Advertising* 23 (June 1994): 49–64; Michael R. Solomon, Richard Ashmore and Laura Longo, 'The Beauty Match-up Hypothesis: Congruence between Types of Beauty and Product Images in Advertising', *Journal of Advertising* 21 (December 1992): 23–34.

Chapter 7

The self

Gareth, a marketing director in his thirties, is a happily married man, and his two children aged four and three provide immense joy in his life. However, at 36 he feels younger than his years, and somewhat anxious about his totally family-oriented life – he has a nice house, a magnificent garden and takes regular family holidays in rural France. But he has begun to feel the loss of his previous, extravagant, carefree life, one in which he perceived himself to be a well-dressed, admired individual of good taste and discernment who always turned heads when he entered the room. He is apprehensive that his 'Gareth the family man' role has totally taken over his life's spirit. It's a life he loves and one which has his complete commitment, but one which he also views as 'prudent and sensible'.

Some months into the development of these feelings, Gareth is contacted by his company's personnel department about replacing his company car. Three years earlier he had selected a sensible Audi 80 with the needs of the family in mind. In the meantime, his wife has bought a Volvo Estate which is always used for family travel. He has an exorbitant budget allocated to car purchase, due to his long-term commitment and excellent contribution to company performance over the last 18 months. As a result he can select almost any car he desires. After a prolonged search and extensive thought he decides on a Porsche Boxer.

The Porsche Boxer, a well-designed and admired car for the driver of good taste and discernment, has the image of a sporty, confident, powerful individual. The current press campaign displays a successful 30-something man being admired at the traffic lights, in the office car parks *and* at the local school collecting his children. Whilst driving home Gareth plays his CD collection at full volume, exceeds the legal speed limit when he believes it is 'safe' to do so, and generally feels more like the much-revered Gareth who graduated 15 years ago.

Carolyn Strong, University of Wales, Cardiff

Perspectives on the self

Gareth is not alone in feeling that his self-image and possessions affect his 'value' as a person. Consumers' insecurities about their appearance are rampant: it has been estimated that 72 per cent of men and 85 per cent of women are unhappy with at least one aspect of their appearance.[1] Many products, from cars to aftershave, are bought because the person is trying to highlight or hide some aspect of the self. In this chapter, we'll focus on how consumers' feelings about themselves shape their consumption habits, particularly as they strive to fulfil their society's expectations about how a male or female should look and act.

Does the self exist?

The 1980s were called the 'Me Decade' because for many this time was marked by an absorption with the self. While it seems natural to think about each consumer having a self, this concept is actually a relatively new way of regarding people and their relationship to society. The idea that each human life is unique, rather than a part of a group, developed in late medieval times (between the eleventh and fifteenth centuries in Europe). The notion that the self is an object to be pampered is even more recent. In addition, the emphasis on the unique nature of the self is much greater in western societies.[2] Many Eastern cultures by contrast stress the importance of a collective self, where the person's identity is derived in large measure from his or her social group.

Both Eastern and Western cultures see the self as divided into an inner, private self and an outer, public self. But where they differ is in terms of which part is seen as the 'real you'. The West tends to subscribe to an independent construal of the self which emphasizes the inherent separateness of each individual. Non-Western cultures, in contrast, tend to focus on an interdependent self where one's identity is largely defined by the relationships one has with others.[3]

For example, a Confucian perspective stresses the importance of 'face' – others' perceptions of the self and maintaining one's desired status in their eyes. One dimension of face is *mien-tzu* – reputation achieved through success and ostentation. Some Asian cultures developed explicit rules about the specific garments and even colours that certain social classes and occupations were allowed to display, and these live on today in Japanese style manuals which provide very detailed instructions for dressing and for addressing a particular individual.[4] That orientation is at odds with such Western practices as 'casual Fridays', which encourage employees to express their unique selves. To illustrate these cross-cultural differences further, a recent Roper Starch Worldwide survey compared consumers in 30 countries to see which were the most and least vain. Women living in Venezuela topped the charts: 65 per cent said they thought about their appearance all the time.[5] Other high-scoring countries included Russia and Mexico. The lowest scorers lived in the Philippines and Saudi Arabia (where only 28 per cent of consumers surveyed agreed with this statement).

The self can be understood from many different theoretical vantage-points. As discussed in Chapter 4, a psychoanalytical or Freudian perspective regards the self as a system of competing forces riddled with conflict. In Chapter 3 we also noted that behaviourists tend to regard the self as a collection of conditioned responses. From a cognitive orientation, the self is an information-processing system, an organizing force that serves as a nucleus around which new information is processed.[6]

Self-concept

▶ The **self-concept** refers to the beliefs a person holds about his or her attributes, and how he or she evaluates these qualities. While one's overall self-concept may be positive, there are certainly parts of the self that are evaluated more positively than others. For example, Gareth felt better about his professional identity than he did about his pending 'middle age' identity.

Components of the self-concept

The self-concept is a very complex structure. It is composed of many attributes, some of which are given greater emphasis when the overall self is being evaluated. Attributes of self-concept can be described along such dimensions as their content (e.g. facial attractiveness vs. mental aptitude), positivity or negativity (i.e. self-esteem), intensity, stability over time and accuracy (i.e. the degree to which one's self-assessment corresponds to reality).[7] As we'll see later in the chapter, consumers' self-assessments can be quite distorted, especially with regard to their physical appearance.

Self-esteem

Self-esteem refers to the positivity of a person's self-concept. People with low self-esteem do not expect that they will perform very well, and they will try to avoid embarrassment, failure or rejection. In developing a new line of snack cakes, for example, Sara Lee found that consumers low in self-esteem preferred portion-controlled snack items because they felt they lacked self-control.[8] In contrast, people with high self-esteem expect to be successful, will take more risks and are more willing to be the centre of attention.[9] Self-esteem is often related to acceptance by others. As you probably remember, teenagers who are members of high-status groups have higher self-esteem than their excluded classmates.[10]

Marketing communications can influence a consumer's level of self-esteem. Exposure to ads can trigger a process of *social comparison*, where the person tries to evaluate his or her self by comparing it to the people depicted in these artificial images. This form of comparison appears to be a basic human motive, and many marketers have tapped into this need by supplying idealized images of happy, attractive people who just happen to be using their products.

A recent study illustrates the social comparison process. It showed that female college students do tend to compare their physical appearance with advertising models. Furthermore, study participants who were exposed to beautiful women in advertisements afterwards expressed lowered satisfaction with their own appearance, as compared to controls.[11] Another study demonstrated that young women's perceptions of their own body shapes and sizes can be altered after being exposed to as little as 30 minutes of television programming.[12]

Self-esteem advertising attempts to change product attitudes by stimulating positive feelings about the self.[13] One strategy is to challenge the consumer's self-esteem and then show a linkage to a product that will provide a remedy. For example, the US Marine Corps uses this strategy with its theme targeted at young men: 'If you have what it takes ...'. Another strategy is outright flattery, as when Virginia Slims cigarettes proclaim to women, 'You've come a long way, baby'.

Sometimes such compliments are derived by comparing the person to others. For instance, many consumers are socialized to consider body odour repulsive and are motivated to protect their self-image by denying the existence of these odours in themselves. This attitude explains the success of the theme of Dial soap's advertising: 'Aren't you glad you use Dial, don't you wish everyone did?'[14]

Real and ideal selves

Self-esteem is influenced by a process where the consumer compares his or her actual standing on some attribute to some ideal. A consumer might ask 'Am I as attractive as I would like to be?', 'Do I make as much money as I should?', and so on. The **ideal self** is a person's conception of how he or she would like to be, while the **actual self** refers to our more realistic appraisal of the qualities we have or lack.

The ideal self is partly moulded by elements of the consumer's culture, such as heroes or people depicted in advertising, who serve as models of achievement or appearance.[15] Products may be purchased because they are believed to be instrumental in helping us achieve these goals. Some products are chosen because they are perceived to be consistent with the consumer's actual self, while others are used to help reach the standard set by the ideal self.

Fantasy: bridging the gap between the selves

While most people experience a discrepancy between their real and ideal selves, for some consumers this gap is larger than for others. These people are especially good targets for marketing communications that employ *fantasy* appeals.[16] A **fantasy** or daydream is a self-induced shift in consciousness, which is sometimes a way of compensating for a lack of external stimulation or of escaping from problems in the real world.[17] Many products and services are successful because they appeal to consumers' tendency to fantasize. These marketing strategies allow us to extend our vision of ourselves by placing us in unfamiliar, exciting situations or by permitting us to try interesting or provocative roles. And with today's technology, like *Cosmopolitan*'s online makeover (*virtualmakeover.com*) or the virtual preview of sunglass styles superimposed on your scanned photo at *rayban.com*, consumers can even experiment with different looks before actually taking the plunge in the real world.[18]

Multiple selves

In a way, each of us really is a number of different people – your mother probably would not recognize the 'you' that emerges while you're on holiday with a group of friends! We have as many selves as we do different social roles. Depending on the situation, we act differently, use different products and services, and we even vary in terms of how much we like ourselves. A person may require a different set of products to play a desired role: she may choose a sedate, understated perfume when she is being her professional self, but splash on something more provocative on Saturday night as she becomes her *femme fatale* self. The dramaturgical perspective on consumer behaviour views people much like actors who play different roles. We each play many roles, and each has its own script, props and costumes.[19]

The self can be thought of as having different components, or *role identities*, and only some of these are active at any given time. Some identities (e.g. husband, boss, student) are more central to the self than others, but other identities (e.g. stamp col-

This is not normal.
(Despite what you see at the Oscars'.)

Celebrity images of the thin and beautiful may be glamorous to look at, but these images also influence our sense of who the 'idea self' might be. This ad from a weight loss online community tries to point out that an exaggerated sense of thin is not particularly normal.

lector, dancer or advocate for greater equality in the workplace) may be dominant in specific situations. For example, executives in a survey undertaken in the US, UK and some Pacific Rim countries said that different aspects of their personalities come into play depending on whether they are making purchase decisions at home or at work. Not surprisingly, they report being less time-conscious, more emotional and less disciplined in their home roles.[20]

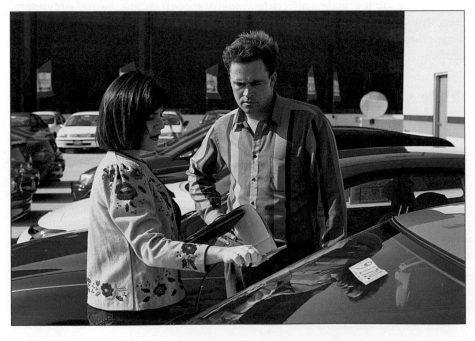

This photo shows the working woman in one of her many (relatively new) roles.

Symbolic interactionism

If each person potentially has many social selves, how does each develop and how do we decide which self to 'activate' at any point in time? The sociological tradition of **symbolic interactionism** stresses that relationships with other people play a large part in forming the self.[21] This perspective maintains that people exist in a symbolic environment, and the meaning attached to any situation or object is determined by the interpretation of these symbols. As members of society, we learn to agree on shared meanings. Thus, we 'know' that a red light means stop, or that McDonald's 'golden arches' mean fast food.

Like other social objects, the meanings of consumers themselves are defined by social consensus. The consumer interprets his or her own identity, and this assessment is continually evolving as he or she encounters new situations and people. In symbolic interactionist terms, we *negotiate* these meanings over time. Essentially the consumer poses the question: 'Who am I in this situation?' The answer to this question is greatly influenced by those around us: 'Who do *other people* think I am?' We tend to pattern our behaviour on the perceived expectations of others in a form of *self-fulfilling prophecy*. By acting the way we assume others expect us to act, we may confirm these perceptions. This pattern of self-fulfilling behaviour is often expressed in our 'gendered roles', as we will see later in this chapter.

The looking-glass self

This process of imagining the reactions of others towards us is known as 'taking the role of the other', or the **looking-glass self**.[22] According to this view, our desire to define ourselves operates as a sort of psychological sonar: we take readings of our own identity by 'bouncing' signals off others and trying to project what impression they have of us. The looking-glass image we receive will differ depending upon whose views we are considering.

Like the distorted mirrors in a funfair, our appraisal of who we are can vary, depending on whose perspective we are taking and how accurately we are able to predict their evaluations of us. A successful man like Gareth may have doubts about his role as a middle-aged 'family man' as it conflicts with his earlier self-image as dapper and carefree (whether these perceptions are true or not). A self-fulfilling prophecy may be at work here, since these 'signals' can influence Gareth's actual behaviour. If he doesn't believe he's dapper, he may choose clothing and behaviours that actually make him less dapper. On the other hand, his self-confidence in a professional setting may cause him to assume that others hold his 'executive self' in even higher regard than they actually do (we've all known people like that!).

Self-consciousness

There are times when people seem to be painfully aware of themselves. If you have ever walked into a class in the middle of a lecture and noticed that all eyes were on you, you can understand this feeling of *self-consciousness*. In contrast, consumers sometimes behave with shockingly little self-consciousness. For example, people may do things in a stadium, a riot or a student party that they would never do if they were highly conscious of their behaviour.[23]

Some people seem in general to be more sensitive to the image they communicate to others (on the other hand, we all know people who act as if they're oblivious to the impression they are making!). A heightened concern about the nature of one's public 'image' also results in more concern about the social appropriateness of products and consumption activities.

Several measures have been devised to measure this tendency. Consumers who score high on a scale of *public self-consciousness*, for example, are also more interested in clothing and are heavier users of cosmetics.[24] A similar measure is *self-monitoring*. High self-monitors are more attuned to how they present themselves in their social environments, and their product choices are influenced by their estimates of how these items will be perceived by others.[25] Self-monitoring is assessed by consumers' extent of agreement with such items as 'I suppose I put on a show to impress or entertain others', or 'I would probably make a good actor'.[26] High self-monitors are more likely than low self-monitors to evaluate products consumed in public in terms of the impressions they make on others.[27] Similarly, some recent research has looked at aspects of *vanity*, such as a fixation on physical appearance or on the achievement of personal goals. Perhaps not surprisingly, groups like body-builders and fashion models tend to score higher on this dimension.[28]

Consumption and self-concept

By extending the dramaturgical perspective a bit further, it is easy to see how the consumption of products and services contributes to the definition of the self. For an actor to play a role convincingly, he or she needs the correct props, stage setting, and so on. Consumers learn that different roles are accompanied by *constellations* of products and activities which help to define these roles.[29] Some 'props' are so important to the roles we play that they can be viewed as a part of the *extended self*, a concept to be discussed shortly.

Products that shape the self: you are what you consume

Recall that the reflected self helps to shape self-concept, which implies that people see themselves as they imagine others see them. Since what others see includes a person's clothing, jewellery, furniture, car, and so on, it stands to reason that these products also help to determine the perceived self. A consumer's products place him or her in a social role, which helps to answer the question 'Who am I *now*?'

People use an individual's consumption behaviours to help them make judgements about that person's social identity. In addition to considering a person's clothes, grooming habits, and so on, we make inferences about personality based on a person's choice of leisure activities (e.g. squash vs. soccer), food preferences (e.g. vegetarians vs. 'steak and chips' people), cars, home decorating choices, and so on. People who are shown pictures of someone's sitting room, for example, are able to make surprisingly accurate guesses about his or her personality.[30] In the same way that a consumer's use of products influences others' perceptions, the same products can help to determine his or her *own* self-concept and social identity.[31]

A consumer exhibits *attachment* to an object to the extent that it is used by that person to maintain his or her self-concept.[32] Objects can act as a sort of security blanket by reinforcing our identities, especially in unfamiliar situations. For example, students who decorate their room or house with personal items are less likely to drop out. This coping process may protect the self from being diluted in an unfamiliar environment.[33]

The use of consumption information to define the self is especially important when an identity is yet to be adequately formed, something that occurs when a consumer plays a new or unfamiliar role. **Symbolic self-completion theory** predicts that people who have an incomplete self-definition tend to complete this identity by acquiring and displaying symbols associated with it.[34] Adolescent boys may use 'macho' products like cars and cigarettes to bolster their developing masculinity: these items act as a 'social crutch' to be leaned on during a period of uncertainty about identity.

Loss of self

The contribution of possessions to self-identity is perhaps most apparent when these treasured objects are lost or stolen. One of the first acts performed by institutions that want to repress individuality and encourage group identity, such as prisons or convents, is to confiscate personal possessions.[35] Victims of burglaries and natural disasters commonly report feelings of alienation, depression or of being 'violated'. One consumer's comment after being robbed is typical: 'It's the next worse thing to being bereaved; it's like being raped.'[36] Burglary victims exhibit a diminished sense of community, reduced sense of privacy and take less pride in their house's appearance than do their neighbours.[37]

The dramatic impact of product loss is highlighted by studying post-disaster conditions, when consumers may literally lose almost everything but the clothes on their backs following a fire, hurricane, flood or earthquake. Some people are reluctant to undergo the process of recreating their identity by acquiring all new possessions. Interviews with disaster victims reveal that some are reluctant to invest the self in new possessions and so become more detached about what they buy. This comment from a woman in her fifties is representative of this attitude: 'I had so much love tied up in my things. I can't go through that kind of loss again. What I'm buying now won't be as important to me.'[38]

Self/product congruence

Because many consumption activities are related to self-definition, it is not surprising to learn that consumers demonstrate consistency between their values (see Chapter 4) and the things they buy.[39] **Self-image congruence models** predict that products will be chosen when their attributes match some aspect of the self.[40] These models assume a process of cognitive matching between these attributes and the consumer's self-image.[41]

While results are somewhat mixed, the ideal self appears to be more relevant as a comparison standard for highly expressive social products such as perfume. In contrast, the actual self is more relevant for everyday, functional products. These standards are also likely to vary by usage situation. For example, a consumer might want a functional, reliable car to commute to work everyday, but a flashier model with more 'zing' when going out on a date in the evening. Sadly, there are examples of people using products wherein the goal of enhancing the ideal self ends up conflicting with and damaging the actual self. The bodybuilding craze that has swept through the US and the north-east of England has resulted in an increasing number of young men using anabolic steroids for bodybuilding. This steroid use may 'bulk up' the physique (and provide a faster attainment of the ideal self), but it also damages the actual self, since the steroids cause male infertility.[42]

Research tends to support the idea of congruence between product usage and self-image. One of the earliest studies to examine this process found that car owners' ratings of themselves tended to match their perceptions of their cars – drivers of the sporty Pontiac model saw themselves as more active and flashier than did Volkswagen drivers.[43] Congruity has also been found between consumers and their most preferred brands of beer, soap, toothpaste and cigarettes relative to their least preferred brands, as well as between consumers' self-images and their favourite shops.[44] Some specific attributes that have been found to be useful in describing some of the matches between consumers and products include rugged/delicate, excitable/calm, rational/emotional and formal/informal.[45]

While these findings make some intuitive sense, we cannot blithely assume that consumers will always buy products whose characteristics match their own. It is not clear that consumers really see aspects of themselves in down-to-earth, functional products that don't have very complex or human-like images. It is one thing to consider a brand personality for an expressive, image-oriented product like perfume and quite another to impute human characteristics to a toaster.

Another problem is the old 'chicken-and-egg' question: do people buy products because the products are seen as similar to the self, or do they *assume* that these products must be similar because they have bought them? The similarity between a person's self-image and the images of products purchased does tend to increase with ownership, so this explanation cannot be ruled out.

The extended self

As noted earlier, many of the props and settings consumers use to define their social roles in a sense become a part of their selves. Those external objects that we consider a part of us comprise the **extended self**. In some cultures, people literally incorporate objects into the self – they lick new possessions, take the names of conquered enemies (or in some cases eat them) or bury the dead with their possessions.[46] We don't usually go that far, but many people do cherish possessions as if they were a part of them. Many material objects, ranging from personal possessions and pets to national monuments or landmarks, help to form a consumer's identity. Just about everyone can name a valued possession that has a lot of the self 'wrapped up' in it, whether it is a treasured photograph, a trophy, an old shirt, a car or a cat. Indeed, it is often possible to construct a pretty accurate 'biography' of someone just by cataloguing the items on display in his or her bedroom or office.

In one study on the extended self, people were given a list of items that ranged from electronic equipment, facial tissues and television programmes to parents,

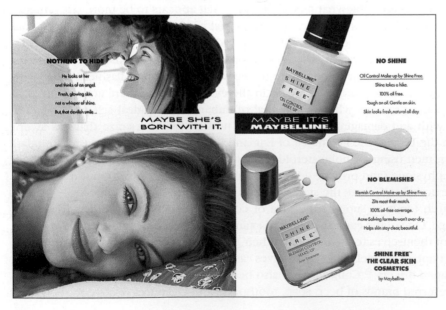

Blending self-concepts with product attributes, Maybelline evokes images of the real and ideal self.

body parts and favourite clothes. They were asked to rate each in terms of its closeness to the self. Objects were more likely to be considered a part of the extended self if 'psychic energy' was invested in them by expending effort to obtain them or because they were personalized and kept for a long time.[47]

Four levels of the extended self were described. These range from very personal objects to places and things that allow people to feel like they are rooted in their larger social environments:[48]

- *Individual level.* Consumers include many of their personal possessions in self-definition. These products can include jewellery, cars, clothing, and so on. The saying 'You are what you wear' reflects the belief that one's things are a part of what one is.

- *Family level.* This part of the extended self includes a consumer's residence and its furnishings. The house can be thought of as a symbolic body for the family and often is a central aspect of identity.

- *Community level.* It is common for consumers to describe themselves in terms of the neighbourhood or town from which they come. For farming families or residents with close ties to a community, this sense of belonging is particularly important.

- *Group level.* Our attachments to certain social groups can be considered a part of self. A consumer may feel that landmarks, monuments or sports teams are a part of the extended self.

Gender roles

Sexual identity is a very important component of a consumer's self-concept. People often conform to their culture's expectations about how those of their gender should act, dress, speak, and so on. Of course, these guidelines change over time, and they can differ radically across societies. Some societies are highly dichotomized, with little tolerance for deviation from gender norms. In other societies this is not the case, and greater freedom in behaviour, including behaviour stemming from sexual orientation, is allowed. In certain societies, lip-service is paid to gender equality, but inequalities are just under the surface; in others, there is greater sharing of power, of resources and of decision-making. To the extent that our culture is everything that we learn, then virtually all aspects of the consumption process must be affected by culture. It is not always clear to what extent sex differences are innate vs. culturally shaped – but they're certainly evident in many consumption decisions![49]

Consider the gender differences market researchers have observed when comparing the food preferences of men and women. Women eat more fruit; men are more likely to eat meat. As one food writer put it, 'Boy food doesn't grow. It is hunted or killed.' Men are more likely to eat Frosted Flakes or Corn Flakes, while women prefer multigrain cereals. Men are more likely than women to consume soft drinks, while women account for the bulk of sales of bottled water. The sexes also differ sharply in the quantities of food they eat: when researchers at Hershey's discovered that women eat smaller amounts of sweets, the company created a white chocolate confection called Hugs, one of the most successful food launches of all time.

Gender differences in socialization

A society's assumptions about the proper roles of men and women are communicated in terms of the ideal behaviours that are stressed for each sex (in advertising, among other places). It is likely, for instance, that many women eat smaller quantities because they have been 'trained' to be more delicate and dainty.

Gender goals and expectations

▶ In many societies, males are controlled by **agentic goals**, which stress self-assertion
▶ and mastery. Females, on the other hand, are taught to value **communal goals**, such as affiliation and the fostering of harmonious relations.[50]

Every society creates a set of expectations regarding the behaviours appropriate for men and women, and finds ways to communicate these priorities. This training begins very young: even children's birthday stories reinforce sex roles. A recent analysis showed that while stereotypical depictions have decreased over time, female characters in children's books are still far more likely to take on nurturant roles such as baking and gift-giving. The adult who prepares the birthday celebration is almost always the mother – often no adult male is present at all. On the other hand, the male figure in these stories is often cast in the role of a miraculous provider of gifts.[51]

Macho marketers?

Marketing has historically been largely defined by men, so it still tends to be dominated by male values. Competition rather than co-operation is stressed, and the language of warfare and domination is often used. Strategists often use distinctly masculine concepts: 'market penetration' or 'competitive thrusts', for example. Marketing articles in academic journals also emphasize agentic rather than communal goals. The most pervasive theme is power and control over others. Other themes include instrumentality (manipulating people for the good of an organization) and competition.[52] This bias may diminish in years to come, as more marketing researchers begin to stress such factors as emotions and aesthetics in purchase decisions, and as increasing numbers of women graduate in marketing!

Gender vs. sexual identity

Sex role identity is a state of mind as well as body. A person's biological gender (i.e.
▶ male or female) does not totally determine whether he or she will exhibit **sex-typed traits**, or characteristics that are stereotypically associated with one sex or the other. A consumer's subjective feelings about his or her sexuality are crucial as well.[53]

Unlike maleness and femaleness, masculinity and femininity are *not* biological characteristics. A behaviour considered masculine in one culture may not be viewed as such in another. For example, the norm in northern Europe, and in Scandinavia in particular, is that men are stoic, while cultures in southern Europe and in Latin America allow men to show their emotions. Each society determines what 'real' men and women should and should not do.

Sex-typed products

Many products also are *sex-typed*: they take on masculine or feminine attributes, and consumers often associate them with one sex or another.[54] The sex-typing of products is often created or perpetuated by marketers (e.g. Princess telephones, boys' and girls' toys, and babies' colour-coded nappies). Even brand names appear to be

Table 7.1 Sex-typed products

Masculine	Feminine
Pocket knife	Scarf
Tool kit	Baby oil
Shaving cream	Bedroom slippers
Briefcase	Hand lotion
Camera (35 mm)	Clothes dryer
Stereo system	Food processor
Scotch	Wine
Wall paint	Facial tissues

Source: Adapted from Kathleen Debevec and Easwar Iyer, 'Sex Roles and Consumer Perceptions of Promotions, Products, and Self: What Do We Know and Where Should We Be Headed', in *Advances in Consumer Research* 13, ed. Richard J. Lutz (Provo, UT: Association for Consumer Research, 1986): 210–14.

sex-typed: those containing alphanumerics (e.g. Formula 409, 10W40, Clorox 2) are assumed to be technical and hence masculine.[55] Our gender also seems to influence the instrumentality of the products we buy. Studies have shown that men tend to buy instrumental and leisure items impulsively, projecting independence and activity, while women tend to buy symbolic and self-expressive goods concerned with appearance and emotional aspects of self. Other research has shown, for example, that men take a more self-oriented approach to buying clothes, stressing its use as expressive symbols of personality and functional benefits, whilst women have 'other-oriented' concerns, choosing to use clothes as symbols of their social and personal interrelatedness with others.[56] Some sex-typed products are listed in Table 7.1.

Androgyny

Masculinity and femininity are not opposite ends of the same dimension. **Androgyny** refers to the possession of both masculine and feminine traits.[57] Researchers make a distinction between *sex-typed people*, who are stereotypically masculine or feminine, and *androgynous people*, whose mixture of characteristics allows them to function well in a variety of social situations.

Differences in sex-role orientation can influence responses to marketing stimuli, at least under some circumstances.[58] For example, research evidence indicates that females are more likely to undergo elaborate processing of message content, so they tend to be more sensitive to specific pieces of information when forming a judgement, while males are more influenced by overall themes.[59] In addition, women with a relatively strong masculine component in their sex-role identity prefer ad portrayals that include non-traditional women.[60] Some research indicates that sex-typed people are more sensitive to the sex-role depictions of characters in advertising, although women appear to be more sensitive to gender role relationships than are men.

In one study, subjects read two versions of a beer advertisement, couched in either masculine or feminine terms. The masculine version contained phrases like 'X Beer has the strong aggressive flavour that really asserts itself with good food and good company ...', while the feminine version made claims like 'Brewed with tender care, X Beer is a full-bodied beer that goes down smoothly and gently ...'. People who rated themselves as highly masculine or highly feminine preferred the version that was described in (respectively) very masculine or feminine terms.[61] Sex-

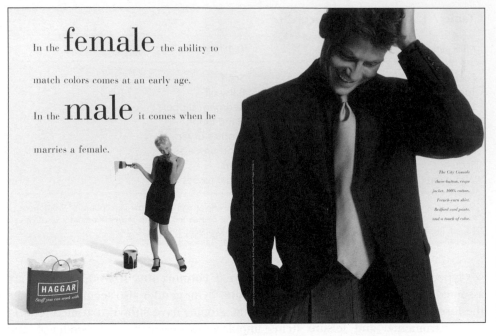

In the **female** the ability to match colors comes at an early age. In the **male** it comes when he marries a female.

The City Casuals three-button, crepe jacket, 100% cotton, French-yarn shirt, Bedford cord pants and a touch of color.

HAGGAR
Stuff you can work with

In spite of many changes in 'gendered behaviour' over the past years, some sex-role stereotypes continue to endure.
Used with permission.

typed people in general are more concerned with ensuring that their behaviour is consistent with their culture's definition of gender appropriateness.

Female gender roles

Gender roles for women are changing rapidly. Social changes, such as the dramatic increase in the proportion of women in waged work, have led to an upheaval in the way women are regarded by men, the way they regard themselves and in the products they choose to buy. Modern women now play a greater role in decisions regarding traditionally male purchases. For example, more than 60 per cent of new car buyers under the age of 50 are female, and women even buy almost half of all condoms sold.[62]

Segmenting women

In the 1949 movie *Adam's Rib*, Katharine Hepburn played a stylish and competent lawyer. This film was one of the first to show that a woman can have a successful career and still be happily married. Historically, married women have worked outside the home, especially during wartime. However, the presence of women in a position of authority is a fairly recent phenomenon. The evolution of a new mana-

Multicultural dimensions

One of the most marked changes in gender roles is occurring in Japan. Traditional Japanese wives stay at home and care for their children while their husbands work late and entertain clients. The good Japanese wife is expected to walk two paces behind her husband. However, these patterns are changing as women are less willing to live vicariously through their husbands. More than half of Japanese women aged between 25 and 29 are either working or looking for a job.[63] Japanese marketers and advertisers are beginning to depict women in professional situations (though still usually in subservient roles), and even to develop female market segments for such traditionally male products as cars.

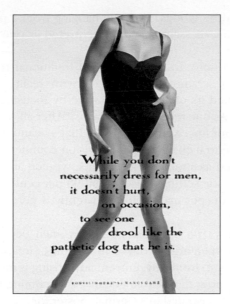

While you don't necessarily dress for men, it doesn't hurt, on occasion, to see one drool like the pathetic dog that he is.

This ad illustrates the 'men-bashing' approach taken by some advertisers who are trying to appeal to women.
Advertising Age (1994).
Photo courtesy of Goldsmith/Jeffrey and Bodyslimmers.

gerial class of women has forced marketers to change their traditional assumptions about women as they target this growing market.

Ironically, it seems that in some cases marketers have overcompensated for their former emphasis on women as housewives. Many attempts to target the vast market of females employed outside the home tend to depict all these women in glamorous, executive positions. This portrayal ignores the fact that the majority of women do not hold such jobs, and that many work because they have to, rather than for self-fulfilment. This diversity means that not all women should be expected to respond to marketing campaigns that stress professional achievement or the glamour of the working life.

Whether or not they work outside the home, many women have come to value greater independence and respond positively to marketing campaigns that stress the freedom to make their own lifestyle decisions. American Express has been targeting women for a long time, but the company found that its 'Do you know me?' campaign did not appeal to women as much as to men. A campaign aimed specifically at women featured confident women using their American Express cards. By depicting women in active situations, the company greatly increased its share of the woman's credit card market.[64]

Cheesecake: the depiction of women in advertising

As implied by the ads for Virginia Slims cigarettes – 'You've come a long way, baby!' – attitudes about female sex roles changed remarkably during the twentieth century. Still, women continue to be depicted by advertisers and the media in stereotypical ways. Analyses of ads in such magazines as *Time*, *Newsweek*, *Playboy* and even *Ms*. have shown that the large majority of women included were presented as sex objects (so-called 'cheesecake' ads) or in traditional roles.[65] Similar findings have been obtained in both the UK and the US.[66] One of the biggest culprits may be rock videos, which tend to reinforce traditional women's roles.

Ads may also reinforce negative stereotypes. Women are often portrayed as stupid, submissive, temperamental, or as sexual objects who exist solely for the pleasure of men. An ad for Newport cigarettes illustrates how the theme of female submission may be perpetuated. The copy 'Alive with pleasure!' is accompanied by a photo of a woman in the woods, playfully hanging from a pole being carried by two men. The underlying message may be interpreted as two men bringing home their captured prey.[67]

Although women continue to be depicted in traditional roles, this situation is changing as advertisers scramble to catch up with reality. For example, Avon Products is trying to shed its old-fashioned image by focusing on the concerns of contemporary women. As one recent ad proclaims, 'After all, you have more on your mind than what's on your lips. And Avon thinks that's beautiful.'[68] Women are now as likely as men to be central characters in television commercials. Still, while males are increasingly depicted as spouses and parents, women are still more likely than men to be seen in domestic settings. Also, about 90 per cent of all narrators in commercials are male. The deeper male voice apparently is perceived as more authoritative and credible.[69]

Some ads now feature *role reversal*, where women occupy traditional men's roles. In other cases, women are portrayed in romantic situations, but they tend to be more sexually dominant. Ironically, current advertising is more free to emphasize traditional female traits now that sexual equality is becoming more of an accepted fact. This freedom is demonstrated in a German poster for a women's magazine. The caption reads 'Today's women can sometimes show weakness, because they are strong'.

MARKETING PITFALL

Marketers continue to grapple with ways to entice female customers for traditionally male-oriented products, such as cars and computers, without offending them. One early effort by Tandy Corp. illustrates the potential for these efforts to backfire. When the company decided to market personal computers to women in 1990, it did so by packaging them with software for doing such 'feminine' tasks as making Christmas lists, taking inventories of silverware and china, and generating recipes. Women were not amused by the homemaker stereotype, and the campaign failed.[70]

This German ad for New West cigarettes features a gay wedding. The headline focuses on the brand's strong taste, depicting it as the choice of fearless individuals.
Advertising Age (Global Gallery), 8 March 1993, p. 40.
Photo: Scholz & Friends, Hamburg.

Male sex roles

While the traditional conception of the ideal male as a tough, aggressive, muscular man who enjoys 'manly' sports and activities is not dead, society's definition of the male role is evolving. Men in the late 1990s were allowed to be more compassionate and to have close friendships with other men. In contrast to the depiction of macho men who do not show feelings, some marketers were promoting men's 'sensitive' side. An emphasis on male bonding was the centrepiece of many ad campaigns, especially for beers.[71]

The prototype of the 'new man' was expressed in the positioning statement for Paco Rabanne Pour Homme, an aftershave that attempted to focus on this new lifestyle: 'Paco Rabanne Pour Homme is a prestige men's fragrance for the male who is not a clichéd stereotype, the man who understands and accepts the fluidity of male/female relationships.' The ideal personality of the target consumer for the aftershave was described by the company with adjectives like confident, independent, romantic, tender and playful.[72]

MARKETING OPPORTUNITY

Marketing opportunity

As sex roles for males evolve, formerly 'feminine products' such as fragrances and hair colouring are being marketed to men. Even nail polish is slowly making its way onto men's bathroom shelves – the Hard Candy line offers its Candy Man collection, which includes a metallic gold called Cowboy and a forest green shade named Oedipus. And, responding to pressures felt by many men to look younger, ads aimed at getting men to remove grey hair have tripled over the past decade. Roper Starch Worldwide reports that 36 per cent of men have either tried colouring their hair or were open to it. L'Oréal's new Feria line for men's hair includes new hues like Camel (brownish orange) and Cherry Cola. Other vanity products introduced in recent years include Bodyslimmers underwear that sucks in the waist, and Super Shaper Briefs that round out the buttocks (for an extra $5 the buyer can get an 'endowment pad' that slips in the front . . .).[73]

Men in Japan are taking it a step further: it's fashionable for everyone from high school students to professional baseball players to tweeze their eyebrows. Others are putting mud packs on their cheeks and using hairpins, and market researchers are starting to see an interest among men in wearing foundation make-up. These choices illustrate the lengths to which one sex will go to please the other: the men are apparently trying to compete with the large number of boyish, clean-cut actors and singers who are now the rage among young Japanese women.[74]

The joys of fatherhood

Males' lifestyles are changing to allow greater freedom of expression in clothing choices, hobbies such as cooking, and so on. Men are getting more involved in bringing up children, and advertising campaigns for such companies as Kodak, Omega watches and Pioneer electronics stress the theme of fatherhood.[75] Still, this change is coming slowly. A commercial for 7–11 stores (a corner shop chain in America and western Europe) showed two men out for a walk, each with a pushchair. As they neared a 7–11, they began to push faster until they were racing each other. The campaign's creative director explained, 'We showed them engaged in a competition to make it easier for men to accept the concept of taking care of children.'[76]

Beefcake: the depiction of men in advertising

Men as well as women are often depicted in a negative fashion in advertising. They frequently come across as helpless or bumbling. As one advertising executive put it, 'The woman's movement raised consciousness in the ad business as to how women can be depicted. The thought now is, if we can't have women in these old-fashioned traditional roles, at least we can have men being dummies.'[77]

Just as advertisers are criticized for depicting women as sex objects, so the same accusations can be made about how males are portrayed – a practice correspondingly known as 'beefcake'.[78] An ad campaign for Sansabelt trousers featured the theme 'What women look for in men's pants'. Ads feature a woman who confides, 'I always lower my eyes when a man passes [pause] to see if he's worth following.' One female executive commented, 'turnabout is fair play ... If we can't put a stop to sexism in advertising ... at least we can have some fun with it and do a little leering of our own.'[79]

Gay and lesbian consumers

Gay and lesbian consumers are still largely ignored by marketers. This situation is starting to change, however, as some marketers are acknowledging the upmarket demographic profile of these consumers.[80] IKEA, the Swedish furniture retailer with outlets throughout Europe and in several major US cities, broke new ground by running a TV spot featuring a gay male couple purchasing a dining-room table at the shop.[81] Other major companies making an effort to market to homosexuals include AT&T, Anheuser-Busch, Apple Computers, Benetton, Philip Morris, Seagram and Sony.[82] Gay consumers can even get their own credit card – a Rainbow Visa card issued by Travelers Bank USA. Using tennis star Martina Navratilova as its spokeswoman, users of the card benefit such groups as the National Center for Lesbian Rights. The card allows people who don't qualify based on income to apply with a same-sex partner.[83]

The percentage of the population that is gay and lesbian is difficult to determine, and efforts to measure this group have been controversial.[84] However, the respected research company Yankelovich Partners Inc., which has tracked consumer values and attitudes since 1971 in its annual Monitor™ survey, now includes a question about sexual identity in its survey. This study was virtually the first to use a sample that reflects the population as a whole instead of polling only smaller or biased groups (such as readers of gay publications) whose responses may not be representative of all consumers. About 6 per cent of respondents identified themselves as gay/homosexual/lesbian.

As civil rights gains are made by gay activists, the social climate is becoming more favourable for firms targeting this market segment.[85] In one of the first academic studies in this field, the conclusion was that gays and lesbians did not qualify as a market segment because they did not satisfy the traditional criteria of being identifiable, accessible and of sufficient size.[86] Subsequent studies have argued that the segmentation criteria rely on outdated assumptions regarding the nature of consumers, marketing activities and the ways in which media are used in the contemporary marketplace. Here, the argument is that identifiability is an unreliable construct for socially subordinated groups, and really isn't the issue anyway. How marketers segment (by race, ethnicity, gender or, in this case, sexuality) isn't as important as whether the group itself expresses consumption patterns in identifiable ways. Similarly, the accessibility criterion continues with the assumption of active marketers who contact passive consumers. This criterion also needs to take

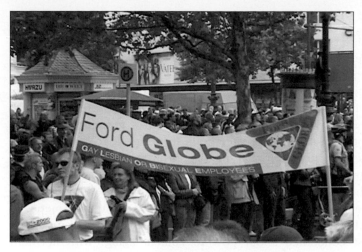

As gays and lesbians continue to become more socially intergrated into the mainstream of European cultures, many companies (large and small) are also becoming more visible and open in their support of this social movement. This photo, taken at the Gay & Lesbian Parade in Berlin in June 2001, shows the involvement and support of Ford in the day's celebrations.
Photo: Gary Bamossy

into account the dramatic changes in media over the past two decades, in particular the use of speciality media by marketers to access special-interest segments. Gay consumers are also active web surfers: the website **Gay.com** attracts one million consumers a month. As many as 65 per cent of gay and lesbian internet users go online more than once a day and over 70 per cent make purchases online.[87] Finally, sufficient size assumes separate campaigns are necessary to reach each segment, an assumption that ignores consumers' ability and willingness to explore multiple media.[88]

At least in some parts of the US and Europe, homosexuality appears to be becoming more mainstream and accepted. Mattel even sells an Earring Magic Ken doll, complete with *faux*-leather vest, lavender mesh shirt and two-tone hair (though the product has become a favourite of gay men, the company denied it was targeted to that group).

MARKETING OPPORTUNITY

Lesbian consumers have recently been in the cultural spotlight, perhaps due in part to the actions of such high-profile cultural figures as Martina Navratilova, singers k.d. lang and Melissa Etheridge, and actress Ellen deGeneres. Whatever the reason, American Express, Stolichnaya vodka, Atlantic Records and Naya bottled water are among those corporations now running ads in lesbian publications (an ad for American Express Travellers Cheques for Two shows two women's signatures on a cheque). Acting on research that showed that lesbians are four times as likely to own one of their cars, Subaru of America recently began to target this market as well.[89]

Body image

▶ A person's physical appearance is a large part of his or her self-concept. **Body image** refers to a consumer's subjective evaluation of his or her physical self. As was the case with the overall self-concept, this image is not necessarily accurate. A man may think of himself as being more muscular than he really is, or a woman may think she is fatter than is the case. In fact, it is not uncommon to find marketing strategies that exploit consumers' tendencies to distort their body images by preying upon insecurities about appearance, thereby creating a gap between the real and the ideal physical self and, consequently, the desire to purchase products and services to narrow that gap.

Body cathexis

▶ A person's feelings about his or her body can be described in terms of **body cathexis**. Cathexis refers to the emotional significance of some object or idea to a person, and some parts of the body are more central to self-concept than others. One study of young adults' feelings about their bodies found that these respondents were most satisfied with their hair and eyes and had least positive feelings about their waists. These feelings were related to consumption of grooming products. Consumers who were more satisfied with their bodies were more frequent users of such 'preening' products as hair conditioner, hairdryers, aftershave, artificial tanning products, toothpaste and pumice soap.[90] In a large-scale study of older women in six European countries, the results showed that women would like to 'grow old beautifully', and that they were prepared to follow diets, exercise and use cosmetics to reach this goal. Wrinkles were the biggest concern, and Greek and Italian women were by far the most concerned about how to combat aging, with northern European women expressing more agreement with the statement that aging was natural and inevitable.[91]

Ideals of beauty

A person's satisfaction with the physical image he or she presents to others is affected by how closely that image corresponds to the image valued by his or her culture. In fact, infants as young as two months show a preference for attractive faces.[92] An ▶ **ideal of beauty** is a particular model, or exemplar, of appearance. Ideals of beauty for both men and women may include physical features (e.g. big breasts or small, bulging muscles or not) as well as clothing styles, cosmetics, hairstyles, skin tone (pale vs. tan) and body type (petite, athletic, voluptuous, etc.).

Is beauty universal?

Recent research indicates that preferences for some physical features over others are 'wired in' genetically, and that these reactions tend to be the same among people around the world. Specifically, people appear to favour features associated with good health and youth, attributes linked to reproductive ability and strength. Men

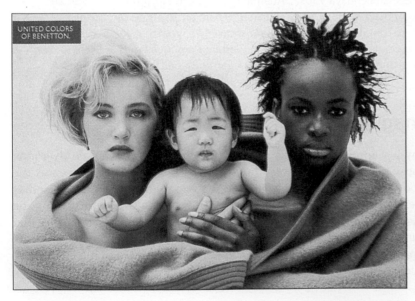

As suggested by this Benetton ad, a global perspective on ideals of beauty is resulting in more ways to be considered attractive.

Photo by Oliviero Toscani for Benetton.

are also more likely to use a woman's body shape as a sexual cue, and it has been theorized that this is because feminine curves provide evidence of reproductive potential. During puberty a typical female gains almost 15 kg of 'reproductive fat' around hips and thighs which supplies the approximately 80,000 extra calories needed for pregnancy. Most fertile women have waist : hip ratios of 0.6 : 0.8, an hourglass shape that happens to be the one men rank highest. Even though preferences for total weight change, waist : hip ratios tend to stay in this range – even the superthin model Twiggy (who pioneered the 'waif' look decades before Kate Moss!) had a ratio of 0.73.[93] Other positively valued female characteristics include a higher forehead than average, fuller lips, a shorter jaw and a smaller chin and nose. Women, on the other hand, favour men with a heavy lower face, those who are slightly above average height and those with a prominent brow.

Of course, the way these faces are 'packaged' still varies enormously, and that's where marketers come in. Advertising and other forms of mass media play a significant role in determining which forms of beauty are considered desirable at any point in time. An ideal of beauty functions as a sort of cultural yardstick. Consumers compare themselves to some standard (often advocated by the fashion media) and are dissatisfied with their appearance to the extent that it doesn't match up to it. These mass media portrayals have been criticized not only on social grounds, but on issues of health as well. In a study of New Zealand print advertisements over the period 1958–88, the findings confirmed that advertising models became thinner and less curvaceous over the 30-year period, resulting in contemporary models being approximately 8.5 kg lighter than they would be if they had the same body shape as models of the late 1950s. To achieve the currently fashionable body shape, a young woman of average height would have to weigh approximately 42 kg, which is far below the recommended level for good health.[94]

Ideals of beauty over time

While beauty may be only skin deep, throughout history and across cultures women in particular have worked very hard to attain it. They have starved themselves, painfully bound their feet, inserted plates into their lips, spent countless hours under hairdryers, in front of mirrors and beneath ultraviolet lights, and have undergone breast reduction or enlargement operations to alter their appearance and meet their society's expectations of what a beautiful woman should look like.

Periods of history tend to be characterized by a specific 'look', or ideal of beauty. American history can be described in terms of a succession of dominant ideals. For example, in sharp contrast to today's emphasis on health and vigour, in the early 1800s it was fashionable to appear delicate to the point of looking ill. The poet John Keats described the ideal woman of that time as 'a milk white lamb that bleats for man's protection'. Other looks have included the voluptuous, lusty woman as epitomized by Lillian Russell, the athletic Gibson Girl of the 1890s, and the small, boyish flapper of the 1920s as exemplified by Clara Bow.[95]

Throughout much of the nineteenth century, the desirable waistline for American women was 18 inches, a circumference that required the use of corsets pulled so tight that they routinely caused headaches, fainting fits, and possibly even the uterine and spinal disorders common among women of the time. While modern women are not quite as 'straitlaced', many still endure such indignities as high heels, body waxing, eye-lifts and liposuction. In addition to the millions spent on cosmetics, clothing, health clubs and fashion magazines, these practices remind us that – rightly or wrongly – the desire to conform to current standards of beauty is alive and well.

The ideal body type of Western women has changed radically over time, and these

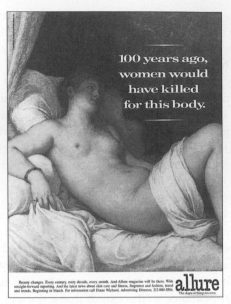

100 years ago, women would have killed for this body.

Beauty changes. Every century, every decade, every month. And Allure magazine will be there. With straight-forward reporting. And the latest news about skin care and fitness, fragrance and fashion, travel and trends. Beginning in March. For information call Diane Wichard, Advertising Director, 212-880-5934.   **allure**   The shape of things to come.

Allure magazine reminds us that ideals of beauty change over time.
Condé Nast Publications, Inc.

changes have resulted in a realignment of *sexual dimorphic markers* – those aspects of the body that distinguish between the sexes. For example, analyses of the measurements of *Playboy* centrefolds over a 20-year period from 1958 to 1978 show that these ideals got thinner and more muscular. The average hip measurement went from 36 inches in 1958 to just over 34 inches in 1978. Average bust size shrank from almost 37 inches in 1958 to about 35 inches in 1978.[96]

The first part of the 1990s saw the emergence of the controversial 'waif' look, where successful models (notably Kate Moss) were likely to have bodies resembling those of young boys. More recently, the pendulum seems to be shifting back a bit, as the more buxom 'hourglass figure' popular in the 1950s (exemplified by the Marilyn Monroe ideal) has reappeared.[97] One factor leading to this change has been the opposition to the use of super-thin models by feminist groups, who charge that these role models encourage starvation diets and eating disorders among women who want to emulate the look.[98] These groups have advocated boycotts against companies like Coca-Cola and Calvin Klein who have used wafer-thin models in their advertising. Some protesters have even taken to pasting stickers over these ads that read 'Feed this woman', or 'Give me a cheeseburger'.

We can also distinguish among ideals of beauty for men in terms of facial features, musculature and facial hair – who could confuse Tom Cruise with Mr Bean? In fact, one recent national survey which asked both men and women to comment on male aspects of appearance found that the dominant standard of beauty for men is a strongly masculine, muscled body – though women tend to prefer men with less muscle mass than men themselves strive to attain.[99] Advertisers appear to have the males' ideal in mind – a recent study of men appearing in advertisements found that most sport the strong and muscular physique of the male stereotype.[100]

Working on the body

Because many consumers are motivated to match up to an ideal appearance, they often go to great lengths to change aspects of their physical selves. From cosmetics to plastic surgery, tanning salons to diet drinks, a multitude of products and services are directed towards altering or maintaining aspects of the physical self in order to

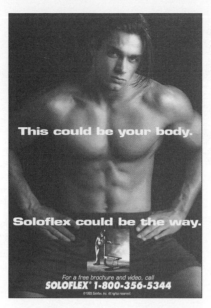

Could this really be your body? Physical self-concept and improving one's appearance are important motivations in consumer behaviour.

present a desirable appearance. It is difficult to overstate the importance of the physical self-concept (and the desire by consumers to improve their appearance) to many marketing activities.

Sizeism

As reflected in the expression 'you can never be too thin or too rich', many Western societies have an obsession with weight. Even primary school children perceive obesity as worse than being disabled.[101] The pressure to be slim is continually reinforced both by advertising and by peers. Americans in particular are preoccupied by what they weigh. They are continually bombarded by images of thin, happy people.

How realistic are these appearance standards? There is a small consumer movement urging people to stop judging people by the pound – a coalition of pro-fat groups holds an International No-Diet Day, and a group in Seattle held a scale-smashing event.[102] Still, many consumers focus on attaining an unrealistic ideal weight, sometimes by relying on height and weight charts which show what one should weigh. These expectations are communicated in subtle ways. Even fashion dolls, such as the ubiquitous Barbie, reinforce the ideal of thinness. The dimensions of these dolls, when extrapolated to average female body sizes, are unnaturally long and thin.[103] In spite of Americans' obsession about weight, as a country they continue to have a greater percentage of obesity in the general population relative to all European countries, as shown in Figure 7.1. Within Europe, Greek, Spanish, British and German men lead the European Union in measures of obesity.[104]

Body image distortions

While many people perceive a strong link between self-esteem and appearance, some consumers unfortunately exaggerate this connection even more, and sacrifice greatly to attain what they consider to be a desirable body image. Women tend to be taught to a greater degree than men that the quality of their bodies reflects their self-worth, so it is not surprising that most major distortions of body image occur among females.

Men do not tend to differ in ratings of their current figure, their ideal figure and the figure they think is most attractive to women. In contrast, women rate both the

Figure 7.1 Body mass index for selected countries

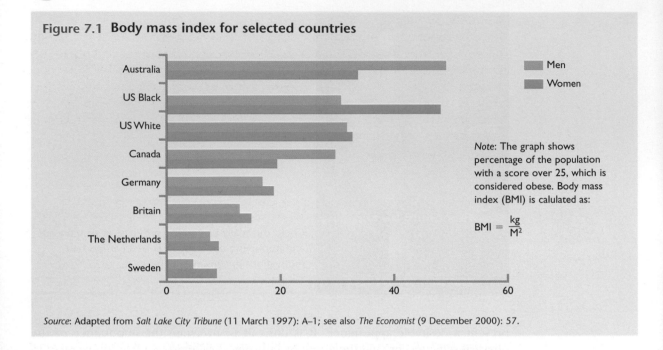

Note: The graph shows percentage of the population with a score over 25, which is considered obese. Body mass index (BMI) is calulated as:

$$BMI = \frac{kg}{M^2}$$

Source: Adapted from *Salt Lake City Tribune* (11 March 1997): A–1; see also *The Economist* (9 December 2000): 57.

figure they think is most attractive to men and their ideal figure as much thinner than their actual figure.[105] In one survey, two-thirds of college women admitted resorting to unhealthy behaviour to control weight. Advertising messages that convey an image of slimness help to reinforce these activities by arousing insecurities about weight.[106]

A distorted body image has been linked to the rise of eating disorders, which are particularly prevalent among young women. People with anorexia regard them-selves as fat, and starve themselves in the quest for thinness. This condition may be accompanied by bulimia, which involves two stages: first, binge eating occurs (usually in private), where more than 5000 calories may be consumed at one time. The binge is then followed by induced vomiting, abuse of laxatives, fasting and/or overly strenuous exercise – a 'purging' process that reasserts the woman's sense of control.

Most eating disorders are found in white, teenaged girls and students. Victims often have brothers or fathers who are hypercritical of their weight. In addition, binge eating may be encouraged by one's peers. Groups such as athletic teams and social clubs at school may develop positive norms regarding binge eating. In one study of a female social club, members' popularity within the group increased the more they binged.[107]

Eating disorders do affect some men as well. They are common among male ath-letes who must also conform to various weight requirements, such as jockeys, boxers and male models.[108] In general, though, most men who have distorted body images consider themselves to be too light rather than too heavy: society has taught them that they must be muscular to be masculine. Men are more likely than women to express their insecurities about their bodies by becoming addicted to exercise. In fact, striking similarities have been found between male compulsive runners and female anorexics. These include a commitment to diet and exercise as a central part of one's identity and susceptibility to body image distortions.[109]

Cosmetic surgery

American consumers are increasingly electing to have cosmetic surgery to change a poor body image.[110] More than half a million cosmetic surgical procedures are performed in the US every year, and this number continues to grow.[111] There is no longer much (if any) psychological stigma associated with having this type of operation: it is commonplace and accepted among many segments of consumers.[112] In fact, men now account for as many as 20 per cent of plastic surgery patients. Popular operations include the implantation of silicon pectoral muscles (for the chest) and even calf implants to fill out 'chicken legs'.[113]

Multicultural dimensions

Belly button reconstruction is now a popular form of cosmetic surgery in Japan, as women strive for the perfect navel they can show off as they wear the midriff fashions now popular there. The navel is an important part of Japanese culture, and mothers often save a baby's umbilical cord. In Japanese, a 'bent navel' is a grouch, and the phrase which would roughly mean 'give me a break' translates as 'yeah, and I brew tea in my belly button'. A popular insult among children: 'Your mother has an outie [protruding belly button].'[114]

Many women turn to surgery either to reduce weight or to increase sexual desirability. The use of liposuction, where fat is removed from the thighs with a vacuum-like device, has almost doubled since it was introduced in the United States in 1982.[115] Some women believe that larger breasts will increase their allure and undergo breast augmentation procedures. Although some of these procedures have generated controversy due to possible negative side effects, it is unclear whether potential medical problems will deter large numbers of women from choosing surgical options to enhance their (perceived) femininity. The importance of breast size to self-concept resulted in an interesting and successful marketing strategy undertaken by an underwear company. While conducting focus groups on bras, an analyst noted that small-chested women typically reacted with hostility when discussing the subject. They would unconsciously cover their chests with their arms as they spoke and felt that their needs were ignored by the fashion industry. To meet this overlooked need, the company introduced a line of A-cup bras called 'A-OK' and depicted wearers in a positive light. A new market segment was born. Other companies are going in the opposite direction by promoting bras that create the illusion of a larger cleavage. In Europe and the US, both Gossard and Playtex are aggressively marketing specially designed bras offering 'cleavage enhancement' which use a combination of wires and internal pads to create the desired effect. Recently, the market for women's bras has had to contend with at least one natural development: unaugmented breasts (no surgery) are getting bigger by themselves, as a result of using the pill and changes in diet. The average cup size in Britain has grown from 34B to 36C over the past 30 years, and bra designers such as Bioform and Airotic, and retailers such as Knickerbox and Victoria's Secret, have all responded with new product offerings to meet what they consider to be a long-term market trend.[116]

Body decoration and mutilation

The body is adorned or altered in some way in every culture. Decorating the self serves a number of purposes.[117]

● *To separate group members from non-members.* The Chinook Indians of North America used to press the head of a newborn baby between two boards for a year,

Multicultural dimensions

Cosmetic surgeons often try to mould their patients into a standard ideal of beauty, using the features of such Caucasian classic beauties as Grace Kelly or Katharine Hepburn as a guide. The aesthetic standard used by surgeons is called the *classic canon*, which spells out the ideal relationships between facial features. For example, it states that the width of the base of the nose should be the same as the distance between the eyes.

However, this standard applies to the Caucasian ideal, and is being revised as people from other ethnic groups are demanding less rigidity in culture's definition of what is beautiful. Some consumers are rebelling against the need to conform to the Western ideal. For example, a rounded face is valued as a sign of beauty by many Asians, and thus giving cheek implants to an Asian patient would remove much of what makes her face attractive.

Some surgeons who work on African-Americans are trying to change the guidelines they use when sculpting features. For example, they argue that an ideal African-American nose is shorter and has a more rounded tip than does a Caucasian nose. Doctors are beginning to diversify their 'product lines', offering consumers a broader assortment of features that better reflect the diversity of cultural ideals of beauty in a heterogeneous society.[118]

Racial differences in beauty ideals also surfaced in a recent study of teenagers. White girls who were asked to describe the 'ideal' girl agreed she should be 5 ft 7 ins, weigh between 45 and 50 kg, and have blue eyes and long, flowing hair – in other words, she should look a lot like a Barbie doll. Almost 90 per cent of the girls in this study said they were dissatisfied with their weight.

In contrast, 70 per cent of the black girls in the same study responded that they were *satisfied* with their weight. They were much less likely to use physical characteristics to describe the ideal girl, instead emphasizing someone who has a personal sense of style and who gets along with others. It was only when prodded that they named such features as fuller hips, large thighs and a small waist, which, the authors of the study say, are attributes valued by black men.[119]

permanently altering its shape. In our society, teenagers go out of their way to adopt distinctive hair and clothing styles that will distinguish them from adults.

● *To place the individual in the social organization*. Many cultures engage in rites of passage at puberty when a boy symbolically becomes a man. Young men in Ghana paint their bodies with white stripes to resemble skeletons to symbolize the death of their child status. In Western culture, this rite may involve some form of mild self-mutilation or engaging in dangerous activities.

● *To place the person in a gender category*. The Tchikrin Indians of South America insert a string of beads in a boy's lip to enlarge it. Western women wear lipstick to enhance femininity. At the turn of the century, small lips were fashionable because they represented women's submissive role at that time.[120] Today, big, red lips are provocative and indicate an aggressive sexuality. Some women, including a number of famous actresses and models, have collagen injections or lip inserts to create large, pouting lips (known in the modelling industry as 'liver lips').[121]

● *To enhance sex-role identification*. Wearing high heels, which podiatrists agree are a prime cause of knee and hip problems, backaches and fatigue, can be compared with the traditional Oriental practice of foot-binding to enhance femininity. As one doctor observed, 'When they [women] get home, they can't get their high-heeled shoes off fast enough. But every doctor in the world could yell from now until Doomsday, and women would still wear them.'[122]

- *To indicate desired social conduct.* The Suya of South America wear ear ornaments to emphasize the importance placed in their culture on listening and obedience. In Western society gay men may wear an earring to signal how they expect to be treated.

- *To indicate high status or rank.* The Hidates Indians of North America wear feather ornaments that indicate how many people they have killed. In our society, some people wear glasses with clear lenses, even though they do not have eye problems, to increase their perceived status.

- *To provide a sense of security.* Consumers often wear lucky charms, amulets, rabbits' feet and so on to protect them from the 'evil eye'. Some modern women wear a 'mugger whistle' around their necks for a similar reason.

Tattoos

Tattoos – both temporary and permanent – are a popular form of body adornment. This body art can be used to communicate aspects of the self to onlookers and may serve some of the same functions that other kinds of body painting do in primitive cultures. In fact, much of the recent literature and discourse on tattoos centres on the theme of users as 'Modern Primitives'.[123] Tattoos (from the Tahitian *ta-tu*) have deep roots in folk art. Until recently, the images were crude and were primarily either death symbols (e.g. a skull), animals (especially panthers, eagles and snakes), pin-up women or military designs. More current influences include science fiction themes, Japanese symbolism and tribal designs.

A tattoo may be viewed as a fairly risk-free (?) way of expressing an adventurous side of the self. Tattoos have a long history of association with people who are social outcasts. For example, the faces and arms of criminals in sixth-century Japan were tattooed as a way of identifying them, as were Massachusetts prison inmates in the nineteenth century. These emblems are often used by marginal groups, such as bikers or Japanese *yakuze* (gang members), to express group identity and solidarity.

Body piercing

Decorating the body with various kinds of metallic inserts has evolved from a practice associated with some fringe groups to become a popular fashion statement.

Body decoration can be permanent, or (hopefully!) temporary, in order to distinguish oneself, shock others, signify group membership, or express a particular mood or message.

Piercings can range from a hoop protruding from a navel to scalp implants, where metal posts are inserted in the skull (do not try this at home!). Publications such as *Piercing Fans International Quarterly* are seeing their circulations soar and websites featuring piercings and piercing products are attracting numerous followers. This popularity is not pleasing to hard-core piercing fans, who view the practice as a sensual consciousness-raising ritual and are concerned that now people just do it because it's trendy. As one customer waiting for a piercing remarked, 'If your piercing doesn't mean anything, then it's just like buying a pair of platform shoes.'[124]

Chapter summary

- Consumers' *self-concepts* are reflections of their attitudes towards themselves. Whether these attitudes are positive or negative, they will help to guide many purchase decisions; products can be used to bolster self-esteem or to 'reward' the self.

- Many product choices are dictated by the similarity the consumer perceives between his or her personality and attributes of the product. The *symbolic interactionist perspective* on the self implies that each of us actually has many selves, and a different set of products is required as props to play each. Many things other than the body can also be viewed as part of the self. Valued objects, car, homes and even attachments to sports teams or national monuments are used to define the self, when these are incorporated into the extended self.

- A person's *sex-role identity* is a major component of self-definition. Conceptions about masculinity and femininity, largely shaped by society, guide the acquisition of 'sex-typed' products and services.

- Advertising and other media play an important role in socializing consumers to be male and female. While traditional women's roles have often been perpetuated in advertising depictions, this situation is changing somewhat. The media do not always portray men accurately either.

- Sometimes these activities are carried to an extreme, as people try too hard to live up to cultural ideals. One example is found in eating disorders, where women in particular become obsessed with thinness.

- A person's conception of his or her body also provides feedback to self-image. A culture communicates certain ideals of beauty, and consumers go to great lengths to attain these. Many consumer activities involve manipulating the body, whether through dieting, cosmetic surgery, tattooing, or so forth.

KEY TERMS

Actual self (*p. 191*)
Agentic goals (*p. 198*)
Androgyny (*p. 199*)
Body cathexis (*p. 206*)
Body image (*p. 205*)
Communal goals (*p. 198*)
Extended self (*p. 196*)
Fantasy (*p. 191*)
Ideal of beauty (*p. 206*)

Ideal self (*p. 191*)
Looking-glass self (*p. 193*)
Self-concept (*p. 190*)
Self-image congruence models
   (*p. 195*)
Sex-typed traits (*p. 198*)
Symbolic interactionism (*p. 193*)
Symbolic self-completion theory
   (*p. 194*)

For additional material see the companion website at:
www.booksites.net/solomon_euro

Consumer behaviour challenge

1. How might the creation of a self-conscious state be related to consumers who are trying on clothing in changing rooms? Does the act of preening in front of a mirror change the dynamics by which people evaluate their product choices? Why?

2. Is it ethical for marketers to encourage infatuation with the self?

3. List three dimensions by which the self-concept can be described.

4. Compare and contrast the real vs. the ideal self. List three products for which each type of self is likely to be used as a reference point when a purchase is considered.

5. Watch a series of ads featuring men and women on television. Try to imagine the characters with reversed roles (i.e. the male parts played by women, and vice versa). Can you see any differences in assumptions about sex-typed behaviour?

6. To date, the bulk of advertising targeted at gay consumers has been placed in exclusively gay media. If it was your decision, would you consider using mainstream media to reach gays, who constitute a significant proportion of the general population? Or, bearing in mind that members of some targeted segments have serious objection to this practice, especially when the product (e.g. alcohol, cigarettes) may be viewed as harmful in some way, do you think gays should be singled out at all by marketers?

7. Do you agree that marketing strategies tend to have a male-oriented bias? If so, what are some possible consequences for specific marketing activities?

8. Construct a 'consumption biography' of a friend or family member. Make a list and/or photograph his or her favourite possessions, and see if you or others can describe this person's personality just from the information provided by this catalogue.

9. Some consumer advocates have protested at the use of super-thin models in advertising, claiming that these women encourage others to starve themselves in order to attain the 'waif' look. Other critics respond that the media's power to shape behaviour has been overestimated, and that it is insulting to people to assume that they are unable to separate fantasy from reality. What do you think?

Notes

1. Daniel Goleman, 'When Ugliness is Only in Patient's Eye, Body Image Can Reflect Mental Disorder', *New York Times* (2 October 1991): C13.
2. Harry C. Triandis, 'The Self and Social Behavior in Differing Cultural Contexts', *Psychological Review* 96 (1989) 3: 506–20; H. Markus and S. Kitayamak, 'Culture and the Self: Implications for Cognition, Emotion, and Motivation', *Psychological Review* 98 (1991): 224–53.
3. Markus and Kitayama, 'Culture and the Self': 224–53.
4. Nancy Wong and Aaron Ahuvia, 'A Cross-Cultural Approach to Materialism and the Self', in Dominique Bouchet, ed., *Cultural Dimensions of International Marketing* (Odense University, Denmark, 1995): 68–89.
5. Lisa M. Keefe, 'You're so Vain', *Marketing News* (28 February 2000): 8.

6. Anthony G. Greenwald and Mahzarin R. Banaji, 'The Self as a Memory System: Powerful, but Ordinary', *Journal of Personality and Social Psychology* 57 (1989)1: 41–54; Hazel Markus, 'Self Schemata and Processing Information About the Self', *Journal of Personality and Social Psychology* 35 (1977): 63–78.

7. Morris Rosenberg, *Conceiving the Self* (New York: Basic Books, 1979); M. Joseph Sirgy, 'Self-Concept in Consumer Behavior: A Critical Review', *Journal of Consumer Research* 9 (December 1982): 287–300.

8. Emily Yoffe, 'You Are What You Buy', *Newsweek* (4 June 1990): 59.

9. Roy F. Baumeister, Dianne M. Tice and Debra G. Hutton, 'Self-Presentational Motivations and Personality Differences in Self-Esteem', *Journal of Personality* 57 (September 1989): 547–75; Ronald J. Faber, 'Are Self-Esteem Appeals Appealing?', *Proceedings of the 1992 Conference of the American Academy of Advertising*, ed. Leonard N. Reid (1992): 230–5.

10. B. Bradford Brown and Mary Jane Lohr, 'Peer-Group Affiliation and Adolescent Self-Esteem: An Integration of Ego Identity and Symbolic-Interaction Theories', *Journal of Personality and Social Psychology* 52 (1987) 1: 47–55.

11. Marsha L. Richins, 'Social Comparison and the Idealized Images of Advertising', *Journal of Consumer Research* 18 (June 1991): 71–83; Mary C. Martin and Patricia F. Kennedy, 'Advertising and Social Comparison: Consequences for Female Preadolescents and Adolescents', *Psychology & Marketing* 10 (November/December 1993) 6: 513–30.

12. Philip N. Myers, Jr and Frank A. Biocca, 'The Elastic Body Image: The Effect of Television Advertising and Programming on Body Image Distortions in Young Women', *Journal of Communication* 42 (Summer 1992): 108–33.

13. Jeffrey F. Durgee, 'Self-Esteem Advertising', *Journal of Advertising* 14 (1986) 4: 21.

14. Ernest Dichter, *Handbook of Consumer Motivations* (New York: McGraw-Hill, 1964).

15. Sigmund Freud, *New Introductory Lectures in Psychoanalysis* (New York: Norton, 1965).

16. Harrison G. Gough, Mario Fioravanti and Renato Lazzari, 'Some Implications of Self versus Ideal-Self Congruence on the Revised Adjective Check List', *Journal of Personality and Social Psychology* 44 (1983) 6: 1214–20.

17. Steven Jay Lynn and Judith W. Rhue, 'Daydream Believers', *Psychology Today* (September 1985): 14.

18. Bruce Headlam, 'Ultimate Product Placement: Your Face Behind the Ray-Bans', *New York Times* (25 June 1998): E4.

19. Erving Goffman, *The Presentation of Self in Everyday Life* (Garden City, NY: Doubleday, 1959); Michael R. Solomon, 'The Role of Products as Social Stimuli: A Symbolic Interactionism Perspective', *Journal of Consumer Research* 10 (December 1983): 319–29.

20. Julie Skur Hill, 'Purchasing Habits Shift for Execs', *Advertising Age* (27 April 1992): 1–16.

21. George H. Mead, *Mind, Self and Society* (Chicago: University of Chicago Press, 1934).

22. Charles H. Cooley, *Human Nature and the Social Order* (New York: Scribner's, 1902).

23. J. G. Hull and A. S. Levy, 'The Organizational Functions of the Self: An Alternative to the Duval and Wicklund Model of Self-Awareness', *Journal of Personality and Social Psychology* 37 (1979): 756–68; Jay G. Hull, Ronald R. Van Treuren, Susan J. Ashford, Pamela Propsom and Bruce W. Andrus, 'Self-Consciousness and the Processing of Self-Relevant Information', *Journal of Personality and Social Psychology* 54 (1988) 3: 452–65.

24. Arnold W. Buss, *Self-Consciousness and Social Anxiety* (San Francisco: W. H. Freeman, 1980); Lynn Carol Miller and Cathryn Leigh Cox, 'Public Self-Consciousness and Makeup Use', *Personality and Social Psychology Bulletin* 8 (1982) 4: 748–51; Michael R. Solomon and John Schopler, 'Self-Consciousness and Clothing', *Personality and Social Psychology Bulletin* 8 (1982) 3: 508–14.

25. Morris B. Holbrook, Michael R. Solomon and Stephen Bell, 'A Re-Examination of Self-Monitoring and Judgments of Furniture Designs', *Home Economics Research Journal* 19 (September 1990): 6–16; Mark Snyder and Steve Gangestad, 'On the Nature of Self-Monitoring: Matters of Assessment, Matters of Validity', *Journal of Personality and Social Psychology* 51 (1986): 125–39.

26. Snyder and Gangestad, 'On the Nature of Self-Monitoring'.

27. Timothy R. Graeff, 'Image Congruence Effects on Product Evaluations: The Role of Self-Monitoring and Public/Private Consumption', *Psychology & Marketing* 13(5) (August 1996): 481–99.

28. Richard G. Netemeyer, Scot Burton and Donald R. Lichtenstein, 'Trait Aspects of Vanity: Measurement and Relevance to Consumer Behavior', *Journal of Consumer Research* 21 (March 1995): 612–26.

29. Michael R. Solomon and Henry Assael, 'The Forest or the Trees?: A Gestalt Approach to Symbolic Consumption', in Jean Umiker-Sebeok, ed., *Marketing and Semiotics: New Directions in the Study of Signs for Sale* (Berlin: Mouton de Gruyter, 1987): 189–218.

30. Jack L. Nasar, 'Symbolic Meanings of House Styles', *Environment and Behavior* 21 (May 1989): 235–57; E. K. Sadalla, B. Verschure and J. Burroughs, 'Identity Symbolism in Housing', *Environment and Behavior* 19 (1987): 599–87.

31. Michael R. Solomon, 'The Role of Products as Social Stimuli: A Symbolic Interactionism Perspective', *Journal of Consumer Research* 10 (December

1983): 319-28; Robert E. Kleine III, Susan Schultz-Kleine and Jerome B. Kernan, 'Mundane Consumption and the Self: A Social-Identity Perspective', *Journal of Consumer Psychology* 2 (1993) 3: 209-35; Newell D. Wright, C. B. Claiborne and M. Joseph Sirgy, 'The Effects of Product Symbolism on Consumer Self-Concept', in John F. Sherry, Jr and Brian Sternthal, eds, *Advances in Consumer Research* 19 (Provo, UT: Association for Consumer Research, 1992): 311-18; Susan Fournier, 'A Person-Based Relationship Framework for Strategic Brand Management', PhD dissertation, University of Florida, 1994.

32. A. Dwayne Ball and Lori H. Tasaki, 'The Role and Measurement of Attachment in Consumer Behavior', *Journal of Consumer Psychology* 1 (1992) 2: 155-72.

33. William B. Hansen and Irwin Altman, 'Decorating Personal Places: A Descriptive Analysis', *Environment and Behavior* 8 (December 1976): 491-504.

34. R. A. Wicklund and P. M. Gollwitzer, *Symbolic Self-Completion* (Hillsdale, NJ: Lawrence Erlbaum, 1982).

35. Erving Goffman, *Asylums* (New York: Doubleday, 1961).

36. Quoted in Floyd Rudmin, 'Property Crime Victimization Impact on Self, on Attachment, and on Territorial Dominance', *CPA Highlights, Victims of Crime Supplement* 9 (1987) 2: 4-7.

37. Barbara B. Brown, 'House and Block as Territory', paper presented at the Conference of the Association for Consumer Research, San Francisco, 1982.

38. Quoted in Shay Sayre and David Horne, 'I Shop, Therefore I Am: The Role of Possessions for Self Definition', in Shay Sayre and David Horne, eds, *Earth, Wind, and Fire and Water: Perspectives on Natural Disaster* (Pasadena, CA: Open Door Publishers, 1996): 353-70.

39. Deborah A. Prentice, 'Psychological Correspondence of Possessions, Attitudes, and Values', *Journal of Personality and Social Psychology* 53 (1987) 6: 993-1002.

40. Sak Onkvisit and John Shaw, 'Self-Concept and Image Congruence: Some Research and Managerial Implications', *Journal of Consumer Marketing* 4 (Winter 1987): 13-24. For a related treatment of congruence between advertising appeals and self-concept, see George M. Zinkhan and Jae W. Hong, 'Self-Concept and Advertising Effectiveness: A Conceptual Model of Congruency, Conspicuousness, and Response Mode', in Rebecca H. Holman and Michael R. Solomon, eds, *Advances in Consumer Research* 18 (Provo, UT: Association for Consumer Research, 1991): 348-54.

41. C. B. Claiborne and M. Joseph Sirgy, 'Self-Image Congruence as a Model of Consumer Attitude Formation and Behavior: A Conceptual Review and Guide for Further Research', paper presented at the Academy of Marketing Science Conference, New Orleans, 1990.

42. Liz Hunt, 'Rise in Infertility Linked to Craze for Body Building', *The Independent* (12 July 1995): 12.

43. Al E. Birdwell, 'A Study of Influence of Image Congruence on Consumer Choice', *Journal of Business* 41 (January 1964): 76-88; Edward L. Grubb and Gregg Hupp, 'Perception of Self, Generalized Stereotypes, and Brand Selection', *Journal of Marketing Research* 5 (February 1986): 58-63.

44. Ira J. Dolich, 'Congruence Relationship Between Self-Image and Product Brands', *Journal of Marketing Research* 6 (February 1969): 80-4; Danny N. Bellenger, Earle Steinberg and Wilbur W. Stanton, 'The Congruence of Store Image and Self Image as it Relates to Store Loyalty', *Journal of Retailing* 52 (1976) 1: 17-32; Ronald J. Dornoff and Ronald L. Tatham, 'Congruence between Personal Image and Store Image', *Journal of the Market Research Society* 14 (1972) 1: 45-52.

45. Naresh K. Malhotra, 'A Scale to Measure Self-Concepts, Person Concepts, and Product Concepts', *Journal of Marketing Research* 18 (November 1981): 456-64.

46. Ernest Beaglehole, *Property: A Study in Social Psychology* (New York: Macmillan, 1932).

47. M. Csikszentmihalyi and Eugene Rochberg Halton, *The Meaning of Things: Domestic Symbols and the Self* (Cambridge, MA: Cambridge University Press, 1981).

48. Russell W. Belk, 'Possessions and the Extended Self', *Journal of Consumer Research* 15 (September 1988): 139-68.

49. Janeen Arnold Costa, 'Introduction', in J. A. Costa, ed., *Gender Issues and Consumer Behavior* (Thousand Oaks: Sage Publications, 1994).

50. Joan Meyers Levy, 'The Influence of Sex Roles on Judgment', *Journal of Consumer Research* 14 (March 1988): 522-30.

51. Kimberly J. Dodson and Russell W. Belk, 'Gender in Children's Birthday Stories', in Janeen Costa, ed., *Gender, Marketing, and Consumer Behavior* (Salt Lake City, UT: Association for Consumer Research, 1996): 96-108.

52. Elizabeth C. Hirschman, 'A Feminist Critique of Marketing Theory: Toward Agentic-Communal Balance', working paper, School of Business, Rutgers University, New Brunswick, NJ, 1990.

53. Eileen Fischer and Stephen J. Arnold, 'Sex, Gender Identity, Gender Role Attitudes, and Consumer Behavior', *Psychology & Marketing* 11 (March/April 1994) 2: 163-82.

54. Kathleen Debevec and Easwar Iyer, 'Sex Roles and Consumer Perceptions of Promotions, Products, and Self: What Do We Know and Where Should We Be Headed', in Richard J. Lutz, ed., *Advances in*

Consumer Research 13 (Provo, UT: Association for Consumer Research, 1986): 210–14; Joseph A. Bellizzi and Laura Milner, 'Gender Positioning of a Traditionally Male-Dominant Product', *Journal of Advertising Research* (June/July 1991): 72–9.

55. Janeen Arnold Costa and Teresa M. Pavia, 'Alpha-Numeric Brand Names and Gender Stereotypes', *Research in Consumer Behavior* 6 (1993): 85–112.

56. Helga Dittmar, Jane Beattie and Susanne Friese, 'Gender Identity and Material Symbols: Objects and Decision Considerations in Impulse Purchases', *Journal of Economic Psychology* 16 (1995): 491–511; Jason Cox and Helga Dittmar, 'The Functions of Clothes and Clothing (Dis)Satisfaction: A Gender Analysis Among British Students', *Journal of Consumer Policy* 18 (1995): 237–65.

57. Sandra L. Bem, 'The Measurement of Psychological Androgyny', *Journal of Consulting and Clinical Psychology* 42 (1974): 155–62; Deborah E. S. Frable, 'Sex Typing and Gender Ideology: Two Facets of the Individual's Gender Psychology That Go Together', *Journal of Personality and Social Psychology* 56 (1989) 1: 95–108.

58. See D. Bruce Carter and Gary D. Levy, 'Cognitive Aspects of Early Sex-Role Development: The Influence of Gender Schemas on Preschoolers' Memories and Preferences for Sex-Typed Toys and Activities', *Child Development* 59 (1988): 782–92; Bernd H. Schmitt, France Le Clerc and Laurette Dube-Rioux, 'Sex Typing and Consumer Behavior: A Test of Gender Schema Theory', *Journal of Consumer Research* 15 (June 1988): 122–7.

59. Carol Gilligan, *In a Different Voice: Psychological Theory and Women's Development* (Cambridge, MA: Harvard University Press, 1982); Joan Meyers-Levy and Durairaj Maheswaran, 'Exploring Differences in Males' and Females' Processing Strategies', *Journal of Consumer Research* 18 (June 1991): 63–70.

60. Lynn J. Jaffe and Paul D. Berger, 'Impact on Purchase Intent of Sex-Role Identity and Product Positioning', *Psychology & Marketing* (Fall 1988): 259–71; Lynn J. Jaffe, 'The Unique Predictive Ability of Sex-Role Identity in Explaining Women's Response to Advertising', *Psychology & Marketing* 11 (September/October 1994) 5: 467–82.

61. Leila T. Worth, Jeanne Smith and Diane M. Mackie, 'Gender Schematicity and Preference for Gender-Typed Products', *Psychology & Marketing* 9 (January 1992): 17–30.

62. Julie Candler, 'Woman Car Buyer – Don't Call Her a Niche Anymore', *Advertising Age* (21 January 1991): S-8; see also Robin Widgery and Jack McGaugh, 'Vehicle Message Appeals and the New Generation Woman', *Journal of Advertising Research* (September/October 1993): 36–42; Blayne Cutler, 'Condom Mania', *American Demographics* (June 1989): 17.

63. Laurel Anderson and Marsha Wadkins, 'The New Breed in Japan: Consumer Culture', unpublished manuscript, Arizona State University, Tempe, 1990; Doris L. Walsh, 'A Familiar Story', *American Demographics* (June 1987): 64.

64. B. Abrams, 'American Express is Gearing New Ad Campaign to Women', *Wall Street Journal* (4 August 1983): 23.

65. 'Ads' Portrayal of Women Today is Hardly Innovative', *Marketing News* (6 November 1989): 12; Jill Hicks Ferguson, Peggy J. Kreshel and Spencer F. Tinkham, 'In the Pages of *Ms*.: Sex Role Portrayals of Women in Advertising', *Journal of Advertising* 19 (1990) 1: 40–51.

66. Richard Elliott, Abigail Jones, Andrew Benfield and Matt Barlow, 'Overt Sexuality in Advertising: A Discourse Analysis of Gender Responses', *Journal of Consumer Policy* 18 (1995): 187–217. Sonia Livingstone and Gloria Greene, 'Television Advertisements and the Portrayal of Gender', *British Journal of Social Psychology* 25 (1986): 149–54; for one of the original articles on this topic, see L. Z. McArthur and B. G. Resko, 'The Portrayal of Men and Women in American Television Commercials', *Journal of Social Psychology* 97 (1975): 209–20.

67. Richard Edel, 'American Dream Vendors', *Advertising Age* (9 November 1988): 153.

68. Stuart Elliott, 'Avon Products is Abandoning Its Old-Fashioned Image in an Appeal to Contemporary Women', *New York Times* (27 April 1993): D21.

69. Daniel J. Brett and Joanne Cantor, 'The Portrayal of Men and Women in U.S. Television Commercials: A Recent Content Analysis and Trends Over 15 Years', *Sex Roles* 18 (1988): 595–609.

70. Kyle Pope, 'High-Tech Marketers Try to Attract Women Without Causing Offense', *Wall Street Journal* (17 March 1994): B1 (2).

71. Gordon Sumner, 'Tribal Rites of the American Male', *Marketing Insights* (Summer 1989): 13.

72. Margaret G. Maples, 'Beefcake Marketing: The Sexy Sell', *Marketing Communications* (April 1983): 21–5.

73. Jim Carlton, 'Hair-Dye Makers, Sensing a Shift, Step Up Campaigns Aimed at Men', *Wall Street Journal Interactive Edition* (17 January 2000); Yochi Dreazen, (no headline), *Wall Street Journal Interactive Edition* (8 June 1999); Cyndee Miller, 'Cosmetics Makers to Men: Paint Those Nails', *Marketing News* (12 May 1997): 14 (2).

74. Yumiko Ono, (no headline), *Wall Street Journal Interactive Edition* (11 March 1999).

75. 'Changing Conceptions of Fatherhood', *USA Today* (May 1988): 10.

76. Quoted in Kim Foltz, 'In Ads, Men's Image Becomes Softer', *New York Times* (26 March 1990): D12.

77. Quoted in Jennifer Foote, 'The Ad World's New Bimbos', *Newsweek* (25 January 1988): 44.

78. Maples, 'Beefcake Marketing'.

79. Quoted in Lynn G. Coleman, 'What Do People Really Lust After in Ads?', *Marketing News* (6 November 1989): 12.

80. Riccardo A. Davis, 'Marketers Game for Gay Events', *Advertising Age* (30 May 1994): S-1 (2); Cyndee Miller, 'Top Marketers Take Bolder Approach in Targeting Gays', *Marketing News* (4 July 1994): 1 (2); see also Douglas L. Fugate, 'Evaluating the US Male Homosexual and Lesbian Population as a Viable Target Market Segment', *Journal of Consumer Marketing* 10 (1993) 4: 46–57; Laura M. Milner, 'Marketing to Gays and Lesbians: A Review', unpublished manuscript, the University of Alaska, 1990.

81. Kate Fitzgerald, 'IKEA Dares to Reveal Gays Buy Tables, Too', *Advertising Age* (28 March 1994): 3(2); Miller, 'Top Marketers Take Bolder Approach in Targeting Gays': 1(2); Paula Span, 'ISO the Gay Consumer', *Washington Post* (19 May 1994): D1 (2).

82. Kate Fitzgerald, 'AT&T Addresses Gay Market', *Advertising Age* (16 May 1994): 8.

83. James S. Hirsch, 'New Credit Cards Base Appeals on Sexual Orientation and Race', *Wall Street Journal* (6 November 1995): B1 (2).

84. Projections of the incidence of homosexuality in the general population are often influenced by assumptions of the researchers, as well as the methodology they employ (e.g. self-report, behavioural measures, fantasy measures). For a discussion of these factors, see Edward O. Laumann, John H. Gagnon, Robert T. Michael and Stuart Michaels, *The Social Organization of Homosexuality* (Chicago: University of Chicago Press, 1994).

85. Lisa Peñaloza, 'We're Here, We're Queer, and We're Going Shopping! A Critical Perspective on the Accommodation of Gays and Lesbians in the U.S. Marketplace', *Journal of Homosexuality* 31(1/2) (1966): 9–41.

86. D. L. Fugate, 'Evaluating the U.S. Male Homosexual and Lesbian Population as a Viable Target Market Segment: A Review with Implications', *Journal of Consumer Marketing* 10 (4) (1993): 46–57. See also Laumann, Gagnon, Michael and Michaels, *The Social Organization of Homosexuality*.

87. Laura Koss-Feder, 'Out and About', *Marketing News* (25 May 1998): 1(2); Rachel X. Weissman, 'Gay Market Power', *American Demographics* 21 (June 1999) 6: 32–3.

88. Peñaloza, 'We're Here, We're Queer, and We're Going Shopping!'

89. Michael Wilke, 'Subaru Adds Lesbians to Niche Marketing Drive', *Advertising Age* (4 March 1996): 8.

90. Dennis W. Rook, 'Body Cathexis and Market Segmentation', in Michael R. Solomon, ed., *The Psychology of Fashion* (Lexington, MA: Lexington Books, 1985): 233–41.

91. 'Nederlandse vrouw krijt lachend rimpels', *De Telegraaf* (26 April 1997): TA5.

92. Jane E. Brody, 'Notions of Beauty Transcend Culture, New Study Suggests', *New York Times* (21 March 1994): A14.

93. Geoffrey Cowley, 'The Biology of Beauty', *Newsweek* (3 June 1996): 61–6.

94. Michael Fay and Christopher Price, 'Female Body-Shape in Print Advertisements and the Increase in Anorexia Nervosa', *European Journal of Marketing* 28 (1994): 12.

95. Lois W. Banner, *American Beauty* (Chicago: The University of Chicago Press, 1980); for a philosophical perspective, see Barry Vacker and Wayne R. Key, 'Beauty *and* the Beholder: The Pursuit of Beauty Through Commodities', *Psychology & Marketing* (10 November/ December 1993) 6: 471–94.

96. David M. Garner, Paul E. Garfinkel, Donald Schwartz and Michael Thompson, 'Cultural Expectations of Thinness in Women', *Psychological Reports* 47 (1980): 483–91.

97. Kathleen Boyes, 'The New Grip of Girdles is Lightened by Lycra', *USA Today* (25 April 1991): 6D.

98. Stuart Elliott, 'Ultrathin Models in Coca-Cola and Calvin Klein Campaigns Draw Fire and a Boycott Call', *New York Times* (26 April 1994): D18; Cyndee Miller, 'Give Them a Cheeseburger', *Marketing News* (6 June 1994): 1 (2).

99. Jill Neimark, 'The Beefcaking of America', *Psychology Today* (November/December 1994): 32 (11).

100. Richard H. Kolbe and Paul J. Albanese, 'Man to Man: A Content Analysis of Sole-Male Images in Male-Audience Magazines', *Journal of Advertising* 25(4) (Winter 1996): 1–20.

101. 'Girls at 7 Think Thin, Study Finds', *New York Times* (11 February 1988): B9.

102. Sarah McBride, 'Turn On! Tune In! Eat Up!: Antidiet Trend Gets Militant', *Wall Street Journal Interactive Edition* (2 May 1997).

103. Elaine L. Pedersen and Nancy L. Markee, 'Fashion Dolls: Communicators of Ideals of Beauty and Fashion', paper presented at the International Conference on Marketing Meaning, Indianapolis, IN, 1989; Dalma Heyn, 'Body Hate', *Ms.* (August 1989): 34; Mary C. Martin and James W. Gentry, 'Assessing the Internalization of Physical Attractiveness Norms', *Proceedings of the American Marketing Association Summer Educators' Conference* (Summer 1994): 59–65.

104. 'So Germans can be gourmets too', *The Economist* (9 December 2000): 57. See also The European Commission, and Eurostat.

105. Debra A. Zellner, Debra F. Harner and Robbie I. Adler, 'Effects of Eating Abnormalities and Gender on Perceptions of Desirable Body Shape', *Journal of Abnormal Psychology* 98 (February 1989): 93–6.

106. Robin T. Peterson, 'Bulimia and Anorexia in an Advertising Context', *Journal of Business Ethics* 6 (1987): 495–504.

107. Christian S. Crandall, 'Social Contagion of Binge Eating', *Journal of Personality and Social Psychology* 55 (1988): 588–98.

108. Judy Folkenberg, 'Bulimia: Not For Women Only', *Psychology Today* (March 1984): 10.

109. Eleanor Grant, 'The Exercise Fix: What Happens When Fitness Fanatics Just Can't Say No?', *Psychology Today* 22 (February 1988): 24.

110. John W. Schouten, 'Selves in Transition: Symbolic Consumption in Personal Rites of Passage and Identity Reconstruction', *Journal of Consumer Research* 17 (March 1991): 412–25.

111. Monica Gonzalez, 'Want a Lift?', *American Demographics* (February 1988): 20.

112. Annette C. Hamburger and Holly Hall, 'Beauty Quest', *Psychology Today* (May 1988): 28.

113. Emily Yoffe, 'Valley of the Silicon Dolls', *Newsweek* (26 November 1990): 72.

114. Norihiko Shirouzu, 'Reconstruction Boom in Tokyo: Perfecting Imperfect Bellybuttons', *Wall Street Journal* (4 October 1995): B1.

115. Keith Greenberg, 'What's Hot: Cosmetic Surgery', *Public Relations Journal* (June 1988): 23.

116. 'Bra Wars', *The Economist* (2 December 2000): 64.

117. Ruth P. Rubinstein, 'Color, Circumcision, Tattoos, and Scars', in Solomon, ed., *The Psychology of Fashion*: 243–54; Peter H. Bloch and Marsha L. Richins, 'You Look "Mahvelous": The Pursuit of Beauty and Marketing Concept', *Psychology & Marketing* 9 (January 1992): 3–16.

118. Kathy H. Merrell, 'Saving Faces', *Allure* (January 1994): 66 (2).

119. 'White Weight', *Psychology Today* (September/October 1994): 9.

120. Sondra Farganis, 'Lip Service: The Evolution of Pouting, Pursing, and Painting Lips Red', *Health* (November 1988): 48–51.

121. Michael Gross, 'Those Lips, Those Eyebrows: New Face of 1989 (New Look of Fashion Models)', *New York Times Magazine* (13 February 1989): 24.

122. Quoted in 'High Heels: Ecstasy's Worth the Agony', *New York Post* (31 December 1981).

123. Mike Featherstone, ed., *Body Modification* (Thousand Oaks, CA: Sage Publications, Inc., 2000); Anne M. Velliquette, and Jeff B. Murray, 'The New Tattoo Subculture', in *Mapping the Social Landscape: Readings in Sociology*, ed. Susan Ferguson (Mountain View, CA: Mayfield Publishing Company, 1999): 56–68; Anne M. Velliquette, Jeff B. Murray and Elizabeth H. Creyer, 'The Tattoo Renaissance: An Ethnographic Account of Symbolic Consumer Behavior', in *Advances in Consumer Research* 25, ed. Joseph W. Alba and J. Wesley Hutchinson (Provo, UT: Association for Consumer Research, 1998): 461–7; Anne M. Velliquette, 'Modern Primitives: The Role of Product Symbolism in Lifestyle Cultures and Identity', dissertation, University of Arkansas Press, 2000; Margo DeMello, *Bodies of Inscription: A Cultural History of the Modern Tattoo Community* (Durham, NC: Duke University Press, 2000; Anne Veliquette and Gary Bamossy, 'Modern Primitives: The Role of the Body and Product Symbolism in Lifestyle Cultures and Identity' (Association for Consumer Research, Berlin, 20–23 June 2001, forthcoming).

124. Quoted in Wendy Bounds, 'Body-Piercing Gets Under America's Skin', *Wall Street Journal* (4 April 1994): B1 (2), B4.

CASE STUDY 1

Attention to and perception of cinema commercials

CHRISTIAN ALSTED, Alsted Marketing Research, Copenhagen

In a recent survey carried out among Danish cinema-goers it was demonstrated that 93 per cent of them were seated before the first commercial was shown. Also, on-going research has demonstrated much higher recall and understanding of basic intended messages in cinema advertising than in TV commercials. In short, Danish cinema-goers love to watch the commercials before a movie, which is not the case for TV commercials. Therefore it is likely that commercials aired in cinemas have much more potential for influencing viewers than TV commercials have. Up until now, no explanations of this phenomenon had been provided.

In an attempt to clarify this issue, six measures were made of certain commercials which were aired for the first time simultaneously in cinemas and on TV. In addition to a simple ad recollection test, the quality of respondents' memory was measured. Did respondents understand the messages of the commercials? Results from these measurements indicate that cinema commercials have three times the communication value of their TV-aired counterparts (see Figure 1).

The survey thus demonstrated that audiences in cinemas are mentally more ready to process new stimuli. It was also shown that this cinema context has a positive effect on the commercials in the cinemas. Viewing commercials in cinemas is a part of the overall 'cinema experience' and a conscious or subconscious transfer occurs

Figure 1
Communication value, 13–29-year-olds: comparison between six commercials shown on television and in the cinema

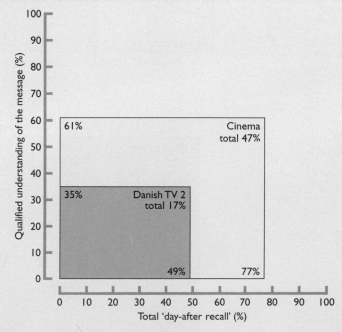

Cinema has 2.8 times better communication value than television

CASE STUDY 1 continued

from viewers' positive expectations towards the movie they are about to see, to the commercial.

When it was subsequently qualitatively examined which specific qualities viewers associate with cinema commercials, six different values were detected: high quality, opening, entertainment, actions, novelty, luxury. The positive associations with cinema commercials are transferred to the advertised products. In other words the products advertised are met with a positive attitude and can rely on a positive initial reception by viewers.

When the lights go out and the commercials start, an instant and drastic increase in attention among the audience can be observed (see Figure 2). This heightened attention reaches its first peak in the beginning of the set of commercials and then flattens out. This contrasts with the attention pattern found with TV commercials where attention is more fragmented. With TV it is more a case of floating peaks and troughs in the attention of the audience (see Figure 3).

**Figure 2
Excitement
curve/arousal –
cinema**

*Source: Cinema Quality –
Alsted Research*, Spring
1994

**Figure 3
Excitement
curve/arousal –
television**

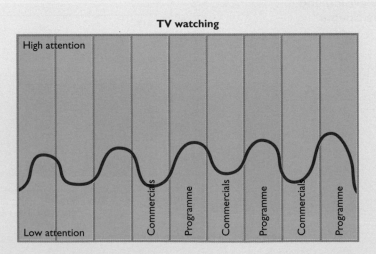

*Source: Cinema Quality –
Alsted Research*, Spring
1994

Going to the cinema is seen as an 'event', and viewing the advertisements is considered as part of this event. This is important because 'events' are associated with positive expectations. The event itself can be split into three parts (Figure 2). First there is the warm-up with commercials. Then trailers ensue which are also important. They are seen less as 'commercials' for coming films and more as 'appetisers' of coming cultural events. Finally, there is the film. In this tripartite construct all parts are important. Young people, in particular, see commercials and trailers as a good warm-up to the film. Many young people perceive cinema commercials as good entertainment and link the fact of advertising in the cinema to a luxurious, high quality, entertaining and/or exciting image of the advertised product.

Questions

1 For which kind of products would you think that the transfer of meaning from the 'film-viewing' event to the advertised product is especially successful?

2 The focus of attention was found to be crucial in this study. Focus on the advertisements is high in the cinema situation and low in the TV situation. Which other concept from psychological theory is reminiscent of this?

3 Which factors of attraction and distraction may be decisive for the experience of the cinema-going event?

4 What general conclusions could be drawn from this case, concerning consumers' 'consumption' of advertisements?

CASE STUDY 2

Quorn – neither fish, flesh nor fowl

ANDERS BENGTSSON and JACOB ÖSTBERG, Lund University

Eating habits have changed at a remarkable speed over the last couple of years for many parts of the population. This is especially evident among young people, where the trend has been away from meat-based diets and towards different vegetarian alternatives. A number of different reasons are usually posed for avoidance of meat. On the one hand there is increased health awareness among consumers: avoiding meat in your diet is sometimes portrayed as having beneficial influences on your health. Red meat especially has been posed as having negative effects on health whereas poultry and fish have been put in a better position. On the other hand there are consumers whose avoidance of meat is motivated by concern for the well-being of the animals. This last stance has been fuelled lately by reports of the poor circumstances under which many animals are kept. It is quite common for consumers to combine these two positions in different ways, staying away from meat consumption both for health and for animal rights reasons.

Another trend among consumers is towards convenience: sales of ready-made meals and semi-manufactured products are soaring. Even though there is an increased focus on convenience above all and many new product launches, there are very few vegetarian alternatives on the market. This is peculiar in light of more consumers turning towards vegetarianism and vegetarians' frequent laments over the trouble of preparing convenient vegetarian solutions that fulfill the necessary nutritional requirements.

Back in the 1960s, many nutritionists predicted that the population of the world would increase at such a speed that there would be a shortage of food rich in proteins. Various research projects were therefore initiated to discover new ways of growing food with high protein content. In 1967, a number of British researchers discovered an organism that was growing naturally in a garden. The organism was the microscopic fungus called *Fusarium venenatum*. After several years of laboratory research, they managed to control the growth of the fungus mycelia and create a myco protein. This is the base for the product that today is called Quorn, which is produced by Marlow Foods in Great Britain. The most convenient way to grow Quorn is in fact not in a garden but rather in big silos through a fermentation process. The mycelia are grown in 60-metre-tall silos where fermentation is controlled by glucose, oxygen, nitrogen and minerals. The mycelia are continually harvested and centrifugalized to a dough. Egg white is then added to the dough to bind the myco protein's threads in order to create a texture similar to that of meat. The pure Quorn product has a neutral taste but can be flavoured to imitate the taste of fish, flesh or fowl. Marlow Foods co-operates with various retailers who sell the Quorn products endorsed by their own store brands. Quorn was launched nationally in the British market in 1994 and has since been launched in Ireland, the Netherlands, Switzerland, Belgium and Sweden. In 2001, Marlow Foods is preparing to launch Quorn in the American market.

In 1999, Kooperativa Förbundet (KF), which is the second largest food retailer in Sweden, introduced Quorn into the Swedish market. KF is a consumer co-op that operates hypermarkets and supermarkets as well as discount stores in Sweden. All of the different store concepts have a highly centralized management that guarantees complete store coverage of new product introductions. KF introduced Quorn in various ready-made meal versions endorsed by its own store brand, Signum, which is positioned as an upmarket store brand. The Signum brand has been heavily promoted with TV advertising, evoking the meaning of carefully selected primary produce. In the commercials, scenes from southern Europe are typically shown and the best primary produce is selected and then shipped in Signum trucks to Sweden.

When KF introduced Quorn into the Swedish market it was a completely new product that had not been sold there before. Quorn was therefore a new ingredient that consumers had little knowledge about. However, KF chose not to focus on the novelty of Quorn in its introduction in the Swedish market. Instead, they positioned it as a conventional frozen, ready-made meal. The Quorn ready-made meals were just quietly put in the grocery stores' frozen-food displays next to other ready-made meals. The packages were also designed to look just like any ready-made meal. Very little information was provided to consumers about this novelty product. The only source provided by KF was a folder with a couple of Quorn recipes. In this folder, KF claimed that Quorn is modern food for aware people.

Even though Quorn is a vegetable product it was not as a vegetarian dish that KF introduced the ready-made meals. Rather, the different dishes of ready-made meals were introduced as non-meat products. The names of the different dishes make it easy for consumers to associate the ready-made meals with common meat dishes. For instance, the Quorn Stroganoff dish with rice evokes associations with the traditional dish Korv Stroganoff, where Korv is Swedish for 'sausage'. Initially Quorn was introduced only in ready-made meals. Later on KF launched pure Quorn as mince and in pieces to make it possible for consumers to create their own dishes with Quorn as an ingredient. KF has now introduced the product in 17 different versions in the Swedish market.

Questions

1 Give examples of some alternative strategies of introducing Quorn in the Swedish market.

2 Give some reasons for and against choosing the alternative strategies proposed in question 1 as well as the strategy chosen by KF.

3 Discuss the way in which KF designed the packages.

4 Discuss the possibility that consumers may interpret Quorn as a generic term referring to a product rather than a brand name. Discuss also the potential drawbacks for Marlow Foods if consumers use Quorn in the same way that they use the terms fish, flesh or fowl.

CASE STUDY 3

'The medium is the message ... *or* are you what you drink?'

The impact of self-monitoring on image congruence and product/brand evaluation

MARGARET K. HOGG and ALASTAIR J. COX, Manchester School of Management

Context

The drinks market for young adults in the UK is characterized by innovation as well as by sharp swings in tastes and trends, with the rapid diffusion of new or fashionable products. This is clearly illustrated by the rapid growth in retail sales of alcoholic soft drinks since their launch in the UK in June 1995 (Mintel 1996). Within this market it is possible to segment drinks brands by their flavour, alcoholic strength and packaging. The early entrants and market leaders were alcoholic lemonades although there has recently been a shift towards alcoholic sodas. Most of the brands sold in this category in the UK are comparable to premium bottled lagers with between 4 and 5% ABV (alcohol by volume). Although some brands are available in 330 ml bottles and cans, most drinks brands in this category are sold in glass bottles. Most alcoholic drinks have both a heavy usage and penetration rate in age groups that are under 34, and are particularly strong in age groups below 24. These drinks, regarded as a refreshing alternative to beer, are associated with fashion and young people (Mintel 1996). A recent introduction into this market was a range of products which contained extracts from plants (such as caffeine, guarana and damiana). The naturally based stimulants in these alcopops were intended to give drinkers added vitality and energy as they spent the night clubbing and dancing.

Scenario

Vicky, Katherine, Chloe, Daniel and Robert were sitting around chatting, as they often did, after supper on a Sunday evening. Usually they talked about the last football match which the lads had been to, or the latest film they had all seen. However, on this occasion the discussion had started to get rather heated, and they were now close to having a real argument. Last time this had happened, they had ended up with a row about vegetarianism and animal testing. This time, it had begun with an off-the-cuff remark from Rob about the recent craze for alcoholic lemonades, which he had dismissed as 'nasty, fizzy drinks'.

The previous evening, while out clubbing, Chloe had tried one of the new 'alcopop' products which contained natural stimulants and which were meant to keep clubbers going all night. Rob hadn't meant to start an argument, with his remark to Chloe:

Rob: How can anyone bear to be seen drinking that stuff – it's got a dreadful image, and it's an awful drink, not to put too fine a point on it ...

Chloe: Excuse me, it's not awful. If you must know – I rather liked it. Anyway when did you try it?

Rob: No way, I wouldn't be seen dead drinking that stuff.

Chloe: So how would you know what it's like then? How can you say it's awful when you haven't even tried it?

Rob: Everyone knows those alcopops are horribly sweet and sickly; and anyway, they're all women's drinks.

Chloe: I don't see how you can say that when you admit you have not even tasted them.

[Katherine tried to calm things down a little, by moving the discussion away from the strictly personal, onto a more general level.]

Katherine: Alright, alright, alright – no need to get quite so cross. Surely, Chloe though, it's pretty obvious that what you drink reflects the type of person you are: financially, socially and probably sexually, even if it is only subconsciously.

[However, Katherine only succeeded in making Chloe even more mad, and Vicky quite scathing.]

Chloe: Well that just doesn't make any sense.

Vicky: It doesn't make any sense to me either. I think it's pretty obvious that some people are just more susceptible to media manipulation and fashion trends than others – but they're just sad people really.

Katherine: No, I think you've both got it wrong. It's obvious, surely – we all behave differently according to the situation we are in. I mean I change the way I behave to fit in, especially when I am out with some of my more flamboyant friends.

Vicky: Now why on earth do you do that, Katherine, what's the point? You are who you are, surely?

Katherine: Well I think the way I behave does depend on who I am with – an awful lot depends on the type of people you're with for instance, and the place you're in – whether it's a bar or a club. It's also important where the place is, its location and whether it has a dress code. I mean these are all mixed up together and you behave accordingly.

Daniel: Vicky look, I now when I'm out with my mates I would look really stupid if I ordered whisky when everyone else was drinking lager – I'd just look and feel a right idiot.

Katherine: That's it, Dan, that's precisely the point I'm trying to make. Like, for instance, when I'm in a wine bar or restaurant I would almost always choose wine or cocktails to drink, but when I'm in a pub I usually drink beer . . . I mean you want to make sure you're not out of place by the way you are behaving or by what you're drinking. It's rather like what you wear, it's everything . . . honestly, Vicky.

Daniel: Oh, come on, Vicky, you've got to admit Katherine's right you know. People choose drinks which fit into the kind of places they are in and the people they're with.

Vicky: Look, I think that might have been true in the eighties, when it was all image, mobile phones and bottles of Budweiser. But I think it's a lot different now, there's much more sense of a free spirit and of free choice.

Daniel: I don't know that you can really say that, Vicky – not really, I mean look at Chloe. Chloe, you wouldn't drink beer from a pint glass in a trendy bar now would you? You'd look like an old man with a pint glass in your hand. You wouldn't want people to associate you with that type of image would you?

Chloe: Of course I wouldn't drink a pint in a trendy bar, but that's because it would probably get spilt everywhere. Anyway I have never really liked the taste of those beers and lagers. I really can't say that I'm interested in what other people think about what I drink, and I find it hard to believe that other people are really seriously interested in what I drink.

Robert: Chloe, I really think you're quite wrong, you know. You're really completely missing the point here. You can definitely read meanings into people's product or brand choices, certainly some of their choices, anyway. Look at alcopops for instance. They are definitely a woman's drink. They've got such a female image, though you certainly won't see many older women drinking alcopops and you definitely don't see many blokes drinking them either. That's why it would look rather odd for me to stand at a bar drinking alcopops.

Chloe: Don't be so ridiculous Rob – how can you read so much into one bottle of alcopops? You'll be saying next that the clothes I wear and the music I listen to send messages about me – that's really nonsense. What about these jeans, for instance – what meaning can you see in this pair of blue jeans?

Rob: Well for a start, they're Levi 501s which are about as trendy as you can get in branded jeans – apart from the designer labels like Calvin Klein and Armani.

Chloe: Well, you see you're wrong. I chose this pair of branded jeans simply for the cut and the quality. I am not worried about what people think the label says about me, and I am not really bothered about what you all think of me wearing this brand of jeans . . . as long as you think they suit me and fit well.

Katherine: But Chloe, I really can't imagine you in an ordinary pair of jeans, I mean would you buy ordinary jeans – say from the market or from a department store? I bet you never have.

Chloe: But that's my point, surely. I wouldn't buy jeans which didn't have the cut and quality I wanted, and these just happen to be the brand I like.

Katherine: Well, Chloe maybe you're the exception to the rule, but I definitely think people's choices of things like jeans and drinks (not to mention cars) are influenced by the people around them, even if it is only subconsciously. Everything changes depending on the people you associate with and the situation you're in.

Vicky: Oh come on Katherine, now that really is a ridiculous idea – it's an incredible notion to suggest that everyone changes all the time – I mean, you might change your behaviour slightly to fit in, but you're still the same person underneath after all. I know I am, and I am sure you are.

[At this point, Daniel decided to try another tack.]

Daniel: OK Vicky and Chloe, why don't we try looking at it another way, and then you might be able to see what Katherine, Rob and I are trying to get at. Let's assume you're at that popular bar in the centre of town – it's busy as it always is on a Saturday night. You're planning to spend a couple of hours there before meeting up with some friends and going on to a club. Imagine you are just about to go up and buy a drink. There are lots of people around who will be able to see what brand you choose to drink – what influences your choice of drink in those circumstances?

Vicky: Well it depends . . .

Daniel : Yes, but what on . . .

Vicky: Well I don't know – how I feel I suppose, what I feel like drinking, how much I've already had to drink, what's available, what I can afford – oh, I don't know, lots of things . . .

Daniel: What about you Chloe, like last night for instance, what made you choose the new alcopops drink?

Chloe: Someone else bought it for me, actually, and I did not like to refuse it. It was not necessarily something that I would have chosen myself. I am not very keen on fizzy drinks if I am going dancing. But it was OK – a bit sweet maybe, but not bad; and besides it didn't cost me anything. I switched back to one of those bottled beers afterwards, I must admit – it certainly tasted a lot better, though it is a bit expensive for what you get. It was the same stuff you are drinking now Rob. By the way Rob, what made you choose that brand?

By the end of this case study, you should be able to:

● Define and illustrate symbolic consumption.

● Define and evaluate the role of self-monitoring in consumer behaviour.

● Recognize and explain the situational factors which influence product and brand choices.

● Identify the meanings and interpretations which consumers often associate with their choice of products and brands.

● Access the impact of symbolic consumption on consumer behaviour.

Class preparation: It is recommended that you should have at least read the chapters in Part B. In particular, Chapter 7 ('The self') will provide some useful concepts and theory for analysis and discussion.

Questions

1 What are the factors which influence product/brand evaluation and choice in this case study?

2 Assess the importance of self-image and product image in product/brand evaluation and choice.

3 To what extent can the 'self-image congruence models' discussed in Chapter 7 help us understand the interaction between consumers and product/brands in this case study?

4 Discuss the different levels of self-monitoring displayed by Katherine, Vicky, Chloe, Daniel and Robert (review *symbolic interactionism and self-consciousness* in Chapter 7).

5 How far can the products and brands in this case study be seen as social stimuli and/or as responses?

6 Why is symbolic consumption so central to our understanding of consumer behaviour?

Exercises

1 **Preliminary task**. As preparation for the class, prepare short market research reports on the market for alcopops in Europe, using industry reports and concentrating particularly on the consumer behaviour aspects when reporting your findings.

2 **Follow-up task**. After the class discussion of the case material, work in small groups to undertake some market research of your own, by interviewing ten users and ten non-users of alcopops, around the themes identified in the class discussion.

Notes

The authors acknowledge the support of *GSM Marketing* Leeds and *Hard Times* Leeds for the research project on which this case study material is based. © Hogg and Cox, January 1998

1. This background information is based on company documents (personal correspondence) and a Mintel report (1996) on the alcoholic soft drinks industry.

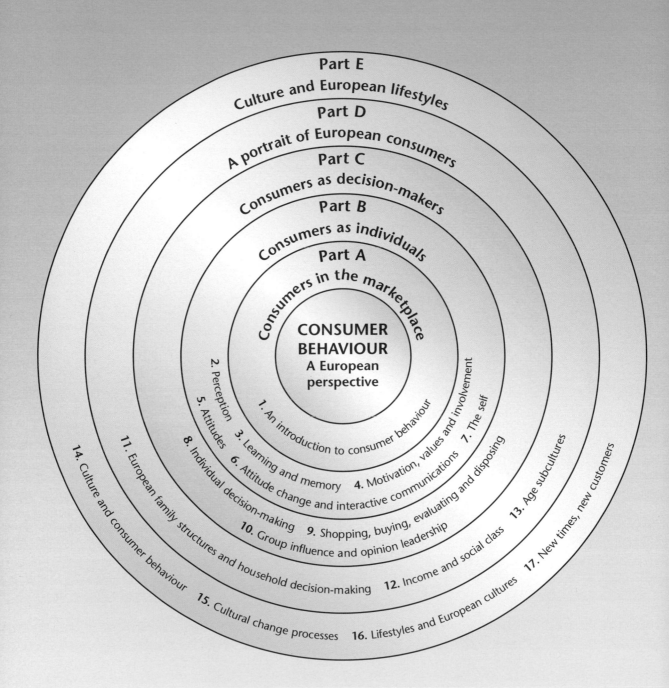

Part E
Culture and European lifestyles

Part D
A portrait of European consumers

Part C
Consumers as decision-makers

Part B
Consumers as individuals

Part A
Consumers in the marketplace

CONSUMER
BEHAVIOUR
A European
perspective

1. An introduction to consumer behaviour

2. Perception
3. Learning and memory
4. Motivation, values and involvement
7. The self

5. Attitudes
6. Attitude change and interactive communications

8. Individual decision-making
9. Shopping, buying, evaluating and disposing

10. Group influence and opinion leadership

11. European family structures and household decision-making
12. Income and social class
13. Age subcultures

14. Culture and consumer behaviour
15. Cultural change processes
16. Lifestyles and European cultures
17. New times, new customers

Part C

CONSUMERS AS DECISION-MAKERS

This part explores how we make consumption decisions and discusses the many influences exerted by others in this process. Chapter 8 focuses on the basic sequence of steps we undergo when making a decision. Chapter 9 considers how the particular situation we find ourselves in affects these decisions and how we go about evaluating what we've bought afterwards. Chapter 10 provides an overview of group processes and discusses the reasons we are motivated to conform to the expectations of our fellow group members. It also considers how some individuals in particular (called 'opinion leaders') are likely to influence the consumption behaviour of others in a group.

Chapter 8

Individual decision-making

Andy has had enough. He can no longer bear to go on watching TV on his tiny, antiquated, black-and-white set. It was bad enough trying to see the graphics of the possible answers to questions on *Who Wants to be a Millionaire?* The final straw was when he couldn't tell Manchester United from Ajax during last Wednesday night's football match! When he went next door to watch the second half on Mark's big set, he really realized what he had been missing. Budget or not, it was time to act. A man has to have his priorities.

Andy thinks he'll probably get a good selection (at an affordable price) in one of those new warehouse stores. Arriving at the London Appliance Emporium, Andy heads straight for the Video Zone – barely noticing the rows of toasters, microwave ovens and stereos en route. Within minutes, he's intercepted by a smiling salesman wearing a cheap suit. Even though he could use some help, Andy tells the salesman he's just browsing – these guys don't know what they're talking about, and they're only interested in closing a sale, no matter what.

Andy starts to examine some of the features on the 52 cm colour sets. He knows his friend Carol has a set by Prime Wave which she really likes, and his sister Diane has warned him to stay away from the Kamashita. Although Andy finds a Prime Wave model with lots of features such as a sleep timer, on-screen programming menu, cable compatible tuner and remote control, he chooses the less expensive Precision 2000X because it has one feature that really catches his fancy: stereo broadcast reception. Later that day, Andy is a happy man as he sits in his easy chair, watching *Arrowsmith* on video. If he's going to be a couch potato, he's doing it in style . . .

Consumers as problem-solvers

A consumer purchase is a response to a problem, which in Andy's case is the perceived need for a new TV. His situation is similar to that encountered by consumers virtually every day of their lives. He realizes that he wants to make a purchase, and he goes through a series of steps in order to make it. These steps can be described as (1) problem recognition, (2) information search, (3) evaluation of alternatives, and (4) product choice. Of course, after the decision is made, the quality of that decision affects the final step in the process, when learning occurs based on how well the choice worked out. This learning process influences the likelihood that the same choice will be made the next time the need for a similar decision occurs.

An overview of this decision-making process is shown in Figure 8.1. This chapter begins by considering various approaches consumers use when faced with a purchase decision. It then focuses on three of the steps in the decision process: how consumers recognize the problem, or need for a product; their search for information about product choices; and the ways in which they evaluate alternatives to arrive at a decision. Chapter 9 considers influences in the actual purchase situation, as well as the person's satisfaction with the decision.

Since some purchase decisions are more important than others, the amount of effort we put into each differs. Sometimes the decision-making process is done almost automatically: we seem to make snap judgements based on very little information. At other times, reaching a purchase decision begins to resemble a full-time job. A person may spend literally days or weeks thinking about an important purchase such as a new home, even to the point of obsession.

Perspectives on decision-making

Traditionally, consumer researchers have approached decision-makers from a **rational perspective**. In this view, people calmly and carefully integrate as much information as possible with what they already know about a product, painstakingly weigh the pluses and minuses of each alternative, and arrive at a satisfactory decision. This process implies that steps in decision-making should be carefully studied by marketing managers in order to understand how information is obtained, how beliefs are formed, and what product choice criteria are specified by consumers. Products can then be developed that emphasize appropriate attributes, and promotional strategies can be tailored to deliver the types of information that are most likely to be desired in the most effective formats.[1]

While the steps in decision-making are followed by consumers for some purchases, such a process is not an accurate portrayal of many purchase decisions.[2] Consumers simply do not go through this elaborate sequence for every decision. If they did, their entire lives would be spent making such decisions, leaving them very little time to enjoy the things they eventually decide to buy.

Researchers are now beginning to realize that decision-makers actually possess a repertoire of strategies. A consumer evaluates the effort required to make a particular choice, and then he or she chooses a strategy best suited to the level of effort

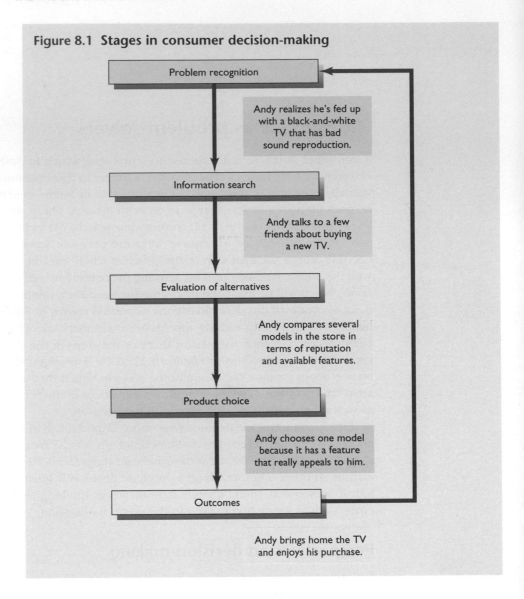

Figure 8.1 Stages in consumer decision-making

Problem recognition

Andy realizes he's fed up with a black-and-white TV that has bad sound reproduction.

Information search

Andy talks to a few friends about buying a new TV.

Evaluation of alternatives

Andy compares several models in the store in terms of reputation and available features.

Product choice

Andy chooses one model because it has a feature that really appeals to him.

Outcomes

Andy brings home the TV and enjoys his purchase.

required. This sequence of events is known as *constructive processing*. Rather than use a big club to swat a fly, consumers tailor their degree of cognitive 'effort' to the task at hand.[3]

Some decisions are made under conditions of low involvement, as discussed in Chapter 4. In many of these situations, the consumer's decision is a learned response to environmental cues (see Chapter 3), as when he or she decides to buy on impulse something that is promoted as a 'special offer' in a shop. A concentration on these types of decision can be described as the **behavioural influence perspective**. Under these circumstances, managers must concentrate on assessing the characteristics of the environment, such as the design of a retail outlet or whether a package is enticing, that influence members of a target market.[4]

In other cases, consumers are highly involved in a decision, but still the selections made cannot be explained entirely rationally. For example, the traditional approach is hard-pressed to explain a person's choice of art, music or even a spouse. In these cases, no single quality may be the determining factor. Instead, the **experiential perspective** stresses the gestalt, or totality, of the product or service. Marketers in these areas focus on measuring consumers' affective responses to products or services, and develop offerings that elicit appropriate subjective reactions.

Types of consumer decisions

One helpful way to characterize the decision-making process is to consider the amount of effort that goes into the decision each time it must be made. Consumer researchers have found it convenient to think in terms of a continuum, which is anchored at one end by **habitual decision-making** and at the other extreme by **extended problem-solving**. Many decisions fall somewhere in the middle and are characterized by **limited problem-solving**. This continuum is presented in Figure 8.2.

Extended problem-solving

Decisions involving extended problem-solving correspond most closely to the traditional decision-making perspective. As indicated in Table 8.1, the extended problem-solving process is usually initiated by a motive that is fairly central to the self-concept (see Chapter 7), and the eventual decision is perceived to carry a fair degree of risk. The consumer tries to collect as much information as possible, both from memory (internal search) and from outside sources (external search). Based on the importance of the decision, each product alternative is carefully evaluated. The evaluation is often done by considering the attributes of one brand at a time and seeing how each brand's attributes shape up to some set of desired characteristics.

Limited problem-solving

Limited problem-solving is usually more straightforward and simple. Buyers are not as motivated to search for information or to evaluate each alternative rigorously. People instead use simple *decision rules* to choose among alternatives. These cognitive shortcuts (more about these later) enable them to fall back on general guidelines, instead of having to start from scratch every time a decision is to be made.

Habitual decision-making

Both extended and limited problem-solving modes involve some degree of information search and deliberation, though they vary in the degree to which these activi-

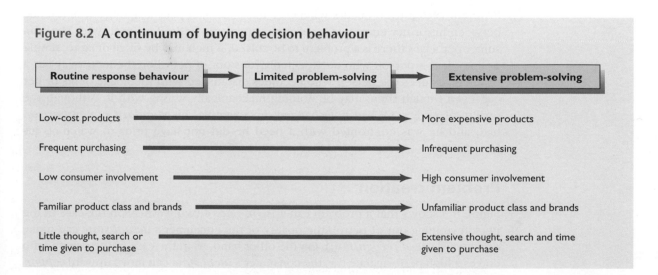

Figure 8.2 A continuum of buying decision behaviour

| Routine response behaviour | → | Limited problem-solving | → | Extensive problem-solving |

Low-cost products ——————————→ More expensive products

Frequent purchasing ——————————→ Infrequent purchasing

Low consumer involvement ——————————→ High consumer involvement

Familiar product class and brands ——————————→ Unfamiliar product class and brands

Little thought, search or time given to purchase ——————————→ Extensive thought, search and time given to purchase

Table 8.1 Characteristics of limited vs. extended problem-solving

	Limited problem-solving	Extended problem-solving
Motivation	Low risk and involvement	High risk and involvement
Information search	Little search	Extensive search
	Information processed passively	Information processed actively
	In-store decision likely	Multiple sources consulted prior to store visits
Alternative evaluation	Weakly held beliefs	Strongly held beliefs
	Only most prominent criteria used	Many criteria used
	Alternatives perceived as basically similar	Significant differences perceived among alternatives
	Non-compensatory strategy used	Compensatory strategy used
Purchase	Limited shopping time; may prefer self-service	Many outlets shopped if needed
	Choice often influenced by store displays	Communication with store personnel often desirable

ties are undertaken. At the other end of the choice continuum, however, are decisions that are made with little or no conscious effort. Many purchase decisions are so routinized that we may not realize we've made them until we look in our shopping trolleys. Choices characterized by *automaticity* are performed with minimal effort and without conscious control.[5] While this kind of thoughtless activity may seem dangerous or at best stupid, it is actually quite efficient in many cases. The development of habitual, repetitive behaviour allows consumers to minimize the time and energy spent on mundane purchase decisions.

Problem recognition

▶ **Problem recognition** occurs whenever the consumer sees a significant difference between his or her current state of affairs and some desired or ideal state. The consumer perceives there is a problem to be solved, which may be small or large, simple or complex. A person who unexpectedly runs out of petrol on the motorway has a problem, as does the person who becomes dissatisfied with the image of his or her car, even though there may be nothing mechanically wrong with it. Although the quality of Andy's TV had not changed, for example, his *standard of comparison* had, and he was confronted with a need he did not have prior to watching his friend's TV.

Problem creation

Figure 8.3 shows that a problem can arise in one of two ways. As in the case of the person running out of petrol, the quality of the consumer's *actual state* can move downward (*need recognition*). On the other hand, as in the case of the person who craves a high-performance car, the consumer's *ideal state* can move upward (*oppor-*

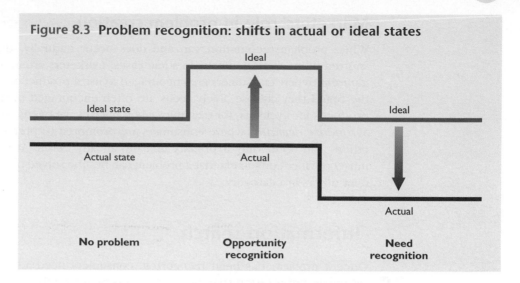

Figure 8.3 Problem recognition: shifts in actual or ideal states

tunity recognition). Either way, a gulf occurs between the actual state and the ideal state.[6] In Andy's case, a problem was perceived as a result of opportunity recognition: his ideal state in terms of television reception quality was altered.

Need recognition can occur in several ways. The quality of the person's actual state can be diminished simply by running out of a product, by buying a product that turns out not to satisfy needs adequately, or by creating new needs (e.g. buying a house can set off an avalanche of other choices, since many new things will be needed to furnish the house). Opportunity recognition often occurs when a consumer is exposed to different or better quality products. This shift often occurs because the person's circumstances have somehow changed, as when an individual goes to college or gets a new job. As the person's frame of reference shifts, purchases are made to adapt to the new environment.

MARKETING PITFALL

A common structure for advertisements has been to present a person who has a physical or social problem, and then 'miraculously' show how the product will resolve it. Some marketers have gone so far as to invent a problem and then offer a remedy for it. In the 1940s, for example, the Talon zipper was touted as a cure for 'gaposis', the horrifying condition that develops when puckers appear around the buttons on a woman's skirt. Listerine, a mouthwash, which was originally sold to fight dandruff, carried warnings about 'bottle bacillus', which caused 'infectious dandruff'. Geritol gave us a remedy for 'tired blood', and Wisk detergent drew our attention to the shame of 'ring around the collar'.[7]

Even when real problems are depicted in ads, the offered solutions are sometimes too simplistic, implying that the problem will disappear if the product is used. One analysis of over 1000 television ads found that about 80 per cent suggest that the problem will be resolved within seconds or minutes of using the product. In addition, 75 per cent of the ads make definite claims that the product will solve the problem, and over 75 per cent imply that this solution is a one-step process – all the consumer needs to do is buy the product, and the problem will go away.[8] Consumers, however, are becoming more cynical and less susceptible to such claims. As many marketers are discovering, consumers of the new millennium are more receptive to realistic ads that provide solid information about the product. In addition, both the government and consumer groups are now taking a more active interest in product claims, and marketers are more cautious about the content of their ads.

Marketers' role in problem creation

While problem recognition can and does occur naturally, this process is often spurred by marketing efforts. In some cases, marketers attempt to create *primary demand*, where consumers are encouraged to use a product or service regardless of the brand they choose. Such needs are often encouraged in the early stages of a product's life cycle, as, for example, when microwave ovens were first introduced. *Secondary demand*, where consumers are prompted to prefer a specific brand to others, can occur only if primary demand already exists. At this point, marketers must convince consumers that a problem can best be solved by choosing their brand over others in a category.

Information search

Once a problem has been recognized, consumers need adequate information to resolve it. **Information search** is the process by which the consumer surveys his or her environment for appropriate data to make a reasonable decision. This section will review some of the factors involved in this search.

Types of information search

A consumer may explicitly search the marketplace for specific information after a need has been recognized (a process called *pre-purchase search*). On the other hand, many consumers, especially veteran shoppers, enjoy browsing just for the fun of it, or because they like to stay up-to-date on what's happening in the marketplace. They are engaging in *ongoing search*.[9] Some differences between these two search modes are described in Table 8.2.

Table 8.2 A framework for consumer information search

	Pre-purchase search	Ongoing search
Determinants	Involvement in the purchase Market environment Situational factors	Involvement with the product Market environment Situational factors
Motives	Making better purchase decisions	Building a bank of information for future use Experiencing fun and pleasure
Outcomes	Increased product and market knowledge Better purchase decisions Increased satisfaction with the purchase outcome	Increased product and market knowledge, leading to • future buying efficiencies • personal influence Increased impulse buying Increased satisfaction from search and other outcomes

Source: Peter H. Bloch, Daniel L. Sherrell and Nancy M. Ridgway, 'Consumer Search: An Extended Framework', *Journal of Consumer Research* 13 (June 1986): 120. Reprinted with permission by The University of Chicago Press.

This ad for Arm & Hammer demonstrates the strategy of identifying new problems an existing product can solve.
Church & Dwight Co., Inc.

Internal vs. external search

Information sources can roughly be broken down into two kinds: internal and external. As a result of prior experience and simply living in a consumer culture, each of us often has some degree of knowledge about many products already in memory. When confronted with a purchase decision, we may engage in *internal search* by scanning our own memory banks to assemble information about different product alternatives (see Chapter 3). Usually, though, even the most market-aware of us needs to supplement this knowledge with external search, where information is obtained from advertisements, friends, or just plain people-watching.

Deliberate vs. 'accidental' search

Our existing knowledge of a product may be the result of *directed learning*, where on a previous occasion we had already searched for relevant information or experienced some of the alternatives. A parent who bought a birthday cake for one child last month, for example, probably has a good idea of the best kind to buy for another child this month.

Alternatively, we may have acquired information in a more passive manner. Even though a product may not be of interest, exposure to advertising, packaging and sales promotion activities may result in *incidental learning*. Mere exposure over time to conditioned stimuli and observations of others results in the learning of much material which may not be needed for some time after the fact, if ever. For marketers, this result is a benefit of steady, 'low-dose' advertising, since product associations are established and maintained until the time they are needed.[10]

In some cases, we may be so expert about a product category (or at least believe we are) that no additional search is undertaken. Frequently, however, our existing state of knowledge is not satisfactory to make an adequate decision, and we must look elsewhere for more information. The sources we consult for advice vary: they may be impersonal and marketer-dominated sources, such as retailers and catalogues; they may be friends and family members; or they may be unbiased third parties such as *Which?* magazine or other consumer reports which are published in a number of European countries.[11]

Cybermediaries

As anyone who's ever typed a phrase like 'home theatres' into a search engine knows, the Web delivers enormous amounts of product and retailer information in seconds. In fact, the biggest problem surfers face these days is narrowing down their choices, not increasing them. In cyberspace, simplification is key. Some people even use web filters like ***intermute.com*** to remove soundtracks, pop-up frames and other distractions from the sites they find.

With the tremendous number of websites available, and the huge number of people surfing the Web each day, how can people organize information and decide where to click? One type of business that is growing to meet this demand is called a *cybermediary*. This is an intermediary that helps to filter and organize online market information so that customers can identify and evaluate aternatives more efficiently.[12] Cybermediaries take different forms.[13] *Directories* and *portals* such as Yahoo! or ***fashionmall.com*** are general services that tie together a large variety of different sites. *Website evaluators* reduce the risk to consumers by reviewing sites and recommending the best ones. For example, Point Communications selects sites that it designates as Top 5% of the Web. *Forums, fan clubs* and *user groups* offer product-related discussions to help customers sift through options.

Intelligent agents are sophisticated software programs that use *collaborative filtering* technologies to learn from past user behaviour in order to recommend new purchases. For example, when you let ***Amazon.com*** suggest a new book, it's using an intelligent agent to suggest novels based on what you and others like you have bought in the past. This approach was introduced in 1995 (the Stone Ages in web time!) by Firefly to make recommendations for taste-based products like music, books and films.[14] Now, a variety of 'shopping bots' are available to act as online purchasing shopping agents, including ***clickthebutton.com***, ***mysimon.com*** and ***dealtime.com***. Collaborative filtering is still in its infancy. In the next few years, expect to see many new web-based methods to simplify the consumer decision-making process. Now if only someone could come up with an easier way to pay for all the great stuff you find courtesy of shopping bots!

The economics of information

The traditional decision-making perspective incorporates the *economics-of-information* approach to the search process: it assumes that consumers will gather as much data as is needed to make an informed decision. Consumers form expectations of the value of additional information and continue to search to the extent that the rewards of doing so (what economists call the *utility*) exceed the costs. This utilitarian assumption implies that the most valuable units of information will be collected first. Additional pieces will be absorbed only to the extent that they are seen as adding to what is already known.[15] In other words, people will put themselves out to collect as much information as possible, as long as the process of gathering it is not too onerous or time-consuming.[16] Variety-seeking can influence a consumer to switch from their favourite product to a less pleasurable item. This can even occur before an individual becomes satiated or tired of their favourite product. Explanations of this phenomenon stem from research that supports the idea that consumers are willing to trade enjoyment for variety and that variety-seeking is a

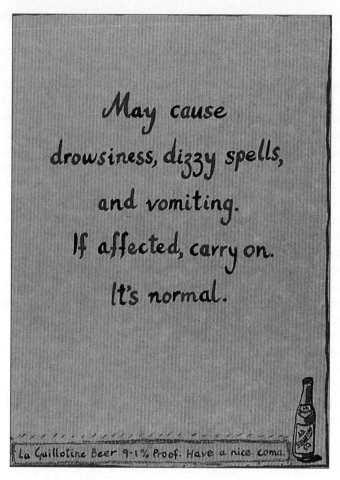

This Singaporean beer ad reminds us that not all product decisions are made rationally.

choice strategy that occurs as a result of pleasurable memories of ringing the changes.[17]

Do consumers always search rationally?

This assumption of rational search is not always supported. The amount of external search for most products is surprisingly small, even when additional information would most likely benefit the consumer. For example, lower-income shoppers, who have more to lose by making a bad purchase, actually search *less* prior to buying than do more affluent people.[18] Like our friend Andy, some consumers typically visit only one or two stores and rarely seek out unbiased information sources prior to making a purchase decision, especially when little time is available to do so.[19] This pattern is especially prevalent for decisions regarding durables like appliances or cars, even when these products represent significant investments. One study of Australian car buyers found that more than a third had made only one or two trips to inspect cars prior to buying one. Finally, there is some evidence that even having information available on the package does not necessarily mean that consumers make use of it. Environmentally friendly products in Finland are beginning to carry the Nordic Environmental Label to assist consumers in their choice of environmentally safe products. In a study which asked Finnish consumers to evaluate detergent and batteries choices, little use and little trust were given to the 'green label' on the packages, in spite of the positive attitudes that Finnish citizens have towards the environment. The results suggest that marketers have a long way to go in order to provide clear, easily comprehensible and unbiased information regarding 'green' products.[20]

This tendency to avoid external search is less prevalent when consumers consider the purchase of symbolic items, such as clothing. In those cases, not surprisingly, people tend to do a fair amount of external search, although most of it involves seeking the opinions of peers.[21] While the stakes may be lower financially, these self-expressive decisions may be seen as having dire social consequences if the wrong choice is made. The level of perceived risk, a concept to be discussed shortly, is high.

In addition, consumers are often observed to engage in *brand-switching*, even if their current brand satisfies their needs. For example, researchers for the British brewer Bass Export who were studying the American beer market discovered a consumer trend towards having a repertoire of 2–6 favourite brands, rather than sticking to just one. This preference for brand-switching led the firm to begin exporting their Tennent's 1885 lager to the US, positioning the brew as an alternative to young drinkers' usual favourite brands.[22]

Sometimes, it seems that people just plain like to try new things – they are interested in variety-seeking, in which the priority is to vary one's product experiences, perhaps as a form of stimulation or to reduce boredom. *Variety-seeking* is especially likely to occur when people are in a good mood, or when there is relatively little stimulation elsewhere in their environment.[23] In the case of foods and beverages, variety-seeking can occur due to a phenomenon known as *sensory-specific satiety*. Put simply, this means that the pleasantness of a food just eaten drops while the pleasantness of uneaten foods remains unchanged.[24] So even though we have favourites we still like to sample other possibilities. Ironically, consumers actually may switch to less-preferred options for variety's sake even though they enjoy the more familiar option more.[25] On the other hand, when the decision situation is ambiguous or when there is little information about competing brands, consumers tend to opt for the safe choice by selecting familiar brands and maintaining the status quo.

Brand familiarity influences confidence about a brand, which in turn affects purchase intention.[26] Still, the tendency of consumers to shift brand choices over time means that marketers can never relax in the belief that once they have won a customer, he or she is necessarily theirs forever.[27]

Biases in the decision-making process

Consider the following scenario: you've been given a free ticket to the finals of a world-class tennis tournament. At the last minute, a snowstorm makes getting to the stadium dangerous. Would you go? Now, assume the same final and the same snowstorm, but this time you have paid handsomely for the ticket. Would you go?

Analyses of people's responses to this situation and to others illustrate principles of *mental accounting*, where decisions are influenced by the way a problem is posed (called *framing*), and by whether it is put in terms of gains or losses.[28] For example, people are more likely to risk their personal safety in the storm if they paid for the tennis ticket. Only the most diehard fan would fail to recognize that this is an irrational choice, since the risk to the person is the same regardless of whether he or she got a great deal on the ticket. This decision-making bias is called the *sunk-cost fallacy* – having paid for something makes us reluctant to waste it.

Another bias is known as *loss aversion*. People place much more emphasis on loss than they do on gain. For example, for most people losing money is more unpleasant than gaining money is pleasant. *Prospect theory*, a descriptive model of choice, finds that utility is a function of gains and losses, and risk differs when the consumer faces options involving gains vs. those involving losses.[29]

To illustrate this bias, consider the following. For each, would you take the safe bet or choose to gamble?

> *Option 1.* You're given £30 and then offered a chance to flip a coin: Heads you win £9, tails you lose £9.

> *Option 2.* You're given a choice of getting £30 outright or accepting a coin flip that will win you either £39 or £21.

In one study, 70 per cent of those given option 1 chose to gamble, compared to just 43 per cent of those offered option 2. Yet the odds are the same for both options! The difference is that people prefer 'playing with the house money'; they are more willing to take risks when they perceive they're using someone else's resources. So, contrary to a rational decision-making perspective, we value money differently depending on its source. This explains why someone might choose to spend a big bonus on a frivolous purchase, while they would never consider taking that amount from their savings account for the same purpose.

Finally, research in mental accounting demonstrates that extraneous charac-teristics of the choice situation can influence our selections, even though they shouldn't if we were rational decision-makers. As one example, participants in a survey were provided with one of two versions of this scenario:

> You are lying on the beach on a hot day. All you have to drink is iced water. For the last hour you have been thinking about how much you would enjoy a nice cold bottle of your favourite brand of beer. A companion gets up to go and make a phone call and offers to bring back a beer from the only place nearby where beer is sold (either a smart hotel or a small, run-down grocery store, depending on the version you're given). He says that the beer might be expensive and so asks how much you are willing to pay for it. What price do you tell him?

In this survey, the median price given by participants who were in the 'smart hotel' version was the equivalent of $2.65, while those given the cheaper 'grocery store version' were only willing to pay $1.50! In both versions the consumption act is the same, the beer is the same and no 'atmosphere' is consumed since the beer is being brought back to the beach.[30] So much for rational decision-making!

How much search occurs?

As a general rule, search activity is greater when the purchase is important, when there is a need to learn more about the purchase and/or when the relevant infor-mation is easily obtained and utilized.[31]

Consumers differ in the amount of search they tend to undertake, regardless of the product category in question. All things being equal, younger, better-educated people who enjoy the shopping/fact-finding process tend to conduct more infor-mation search. Women are more inclined to search than men, as are those who place greater value on style and the image they present.[32]

The consumer's prior expertise
Should prior product knowledge make it more or less likely that consumers will engage in search? Product experts and novices use very different procedures during decision-making. Novices who know little about a product should be the most motivated to find out more about it. However, experts are more familiar with the

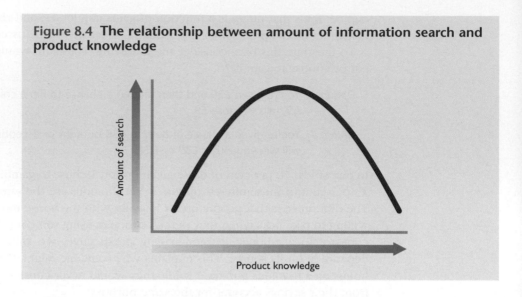

Figure 8.4 **The relationship between amount of information search and product knowledge**

product category, so they should be able to understand better the meaning of any new product information they might acquire.

So, who searches more? The answer is neither: search tends to be greatest among those consumers who are *moderately* knowledgeable about the product. There is an inverted-U relationship between knowledge and external search effort, as shown in Figure 8.4. People with very limited expertise may not feel they are capable of searching extensively. In fact, they may not even know where to start. Andy, who did not spend a lot of time researching his purchase, is representative of this situation. He visited one store, and he only looked at brands with which he was already familiar. In addition, he focused on only a small number of product features.[33]

The *type* of search undertaken by people with varying levels of expertise differs as well. Because experts have a better sense of what information is relevant to the decision, they tend to engage in *selective search*, which means their efforts are more focused and efficient. In contrast, novices are more likely to rely on the opinions of others and to rely on 'non-functional' attributes, such as brand name and price, to distinguish between alternatives. They may also process information in a 'top-down' rather than a 'bottom-up' manner, focusing less on details than on the big picture. For instance, they may be more impressed by the sheer amount of technical information presented in an ad than by the actual significance of the claims made.[34]

Perceived risk

As a rule, purchase decisions that involve extensive search also entail some kind of **perceived risk**, or the belief that the product has potentially negative consequences. Perceived risk may be present if the product is expensive or is complex and difficult to understand. Alternatively, perceived risk can be a factor when a product choice is visible to others, and we run the risk of embarrassment if the wrong choice is made.

Figure 8.5 lists five basic kinds of risk – including both objective (e.g. physical danger) and subjective factors (e.g. social embarrassment) – as well as the products that tend to be affected by each type. As this figure notes, consumers with greater 'risk capital' are less affected by perceived risks associated with the products. For example, a highly self-confident person would be less worried about the social risk

Figure 8.5 Five types of perceived risk

	Buyers most sensitive to risk	Purchases most subject to risk
Monetary risk	Risk capital consists of money and property. Those with relatively little income and wealth are most vulnerable.	High-price items that require substantial expenditures are most subject to this form of risk.
Functional risk	Risk capital consists of alternate means of performing the function or meeting the need. Practical consumers are most sensitive.	Products or services whose purchase and use requires the buyer's exclusive commitment and precludes redundancy are most sensitive.
Physical risk	Risk capital consists of physical vigour, health and vitality. Those who are elderly, frail, or in ill health are most vulnerable.	Mechanical or electrical goods (such as vehicles or flammables), drugs and medical treatment, and food and beverages are most sensitive.
Social risk	Risk capital consists of self-esteem and self-confidence. Those who are insecure and uncertain are most sensitive.	Socially visible or symbolic goods, such as clothes, jewellery, cars, homes, or sports equipment are most subject to it.
Psychological risk	Risk capital consists of affiliations and status. Those lacking self-respect or attractiveness to peers are most sensitive.	Expensive personal luxuries that may engender guilt; durables; and services whose use demands self-discipline or sacrifice are most sensitive.

Minolta features a No-Risk Guarantee as a way of reducing the perceived risk in buying an office copier.

Courtesy of Minolta Corporation.

inherent in a product, while a more vulnerable, insecure consumer might be reluctant to take a chance on a product that might not be accepted by peers.

Marketing opportunity

The spread of the HIV virus has created a boom in home-testing kits which encourage people to find out if they have been infected in a less threatening environment than a clinic or a doctor's surgery. The typical kit allows the consumer to send a blood sample to a testing lab, and results are returned in 3–7 days. While high-risk groups such as adolescents and gay men are most likely to need the kits, some speculate that sales will come primarily from the 'worried well', those who are less likely to be infected in the first place. Companies are taking different approaches, ranging from humorous to provocative to serious, as they try to find the best way to reach people who are unlikely to go to a clinic to be tested. In one ad for Home Access, the copy (targeted at young straight males) reads: 'Nothing arouses a woman like knowing you're responsible'.[35]

Evaluation of alternatives

Much of the effort that goes into a purchase decision occurs at the stage where a choice must be made from the available alternatives. After all, modern consumer society abounds with choice. In some cases, there may be dozens of different brands (as in cigarettes) or different variations of the same brand (as in shades of lipstick), each clamouring for our attention.

Just for fun, ask a friend to name all the brands of perfume she can think of. The

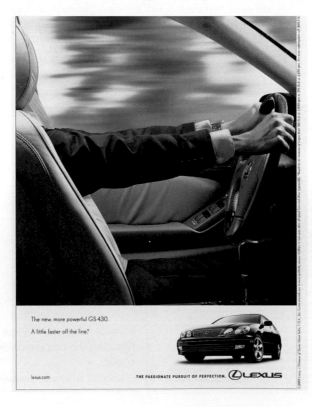

The new, more powerful GS 430.

A little faster off the line.*

lexus.com

THE PASSIONATE PURSUIT OF PERFECTION. *LEXUS*

Focusing on the car buyer's sense of self-confidence and self-esteem, this Lexus ad makes a subtle appeal to reducing social risk.
Image © 2000 Chris Wimpey Photography. Created by: Team One Advertising.

odds are she will reel off three to five names quickly, then pause before coming up with a few more. It is likely that the first set of brands will be those with which she is highly familiar, and she probably wears one or more of these. The list may also contain one or two brands that she does not like and would perhaps like to forget. Note also that there are many, many more brands on the market that she did not name at all.

If your friend were to go to a shop to buy perfume, she would probably consider buying some or most of the brands she listed initially. She might also consider a few others if these were forcefully brought to her attention while in the shop – for example, if she were approached by an employee who was spraying scent samples on shoppers, which is a common occurrence in some department stores.

Identifying alternatives

How do we decide which criteria are important, and how do we narrow down product alternatives to an acceptable number and eventually choose one in preference to the others? The answer varies depending upon the decision-making process used. A consumer engaged in extended problem-solving may carefully evaluate several brands, while someone making a habitual decision may not consider any alternatives to their normal brand. Some evidence indicates that more extended processing occurs in situations where negative emotions are aroused due to conflicts among the choices available.[36]

The alternatives actively considered during a consumer's choice process are his or her **evoked set**. The evoked set is composed of those products already in memory (the retrieval set), plus those prominent in the retail environment. For example, recall that Andy did not know much about the technical aspects of television sets and had only a few major brands in memory. Of these, two were acceptable possibilities and one was not. The alternatives that the consumer is aware of but would not consider buying are his or her *inept set*, while those not under consideration at all comprise the *inert set*. You can easily guess in which set a marketer wants its brand to appear! These categories are depicted in Figure 8.6.

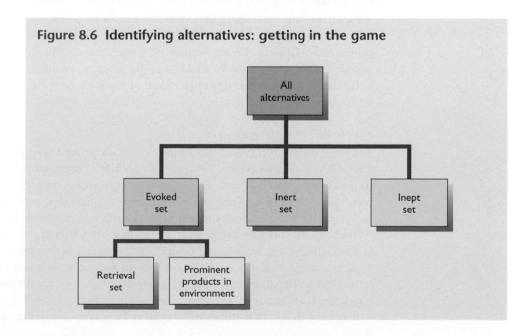

Figure 8.6 Identifying alternatives: getting in the game

Consumers often include a surprisingly small number of alternatives in their evoked set. One study combined results from several large-scale investigations of consumers' evoked sets and found that the number of products included in these sets was limited, although there were some marked variations by product category and across countries. For example, the average evoked set size for American beer consumers was one or two, while Canadian consumers typically considered seven brands. In contrast, while car buyers in Norway studied two alternatives, American consumers on average looked at more than eight models before making a decision.[37]

For obvious reasons, a marketer who finds that her or his brand is not in the evoked set of a target market has cause to worry. A product is not likely to be placed in the evoked set after it has previously been considered and rejected. Indeed, a new brand is more likely to be added to the evoked set than is an existing brand that was previously considered but passed over, even after additional positive information has been provided for that brand.[38] For marketers, this unwillingness to give a rejected product a second chance underscores the importance of ensuring that it performs well from the time it is introduced.

Product categorization

Remember that when consumers process product information, they do not do so in a vacuum. Instead, a product stimulus is evaluated in terms of what people already know about a product or those things to which it is similar. A person evaluating a particular 35 mm camera will most likely compare it to other 35 mm cameras rather than to a Polaroid camera, and the consumer would certainly not compare it to a slide projector or a VCR. Since the category in which a product is placed determines the other products it will be compared to, *categorization* is a crucial determinant of how a product is evaluated.

The products in a consumer's evoked set are likely to be those that share similar features. It is important to understand how this knowledge is represented in a consumer's **cognitive structure**, which refers to a set of factual knowledge about products (i.e. beliefs) and the way these beliefs are organized in people's minds.[39] These knowledge structures were discussed in Chapter 4. One reason is that marketers want to ensure that their products are correctly grouped. For example, General Foods brought out a new line of Jell-O flavours such as Cranberry Orange which it called 'Jell-O Gelatin Flavors for Salads'. Unfortunately, the company discovered that people would use it only for salad since the name encouraged them to put the product in their 'salad' structure rather than in their 'dessert' structure. The line had to be dropped.[40]

Levels of categorization

Not only do people group things into categories, but these groupings occur at different levels of specificity. Typically, a product is represented in a cognitive structure at one of three levels. To understand this idea, consider how someone might respond to these questions about an ice cream cone: what other products share similar characteristics, and which would be considered as alternatives to eating a cone?

These questions may be more complex than they first appear. At one level, a cone is similar to an apple, because both could be eaten as a dessert. At another level, a cone is similar to a piece of pie, since both are eaten as a dessert and both are fattening. At still another level, a cone is similar to an ice cream sundae. Both are eaten for dessert, are made of ice cream and are fattening.

It is easy to see that the items a person associates with, say, the category 'fatten-

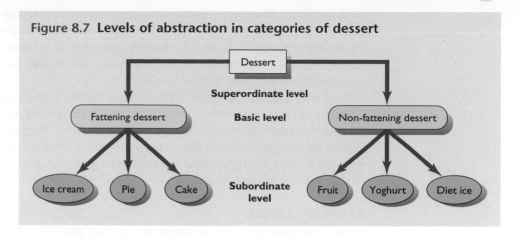

Figure 8.7 **Levels of abstraction in categories of dessert**

ing dessert' influence the choices he or she will make about what to eat after dinner. The middle level, known as a *basic level category*, is typically the most useful in classifying products, since items grouped together tend to have a lot in common, but still permit a range of alternatives to be considered. The broader *superordinate category* is more abstract, while the more specific *subordinate category* often includes individual brands.[41] These three levels are depicted in Figure 8.7.

Of course, not all items fit equally well into a category. Apple pie is a better example of the subordinate category 'pie' than is rhubarb pie, even though both are types of pie. Apple pie is thus more *prototypical*, and would tend to be considered first, especially by category novices. In contrast, pie experts will tend to have knowledge about both typical and atypical category examples.[42]

Strategic implications of product categorization

Product categorization has many strategic implications. The way a product is grouped with others has very important ramifications for determining both its competitors for adoption and what criteria will be used to make this choice.

Product positioning

The success of a *positioning strategy* often hinges on the marketer's ability to convince the consumer that his or her product should be considered within a given category. For example, the orange juice industry tried to reposition orange juice as a drink that could be enjoyed all day long ('It's not just for breakfast anymore'). On the other hand, soft drink companies are now attempting the opposite by portraying carbonated drinks as suitable for breakfast consumption. They are trying to make their way into consumers' 'breakfast drink' category, along with orange juice, grapefruit juice and coffee. Of course, this strategy can backfire, as Pepsi-Cola discovered when it introduced Pepsi A.M. and positioned it as a coffee substitute. The company did such a good job of categorizing the drink as a morning beverage that consumers wouldn't drink it at any other time and the product failed.[43]

Identifying competitors

At the abstract, superordinate level, many different product forms compete for membership. Both bowling and the ballet may be considered as subcategories of 'entertainment' by some people, but many would not necessarily consider the substitution of one of these activities for the other. Products and services that on the surface are quite different, however, actually compete with each other at a broad level for consumers' discretionary money. While football or the ballet may not be a likely trade-off for many people, it is feasible, for example, that an orchestral concert might try to lure season-ticketholders to the ballet by positioning itself as an equivalent member of the category 'cultural event'.[44]

Consumers are often faced with choices between non-comparable categories, where a number of attributes exist that cannot be directly related to one another (the old problem of comparing apples and oranges). The comparison process is easier when consumers can derive an overlapping category that encompasses both items (e.g. entertainment, value, usefulness) and then rate each alternative in terms of that superordinate category.[45]

Exemplar products

As we saw with the case of apple vs. rhubarb pie, if a product is a really good example of a category it is more familiar to consumers, and is more easily recognized and recalled.[46] Judgements about category attributes tend to be disproportionately influenced by the characteristics of category exemplars.[47] In a sense, brands that are strongly associated with a category 'call the shots' by defining the evaluative criteria that should be used to evaluate all category members.

Being a bit less than prototypical is not necessarily a bad thing, however. Products that are moderately unusual within their product category may stimulate more information-processing and positive evaluations, since they are neither so familiar that they will be taken for granted nor so discrepant that they will be dismissed.[48] A brand that is strongly discrepant may occupy a unique niche position, while those that are moderately discrepant remain in a distinct position within the general category.[49]

Locating products

Product categorization may affect consumers' expectations regarding the places they can locate a desired product. If products do not clearly fit into categories (e.g. is a *carpet* furniture?), consumers' ability to find them or make sense of them may be diminished. For instance, a frozen dog food that had to be thawed and cooked failed in the market partly because people could not adapt to the idea of buying dog food in the 'frozen foods for people' section of their supermarket.

Product choice: selecting among alternatives

Once the relevant options from a category have been assembled and evaluated, a choice must be made among them.[50] Recall that the decision rules guiding choice can range from very simple and quick strategies to complicated processes requiring a lot of attention and cognitive processing. The choice can be influenced by integrating information from such sources as prior experience with the product, information present at the time of purchase and beliefs about the brands that have been created by advertising.[51]

Evaluative criteria

When Andy was looking at different television sets, he focused on one or two product features while completely ignoring several others. He narrowed down his choice by considering only two specific brand names, and from the Prime Wave and Precision models he chose one that had a stereo capability.

▶   **Evaluative criteria** are the dimensions used to judge the merits of competing options. In comparing alternative products, Andy could have chosen from among any number of criteria, ranging from very functional attributes ('does this TV come with remote control?') to experiential ones ('does this TV's sound reproduction make me imagine I'm in a concert hall?').

Another important point is that criteria on which products *differ* from one another carry more weight in the decision process than do those where the alternatives are *similar*. If all brands being considered rate equally well on one attribute (e.g. if all TVs come with remote control), consumers will have to find other reasons to choose one over another. The attributes actually used to differentiate among choices are called *determinant attributes*.

Marketers can play a role in educating consumers about which criteria should be used as determinant attributes. For example, consumer research indicated that many consumers view the use of natural ingredients as a determinant attribute. The result was promotion of a toothpaste made from baking soda, which the company already manufactured for its Arm & Hammer brand.[52]

The decision about which attributes to use is the result of *procedural learning*, where a person undergoes a series of cognitive steps before making a choice. These steps include identifying important attributes, remembering whether competing brands differ on those attributes, and so on. In order for a marketer to recommend a new decision criterion effectively, his or her communication should convey three pieces of information:[53]

1   It should point out that there are significant differences between brands on the attribute.

2   It should supply the consumer with a decision-making rule, such as *if* (deciding among competing brands), *then* ... (use the attribute as a criterion).

3   It should convey a rule that can be easily integrated with how the person has made this decision in the past. Otherwise, the recommendation is likely to be ignored, since it requires too much mental work.

Claiming the product is 'full of strength', this ad for Pucko, a Swedish chocolate drink, emphasizes an evaluation criterion based on nutritional value, whereas American consumers might evaluate a similar product based on taste or calorie content.
Photographer: Kurt Wass. Forsman and BodenFors.

Heuristics: mental shortcuts

Do we actually perform complex mental calculations every time we make a purchase decision? Of course not! To simplify decisions, consumers often employ decision rules that allow them to use some dimensions as substitutes for others. For example, Andy relied on certain assumptions as substitutes for prolonged information search. In particular, he assumed that the selection at the London Appliance Emporium would be more than sufficient, so he did not bother to investigate any of Emporium's competitors. This assumption served as a shortcut to more extended information processing.[54]

▶ Especially where limited problem-solving occurs prior to making a choice, consumers often fall back on **heuristics**, or mental rules-of-thumb, that lead to a speedy decision. These rules range from the very general (e.g. 'Higher priced products are higher quality products' or 'Buy the same brand I bought last time') to the very specific (e.g. 'Buy Silver Spoon, the brand of sugar my mother always bought').[55]

Sometimes these shortcuts may not be in consumers' best interests. A consumer who personally knows one or two people who have had problems with a particular make of car might assume he or she would have similar trouble with it and thus overlook the model's overall excellent repair record.[56] The influence of such assumptions may be enhanced if the product has an unusual name, which makes it *and* the experiences with it more distinctive.[57]

Relying on a product signal

One frequently used shortcut is the tendency to infer hidden dimensions of products from observable attributes. The aspect of the product that is visible acts as a *signal* of some underlying quality. Such inferences explain why someone trying to sell a used car takes great pains to be sure the car's exterior is clean and shiny: potential buyers often judge the vehicle's mechanical condition by its appearance, even though this means they may drive away in a shiny, clean death trap.[58]

When product information is incomplete, judgements are often derived from beliefs about *covariation*, or perceived associations among events which may or may not actually influence one another.[59] For example, a consumer may form an association between product quality and the length of time a manufacturer has been in business. Other signals or attributes believed to coexist with good or bad products include well-known brand names, country of origin, price, and the retail outlets that carry the product.

Unfortunately, consumers tend to be poor estimators of covariation. Their beliefs persist despite evidence to the contrary. Similar to the consistency principle discussed in Chapter 5, people tend to see what they are looking for. They will look for product information that confirms their guesses. In one experiment, consumers sampled four sets of products to determine if price and quality were related. Those who believed in this relationship prior to the study elected to sample higher-priced products, thus creating a sort of self-fulfilling prophecy.[60]

Market beliefs: is it better if I have to pay more for it?

Consumers often form assumptions about companies, products and shops. These
▶ **market beliefs** then become the shortcuts that guide their decisions – whether or not they are accurate.[61] Recall, for instance, that Andy chose to shop at a large 'electronics supermarket' because he *assumed* the selection would be better than if he went to a specialized shop. A large number of market beliefs have been identified. Some of these are listed in Table 8.3. How many do you share?

Table 8.3 Common market beliefs

Brand	All brands are basically the same.
	Generic products are just name brands sold under a different label at a lower price.
	The best brands are the ones that are purchased the most.
	When in doubt, a national brand is always a safe bet.
Store	Specialized shops are good places to familiarize yourself with the best brands; but once you know what you want, it's cheaper to buy it at a discount outlet.
	A store's character is reflected in its window displays.
	Sales people in specialized shops are more knowledgeable than other sales personnel.
	Larger stores offer better prices than small stores.
	Locally owned stores give the best service.
	A store that offers a good value on one of its products probably offers good values on all of its items.
	Credit and return policies are most lenient at large department stores.
	Stores that have just opened usually charge attractive prices.
Prices/Discounts/Sales	Sales are typically run to get rid of slow-moving merchandise.
	Stores that are constantly having sales don't really save you money.
	Within a given store, higher prices generally indicate higher quality.
Advertising and sales promotion	'Hard-sell' advertising is associated with low-quality products.
	Items tied to 'giveaways' are not good value (even with the freebie).
	Coupons represent real savings for customers because they are not offered by the store.
	When you buy heavily advertised products, you are paying for the label, not for higher quality.
Product/Packaging	Largest-sized containers are almost always cheaper per unit than smaller sizes.
	New products are more expensive when they're first introduced; prices tend to settle down as time goes by.
	When you are not sure what you need in a product, it's a good idea to invest in the extra features, because you'll probably wish you had them later.
	In general, synthetic goods are lower in quality than goods made of natural materials.
	It's advisable to stay away from products when they are new to the market; it usually takes the manufacturer a little time to work the bugs out.

Source: Adapted from Calvin P. Duncan, 'Consumer Market Beliefs: A Review of the Literature and an Agenda for Future Research', in Marvin E. Goldberg, Gerald Gorn and Richard W. Pollay, eds., *Advances in Consumer Research* 17 (Provo, UT: Association for Consumer Research, 1990): 729–35.

Do higher prices mean higher quality? The assumption of a *price–quality relationship* is one of the most pervasive market beliefs.[62] Novice consumers may in fact consider price as the *only* relevant product attribute. Experts also consider this information, although in these cases price tends to be used for its informational value, especially for products (e.g. pure new wool) that are known to have wide quality variations in the marketplace. When this quality level is more standard or strictly regulated (e.g. Harris Tweed sports jackets), experts do not weigh price in their decisions. For the most part, this belief is justified: you do tend to get what you pay for. However, let the buyer beware: the price–quality relationship is not always justified.[63]

Country of origin as a product signal

Modern consumers choose among products made in many countries. European consumers may buy Italian or Brazilian shoes, Japanese cars, clothing imported from Taiwan or microwave ovens built in South Korea. Consumers' reactions to these imports are mixed. In some cases, people have come to assume that a product made overseas is of better quality (e.g. cameras, cars), while in other cases the knowledge that a product has been imported tends to lower perceptions of product quality (e.g. apparel).[64] In general, people tend to rate their own country's products more favourably than do foreigners, and products from industrialized countries are better rated than are those from developing countries.

As briefly discussed in Chapter 6 when we were talking about persuasive communication, a product's *country of origin* in some cases is an important piece of information in the decision-making process.[65] A product's origin, then, is often used as a signal of quality. Certain items are strongly associated with specific countries, and products from those countries often attempt to benefit from these linkages. Country of origin can function as a *stereotype* – a knowledge structure based on inferences across products. These stereotypes may be biased or inaccurate, but they do play a constructive role in simplifying complex choice situations.[66] For example, a Brazilian soft drinks company is now trying to market a beverage it is calling Samba in the US. Samba is made from the guaraná berry, and this sweet, flowery-tasting soft drink is extremely popular in Brazil. The company is capitalizing on the carefree, partying image that many Americans have of Brazilians to get them to try it. In its commercials, a scantily clad woman says, 'In Brazil we do things a little differently. We laugh a little more, wear a little less and dance the samba. Dance the dance. Drink the drink.'[67]

MARKETING OPPORTUNITY

The growing popularity of *faux* Irish pubs around the world attests to the power of country stereotypes to influence consumers' preferences. About 800 Irish-themed pubs have been opened in countries including South Africa, Italy, Hong Kong and Russia. The Irish brewer Guinness PLC encourages the establishment of these outputs, since an Irish

Photo: Bernard Wolf.

pub is mere blarney without Guinness on tap. The company helps owners design the pub and even assists in locating Irish bar staff to dispense its thick brew. As one Guinness executive explained, 'We've created a mythology of an Irish ambience.'[68] Since Guinness launched its Irish Pub Concept in 1992 it has helped over 1250 entrepreneurs in 36 countries establish their own Irish pubs. Aspiring publicans can choose from five pre-set designs: Victorian Dublin, Irish Brewery Pub, Irish Pub Shop, Irish County Cottage or Gaelic.

Multicultural dimensions

Japanese consumers have a strong interest in European and American products, and other countries work hard to cultivate a favourable image in the discriminating Japanese market. Dentsu, the largest Japanese advertising agency, has conducted several studies for the Commission of the European Communities to determine how Japanese consumers perceive European countries, the US and some Asian countries, and how they evaluate products from those countries.

The study involved personal interviews with 1600 consumers ranging in age from 15 to 59. Respondents rated countries on such overall dimensions as 'rich in history/tradition', 'abundant natural scenery' and 'would like to visit', as well as on product-related characteristics, such as 'high-quality, performance products' and 'well-designed, stylish products'. The results showed that the Japanese public associates Europe with history, tradition and well-designed products, while American advanced technology and agriculture are highly rated (products from South Korea and Taiwan tended to be rated lower than those from the US or Europe).

Overall, respondents told the researchers that foreign products (i.e. non-Japanese) are well regarded in terms of style, but are assumed to be lower in technological sophistication than most Japanese products. There was also a widespread feeling that many non-Japanese products are not well suited to Japanese needs. These consumers felt that many foreign goods are too expensive and need more thorough after-sales service.

Figure 8.8 Perceptual positioning by country of origin among Japanese consumers

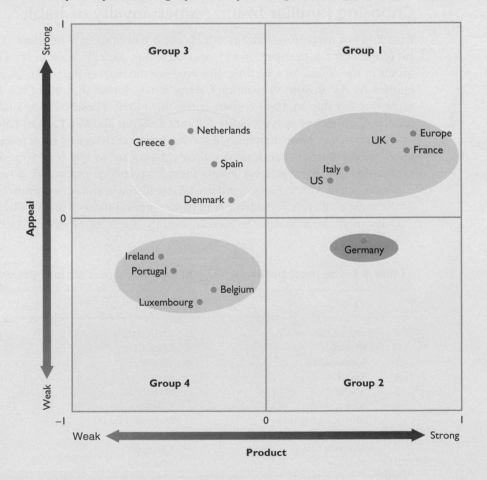

A perceptual map (these were described in Chapter 2) summarizing Japanese consumers' images of European countries and the US is shown in Figure 8.8. The five countries in Group 1 have the most 'image wealth': they are strong in both overall appeal and in ratings of product quality. Germany is the sole country in Group 2, indicating that its products are better regarded than is the country as a whole. The countries in Group 3 have positive images, but have yet to transfer these good feelings to their products. Finally, the countries in Group 4 appear to have their work cut out if they hope to win over the hearts and wallets of Japanese consumers.[69]

Recent evidence indicates that learning of a product's country of origin is not necessarily good or bad. Instead, it has the effect of stimulating the consumer's interest in the product to a greater degree. The purchaser thinks more extensively about the product and evaluates it more carefully.[70] The origin of the product thus can act as a product attribute which combines with other attributes to influence evaluations.[71] In addition, the consumer's own expertise with the product category moderates the effects of this attribute. When other information is available, experts tend to ignore country-of-origin information while novices continue to rely upon it. However, when other information is unavailable or ambiguous, both experts and novices will rely on this attribute to make a decision.[72]

Choosing familiar brand names: loyalty or habit?

Branding is a marketing strategy which often functions as a heuristic. People form preferences for a favourite brand, and then they literally may never change their minds in the course of a lifetime. In a study of the market leaders in 30 product categories by the Boston Consulting Group, it was found that 27 of the brands that were number one in 1930 remain at the top today. These include such perennial American favourites as Ivory Soap, Campbell's Soup and Gold Medal Flour.[73]

A brand that exhibits that kind of staying power is treasured by marketers, and for good reason. Brands that dominate their markets are as much as 50 per cent more profitable than their nearest competitors.[74] A survey on brand power in Asia, Australia, South Africa, Europe and the US calculated brand scores to produce the list of the most positively regarded brand names around the world given in Table 8.4.[75]

Consumers' attachments to certain brands, such as Marlboro, Coca-Cola and

Table 8.4 The most positively regarded brand names around the world

	1990	*1996*
1	Coca-Cola	McDonald's
2	Kellogg's	Coca-Cola
3	McDonald's	Disney
4	Kodak	Kodak
5	Marlboro	Sony
6	IBM	Gillette
7	American Express	Mercedes-Benz
8	Sony	Levi's
9	Mercedes-Benz	Microsoft
10	Nescafé	Marlboro

Levi's, are so powerful that this loyalty is often considered as a positive product attribute in and of itself. Brand equity actually can be quantified in terms of *good-will*, defined as the difference between the market value and the book value of a brand. Recently, the British company Grand Metropolitan decided to record brand names it had acquired on its balance sheets, including these intangible assets in its financial reports to shareholders.[76] Marlboro is the most valuable brand name in the world. It was recently valued at $31.2 billion.[77]

Inertia: the fickle customer

Many people tend to buy the same brand almost every time they go to a shop. This consistent pattern is often due to **inertia**, where a brand is bought out of habit merely because less effort is required. If another product is introduced which for some reason is easier to buy (e.g. it is cheaper, or the original product is out of stock), the consumer will not hesitate to do so. A competitor who is trying to change a buying pattern based on inertia can do so quite easily, because little resistance to brand-switching will be encountered if the right incentive is offered. Since there is little or no underlying commitment to the product, such promotional tools as point-of-purchase displays, extensive couponing or noticeable price reductions may be sufficient to 'unfreeze' a consumer's habitual pattern.

Brand loyalty: a 'friend', tried and true

This kind of fickleness will not occur if true **brand loyalty** exists. In contrast to inertia, brand loyalty is a form of repeat purchasing behaviour reflecting a *conscious* decision to continue buying the same brand.[78] For brand loyalty to exist, a pattern of repeat purchase must be accompanied by an underlying positive attitude towards the brand. Brand loyalty may be initiated by customer preference based on objective reasons, but after the brand has existed for a long time and is heavily advertised it can also create an emotional attachment, either by being incorporated into the consumer's self-image or because it is associated with prior experiences.[79] Purchase decisions based on brand loyalty also become habitual over time, though in these cases the underlying commitment to the product is much firmer.

Compared to inertia, where the consumer passively accepts a brand, a brand-loyal consumer is actively (sometimes passionately) involved with his or her favourite. Because of the emotional bonds that can be created between brand-loyal consumers and products, 'true-blue' users react more vehemently when these products are altered, redesigned or withdrawn.[80] Recall, for example, the national call-in campaigns, boycotts and other protests when Coca-Cola replaced its tried-and-true formula with New Coke.

In recent years, marketers have struggled with the problem of *brand parity*, which refers to consumers' beliefs that there are no significant differences between brands. For example, one survey found that more than 70 per cent of consumers worldwide believe that all paper towels, soaps and crisps are alike.[81] Some analysts even proclaimed that brand names are dead, killed off by own-label or generic products which offer the same value for less money.

However, the reports of this death appear to be premature – major brands are making a comeback. This renaissance is attributed to information overload – with too many alternatives (many of them unfamiliar names) to choose from, people are looking for a few clear signals of quality. Following a period in the late 1980s and early 1990s when people had strong doubts about the ability of large companies to produce quality products, more recent surveys indicate consumers are slowly beginning to trust major manufacturers again.[82] Brand names are very much alive.

Table 8.5 Hypothetical alternatives for a television set

Attribute	Importance ranking	Brand ratings		
		Kamashita	Prime Wave	Precision
Size of screen	1	Excellent	Excellent	Excellent
Stereo broadcast capability	2	Good	Poor	Excellent
Brand reputation	3	Poor	Excellent	Excellent
On-screen programming	4	Poor	Excellent	Poor
Cable-ready capability	5	Good	Good	Good
Sleep timer	6	Good	Excellent	Poor

Decision rules

Consumers consider sets of product attributes by using different rules, depending upon the complexity of the decision and the importance of the decision to them. As we have seen, in some cases these rules are quite simple: people simply rely on a 'shortcut' to make a choice. In other cases, though, more effort and thought is put into carefully weighing alternatives before coming to a decision.

One way to differentiate among decision rules is to divide them into those that are *compensatory* vs. those that are *non-compensatory*. To aid the discussion of some of these rules, the attributes of TV sets considered by Andy are summarized in Table 8.5. Now, let's see how some of these rules result in different brand choices.

Non-compensatory decision rules

Simple decision rules are **non-compensatory**, meaning that a product with a low standing on one attribute cannot make up for this position by being better on another. In other words, people simply eliminate all options that do not meet some basic standards. A consumer like Andy who uses the decision rule 'Only buy well-known brand names' would not consider a new brand, even if it was equal or superior to existing ones. When people are less familiar with a product category or are not very motivated to process complex information, they tend to use simple, non-compensatory rules, which are summarized below:[83]

When the *lexicographic rule* is used, the brand that is the best on the most important attribute is selected. If two or more brands are seen as being equally good on that attribute, the consumer then compares them on the second most important attribute. This selection process goes on until the tie is broken. In Andy's case, since both the Prime Wave and Precision models were tied on his most important attribute (a 52 cm screen), the Precision was chosen because of its rating on his second most important attribute – its stereo capability.

Using the *elimination-by-aspects rule*, brands are also evaluated on the most important attribute. In this case, though, specific cut-offs are imposed. For example, if Andy had been more interested in having a sleep timer on his TV (i.e. if it had had a higher importance ranking), he might have stipulated that his choice 'must have a sleep timer'. Since the Prime Wave model had one and the Precision did not, the Prime Wave would have been chosen.

While the two former rules involve processing by attribute, the *conjunctive rule* entails processing by brand. As with the elimination-by-aspects procedure, cut-offs are established for each attribute. A brand is chosen if it meets all the cut-offs, while failure to meet any one cut-off means it will be rejected. If none of the brands meets all the cut-offs, the choice may be delayed, the decision rule may be changed or the cut-offs may be modified.

If Andy had stipulated that all attributes had to be rated 'good' or better, he would not have been able to choose any of the options. He might then have modified his decision rule, conceding that it was not possible to attain these high standards in the price range he was considering. In this case, Andy might have decided that he could live without on-screen programming, so the Precision model could again be considered.

Compensatory decision rules

Unlike non-compensatory decision rules, **compensatory decision rules** give a product a chance to make up for its shortcomings. Consumers who employ these rules tend to be more involved in the purchase, and thus are willing to exert the effort to consider the entire picture in a more exacting way. The willingness to offset good product qualities against bad ones can result in quite different choices. For example, if Andy had not been concerned about having stereo reception, he might have chosen the Prime Wave model. But because this brand did not feature this highly ranked attribute, it didn't stand a chance when he used a non-compensatory rule.

Two basic types of compensatory rules have been identified. When using the *simple additive rule*, the consumer merely chooses the alternative having the largest number of positive attributes. This choice is most likely to occur when his or her ability or motivation to process information is limited. One drawback to this approach for the consumer is that some of these attributes may not be very meaningful or important. An ad containing a long list of product benefits may be persuasive, despite the fact that many of the benefits included are actually standard within the product class and aren't determinant attributes at all.

The more complex version is known as the *weighted additive rule*.[84] When using this rule, the consumer also takes into account the relative importance of positively rated attributes, essentially multiplying brand ratings by importance weights. If this process sounds familiar, it should. The calculation process strongly resembles the multiattribute attitude model described in Chapter 5.

Chapter summary

- Consumers are faced with the need to make decisions about products all the time. Some of these decisions are very important and entail great effort, while others are made more or less automatically.

- Perspectives on decision-making range from a focus on habits that people develop over time to novel situations involving a great deal of risk, where consumers must carefully collect and analyse information prior to making a choice.

- A typical decision process involves several steps. The first is *problem recognition*, where the consumer first realizes that some action must be taken. This realization may be prompted in a variety of ways, ranging from the actual malfunction of a current purchase to a desire for new things based on exposure to different circumstances or advertising that provides a glimpse into what is needed to 'live the good life'.

- Once a problem has been recognized and is seen as sufficiently important to warrant some action, *information search* begins. This search may range from simply scanning memory to determine what has been done to resolve the problem in the past, to extensive fieldwork where the consumer consults a variety of sources to amass as much information as possible. In many cases, people engage in surprisingly little search. Instead, they rely on various mental shortcuts, such as brand names or price, or they may simply imitate others.

● In the *evaluation of alternatives* stage, the product alternatives that are considered comprise the individual's evoked set. Members of the *evoked set* usually share some characteristics; they are categorized similarly. The way products are mentally grouped influences which alternatives will be considered, and some brands are more strongly associated with these categories than are others (i.e. they are more prototypical).

● When the consumer eventually must make a *product choice* from among alternatives, a number of decision rules may be used. *Non-compensatory rules* eliminate alternatives that are deficient on any of the criteria the consumer has chosen to use. *Compensatory rules*, which are more likely to be applied in high-involvement situations, allow the decision-maker to consider each alternative's good and bad points more carefully to arrive at the overall best choice.

● Very often *heuristics*, or mental rules-of-thumb, are used to simplify decision-making. In particular, people develop many market beliefs over time. One of the most common beliefs is that price is positively related to quality. Other heuristics rely on well-known brand names or a product's country of origin as signals of product quality. When a brand is consistently purchased over time, this pattern may be due to true *brand loyalty*, or simply to *inertia* because it's the easiest thing to do.

KEY TERMS

Behavioural influence perspective (*p. 236*)
Brand loyalty (*p. 259*)
Cognitive structure (*p. 250*)
Compensatory decision rules (*p. 261*)
Evaluative criteria (*p. 253*)
Evoked set (*p. 249*)
Experiential perspective (*p. 236*)
Extended problem-solving (*p. 237*)
Habitual decision-making (*p. 237*)

Heuristics (*p. 254*)
Inertia (*p. 259*)
Information search (*p. 240*)
Limited problem-solving (*p. 237*)
Market beliefs (*p. 254*)
Non-compensatory decision rule (*p. 260*)
Perceived risk (*p. 246*)
Problem recognition (*p. 238*)
Rational perspective (*p. 235*)

For additional material see the companion website at:
www.booksites.net/solomon_euro

Consumer behaviour challenge

1. If people are not always rational decision-makers, is it worth the effort to study how they reach decisions? What techniques might be employed to understand experiential consumption and to translate this knowledge into marketing strategy?

2. List three product attributes that can be used as quality signals and provide an example of each.

3. Explain the 'evoked set'. Why is it difficult to place a product in a consumer's evoked set after it has already been rejected? What strategies might a marketer use in an attempt to accomplish this goal?

4. Define the three levels of product categorization described in the chapter. Draw a diagram of these levels for a health club.

5. Discuss two different non-compensatory decision rules and highlight the difference(s) between them. How might the use of one rule vs. another result in a different product choice?

6. Choose a friend or parent who purchases groceries on a regular basis and keep a log of their purchases of common consumer products over the term. Can you detect any evidence of brand loyalty in any categories based on consistency of purchases? If so, talk to the person about these purchases. Try to determine if his or her choices are based on true brand loyalty or on inertia. What techniques might you use to differentiate between the two?

7. Find a person who is about to make a major purchase. Ask that person to make a chronological list of all the information sources consulted prior to making a decision. How would you characterize the types of sources used (i.e. internal vs. external, media vs. personal, etc.)? Which sources appeared to have the most impact on the person's decision?

8. Perform a survey of country-of-origin stereotypes. Compile a list of five countries and ask people what products they associate with each. What are their evaluations of the products and likely attributes of these different products? The power of a country stereotype can also be demonstrated in another way. Prepare a brief description of a product, including a list of features, and ask people to rate it in terms of quality, likelihood of purchase, and so on. Make several versions of the description, varying only the country from which it comes. Do ratings change as a function of the country of origin?

9. Ask a friend to 'talk through' the process he or she used to choose one brand over others during a recent purchase. Based on this description, can you identify the decision rule that was most likely employed?

10. Consider the five types of perceived risk in Figure 8.5 of this chapter within the context of making a decision to purchase a new diamond. Review the following websites, and discuss the kinds of risk you would consider in buying a diamond on the Web: *www.diamond.com*, *www.mondera.com*, *www.bluenile.com*.

Notes

1. John C. Mowen, 'Beyond Consumer Decision Making', *Journal of Consumer Marketing* 5 (1988) 1: 15–25.

2. Richard W. Olshavsky and Donald H. Granbois, 'Consumer Decision Making – Fact or Fiction', *Journal of Consumer Research* 6 (September 1989): 93–100.

3. James R. Bettman, 'The Decision Maker Who Came In from the Cold', Presidential Address, in Leigh McAllister and Michael Rothschild, eds, *Advances in Consumer Research* 20 (Provo, UT: Association for Consumer Research, in press); John W. Payne, James R. Bettman and Eric J. Johnson, 'Behavioral Decision Research: A Constructive Processing Perspective', *Annual Review of Psychology* 4 (1992): 87–131; for an overview of recent developments in

individual choice models, see Robert J. Meyer and Barbara E. Kahn, 'Probabilistic Models of Consumer Choice Behavior', in Thomas S. Robertson and Harold H. Kassarjian, eds, *Handbook of Consumer Behavior* (Englewood Cliffs, NJ: Prentice-Hall, 1991): 85–123.

4. Mowen, 'Beyond Consumer Decision Making'; Kordelia Spies, Friedrich Hesse and Kerstin Loesch, 'Store Atmosphere, Mood and Purchasing Behavior', *International Journal of Research in Marketing* 14 (1997): 1–17; José M. M. Bloemer and Hans D. P. Kasper, 'The Complex Relationship between Consumer Satisfaction and Brand Loyalty', *Journal of Economic Psychology* 16 (1995): 311–29.

5. Joseph W. Alba and J. Wesley Hutchinson, 'Dimensions of Consumer Expertise', *Journal of Consumer Research* 13 (March 1988): 411–54; Jouni T. Kujala and Michael D. Johnson, 'Price Knowledge and Search Behavior for Habitual, Low Involvement Food Purchases', *Journal of Economic Psychology* 14 (1993): 249–65.

6. Gordon C. Bruner III and Richard J. Pomazal, 'Problem Recognition: The Crucial First Stage of the Consumer Decision Process', *Journal of Consumer Marketing* 5 (1988) 1: 53–63.

7. Ross K. Baker, 'Textually Transmitted Diseases', *American Demographics* (December 1987): 64.

8. Julia Marlowe, Gary Selnow and Lois Blosser, 'A Content Analysis of Problem-Resolution Appeals in Television Commercials', *Journal of Consumer Affairs* 23 (1989) 1: 175–94.

9. Peter H. Bloch, Daniel L. Sherrell and Nancy M. Ridgway, 'Consumer Search: An Extended Framework', *Journal of Consumer Research* 13 (June 1986): 119–26.

10. Girish Punj, 'Presearch Decision Making in Consumer Durable Purchases', *Journal of Consumer Marketing* 4 (Winter 1987): 71–82.

11. H. Beales, M. B. Jagis, S. C. Salop and R. Staelin, 'Consumer Search and Public Policy', *Journal of Consumer Research* 8 (June 1981): 11–22.

12. Michael Porter, *Competitive Advantage* (New York: Free Press, 1985).

13. Material in this section adapted from Michael R. Solomon and Elnora W. Stuart, *Welcome to Marketing.com: The Brave New World of E-Commerce* (Englewood Cliffs, NJ: Prentice Hall, 2001).

14. Phil Patton, 'Buy Here, and We'll Tell You What You Like', *The New York Times on the Web* (22 September 1999).

15. Itamar Simonson, Joel Huber and John Payne, 'The Relationship Between Prior Brand Knowledge and Information Acquisition Order', *Journal of Consumer Research* 14 (March 1988): 566–78.

16. John R. Hauser, Glen L. Urban and Bruce D. Weinberg, 'How Consumers Allocate Their Time When Searching for Information', *Journal of Marketing Research* 30 (November 1993): 452–66; George J. Stigler, 'The Economics of Information', *Journal of Political Economy* 69 (June 1961): 213–25.

17. Rebecca K. Ratner, Barbara E. Kahn and Daniel Kahneman, 'Choosing Less-Preferred Experiences for the Sake of Variety', *Journal of Consumer Research* 26 (June 1999): 1–15.

18. Cathy J. Cobb and Wayne D. Hoyer, 'Direct Observation of Search Behaviour', *Psychology & Marketing* 2 (Fall 1985): 161–79.

19. Sharon E. Beatty and Scott M. Smith, 'External Search Effort: An Investigation across Several Product Categories', *Journal of Consumer Research* 14 (June 1987): 83–95; William L. Moore and Donald R. Lehmann, 'Individual Differences in Search Behavior for a Nondurable', *Journal of Consumer Research* 7 (December 1980): 296–307.

20. Geoffrey C. Kiel and Roger A. Layton, 'Dimensions of Consumer Information Seeking Behavior', *Journal of Marketing Research* 28 (May 1981): 233–9; see also Narasimhan Srinivasan and Brian T. Ratchford, 'An Empirical Test of a Model of External Search for Automobiles', *Journal of Consumer Research* 18 (September 1991): 233–42; Mari Niva, Eva Heiskanen and Päivi Timonen, 'Environmental Information in Consumer Decision Making', *National Consumer Research Centre* (Helsinki, July 1996).

21. David F. Midgley, 'Patterns of Interpersonal Information Seeking for the Purchase of a Symbolic Product', *Journal of Marketing Research* 20 (February 1983): 74–83.

22. Cyndee Miller, 'Scotland to U.S.: "This Tennent's for You"', *Marketing News* (29 August 1994): 26.

23. Satya Menon and Barbara E. Kahn, 'The Impact of Context on Variety Seeking in Product Choices', *Journal of Consumer Research* 22 (December 1995): 285–95; Barbara E. Kahn and Alice M. Isen, 'The Influence of Positive Affect on Variety Seeking among Safe, Enjoyable Products', *Journal of Consumer Research* 20 (September 1993): 257–70.

24. J. Jeffrey Inman, 'The Role of Sensory-Specific Satiety in Consumer Variety Seeking Among Flavors', unpublished manuscript, A. C. Nielsen Center for Marketing Research, University of Wisconsin-Madison, July 1999.

25. Ratner, Kahn, and Kahneman, 'Choosing Less-Preferred Experiences for the Sake of Variety'.

26. Michael Laroche, Chankon Kim and Lianxi Zhou, 'Brand Familiarity and Confidence as Determinants of Purchase Intention: An Empirical Test in a Multiple Brand Context', *Journal of Business Research* 37 (1996): 115–120.

27. Barbara E. Kahn, 'Understanding Variety-Seeking Behavior From a Marketing Perspective', unpublished manuscript, University of Pennsylvania, University Park, 1991; Leigh McAlister and Edgar A. Pessemier, 'Variety-Seeking Behavior: An Interdisciplinary Review', *Journal of Consumer Research* 9

(December 1982): 311–22; Fred M. Feinberg, Barbara E. Kahn and Leigh McAlister, 'Market Share Response When Consumers Seek Variety', *Journal of Marketing Research* 29 (May 1992): 228–37; Kahn and Isen, 'The Influence of Positive Affect on Variety Seeking Among Safe, Enjoyable Products'.

28. Gary Belsky, 'Why Smart People Make Major Money Mistakes', *Money* (July 1995): 76 (10); Richard Thaler and Eric J. Johnson, 'Gambling with the House Money or Trying to Break Even: The Effects of Prior Outcomes on Risky Choice', *Management Science* 36 (June 1990): 643–60; Richard Thaler, 'Mental Accounting and Consumer Choice', *Marketing Science* 4 (Summer 1985): 199–214.

29. Daniel Kahneman and Amos Tversky, 'Prospect Theory: An Analysis of Decision under Risk', *Econometrica* 47 (March 1979): 263–91; Timothy B. Heath, Subimal Chatterjee and Karen Russo France, 'Mental Accounting and Changes in Price: The Frame Dependence of Reference Dependence', *Journal of Consumer Research* 22 (1) (June 1995): 90–7.

30. Quoted in Thaler, 'Mental Accounting and Consumer Choice': 206.

31. Girish N. Punj and Richard Staelin, 'A Model of Consumer Search Behavior for New Automobiles', *Journal of Consumer Research* 9 (March 1983): 366–80.

32. Cobb and Hoyer, 'Direct Observation of Search Behavior'; Moore and Lehmann, 'Individual Differences in Search Behavior for a Nondurable'; Punj and Staelin, 'A Model of Consumer Search Behavior for New Automobiles'.

33. James R. Bettman and C. Whan Park, 'Effects of Prior Knowledge and Experience and Phase of the Choice Process on Consumer Decision Processes: A Protocol Analysis', *Journal of Consumer Research* 7 (December 1980): 234–48.

34. Alba and Hutchinson, 'Dimensions of Consumer Expertise'; Bettman and Park, 'Effects of Prior Knowledge and Experience and Phase of the Choice Process on Consumer Decision Processes'; Merrie Brucks, 'The Effects of Product Class Knowledge on Information Search Behavior', *Journal of Consumer Research* 12 (June l985): 1–16; Joel E. Urbany, Peter R. Dickson and William L. Wilkie, 'Buyer Uncertainty and Information Search', *Journal of Consumer Research* 16 (September 1989): 208–15.

35. Cyndee Miller, 'HIV Kits Target Untested Market', *Marketing News* (20 January 1997): 1, 11.

36. Mary Frances Luce, James R. Bettman and John W. Payne, 'Choice Processing in Emotionally Difficult Decisions', *Journal of Experimental Psychology* 23(2) (1997): 384–405.

37. John R. Hauser and Birger Wernerfelt, 'An Evaluation Cost Model of Consideration Sets', *Journal of Consumer Research* 16 (March 1990): 393–408.

38. Robert J. Sutton, 'Using Empirical Data to Investigate the Likelihood of Brands Being Admitted or Readmitted Into an Established Evoked Set', *Journal of the Academy of Marketing Science* 15 (Fall 1987): 82.

39. Alba and Hutchison, 'Dimensions of Consumer Expertise'; Joel B. Cohen and Kunal Basu 'Alternative Models of Categorization: Toward a Contingent Processing Framework', *Journal of Consumer Research* 13 (March 1987): 455–72.

40. Robert M. McMath, 'The Perils of Typecasting', *American Demographics* (February 1997): 60.

41. Eleanor Rosch, 'Principles of Categorization', in E. Rosch and B. B. Lloyd, eds, *Recognition and Categorization* (Hillsdale, NJ: Lawrence Erlbaum, 1978).

42. Michael R. Solomon, 'Mapping Product Constellations: A Social Categorization Approach to Symbolic Consumption', *Psychology & Marketing* 5 (1988) 3: 233–58.

43. Robert M. McMath, 'The Perils of Typecasting', *American Demographics* (February 1997): 60.

44. Elizabeth C. Hirschman and Michael R. Solomon, 'Competition and Cooperation Among Culture Production Systems', in Ronald F. Bush and Shelby D. Hunt, eds, *Marketing Theory: Philosophy of Science Perspectives* (Chicago: American Marketing Association, 1982): 269–72.

45. Michael D. Johnson, 'The Differential Processing of Product Category and Noncomparable Choice Alternatives', *Journal of Consumer Research* 16 (December 1989): 300–9.

46. Mita Sujan, 'Consumer Knowledge: Effects on Evaluation Strategies Mediating Consumer Judgments', *Journal of Consumer Research* 12 (June 1985): 31–46.

47. Rosch, 'Principles of Categorization'.

48. Joan Meyers-Levy and Alice M. Tybout, 'Schema Congruity as a Basis for Product Evaluation', *Journal of Consumer Research* 16 (June 1989): 39–55.

49. Mita Sujan and James R. Bettman, 'The Effects of Brand Positioning Strategies on Consumers' Brand and Category Perceptions: Some Insights from Schema Research', *Journal of Marketing Research* 26 (November 1989): 454–67.

50. Cf. William P. Putsis, Jr and Narasimhan Srinivasan, 'Buying or Just Browsing? The Duration of Purchase Deliberation', *Journal of Marketing Research* 31 (August 1994): 393–402.

51. Robert E. Smith, 'Integrating Information from Advertising and Trial: Processes and Effects on Consumer Response to Product Information', *Journal of Marketing Research* 30 (May 1993): 204–19.

52. Jack Trout, 'Marketing in Tough Times', *Boardroom Reports* (October 1992) 2: 8.

53. Amna Kirmani and Peter Wright, 'Procedural Learning, Consumer Decision Making and Marketing Communication', in *Marketing Letters* (1992); Michael R. Solomon, Sarah Drenan and Chester A. Insko, 'Popular Induction: When is Consensus

Information Informative?', *Journal of Personality* 49 (1981) 2: 212–24.

54. Robert A. Baron, *Psychology: The Essential Science* (Boston: Allyn & Bacon, 1989); Valerie S. Folkes, 'The Availability Heuristic and Perceived Risk', *Journal of Consumer Research* 15 (June 1989): 13–23; Daniel Kahneman and Amos Tversky, 'Prospect Theory: An Analysis of Decision Under Risk', *Econometrica* 47 (1979): 263–91.

55. Wayne D. Hoyer, 'An Examination of Consumer Decision Making for a Common Repeat Purchase Product', *Journal of Consumer Research* 11 (December 1984): 822–9; Calvin P. Duncan, 'Consumer Market Beliefs: A Review of the Literature and an Agenda for Future Research', in *Advances in Consumer Research* 17, ed. Marvin E. Goldberg, Gerald Gorn and Richard W. Pollay (Provo, UT: Association for Consumer Research, 1990): 729–35; Frank Alpert, 'Consumer Market Beliefs and Their Managerial Implications: An Empirical Examination', *Journal of Consumer Marketing* 10 (1993) 2: 56–70.

56. Solomon, Drenan and Insko, 'Popular Induction'.

57. Folkes, 'The Availability Heuristic and Perceived Risk'.

58. Beales *et al.*, 'Consumer Search and Public Policy'.

59. Gary T. Ford and Ruth Ann Smith, 'Inferential Beliefs in Consumer Evaluations: An Assessment of Alternative Processing Strategies', *Journal of Consumer Research* 14 (December 1987): 363–71; Deborah Roedder John, Carol A. Scott and James R. Bettman, 'Sampling Data for Covariation Assessment: The Effects of Prior Beliefs on Search Patterns', *Journal of Consumer Research* 13 (June 1986): 38–47; Gary L. Sullivan and Kenneth J. Berger, 'An Investigation of the Determinants of Cue Utilization', *Psychology & Marketing* 4 (Spring 1987): 63–74.

60. John *et al.*, 'Sampling Data for Covariation Assessment'.

61. Duncan, 'Consumer Market Beliefs'.

62. Chr. Hjorth Andersen, 'Price as a Risk Indicator', *Journal of Consumer Policy* 10 (1987): 267–81.

63. David M. Gardner, 'Is There a Generalized Price–Quality Relationship?', *Journal of Marketing Research* 8 (May 1971): 241–3; Kent B. Monroe, 'Buyers' Subjective Perceptions of Price', *Journal of Marketing Research* 10 (1973): 70–80.

64. Durairaj Maheswaran, 'Country of Origin as a Stereotype: Effects of Consumer Expertise and Attribute Strength on Product Evaluations', *Journal of Consumer Research* 21 (September 1994): 354–65; Ingrid M. Martin and Sevgin Eroglu, 'Measuring a Multi-Dimensional Construct: Country Image', *Journal of Business Research* 28 (1993): 191–210; Richard Ettenson, Janet Wagner and Gary Gaeth, 'Evaluating the Effect of Country of Origin and the "Made in the U.S.A." Campaign: A Conjoint Approach', *Journal of Retailing* 64 (Spring 1988): 85–100; C. Min Han and Vern Terpstra, 'Country-of-Origin Effects for Uni-National & Bi-National

Products', *Journal of International Business* 19 (Summer 1988): 235–55; Michelle A. Morganosky and Michelle M. Lazarde, 'Foreign-Made Apparel: Influences on Consumers' Perceptions of Brand and Store Quality', *International Journal of Advertising* 6 (Fall 1987): 339–48.

65. See Richard Jackson Harris, Bettina Garner-Earl, Sara J. Sprick and Collette Carroll, 'Effects of Foreign Product Names and Country-of-Origin Attributions on Advertisement Evaluations', *Psychology & Marketing* 11 (March/April 1994) 2: 129–45; Terence A. Shimp, Saeed Samiee and Thomas J. Madden, 'Countries and Their Products: A Cognitive Structure Perspective', *Journal of the Academy of Marketing Science* 21 (Fall 1993) 4: 323–30. For an excellent review of the country-of-origin literature, see Nicholas Papadopoulos and Louise Heslop, *Product and Country Images: Research and Strategy* (New York: The Haworth Press, 1993). See also Israel D. Nebenzahl, Eugene D. Jaffe and Shlomo I. Lampert, 'Towards a Theory of Country Image Effect on Product Evaluation', *Management International Review* 37 (1997): 27–49; Johny K. Johansson, 'Why Country of Origin Effects are Stronger than Ever', *Association for Consumer Research*, European Conference, Stockholm, June 1997; Basil Englis and Anna Olofsson (eds), in press; Allan Jaeger, 'Crafting the Image of the Netherlands Abroad', *The Netherlander* (31 May 1997): 13.

66. Maheswaran, 'Country of Origin as a Stereotype'.

67. Joshua Levine, 'The Dance Drink', *Forbes* (12 September 1994): 232.

68. Quoted in Howard Banks, 'We'll Provide the Shillelaghs', *Forbes* (8 April 1996): 68 (2), p. 72; see also Brendan I. Koerner, 'Spreading the Taste of Ireland', *U.S. News & World Report* (24 February 1997): 15. For an ethnographic study of the 'authenticity' of Irish pubs, see Michael R. Solomon, Caroline K. Lego, Natalie T. Quilty and Stephanie L. Wright, 'A Thirst for the Real Thing in Themed Retail Environments: Consuming Authenticity in Irish Pubs', *Proceedings of the Society for Marketing Advances* (2000).

69. *Images of Europe: A Survey of Japanese Attitudes Toward European Products*, Report prepared by Dentsu Inc. for the Commission of the European Communities, Brussels, 1994.

70. Sung-Tai Hong and Robert S. Wyer, Jr, 'Effects of Country-of-Origin and Product–Attribute Information on Product Evaluation: An Information Processing Perspective', *Journal of Consumer Research* 16 (September 1989): 175–87; Marjorie Wall, John Liefeld and Louise A. Heslop, 'Impact of Country-of-Origin Cues on Consumer Judgments in Multi-Cue Situations: A Covariance Analysis', *Journal of the Academy of Marketing Science* 19 (1991) 2: 105–13. For a recent example which shows that country of origin does favourably influence Russian consumers

in an unexpected way, see Guy Chazan 'Foreign Products Get Russian Makeovers', *Wall Street Journal* (16 January 2001): A23.

71. Wai-Kwan Li and Robert S. Wyer, Jr, 'The Role of Country of Origin in Product Evaluations: Informational and Standard-of-Comparison Effects', *Journal of Consumer Psychology* 3(2) (1994): 187–212.

72. Maheswaran, 'Country of Origin as a Stereotype'.

73. Richard W. Stevenson, 'The Brands With Billion-Dollar Names', *New York Times* (28 October 1988): A1.

74. Ronald Alsop, 'Enduring Brands Hold Their Allure by Sticking Close to Their Roots', *Wall Street Journal* centennial edn (1989): B4.

75. 'Assessing Brands: Broad, Deep, Long and Heavy', *The Economist* (16 November 1996): 84–5.

76. 'What's in a Name?', *The Economist* (27 August 1988): 62.

77. Stuart Elliott, 'What's in a Name? Perhaps Billions', *New York Times* (12 August 1992): D6.

78. Jacob Jacoby and Robert Chestnut, *Brand Loyalty: Measurement and Management* (New York: Wiley, 1978).

79. Anne B. Fisher, 'Coke's Brand Loyalty Lesson', *Fortune* (5 August 1985): 44.

80. Jacoby and Chestnut, *Brand Loyalty*.

81. Ronald Alsop, 'Brand Loyalty is Rarely Blind Loyalty', *Wall Street Journal* (19 October 1989): B1.

82. Betsy Morris, 'The Brand's the Thing', *Fortune* (4 March 1996): 72 (8).

83. C. Whan Park, 'The Effect of Individual and Situation Related Factors on Consumer Selection of Judgmental Models', *Journal of Marketing Research* 13 (May 1976): 144–51.

84. Joseph W. Alba and Howard Marmorstein, 'The Effects of Frequency Knowledge on Consumer Decision Making', *Journal of Consumer Research* 14 (June 1987): 14–25.

Chapter 9

Shopping, buying, evaluating and disposing

Helmut's old VW barely resembled a car any more. His friends at the last Green Party meeting commented on the fading Greenpeace sticker on the windscreen and the growing oil spots on the road under his old car. They had also discussed with great enthusiasm the new ecologically sound hybrid cars soon to be introduced on the German market and suggested that Helmut ought to think about getting one. His colleagues at the bank where he worked joked about his car making theirs look bad in the staff car park. With the coming of spring Helmut's heart turned to love – and sports cars. After much encouragement from his work colleagues, he replaced his faithful old Beetle with a new BMW. Both he and his friends were elated. The staff car park was much improved and his problems were over – or so he thought. The old VW was still in his garage and he could not decide whether to sell it for a few hundred euros which he could use now, or have the car recycled at a significant cost. The next Green Party meeting was at hand and, recalling their advice, he wondered whether he should have opted for a less stylish, hybrid car. His anxiety was so high about being 'exposed' as a closet yuppie that he even considered driving the old VW to the meeting, if it would start. He could not help wondering whether he had done the right thing in buying the BMW, but it seemed like such a good idea at the time.

Suzanne Beckmann, Copenhagen Business School

Introduction

Helmut's dilemma highlights the importance of the purchase situation (it is spring, one wants to feel more 'seductive') and the post-purchase evaluation (was it the right choice?). On top of this, the experience of service linked to the act of purchasing and evaluating the purchase play central roles. In a recent British poll, 80 per cent of consumers said that they would change suppliers if they were unhappy with the service; and 86 per cent said that they expect better service today than they did five years ago.[1] Furthermore, the issue of environmental friendliness is becoming more and more important for many purchase decisions, just as it was for Helmut, even though environmentalism in this case was overruled by other desires.

Helmut's experience illustrates some of the concepts to be discussed in this chapter. Making a purchase is often not a simple, routine matter of going to a store and picking out something. As illustrated in Figure 9.1, a consumer's choices are affected by many personal factors, such as mood, time pressure and the particular situation or context for which the product is needed. In some situations, like the purchase of a car or a home, the salesperson or the reference group (which we will discuss in Chapter 10) play a pivotal role in the final choice. And today people are using the Web to arm themselves with product and price information before they even enter a dealership or a shop, which puts added pressure on retailers to deliver the value they expect.

The store environment also exerts a major influence: shopping is like a stage performance, with the customer involved either as a member of the audience or as an active participant. The quality of the performance is affected by the other *cast members* (salespeople or other shoppers), as well as by the *setting* of the play (the image of a particular store and the 'feeling' it imparts) and *props* (store fittings and promotional material which try to influence the shopper's decisions).

In addition, the consumer activity *per se* occurs *after* a product has been pur-

Figure 9.1 Issues related to purchase and post-purchase activities

chased and brought home. After using a product, the consumer must decide whether he or she is satisfied with it. The satisfaction process is especially important to marketers, who realize that the key to success is not selling a product once, but rather forging a relationship with the consumer so that he or she will continue to buy in the future. Finally, just as Helmut thought about the resale of his car, we must also consider how consumers go about disposing of products and how secondary markets (e.g. second-hand car dealers) often play a pivotal role in product acquisition. This chapter considers many issues related to purchase and post-purchase phenomena.

Antecedent states

A person's mood or physiological condition at the time of purchase can have a major impact on what is bought and can also affect how products are evaluated.[2] One reason is that behaviour is directed towards certain goal states, as was discussed in Chapter 3. In addition, the person's particular social identity, or the role that is being played at a given time, will be influential.[3]

Situational effects: mood and consumption situations

A consumer's mood will have an impact on purchase decisions. For example, stress can reduce a consumer's information-processing and problem-solving abilities.[4] Two dimensions determine whether a shopper will react positively or negatively to a store environment: *pleasure* and *arousal*. A person can enjoy or not enjoy a situation, and he or she can feel stimulated or not. As Figure 9.2 indicates, different combinations of pleasure and arousal levels result in a variety of emotional states. For example, an arousing situation can be either distressing or exciting, depending on

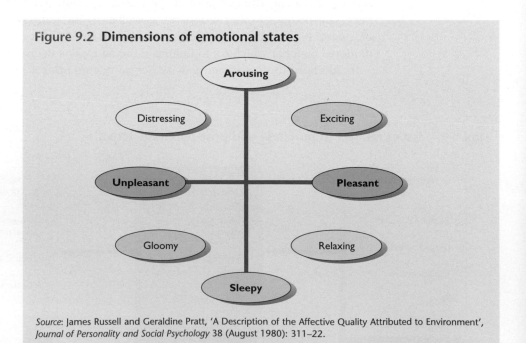

Figure 9.2 Dimensions of emotional states

Source: James Russell and Geraldine Pratt, 'A Description of the Affective Quality Attributed to Environment', *Journal of Personality and Social Psychology* 38 (August 1980): 311–22.

whether the context is positive or negative (e.g. a street riot vs. a street festival). Maintaining an upbeat mood in a pleasant context is one factor behind the success of theme parks such as Disneyland, which try to provide consistent doses of carefully calculated stimulation to patrons.[5]

A specific mood is some combination of these two factors. For example, the state of happiness is high in pleasantness and moderate in arousal, while elation would be high on both dimensions.[6] In general, a mood state (either positive or negative) biases judgements of products and services in that direction.[7] Put simply, consumers like things better when they are in a good mood (this may explain the popularity of the business lunch!).

Moods can be affected by store design, the weather or other factors specific to the consumer. In addition, music and television programming can affect mood; this has important consequences for commercials.[8] When consumers hear happy music or watch happy programmes, they have more positive reactions to commercials and products, especially when the marketing appeals are aimed at arousing emotional reactions.[9]

A *consumption situation* is defined by factors over and above characteristics of the person and of the product. Situational effects can be behavioural (e.g. entertaining friends) or perceptual (e.g. being depressed, or feeling pressed for time).[10] Common sense tells us that people tailor their purchases to specific occasions or that the way we feel at a specific point in time affects what we feel like buying or doing.

One reason for this variability is that the role a person plays at any time is partly determined by his or her *situational self-image*: 'Who am I right now?' (cf. Chapter 7).[11] Someone trying to impress his girlfriend by playing the role of 'man-about-town' may spend more lavishly, ordering champagne rather than beer and buying flowers – purchases he would never consider when he is with his male friends in a pub and playing the role of 'one of the boys'. As this example demonstrates, knowledge of what consumers are doing at the time a product is consumed may improve predictions of product and brand choice.[12] As one renowned European consumer researcher has pointed out, the question '*where* is consumer behaviour?' has been surprisingly little investigated.[13]

MARKETING PITFALL

Sometimes a marketing strategy can work too well. This is the case with Nabisco's Grey Poupon mustard brand, which the company has successfully positioned as a premium product in the USA. The problem is that consumers tend to save the brand for special occasions rather than spreading the mustard on just any old sandwich.

Grey Poupon's 'special' cachet is due to its long-running ad campaign, in which toffee-nosed aristocrats pass the mustard through the windows of their limousines. The campaign is so well known that the familiar tag line 'Pardon me, would you have any Grey Poupon?' was even repeated in the movie *Wayne's World*.

To dig themselves out of this situational hole, the brand's advertising agency developed a new advertising campaign, with magazine ads featuring simpler occasions, such as a picnic. In the ad shown overleaf, readers are reminded to 'Poupon the potato salad' or 'class up the cold cuts'.[14]

Nabisco, Inc.

Situational segmentation

By systematically identifying important usage situations, market segmentation strategies can be developed to position products that will meet the specific needs arising from these situations.[15] Many product categories are amenable to this form of segmentation. For example, consumers' furniture choices are often tailored to specific settings. We prefer different styles for a town flat, a country cottage or an executive suite. The South African ad for Volkswagen shown here emphasizes the versatility of the Volkswagen bus for different situations.

Table 9.1 gives one example of how situations can be used to fine-tune a segmentation strategy. By listing the major contexts where a product is used (e.g. skiing and sunbathing, for a suntan lotion) and the different users of the product, a matrix can be constructed that identifies specific product features which should be emphasized for each situation. Furthermore, our brand loyalty may be dependent on the situation. French research has demonstrated how our brand loyalty within product

This South African ad for Volkswagen emphasizes that brand criteria can differ depending upon the situation in which the product will be used.
Courtesy of Volkswagen of South Africa.

Table 9.1 A person–situation–segmentation matrix for suntan lotion

Situation	Young children Fair skin Dark skin	Teenagers Fair skin Dark skin	Adult women Fair skin Dark skin	Adult men Fair skin Dark skin	Benefits/features
Beach/boat sunbathing	Combined insect repellent		Summer perfume		a. Product serves as windburn protection b. Formula and container can stand heat c. Container floats and is distinctive (not easily lost)
Home–poolside sunbathing			Combined moisturizer		a. Product has large pump dispenser b. Product won't stain wood, concrete, furnishings
Sunlamp bathing			Combined moisturizer and massage oil		a. Product is designed specifically for type of lamp b. Product has an artificial tanning ingredient
Snow skiing			Winter perfume		a. Product provides special protection from special light rays and weather b. Product has antifreeze formula
Person benefit/ features	Special protection a. Protection is critical b. Formula is non-poisonous	Special protection a. Product fits in jeans pocket b. Product used by Female perfume opinion leaders	Special protection Female perfume	Special protection Male perfume	

Source: Adapted from Peter R. Dickson, 'Person–Situation: Segmentation's Missing Link', *Journal of Marketing* 46 (Fall 1982): 62.

categories such as fruit juice, cheese or coffee depends on whether our situation is one of the following: shopping for a reception for friends, running out of the product ourselves, or the shop having run out of stock.[16]

Social and physical surroundings

A consumer's physical and social environment can make a big difference in motives for product purchase and usage and also affect how the product is evaluated. Important cues include the person's physical surroundings, as well as the amount and type of other consumers also present in that situation. Dimensions of the physical environment, such as decor, smells, and even temperature, can significantly influence consumption. One study found that the use of scents in the retail environment can increase the pleasure and hedonic values derived from shopping.[17]

As we shall see in the next chapter, many of a consumer's purchase decisions are significantly affected by the groups or social settings in which these occur. In some cases, the presence or absence of other patrons ('*co-consumers*') in a setting can be a determinant attribute (cf. the discussion in Chapter 8), such as when an exclusive resort or boutique promises to provide privacy to privileged customers. At other times, the presence of others can have positive value. A sparsely attended football match or an empty bar can be depressing sights.

The presence of large numbers of people in a consumer environment increases arousal levels, so a consumer's subjective experience of a setting tends to be more intense. This polarization, however, can be both positive and negative. While the presence of other people creates a state of arousal, the consumer's actual experience depends on his or her *interpretation of* and *reaction to* this arousal. Crowding may result in avoidance (leaving the store earlier), aggressiveness (rushing others), opportunism (using the extra time to find bargains) or self-blame (for coming into the store at the wrong hour).[18] Hence, it is important to distinguish between *density* and *crowding* for this reason. The former term refers to the actual number of people occupying a space, while the psychological state of crowding exists only if a negative affective state occurs as a result of this density.[19] For example, 100 students packed into a classroom designed for 75 may be unpleasant for all concerned, but the same number of people jammed together at a party occupying a room of the same size might just make for a great party.

In addition, the type of consumers who patronize a store or service can serve as a store attribute. We may infer something about a store by examining its customers. For this reason, some restaurants require men to wear a jacket for dinner, and bouncers of some 'hot' nightspots hand-pick patrons based on whether they have the right 'look' for the club. To paraphrase the comedian Groucho Marx, 'I would never join a club that would have me for a member.'

Temporal factors

Time is one of consumers' most limiting resources. We talk about 'making time' or 'spending time', and we are frequently reminded that 'time is money'. Our perspectives on time can affect many stages of decision-making and consumption, such as needs that are stimulated, the amount of information search we undertake, and so on. Common sense tells us that more careful information search and deliberation occurs when we have the luxury of taking our time. A meticulous shopper who would normally check the price of an item in three different shops before buying it might be found running through the mall at Christmas just before closing time, frantically scooping up anything left on the shelves that might serve as a last-minute gift.

Economic time

Time is an economic variable: it is a resource that must be divided among activities.[20] Consumers try to maximize satisfaction by allocating time to the appropriate combination of tasks. Of course, people's allocation decisions differ: we all know people who seem to play all of the time, and others who are workaholics. An individual's priorities determine his or her **time style**.[21] Time style, it has been suggested, incorporates such dimensions as economic time, past orientation, future orientation, time submissiveness and time anxiety.[22]

Many consumers believe they are more pressed for time than ever before. This feeling may, however, be due more to perception than to fact. People may simply have more options for spending their time and feel pressured by the weight of it all. The average working day at the turn of the century was 10 hours (6 days per week), and women did 27 hours of housework per week, compared to under 5 hours now.

Of course, one reason for this difference is that men are sharing these burdens more.[23] This sense of *time poverty* has made consumers very responsive to marketing innovations that allow them to save time. More and more companies, and in Denmark even some kindergartens, offer to do the shopping and other daily chores for busy families during working hours, so that the whole evening can be devoted to family activities. New online business concepts based on improved delivery are popping up all over the Web. Delivery of videos, groceries, dry cleaning or developed photos to customers' doors are a few of the new time-saving online possibilities.[24] In a British pilot project, the Safeway grocery chain is providing 200 consumers with personal organizers to create shopping lists. By using frequent shopper data, the device can suggest items to replenish based on past purchase patterns. A 'smart refrigerator' developed by Frigidaire comes with a bar code scanner so that consumers can order a fresh bottle of salad dressing, ketchup or other frequently used items by scanning the used container across the door. The refrigerator picks up the bar code and automatically orders a fresh supply from the grocery store (cf. also the Electrolux refrigerator described in Chapter 15).[25]

With the increase in time poverty, researchers are also noting a rise in *polychronic activity*, where consumers do more than one thing at a time.[26] One area where this type of activity is especially prevalent is eating. Many consumers often do not allocate a specific time to dining, but do something else while eating. As one food industry executive commented, 'We've moved beyond grazing and into gulping.'[27] On the other hand, counter-trends of slow food are also found among other segments. A new 'slow food movement' originating in Italy and spreading via France to several European countries and even the United States witnesses a cultural resistance to the dissolving of cooking and eating a meal as a social event.

Psychological time

The psychological dimension of time, or how it is experienced, is an important actor in *queuing theory*. A consumer's experience of waiting can radically influence his or her perceptions of service quality. Although we assume that something must be good if we have to wait for it, the negative feelings aroused by long waits can quickly deter customers.[28] For example, it seems that the longer the wait, the more we like to wait alone rather than with others, presumably because for a short wait it is pleasant to have others to talk to, but the longer the waiting time, the more we perceive our fellow waiters as the main reason for the delay.[29] There are large cross-cultural differences in the acceptance of waiting time. Some 20 per cent of Sicilians consider a waiting time of 30 minutes for a dental appointment reasonable, and the average waiting time at a bank counter is 24 minutes.[30] What do you think?

Marketers have adopted a variety of 'tricks' to minimize psychological waiting time. These techniques range from altering customers' perceptions of a queue's length to providing distractions that divert attention away from waiting.[31] However, one study concluded that differences in queuing systems had only a minor effect on perceived waiting time compared to differences in waiting environment attractiveness and actual waiting time.[32]

- One hotel chain, after receiving numerous complaints about the wait for lifts, installed mirrors near the lift entrances. People's natural tendency to check their appearance reduced complaints, even though the actual waiting time was unchanged.

- Airline passengers often complain of the time they have to wait to claim their baggage. In one airport, it would take them one minute to walk from the plane to the baggage carousel where they would wait seven minutes for their luggage. By changing the layout so that the walk to the carousel took six minutes and bags arrived two minutes after that, complaints were almost entirely eliminated. More and more airlines are introducing 'ticketless flights' and self-check-in procedures in order to cut costs but also to avoid the annoying queues at the check-in counter.

● Automated check-out cashier registers are being tested in a variety of countries and contexts. One Swedish study found that many customers in both a grocery store and a library embraced the new technique in spite of its 'impersonal character' because they found it easy and quicker to use (after a period of adaptation), even if the actual time saving was not that significant.[33]

Multicultural dimensions

Even though the western time concept may become more and more dominant, at least in the international business world, this conception of time is far from universal. Large cultural differences exist in terms of people's time perspectives.[34] Some cultures run on procedural time and ignore the clock completely. People decide to do something 'when the time is right'. Much of the world appears to live on 'event time': for example, in Burundi people might arrange to meet when the cows return from the watering hole, while in Madagascar the response if someone asks how long it takes to get to the market might be 'the time it takes to cook rice'.[35]

Alternatively, in circular or cyclic time, people are governed by natural cycles, such as the regular occurrence of the seasons (a perspective found in many Latino cultures). To these consumers, the notion of the future does not make sense, because that time will be much like the present. Since the concept of future value does not exist, these consumers often prefer to buy an inferior product that is available now to waiting for a better one that will become available later. Also, it is hard to convince people who function on circular time to buy insurance or save for the future.

A social scientist recently compared the pace of life in 31 cities around the world as part of a study of time styles. He and his assistants timed how long it takes pedestrians to walk 60 feet and postal clerks to sell a stamp. Based on these responses, the fastest countries were claimed to be:

1. Switzerland, 2. Ireland, 3. Germany, 4. Japan, 5. Italy

and the slowest countries:

31. Mexico, 30. Indonesia, 29. Brazil, 28. El Salvador, 27. Syria.

Obviously, such national results depend on the actual place of measurement: consider, for example, the difference of Sicilian time compared with Milan time.[36]

Social time

Social time has been proposed as an important but overlooked time dimension in consumer behaviour.[37] Social time refers to the time in relation to social processes and rhythms and schedules in society. It takes into account how determined our lives are by interrelated temporal phenomena, such as working hours, opening hours, eating hours and other institutionalized schedules.

To most western consumers, time is something that is neatly compartmentalized: we wake up in the morning, go to school or work, come home, eat, go out, go to bed, then do it all over again. This perspective is called linear separable time (or Christian time): events proceed in an orderly sequence and different times are well defined: 'There's a time and a place for everything'. In this worldwide 'modernized' conception of time, there is a clear sense of past, present and future, and the pres-

**Figure 9.3
Drawings of
time**

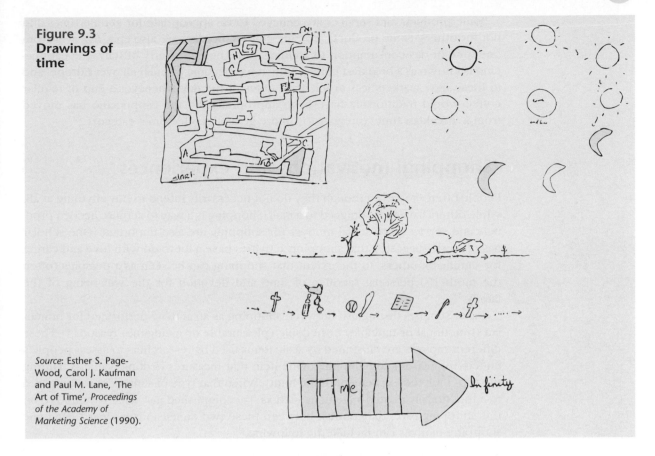

Source: Esther S. Page-
Wood, Carol J. Kaufman
and Paul M. Lane, 'The
Art of Time', *Proceedings
of the Academy of
Marketing Science* (1990).

ent is preferred to the past, whereas the future is generally rated better than the present.[38] Many activities are performed as the means to an end that will occur at a future point, as when people 'save for a rainy day'.

But even in North European and American cultures, the very linear and compartmentalized chronological time is not hegemonic, as indicated by the above-mentioned psychological time patterns, which call for a more relativistic and complex approach to time structures in societies most influenced by economic time concepts.[39]

When groups of university students were asked to draw a picture of time, the resulting sketches (Figure 9.3) illustrated some of these different temporal perspectives.[40] The drawing at the top represents procedural time: there is a lack of direction from left to right and little sense of past, present and future. The two drawings in the middle denote cyclical time, with regular cycles designated by markers. The bottom drawing represents linear time, with a segmented time line moving from left to right in a well-defined sequence.

**MARKETING
PITFALL**

An emphasis on speed resulted in some serious public relations problems for the American pizza delivery company Domino's Pizza, which guarantees delivery within 30 minutes. Critics claimed that this policy encouraged reckless driving and backed up this charge with some damaging statistics. In 1989, more than a dozen lawsuits, stemming from death or serious injuries caused by delivery people rushing to make the half-hour deadline, were filed against the company. The employee death rate was 50 per 100,000, equal to that suffered in the mining industry.[41] Domino's no longer offers the guarantee.

Some products and services are believed to be appropriate for certain times and not for others. Some products crossing cultural borders are also crossing over from one time of day consumption to another. In its home country of Italy, the cappuccino is known as a breakfast coffee. Now it has become popular all over Europe, and in these new markets it is drunk at all times of the day whenever a cup of regular coffee would traditionally have been appropriate. So the cappuccino has moved from a 'breakfast time' category to a more general 'coffee time' category.[42]

Shopping: motivations and experiences

People often shop even though they do not necessarily intend to buy anything at all, while others have to be dragged to a mall. Shopping is a way to acquire needed products and services, but social motives for shopping are also important. One scholar has recently suggested that shopping activities have a lot to do with love and caring for significant others, to the extent that shopping can be seen as a person's (often the mother's) personal sacrifice of time and devotion for the well-being of the family.[43]

Other scholars distinguish between shopping as an activity performed for utilitarian (functional or tangible) or hedonic (pleasurable or intangible) reasons.[44] These different motives are illustrated by scale items used by researchers to assess people's underlying reasons for shopping. One item that measures hedonic value is 'During the trip, I felt the excitement of the hunt'. When that type of sentiment is compared to a functionally related statement such as 'I accomplished just what I wanted to on this shopping trip', the contrast between these two dimensions is clear.[45] Hedonic shopping motives can include the following:[46]

- *Anticipated utility*: Desire for innovative products, expectations of benefits or hedonistic states which will be provided by the product to be acquired.

- *Role enactment*: Taking on the culturally prescribed roles regarding the conduct of shopping activity, such as careful product and price comparisons, possibly discussed with other shoppers.

- *Choice optimization*: Desire to find the absolutely best buy.

- *Negotiation*: To seek economic advantages and sports-like pleasure through bargaining interactions with sellers in a 'bazaar atmosphere'.

- *Affiliation*: Shopping centres are a natural place to affiliate. The shopping arcade has become a central meeting place for teenagers. It also represents a controlled, secure environment for other groups, such as the elderly.

- *Power and authority*: Entering a power game with the sales personnel and maybe feeling superior to the personnel. As every salesperson knows, some people love the experience of being waited on, even though they may not necessarily buy anything. One men's clothing salesman offered this advice: 'remember their size, remember what you sold them last time. Make them feel important! If you can make people feel important, they are going to come back. Everybody likes to feel important!'[47]

- *Stimulation*: Searching for new and interesting things offered in the marketplace – shopping just for fun.

Do people hate to shop or love it? It varies. Consumers can be segmented in terms of their **shopping orientation**, or general attitudes about shopping. These orientations may vary depending on the particular product categories and store types considered. Many people feel insecure about shopping for a car, but they may love to browse in record stores. Several shopping types have been identified, although the following list does not cover the whole range of possibilities:[48]

- *The economic shopper*: a rational, goal-oriented shopper who is primarily interested in maximizing the value of his or her money.
- *The personalized shopper*: a shopper who tends to form strong attachments to store personnel ('I shop where they know my name').
- *The ethical shopper*: a shopper who likes to help out the underdog and will support local shops rather than chainstores.
- *The apathetic shopper*: one who does not like to shop and sees it as a necessary but unpleasant chore.
- *The recreational shopper*: a person who views shopping as a fun, social activity – a preferred way to spend leisure time.

Given what we said above, however, one type of shopper is missing from this list: *the hate-to-shop shopper*. S/he is emerging from research on a variety of examples of the aversive side of shopping, including the hassle of finding a parking space, shopping with one's girl- or boyfriend with completely different shopping motivations, dealing with the fact that just when you've made a purchase you find something better or less expensive, or coping with intruding 'can-I-help-you' sales assistants.[49]

Multicultural dimensions

Who loves to shop the most? In a survey of women around the world, over 60 per cent said they enjoy shopping for clothes in every country except Hong Kong, where only 39 per cent responded so positively. The 'Born to Shop' prize goes to Latin Americans: over 80 per cent of women in countries like Brazil and Colombia agree that clothes shopping is a favourite activity. Other high-scoring countries include France, Italy and Japan. In comparison, only 61 per cent of American women said they like or love to go clothes shopping. Reflecting the casual trend that's swept the country in recent years, the survey indicates that American women are more likely to say that they are not as interested in clothing as they used to be, are more willing to be slightly underdressed at a party rather than slightly overdressed, and are more willing to wear one comfortable outfit all day long than change clothes to fit each occasion. Almost everywhere in the world, women agreed that store displays are the most important source of information about clothing. Two exceptions are German women, who ranked fashion magazines highest, and Mexican women, who reported that their families are the best place to learn about what to wear.[50]

Trends in the purchase environment

We see bumper stickers and T-shirts everywhere: 'Shop 'til you drop', 'When the going gets tough, the tough go shopping', 'Born to shop'. Like it or not, shopping is a major activity for many consumers. The competition for shoppers amongst retailers is getting tougher. Retailers must now offer something extra to lure shoppers, whether that something is excitement or just plain bargains.[51] One prominent trend is the tendency to blur the boundaries between types of outlet. For example, supermarket and hypermarket chains are now posing a serious threat to the petrol companies by taking larger and larger shares of their market (in France, the supermarkets' share is about 50 per cent).[52] In Denmark and other countries, the petrol stations are striking back, increasing their share of the market for daily groceries.

Another European trend is the increase of trade from kiosks, smaller stores with extended opening hours carrying a small selection of daily goods as well as snack products, sweets, newspapers, etc., sometimes more or less like the 7–11 concept imported from the United States. In many countries, such kiosks are well established and are often run by Middle Eastern or North African immigrants. But in countries such as Finland, where the introduction of kiosks is more recent, it has created a whole new situation for a certain part of the retail system.[53]

In order to be able to compete in the European single market, many retail chains have undergone an internationalization process. For example, of the top 25 European retail chains of daily goods, only one (no. 25) is not internationalized or at least participating in an international network of co-operating chains. The ten biggest companies control 30 per cent of the turnover in daily goods in Europe, and the concentration is growing.[54]

Store loyalty

In this turbulent environment, store-loyal consumers are highly valued by retailers. They will routinely visit a small set of stores without considering others or doing much in the way of comparative pre-purchase search. However, consumers now have an abundance of choices regarding where to shop, including the electronic alternatives. For this reason, people do not tend to be as store-loyal as they once were.[55] In Great Britain, the retail chain Tesco was the biggest spender on marketing among British retailers in 1990–4. Together with the introduction of a customer loyalty card, their marketing strategy helped them to take over from their rival Sainsbury as the biggest British retailer. Sainsbury finally gave up its initial resistance to the introduction of loyalty cards in 1996. Their new card became an instant success: between June and August of that year they issued more than 5 million loyalty cards and gained 1 per cent market share increase.[56]

E-commerce: clicks vs. bricks

As more and more websites pop up to sell everything from refrigerator magnets to cars, marketers are hotly debating how this new **cyberspace** marketplace will affect how they conduct business.[57] In particular, many are losing sleep wondering whether e-commerce is destined to replace traditional retailing, work in concert with it, or perhaps even fade away to become another fad your children will laugh about someday. That's unlikely, even though the predictions concerning the e-revolution so far have tended to grossly overestimate the growth rapidity. Even in the most 'advanced' e-commercial markets like the USA, the share of turnover is still only a few per cent of the total market exchanges taking place. And the largest proportion is still accounted for by the business-to-business market. A Swedish survey indicates that searching for product and service information are more important aspects of their internet behaviour than actual purchases. Only 9 per cent want to buy food (and a mere 1 per cent had actually tried it), and even the highest scoring purchase types like travel and ticket purchase do not exceed 30 per cent.[58] But there are obvious differences between the older and younger segments concerning these matters. The e-market will become more and more important – however, it will not come overnight and not to the same extent in all sectors. So far the obvious e-commerce failures in consumer markets have largely exceeded the number of successes.

For marketers, the growth of online commerce is a sword that cuts both ways: on the one hand, they can reach customers around the world even if they're physically located 100 miles from nowhere. On the other hand, it also means that their competition now comes not only from the store across the street, but from thousands of websites spanning the globe. A second problem is that offering products directly to consumers has the potential to cut out the middleman – the loyal store-based retailers who carry the firm's products and who sell them at a marked-up price.[59] The 'clicks vs. bricks' dilemma is raging in the marketing world.

So, can you have your cake and eat it too? Coca-Cola thinks so, with its new 'think local, act local' strategy based on a philosophy of getting closer to the consumers. A Danish–Swedish–Norwegian–Finnish (probably as local as Coca-Cola gets!) campaign featuring an Indiana Jones-inspired adventure quiz has as its primary purpose to get teenagers to log on to the Coca-Cola website in order to participate in a quiz with adventurous travels as prizes. 'If we want to communicate on the teens premises, we have to make an active use of the internet and SMS media', says one executive.[60] Another possibility for reaching the youngster markets is product placement in the chat rooms. For example, a virtual rose given to a fellow chatter could be from a branded chain of florists. Or the chat environment can be constructed as a cruise ship with various branded services and games available for the chatters.[61] But more serious purposes have also demonstrated their abilities to utilize the net. A Danish anti-cancer organization supporting research and cancer patients has a website where visitors can give a small gift by clicking on a button. Immediately 'thank you' appears with six banners referring to sponsoring companies who paid for the small gift, encouraging the visitor to visit the sponsors. This format has produced a much higher rate of banner-clicking than normal commercial banners.[62]

So, what makes e-commerce sites successful? According to a survey by NPD Online, 75 per cent of online shoppers surveyed said that good customer service would make them shop at the site again.[63] And many successful e-tailers are learning that using technology to provide extra value for customers is attracting and keeping customers. A variety of online banking services are becoming very popular. And estate agents can provide much more information, e.g. floor plans and more appealing photographs of homes for sale, than has been possible through the traditional print media. Interactive TV is letting home viewers provide input to the videos played on MTV and to play along on *Who Wants to be a Millionaire?*. Soon MTV viewers will be able to use their remote controls to purchase the CDs that go with the music videos they are seeing.

From the consumer's perspective, electronic marketing has increased convenience by breaking down many of the barriers caused by time and location. You can shop 24 hours a day without leaving home, you can read today's newspaper without getting drenched picking up a hard copy in a rainstorm, and you don't have to wait for the 6 o'clock news to find out what the weather will be like tomorrow – at home or around the globe. And, with the increasing use of hand-held devices and wireless communications, you can get that same information – from stock quotes to the weather – even when you're away from your computer. In Figure 9.4, the major domains in the development of consumer possibilities in cyberspace are depicted.

Consumer experiences in cyberspace can be analysed according to two dimensions: *telepresence* and *bricolage*.[64] Telepresence expresses the degree to which the consumer feels immersed in the virtual environment, the time spent there and the positive feelings generated, whereas bricolage (a French word meaning getting by with whatever is at hand) is an indication of the interactive medium's possibilities for the consumer to be in control of the information gathered and used, presumably leading to a higher degree of involvement in and retention of the information.

Figure 9.4 **Everyday life of a consumer in cyberspace**

| Areas of emphasis in the 1980s | Emerging areas (1990s) | Futuristic |

Source: Alladi Venkatesh, 'Cybermarketscapes and Consumer Freedoms and Identities', *European Journal of Marketing* 32(7/8) (1998): 664–76. Used by permission.

However, all is not perfect in the virtual world. E-commerce does have its limitations. Security is one important concern. We hear horror stories of consumers whose credit cards and other identity information have been stolen. While an individual's financial liability in most theft cases is limited to approximately 60 euros, or £40, the damage to one's credit rating can last for years. Some shady companies are making money by prying and then selling personal information to others – one company promotes itself as 'an amazing new tool that allows you to find out EVERYTHING you ever wanted to know about your friends, family, neighbors, employees, and even your boss!'[65] Pretty scary. Almost daily we hear of hackers getting into a business or even a government website and causing havoc. Businesses risk the loss of trade secrets and other proprietary information. Many must spend significant amounts to maintain security and conduct regular audits to ensure the integrity of their sites.

Other limitations of e-commerce relate to the actual shopping experience. While it may be satisfactory to buy a computer or a book on the Internet, buying clothing and other items where touching the item or trying it on is essential may be less attractive. Even though most companies have very liberal return policies, consumers can still get stuck with large delivery and return shipping charges for items that don't fit or simply aren't the right colour. Some of the pros and cons of e-commerce

Table 9.2 Pros and cons of e-commerce

Benefits of e-commerce	Limitations of e-commerce
For the consumer	**For the consumer**
Shop 24 hours a day	Lack of security
Less travelling	Fraud
Can receive relevant information in seconds from any location	Can't touch items
More choice of products	Exact colours may not reproduce on computer monitors
More products available to less-developed countries	Expensive to order and then return
Greater price information	Potential breakdown of human relationships
Lower prices so that less affluent can purchase	
Participate in virtual auctions	
Fast delivery	
Electronic communities	
For the marketer	**For the marketer**
The world is the marketplace	Lack of security
Decreases costs of doing business	Must maintain site to reap benefits
Very specialized businesses can be successful	Fierce price competition
Real-time pricing	Conflicts with conventional retailers
	Legal issues not resolved

Source: Adapted from Michael R. Solomon and Elnora W. Stuart, *Welcome to Marketing.Com: The Brave New World of E-Commerce* (Englewood Cliffs, NJ: Prentice Hall, 2001).

are summarized in Table 9.2. It's clear that traditional shopping isn't quite dead yet – the winners in the future retail scene will be those who can create a high degree of synergy between their online and offline outlets.[66] Hence, bricks-and-mortar retailers do need to work harder to give shoppers something they can't get in the virtual world – a stimulating or pleasant environment in which to browse. Now let's consider how they're doing that.

Servicescapes: retailing as theatre

Shopping can no longer be regarded as a simple act of purchasing.[67] A retail culture has arisen,[68] where the act of shopping has taken on new entertainment and/or experiential dimensions as retailers compete for customers' attention, not to speak of their loyalty. The act of shopping ties into a number of central existential aspects of human life such as sexuality.[69] Furthermore, the customer may not be regarded as a passive recipient of the offerings of the purchase environment but rather as an active co-creator of this very environment and the meanings attached to it,[70] in a situation analogous to the focus among 'marketing mavens' (see next chapter) on flexibility in the area of product supply and tailor-made marketing mixes for the individual consumer.[71] One of the most obvious trends in the retailing sector in Europe is the construction of shopping malls, most often modelled on American prototypes. In the US today, the mall is often a focal point in a community: 94 per cent of adults visit a mall at least once a month and more than half of all retail purchases (excluding cars and petrol) are made in a mall.[72] Malls are also flourishing in Europe, where, once introduced into an area, they often bring with them a whole new combination of leisure activities, shopping and social encounters in safe environments.[73]

Malls are becoming giant entertainment centres, almost to the point where their traditional retail occupants sometimes seem like an afterthought.[74] It is now common to find features such as carousels, miniature golf or batting cages in a suburban mall. As one retailing executive put it, 'Malls are becoming the new mini-amusement parks.'[75] The importance of creating a positive, vibrant and interesting image has led innovative marketers to blur the line between shopping and the theatre. Shopping malls and individual stores have to create environments that stimulate people and allow them to shop and be entertained at the same time.[76] Themed shopping centres and stores bear witness to the multitude of styles that flourish in the attempt to attract consumers who seek more than just a distribution outlet.[77] The Hard Rock Café, established in London over 25 years ago, now has over 45 restaurants around the world, and has become a sort of pilgrimage place in itself. Some consumers make a point of collecting as many Hard Rock Café merchandise items (T-shirts, etc.) from as many HRCs in the world as possible.

The classic European counterpart to the American malls is the department store.[78] The first department stores can be seen as marking the introduction of a modern consumer culture, nourished by dreams of abundance.[79] Department stores often hold elaborate store-wide promotions based, for example, on the culture of a selected country. During these events the entire store is transformed, with each department featuring unusual merchandise from the country. These promotions are accompanied by lavish parties, food and entertainment associated with that country.

The following are a few examples of 'performers' in the retailing theatre:

● A Dutch internet bank, ING, has turned the ground floor of its office in Toronto, Canada, into a stylish café, complete with counter, armchairs, sofas and background music. But in addition to the variety of coffees, the blackboard behind the counter also announces interest rates in various savings accounts and other banking information.[80]

● The Powerscourt Townhouse Centre in Dublin succeeded in merging a variety of styles and features, including a grand piano on a stage in the central hall, to make a sort of new version of a Victorian marketplace atmosphere. Unlike the Mall of America, it does not appear as a carefully planned environment but rather a happy blend of many consumption opportunities including an Italian restaurant, a modern hairstylist, an antique shop, etc. in a stylish classical setting.[81]

● American malls, the new 'retail-entertainment complexes', have also attracted a lot of attention among European retail environment designers and academics in the last few years. Minneapolis's Mall of America, the largest one in the United States, is organized around a complete amusement park (Camp Snoopy) as well as a Lego playing/exhibition area. Furthermore, it comprises 400 stores, 45 restaurants, 9 discos and 14 cinemas and ranks among the foremost *tourist attractions* in the USA. It has a complete aquatic theme park (Underwater World) as well as a number of other featured themed environments including Planet Hollywood and Rainforest Café, and an Italian restaurant, Tutti Benucci, built upon the image of a classical 1950s southern Italian restaurant by Mr Benucci himself, using his family photos as wall decoration and his grandmother's and mother's recipes in the kitchen. The only thing is, Mr Benucci never really existed but was created by a marketing department . . .[82]

Store image

With so many stores competing for customers, how do consumers select one rather

Multicultural dimensions

American retailers, including Blockbuster Video, Original Levi's stores, Foot Locker, Toys'R'Us and The Gap, are exporting their version of the dynamic retail environment to Europe – with some adaptations. These 'invasions' often begin in Britain, since cultural differences seem smaller, bureaucratic hurdles lower and personnel costs reduced. The Gap found that it needed to stock smaller sizes than in the US, and that many of its European customers prefer darker colours. Also, some retailers have done away with the 'greeters' who stand at the entrance in many American stores – Europeans tend to find them intimidating.[83]

Hard Rock Café: one of the oldest and most well-established themed consumer environments.
Photo by Karen Malene Andreasen.

than another? Like products, stores may be thought of as having 'personalities'. Some stores have very clearly defined images (either good or bad); others tend to blend into the crowd. They may not have anything distinctive about them and may be overlooked for this reason. This personality, or **store image**, is composed of many different factors. The design and general image of the store is central to the perception of the goods displayed there, whether we are talking about fashion,[84] food products[85] or any other type of good. Store features, coupled with such consumer characteristics as shopping orientation, help to predict which shopping outlets people will prefer.[86] Some of the important dimensions of a store's profile are location, merchandise suitability and the knowledge and congeniality of the sales staff.[87]

When shoppers think about stores, they may not say, 'Well, that place is fairly good in terms of convenience, the salespeople are acceptable and service is good.' They are more likely to say, 'That place gives me the creeps', or 'I always enjoy shopping there'. Consumers evaluate stores in terms of both their specific attributes *and* a global evaluation, or the **store gestalt** (see Chapter 2).[88] This overall feeling may have more to do with such intangibles as interior design and the types of people one finds in the store than with such aspects as returns policies or credit availability. As a result, some stores are likely to be consistently in consumers' minds, while others will never be considered.

Because a store's gestalt is now recognized as a very important aspect of the retailing mix, attention is increasingly paid to **atmospherics**, or the 'conscious designing of space and its various dimensions to evoke certain effects in buyers'.[89] These dimensions include colours, scents and sounds. For any store or any shopping centre, one may think of this process as a careful *orchestration* of the various elements, each playing their part to form a whole.[90]

Many elements of store design can be cleverly controlled to attract customers and produce desired effects on consumers. Light colours impart a feeling of spaciousness and serenity, and signs in bright colours create excitement. Stores done out in red tend to make people tense, while a blue decor imparts a calmer feeling.[91] In one subtle but effective application, fashion designer Norma Kamali replaced fluorescent lights with pink ones in department store changing rooms. The light had the effect of flattering the face and banishing wrinkles, making female customers more willing to try on (and buy) the company's bathing suits.[92]

In addition to visual stimuli, all sorts of cues can influence behaviours. For example, music can affect eating habits.[93] A study found that diners who listened to loud, fast music ate more food. In contrast, those who listened to Mozart or Brahms ate less and more slowly. The researchers concluded that diners who choose soothing music at mealtimes can increase weight loss by at least 5 lb a month![94]

In-store decision-making

Despite all their efforts to 'pre-sell' to consumers through advertising, marketers are increasingly recognizing the significant degree to which many purchases are influenced by the store environment. A Danish survey indicated that nine out of ten customers did not plan the purchase of at least one third of the goods they acquired.[95] The proportion of unplanned purchases is even higher for some product categories. For the US market it is estimated that the purchase of 85 per cent of sweets and chewing gum, almost 70 per cent of cosmetics and 75 per cent of oral hygiene purchases is unplanned.[96]

Impulse buying

When a shopper is prompted to buy something while in a shop, one of two different processes may be at work: *unplanned buying* may occur when a person is unfamiliar with a store's layout or perhaps when under some time pressure; or a person may be reminded to buy something by seeing it on a shelf.[97]

In contrast, **impulse buying** occurs when the person experiences a sudden urge that he or she cannot resist.[98] For this reason, so-called impulse items such as sweets and chewing gum are conveniently placed near the checkout. Similarly, many supermarkets have installed wider aisles to encourage browsing, and the widest tend to contain products with the highest margin. Low mark-up items that are purchased regularly tend to be stacked high in narrower aisles, to allow shopping trolleys to speed through.[99] A more recent high-tech tool has been added to encourage impulse buying: a device called 'The Portable Shopper', a personal scanning gun which allows customers to ring up their own purchases as they shop. The gun was initially developed for Albert Heijn, the Netherlands' largest grocery chain, to move customers through the store more quickly. It is now in use in over 150 groceries worldwide.[100]

One particular type of occasion where a lot of impulse buying goes on is the seasonal sales, which appeal especially to younger and price-conscious shoppers according to one British study.[101] In general, shoppers can be categorized in terms of how much advance planning they do. *Planners* tend to know what products and specific brands they will buy beforehand, *partial planners* know they need certain products, but do not decide on specific brands until they are in the store, and *impulse purchasers* do no advance planning whatsoever.[102] Figure 9.5 was drawn by a consumer who participated in a study on consumers' shopping experiences and who was asked to sketch a typical impulse purchaser.

Point-of-purchase stimuli

Because so much decision-making apparently occurs while the shopper is in the purchasing environment, retailers are beginning to pay more attention to the amount of information in their stores, as well as to the way it is presented. It has been estimated that impulse purchases increase by 10 per cent when appropriate

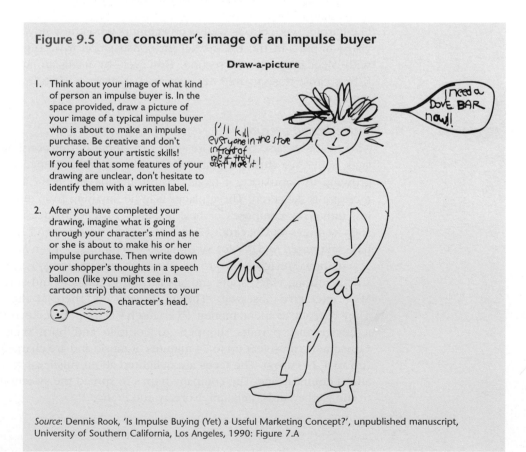

Figure 9.5 One consumer's image of an impulse buyer

Draw-a-picture

1. Think about your image of what kind of person an impulse buyer is. In the space provided, draw a picture of your image of a typical impulse buyer who is about to make an impulse purchase. Be creative and don't worry about your artistic skills! If you feel that some features of your drawing are unclear, don't hesitate to identify them with a written label.

2. After you have completed your drawing, imagine what is going through your character's mind as he or she is about to make his or her impulse purchase. Then write down your shopper's thoughts in a speech balloon (like you might see in a cartoon strip) that connects to your character's head.

Source: Dennis Rook, 'Is Impulse Buying (Yet) a Useful Marketing Concept?', unpublished manuscript, University of Southern California, Los Angeles, 1990: Figure 7.A displays are used. Consumers' images of a good-value-for-money purchase are in many cases not induced by careful price examinations but by powerful and striking in-store information.[103] Each year, American companies spend more than $13 billion on **point-of-purchase stimuli (POP)**. A point-of-purchase stimulus can be an elaborate product display or demonstration, a coupon-dispensing machine, or someone giving out free samples of a new biscuit in the grocery aisle.

Much of the growth in point-of-purchase activity has been in new electronic technologies.[104] Videotronic, a German hardware producer, has specialized in compact in-store video displays. The newest feature is a touch-screen selection of various information which eventually provokes scent to appear.[105] The Point-of-Purchase Radio Corporation offers in-store radio networks which are now used by about 60 grocery chains.[106] Some shopping trolleys have a small screen that displays advertising, which is keyed to the specific areas of the store through which the trolley is wheeled.[107] New interactive possibilities seem to enhance the effectiveness of POP information systems,[108] although the effect of in-store advertising and other POP continues to be difficult to assess. High-tech solutions such as hand-held computers which will process filmed as well as alphanumerical data are used by Reebok to show whether their in-store efforts are used correctly and which type works best in comparison to competitors.[109]

In-store *displays* are another commonly used device to attract attention in the store environment. While most displays consist of simple racks that dispense the product and/or related coupons, some highlight the value of regarding retailing as theatre by supplying the 'audience' with elaborate performances and scenery. For example, POP displays are one of the most important tools in the annual toy acquisition peak before Christmas, and the winners are the large and established brands like Barbie, Lego, etc. as well as newcomers who know how to make an impressive visual impact. In the UK market for construction toys, Lego has long dominated, with Meccano a distant second. However, by using an aggressive POP strategy, K'Nex came close to a 20 per cent market share in 1996 from a standing start that same year.[110]

Place-based media

Advertisers are also being more aggressive about hitting consumers with their messages, wherever they may be. *Place-based media* is a specialized medium that is growing in popularity: it targets consumers based on the locations in which the message is delivered. These places may be anything from airports, doctors' surgeries, university campuses or health clubs. Turner Broadcasting System has begun such ventures as Checkout Channel for grocery stores and Airport Channel, and it has even tested McDTV for McDonald's restaurants.[111] Even MTV is getting in on the act: its new Music Report, to be shown in record stores, is a two-hour 'video capsule' featuring video spots and ads for music retailers and corporate sponsors. An MTV executive observed, 'They're already out there at the retail environment. They're ready to spend money.'[112] A Dutch CD shop, Free Record Shop, has installed a device that permits shoppers to compile and burn their own CD in-store. Consumers can select up to 74 minutes of music and are charged a per-song amount (up to 1.23 euros). The teens are delighted about this legal way of making personalized compilations. The company hopes to spread the system to their other stores in the Netherlands, Belgium, Norway and France.[113]

The salesperson

One of the most important in-store factors is the salesperson, who attempts to influence the buying behaviour of the customer.[114] This influence can be understood in terms of **exchange theory**, which stresses that every interaction involves an exchange of value. Each participant gives something to the other and hopes to receive something in return.[115]

What 'value' does the customer look for in a sales interaction? There are a variety of resources a salesperson might offer. He or she, for example, might offer expertise about the product to make the shopper's choice easier. Alternatively, the customer may be reassured because the salesperson is an admired or likeable person whose tastes are similar and is seen as someone who can be trusted.[116] In fact, research data attest to the impact of a salesperson's appearance on sales effectiveness. In sales, as in much of life, attractive people appear to hold the upper hand.[117]

A buyer/seller situation is like many other dyadic encounters (two-person groups): it is a relationship where some agreement must be reached about the roles of each participant, when a process of *identity negotiation* occurs.[118] For example, if the salesperson immediately establishes him- or herself as an all-knowing expert (and the customer accepts this position), the salesperson is likely to have more influence over the customer through the course of the relationship. Some of the factors that help to determine a salesperson's role (and relative effectiveness) are his or her age, appearance, educational level and motivation to sell.[119]

In addition, more effective salespersons usually know their customers' traits and preferences better than do ineffective salespersons, since this knowledge allows them to adapt their approach to meet the needs of the specific customer.[120] The ability to be adaptable is especially vital when customers and salespeople differ in terms of their *interaction styles*.[121] Consumers, for example, vary in the degree of assertiveness they bring to interactions. At one extreme, non-assertive people believe that complaining is not socially acceptable and may be intimidated in sales situations. Assertive people are more likely to stand up for themselves in a firm but non-threatening way, while aggressives may resort to rudeness and threats if they do not get their way.[122]

Post-purchase satisfaction

Consumer satisfaction/dissatisfaction (CS/D) is determined by the overall feelings, or attitude, a person has about a product after it has been purchased. Consumers are engaged in a constant process of evaluating the things they buy as these products are integrated into their daily consumption activities.[123] Customer satisfaction has a real impact on profitability: a recent study conducted among a large sample of Swedish consumers found that product quality affects customer satisfaction, which in turn results in increased profitability among firms who provide quality products.[124] Quality is more than a marketing 'buzzword'.

Perceptions of product quality

Just what do consumers look for in products? The answer's easy: they want quality and value. Especially because of foreign competition, claims of product quality have become strategically crucial to maintaining a competitive advantage.[125] Consumers use a number of cues to infer quality, including brand name, price, and even their own estimates of how much money has been put into a new product's advertising campaign.[126] These cues, as well as others such as product warranties and follow-up letters from the company, are often used by consumers to relieve perceived risk and assure themselves that they have made smart purchase decisions.[127]

What is quality?

In *Zen and the Art of Motorcycle Maintenance*, a cult book from the mid-1970s, the hero literally goes mad trying to work out the meaning of quality.[128] Marketers appear to use the word 'quality' as a catch-all term for 'good'. Because of its wide and imprecise usage, the attribute 'quality' threatens to become a meaningless claim. If everyone has it, what good is it?

One way to define quality is to establish uniform standards to which products from around the world must conform. This is the intent of the International Standards Organization, a Geneva-based organization that does just that. A set of quality criteria were initially developed in 1987 to regulate product quality. The broad set of guidelines are known as **ISO standards**. These standards exist in different versions and cover issues related to the manufacture and installation of products, post-sale servicing but also sustainability and environmentally friendly production processes.

The importance of expectations

Global standards for quality help to ensure that products work as promised, but consumers' evaluations of those products are a bit more complex. Satisfaction or dissatisfaction is more than a reaction to the actual performance quality of a product or service. First of all, satisfaction is not just a matter of functional but also of the hedonic performance of the product – something which may be more difficult for the producer to ensure beforehand. When we buy a book, we expect to get more from it than that the pages get loose.[129]

Satisfaction is then highly influenced by prior expectations regarding all aspects of quality. According to the **expectancy disconfirmation model**, consumers form beliefs about product performance based upon prior experience with the product and/or communications about the product that imply a certain level of quality.[130] When something performs the way we thought it would, we may not think much about it. If, on the other hand, it fails to live up to expectations, negative affect may result. And if performance exceeds our expectations, we are satisfied and pleased.

To understand this perspective, think about different types of restaurant. People expect to be provided with sparkling clear glassware in high-class restaurants, and they might become upset if they are offered a grimy glass. On the other hand, we may not be surprised to find fingerprints on our mug at a local 'greasy spoon'; we may even shrug it off because it contributes to the place's 'charm'. An important lesson emerges for marketers from this perspective: don't overpromise.[131]

One approach to customer satisfaction, known as the *Kano-model*, operates with three kinds of expectation: basis, performance and enthusiasm expectations. The first includes the implicit and taken-for-granted qualities expected from a product. If these are not satisfied, the product will never be able to live up to the customer's requirements, but even if fulfilled, they do not profile the product because these qualities are taken for granted as a minimum. For the performance expectations satisfaction is proportional to how well the product lives up to the expectations. Such quality requirements are often specified and articulated by the customer. In fact, it is wrong to call the enthusiasm-related product features expectations, since their essential character is that they are *not* expected by the customer. Therefore, such positive surprises can lead to a very great feeling of satisfaction, since the product quality was even better than expected.[132] Furthermore, research evidence indicates that product experience is important for customer satisfaction. When people have no experiences they are relatively easy to satisfy, but with growing experience they become harder to satisfy. Then, when they reach a certain level of experience, satisfaction again becomes easier to obtain, since consumers are now 'experts' and this facilitates choice and generates more realistic expectations.[133]

Furthermore, satisfaction levels are determined not only by the product purchased but also by the expectations about the quality of alternatives that were *not* purchased. In other words, the higher the expectations about unselected alternatives, the lower the level of satisfaction with the chosen good.[134] A general conclusion which one should draw from such a discussion is that consumer goals may be multiple and the product or service offer so complex to evaluate that any measurement of satisfaction must be used with caution.[135]

Quality and product failures

The power of quality claims is most evident when they are not fulfilled, as when a company's product fails. Here, consumers' expectations are dashed, and dissatisfaction results. In these situations, marketers should immediately take steps to reassure customers. When the company confronts the problem candidly, consumers are often willing to forgive and forget, as was the case with Perrier when traces of benzene were found in the water.

Acting on dissatisfaction

If a person is not happy with a product or service, what can be done? Essentially, a consumer can take one or more different courses of action:[136]

1 *Voice response*. The consumer can appeal directly to the retailer for redress (e.g. a refund).

2 *Private response*. The consumer can express dissatisfaction about the store or product to friends and/or boycott the store. As will be discussed in Chapter 10, negative word of mouth (WOM) can be very damaging to a store's reputation.

3 *Third-party response*. The consumer can take legal action against the merchant, register a complaint with the Ombudsman, or perhaps write a letter to a newspaper.

A number of factors influence which route is taken. The consumer may in general be assertive or meek. Action is more likely to be taken for expensive products such as household durables, cars and clothing than for inexpensive products.[137] Also, if the consumer does not believe that the store will respond positively to a complaint, the person will be more likely to switch brands than fight.[138] Ironically, marketers should *encourage* consumers to complain to them: people are more likely to spread the word about unresolved negative experiences to their friends than they are to boast about positive occurrences.[139] Moreover, consumers are more likely to spread negative information about a bad service than they are to spread information about a succesful complaint handling. Complaint management is thus not as good an alternative as high-quality service in the first place.[140]

Product disposal

Because people often do form strong attachments to products, the decision to dispose of something may be a painful one. One function performed by possessions is to serve as anchors for our identities: our past lives on in our things.[141] This attachment is exemplified by the Japanese, who ritually 'retire' worn-out sewing needles, chopsticks and even computer chips by burning them as thanks for good service.[142]

Although some people have more trouble than others in discarding things, even a 'magpie' does not keep everything. Consumers must often dispose of things, either because they have fulfilled their designated functions, or possibly because they no longer fit with consumers' views of themselves. Concern about the environment coupled with a need for convenience has made ease of product disposal a key attribute in categories from razors to nappies. Since we will deal with recycling and environmentalism in a later chapter, we will only briefly address other aspects of product disposal here.

Disposal options

When a consumer decides that a product is no longer of use, several choices are available. The person can either (1) keep the item, (2) temporarily dispose of it, or (3) permanently dispose of it. In many cases, a new product is acquired even though the old one still functions. Some reasons for this replacement include a desire for new features, a change in the person's environment (e.g. a refrigerator is the wrong colour for a freshly painted kitchen) or a change in the person's role or self-image.[143] Figure 9.6 provides an overview of consumers' disposal options. Compared to the original scheme, we have added the opportunity of 'to be recycled' in the lower left corner. This is interesting because it bears witness to the fact that thinking about recycling as a 'natural' thing to do is a rather recent occurrence.

MARKETING OPPORTUNITY

Some enterprising entrepreneurs have found profitable ways to encourage recycling by creating fashion items out of recycled materials. Two young jewellery designers in New York created a fad by making necklaces out of old bottle caps. They even pay homeless people to collect the caps. A company called Little Earth Productions Inc. makes all its products from recycled materials. They sell backpacks decorated with old licence plates, a shoulder bag made from rubber and hubcaps, and even purses crafted from discarded tuna cans.[144]

Lateral cycling: junk vs. 'junque'

Interesting consumer processes occur during **lateral cycling**, where already purchased objects are sold to others or exchanged for yet other things. Many purchases are made second-hand, rather than new. The reuse of other people's things is especially important in our throw-away society because, as one researcher put it, 'there is no longer an "away" to throw things to'.[145]

Flea markets, garage sales, classified advertisements, bartering for services, hand-me-downs and the black market all represent important alternative marketing systems which operate in addition to the formal marketplace. In the US the number of used-merchandise retail establishments has grown at about ten times the rate of other

Figure 9.6 Consumers' disposal options

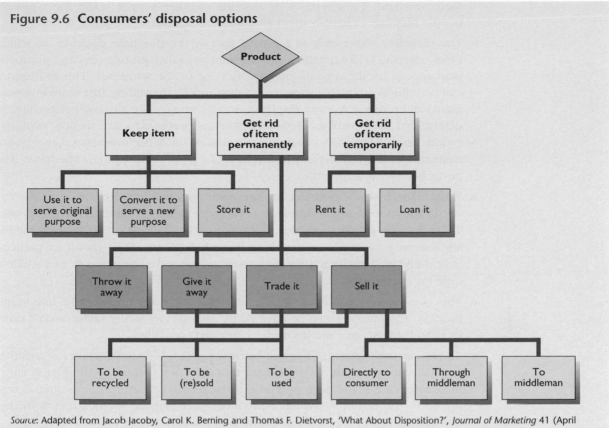

Source: Adapted from Jacob Jacoby, Carol K. Berning and Thomas F. Dietvorst, 'What About Disposition?', *Journal of Marketing* 41 (April 1977): 23.

stores.[146] While traditional marketers have paid little attention to the second-hand market, factors such as concern about the environment, demands for quality and cost and fashion consciousness are conspiring to make these 'secondary' markets more important.[147] Interest in antiques, period accessories and specialized magazines catering for this niche is increasing. Other growth areas include markets for used computers and ski swaps, where used ski equipment is exchanged. A new generation of second-hand shopkeepers is developing markets for everything from used office equipment to cast-off kitchen sinks. Many are non-profit ventures started with government funding. These efforts remind us that recycling is actually the last step in the familiar mantra of the environmental movement: reduce, reuse, recycle. Only if no use is found for an item should it be shredded and made into something else.

Chapter summary

- The *act of purchase* can be affected by many factors. These include the consumer's antecedent state (e.g. his/her mood, time pressure or attitude to shopping). Time is an important resource which often determines how much effort and search will go into a decision. Mood can be affected by the degree of pleasure and arousal present in a store environment.

- The *usage context* of a product can be a basis for segmentation: consumers look for different product attributes depending on the use to which they intend to put their purchase. The presence or absence of other people – and the types of people they are – can also affect a consumer's decisions.

● The *shopping experience* is a pivotal part of the purchase decision. In many cases, retailing is like theatre – the consumer's evaluation of stores and products may depend on the type of 'performance' he or she witnesses. This evaluation can be influenced by the actors (e.g. salespeople), the setting (the store environment) and props (e.g. store displays). A *store image*, like a brand personality, is determined by a number of factors, such as perceived convenience, sophistication, knowledgeability of salespeople, and so on. With increasing competition from non-store alternatives, the creation of a positive shopping experience has never been more important.

● Since many purchase decisions are not made until the time the consumer is actually in the store, *point-of-purchase* (POP) stimuli are very important sales tools. These include product samples, elaborate package displays, place-based media and in-store promotional materials such as 'shelf talkers'. POP stimuli are particularly useful in stimulating impulse buying, where a consumer yields to a sudden urge for a product.

● The consumer's encounter with a salesperson is a complex and important process. The outcome can be affected by such factors as the salesperson's similarity to the customer and his or her perceived credibility.

● *Consumer satisfaction* is determined by the person's overall feeling towards the product after purchase. Many factors influence perceptions of product quality, including price, brand name and product performance. Satisfaction is often determined by the degree to which a product's performance is consistent with the consumer's prior expectations of how well it will function.

● *Product disposal* is an increasingly important problem. Recycling is one option which will continue to be stressed as consumers' environmental awareness grows. Products may also be introduced by consumers into secondary markets during a process of *lateral cycling*, which occurs when objects are bought and sold second-hand, 'fenced' or bartered.

KEY TERMS

Atmospherics (*p. 286*)

Consumer satisfaction/dissatisfaction (CS/D) (*p. 289*)

Cyberspace (*p. 280*)

Exchange theory (*p. 289*)

Expectancy disconfirmation model (*p. 290*)

Impulse buying (*p. 286*)

ISO standards (*p. 290*)

Lateral cycling (*p. 292*)

Point-of-purchase stimuli (POP) (*p. 288*)

Shopping orientation (*p. 278*)

Store gestalt (*p. 286*)

Store image (*p. 285*)

Time style (*p. 274*)

Consumer behaviour challenge

1. Discuss some of the motivations for shopping as described in the chapter. How might a retailer adjust his or her strategy to accommodate these motivations?

2. What are the positive and negative aspects of requiring employees who interact with customers to wear some kind of uniform or to impose a dress code in the office?

3. The store environment is heating up as more and more companies put their promotional means into point-of-purchase efforts. Shoppers are now confronted by videos at the checkout, computer monitors attached to their shopping trolleys, and so on. Place-based media expose us to ads in non-shopping environments. Do you feel that these innovations are unacceptably intrusive? At what point might shoppers rebel and demand some peace while shopping? Do you see any market potential in the future for stores that 'counter-market' by promising a 'hands-off' shopping environment?

4. List the five stages of a long-term service relationship. How can a practitioner of relationship marketing incorporate each stage into his or her strategy?

5. Discuss the concept of 'time style'. Based on your own experiences, how might consumers be segmented in terms of their time styles?

6. Compare and contrast different cultures' conceptions of time. What are the implications for marketing strategy within each of these frameworks?

7. Conduct naturalistic observation at a local mall, shopping centre or supermarket. Sit in a central location and observe the activities of mall staff and customers. Keep a log of the non-retailing activity you observe (e.g. special performances, exhibits, socializing, etc.). Does this activity enhance or detract from business conducted at the mall?

8. Select three competing clothing shops in your area and conduct a store image study for each one. Ask a group of consumers to rate each store on a set of attributes and plot these ratings on the same graph. Based on your findings, are there any areas of competitive advantage or disadvantage you could bring to the attention of store management? (This technique was described in Chapter 5.)

9. Using Table 9.1 as a model, construct a person–situation–segmentation matrix for a brand of perfume.

Notes

1. 'Consumers Hit at Poor Service', *Marketing* (5 December 1996): 4.

2. Laurette Dube and Bernd H. Schmitt, 'The Processing of Emotional and Cognitive Aspects of Product Usage in Satisfaction Judgments', in Rebecca H. Holman and Michael R. Solomon, eds, *Advances in Consumer Research* 18 (Provo, UT: Association for Consumer Research, 1991): 52–6; Lalita A. Manrai and Meryl P. Gardner, 'The Influence of Affect on Attributions for Product Failure', in ibid.: 249–54.

3. Peter J. Burke and Stephen L. Franzoi, 'Studying Situations and Identities Using Experimental Sampling Methodology', *American Sociological Review* 53 (August 1988): 559–68.

4. Kevin G. Celuch and Linda S. Showers, 'It's Time To Stress *Stress*: The Stress-Purchase/Consumption

Relationship', in Holman and Solomon, eds, *Advances in Consumer Research* 18: 284–9; Lawrence R. Lepisto, J. Kathleen Stuenkel and Linda K. Anglin, 'Stress: An Ignored Situational Influence', in ibid.: 296–302.

5. See Eben Shapiro, 'Need a Little Fantasy? A Bevy of New Companies Can Help', *New York Times* (10 March 1991): F4.

6. John D. Mayer and Yvonne N. Gaschke, 'The Experience and Meta-Experience of Mood', *Journal of Personality and Social Psychology* 55 (July 1988): 102–11.

7. Meryl Paula Gardner, 'Mood States and Consumer Behavior: A Critical Review', *Journal of Consumer Research* 12 (December 1985): 281–300; Scott Dawson, Peter H. Bloch and Nancy M. Ridgway, 'Shopping Motives, Emotional States, and Retail

Outcomes', *Journal of Retailing* 66 (Winter 1990): 408–27; Patricia A. Knowles, Stephen J. Grove and W. Jeffrey Burroughs, 'An Experimental Examination of Mood States on Retrieval and Evaluation of Advertisement and Brand Information', *Journal of the Academy of Marketing Science* 21 (April 1993); Paul W. Miniard, Sunil Bhatla and Deepak Sirdeskmuhk, 'Mood as a Determinant of Postconsumption Product Evaluations: Mood Effects and Their Dependency on the Affective Intensity of the Consumption· Experience', *Journal of Consumer Psychology* 1 (1992) 2: 173–95; Mary T. Curren and Katrin R. Harich, 'Consumers' Mood States: The Mitigating Influence of Personal Relevance on Product Evaluations', *Psychology & Marketing* 11 (March/April 1994) 2: 91–107; Gerald J. Gorn, Marvin E. Rosenberg and Kunal Basu, 'Mood, Awareness, and Product Evaluation', *Journal of Consumer Psychology* 2 (1993) 3: 237–56.

8. Gordon C. Bruner, 'Music, Mood, and Marketing', *Journal of Marketing* 54 (October 1990): 94–104; Basil G. Englis, 'Music Television and its Influences on Consumers, Consumer Culture, and the Transmission of Consumption Messages', in Holman and Solomon, eds, *Advances in Consumer Research* 18; see also Steve Oakes, 'Examining the Relationships Between Background Musical Tempo and Perceived Duration Using Different Versions of a Radio Ad', in B. Dubois, T. Lowrey, L. J. Shrum and M. Vanhuele, eds, *European Advances in Consumer Research* 4 (Provo, UT: Association of Consumer Research, 1999): 40–4.

9. Marvin E. Goldberg and Gerald J. Gorn, 'Happy and Sad TV Programs: How They Affect Reactions to Commercials', *Journal of Consumer Research* 14 (December 1987): 387–403; Gorn, Goldberg and Basu, 'Mood, Awareness, and Product Evaluation': 237–56; Mary T. Curren and Katrin R. Harich, 'Consumers' Mood States: The Mitigating Influence of Personal Relevance on Product Evaluations', *Psychology & Marketing* 11 (March/April 1994) 2: 91–107.

10. Pradeep Kakkar and Richard J. Lutz, 'Situational Influence on Consumer Behavior: A Review', in Harold H. Kassarjian and Thomas S. Robertson, eds, *Perspectives in Consumer Behavior*, 3rd edn (Glenview, IL: Scott, Foresman and Company, 1981): 204–14.

11. Carolyn Turner Schenk and Rebecca H. Holman, 'A Sociological Approach to Brand Choice: The Concept of Situational Self-Image', in Jerry C. Olson, ed., *Advances in Consumer Research* 7 (Ann Arbor, MI: Association for Consumer Research, 1980): 610–14.

12. Russell W. Belk, 'An Exploratory Assessment of Situational Effects in Buyer Behavior', *Journal of Marketing Research* 11 (May 1974): 156–63; U. N. Umesh and Joseph A. Cote, 'Influence of Situational Variables on Brand-Choice Models', *Journal of Business Research* 16 (1988) 2: 91–9; see also J. Wesley Hutchinson and Joseph W. Alba, 'Ignoring Irrelevant Information: Situational Determinants of Consumer Learning', *Journal of Consumer Research* 18 (December 1991): 325–45.

13. Gordon Foxall, 'Science and Interpretation in Consumer Research: A Radical Behaviorist Perspective', *European Journal of Marketing* 29(9) (1995): 1–90; Gordon Foxall, 'The Consumer Situation as Interpretive Device', in Flemming Hansen, ed., *European Advances in Consumer Research* 2 (Provo, UT: Association for Consumer Research, 1995): 104–8.

14. Laura Bird, 'Grey Poupon Tones Down Tory Image', *Wall Street Journal* (22 July 1994): B2.

15. Peter R. Dickson, 'Person–Situation: Segmentation's Missing Link', *Journal of Marketing* 46 (Fall 1982): 56–64.

16. Bernard Dubois and Gilles Laurent, 'A Situational Approach to Brand Loyalty', in E. Arnould and L. Scott, eds, *Advances in Consumer Research* 26 (Provo, UT: Association for Consumer Research, 1999): 657–63.

17. Anja Stöhr, 'Air-Design: Exploring the Role of Scents in Retail Environments', in B. Englis and A. Olofsson, eds, *European Advances in Consumer Research* 3 (Provo, UT: Association for Consumer Research, 1998): 126–32.

18. Delphine Dion, 'A Theoretical and Empirical Study of Retail Crowding', in Dubois, Lowrey, Shrum and Vanhuele, eds, *European Advances in Consumer Research* 4: 51–7.

19. Daniel Stokols, 'On the Distinction Between Density and Crowding: Some Implications for Future Research', *Psychological Review* 79 (1972): 275–7.

20. Carol F. Kaufman, Paul M. Lane and Jay D. Linquist, 'Exploring More Than 24 Hours a Day: A Preliminary Investigation of Polychronic Time Use', *Journal of Consumer Research* 18 (December 1991): 392–401.

21. Michelle M. Bergadaà, 'The Role of Time in the Action of the Consumer', *Journal of Consumer Research* 17 (December 1990): 289–302; see also Laurence P. Feldman and Jacob Hornik, 'The Use of Time: An Integrated Conceptual Model', *Journal of Consumer Research* 7 (March 1981): 407–19.

22. Jean-Claude Usunier and Pierre Valette-Florence, 'Individual Time Orientation: A Psychometric Scale', *Time and Society* 3(2) (1994): 219–41.

23. Robert J. Samuelson, 'Rediscovering the Rat Race', *Newsweek* (15 May 1989): 57.

24. Jared Sandberg, 'NoChores.com', *Newsweek* (30 August 1999): 30 (2).

25. Jack Neff, 'Dawn of the Online Icebox', *Ad Age* (15 March 1999): 17.

26. Kaufman Lane and Lindquist, 'Exploring More Than 24 Hours a Day'.

27. Quoted in 'Fast Food? It Just Isn't Fast Enough Anymore', *New York Times* (6 December 1989): A1.

28. Agnès Durande-Moreau and Jean-Claude Usunier, 'Individual Time-Styles and Customer Satisfaction: The Case of the Waiting Experience', in *Marketing for an Expanding Europe*, Proceedings of the 25th EMAC Conference, ed. J. Berács, A. Bauer and J. Simon (Budapest: Budapest University of Economic Sciences, 1996): 371–90; cf. also Shirley Taylor, 'Waiting for Service: The Relationship Between Delays and Evaluations of Service', *Journal of Marketing* 58 (April 1994): 56–69.

29. Ad Pruyn and Ade Smidts, 'Customers' Reactions to Waiting: Effects of the Presence of "Fellow Sufferers" in the Waiting Room', in E. Arnould and L. Scott, eds, *Advances in Consumer Research* 26 (Provo, UT: Association for Consumer Research, 1999): 211–16.

30. Quoted in Gabriele Morello, 'Sicilian Time', *Time and Society* 6(1) (1997): 55–69. However, Morello concludes that in spite of such indications of traditional time perceptions, modernization is showing up in changed paces and attitudes towards time also in Sicily.

31. David H. Maister, 'The Psychology of Waiting Lines', in John A. Czepiel, Michael R. Solomon and Carol F. Surprenant, eds, *The Service Encounter: Managing Employee/Customer Interaction in Service Businesses* (Lexington, MA: Lexington Books, 1985): 113–24.

32. A. T. H. Pruyn and A. Smids, 'Customers' Evaluations of Queues: Three Exploratory Studies', in W. F. van Raaij and G. Bamossy, eds, *European Advances in Consumer Research* 1 (Provo, UT: Association for Consumer Research, 1993): 371–82.

33. Johan Anselmsson, 'Customer-Perceived Service Quality and Technology-Based Self-Service', doctoral dissertation, Lund University, 2001.

34. Robert J. Graham, 'The Role of Perception of Time in Consumer Research', *Journal of Consumer Research* 7 (March 1981): 335–42.

35. Alan Zarembo, 'What if There Weren't Any Clocks to Watch?', *Newsweek* (30 June 1997): 14; based on research reported in Robert Levine, *A Geography of Time: The Temporal Misadventures of a Social Psychologist, or How Every Culture Keeps Time Just a Little Bit Differently* (New York: Basic Books, 1997).

36. Cf. Morello, 'Sicilian Time'.

37. Sigmund Grønmo, 'Concepts of Time: Some Implications for Consumer Research', in Thomas K. Srull, ed., *Advances in Consumer Research* 16 (Provo, UT: Association for Consumer Research 1989): 339–45.

38. Gabriele Morello and P. van der Reis, 'Attitudes Towards Time in Different Cultures: African Time and European Time', *Proceedings of the Third Symposium on Cross-Cultural Consumer and Business Studies* (Honolulu: University of Hawaii, 1990); Gabriele Morello, 'Our Attitudes Towards Time', *Forum* 96/2 (European Forum for Management Development, 1996): 48–51.

39. Gary Davies, 'What Should Time Be?', *European Journal of Marketing* 28(8/9) (1994): 100–13.

40. Esther S. Page-Wood, Carol J. Kaufman and Paul M. Lane, 'The Art of Time', in *Proceedings of the Academy of Marketing Science* (1990).

41. Eric N. Berg, 'Fight on Quick Pizza Delivery Grows', *New York Times* (29 August 1989): D6.

42. Søren Askegaard and Tage Koed Madsen, 'The Local and the Global: Traits of Homogeneity and Heterogeneity in European Food Cultures', *International Business Review* 7(6) (1998): 549–68; for a thorough discussion of food culture, see Claude Fischler, *L'Homnivore* (Paris: Odile Jacob, 1990).

43. Daniel Miller, *A Theory of Shopping* (Cambridge: Polity Press, 1998).

44. For a scale that was devised to assess these dimensions of the shopping experience, see Barry J. Babin, William R. Darden and Mitch Griffin, 'Work and/or Fun: Measuring Hedonic and Utilitarian Shopping Value', *Journal of Consumer Research* 20 (March 1994): 644–56.

45. Ibid.

46. Adapted from Andrea Groeppel-Klein, Eva Thelen and Christoph Antretter, 'The Impact of Shopping Motives on Store Assessment', in Dubois, Lowrey, Shrum and Vanhuele, eds, *European Advances in Consumer Research* 4: 63–72.

47. Quoted in Robert C. Prus, *Making Sales: Influence as Interpersonal Accomplishment* (Newbury Park, CA: Sage Library of Social Research, Sage Publications, Inc., 1989): 225.

48. Gregory P. Stone, 'City Shoppers and Urban Identification: Observations on the Social Psychology of City Life', *American Journal of Sociology* 60 (1954): 36–45; Danny Bellenger and Pradeep K. Korgaonkar, 'Profiling the Recreational Shopper', *Journal of Retailing* 56 (1980) 3: 77–92.

49. Stephen Brown and Rhona Reid, 'Shoppers on the Verge of a Nervous Breakdown', in S. Brown and D. Turley, eds, *Consumer Research: Postcards from the Edge* (London: Routledge, 1997): 79–149.

50. 'A Global Perspective . . . on Women & Women's Wear', *Lifestyle Monitor* 14 (Winter 1999/2000): Cotton Inc., 8–11.

51. Nina Gruen, 'The Retail Battleground: Solutions for Today's Shifting Marketplace', *Journal of Property Management* (July–August 1989): 14.

52. 'Petrol Selling: Pump Action', *The Economist* (27 January 1996): 62.

53. Personal communication with a Finnish reviewer.

54. 'Slaget om Europa', *Jyllands Posten* (12 February 1997).

55. Arieh Goldman, 'The Shopping Style Explanation for Store Loyalty', *Journal of Retailing* 53 (Winter 1977–8): 33–46, 94; Robert B. Settle and Pamela L. Alreck, 'Hyperchoice Shapes the Marketplace', *Marketing Communications* (May 1988): 15.

56. 'Kundekort som konkurrencevåben', *Export* 36 (6 September 1996): 4–6.

57. Some material in this section was adapted from Michael R. Solomon and Elnora W. Stuart, *Welcome to Marketing.Com: The Brave New World of E-Commerce* (Englewood Cliffs, NJ: Prentice Hall, 2001).

58. Mikael Lundström, 'E-handel inget för Svensson', *Info* 8 (2000): 52–4.

59. Rebecca K. Ratner, Barbara E. Kahn and Daniel Kahneman, 'Choosing Less-Preferred Experiences for the Sake of Variety', *Journal of Consumer Research* 26 (June 1999): 1–15.

60. *Markedsføring* (25 November 2000): 18.

61. *Markedsføring* (25 September 2000): 22.

62. *Markedsføring* (9 November 2000): 14.

63. Jennifer Gilbert, 'Customer Service Crucial to Online Buyers', *Advertising Age* (13 September 1999): 52.

64. Chuan-Fong Shih, 'Conceptualizing Consumer Experiences in Cyberspace', *European Journal of Marketing* 32(7/8) (1998): 655–63.

65. Quoted in Timothy L. O'Brien, 'Aided by Internet, Identity Theft Soars', *New York Times on the Web* (accessed 3 April 2000).

66. *Markedsføring* (17 February 2000): 20.

67. An excellent collection of articles on this topic is found in Pasi Falk and Colin Campbell, eds, *The Shopping Experience* (London: Sage, 1997).

68. C. Gardner and J. Sheppard, *Consuming Passion: The Rise of Retail Culture* (London: Unwin Hyman, 1989).

69. Stephen Brown, 'Sex 'n' Shopping', Working Paper 9501 (University of Stirling: Institute for Retail Studies, 1995); see also Stephen Brown, 'Consumption Behaviour in the Sex 'n' Shopping Novels of Judith Krantz: A Post-structuralist Perspective', in Kim P. Corfman and John G. Lynch, Jr, eds, *Advances in Consumer Research* 23 (Provo, UT: Association for Consumer Research, 1996): 43–8.

70. Véronique Aubert-Gamet, 'Twisting Servicescapes: Diversion of the Physical Environment in a Re-Appropriation Process', *International Journal of Service Industry Management* 8(1) (1997): 26–41.

71. Stephen Brown, *Postmodern Marketing* (London: Routledge, 1995), discussion on pp. 50ff.; Lars Thøger Christensen and Søren Askegaard, 'Flexibility in the Marketing Organization: The Ultimate Consumer Orientation or Ford Revisited?', *Marketing Today and for the 21st Century*, Proceedings of the XIV EMAC Conference, ed. Michelle Bergadaà (Cergy-Pontoise: ESSEC, 1995): 1507–14.

72. For a study of consumer shopping patterns in a mall that views the mall as an ecological habitat, see Peter N. Bloch, Nancy M. Ridgway and Scott A. Dawson, 'The Shopping Mall as Consumer Habitat', *Journal of Retailing* 70 (1994): 1: 23–42.

73. Turo-Kimmo Lehtonen and Pasi Mäenpää, 'Shopping in the East Centre Mall', in Falk and Campbell, eds, *The Shopping Experience*: 136–65.

74. See for instance Fabian Csaba, *Designing the Retail-Entertainment Complex: A Marketing Ethnography of the Mall of America*, doctoral dissertation, Odense University, School of Business and Economics, 1998.

75. Quoted in Jacquelyn Bivins, 'Fun and Mall Games', *Stores* (August 1989): 35.

76. Sallie Hook, 'All the Retail World's a Stage: Consumers Conditioned to Entertainment in Shopping Environment', *Marketing News* 21 (31 July 1987): 16.

77. Stephen Brown, 'Marketing as Multiplex: Screening Postmodernism', *European Journal of Marketing* 28(8/9) (1994): 27–51.

78. David Chaney, 'The Department Store as a Cultural Form', *Theory, Culture and Society* 1(3) (1983): 22–31.

79. Cecilia Fredriksson, 'The Making of a Swedish Department Store Culture', in Falk and Campbell, eds, *The Shopping Experience* 111–35.

80. 'ING Uses the Soft Sell for Online Banking Unit', *Wall Street Journal* (17 October 2000): A18.

81. Pauline Maclaran and Lorna Stevens, 'Romancing the Utopian Marketplace', in S. Brown, A. M. Doherty and B. Clarke, eds, *Romancing the Market* (London: Routledge, 1998): 172–86.

82. Patrick Hetzel, 'When Hyperreality, Reality, Fiction and Non-Reality are Brought Together: A Fragmented Vision of the Mall of America Through Personal Interpretation', in Englis and Olofsson, eds, *European Advances in Consumer Research* 3: 261–6; see also Csaba, *Designing the Retail-Entertainment Complex*.

83. 'Enticing Europe's Shoppers: U.S. Way of Dressing and of Retailing Spreading Fast', *New York Times* (24 April 1996): D1(2).

84. Patrick Hetzel and Veronique Aubert, 'Sales Area Design and Fashion Phenomena: A Semiotic Approach', in van Raaij and Bamossy, eds, *European Advances in Consumer Research* 1: 522–33.

85. Søren Askegaard and Güliz Ger, 'Product-Country Images as Stereotypes: A Comparative Analysis of the Image of Danish Food Products in Germany and Turkey', *MAPP Working Paper* 45 (Aarhus: The Aarhus School of Business, 1997).

86. Susan Spiggle and Murphy A. Sewall, 'A Choice Sets Model of Retail Selection', *Journal of Marketing* 51 (April 1987): 97–111; William R. Darden and Barry J. Babin, 'The Role of Emotions in Expanding the Concept of Retail Personality', *Stores* 76 (April 1994) 4: RR7–RR8.

87. Most measures of store image are quite similar to other attitude measures, as discussed in Chapter 5. For a slightly dated but good state-of-the-art bibliography of store image studies, see Mary R. Zimmer and Linda L. Golden, 'Impressions of Retail Stores: A Content Analysis of Consumer Images', *Journal of Retailing* 64 (Fall 1988): 265–93.

88. Ibid.

89. Philip Kotler, 'Atmospherics as a Marketing Tool', *Journal of Retailing* (Winter 1973–4): 10–43, 48–64, 50; for a review of some recent research, see Peter McGoldrick and Christos Pieros, 'The Atmospherics–Customer Behaviour Relationship: Role of Response Moderators', in Berács, Bauer and Simon, eds, *Marketing for an Expanding Europe*: 735–53.

90. Fabian Csaba and Søren Askegaard, 'Malls and the Orchestration of the Shopping Experience in a Historical Perspective', in Arnould and Scott, eds, *Advances in Consumer Research* 26: 34–40.

91. Joseph A. Bellizzi and Robert E. Hite, 'Environmental Color, Consumer Feelings, and Purchase Likelihood', *Psychology & Marketing* 9 (September/October 1992) 5: 347–63.

92. Deborah Blumenthal, 'Scenic Design for In-Store Try-Ons', *New York Times* (9 April 1988).

93. Judy I. Alpert and Mark I. Alpert, 'Music Influences on Mood and Purchase Intentions', *Psychology & Marketing* 7 (Summer 1990): 109–34.

94. Brad Edmondson, 'Pass the Meat Loaf', *American Demographics* (January 1989): 19.

95. 'Butikken er en slagmark', *Berlingske Tidende* (15 July 1996): 3.

96. Marianne Meyer, 'Attention Shoppers!', *Marketing and Media Decisions* 23 (May 1988): 67.

97. Easwar S. Iyer, 'Unplanned Purchasing: Knowledge of Shopping Environment and Time Pressure', *Journal of Retailing* 65 (Spring 1989): 40–57; C. Whan Park, Easwar S. Iyer and Daniel C. Smith, 'The Effects of Situational Factors on In-Store Grocery Shopping', *Journal of Consumer Research* 15 (March 1989): 422–33.

98. Francis Piron, 'Defining Impulse Purchasing', in Holman and Solomon, eds, *Advances in Consumer Research* 18: 509–14; Dennis W. Rook, 'The Buying Impulse', *Journal of Consumer Research* 14 (September 1987): 189–99.

99. Michael Wahl, 'Eye POPping Persuasion', *Marketing Insights* (June 1989): 130.

100. 'Zipping Down the Aisles', *New York Times Magazine* (6 April 1997).

101. Peter McGoldrick, Erica J. Betts and Kathleen A. Keeling, 'Antecedents of Spontaneous Buying Behaviour During Temporary Markdowns', in Arnould and Scott, eds, *Advances in Consumer Research*, vol. 26: 26–33.

102. Cathy J. Cobb and Wayne D. Hoyer, 'Planned Versus Impulse Purchase Behavior', *Journal of Retailing* 62 (Winter 1986): 384–409; Easwar S. Iyer and Sucheta S. Ahlawat, 'Deviations from a Shopping Plan: When and Why Do Consumers Not Buy as Planned', in Melanie Wallendorf and Paul Anderson, eds, *Advances in Consumer Research* 14: 246–9.

103. Andrea Groeppel-Klein, 'The Influence of the Dominance Perceived at the Point-of-Sale on the Price-Assessment', in Englis and Olofsson, eds, *European Advances in Consumer Research* 3: 304–11.

104. William Keenan, Jr, 'Point-of-Purchase: From Clutter to Technoclutter', *Sales and Marketing Management* 141 (April 1989): 96.

105. *Markedsføring* 13 (1999): 24.

106. Meyer, 'Attention Shoppers!'

107. Cyndee Miller, 'Videocart Spruces Up for New Tests', *Marketing News* (19 February 1990): 19; William E. Sheeline, 'User-Friendly Shopping Carts', *Fortune* (5 December 1988): 9.

108. Bernard Swoboda, 'Multimedia Customer Information Systems at the Point of Sale: Selected Results of an Impact Analysis', in Englis and Olofsson, eds, *European Advances in Consumer Research* 3: 239–46.

109. 'Effective Demands', *Marketing* (5 December 1996): 34–8.

110. 'A Never-Ending Toy Story', *Marketing* (5 December 1996): 33.

111. John P. Cortez, 'Media Pioneers Try to Corral On-the-Go Consumers', *Advertising Age* (17 August 1992): 25.

112. Cyndee Miller, 'MTV "Video Capsule" Features Sports for Music Retailers, Corporate Sponsors', *Marketing News* (3 February 1992): 5.

113. 'Dutch Shop Lets Clients Burn Own CD's', *Wall Street Journal* 14 November 2000: B10.

114. See Robert B. Cialdini, *Influence: Science and Practice*, 2nd edn (Glenview, IL: Scott, Foresman and Company, 1988).

115. Richard P. Bagozzi, 'Marketing as Exchange', *Journal of Marketing* 39 (October 1975): 32–9; Peter M. Blau, *Exchange and Power in Social Life* (New York: Wiley, 1964); Marjorie Caballero and Alan J. Resnik, 'The Attraction Paradigm in Dyadic Exchange', *Psychology & Marketing* 3 (1986) 1: 17–34; George C. Homans, 'Social Behavior as Exchange', *American Journal of Sociology* 63 (1958): 597–606; Paul H. Schurr and Julie L. Ozanne, 'Influences on Exchange Processes: Buyers' Preconceptions of a Seller's Trustworthiness and Bargaining Toughness', *Journal of Consumer Research* 11 (March 1985): 939–53; Arch G. Woodside and J. W. Davenport, 'The Effect of Salesman Similarity and Expertise on Consumer Purchasing Behavior', *Journal of Marketing Research* 8 (1974): 433–6.

116. Paul Busch and David T. Wilson, 'An Experimental Analysis of a Salesman's Expert and Referent Bases of

Social Power in the Buyer–Seller Dyad', *Journal of Marketing Research* 13 (February 1976): 3–11; John E. Swan, Fred Trawick, Jr, David R. Rink and Jenny J. Roberts, 'Measuring Dimensions of Purchaser Trust of Industrial Salespeople', *Journal of Personal Selling and Sales Management* 8 (May 1988): 1.

117. For a recent study in this area, see Peter H. Reingen and Jerome B. Kernan, 'Social Perception and Interpersonal Influence: Some Consequences of the Physical Attractiveness Stereotype in a Personal Selling Setting', *Journal of Consumer Psychology* 2 (1993) 1: 25–38.

118. Mary Jo Bitner, Bernard H. Booms and Mary Stansfield Tetreault, 'The Service Encounter: Diagnosing Favorable and Unfavorable Incidents', *Journal of Marketing* 54 (January 1990): 7–84; Robert C. Prus, *Making Sales* (Newbury Park, CA: Sage Publications, 1989); Arch G. Woodside and James L. Taylor, 'Identity Negotiations in Buyer–Seller Interactions', in Elizabeth C. Hirschman and Morris B. Holbrook, eds, *Advances in Consumer Research* 12 (Provo, UT: Association for Consumer Research, 1985): 443–9.

119. Gilbert A. Churchill, Jr, Neil M. Ford, Steven W. Hartley and Orville C. Walker, Jr, 'The Determinants of Salesperson Performance: A Meta-Analysis', *Journal of Marketing Research* 22 (May 1985): 103–18.

120. Siew Meng Leong, Paul S. Busch and Deborah Roedder John, 'Knowledge Bases and Salesperson Effectiveness: A Script-Theoretic Analysis', *Journal of Marketing Research* 26 (May 1989): 164; Harish Sujan, Mita Sujan and James R. Bettman, 'Knowledge Structure Differences Between More Effective and Less Effective Salespeople', *Journal of Marketing Research* 25 (February 1988): 81–6; Robert Saxe and Barton Weitz, 'The SOCCO Scale: A Measure of the Customer Orientation of Salespeople', *Journal of Marketing Research* 19 (August 1982): 343–51; David M. Szymanski, 'Determinants of Selling Effectiveness: The Importance of Declarative Knowledge to the Personal Selling Concept', *Journal of Marketing* 52 (January 1988): 64–77; Barton A. Weitz, 'Effectiveness in Sales Interactions: A Contingency Framework', *Journal of Marketing* 45 (Winter 1981): 85–103.

121. Jagdish M. Sheth, 'Buyer–Seller Interaction: A Conceptual Framework', in *Advances in Consumer Research* (Cincinatti, OH: Association for Consumer Research, 1976): 382–6; Kaylene C. Williams and Rosann L. Spiro, 'Communication Style in the Salesperson–Customer Dyad', *Journal of Marketing Research* 22 (November 1985): 434–42.

122. Marsha L. Richins, 'An Analysis of Consumer Interaction Styles in the Marketplace', *Journal of Consumer Research* 10 (June 1983): 73–82.

123. Rama Jayanti and Anita Jackson, 'Service Satisfaction: Investigation of Three Models', in Holman and Solomon, eds, *Advances in Consumer Research* 18: 603–10; David K. Tse, Franco M. Nicosia and Peter C. Wilton, 'Consumer Satisfaction as a Process', *Psychology & Marketing* 7 (Fall 1990): 177–93.

124. Eugene W. Anderson, Claes Fornell and Donald R. Lehmann, 'Customer Satisfaction, Market Share, and Profitability: Findings from Sweden', *Journal of Marketing* 58 (July 1994) 3: 53–66.

125. Robert Jacobson and David A. Aaker, 'The Strategic Role of Product Quality', *Journal of Marketing* 51 (October 1987): 31–44; for a recent review of issues regarding the measurement of service quality, see J. Joseph Cronin, Jr and Steven A. Taylor, 'Measuring Service Quality: A Reexamination and Extension', *Journal of Marketing* 56 (July 1992): 55–68.

126. Anna Kirmani and Peter Wright, 'Money Talks: Perceived Advertising Expense and Expected Product Quality', *Journal of Consumer Research* 16 (December 1989): 344–53; Donald R. Lichtenstein and Scot Burton, 'The Relationship Between Perceived and Objective Price-Quality', *Journal of Marketing Research* 26 (November 1989): 429–43; Akshay R. Rao and Kent B. Monroe, 'The Effect of Price, Brand Name, and Store Name on Buyers' Perceptions of Product Quality: An Integrative Review', *Journal of Marketing Research* 26 (August 1989): 351–57.

127. Shelby Hunt, 'Post-Transactional Communication and Dissonance Reduction', *Journal of Marketing* 34 (January 1970): 46–51; Daniel E. Innis and H. Rao Unnava, 'The Usefulness of Product Warranties for Reputable and New Brands', in Holman and Solomon, eds, *Advances in Consumer Research* 18: 317–22; Terence A. Shimp and William O. Bearden, 'Warranty and Other Extrinsic Cue Effects on Consumers' Risk Perceptions', *Journal of Consumer Research* 9 (June 1982): 38–46.

128. Morris Holbrook and Kim Corfman, 'Quality and Value in the Consumption Experience: Phaedrus Rides Again', in J. Jacoby and J. C. Olson, eds, *Perceived Quality: How Consumers View Stores and Merchandise* (Lexington, MA: D. C. Heath & Co., 1985): 31–57; Robert M. Pirsig, *Zen and the Art of Motorcycle Maintenance: An Inquiry into Values* (New York: Bantam Books, 1974).

129. Mia Stokmans, 'The Relation Between Postpurchase Evaluations and Consumption Experiences of Hedonic Products: A Case of Reading Fiction', in Englis and Olofsson, eds, *European Advances in Consumer Research* 3: 139–45.

130. W. F. van Raaij, 'The Formation and Use of Expectations in Consumer Decision Making', in T. S. Robertson and H. H. Kassarjian, eds, *Handbook of Consumer Behavior* (Englewood Cliffs, NJ: Prentice-Hall, 1991): 401–18.

131. John W. Gamble, 'The Expectations Paradox: The More You Offer The Customer, The Closer You Are to Failure', *Marketing News* (14 March 1988): 38.

132. Franz Bailom, Hans H. Hinterhuber, Kurt Matzler and Elmar Sauerwein, 'Das Kano-Modell der Kundenzufriedenheit', *Marketing ZFP* 2 (2nd quarter 1996): 117–26.

133. Marit G. Engeset, Kjell Grønhaug and Morten Heide, 'The Impact of Experience on Customer Satisfaction as Measured in Direct Surveys', in *Marketing for an Expanding Europe*, Proceedings of the 25th EMAC Conference, ed. Berács, Bauer and Simon: 403–17.

134. Andreas Herrmann, Frank Huber and Christine Braunstein, 'A Regret Theory Approach to Assessing Customer Satisfaction when Alternatives Are Considered', in Dubois, Lowrey, Shrum and Vanhuele, eds, *European Advances in Consumer Research* 4 82–8.

135. Kjell Grønhaug and Alladi Venkatesh, 'Products and Services in the Perspectives of Consumer Socialisation', *European Journal of Marketing* 21(10) (1987); Folke Ölander, 'Consumer Satisfaction – A Sceptic's View', in H. K. Hunt, ed., *Conceptualization and Measurement of Consumer Satisfaction and Dissatisfaction* (Cambridge, MA: Marketing Science Institute, 1977): 453–88.

136. Mary C. Gilly and Betsy D. Gelb, 'Post-Purchase Consumer Processes and the Complaining Consumer', *Journal of Consumer Research* 9 (December 1982): 323–8; Diane Halstead and Cornelia Dröge, 'Consumer Attitudes Toward Complaining and the Prediction of Multiple Complaint Responses', in Holman and Solomon, eds, *Advances in Consumer Research* 18 (Provo, UT: Association for Consumer Research, 1991): 210–16; Jagdip Singh, 'Consumer Complaint Intentions and Behavior: Definitional and Taxonomical Issues', *Journal of Marketing* 52 (January 1988): 93–107.

137. Alan Andreasen and Arthur Best, 'Consumers Complain – Does Business Respond?', *Harvard Business Review* 55 (July–August 1977): 93–101.

138. Ingrid Martin, 'Expert–Novice Differences in Complaint Scripts', in Holman and Solomon, eds, *Advances in Consumer Research* 18: 225–31; Marsha L. Richins, 'A Multivariate Analysis of Responses to Dissatisfaction', *Journal of the Academy of Marketing Science* 15 (Fall 1987): 24–31.

139. John A. Schibrowsky and Richard S. Lapidus, 'Gaining a Competitive Advantage by Analyzing Aggregate Complaints', *Journal of Consumer Marketing* 11 (1994) 1: 15–26.

140. Veronica Liljander, 'Consumer Satisfaction with Complaint Handling Following a Dissatisfactory Experience with Car Repair', in Dubois, Lowrey, Shrum and Vanhuele, eds, *European Advances in Consumer Research* 4: 270–5.

141. Russell W. Belk, 'The Role of Possessions in Constructing and Maintaining a Sense of Past', in Marvin E. Goldberg, Gerald Gorn and Richard W. Pollay, eds, *Advances in Consumer Research* 17 (Provo, UT: Association for Consumer Research, 1989): 669–76.

142. David E. Sanger, 'For a Job Well Done, Japanese Enshrine the Chip', *New York Times* (11 December 1990): A4.

143. Jacob Jacoby, Carol K. Berning and Thomas F. Dietvorst, 'What About Disposition?', *Journal of Marketing* 41 (April 1977): 22–8.

144. 'Incentive Schemes: Jam Today', *The Economist* (12 April 1997): 67.

145. John F. Sherry, Jr, 'A Sociocultural Analysis of a Midwestern American Flea Market', *Journal of Consumer Research* 17 (June 1990): 13–30.

146. Diane Crispell, 'Collecting Memories', *American Demographics* (November 1988): 38–42.

147. Allan J. Magrath, 'If Used Product Sellers Ever Get Organized, Watch Out', *Marketing News* (25 June 1990): 9; Kevin McCrohan and James D. Smith, 'Consumer Participation in the Informal Economy', *Journal of the Academy of Marketing Science* 15 (Winter 1990): 62.

Group influence and opinion leadership

It was December and Björn had been thinking of snowboards all day after seeing an ad for a store called Summit in the morning newspaper with the headline 'Sweaty feet free of charge'. Maybe he could ask his dad if he could have a snowboard for Christmas? How could he convince him? Well, most of his friends had one, and it would make winter holidays in the Swedish mountains with the family much more fun. He couldn't bear the thought of coming back and telling his friends he had been downhill skiing! And it wouldn't be as expensive because the ad said that if you bought the snowboard now, you would get the boots free.

Björn thought about what clothes to wear. Snowboarders used to wear baggy, knitted clothes which absorbed the snow. But not any more. Goretex is definitely the best material. Maybe his grandmother would pitch in on a jacket? She liked to see him happy and definitely knew that quality matters. If he bought a good, high-tech jacket, it could also be used for mountain climbing. According to his friends, the best brand was Vampire. The Swedish national snowboard team uses Goldwin, and Ingemar Stenmark, the famous skier, is involved in that design. Björn had read about cross-over trends in a sports magazine, that is, that clothing styles for skiers and snowboarders were becoming more similar.

Björn wondered if the snowboard brands in the ad were any good. He would ask his friends and also the salespeople at Summit. The famous Swedish snowboarder Ingmar Backman apparently used Four Square and United Rewind. Of course, the snowboard and brand depended on whether he was going to practise alpine, halfpipe or boarder-cross. Bright colours were out: he definitely wanted a black snowboard. He could just see himself snowboarding at Riksgränsen, on the border of northern Sweden.

Karin Ekström, Göteborg University

Introduction

Skiing and snowboarding are an important part of Björn's identity, and his friends influence many of his buying decisions. Fellow snowboarders are united in their consumption choices so that total strangers feel an immediate bond with each other when they meet.

Humans are social animals. We all belong to groups, try to please others and pick up cues about how to behave by observing the actions of those around us. In fact, our desire to 'fit in' or to identify with desirable individuals or groups is the primary motivation for many of our purchases and activities. We often go to great lengths to please the members of a group whose acceptance we covet.

This chapter focuses on how other people, whether fellow skiers, co-workers, friends and family or just casual acquaintances, influence our purchase decisions. It considers how our preferences are shaped by our group memberships, by our desire to please or be accepted by others, even by the actions of famous people whom we've never even met. Finally, it explores why some people are more influential than others in affecting consumers' product preferences, and how marketers go about finding those people and enlisting their support in the persuasion process.

Reference groups

Björn doesn't model himself on *any* snowboarder – only the people with whom he really identifies can exert that kind of influence. For example, Björn primarily identifies with other Swedish snowboarders. Essentially, only the Swedes comprise Björn's *reference group*.

A **reference group** is 'an actual or imaginary individual or group conceived of having significant relevance upon an individual's evaluations, aspirations, or behaviour'.[1] There are three reference group influences: *informational*, *utilitarian* and *value-expressive*. These are described in Table 10.1 and discussed in this chapter.

Types of reference groups

Although two or more people are normally required to form a group, the term 'reference group' is used more loosely to describe *any* external influence that provides social cues.[2] The referent may be a cultural figure and have an impact on many people (e.g. the late Mother Teresa or members of royal families) or a person or group whose influence is confined to the consumer's immediate environment (e.g. Björn's skiing friends). Reference groups that affect consumption can include parents, fellow skiers, motorcycle or other leisure activity enthusiasts, a political party or even sports clubs such as Manchester United and bands such as U2.

Some groups and individuals exert a greater influence than others and for a broader range of consumption decisions. For example, our parents may play a pivotal role in forming our values towards many important issues, such as attitudes about marriage or where to go to college. This **normative influence** helps to set and

Table 10.1 Three forms of reference group influence

Informational influence	The individual seeks information about various brands from an association of professionals or independent group of experts.
	The individual seeks information from those who work with the product as a profession.
	The individual seeks brand-related knowledge and experience (such as how Brand A's performance compares to Brand B's) from those friends, neighbours, relatives or work associates who have reliable information about the brands.
	The brand the individual selects is influenced by observing a seal of approval of an independent testing agency.
	The individual's observation of what experts do (such as observing the type of car that police drive or the brand of television that repairmen buy) influences his or her choice of a brand.
Utilitarian influence	So that he or she satisfies the expectation of fellow work associates, the individual's decision to purchase a particular brand is influenced by their preferences.
	The individual's decision to purchase a particular brand is influenced by the preferences of people with whom he or she has social interaction.
	The individual's decision to purchase a particular brand is influenced by the preferences of family members.
	The desire to satisfy the expectations that others have of him or her has an impact on the individual's brand choice.
Value-expressive influence	The individual feels that the purchase or use of a particular brand will enhance the image others have of him or her.
	The individual feels that those who purchase or use a particular brand possess the characteristics that he or she would like to have.
	The individual sometimes feels that it would be nice to be like the type of person that advertisements show using a particular brand.
	The individual feels that the people who purchase a particular brand are admired or respected by others.
	The individual feels that the purchase of a particular brand would help show others what he or she is or would like to be (such as an athlete, successful business person, good parent, etc.)

Source: Adapted from C. Whan Park and V. Parker Lessig, 'Students and Housewives: Differences in Susceptibility to Reference Group Influence', *Journal of Consumer Research* 4 (September 1977): 102. Reprinted with permission by The University of Chicago Press.

enforce fundamental standards of conduct. In contrast, a Harley-Davidson club might exert **comparative influence**, where decisions about specific brands or activities are affected.[3]

Formal vs. informal groups

A reference group can take the form of a large, formal organization that has a recognized structure, regular meeting times and officers. Or it can be small and informal, such as a group of friends or students living in a dormitory. Marketers tend to have more control over their influencing of formal groups because they are more easily identifiable and accessible.

In general, small, informal groups exert a more powerful influence on individual consumers. These groups tend to be more involved in our day-to-day lives and to be more important to us, because they are high in normative influence. Larger, formal

Multicultural dimensions

'Common man' or 'slice-of-life' depictions, which highlight 'real' people, are more realistic and thus more credible than celebrities or superstars. While we admire perfect people, it can be frustrating to compare ourselves with them and their actually using the product may seem improbable. By including people who are successful but not perfect, consumers' identification with them is often enhanced. This strategy has been successfully employed in the classic 'Dewar's Profiles', a series of ads describing the lifestyles of non-celebrity high achievers who happen to drink Dewar's Scotch Whisky. Since the strategy uses real people from many different walks of life, the company has expanded its ad campaigns to focus on accomplished people in different countries. For example, a Thai ad highlights a successful architect who lives in Bangkok, while a Spanish campaign features a 29-year-old flight instructor, as seen in the ad shown here.[4]

Dewar's has successfully used non-celebrities as endorsers in its 'Profiles' campaign, which is now being adapted to other countries, as this Spanish ad illustrates.
Schenley Industries, Inc.

groups tend to be more product- or activity-specific and thus are high in comparative influence.

Membership vs. aspirational reference groups
While some reference groups consist of people the consumer actually knows, others are composed of people the consumer can *identify with* or admire. Not surprisingly, many marketing efforts that specifically adopt a reference group appeal concentrate on highly visible, widely admired figures, such as well-known athletes.

Identificational reference groups
Since people tend to compare themselves with others who are similar, they are often swayed by knowing how people like themselves conduct their lives. For this reason, many promotional strategies include 'ordinary' people whose consumption activities provide informational social influence. For example, in the campaign for fish consumption discussed in Chapter 4, the endorsing actors performed as very ordinary people to underline the message that special fish dishes are not difficult to prepare or are for high-class gourmets only.[5]

The likelihood that people will become part of a consumer's identificational reference group is affected by several factors, including:

- *Propinquity*: As physical distance between people decreases and opportunities for interaction increase, relationships are more likely to form. Physical nearness is called *propinquity*. An early study of friendship patterns on a housing estate showed this factor's strong effects: residents were much more likely to be friends with the people next door than with those who lived only two doors away. People who lived next to a stairway had more friends than those at the end of a corridor (presumably, they were more likely to bump into people using the stairs).[6] Physical structure has a lot to do with whom we get to know and how popular we are.

- *Mere exposure*: We grow to like persons or things simply as a result of seeing them more often: the *mere exposure phenomenon*.[7] Greater frequency of contact, even if unintentional, may help to determine one's set of local referents. The same effect holds when evaluating works of art, or even political candidates.[8] One study predicted 83 per cent of the winners in a political election solely by the amount of media exposure given to candidates.[9]

- *Group cohesiveness*: The degree to which members of a group are attracted to each other and value their group membership is called cohesiveness. As the value of the group to the individual increases, so too does the likelihood that the group will guide consumption decisions. Smaller groups tend to be more cohesive, because it is more difficult to relate to larger groups of people. By the same token, groups often try to restrict membership to a select few, which increases the value of membership to those who are admitted. Exclusivity of membership is a benefit often touted by credit card companies, book clubs, and so on, even though the actual membership base might be fairly large.

It is an old, established truth in marketing that while the consumer may have no direct contact with reference groups, they can have powerful influences on his or her tastes and preferences, because they provide guidance as to the types of products used by admired people.[10] *Aspirational reference groups* are composed of idealized figures such as successful business people, athletes or performers. Many ads featuring such groups rely on the aspirational reference group perspective to appeal to people who aspire to be successful like the role models depicted in the ad. For example, one study that included business students who aspired to the 'executive' role found a strong relationship between products they associated with their *ideal selves* (see Chapter 7) and those they assumed would be owned or used by executives.[11]

Positive vs. negative reference groups

Reference groups may exert either a positive or a negative influence on consumption behaviours. In most cases, consumers model their behaviour to be consistent with what they think the group expects of them. In some cases, though, a consumer may try to distance him- or herself from other people or groups who function as *avoidance groups*. He or she may carefully study the dress or mannerisms of a disliked group and scrupulously avoid buying anything that might identify him or her with that group.[12] Many consumers find it difficult to express what they want whereas they can quite clearly express what they do not want. In fact, some researchers suggest that the phenomenon of distaste is much more decisive for our consumption choices but harder to study than tastes, since our choices are quite obvious compared to all the non-selected alternatives.[13] For example, rebellious adolescents often resent parental influence and may deliberately do the opposite of what their parents would like as a way of making a statement about their independ-

Many products, especially those targeted at young people, are often touted as a way to take the inside track to popularity. This Brazilian shoe ad proclaims: 'Anyone who doesn't like them is a nerd'.

Used with permission.

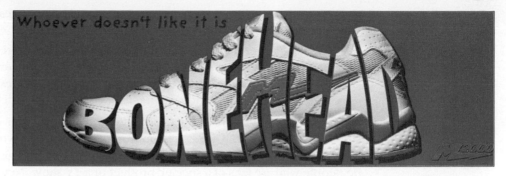

ence. As Romeo and Juliet discovered, nothing makes a partner more attractive than a little parental opposition.

Virtual communities

In ancient times (that is, before the Web was widely accessible), most membership reference groups consisted of people who had face-to-face contact. Now, it's possible to share interests with people whom you've never met – and probably never will. Have you ever heard of the band Widespread Panic? No? Well, the band has never had a music video on MTV or cracked the Billboard Top 200. But it's one of the top 40 touring bands in the USA. How did it get to be so successful? Simple – the group built a virtual community of fans and opened itself up to them. It enlisted listeners to help promote the group in exchange for free tickets and backstage passes. Then, it went virtual: the band lets fans send messages to its recording studio, and hardcore followers can find out vital information like what band members ate for lunch via regular updates on their website.[14]

A **virtual community of consumption** is a collection of people whose online interactions are based upon shared enthusiasm for and knowledge of a specific consumption activity. These anonymous groups grow up around an incredibly diverse set of interests – everything from Barbie dolls to fine wine.

Virtual communities come in many different forms:[15]

- *Multi-User Dungeons (MUD)*. Originally, these were environments where players of fantasy games met. Now they refer to any computer-generated environment where people interact socially through the structured format of role- and game-playing. In a game called EverQuest, on any given night up to 50,000 people can be found roaming around a fantasy land in cyberspace. This is known as a 'massively multiplayer game', which combines the stunning graphics of advanced gaming with the social scene of a chat room. Players create a character as a virtual alter ego, which may be a wise elf or a back-stabbing rogue. The game is also the centre of an active social scene. Players can travel around in groups of six; in many cases they settle into a regular group and spend two to three hours each night online with the same people. One couple even held a virtual wedding while playing. The bride reported, 'We only had one death, a guest who was killed by the guards. It was a lot of fun.'[16] Realizing that the average online player logs 17 hours per week, firms like Sony, Microsoft and Sega are building their own virtual worlds to get a piece of the action. As one game company executive put it, 'This is not a genre of game but a break-through new medium. It provides a completely new social, collaborative shared experience. We're basically in the Internet community business.'[17]

- *Rooms, rings and lists*. These include internet relay chat (IRC), otherwise known as *chat rooms*. *Rings* are organizations of related home pages, and *lists* are groups of people on a single mailing list who share information.

● *Boards*: Online communities can be organized around interest-specific electronic bulletin boards. Active members read and post messages sorted by date and subject. There are boards devoted to musical groups, movies, wind, cigars, cars, comic strips, even fast-food restaurants.

Some communities are created by individuals whose web pages are hosted on sites like *geocities.com*. Others are sponsored by companies who want to give devotees of a product or a lifestyle a congenial place to 'meet'. This could, for example, be people who are fans of a specific product or a TV show. News Digital Media gives Bart Simpson fanatics free Internet access at *simpson.com*. The site is intended to complement the TV show and to give fans a place to congregate.[18] Other than the more global sites at, for example, *geocities.com*, there is a proliferation of national community sites for specific consumer profiles. In Denmark, for example, there are sites for teenage girls (e.g. *surfergirl.dk*), for themes such as relationships (*lovefinder.dk*), or an extremely popular site for medical problems (*netdoktor.dk*).

Virtual communities are still a new phenomenon, but their impact on individuals' product preferences promises to be huge. These loyal consumers are essentially working together to form their tastes, evaluate product quality and even negotiate for better deals with producers. They place great weight on the judgements of their fellow members.

While consumption communities are largely a grass-roots phenomenon founded by consumers for other consumers, these community members can be reached by marketers – if they are careful not to alienate members by being too aggressive or 'commercial'. Using newsgroup archives and search engines, companies can create a detailed profile of any individual consumer who has posted information. Firms like Warner Brothers form communities with fans around the world. The company noticed that many fans of Bugs Bunny, Batman and the Tazmanian Devil were downloading images and sound clips onto their personal web pages and then selling ad space on those pages. Instead of suing its fans, Warner created an online community called ACME City that builds home pages for registered members. Many corporate-sponsored sites build home pages for new members and ask for nothing in return except personal information on a registration form. They can use this information to fine-tune the online experience by making advertising, contests and rewards programmes more relevant.

MARKETING OPPORTUNITY

Some online startups are profiting by creating websites that give people a forum for their opinions about product likes and dislikes. *Epinions.com* was started by several well-known Silicon Valley venture capitalists. This service both rewards and rates product reviewers, in hope of giving them enough incentive to provide useful opinions. Anyone can sign up to give advice on products that fit into the site's 12 categories, and shoppers can rate the reviews on a scale from not useful to very useful. To build credibility, and to eliminate suspicions that they are merely company shills (people posing as satisfied customers), advisers can build a page on the site with photos and personal information. Reviewers earn royalties of from $1 to $3 for every ten times their review is read, and their picture can be featured on the FrontPage if their reviews are widely read. According to one of the founders, the site relies on a 'web of trust' in which viewers and advisers tend to be matched up over time with people whose opinions they have come to trust: 'It mimics the way word-of-mouth works in the real world.' When a recommendation results in a sale, the company earns a referral fee from merchants.[19]

How do people get drawn into consumption communities? Internet users tend to progress from asocial information gathering ('lurkers' are surfers who like to watch but don't participate) to increasingly affiliative social activities. At first they will merely browse the site but later they may well be drawn into active participation.

The intensity of identification with a virtual community depends on two factors. The first is that the more central the activity to a person's self-concept, the more likely he or she will be to pursue active membership in a community. The second is that the intensity of the social relationships the person forms with other members of the virtual community helps to determine the extent of their involvement. As Figure 10.1 shows, combining these two factors creates four distinct member types:

1 *Tourists* lack strong social ties to the group, and maintain only a passing interest in the activity.

2 *Minglers* maintain strong social ties, but are not very interested in the central consumption activity.

3 *Devotees* express strong interest in the activity, but have few social attachments to the group.

4 *Insiders* exhibit both strong social ties and strong interest in the activity.

Devotees and insiders are the most important targets for marketers who wish to exploit communities for promotional purposes. They are the heavy users of virtual communities. And, by reinforcing usage, the community may upgrade tourists and minglers to insiders and devotees.[20] But marketers have only scratched the surface of this intriguing new virtual world.

Virtual consumption communities hold great promise, but there is also great potential for abuse if members can't trust that other visitors are behaving ethically. Many hard-core community members are sensitive to interference from companies, and react negatively when they suspect that another member may in fact be a shill of a marketer who wants to influence evaluations of products on the site.

More generally, e-commerce sites know that consumers give more weight to the opinions of real people, so they are finding ways to let these opinions be included on their websites. This trend of posting customer reviews was started by *Amazon.com* way back in 1995. Now, sellers of computers and other high-priced

Figure 10.1 Virtual communities

Adapted from Robert V. Kozinets, 'E-Tribalized Marketing: The Strategic Implications of Virtual Communities of Consumption', *European Management Journal* 17(3) (June 1999): 252–64 products post customer reviews.[21] A great idea – but in a highly publicized lawsuit Amazon was accused of charging publishers to post positive reviews on the site. The company had to offer refunds for all books it recommended and now Amazon tells customers when a publisher has paid for a prominent display on its site.[22]

A basic topic for discussion is: who owns the net? The outcome of a legal case against the music exchange service Napster, ruling that it was illegal to organize even non-profitable exchange of music files among its users, tends to point in the direction that cyberspace can be patented and owned. However, the reaction among hard-core virtual community people seems to be that there will always be ways of circumventing such attempts to stop the free flows of information within the virtual communities. A similar case is the so-called PotterWar, a website created as a protest against Warner Bros., which holds the rights to Harry Potter related products. They threatened creators of sites such as *HarryPotterNetwork.net* with heavy lawsuits if control of the sites was not given to Warner. It turned out that most of the sites were owned by 12–15-year-olds without the slightest commercial interest. The problem for Warner Bros. and many other producers of cultural products is that on the one hand they like (for good pecuniary reasons) the iconic cult status their products may obtain, but they neglect that part of the love for cultural products is sharing it with other devotees.[23] The big question remains, within as well as outside cyberspace: who owns culture?

When reference groups are important

Reference group influences are not equally powerful for all types of products and consumption activities. For example, products that are not very complex, that are low in perceived risk and that can be tried prior to purchase are less susceptible to personal influence.[24] In addition, the specific impact of reference groups may vary. At times they may determine the use of certain products rather than others (e.g. owning or not owning a computer, eating junk food vs. health food), while at other times they may have specific effects on brand decisions within a product category (e.g. wearing Diesel vs. Calvin Klein jeans, or smoking Marlboro cigarettes instead of a national brand).

Two dimensions that influence the degree to which reference groups are important are whether the purchase is to be consumed publicly or privately and whether it is a luxury or a necessity. As a rule, reference group effects are more robust for purchases that are (1) luxuries rather than necessities (e.g. yachts), since products that are purchased with discretionary income are subject to individual tastes and preferences, while necessities do not offer this range of choices; and (2) socially conspicuous or visible to others (e.g. living-room furniture or clothing), since consumers do not tend to be swayed as much by the opinions of others if their purchases will never be observed by anyone but themselves.[25] The relative effects of reference group influences on some specific product classes are shown in Figure 10.2. This obviously does not mean that a reference group cannot exert influence on the consumption of private necessities.

The power of reference groups

Social power refers to 'the capacity to alter the actions of others'.[26] To the degree that you are able to make someone else do something, whether they do it willingly or not, you have power over that person. The following classification of *power bases* can help us to distinguish among the reasons a person can exert power over

Figure 10.2 Relative reference group influence on purchase decisions

Adapted from William O. Bearden and Michael J. Etzel, 'Reference Group Influence on Product and Brand Purchase Decisions', *Journal of Consumer Research* 9 (September 1982): 185. Reprinted with permission by The University of Chicago Press.

another, the degree to which the influence is allowed voluntarily, and whether this influence will continue to have an effect in the absence of the power source.[27]

Referent power

If a person admires the qualities of a person or a group, he or she will try to imitate those qualities by copying the referent's behaviours (e.g. choice of clothing, cars, leisure activities) as a guide to forming consumption preferences, just as Björn's preferences were affected by his fellow snowboarders. Prominent people in all walks of life can affect people's consumption behaviours by virtue of product endorsements (e.g. top model Cindy Crawford for Omega watches), distinctive fashion statements (e.g. Madonna's use of lingerie as outerwear), or championing causes (e.g. Brigitte Bardot's work against fur). **Referent power** is important to many marketing strategies because consumers voluntarily change behaviours to please or identify with a referent.

Information power

A person can have **information power** simply because he or she knows something others would like to know. Editors of trade publications in the fashion industry often possess power due to their ability to compile and disseminate information that can make or break individual designers or companies. People with information power are able to influence consumer opinion by virtue of their (assumed) access to the 'truth'.

Legitimate power

Sometimes people are granted power by virtue of social agreements, such as the power given to the police and professors. The legitimate power conferred by a

This anti-tobacco advertisement recognizes the role of reference groups. Many teens start smoking due to peer influence. This message uses the same reference group approach to discourage smoking.
Brogan & Partners Convergence Marketing.

uniform is recognized in many consumer contexts, including teaching hospitals, where medical students don white coats to enhance their aura of authority with patients, and organizations where uniforms communicate trustworthiness.[28] This form of power may be 'borrowed' by marketers to influence consumers. For example, an ad featuring a model wearing a nurse's uniform can add an aura of legitimacy or authority to the presentation of the product, as seen in TV advertising campaigns in the babies' nappies market.

Expert power

To attract the casual internet user, U.S. Robotics signed up British physicist Stephen Hawking to endorse its modems. A company executive commented, 'We wanted to generate trust. So we found visionaries who use U.S. Robotics technology, and we let them tell the consumer how it makes their lives more productive.' Hawking, who has Lou Gehrig's (motor neurone) disease and speaks via a synthesizer, says in one TV spot, 'My body may be stuck in this chair, but with the internet my mind can go to the end of the universe.'[29] *Expert power* such as that possessed by Hawking is derived from possessing specific knowledge about a content area; it helps to explain the weight many of us assign to reviews of restaurants, books, movies, cars and so on by critics who specialize in evaluating products on our behalf.[30] This power base also underlies the appeal of television shows, where panels of authorities – often a mix of journalists and professional experts – discuss issues of interest to consumers.

Reward power

When a person or group has the means to provide positive reinforcement (see Chapter 4), that entity will have power over a consumer to the extent that this reinforcement is valued or desired. The reward may be tangible, as occurs when an employee is given a pay rise. Or the reward may be intangible: social approval or acceptance is often what is exchanged in return for moulding one's behaviour to a group or buying the products expected of group members. However, this kind of power is perhaps wearing thin in advertising, since an over-exploitation of reward arguments has left such campaigns with little credibility. The Sprite soft drink campaign under the slogan 'Image is nothing, thirst is everything, obey your thirst' makes fun of other commercials' use of reward power by suggesting something seen as more basic, thirst. However, the slogan in itself paradoxically promises a reward in the form of an image – of somebody who does not fall for cheap tricks.[31]

Coercive power

While coercive power is often effective in the short term, it does not tend to produce permanent attitudinal or behavioural change. Surveillance of some sort is usually required to make people do something they do not wish to do. Fortunately, coercive power is rarely employed in marketing situations, unless you count those annoying calls from telemarketers! However, elements of this power base are evident in fear appeals, intimidation in personal selling, and campaigns that emphasize the negative consequences that can occur if people do not use a product.

Conformity

▶ **Conformity** refers to a change in beliefs or actions as a reaction to real or imagined
▶ group pressure. In order for a society to function, its members develop **norms**, or informal rules that govern behaviour. If such a system of agreements did not evolve, chaos would result. Imagine the confusion if a simple norm such as sitting down to attend class did not exist.

Norms change slowly over time, but there is general agreement within a society about which ones should be obeyed, and we adjust our way of thinking to conform to these norms. A powerful example is the change in our societies' attitudes towards smoking since this practice was first linked with health concerns such as cancer and emphysema in the 1960s. By the mid-1990s some countries had even outlawed smoking in public places. Much of the motivation to begin smoking at an early age is due to peer pressure: the alluring advertising images of smokers as cool, sexy or mature, and obviously also the allure of the forbidden and dangerous which is always tempting for teens, all help to convince many young people that beginning the habit is a path to peer acceptance.

Because the power of advertising to influence attitudes is widely recognized, some groups have tried to fight fire with fire by creating anti-smoking ads that depict smoking as an ugly habit that turns people off. Are these ads effective? One recent study of non-smoking seventh-graders by a pair of consumer researchers examined the kids' perceptions of smokers after being exposed to both cigarette ads and anti-smoking ads. Results were promising: the researchers found that kids who saw the anti-smoking ads were more likely to rate smokers lower in terms of both personal appeal and common sense. These findings imply that it is possible to use advertising to debunk myths about the glamour of smoking, especially if used in tandem with other health education efforts.[32]

Unspoken rules govern many aspects of consumption. In addition to norms regarding appropriate use of clothing and other personal items, we conform to rules that include gift-giving (we expect birthday presents from loved ones and get upset if they do not materialize), sex roles (men are often expected to pick up the bill on a first date) and personal hygiene (we are expected to shower or bathe regularly to avoid offending others).

Types of social influence

Just as the bases for social power can vary, so the process of social influence operates in several ways.[33] Sometimes a person is motivated to model the behaviour of others because this mimicry is believed to yield rewards such as social approval or money. At other times, the social influence process occurs simply because the person honestly does not *know* the correct way to respond and is using the behaviour of the other person or group as a cue to ensure that he or she is responding correctly.[34] **Normative social influence** occurs when a person conforms to meet the expectations of a person or group.

In contrast, **informational social influence** refers to conformity that occurs because the group's behaviour is taken as evidence of reality: if other people respond in a certain way in an ambiguous situation, we may mimic their behaviour because this appears to be the correct thing to do.[35]

Reasons for conformity

Conformity is not an automatic process, and many factors contribute to the likelihood that consumers will pattern their behaviour on others.[36] Among the factors that affect the likelihood of conformity are the following:

- *Cultural pressures*. Different cultures encourage conformity to a greater or lesser degree. The American slogan 'Do your own thing' in the 1960s reflected a movement away from conformity and towards individualism. In contrast, Japanese society is characterized by the dominance of collective well-being and group loyalty over individuals' needs. Most European societies are situated somewhere between these two, in this respect, 'extreme' cultures. In an analysis of the reading of a soft drink TV commercial, Danish consumers stressed the group solidarity that they saw in the ad, an aspect not mentioned at all by the American sample.[37]

- *Fear of deviance*. The individual may have reason to believe that the group will apply *sanctions* to punish behaviour that differs from the group's. It is not unusual to observe adolescents shunning a peer who is 'different' or a corporation passing over a person for promotion because he or she is not a 'team player'.

- *Commitment*. The more a person is dedicated to a group and values membership in it, the more motivated he or she will be to follow the dictates of the group. Rock groupies and followers of religious sects may do anything that is asked of them, and terrorists (or martyrs, depending on the perspective) may be willing to die for the good of their cause. According to the *principle of least interest*, the person or group that is least committed to staying in a relationship has the most power, because that party won't be susceptible to threatened rejection.[38]

- *Group unanimity, size and expertise*. As groups gain in power, compliance increases. It is often harder to resist the demands of a large number of people than just a few, and this difficulty is compounded when the group members are perceived to know what they are talking about.

- *Susceptibility to interpersonal influence*. This trait refers to an individual's need to identify or enhance his or her image in the opinion of significant others. This enhancement process is often accompanied by the acquisition of products the person believes will impress his or her audience, and by the tendency to learn about products by observing how others use them.[39] Consumers who are low on this trait have been called *role relaxed*; they tend to be older, affluent and have high self-confidence. Based on research identifying role-relaxed consumers, Subaru created a communications strategy to reach these people. In one commercial, a man is heard saying, 'I want a car ... Don't tell me about wood panelling, about winning the respect of my neighbours. They're my neighbours. They're not my heroes ...'

Social comparison: 'How am I doing?'

Informational social influence implies that sometimes we look to the behaviour of others to provide a yardstick about reality. **Social comparison theory** asserts that this process occurs as a way of increasing the stability of one's self-evaluation, especially when physical evidence is unavailable.[40] Social comparison even applies to choices for which there is no objectively correct answer. Such stylistic decisions as tastes in music and art are assumed to be a matter of individual choice, yet people often assume that some types are 'better' or more 'correct' than others.[41] If you have ever been responsible for choosing the music to play at a party, you can probably appreciate the social pressure involved in choosing the right 'mix'.

Although people often like to compare their judgements and actions with those of others, they tend to be selective about precisely whom they will use as benchmarks. Similarity between the consumer and others used for social comparison boosts confidence that the information is accurate and relevant (though we may find it more threatening to be outperformed by someone similar to ourselves).[42] We tend to value the views of obviously dissimilar others only when we are reasonably certain of our own.[43]

In general people tend to choose a *co-oriented peer*, or a person of equivalent standing, when undergoing social comparison. For example, a study of adult cosmetics users found that women were more likely to seek information about product choices from similar friends to reduce uncertainty and to trust the judgements of similar others.[44] The same effects have been found for evaluations of products as diverse as men's suits and coffee.[45]

Tactical requests

How do we increase the likelihood that a person will conform to our wishes? The way a request for compliance is phrased or structured can make a difference. One well-known sales tactic is known as the *foot-in-the-door technique*, where the consumer is first asked a small request and then is 'hit' for something bigger.[46] This term is adapted from door-to-door selling. Experienced salespeople know that they are much more likely to make a sale if they first convince a customer to let them into the house to deliver their sales pitch. Once the person has agreed to this small request, it is more difficult to refuse a larger one, since the consumer has legitimized the salesperson's presence by entering into a dialogue. He or she is no longer a threatening stranger at the door.

Other variations on this strategy include the *low-ball technique*, where a person is asked a small favour and is informed after agreeing to it that it will be very costly, or the *door-in-the-face technique*, where a person is first asked to do something extreme (a request that is usually refused) and then is asked to do something smaller. In each of these cases, people tend to go along with the smaller request, possibly because they feel guilty about denying the larger one.[47]

Group effects on individual behaviour

With more people in a group, it becomes less likely that any one member will be singled out for attention. People in larger groups or those in situations where they are likely to be unidentified tend to focus less attention on themselves, so normal restraints on behaviour are reduced. You may have observed that people sometimes behave more wildly at fancy dress parties or partying on, for example, charter holidays than they do normally. This phenomenon is known as **deindividuation**, where individual identities get submerged within a group and a special situation.

There is some evidence that decisions made by groups differ from those made by an individual. In many cases, group members show a greater willingness to consider riskier alternatives following group discussion than they would if each member made his or her own decision with no discussion. This change is known as the **risky shift**.[48]

Several explanations have been advanced to explain this increased riskiness. One possibility is that something similar to social loafing occurs. As more people are involved in a decision, each individual is less accountable for the outcome, so *diffusion of responsibility* occurs.[49] Another explanation is termed the *value hypothesis*. In this case, riskiness is a culturally valued characteristic, and social pressures operate on individuals to conform to attributes valued by society.[50]

Evidence for the risky shift is mixed. A more general effect appears to be that group discussion tends to increase decision polarization. Whichever direction the group members were leaning before discussion began, towards a risky choice or towards a conservative choice, becomes even more extreme in that direction after discussion. Group discussions regarding product purchases tend to create a risky shift for low-risk items, but they yield even more conservative group decisions for high-risk products.[51]

Shopping patterns

Shopping behaviour changes when people do it in groups. For example, people who shop with at least one other person tend to make more unplanned purchases, buy more and cover more areas of a store than those who go alone.[52] These effects are due to both normative and informational social influence. Group members may be convinced to buy something to gain the approval of the others, or they may simply be exposed to more products and stores by pooling information with the group. Shopping as a social activity, as discussed in the previous chapter, is at the core of both the shopping phenomenon and of group influences on consumer behaviour.[53] For these reasons, retailers would be well advised to encourage group shopping activities.

MARKETING OPPORTUNITY

The institution of home shopping parties, as epitomized by Tupperware, capitalizes on group pressure to boost sales.[54] A company representative makes a sales presentation to a group of people who have gathered in the home of a friend or acquaintance. This format is effective because of informational social influence: participants model the behaviour of others who can provide them with information about how to use certain products, especially since the home party is likely to be attended by a relatively homogeneous group (e.g. neighbourhood housewives) that serves as a valuable benchmark. Normative social influence also operates because actions are publicly observed. Pressures to conform may be particularly intense and may escalate as more and more group members begin to 'cave in' (this process is sometimes termed the *bandwagon effect*). In addition, deindividuation and/or the risky shift may be activated: as consumers get caught up in the group, they may find themselves willing to try new products they would not normally consider.

Resistance to influence

Many people pride themselves on their independence, unique style or ability to resist the best efforts of salespeople and advertisers to buy products.[55] Indeed, individuality should be encouraged by the marketing system: innovation creates change and demand for new products and styles.

Anti-conformity vs. independence

It is important to distinguish between *independence* and *anti-conformity*, where defiance of the group is the actual object of behaviour.[56] Some people will go out of their way *not* to buy whatever happens to be in fashion. Indeed, they may spend a lot of time and effort to ensure that they will not be caught in style. This behaviour is a bit of a paradox, since in order to be vigilant about not doing what is expected, one must always be aware of what is expected. In contrast, truly independent people are oblivious to what is expected, they 'march to their own drummers'.

Reactance and the need for uniqueness

People have a deep-seated need to preserve freedom of choice. When they are threatened with a loss of freedom, they try to overcome this loss. This negative emotional state is termed **reactance**.[57] For example, efforts to censor books, television or rock music because some people find the content objectionable may result in an *increased* desire for these products by the public.[58] Similarly, extremely overbearing promotions that tell consumers they must or should use a product may lose customers in the long run, even those who were already loyal to the advertised brand! Reactance is more likely to occur when the perceived threat to one's freedom increases and as the threatened behaviour's importance to the consumer also increases.

If you have ever arrived at a party wearing the same outfit as someone else, you know how upsetting it can be, a reaction resulting from a search for uniqueness.[59] Consumers who have been led to believe they are not unique are more likely to try to compensate by increasing their creativity, or even to engage in unusual experiences. In fact, this is one explanation for the purchase of relatively obscure brands. People may try to establish a unique identity by deliberately *not* buying market leaders.

This desire to carve out a unique identity was the rationale behind Saab's shift from stressing engineering and safety in its marketing messages to appealing to people to 'find your own road'. According to a Saab executive, 'Research companies tell us we're moving into a period where people feel good about their choices because it fits their own self-concept rather than social conventions'.[60]

Word-of-mouth communication

Despite the abundance of formal means of communication (such as newspapers, magazines and television), much information about the world is conveyed by individuals on an informal basis. If you think carefully about the content of your own conversations in the course of a normal day, you will probably agree that much of what you discuss with friends, family members or fellow employees is product-related: whether you compliment someone on her dress and ask her where she bought it, recommend a new restaurant to a friend or complain to your neighbour about the shoddy treatment you got at the bank, you are engaging in **word-of-**

mouth communication (WOM). Recall, for example, that many of Björn's equipment purchases were directly initiated by comments and suggestions from his friends. This kind of communication can be an efficient marketing tool. When the movie *The Blair Witch Project* became a big success, it was almost assured beforehand because of the pre-premiere WOM sparked by a good website and heavy exploitation of the blurring of reality and fiction.

Information obtained from those we know or talk to directly tends to be more reliable and trustworthy than that received through more formal channels, and unlike advertising, it is often backed up by social pressure to conform to these recommendations.[61] Another factor in the importance of WOM is the decline in people's faith in institutions. As traditional endorsers are becoming increasingly problematical to use, celebrities because they can be unreliable and classical authority figures because of the withering of their authority, and, indeed, as people are becoming more cynical about all sorts of commercial communications, they turn to sources which they feel are above commercial exploitation: friends and family.[62] The importance of personal, informal product communication to marketers is further underscored by one advertising executive, who stated, 'Today, 80 per cent of all buying decisions are influenced by someone's direct recommendations.'[63]

The dominance of WOM

In the 1950s communications theorists began to challenge the assumption that advertising is the primary determinant of purchases: it is now generally accepted that advertising is more effective at reinforcing existing product preferences than at creating new ones.[64] Studies in both industrial and consumer purchase settings underscore the idea that while information from impersonal sources is important for creating brand awareness, word-of-mouth is relied upon in the later stages of evaluation and adoption.[65] The more positive information a consumer gets about a product from peers, the more likely it is that he or she will adopt the product.[66] The influence of others' opinions is at times even more powerful than one's own perceptions. In one study of furniture choices, consumers' estimates of how much their friends would like the furniture was a better predictor of purchase than their *own* evaluations.[67]

Factors encouraging WOM

Product-related conversations can be motivated by a number of factors:[68]

- A person might be highly involved with a type of product or activity and enjoy talking about it. Computer hackers, avid bird-watchers and 'fashion plates' seem to share the ability to steer a conversation towards their particular interest.

- A person might be knowledgeable about a product and use conversations as a way to let others know it. Thus, word-of-mouth communication sometimes enhances the ego of the individual who wants to impress others with his or her expertise.

- A person might initiate such a discussion out of a genuine concern for someone else. We are often motivated to ensure that people we care about buy what is good for them, do not waste their money, and so on.

- One way to reduce uncertainty about the wisdom of a purchase is to talk about it. Talking gives the consumer an opportunity to generate more supporting arguments for the purchase and to garner support for this decision from others.

Most WOM campaigns happen spontaneously, as a product begins to develop a regional or a subcultural following, but occasionally a 'buzz' is created intentionally. For example, when launching a new brand of beer, called Black Sheep, bottles were distributed and maximum exposure to opinion leaders in the trade ensured in order to pave the way for a massive word-of-mouth effect, intended as the vehicle carrying the new brand towards success.[69] A similar *word-of-mouth advertising* technique was used when a group of opinion leaders, or 'influencers', were used to market services in the insurance market.[70]

Guerrilla marketing

To promote hip hop albums, Def Jam and other labels start building a buzz months before a release, leaking advance copies to DJs who put together 'mix tapes' to sell on the street. If the kids seem to like a song, *street teams* then push it to club DJs. As the official release date nears, these groups of fans start slapping up posters around the inner city. They plaster telephone poles, sides of buildings and car windscreens with promotions announcing the release of new albums by artists such as Public Enemy, Jay-Z, DMX or L. L. Cool J.[71]

These streetwise strategies started in the mid-1970s, when pioneering DJs promoted their parties through graffiti-style flyers. This type of grass-roots effort epitomizes guerrilla marketing, promotional strategies that use unconventional locations and intensive word-of-mouth campaigns to push products. As Ice Cube observed, 'Even though I'm an established artist, I still like to leak my music to a kid on the street and let him duplicate it for his homies before it hits radio.'[72]

Today, big companies are buying into guerrilla marketing strategies big time. Coca-Cola did it for a Sprite promotion, Nike did it to build interest in a new shoe model.[73] When RCA Records wanted to create a buzz around teen pop singer Christina Aguilera, they hired a team of young people to swarm the Web and chat about her on popular teen sites. They posted information casually, sometimes sounding like fans. Just before one of her albums debuted, RCA also hired a direct marketing company to email electronic postcards filled with song snippets and biographical information to 50,000 web addresses.[74] Guerrilla marketing delivers: the album quickly went to No. 1 in the charts.

Viral marketing

Many students are big fans of hotmail, a free email service. But there's no such thing as a free lunch: hotmail inserts a small ad on every message sent, making each user a salesperson. The company had 5 million subscribers in its first year and continues to grow exponentially.[75] **Viral marketing** refers to the strategy of getting customers to sell a product on behalf of the company that creates it. This approach is particularly well suited to the Web, since emails circulate so easily. According to a study by Jupiter Communications, only 24 per cent of consumers say they learn about new websites in magazine or newspaper ads. Instead, they rely on friends and family for new site recommendations, so viral marketing is their main source of information about new sites. The chief executive of *Gazooba.com*, a company that creates viral marketing promotions, observed that 'the return mail address of a friend is a brand that you trust'.[76] Obviously, given what was discussed above, there may be some ethical problems and limitations as to how much marketers can infiltrate what otherwise is a network of friends/fans, before this particular 'brand that you trust' is no longer trusted.

Efficiency of WOM

Interpersonal transmissions can be quite rapid. The producers of *Batman* showed a trailer to 300 Batman fans months before its release to counteract widespread anger about the casting of Michael Keaton as the hero. The filmmakers attribute the film's eventual huge success to the positive word-of-mouth that quickly spread following the screening.[77]

WOM is especially powerful in cases where the consumer is relatively unfamiliar with the product category. Such a situation would be expected in cases where the product is new (e.g. medication to prevent hair loss) or is technologically complex (e.g. CD players). As one example, the strongest predictor of a person's intention to buy a residential solar water heating system was found to be the number of solar heating users the person knew.[78]

Negative WOM

Word-of-mouth is a two-edged sword that can cut both ways for marketers. Informal discussions among consumers can make or break a product or store. And negative word-of-mouth is weighted *more* heavily by consumers than are positive comments. According to one study, 90 per cent of unhappy customers will not do business with a company again. Each of these people is likely to share their grievance with at least nine other people, and 13 per cent of these disgruntled customers will go on to tell *more than 30* people of their negative experience.[79] Especially when making a decision about trying a new product, the consumer is more likely to pay attention to negative information than positive information and to relate news of this experience to others.[80] Some consumers may even use negative WOM in order to restore their own positive self-image, for example in cases where a product offering is judged not to have corresponded to the person's self. Instead of blaming oneself for a misjudgement which would harm self-images of rationality and being in control, negative WOM may be the outcome.[81] Negative WOM has been shown to reduce the credibility of a firm's advertising, and to influence consumers' attitudes towards a product as well as their intention to buy it.[82] And negative WOM is even easier to spread online. Many dissatisfied customers and disgruntled former employees have been 'inspired' to create websites just to share their tales of woe with others. For example, a website for people to complain about the Dunkin' Donuts chain got to be so popular that the company bought it in order to control the bad press it was getting. It grew out of a complaint by the original owner because he could not get skimmed milk for his coffee.[83] For other protest sites, visit *protest.net* and prepare to be outraged . . .

Rumours

In the 1930s, 'professional rumourmongers' were hired to organize word-of-mouth campaigns to promote clients' products and criticize those of competitors.[84] A **rumour**, even if it has no basis in fact, can be a very dangerous thing. As information is transmitted among consumers, it tends to change. The resulting message ceases to resemble the original.

Figure 10.3 The transmission of misinformation. These drawings provide a classic example of the distortions that can occur as information is transmitted from person to person. As each person reproduces the figure, it gradually changes from an owl to a cat.

Original drawing

Source: Kenneth J. Gergen and Mary Gergen, *Social Psychology* (New York: Harcourt Brace Jovanovich, 1981): 365. Adapted from F.C. Bartlett, *Remembering* (Cambridge: Cambridge University Press, 1932).

Social scientists who study rumours have examined the process by which information gets distorted. The British psychologist Frederic Bartlett used the method of *serial reproduction* to examine this phenomenon. A subject is asked to reproduce a stimulus, such as a drawing or a story. Another subject is given this reproduction and asked to copy that, and so on. This technique is shown in Figure 10.3. Bartlett found that distortions almost inevitably follow a pattern: they tend to change from ambiguous forms to more conventional ones as subjects try to make them consistent with pre-existing schemas. This process, known as *assimilation*, is characterized by *levelling*, where details are omitted to simplify the structure, or *sharpening*, where prominent details are accentuated.

In general, people have been shown to prefer transmitting good news rather than bad, perhaps because they like to avoid unpleasantness or dislike arousing hostility. However, this reluctance does not appear to occur when companies are the topic of conversation. Corporations such as Procter & Gamble and McDonald's have been the subjects of rumours about their products, sometimes with marked effects on sales.

MARKETING PITFALL

After a very successful launching of the combined shampoo and conditioner Wash&Go on the Danish market in January 1990, where the product reached a market share (value) of more than 20 per cent in September that same year, a negative rumour caused a severe blow to its parent company. First, hairdressers complained about problems with doing colourings and perms on clients using the new product. Procter & Gamble denied the complaint, but did not dispel the rumour and soon had to deal with a second rumour: that the use of the product caused significant loss of hair. Their market share fell from 20 to 5 per cent.[85]

Most rumours have some 'kernel of truth', and it is very important for the company facing the rumour to detect it. The silicon in Wash&Go actually did cause problems for certain perm or colouring products, but this was not immediately acknowledged. Instead, the denial of the first rumour without producing substantial factual documentation led to the spreading of the second rumour, perhaps as an attempt to 'get even with' the 'aggressive' marketer. Large foreign companies are often targets of such negative word-of-mouth.[86] Procter & Gamble first tried to ignore the rumour by denial, then to refute it with reference to their own research, a source of information which had little credibility and probably strengthened the rumour rather than weakened it. Only when they asked the state environmental agency to conduct independent tests could Procter & Gamble disprove the rumours and slowly begin to regain the lost market shares.[87]

Rumours are thought to reveal the underlying fears of a society. One of the most (in)famous rumours in modern European history concerned the white slave trade and reflected a tacit anti-Semitism in society. The rumour said that young women were being kidnapped from fitting rooms in Jewish shopkeepers' fashion boutiques in the French city of Orléans to be sent to the Middle East. The rumour in turn generated rumours about an anti-Semitic conspiracy against Jewish businesspeople.[88] Another rumour regarding snakes coming out of teddy bears imported from the Orient was interpreted to signify western consumers' apprehensions about Asian influences. While rumours sometimes die out by themselves, in other instances a company may take direct action to counteract them. A French margarine was rumoured to contain contaminants, and the company addressed this in its advertising by referring to the story as 'The rumour that costs you dearly'.[89]

Multicultural dimensions

Multinational firms are especially prone to damage from rumours, since they may have less control over product quality, content or word-of-mouth. Several marketers in Indonesia, including Nestlé, have been damaged by rumours that their foods contain pork, which is prohibited to the 160 million Muslim consumers in that country. Islamic preachers, or mullahs, responded to these rumours by warning consumers not to buy products that might be tainted with pork fat. Nestlé spent more than $250,000 on an ad campaign to counteract the rumours.[90] In another recent incident in the Middle East, the Egyptian subsidiary of Coca-Cola had to get an edict from Egypt's mufti (top religious authority) certifying that the familiar Coca-Cola script logo does not in fact say 'No Mohammed, No Mecca' in Arabic after a rumour spread about hidden messages. This problem echoed one experienced a few years earlier by Nike, which recalled 38,000 pairs of shoes because its flaming air logo resembled the Arabic script for Allah.[91]

Opinion leadership

Although consumers get information from personal sources, they do not tend to ask *anyone* for advice about purchases. If you decide to buy a new stereo, you are most likely to seek advice from a friend who knows a lot about sound systems. This friend may own a sophisticated system, or he or she may subscribe to specialist magazines and spend time browsing in electronics stores. On the other hand, you may have another friend who has a reputation for being stylish and who spends *his* free time reading fashion and lifestyle magazines and shopping in trendy boutiques. While you might not bring your stereo problem to him, you may take him with you to shop for a new wardrobe.

This so-called opinion leadership is an important influence on a brand's popularity in many categories. The market for sports accessories is among these, where both celebrity endorsements (see Chapter 6) and sponsorship in order to form opinions are major marketing tools. The American Gatorade sports drink company made its entrance on the British market on an exclusive opinion leadership basis, sponsoring sports events and professionals like the captain of the national cricket team, but without any major promotion of the product itself. This suspense strategy created curiosity, interest and inquiries, and probably pre-shaped a lot of opinion leaders' opinions about the product before its major launch in distribution outlets.[92]

The nature of opinion leadership

Everyone knows people who are knowledgeable about products and whose advice is taken seriously by others. These individuals are **opinion leaders**. An opinion leader is a person who is frequently able to influence others' attitudes or behaviours.[93] Opinion leaders are extremely valuable information sources for a number of reasons:

- They are technically competent and thus are convincing because they possess expert power.[94]

- They have pre-screened, evaluated and synthesized product information in an unbiased way, so they possess knowledge power.[95] Unlike commercial endorsers, opinion leaders do not represent the interests of one company. They are more credible because they have no 'axe to grind'.

- They tend to be socially active and highly interconnected in their community.[96] They are likely to hold office in community groups and clubs and to be active outside the home. As a result, opinion leaders often have legitimate power by virtue of their social standing.

- They tend to be similar to the consumer in terms of their values and beliefs, so they possess referent power. Note that while opinion leaders are set apart by their interest or expertise in a product category, they are more convincing to the extent that they tend to be just slightly higher in terms of status and educational attainment than those they influence, but not so high as to be in a different social class.

- Opinion leaders are often among the first to buy new products, so they absorb much of the risk. This experience reduces uncertainty for others who are not as courageous. And, while company-sponsored communications tend to focus exclusively on the positive aspects of a product, this hands-on experience makes opinion leaders more likely to impart *both* positive *and* negative information about product performance.

This ad for MTV focuses on the importance of young opinion leaders in shaping their friends' preferences.

Viacom International.

Whereas individual behavioural and psychological traits are the most important in identifying opinion leaders, there are some indications that opinion leadership does not function the same way in different cultures. For example, there are cultural differences in how much people rely on impersonal vs. personal information. In a study of opinion leadership in 14 European countries plus the USA and Canada, the countries most characterized by the use of impersonal information seeking (e.g. from consumer magazines, etc.) were Denmark, Norway, Sweden and Finland, whereas the countries least characterized by impersonal information seeking were Italy, Portugal and Spain.[97]

The extent of an opinion leader's influence

When marketers and social scientists initially developed the concept of the opinion leader, it was assumed that certain influential people in a community would exert an overall impact on group members' attitudes. Later work, however, began to question the assumption that there is such a thing as a *generalized opinion leader*, somebody whose recommendations are sought for all types of purchases. Very few people are capable of being expert in a number of fields. Sociologists distinguish between those who are *monomorphic*, or experts in a limited field, and those who are *polymorphic*, or experts in several fields.[98] Even the opinion leaders who are polymorphic tend to concentrate on one broad domain, such as electronics or fashion.

Research on opinion leadership generally indicates that while opinion leaders do exist for multiple product categories, expertise tends to overlap across similar categories. It is rare to find a generalized opinion leader. An opinion leader for home appliances is likely to serve a similar function for home cleaners, but not for cosmetics. In contrast, a *fashion opinion leader* whose primary influence is on clothing choices may also be consulted for recommendations on cosmetics purchases, but not necessarily on microwave ovens.[99]

Opinion leaders vs. other consumer types

Early conceptions of the opinion leader role also assumed a static process: the opinion leader absorbs information from the mass media and in turn transmits these data to opinion receivers. This view has turned out to be oversimplified: it confuses the functions of several different types of consumers. Furthermore, research has shown some evidence that the flow of influence is not one-way but two-way, so that opinion leaders are influenced by the responses of their followers.[100] This would reflect a more complex communication situation as described by the interactive communication model discussed in Chapter 6.

Opinion leaders may or may not be purchasers of the products they recommend. Early purchasers are known as *innovators*. Opinion leaders who are also early purchasers have been termed **innovative communicators**. One study identified a number of characteristics of male university students who were innovative communicators for fashion products. These men were among the first to buy new fashions, and their fashion opinions were incorporated by other students in their own clothing decisions. Other characteristics included:[101]

- They were socially active.
- They were appearance-conscious and narcissistic (i.e. they were quite fond of themselves and self-centred).
- They were involved in rock culture.
- They were heavy magazine readers.
- They were likely to own more clothing, and a broader range of styles, than other students.
- Their intellectual interests were relatively limited.

Opinion leaders are also likely to be **opinion seekers**. They are generally more involved in a product category and actively search for information. As a result, they are more likely to talk about products with others and to solicit others' opinions as well. Contrary to the static view of opinion leadership, most product-related conversation does not take place in a 'lecture' format, where one person does all of the talking. A lot of product-related conversation is prompted by the situation and occurs in the context of a casual interaction rather than as formal instruction.[102] One study, which found that opinion seeking is especially high for food products, revealed that two-thirds of opinion seekers also view themselves as opinion leaders.[103]

Consumers who are expert in a product category may not actively communicate with others, while other consumers may have a more general interest in being involved in product discussions. A consumer category called the **market maven** has been proposed to describe people who are actively involved in transmitting marketplace information of all types. Market mavens are not necessarily interested in certain products and may not necessarily be early purchasers of products. They come closer to the function of a generalized opinion leader because they tend to have a solid overall knowledge of how and where to procure products.[104] A scale that has been used to identify market mavens is shown in Figure 10.4.

In addition to everyday consumers who are influential in influencing others' purchase decisions, a class of marketing intermediary called the surrogate consumer is an active player in many categories. A **surrogate consumer** is a person who is hired to provide input into purchase decisions. Unlike the opinion leader or market maven, the surrogate consumer is usually compensated for this involvement.

Interior decorators, stockbrokers or professional shoppers can all be thought of as surrogate consumers. Whether or not they actually make the purchase on behalf of the consumer, surrogates' recommendations can be enormously influential. The consumer in essence relinquishes control over several or all decision-making functions, such as information search, evaluation of alternatives or the actual purchase. For example, a client may commission an interior decorator, while a broker may be

Figure 10.4 Scale items used to identify market mavens

1. I like introducing new brands and products to my friends.

2. I like helping people by providing them with information about many kinds of products.

3. People ask me for information about products, places to shop, or sales.

4. If someone asked me where to get the best buy on several types of products, I could tell him or her where to shop.

5. My friends think of me as a good source of information when it comes to new products or sales.

6. Think about a person who has information about a variety of products and likes to share this information with others. This person knows about new products, sales, stores, and so on, but does not necessarily feel he or she is an expert on one particular product. How well would you say this description fits you?

Source: Adapted from Lawrence Feick and Linda Price, 'The Market Maven: A Diffuser of Marketplace Information', *Journal of Marketing* 51 (January 1987): 83–7.

entrusted to make crucial buy/sell decisions on behalf of investors. The involvement of surrogates in a wide range of purchase decisions tends to be overlooked by many marketers, who may be mistargeting their communications to end-consumers instead of to the surrogates who are actually sifting through product information.[105]

Identifying opinion leaders

Because opinion leaders are so central to consumer decision-making, marketers are quite interested in identifying influential people for a product category. In fact, many ads are intended to reach these influentials rather than the average consumer, especially if the ads contain a lot of technical information.

Professional opinion leaders

Perhaps the easiest way to find opinion leaders is to target people who are paid to give expert opinions. *Professional opinion leaders* are people such as doctors or scientists who obtain specialized information from technical journals and other practitioners.

Marketers who are trying to gain consumer acceptance for their products sometimes find it easier to try to win over professional opinion leaders, who (they hope) will, in turn, recommend their products to customers. A case in point is the effort by Roc S.A., maker of Europe's leading brand of hypoallergenic lotions, to break into the lucrative American market for skin-care products. Instead of competing head-to-head with the lavish consumer advertising of Revlon or Estée Lauder, the French company decided first to gain medical acceptance by winning over pharmacists and dermatologists. In 1994 the company began advertising in medical journals, and the product was distributed to dermatologists and to pharmacies patronized by patients of dermatologists. A free telephone number was established to provide interested consumers with the names of pharmacies carrying the range.[106]

Of course, this approach may backfire if it is carried to an extreme and compromises the credibility of professional opinion leaders. In several countries, the medical industry has a dubious reputation of 'bribing' doctors with invitations to product presentations disguised as conferences, often held in glamorous places.

Consumer opinion leaders

Since most opinion leaders are everyday consumers and are not formally included in marketing efforts, they are harder to find. A celebrity or an influential industry executive is by definition easy to locate. He or she has national or at least regional visibility or may be listed in published directories. In contrast, opinion leaders tend to operate at the local level and may influence 5–10 consumers rather than an entire market segment. In some cases, companies have been known to identify influentials and involve them directly in their marketing efforts, hoping to create a 'ripple effect' as these consumers sing the company's praises to their friends. Many department stores, for example, have fashion 'panels', usually composed of adolescent girls, who provide input into fashion trends, participate in fashion shows, and so on.

Because of the difficulties involved in identifying specific opinion leaders in a large market, most attempts to do so focus on exploratory studies where the characteristics of representative opinion leaders can be identified and then generalized to the larger market. This knowledge helps marketers to target their product-related information to appropriate settings and media. For example, one attempt to identify financial opinion leaders found that these consumers were more likely to be involved in managing their own finances and tended to use a computer to do so. They were also more likely to follow their investments on a daily basis and to read books and watch television programmes devoted to financial issues.[107]

The self-designating method

The most commonly used technique to identify opinion leaders is simply to ask individual consumers whether they consider themselves to be opinion leaders.

However, there are obvious problems with self-designation. While respondents who report a greater degree of interest in a product category are more likely to be opinion leaders, the results of surveys intended to identify self-designated opinion leaders must be viewed with some scepticism. Some people have a tendency to inflate their own importance and influence, while others who really are influential might not admit to this quality.[108] Just because we transmit advice about products does not mean other people *take* that advice. For someone to be considered a *bona fide* opinion leader, his or her advice must actually be heard and heeded by opinion seekers. An alternative is to select certain group members (*key informants*) who in turn are asked to identify opinion leaders. The success of this approach hinges on locating those who have accurate knowledge of the group and on minimizing their response biases (e.g. the tendency to inflate one's own influence on the choices of others).

While the self-designating method is not as reliable as a more systematic analysis (where individual claims of influence can be verified by asking others whether the person is really influential), it does have the advantage of being easy to administer to a large group of potential opinion leaders. In some cases not all members of a community are surveyed. One of the original measurement scales developed for self-designation of opinion leaders is shown in Figure 10.5.

Sociometry

A web-based service has been created that is based on the popular play *Six Degrees of Separation*. The basic premise of the plot is that everyone on the planet is separated by only six other people. The website (*www.sixdegrees.com*) allows a person to register and provide names and email addresses of other people, so that when the user needs to network a connection is made with others in the database.[109]

This site is a digital version of more conventional **sociometric methods**, which

Figure 10.5 A revised and updated version of the opinion leadership scale

Please rate yourself on the following scales relating to your interactions with friends and neighbours regarding _____.

1. In general, do you talk to your friends and neighbours about _____:

very often				never
5	4	3	2	1

2. When you talk to your friends and neighbours about _____ do you:

give a great deal of information				give very little information
5	4	3	2	1

3. During the past six months, how many people have you told about a new _____?

told a number of people				told no one
5	4	3	2	1

4. Compared with your circle of friends, how likely are you to be asked about new _____?

very likely to be asked				not at all likely to be asked
5	4	3	2	1

5. In discussion of new _____, which of the following happens most?

you tell your friends about _____				your friends tell you about _____
5	4	3	2	1

6. Overall in all of your discussions with friends and neighbours are you:

often used as a source of advice				not used as a source of advice
5	4	3	2	1

Source: Adapted from Terry L. Childers, 'Assessment of the Psychometric Properties of an Opinion Leadership Scale', *Journal of Marketing Research* 23 (May 1986): 184–8; and Leisa Reinecke Flynn, Ronald E. Goldsmith and Jacqueline K. Eastman, 'The King and Summers Opinion Leadership Scale: Revision and Refinement', *Journal of Business Research* 31 (1994): 55–64.

trace communication patterns among group members and allow researchers systematically to map out the interactions that take place among group members. By interviewing participants and asking them whom they go to for product information, those who tend to be sources of product-related information can be identified. While this method is the most precise, it is expensive to implement, since it involves very close study of interaction patterns in small groups. For this reason, sociometric techniques are best applied in a closed, self-contained social setting, such as in hospitals, prisons and army bases, where members are largely isolated from other social networks.

Many professionals and services marketers depend primarily on word-of-mouth to generate business. In many cases consumers recommend a service provider to a friend or fellow worker, and in other cases other businesspeople will make recommendations to their customers.

Sociometric analyses can be used to understand better *referral behaviour* and to locate strengths and weaknesses in terms of how one's reputation is communicated through a community. *Network analysis* focuses on communication in social systems, considers the relations among people in a *referral network* and measures the *tie strength* among them. Tie strength refers to the nature of the bond between people. It can range from strong primary (e.g. one's spouse) to weak secondary (e.g. an acquaintance that one rarely sees). A strong tie relationship may be thought of as a primary reference group: interactions are frequent and important to the individual.

While strong ties are important, weak ties can perform a *bridging function*. This type of connection allows a consumer access between subgroups. For example, you might have a regular group of friends who serve as a primary reference group (strong ties). If you have an interest in tennis, say, one of these friends might introduce you to a group of people who play in the tennis team. As a result, you gain access to their valuable expertise through this bridging function. This referral process demonstrates the strength of weak ties.

Chapter summary

- Consumers belong to or admire many different groups and are often influenced in their purchase decisions by a desire to be accepted by others.

- Individuals have influence in a group to the extent that they possess *social power*; types of power include information power, referent power, legitimate power, expert power, reward power and coercive power.

- We conform to the desires of others for one of two basic reasons. People who model their behaviour on others because they take others' behaviour as evidence of the correct way to act are conforming because of *informational social influence*. Those who conform to satisfy the expectations of others and/or to be accepted by the group are affected by *normative social influence*.

- Group members often do things they would not do as individuals because their identities become merged with the group; they become *deindividuated*.

- Individuals or groups whose opinions or behaviour are particularly important to consumers are *reference groups*. Both formal and informal groups influence the individual's purchase decisions, although the impact of reference group influence is affected by such factors as the conspicuousness of the product and the relevance of the reference group for a particular purchase.

- *Opinion leaders* who are knowledgeable about a product and whose opinions are highly regarded tend to influence others' choices. Specific opinion leaders are somewhat hard to identify, but marketers who know their general characteristics can try to target them in their media and promotional strategies.

- Other influencers include *market mavens*, who have a general interest in marketplace activities, and *surrogate consumers*, who are compensated for their advice about purchases.

- Much of what we know about products comes about through *word-of-mouth communication (WOM)* rather than formal advertising. Product-related information tends to be exchanged in casual conversations.

- While word-of-mouth is often helpful for making consumers aware of products, it can also hurt companies when damaging product *rumours* or negative word-of-mouth occurs.

- *Sociometric methods* are used to trace referral patterns. This information can be used to identify opinion leaders and other influential consumers.

KEY TERMS

Comparative influence (*p. 304*)

Conformity (*p. 313*)

Deindividuation (*p. 316*)

Information power (*p. 311*)

Informational social influence (*p. 314*)

Innovative communicators (*p. 325*)

Market maven (*p. 325*)

Normative influence (*p. 303*)

Normative social influence (*p. 314*)

Norms (*p. 313*)

Opinion leaders (*p. 323*)

Opinion seekers (*p. 325*)

Reactance (*p. 317*)

Reference group (*p. 303*)

Referent power (*p. 311*)

Risky shift (*p. 316*)

Rumour (*p. 320*)

Social comparison theory (*p. 315*)

Sociometric methods (*p. 327*)

Surrogate consumer (*p. 325*)

Viral marketing (*p. 319*)

Virtual community of consumption (*p. 307*)

Word-of-mouth communication (WOM) (*p. 317*)

For additional material see the companion website at:
www.booksites.net/solomon_euro

Consumer behaviour challenge

1 Compare and contrast the five bases of power described in the text. Which are most likely to be relevant for marketing efforts?

2 Why is referent power an especially potent force for marketing appeals? What are factors that help to predict whether reference groups will or will not be a powerful influence on a person's purchase decisions?

3 Discuss some factors that determine the amount of conformity likely to be observed among consumers.

4 Under what conditions are we more likely to engage in social comparison with dissimilar others vs. similar others? How might this dimension be used in the design of marketing appeals?

5 Discuss some factors that influence whether or not membership groups will have a significant influence on a person's behaviour.

6 Why is word-of-mouth communication often more persuasive than advertising?

7 Is there such a thing as a generalized opinion leader? What is likely to determine if an opinion leader will be influential with regard to a specific product category?

8 What is your opinion about the techniques of guerilla marketing and viral marketing? Discuss the pros and cons.

9 The power of unspoken social norms often becomes obvious only when these norms are violated. To witness this result first hand, try one of the following: stand facing the back wall in a lift; serve dessert before the main course; offer to pay cash for dinner at a friend's home; wear pyjamas to class; or tell someone not to have a nice day.

10 Identify a set of avoidance groups for your peers. Can you identify any consumption decisions that are made with these groups in mind?

11 Identify fashion opinion leaders at your university or business school. Do they fit the profile discussed in the chapter?

12 Conduct a sociometric analysis within your dormitory or neighbourhood. For a product category such as music or cars, ask each individual to identify other individuals with whom they share information. Systematically trace all of these avenues of communication, and identify opinion leaders by locating individuals who are repeatedly named as providing helpful information.

Notes

1. Joel B. Cohen and Ellen Golden, 'Informational Social Influence and Product Evaluation', *Journal of Applied Psychology* 56 (February 1972): 54–9; Robert E. Burnkrant and Alain Cousineau, 'Informational and Normative Social Influence in Buyer Behavior', *Journal of Consumer Research* 2 (December 1975): 206–15; Peter H. Reingen, 'Test of a List Procedure for Inducing Compliance with a Request to Donate Money', *Journal of Applied Psychology* 67 (1982): 110–18; C. Whan Park and V. Parker Lessig, 'Students and Housewives: Differences in Susceptibility to Reference Group Influence', *Journal of Consumer Research* 4 (September 1977): 102–10.

2. Kenneth J. Gergen and Mary Gergen, *Social Psychology* (New York: Harcourt Brace Jovanovich, 1981).

3. Harold H. Kelley, 'Two Functions of Reference Groups', in *Basic Studies in Social Psychology*, ed., Harold Proshansky and Bernard Siedenberg (New York: Holt, Rinehart and Winston, 1965): 210-14.

4. David Murrow, 'Dewar's Profiles Travel Well', *Advertising Age* (14 August 1989): 28.

5. 'Flere vil spise mere fisk', *Markedsføring* 18 (1996): 18.

6. L. Festinger, S. Schachter and K. Back, *Social Pressures in Informal Groups: A Study of Human Factors in Housing* (New York: Harper, 1950).

7. R. B. Zajonc, H. M. Markus and W. Wilson, 'Exposure Effects and Associative Learning', *Journal of Experimental Social Psychology* 10 (1974): 248-63.

8. D. J. Stang, 'Methodological Factors in Mere Exposure Research', *Psychological Bulletin* 81 (1974): 1014-25; R. B. Zajonc, P. Shaver, C. Tavris and D. van Kreveid, 'Exposure, Satiation and Stimulus Discriminability', *Journal of Personality and Social Psychology* 21 (1972): 270-80.

9. J. E. Grush, K. L. McKeogh and R. F. Ahlering, 'Extrapolating Laboratory Exposure Research to Actual Political Elections', *Journal of Personality and Social Psychology* 36 (1978): 257-70.

10. A. Benton Cocanaugher and Grady D. Bruce, 'Socially Distant Reference Groups and Consumer Aspirations', *Journal of Marketing Research* 8 (August 1971): 79-81; James E. Stafford, 'Effects of Group Influences on Consumer Brand Preferences', *Journal of Marketing Research* 3 (February 1966): 68-75.

11. Cocanaugher and Bruce, 'Socially Distant Reference Groups and Consumer Aspirations'.

12. Anne F. Jensen and Søren Askegaard, 'In Pursuit of Ugliness - Searching for a Fashion Concept in the Era After Good Taste', *Working Paper in Marketing* 17, School of Business and Economics, Odense University, 1998.

13. Richard Wilk, 'A Critique of Desire: Distaste and Dislike in Consumer Behavior', *Consumption, Culture and Markets* 1(2) (1997): 175-96.

14. Greg Jaffe, 'No MTV for Widespread Panic, Just Loads of Worshipful Fans', *Wall Street Journal Interactive Edition* (17 February 1999).

15. This typology is adapted from material presented in Robert V. Kozinets, 'E-Tribalized Marketing: The Strategic Implications of Virtual Communities of Consumption', *European Management Journal* 17(3) (June 1999): 252-64.

16. Tom Weber, 'Net's Hottest Game Brings People Closer', *Wall Street Journal Interactive Edition* (20 March 2000).

17. Quoted in Marc Gunther, 'The Newest Addiction', *Fortune* (2 August 1999): 122-4, at 123.

18. Laurie J. Flynn, 'Free Internet Service for Simpsons Fans', *New York Times on the Web* (24 January 2000).

19. Bob Tedeschi, 'Product Reviews from Anyone with an Opinion', *New York Times on the Web* (25 October 1999).

20. Kozinets, 'E-Tribalized Marketing'.

21. Bob Tedeschi, 'Online Retailers Find that Customer Reviews Build Loyalty', *New York Times on the Web* (6 September 1999).

22. 'Bookseller Offers Refunds for Advertised Books', *Opelika-Auburn News* (11 February 1999): A11.

23. *Information* (14 February 2001): 2.

24. Jeffrey D. Ford and Elwood A. Ellis, 'A Re-examination of Group Influence on Member Brand Preference', *Journal of Marketing Research* 17 (February 1980): 125-32; Thomas S. Robertson, *Innovative Behavior and Communication* (New York: Holt, Rinehart and Winston, Inc., 1980): chapter 8.

25. William O. Bearden and Michael J. Etzel, 'Reference Group Influence on Product and Brand Purchase Decisions', *Journal of Consumer Research* 9 (1982) 2: 183-94.

26. Gergen and Gergen, *Social Psychology*: 312.

27. J. R. P. French, Jr and B. Raven, 'The Bases of Social Power', in *Studies in Social Power*, ed. D. Cartwright (Ann Arbor, MI: Institute for Social Research, 1959): 150-67.

28. Michael R. Solomon, 'Packaging the Service Provider', *Service Industries Journal* 5 (March 1985): 64-72.

29. Quoted in Tamar Charry, 'Advertising: Hawking, Wozniak Pitch Modems for U.S. Robotics', *New York Times News Service* (1997), accessed 2 May 1997.

30. Cf. Patricia M. West and Susan M. Broniarczyk, 'Integrating Multiple Opinions: The Role of Aspiration Level on Consumer Response to Critic Consensus', *Journal of Consumer Research* 25 (June 1998): 38-51.

31. Lars Thøger Christensen and Søren Askegaard, 'Identities and Images of Products and Organizations: A Semiotic Exercise', *European Journal of Marketing* 35(3/4) (2001): 292-315.

32. Pechmann and S. Cornelia Ratneshwar, 'The Effects of Antismoking and Cigarette Advertising on Young Adolescents' Perceptions of Peers Who Smoke', *Journal of Consumer Research* 21 (September 1994): 2: 236-51.

33. See Robert B. Cialdini, *Influence: Science and Practice*, 2nd edn (New York: Scott, Foresman, 1988) for an excellent and entertaining treatment of this process.

34. For the seminal work on conformity and social influence, see Solomon E. Asch, 'Effects of Group Pressure Upon the Modification and Distortion of Judgments', in D. Cartwright and A. Zander, eds, *Group Dynamics* (New York: Harper and Row,

1953); Richard S. Crutchfield, 'Conformity and Character', *American Psychologist* 10 (1955): 191-8; Muzafer Sherif, 'A Study of Some Social Factors in Perception', *Archives of Psychology* 27 (1935): 187.

35. Burnkrant and Cousineau, 'Informational and Normative Social Influence in Buyer Behavior'.

36. For a recent attempt to measure individual differences in proclivity to conformity, see William O. Bearden, Richard G. Netemeyer and Jesse E. Teel, 'Measurement of Consumer Susceptibility to Interpersonal Influence', *Journal of Consumer Research* 15 (March 1989): 473-81.

37. Douglas B. Holt, Søren Askegaard and Torsten Ringberg, '7ups and Downs', unpublished manuscript, Penn State University.

38. John W. Thibaut and Harold H. Kelley, *The Social Psychology of Groups* (New York: John Wiley, 1959); W. W. Waller and R. Hill, *The Family: A Dynamic Interpretation* (New York: Dryden, 1951).

39. Bearden, Netemeyer and Teel, 'Measurement of Consumer Susceptibility to Interpersonal Influence' Lynn R. Kahle, 'Observations: Role-Relaxed Consumers: A Trend of the Nineties', *Journal of Advertising Research* 35(2) (March/April 1995): 66-71; Lynn R. Kahle and Aviv Shoham, 'Observations: Role-Relaxed Consumers: Empirical Evidence', *Journal of Advertising Research* 35 (3) (May/June 1995): 59-62.

40. Leon Festinger, 'A Theory of Social Comparison Processes', *Human Relations* 7 (May 1954): 117-40.

41. Chester A. Insko, Sarah Drenan, Michael R. Solomon, Richard Smith and Terry J. Wade, 'Conformity as a Function of the Consistency of Positive Self-Evaluation with Being Liked and Being Right', *Journal of Experimental Social Psychology* 19 (1983): 341-58.

42. Abraham Tesser, Murray Millar and Janet Moore, 'Some Affective Consequences of Social Comparison and Reflection Processes: The Pain and Pleasure of Being Close', *Journal of Personality and Social Psychology* 54 (1988) 1: 49-61.

43. L. Wheeler, K. G. Shaver, R. A. Jones, G. R. Goethals, J. Cooper, J. E. Robinson, C. L. Gruder and K. W. Butzine, 'Factors Determining the Choice of a Comparison Other', *Journal of Experimental Social Psychology* 5 (1969): 219-32.

44. George P. Moschis, 'Social Comparison and Informal Group Influence', *Journal of Marketing Research* 13 (August 1976): 237-44.

45. Burnkrant and Cousineau, 'Informational and Normative Social Influence in Buyer Behavior'; M. Venkatesan, 'Experimental Study of Consumer Behavior Conformity and Independence', *Journal of Marketing Research* 3 (November 1966): 384-7.

46. J. L. Freedman and S. Fraser, 'Compliance Without Pressure: The Foot-in-the-Door Technique', *Journal of Personality and Social Psychology* 4 (1966): 195-202.

47. R. B. Cialdini, J. E. Vincent, S. K. Lewis, J. Catalan, D. Wheeler and B. L. Darby, 'Reciprocal Concessions Procedure for Inducing Compliance: The Door-in-the-Face Effect', *Journal of Personality and Social Psychology* 31 (1975): 200-15.

48. Nathan Kogan and Michael A. Wallach, 'Risky Shift Phenomenon in Small Decision-Making Groups: A Test of the Information Exchange Hypothesis', *Journal of Experimental Social Psychology* 3 (January 1967): 75-84; Nathan Kogan and Michael A. Wallach, *Risk Taking* (New York: Holt, Rinehart and Winston, 1964); Arch G. Woodside and M. Wayne DeLozier, 'Effects of Word-of-Mouth Advertising on Consumer Risk Taking', *Journal of Advertising* (Fall 1976): 12-19.

49. Kogan and Wallach, *Risk Taking*.

50. Roger Brown, *Social Psychology* (New York: The Free Press, 1965).

51. David L. Johnson and I. R. Andrews, 'Risky Shift Phenomenon Tested with Consumer Product Stimuli', *Journal of Personality and Social Psychology* 20 (1971): 382-5; see also Vithala R. Rao and Joel H. Steckel, 'A Polarization Model for Describing Group Preferences', *Journal of Consumer Research* 18 (June 1991): 108-18.

52. Donald H. Granbois, 'Improving the Study of Customer In-Store Behavior', *Journal of Marketing* 32 (October 1968): 28-32.

53. Özlem Sandikci and Douglas B. Holt, 'Malling Society: Mall Consumption Practices and the Future of Public Space', in J. F. Sherry, Jr, ed., *ServiceScapes* (Chicago: NTC Business Books, 1998): 305-36; cf. also P. Falk and C. Campbell, eds, *The Shopping Experience* (London: Sage, 1997).

54. Len Strazewski, 'Tupperware Locks in New Strategy', *Advertising Age* (8 February 1988): 30.

55. Gergen and Gergen, *Social Psychology*.

56. L. J. Strickland, S. Messick and D. N. Jackson, 'Conformity, Anticonformity and Independence: Their Dimensionality and Generality', *Journal of Personality and Social Psychology* 16 (1970): 494-507.

57. Jack W. Brehm, *A Theory of Psychological Reactance* (New York: Academic Press, 1966).

58. R. D. Ashmore, V. Ramchandra and R. Jones, 'Censorship as an Attitude Change Induction', paper presented at meetings of Eastern Psychological Association, New York, 1971; R. A. Wicklund and J. Brehm, *Perspectives on Cognitive Dissonance* (Hillsdale, NJ: Lawrence Erlbaum, 1976).

59. C. R. Snyder and H. L. Fromkin, *Uniqueness: The Human Pursuit of Difference* (New York: Plenum Press, 1980).

60. Quoted in Raymond Serafin, 'Non-conformity Sparks Saab', *Advertising Age* (3 April 1995): 27.

61. Johan Arndt, 'Role of Product-Related Conversations in the Diffusion of a New Product', *Journal of Marketing Research* 4 (August 1967): 291-5.

62. 'Word-of-Mouth' to Become True Measure of Ads', *Marketing* (9 February 1995): 7.

63. Quoted in Barbara B. Stern and Stephen J. Gould, 'The Consumer as Financial Opinion Leader', *Journal of Retail Banking* 10 (Summer 1988): 43-52.

64. Elihu Katz and Paul F. Lazarsfeld, *Personal Influence* (Glencoe, IL: Free Press, 1955).

65. John A. Martilla, 'Word-of-Mouth Communication in the Industrial Adoption Process', *Journal of Marketing Research* 8 (March 1971): 173-8; see also Marsha L. Richins, 'Negative Word-of-Mouth by Dissatisfied Consumers: A Pilot Study', *Journal of Marketing* 47 (Winter 1983): 68-78.

66. Arndt, 'Role of Product-Related Conversations in the Diffusion of a New Product'.

67. James H. Myers and Thomas S. Robertson, 'Dimensions of Opinion Leadership', *Journal of Marketing Research* 9 (February 1972): 41-6.

68. James F. Engel, Robert J. Kegerreis and Roger D. Blackwell, 'Word of Mouth Communication by the Innovator', *Journal of Marketing* 33 (July 1969): 15-19.

69. 'Black Sheep of the Theakston Family', *Marketing* (3 December 1992): 24.

70. Kimberley Paterson, 'Giving a Boost to Word-of-Mouth Advertising', *Rough Notes Co. Inc.* (April 1999).

71. Sonia Murray, 'Street Marketing Does the Trick', *Advertising Age* (20 March 2000): S12.

72. Quoted in 'Taking to the Streets', *Newsweek* (2 November 1998): 70-3, at 71.

73. Constance L. Hays, 'Guerrilla Marketing is Going Mainstream', *New York Times on the Web* (7 October 1999).

74. Wayne Friedman, 'Street Marketing Hits the Internet', *Advertising Age* (1 May 2000): 32; Erin White, 'Online Buzz Helps Album Skyrocket to Top of Charts', *Wall Street Journal Interactive Edition* (5 October 1999).

75. Jared Sandberg, 'The Friendly Virus', *Newsweek* (12 April 1999): 65-6.

76. Karen J. Bannan, 'Marketers Try Infecting the Internet', *New York Times on the Web* (22 March 2000).

77. Bill Barol, 'Batmania', *Newsweek* (26 June 1989): 70.

78. Dorothy Leonard-Barton, 'Experts as Negative Opinion Leaders in the Diffusion of a Technological Innovation', *Journal of Consumer Research* 11 (March 1985): 914-26.

79. Chip Walker, 'Word of Mouth', *American Demographics* (July 1995): 38-44.

80. Richard J. Lutz, 'Changing Brand Attitudes through Modification of Cognitive Structure', *Journal of Consumer Research* 1 (March 1975): 49-59; for some suggested remedies to bad publicity, see Mitch Griffin, Barry J. Babin and Jill S. Attaway, 'An Empirical Investigation of the Impact of Negative Publicity on Consumer Attitudes and Intentions', in Rebecca H. Holman and Michael R. Solomon, eds, *Advances in Consumer Research* 18 (Provo, UT: Association for Consumer Research, 1991): 334-41; Alice M. Tybout, Bobby J. Calder and Brian Sternthal, 'Using Information Processing Theory to Design Marketing Strategies', *Journal of Marketing Research* 18 (1981): 73-9.

81. Gulden Asugman, 'An Evaluation of Negative Word-of-Mouth Research for New Extensions', in B. Englis and A. Olofsson, eds, *European Advances in Consumer Research* 3 (Provo, UT: Association for Consumer Research, 1998): 70-5.

82. Robert E. Smith and Christine A. Vogt, 'The Effects of Integrating Advertising and Negative Word-of-Mouth Communications on Message Processing and Response', *Journal of Consumer Psychology* 4(2) (1995): 133-51; Paula Fitzgerald Bone, 'Word-of-Mouth Effects on Short-Term and Long-Term Product Judgments', *Journal of Business Research* 32 (1995): 213-23.

83. 'Dunkin' Donuts Buys Out Critical Web Site', *New York Times on the Web* (27 August 1999).

84. Charles W. King and John O. Summers, 'Overlap of Opinion Leadership Across Consumer Product Categories', *Journal of Marketing Research* 7 (February 1970): 43-50.

85. Jan Møller Jensen, 'A Strategic Framework for Analysing Negative Rumors in the Market Place: The Case of Wash & Go in Denmark', in J. Sirgy, K. D. Bahn and T. Erem, eds, *World Marketing Congress*, 6 (Istanbul: Proceedings of the Sixth Bi-Annual Conference of the Academy of Marketing Science, 1993): 559-63.

86. John F. Sherry, Jr, 'Some Implications of Consumer Oral Tradition for Reactive Marketing', in Thomas Kinnear, ed., *Advances in Consumer Research* 11 (Ann Arbor, MI: Association for Consumer Research, 1984): 741-7.

87. Jensen, 'A Strategic Framework'.

88. This rumour is wonderfully and profoundly analysed in Edgar Morin, *La Rumeur d'Orléans* (Paris: Seuil, 1969).

89. John Leo, 'Psst! Wait 'Till You Hear This: A Scholar Says Rumors Reveal Our Fears and Desires', *Time* (16 March 1987): 76.

90. Sid Astbury, 'Pork Rumors Vex Indonesia', *Advertising Age* (16 February 1989): 36.

91. Mae Ghalwash, 'Squint Hard, Be Creative in Search for Blasphemy in Coca-Cola Logo', *Opelika-Auburn News* (22 May 2000): 2A.

92. 'Beware Yanks Bearing Drinks', *Marketing* (5 March 1992): 23-4.

93. Everett M. Rogers, *Diffusion of Innovations*, 3rd edn (New York: Free Press, 1983).

94. Leonard-Barton, 'Experts as Negative Opinion

Leaders in the Diffusion of a Technological Innovation'; Rogers, *Diffusion of Innovations*.

95. Herbert Menzel, 'Interpersonal and Unplanned Communications: Indispensable or Obsolete?', in Edward Roberts, ed., *Biomedical Innovation* (Cambridge, MA: MIT Press, 1981): 155–63.

96. Meera P. Venkatraman, 'Opinion Leaders, Adopters, and Communicative Adopters: A Role Analysis', *Psychology & Marketing* 6 (Spring 1989): 51–68.

97. Niraj Dawar, Philip M. Parker and Lydia J. Price, 'A Cross-Cultural Study of Interpersonal Information Exchange', *Journal of International Business Studies* (3rd quarter 1996): 497–516.

98. Robert Merton, *Social Theory and Social Structure* (Glencoe, IL: Free Press, 1957).

99. King and Summers, 'Overlap of Opinion Leadership Across Consumer Product Categories'; see also Ronald E. Goldsmith, Jeanne R. Heitmeyer and Jon B. Freiden, 'Social Values and Fashion Leadership', *Clothing and Textiles Research Journal* 10 (Fall 1991): 37–45; J. O. Summers, 'Identity of Women's Clothing Fashion Opinion Leaders', *Journal of Marketing Research* 7 (1970): 178–85.

100. Gerrit Antonides and Gulden Asugman, 'The Communication Structure of Consumer Opinions', in Flemming Hansen, ed., *European Advances in Consumer Research* 2 (Provo, UT: Association for Consumer Research, 1995): 132–7.

101. Steven A. Baumgarten, 'The Innovative Communicator in the Diffusion Process', *Journal of Marketing Research* 12 (February 1975): 12–18.

102. Russell W. Belk, 'Occurrence of Word-of-Mouth Buyer Behavior as a Function of Situation and Advertising Stimuli', in Fred C. Allvine, ed., *Combined Proceedings of the American Marketing Association*, Series No. 33 (Chicago: American Marketing Association, 1971): 419–22.

103. Lawrence F. Feick, Linda L. Price and Robin A. Higie, 'People Who Use People: The Other Side of Opinion Leadership', in Richard J. Lutz, ed., *Advances in Consumer Research* 13 (Provo, UT: Association for Consumer Research, 1986): 301–5.

104. For discussion of the market maven construct, see Lawrence F. Feick and Linda L. Price, 'The Market Maven', *Managing* (July 1985): 10; scale items adapted from Lawrence Feick and Linda Price, 'The Market Maven: A Diffuser of Marketplace Information', *Journal of Marketing* 51 (January 1987): 83–7.

105. Michael R. Solomon, 'The Missing Link: Surrogate Consumers in the Marketing Chain', *Journal of Marketing* 50 (October 1986): 208–18.

106. Andra Adelson, 'A French Skin-Care Line Seeks to Take America by First Winning Over Pharmacists', *New York Times* (14 February 1994): D7.

107. Stern and Gould, 'The Consumer as Financial Opinion Leader'.

108. William R. Darden and Fred D. Reynolds, 'Predicting Opinion Leadership for Men's Apparel Fashions', *Journal of Marketing Research* 1 (August 1972): 324–8. A modified version of the opinion leadership scale with improved reliability and validity can be found in Terry L. Childers, 'Assessment of the Psychometric Properties of an Opinion Leadership Scale', *Journal of Marketing Research* 23 (May 1986): 184–8.

109. 'Connect', *Newsweek* (5 May 1997): 11.

CASE STUDY 4

From *Mille lire* to *Mille et Une Nuits*: inventing 'disposable' books

BENOÎT HEILBRUNN, E.M. Lyon

'A book for the price of an *espresso*' is Marcello Baraghini's idea. In the 1970s, he created a small publishing company called Stampa Alternativa, close to the left wing anti-establishment movements. After beginning with political pamphlets in the 1980s, Baraghini changed his stand and went into publishing luxury hardbacks ranging from art and poetry to music and fairy tales. In 1990, he came up with the idea of launching a series of books with very low production costs (200 lire) which would allow them to be sold at a very low price. The idea of *Mille lire* books was born: paperbacks with no more than 100 pages of text, printed on recycled paper, with no pictures. Fifty thousand copies of each title were printed. The authors published included Freud, Shakespeare, Garcia Lorca, Stendhal and Poe. The books were sold for the price of an espresso: 1000 lire, cheaper than a pack of cigarettes!

What an amazing phenomenon and a very innovative move in a country where the average selling price of a book ranges from 10,000 lire for a paperback to 34,000 lire for a hardback. The success of the *Mille lire* books was inevitable. For example, the *Lettera sulla felicita* translated from Epicurus sold 500,000 copies and was among the Italian best sellers of the year. In 1992, over 2 million *Mille lire* books were sold in Italy. This new concept of books was successful because it created a new category of readers by overcoming the psychological hindrance of high prices. But this phenomenon also influenced the behaviour of regular book buyers, simply because the risk of buying an uninteresting book is considerably reduced with such low prices. This contributed to shift the buying decision criterion from price (which is predominant in the book sector together with the author's reputation or the front cover impact) to situation. People would thus buy a *Mille lire* as they buy an espresso or a pack of cigarettes depending on their consumption situation. The publisher was required to adapt his choice of retail outlets according to these situation factors. It was therefore decided to sell the *Mille lire* in the traditional newsagents on every main street. People waiting for a date, an appointment or a train would be tempted to buy such books on impulse just as they would buy any 'disposable' product such as newspapers, cigarettes or chewing gum. You use them once and throw them away . . .

This new concept of books, which responds to a sudden and rapid decision process, corresponds to the evolution in the status of books in western cultures. In European history, the first printed books were sacred (the first book printed by Gutenberg was a Bible), scarce (only seven copies of Gutenberg's Bible were printed), and very expensive. With the evolution of printing techniques and the increase in paper production, the average production price of books slowly began to decrease which made it possible for books to be more widely available. The democratization of books also meant that the natural place of books gradually shifted from libraries to family homes. The book which had for a long time been collectively read started to become an individual object. Also the evolution of the size of books – and mainly the appearance of paperbacks in the 1960s – allowed books to be

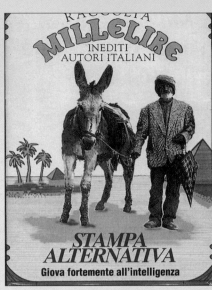

Sample covers of *Mille lire* titles

carried about in a pocket. The rise of such cheap books illustrates three important features of European societies. The first is the individualization of consumption activities which means that the purchase decision for most consumer goods is made individually. This individual choice is also very much influenced by situation variables such as the time and place of consumption, the consumer's mood, the consumer's occupation at the time of purchase, etc. The individualization of societies goes with new lifestyles such as nomadism, consumers tend to have fewer social links and to build autonomous consumption activities. The concept of *Mille lire* books is very representative of this change in society. Depending on his/her situation, mood, available time, the consumer would buy a *Mille lire,* read it and get rid of it. It means that *Mille lire* books may be considered more or less disposable as such items as pens, razors, lighters or even cameras. The main criticism targeted at the *Mille lire* operation was that this would depreciate the concept of the book, making it just another disposable product among so many others. Many people in Italy were shocked at the idea that a book could become consumable merchandise which could be used and then thrown away like any plain object. However, it was argued that this new book concept was aimed at new segments of customers, people who wouldn't buy 'normal' books because of their prohibitive price.

The effect of these books was quite paradoxical because on the one hand they depreciated the idea of culture, being cheap and easily consumed cultural products, and on the other hand, they helped to rediscover ancient authors who were not read any more and also encouraged new people towards reading.

Due to its enormous success in Italy, the idea spread rapidly and crossed the French border. In July 1993, a new collection of similar books was launched by *Mille et Une Nuits* in France, a small and newly born publisher. The concept was slightly adapted and the books were sold for 10 francs.

In France, the situation of the market was quiet. The 'livres de poche' ('pocket books', paperbacks) were celebrating their 30th birthday. The concept of 'pocket book' first appeared there in 1963, with two major characteristics: the books were

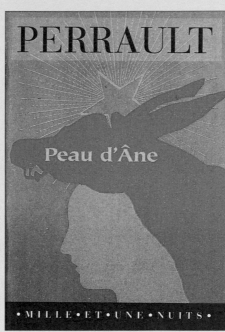

Sample covers of *Mille et Une Nuits* titles

sold at a very low price and their size enabled them to be carried in a pocket, hence the name given to them. This market grew rapidly in France with a great number of collections being created. However, the extension of the concept also saw the price range rapidly widen. Nowadays there are approximately 100 collections of 'livres de poche' with prices ranging from 12 francs to 120 francs. This simply means that the 'livre de poche' no longer represents or federates a unique concept.

The dilution of the original concept allowed a market niche to emerge with very low-priced books such as *Mille et Une Nuits*, which appeared to be the first brand to explicitly pre-empt this market segment. The books launched by *Mille et Une Nuits* contain up to 96 pages (in fact 32, 64 or 96 pages) printed on ecological recycled paper with an illustrated cover, some black and white plates in the text, a presentation of the text, a bibliography and a short presentation of the author's life. The first title to be printed was *Lettre sur le bonheur* (The Letter on Happiness) by Epicurus which had been a tremendous success in Italy. In order to promote and to build the awareness of this new concept, the first title was given as a free supplement (425,000 copies) with an issue of a weekly magazine called *Le Nouvel Observateur* (no. 1496, 14 July 1993). The launch of a whole collection was announced: 12 titles coming out in September 1993. These first titles were new editions of forgotten or out-of-print books by very famous authors such as Maupassant, Baudelaire, Sade, Perrault, Kleist, Cervantes and London.

The positioning of the concept was expressed in the motto written on the last page of each book: 'Mille et Une Nuits propose des chefs-d'oeuvre pour le temps d'une attente, d'un voyage, d'une insomnie.' (Mille et Une Nuits offers you a masterpiece while you wait, a trip, a night). The retail outlets used were bookshops and some superstores and but not the newsagents as in Italy. This simply meant that the *Mille et Une Nuits* products were real books and not newspapers. But very soon the publisher had to face problems due to the choice of such a distribution strategy. First, the margin the booksellers were left with was unusually thin because it amounted to one-third of the retail price (average ratio in this sector) which meant only 3 francs. This was more than three times less that an average paperback, though the storage space needed and effort required to sell them were almost the same. Second, these books were fragile, easily damaged, and the soft cover made it almost impossible to stand them upright. They had to be laid flat on a table, the whole collection taking up a lot of space. Thus, many booksellers were reluctant to promote these books even if the publisher offered to provide them with a counter display, which enabled them to present the entire collection in a very convenient and elegant way.

Despite this reluctance, the launching was a success. The original print run was 25,000 but this was soon increased to 35,000. The collection was distributed in 12,000 bookshops and superstores.

However, the small publisher will soon have to deal with several threats faced by his new product. First, how to avoid being a mere fad product? Second, how to survive competition? Many large publishers were willing to counterattack by launching similar books targeted at different publics. Retailers were also thinking of launching their own brand of cheap books.

Discussion questions

1 What are the main factors of success for this particular product?

2 What would be the lifecycle of such a product? Do you think this product going to last or is it doomed to have a very short lifespan similar to a fad product?

3 Do you think it is possible to build brand loyalty for the publisher? Or loyalty for the product category of cheap books? Why or why not?

4 Is this product transferable to any country in Europe? What factors would be critical success factors in your country? Why? How do you think those factors might differ for other European countries?

CASE STUDY 5

Viral marketing and 'Norman'

SUZANNE BECKMANN, Copenhagen Business School and Saatchi & Saatchi

Viral marketing (VM) is in its essence a communication strategy that uses ideas, slogans, catch-phrases and icons, or a combination thereof, to transmit a message concerning a product as fast and as widespread as possible within a given target group. It is often part of a branding strategy and it usually seeks to address opinion leaders and often also early adopters. VM, if successful, powerfully compounds the benefits of a *first-mover advantage*.

The emergence of VM and consideration of its underlying mechanisms has led to inevitable comparisons with word-of-mouth (WOM) communication. Certainly the principles that underpin both forms of communication are similar. Both depend on a valuable core product and a well-crafted message. In addition, the success of both VM and WOM rely on a network of social relations and a willingness to share consumption-related experiences. Similarity across such key dimensions has led many commentators to claim that VM is no different to WOM. Indeed, Fattah (2000: 88) encourages us to think of the VM concept as 'word-of-mouth advertising on steroids'. The implication is that the two approaches to communication differ only according to the speed with which the message diffuses. But it can be argued that there are other key differences, which have implications for the application of each approach (see Table 1; Beckmann and Bell 2001). These differences are based primarily on the type of media used to diffuse a message – while WOM typically uses personal interaction, VM takes advantage of the internet.

Independent of this, practitioners stress that there are several rules to follow if VM is to be successful. First of all, the core feature of a virus has to be carefully

Table 1 Differences between word of mouth and viral marketing

	Word of mouth	*Viral marketing*
Speed	Moderate	High
Nature of copy	High verbal, low visual	Low verbal, high visual
Control over copy/execution	Relatively low Consumers' story-telling can lead to modifications of the experience	Relatively high Copy remains unchanged as message is propagated
Social/situational influence	Receiver more likely to attend to the message within dyadic communication Allows for both information pull and push	No personal interaction Less pressure on receiver to attend to the message Information push only
Domain of application	Unlimited reach	Reach limited to people with internet access

monitored: survival and reproduction. Without a host, a virus cannot survive and hence cannot be reproduced, because a virus as such is passive. And a virus thrives the better, the more hosts are 'infected'. The internet has a number of features that facilitate infection – at least for certain product categories. Here is a list of strategies suggested by practitioners: be cool enough to create a buzz, put your URL everywhere, make it easy for people to pass it on, flatter them into talking, reward them for passing it on, give away your site, sponsor give-aways on other people's sites, let people 'reprint' your content, and so on.

'Norman' and the Sony MiniDisc

In early August 2000, the website *www.normanrules.com* was launched – an example of VM on the internet. The objective was to increase awareness and sales of Sony's MiniDisc player and the campaign was targeted at the youth market (12–25 years) in the Nordic countries. To create traffic to the site, *normanrules.com* bought a seven months' sponsorship of MTV Top Selection and advertised through radio, free postcards, print and banner ads.

'Norman' is a fictitious anti-hero whose core interests are music and junk food, who basically has no taste in clothes, and who displays a rather weird sense of humour. He is a bit of a nerd, yet somehow likeable.

The website contains a number of themes, all of them with a humorous twist (however, since the content of the website changes regularly in order to keep the audience interested, some of these are temporary). The themes combine the world of entertainment with the universe of a single person, using a slightly sarcastic tonality and animating visitors to the site to become engaged in Norman's world, which is influenced by his liking of the Sony MiniDisc player:

- The *daily life* of Norman displays photographs of an ordinary Norman day from getting up late in the morning until bedtime.
- Norman's favourite *pick-up lines*: a photo gallery of Norman making a fool of himself in a bar by twisting well-known pick-up lines in the wrong direction (e.g. 'What does a girl like you do in a nice bar like this?').
- Norman's *hairstyle*: a how-to-do guide on hair styling, combined with a competition to send in own suggestions.
- Norman's *dancing moves*: animated photographs of Norman dancing, complete with step diagrams.
- *e-cards* to be sent: (introduced this way: 'Your friends will be disgusted – your parents will ground you. Send one now – you will regret it').
- Norman's view on what's hot and what's not.

The virus on *normanrules.com* comes in various forms: e-cards that can be sent after creating them with your own choice of Norman 'cut-outs', competitions, e.g. one where people are asked to send in photographs with strange hair styles (400 participated in this competition, where the first prize was a ball-point pen with a naked lady and the second a Sony MiniDisc), and there is the possibility to download Norman as screensaver or wallpaper. Hence, quite a few techniques of VM are employed. One of the rules, 'Look like a host, not a virus', though, is adapted so that the website does not hide the fact that the sender is Sony MiniDisc, although it does not feature prominently – in order not to insult the target group's intelligence.

The VM strategy for the Sony MiniDisc had the following objectives: increase awareness of the product to an average of 80 per cent in Scandinavia and increase knowledge among the 15–30-year-olds that a MiniDisc can be used to copy music to an average of 50 per cent. The expected number of visitors in the first four weeks was 33,000. The results showed an increase in awareness to 92.25 per cent and an increase in knowledge to 68.75 per cent. In the first four weeks, more than 75,000 unique visitors were registered at the website. Moreover, while the average user session at a website lasts 1.27 minutes and 2.17 minutes at an e-commerce site, the average session at *normanrules.com* lasted 3 minutes.

Questions

1 Viral marketing is often targeted at opinion leaders. Starting from the characteristics of opinion leaders, identify a set of arguments why this is the preferred approach in a branding strategy.

2 Elaborate on the differences between VM and WOM. Then identify examples for both strategies and indicate which one is preferable for a given product/brand.

3 Which characteristics of the youth segment and the consumer culture they live in make viral marketing a persuasive advertising strategy?

4 The viral marketing strategy for the Sony MiniDisc used a fictitious and anti-hero to influence attitudes towards the product. Argue, with regard to the ELM model, whether this strategy targets the central or peripheral route.

Bibliography

Beckmann, Suzanne C. and Bell, Simon (2001), 'Viral marketing = word-of-mouth marketing on the Internet?' (and a case story from the Nordic countries). In: Breivik, Einar, Falkenberg, Andreas W., and Grønhaug, Kjell, eds, *Rethinking European Marketing. Proceedings from the 30th EMAC conference*, Bergen/Norway (CD-ROM, *www.nhh.no/emac*)

Brodie, Richard (1995), *Virus of the Mind*. *http://www.amazon.com/exec/obidos/ISBN%3D0963600117/memecentralA/102-6288262-2731334*

Dawkins, Richard (1976), *The Selfish Gene* (Oxford: Oxford University Press)

Fattah, H. M. (2000), 'Viral marketing is nothing new', *MC Technology Marketing Intelligence* 20 (October): 88–9

Frohlich, Norman and Oppenheimer, Joe (1998), 'Some consequences of e-mail vs. face-to-face communication in experiment', *Journal of Economic Behavior & Organization* 35 (April): 389–403

Herr, Paul M., Kardes, Frank R. and Kim, John (1991), 'Effects of word-of-mouth and product-attribute information on persuasion: an accessibility-diagnosticity perspective', *Journal of Consumer Research* 17 (March): 454–62

Hoffman, Donna L. and Novak, Thomas P. (1996), 'Marketing in hypermedia computer-mediated environments: conceptual foundations', *Journal of Marketing* 60(3): 50ff.

www.profitjump.com
www.marketingclick.com
www.bizjournals.com
www.fastcompany.com
www.drapervc.com

CASE STUDY 6

Triumph of femininity

PER ØSTERGAARD, University of Southern Denmark – Odense University

At the end of the 1980s, the lingerie firm Triumph introduced a new advertising campaign in Denmark. Until then, the standard concept for lingerie ads had been a picture of a beautiful woman in underwear. The woman was always depicted as passive and as if she was being gazed at by a man or waiting for her husband to come home and see her in her new lingerie.

Triumph introduced a new concept. The woman depicted was no longer passive, but doing something for herself. It could be dressing, doing her nails, reading a magazine after taking a bath, eating a sandwich, doing her hair, etc. In each ad there were three to four pictures of the same woman in different situations and different lingerie. Apart from the photos in each ad there was a long text telling a story. Not a story about the woman in the photo, but a general story about the thoughts women of that generation might have. Here are two ads from the campaign, which ran almost unchanged for many years.

The title on all the ads in the campaign is: 'The freedom to be the woman you are' which in Danish is: 'Friheden til at være den pige, man er'.

Gud skabte kvinden . . . God created the woman. The rest she manages herself. Today, we girls luckily decide when we want to be cute little peaches and when we want to steer a crane. Regarding clothes, we dress depending on what mood we are in. From inside to outside.

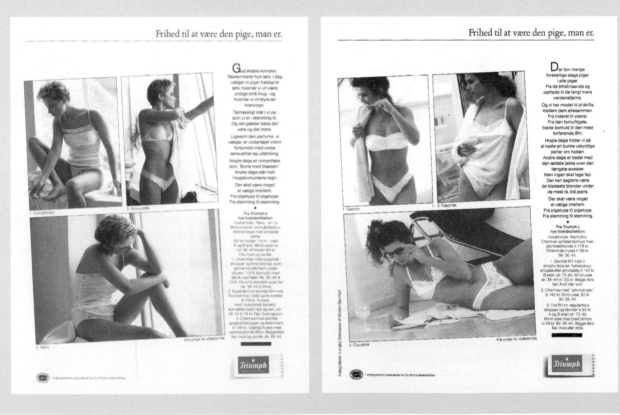

Like the perfume we choose, our underwear is intimately connected with our sensuality and appearance. Some days are romantic like *Gone with the Wind*. Some are devoted to washing the cotton underwear.

There has to be something to choose between. From type of girl to type of girl. From mood to mood.

Der bor mange forskellige ... Inside every girl lives a lot of different girls. From the giggling and the giddying to the far more aloof. From inside to outside. From the most sensible soft cotton to the most seductive bra. Some days we throw a heap of innocent pearls around the neck. Some days are best with the oldest jacket over the longest sweater. But nobody must be mistaken. There can easily be the softest laces under the coolest blue jeans. There has to be something to choose between. From type of girl to type of girl. From mood to mood.

Questions

1 Discuss the self-concept expressed in the respective ads.

2 Explain the female gender roles expressed in the ads.

3 What kind of body image and ideals of beauty are expressed?

4 Discuss how consumption of underwear can be part of grooming rituals.

5 Discuss to what extent you can give underwear as a gift.

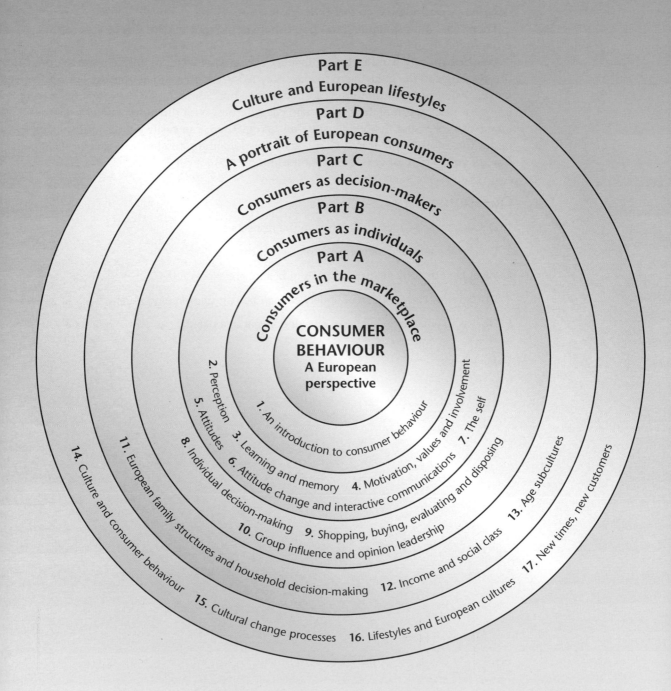

Part E
Culture and European lifestyles

Part D
A portrait of European consumers

Part C
Consumers as decision-makers

Part B
Consumers as individuals

Part A
Consumers in the marketplace

CONSUMER
BEHAVIOUR
A European
perspective

1. An introduction to consumer behaviour

2. Perception 3. Learning and memory 4. Motivation, values and involvement 7. The self

5. Attitudes 6. Attitude change and interactive communications

8. Individual decision-making 9. Shopping, buying, evaluating and disposing

10. Group influence and opinion leadership

11. European family structures and household decision-making 12. Income and social class 13. Age subcultures

14. Culture and consumer behaviour 15. Cultural change processes 16. Lifestyles and European cultures 17. New times, new customers

Part D

A PORTRAIT OF EUROPEAN CONSUMERS

The chapters in this part consider some of the social influences that help to determine who we are, with an emphasis on the various subcultures to which we belong. Chapter 11 provides a discussion of family structures in Europe, and identifies the many instances in which our purchase decisions are made in conjunction with the family. Chapter 12 focuses on factors that define our social classes, and how membership in a social class exerts a strong influence on what we buy with the money we make. Chapter 13 discusses the strong influence that age has on our behaviour as consumers, with an emphasis on the bonds we share with others who were born at roughly the same time.

Chapter 11

European family structures and household decision-making

Saturday is the main shopping day, and Tom is accompanying his mother to the supermarket. He doesn't usually go with her, and he suspects that Sue, his mum, would rather go without him. She spends less and gets home faster without him, she says. And as a single parent, time is one of her scarcest resources! But he's going today anyway, partly to be sure that she picks out the right stuff for his forthcoming birthday party. The Pokémon figures and biscuits were OK last year, but he's almost a teenager now and he plans to push heavily for the right food and decorations. He wants a party with the 'right atmosphere' – maybe some music by Jennifer Lopez, or the newest video game by WWF Smackdown 2. Even though Jennifer's music and the wrestling game are really different sorts of choices, he's seen a lot of them on TV, and his friends at school talk about both all the time. If he could just get his mum to buy *both* the CD and the video game, he would have a better idea of which to play for 'setting the mood' at his party.

First, though, they have to get the family's regular shopping out of the way. Sue gets a little exasperated as Tom tells her about the best type of cat food to get for Martin, the family cat. Finally, at Sue's urging, they move on to the next aisle, where she quickly throws two cans of tuna fish into the trolley. She starts to move on, but from behind her she hears Tom say: 'You're not really going to buy that brand, are you? Don't you know that they still use nets to catch their tuna and those nets kill hundreds of innocent dolphins every year?' This was news to Sue. After getting over her initial irritation at being told how to shop by a child who can't even tidy his room, she realizes that Tom is making a lot of sense. As she puts the offending cans back on the shelf, she remarks, 'Well, Tom, I think I should send you to do the shopping from now on!'

Introduction

Children are becoming a major force in persuading their parents to clean up their act when it comes to the environment. One study showed that one-third of parents have changed their shopping habits to be more environmentally conscious because of information they received from their children. Teenagers have been instrumental in projects ranging from home and school recycling to persuading tuna companies to stop buying tuna caught in nets that also trap dolphins. Many companies are becoming aware of young people's influence in everyday family buying decisions, and some are trying hard to convince 'green teens' that their products are environmentally friendly.[1]

Tom's influence on Sue's choice of an environmentally safe product illustrates that many consumer decisions are made jointly. The individual decision-making process described in detail in Chapter 8 is, in many cases, too simplistic since more than one person may be involved in any stage of the problem-solving sequence, from initial problem recognition and information search to evaluation of alternatives and product choice. For example, the decision to get a pet is often made jointly by family members. The children may be instrumental in persuading their reluctant parents to get a dog or a cat, while the parents may be responsible for the information search to determine what breed to get or where to get it. Then, the entire family may be involved in selecting the puppy or kitten that will soon become another family member.

Whether they are choosing a can of tuna or buying a new PC for the home, consumers commonly work together. This chapter examines issues related to *collective decision-making*, where more than one person is involved in the purchasing process for products or services that may be used by multiple consumers. We focus specifically on one of the most important organizations to which we all claim membership – the family unit. We'll consider how members of a family negotiate among themselves, and how important changes in modern family structure are affecting this process. The chapter concludes by discussing how 'new employees' – children – learn to become consumers.

The family

Constructing and deconstructing the family in Europe

While it might still be too early to draw definite conclusions, it's reasonable to speculate that historians will regard the 1990s as one of the most politically, socially and economically turbulent decades in modern history. Radical political and market changes throughout western and eastern Europe were reflections and outcomes of intense social change in European societies that had been underway since the 1950s. While the extent and pace of change, and the national perceptions of social change, differed from one country to another, it is clear that many of our social institutions altered radically in the second half of the twentieth century, not least the notion of 'family'.

Before moving on to a discussion of the forces that have changed our notions of family, and what these changes mean in terms of consumer behaviour, we need to spend a moment tackling the thorny question 'What is the family, and how do we gather data about it?' There is a great deal of family diversity throughout Europe, and the conceptualization of *family* is based on ideology, popular mythology and conventions that are firmly rooted in each country's historical, political, economic and cultural traditions. Certainly, European governments have had a strong history of requiring regular and up-to-date socio-demographic information on the behaviour of families (birth rates, fertility rates, divorce rates), and about family forms (size, structure and organization). This sort of information is an essential component in governments' policy-making processes.

Yet, despite a long history of international collaboration and the growing need for reliable information about demographic trends in Europe, by the mid-1990s data on households and families in the European Union were still far from comparable.[2] Attempts to standardize data collection methods across countries have had to deal with issues such as national political priorities and ideologies, the centralization and autonomy of the organizations responsible for data collection, and the reluctance of some governments to accept decisions taken at the supranational level. As an example of the problems of comparing families across Europe, consider the problem of dealing with the *age of children living at home*. In most EU member states, no age limit was applied during the 1991 census. However, in Denmark, Finland and Sweden, children were considered as part of the family up to the age of 18, and in Luxembourg to 25. France applied a limit of 25 years until 1982, but this was abolished for the 1991 census, which increased the proportion of lone-parent families by 35 per cent! Eurostat's 1991 census reported that the 'traditional family' (man, woman and children under one roof) made up just 54 per cent of the European population, while their 1996 report (using a new sampling frame and method) concluded that the traditional one-family household is still predominant throughout Europe, comprising 72 per cent of the population. In the report for 2000, the share of a nuclear family (composed of a couple with children) was described as 'gradually declining, but still stands around 55%, with the highest proportions in Ireland and the southern Member States'.[3] As the new millennium unfolds, more standardized and comparable forms of data about the European family will be collected.

MARKETING OPPORTUNITY

Under the same roof: living arrangements in the European Union

Data from the European Community Household Panel (ECHP) are now available which focus on living conditions, income and many aspects of social well-being. Some highlights from this report include the following descriptions:

Household size is getting smaller, with the average size for the 'EU-15 countries' dropping from 2.8 in 1982 to 2.5 in 1998. Multi-generational households still persist: around 30 per cent in Greece, Spain and Portugal, although this figure drops drastically to 5 per cent or less in Denmark, Holland and Sweden. In Spain, Italy, Portugal and Ireland the percentage of individuals living in households where at least one child over the age of 16 is still living with his or her parents amounts to around a third of all individuals. The number of dependent children living with just one of their parents is also growing, as the divorce rates in the EU climb. In 1998, 13 per cent of all dependent children lived with just one parent, compared to 8 per cent in 1983. In the UK, the rate more than doubled in this period, from 11 per cent to 25 per cent. Living alone has become important in the EU (10 per cent of the population), and there is a growth of cohabitation, particularly among young people (70 per cent in Denmark).

Results also suggest that a different pattern of living is emerging between northern countries and southern countries plus Ireland. In the Mediterranean countries and Ireland, children tend to live in the parental home until they are ready to form new, usually legalized, family units. Also, more than one generation share the same household. In northern countries, the transition from the parental home to forming a new family is less straightforward, with living alone and cohabitation periods in between.[4]

From both a statistical as well as a sociological perspective, 'family' is hard to nail down! However, one thing is certain – the concept of family will continue to exist and will manifest itself in varying forms over time and across countries throughout Europe. Figure 11.1 provides an overview of the many components that make up our notion of a European household.

Defining the modern family

Some experts have argued that as traditional family living arrangements decline, people are placing even greater emphasis on the role of siblings, close friends and other relatives to provide companionship and social support.[5] In the US, some people are even joining 'intentional families', groups of strangers who meet regularly for meals and who spend holidays together. Over 500 of these communities currently operate in the US.[6]

Many marketers have focused on the renewed interest in family life brought about by the more flexible definitions of what constitutes a family. While families were indeed out of fashion in the 1960s and 1970s, being seen by some as an infringement on personal freedom, 90 per cent of the respondents in one survey confirmed that

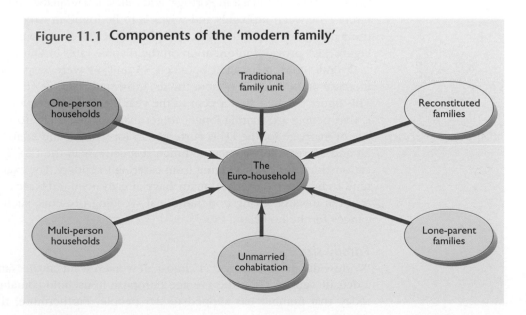

Figure 11.1 **Components of the 'modern family'**

family life was one of the most important things to them.[7] In a radical departure from the old 'affluent singles' days, half of the holidaymakers who stay at Club Med resorts now bring their families along.[8]

▶   The **extended family** was once the most common family unit. It consisted of three generations living together and often included not only the grandparents but
▶   aunts, uncles and cousins. The **nuclear family**, a mother and a father and one or more children (perhaps with a dog thrown in for good measure), became the model family unit over time. However, many changes have occurred since the 1960s.

Just what is a household?

For statistical purposes, Eurostat has implemented the United Nation's definition of the family unit based on the 'conjugal family concept'. *The family* is defined in the narrow sense of a family nucleus as follows: 'The persons within a private or institutional household who are related as husband and wife or as parent and never-married child by blood or adoption'. Thus, a family nucleus comprises a married couple without children or a married couple with one or more never-married children of any age, or one parent with one or more never-married children of any age. The definition tries to take into account whenever possible, couples who report that they are living in consensual unions, regardless of whether they are legally married.
▶   Under the more recent European Community Household Panel, a **family household** is more broadly defined, as a 'shared residence and common housekeeping arrangement'. Marketers are interested in both of these units, not only for their similarities, but as a way of understanding differences. Changes in consumers' family structures, such as cohabitation, delayed marriage and delayed childbirth, the return of mothers to the workforce and the upheaval caused by divorce, often represent opportunities for marketers as normal purchasing patterns become unfrozen and people make new choices about products and brands.[9]

Trends in marriage and divorce in the EU

Since 1960, the EU has seen a trend of falling numbers of marriages and an increase in the number of divorces. Moreover, people are remarrying more often than they did before the 1960s, and men are more likely to form a new family than women. Couples marry youngest in Portugal and oldest in Denmark, and the greatest age difference between husbands and wives is to be found in Greece. Figure 11.2 shows the marriage rates per thousand people for the different countries in the EU, while Figure 11.3 provides information on the divorce rates in European countries.[10]

Overall, consumers aged between 35 and 44 were responsible for the largest increase in the number of households, growing by almost 40 per cent since 1980.[11] This figure reached 50 per cent in the year 2000. An important reason for this shift is that people are waiting longer to get married: according to Eurostat, the average age of marriage for the EU is currently 25 for women and 28 for men (compared to 24 and 26 years for women and men respectively in the US). This trend has implications for businesses, ranging from catering to cutlery. For example, since couples tend to be married later and many have already acquired basic household items, the trend is towards giving non-traditional wedding presents, such as electrical appliances for the home and PCs.[12]

Family size

Worldwide, surveys show that almost all women want smaller families than they did a decade ago. In 1982, the average European household contained 2.8 people, but today that number has slipped to 2.5 people. Furthermore, the current average

Figure 11.2 Cohabitation and marriage rates in the EU per 1000 population, 1970–98

Source: Eurostat, Demographic Statistics.
Note: S – national data.

Figure 11.3 Crude divorce rates per 1000 population in European countries, 1970–98

Source: Eurostat, Demographic Statistics.
Note: S, IS, NO, CH – national data.

number of children per woman is below the generational replacement threshold level, with a fertility rate for Europe of 1.44 children per woman in 1993 (compared to almost double this in 1964). A recent UK study predicts that one in five women born in the 1960s–1980s will remain childless – a halving of the birth rate of their mothers' generation.[13] Family size is dependent on such factors as educational level, the availability of birth control and religion. The **fertility rate** is determined by the number of births per year per 1000 women of childbearing age. Figure 11.4 shows the trends in total fertility rates in EU member states from 1990 and 1998, with projections for 2020.[14]

Marketers keep a close eye on the population's birth rate to gauge how the pattern of births will affect demand for products in the future. Even when a married couple does live with children, families are shrinking. The number of European households comprising one or two people is increasing (from 22 per cent to 26 per cent during 1980–90) and the number of households with four or more people is falling (from 34 per cent to 25 per cent during 1980–90).[15]

The number of unmarried adults and one-person households is steadily rising (they now account for 26 per cent of European households, and are projected to be the fastest growing segment through to the year 2005). In the age group 16–29 years, 31 per cent of European couples living together are not married. This rate varies from a low in Portugal, Italy and Spain (10 per cent), to a high of 73 per cent in Denmark and Sweden.[16] Some marketers are beginning to address the fact that

Figure 11.4 Total fertility rates in EU member states, 1990–98 and projected figures for 2020

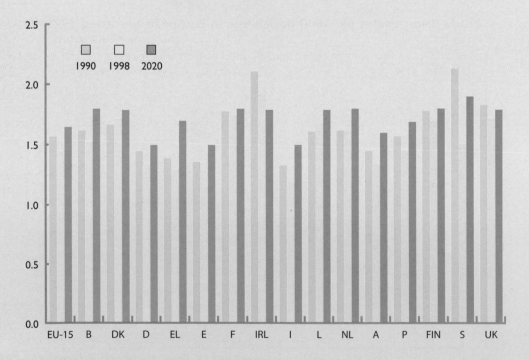

Source: Eurostat, Demographic Statistics.
Note: The total fertility rate is the average number of children that would be born alive to a woman during her lifetime if current fertility rates were to continue.

this group is under-represented in advertising.[17] Gold Blend coffee built a very popular TV ad campaign around a romance between two single neighbours, while Procter & Gamble introduced Folger's Singles 'single-serve' coffee bags for people who live alone and don't need a full pot.[18] On the other hand, many singles report that they avoid buying single-size food portions or eating alone in restaurants since both remind them of their unattached status – they prefer takeaway food.[19]

Single men and women constitute quite different markets. More than half of single men are under the age of 35, while among people over age 65, women account for 80 per cent of one-person households. Europeans are also getting married at a later age – in 1980, men's average age at first marriage was 26, compared to 30 in 2000, while for women age at first marriage has increased from 23 to 27 years. Despite single males' greater incomes, single women dominate many markets because of their spending patterns. Single women are more likely than single men to own a home, and they spend more on housing-related items and furniture. Single men, in contrast, spend more overall in restaurants and on cars. However, these spending patterns are also significantly affected by age: middle-aged single women, for example, spend *more* than their male counterparts on cars.[20]

Who's living at home?

In many cases the nuclear family is being transformed to resemble the old-fashioned extended family. Many adults are being forced to care for parents as well as for children. A growing trend in the US and Europe is for middle-aged couples to be faced with the prospect of caring for both their children and their parents simultaneously. Americans spend on average 17 years caring for their children, but 18 years assisting elderly parents. By 2010, more than 80 per cent of the EU's elderly population (aged 65 and older) will be either living alone or with a partner. Here again, there are marked differences between countries, with 30 per cent or more of the elderly living with, or having some important form of support from, their children in Spain and Portugal, and 5 per cent or less in Denmark, the Netherlands and Sweden.[21] Middle-aged people have been termed '*the sandwich generation*', because they must attend to those above and below them in age. The problem of caring for ageing parents became so acute in Singapore that the government established a Tribunal for the Maintenance of Parents in 1996. A new law now requires adult offspring to take care of their parents, a practice which traditionally is a priority in Asian cultures. Some 200 cases involving neglected parents were heard by the tribunal in its first six months of operation.[22] As the population ages and life expectancies continue to climb in developed countries, the problem of allocating resources to the support of parents will only get worse.

Non-traditional family structures

The ECHP regards any occupied housing unit as a household, regardless of the relationships between the people living there. Thus, one person living alone, three room-mates or two lovers all constitute households. Less traditional households will increase rapidly if these trends persist. One-parent households are increasing steadily throughout Europe (most common in the UK, Denmark and Belgium, least common in Greece). Although these households are in the majority of cases headed by women, there is also an increasing trend for fathers to take on this role.[23] In the US, 10 million children live with a step-parent or with children who are not full brothers or sisters, and 24 per cent of all children live in one-parent families.[24]

MARKETING OPPORTUNITY

Companion animals are often treated as family members. Many people assume pets share our emotions – perhaps that helps to explain why more than three-quarters of domestic cats and dogs receive presents on holidays and birthdays.[25] Over 35 per cent of European households and over 42 per cent of American households own at least one pet.[26] Together, they spend over $30 billion a year on their pets (more than they spend on going to the cinema and home videos combined).[27] In France, there are twice as many dogs and cats as children![28] The inclusion of pets as family members creates many marketing opportunities, ranging from bejewelled collars to professional dogwalkers. Listed below are worldwide samples of some recent attempts to cater to people's pet attachments.[29]

● Macy's department store opened a Petigree shop for dogs and cats. Says one employee, 'You can put your dog in a pink satin party dress or a 1920s flapper dress with fringe'. Other items include a wedding dress for dogs (for $100; the veil is extra), a $48 black dinner jacket or a $30 trench coat.

● A vet in Maryland offers holistic medicine for pets. He features natural foods, acupuncture and chiropractic massages. The vet also sells the Rodeo Drive Fragrance Collection (named after a fashionable street in Beverley Hills), a set of spray colognes for dogs.

● A 25-minute video, *Doggie Adventure*, was produced for dogs. Shot with a camera balanced two feet off the ground, it takes viewers on a romp from a dog's perspective.

● Kennelwood Village, a day-care centre for dogs in St Louis, features a swimming pool (with a lifeguard on duty), tetherball tournaments and whirlpool therapy for arthritic canines.

● In the UK, pet insurance is a £100 million industry, with more than 1 million pets being covered by insurance policies.

● About 85 per cent of Swedish dogs carry health and life insurance.

Effects of family structure on consumption

A family's needs and expenditures are affected by such factors as the number of people (children and adults) in the family, their ages, and whether one, two or more adults are employed outside the home.

Two important factors determining how a couple spend time and money are whether they have children and whether the woman works. Couples with children generally have higher expenses, and not just for the 'basics' such as food and utilities bills. Studies in the UK estimate that the costs of keeping a teenager 'in the style to which they aspire' run close to £66,000, and the costs of getting a child to the teen years is approaching £33,000.[30] In addition, a recently married couple make very different expenditures compared to people with young children, who in turn are quite different from a couple with children in college, and so on. Families with working mothers must often make allowances for such expenses as nursery care and a working wardrobe for the woman.

Multicultural dimensions

The Euro-housewife: considerable differences between EU member states

- The percentage of women aged between 25 and 59 who describe themselves as housewives varies considerably between member states. While the EU average is 33 per cent, it ranges from a high of 60 per cent in Ireland (Spain, Greece, Italy and Luxembourg are also high), to a mere 4 per cent in Denmark.

- Barely 6 per cent of women aged between 25 and 39 without children stay at home, compared with 36 per cent with one child under 5 and 52 per cent with at least two children under 5.

- EU-wide, only 7 per cent of today's housewives stopped working because of marriage – but this number peaked at 15 per cent in Greece and 14 per cent in Spain. However, 42 per cent stopped because of children.

- Family obligations such as housework and caring for children or others are the main reason that 84 per cent of housewives are not looking for work.

- Women are almost twice as likely as men to provide unpaid child care on a daily basis (31 per cent, compared to 16 per cent). In the southern member states, this disparity is even greater (3:1 in Greece, and 5:1 in Portugal). In Denmark and the Netherlands, the difference is much smaller.

- Being a housewife is strongly related to the level of education. Housewives represent 45 per cent of EU women aged from 25 to 59 with lower secondary education, 26 per cent with upper secondary education, and only 13 per cent of women with higher educational levels.[31]

The family life cycle

Recognizing that family needs and expenditures change over time, the concept of the **family life cycle (FLC)** has been widely used by marketers. The FLC combines trends in income and family composition with the changes in demands placed upon this income. As we grow older, our preferences for products and activities tend to change. In many cases, our income levels tend to rise (at least until retirement), so that we can afford more as well. In addition, many purchases that must be made at an early age do not have to be repeated very often. For example, we tend to accumulate durable goods, such as furniture, and only replace them as necessary.

A life cycle approach to the study of the family assumes that pivotal events alter role relationships and trigger new stages of life which modify our priorities. These events include the birth of a first child, the departure of the last child from the house, the death of a spouse, retirement of the principal wage earner and divorce.[32] Movement through these life stages is accompanied by significant changes in expenditures in leisure, food, durables and services, even after the figures have been adjusted to reflect changes in income.[33]

This focus on longitudinal changes in priorities is particularly valuable in predicting demand for specific product categories over time. For example, the money spent by a couple with no children on eating out and holidays will probably be diverted for quite different purchases after the birth of a child. While a number of models have been proposed to describe family life cycle stages, their usefulness has been limited because in many cases they have failed to take into account such important social trends as the changing role of women, the acceleration of alternative lifestyles, childless and delayed-child marriages and single-parent households.

Four variables are necessary to describe these changes: age, marital status, the presence or absence of children in the home, and their ages. In addition, our definition of marital status (at least for the purposes of analysis) must be relaxed to include any couple living together who are in a long-term relationship. Thus, while room-mates might not be considered 'married', a man and woman who have established a household would be, as would two homosexual men or women who have a similar understanding.

When these changes are considered, this approach allows us to identify a set of categories that include many more types of family situations.[34] These categories, which are listed in Table 11.1, are derived by dividing consumers into groups in terms of age, whether there is more than one adult present, and whether there are children. For example, a distinction is made between the consumption needs of people in the full nest I category (where the youngest child is under 6), the full nest II category (where the youngest child is over 6), the full nest III category (where the youngest child is over 6 and the parents are middle-aged), and the delayed full nest (where the parents are in their forties but the youngest child is under 6).

Table 11.1 The family life cycle: an updated view

	Age of head of household		
	Under 35	35–64	Over 64
One adult in household	Bachelor I	Bachelor II	Bachelor III
Two adults in household	Young couple	Childless couple	Older couple
Two adults plus children in household	Full nest I	Delayed full nest	
	Full nest II	Full nest III	

Source: Adapted from Mary C. Gilly and Ben M. Enis, 'Recycling the Family Life Cycle: A Proposal for Redefinition', in Andrew A. Mitchell, ed., Advances in Consumer Research 9 (Ann Arbor, MI: Association for Consumer Research, 1982): 274, Figure 1.

Life cycle effects on buying

As might be expected, consumers classified into these categories show marked differences in consumption patterns. Young bachelors and newlyweds have the most 'modern' sex-role attitudes, are the most likely to exercise regularly, to go to pubs, concerts, the cinema and restaurants, and to go dancing; and they consume more alcohol. Families with young children are more likely to consume health foods such as fruit juice and yogurt, while those made up of single parents and older children buy more junk foods. The monetary value of homes, cars and other durables is lowest for bachelors and single parents, but increases as people go through the full nest and childless couple stages. Perhaps reflecting the bounty of wedding gifts, newlyweds are the most likely to own appliances such as toasters, ovens and electric coffee grinders. Babysitter and day care usage is, of course, highest among single-parent and full nest households, while home maintenance services (e.g. lawnmowing) are most likely to be employed by older couples and bachelors.

The growth of these additional categories creates many opportunities for enterprising marketers. For example, divorced people undergo a process of transition to a new social role. This change is often accompanied by the disposal of possessions linked to the former role and the need to acquire a set of possessions that will help to express the person's new identity as he or she experiments with new lifestyles.[35]

The intimate corporation: family decision-making

The decision process within a household unit in some ways resembles a business conference. Certain matters are put up for discussion, different members may have different priorities and agendas, and there may be power struggles to rival any tale of corporate intrigue. In just about every living situation, whether a conventional family, students sharing a house or apartment, or some other non-traditional arrangement, group members seem to take on different roles just as purchasing agents, engineers, account executives and others do within a company.

Household decisions

▶ Two basic types of decisions are made by families.[36] In a **consensual purchase decision**, the group agrees on the desired purchase, differing only in terms of how it will be achieved. In these circumstances, the family will probably engage in problem-solving and consider alternatives until the means for satisfying the group's goal is found. For example, a household considering adding a dog to the family but concerned about who will take care of it might draw up a chart assigning individuals to specific duties.

▶ Unfortunately, life is not always that easy. In an **accommodative purchase decision,** group members have different preferences or priorities and cannot agree on a purchase that will satisfy the minimum expectations of all involved. It is here that bargaining, coercion, compromise and the wielding of power are all likely to be used to achieve agreement on what to buy or who gets to use it. Family decisions are often characterized by an accommodative rather than a consensual decision. Conflict occurs when there is incomplete correspondence in family members' needs and preferences. While money is the most common source of conflict between marriage partners, television choices come a close second![37] Some specific factors determining the degree of family decision conflict include the following:[38]

- *Interpersonal need* (a person's level of investment in the group). A child in a family situation may care more about what his or her family buys for the house than a university student who is living in student accommodation.

- *Product involvement and utility* (the degree to which the product in question will be used or will satisfy a need): A family member who is an avid coffee drinker will obviously be more interested in the purchase of a new coffeemaker to replace a malfunctioning one than in a similar expenditure for some other item.

- *Responsibility* (for procurement, maintenance, payment, and so on). People are more likely to have disagreements about a decision if it entails long-term consequences and commitments. For example, a family decision about getting a dog may involve conflict regarding who will be responsible for walking and feeding it.

- *Power* (or the degree to which one family member exerts influence over the others in making decisions). In traditional families, the husband tends to have more power than the wife, who in turn has more than the oldest child, and so on. In family decisions, conflict can arise when one person continually uses the power he or she has within the group to satisfy his or her priorities. For example, if Tom believed that his mother was not very likely to buy him both the CD and the WWF game, he might be willing to resort to extreme tactics to influence her, such as giving her the 'silent treatment' or refusing to participate in family chores.

In general, decisions will involve conflict among family members to the extent that they are important or novel and/or if individuals have strong opinions about good and bad alternatives. The degree to which these factors generate conflict determines the type of decision the family will make.[39]

Sex roles and decision-making responsibilities

Traditionally, some buying decisions, termed **autocratic decisions**, were made by one spouse. Men, for instance, often had sole responsibility for selecting a car, while most decorating choices fell to women. Other decisions, such as holiday destinations, were made jointly: these are known as **syncratic decisions**. According to a study conducted by Roper Starch Worldwide, wives tend to have the most say when buying groceries, children's toys, clothes and medicines. Syncratic decisions are common for cars, holidays, homes, appliances, furniture, home electronics, interior design and long-distance phone services. As the couple's education increases, so more decisions are likely to be made together.[40]

Identifying the decision-maker

The nature of consumer decision-making within a particular product category is an important issue for marketers, so that they know whom to target and whether or not they need to reach both spouses to influence a decision. For example, when market research in the 1950s indicated that women were playing a larger role in household purchasing decisions, lawnmower manufacturers began to emphasize the rotary mower over other power mowers. Rotary mowers, which conceal the cutting blades and engine, were often depicted being used by young women and smiling grandmothers to relieve fears of injuries.[41]

Researchers have paid special attention to which spouse plays the role of what has been called the **family financial officer (FFO)**, who keeps track of the family's bills and decides how any surplus funds will be spent. Among newlyweds, this role tends to be played jointly, and then over time one spouse or the other tends to take over these responsibilities.[42] Spouses usually exert significant influence on decision-making, even after one of them has died. An Irish study found that many widows claim to sense the continued presence of their dead husbands, and to conduct 'conversations' with them about household matters![43]

In traditional families (and especially those with low educational levels), women are primarily responsible for family financial management – the man makes it, and the woman spends it.[44] Each spouse 'specializes' in certain activities.[45] The pattern is different among families where spouses adhere to more modern sex-role norms. These couples believe that there should be more shared participation in family maintenance activities. In these cases, husbands assume more responsibility for laundering, house-cleaning, day-to-day shopping and so on, in addition to such traditionally 'male' tasks as home maintenance and waste removal.[46] Of course, cultural background is an important determinant of the dominance of the husband or wife. Husbands tend to be more dominant in decision-making among couples with a strong Mediterranean ethnic identification.[47] Even in northern Europe, the pattern of traditional 'male' and 'female' roles is still fairly strong (see Table 11.2).[48]

Four factors appear to determine the degree to which decisions will be made jointly or by one or the other spouse:[49]

1 *Sex-role stereotypes*. Couples who believe in traditional sex-role stereotypes tend to make individual decisions for sex-typed products (i.e. those considered to be 'masculine' or 'feminine').

Table 11.2 'New man fails to survive into the nineties'

Divisions of household tasks, 1994	Always the woman	Usually the woman	About equal, or both	Usually the man	Always the man	All couples together
Washing and ironing	47	32	18	1	1	100
Deciding what to have for dinner	27	32	35	3	1	100
Looking after sick family members	22	26	45	–	–	100
Shopping for groceries	20	21	52	4	1	100
Small repairs around the house	2	3	18	49	25	100

Source: Nicholas Timmins, 'New Man Fails to Survive into the Nineties', *The Independent* (25 January 1996).

2 *Spousal resources.* The spouse who contributes more resources to the family has the greater influence.

3 *Experience.* Individual decisions are made more frequently when the couple has gained experience as a decision-making unit.

4 *Socio-economic status.* Joint decisions are made more by middle-class families than in either higher- or lower-class families.

Multicultural dimensions

Cultural background plays a big role in determining whether husbands or wives are dominant in the family unit. For example, as we have seen, husbands tend to be more dominant in decision-making among couples with a strong Hispanic ethnic identification.[50] Similarly, Vietnamese-Americans are also more likely to adhere to the traditional model: the man makes the decision for any large purchase, whereas the woman is given a budget to manage the home.[51] In a study comparing marital decision-making in the United States vs. China, American women reported more 'wife decides' situations than did the Chinese.[52] Assumptions about 'who's the boss' are often reflected in advertising and marketing strategies. Here are a few examples to illustrate some cross-cultural differences:

● The Coca-Cola Co. developed a campaign to appeal to Latin American women based on an $800,000 research project the company conducted in Brazil. A motherly female kangaroo was found most likely to appeal to women shopping for their families – and who happen to account for 80 per cent of Coke's $3.5 billion Brazilian sales. The ads were themed 'Mom knows everything', after women in focus groups said they felt the media neglected them even though they were responsible for purchasing all the products in their households.[53]

● A programme in India called Butterfly enlists village medicine men to convince local women to take birth control pills. A big obstacle is that women are not accustomed to making these decisions for themselves. The response of one village resident is typical: 'I have never taken contraceptives. My husband is my master – he will decide.'[54]

● Procter & Gamble produced a commercial for its Ariel laundry detergent in India. A man named Ravi is shown doing the laundry, which is highly unusual in that country. A female voice asks, 'Where's the wife? Are you actually going to wash them? . . . man cannot . . . should not wash clothes . . . [he is] sure to fail.'

▶

● Ads showing men doing housework are risky in Asia as well, even though more Asian women are working outside the home. A South Korean vacuum cleaner ad showed a woman lying on the floor giving herself a facial with slices of cucumber while her husband vacuumed around her. Women there didn't appreciate this ad. As a local ad executive put it, they regarded the ad as a challenge to 'the leadership of women in the home'.[55]

Despite recent changes in decision-making responsibilities, women are still primarily responsible for the continuation of the family's **kin network system**: they perform the rituals intended to maintain ties among family members, both immediate and extended. This function includes such activities as coordinating visits among relatives, phoning and writing to family members, sending greetings cards, making social engagements, and so on.[56] This organizing role means that women often make important decisions about the family's leisure activities, and are more likely to decide with whom the family will socialize.

With many women now working outside the home, men are participating more in housekeeping activities, but women continue to do the lion's share of household chores. Ironically, this even appears to be true when the woman's income actually exceeds her husband's![57] Overall, the degree to which a couple adhere to traditional sex-role norms determines how much their allocation of responsibilities will fall along familiar lines and how their consumer decision-making responsibilities will be allocated.

Heuristics in joint decision-making

The *synoptic ideal* calls for the husband and wife to take a common view and act as joint decision-makers. According to this ideal, they would very thoughtfully weigh alternatives, assign to one another well-defined roles, and calmly make mutually beneficial consumer decisions. The couple would act rationally, analytically, and use as much information as possible to maximize joint utility. In reality, however, spousal decision-making is often characterized by the use of influence or methods that are likely to reduce conflict. A couple 'reaches' rather than 'makes' a decision. This process has been described as 'muddling through'.[58]

One common technique for simplifying the decision-making process is the use of *heuristics* (see Chapter 8). Some decision-making patterns frequently observed when a couple makes decisions about buying a new house illustrate the use of heuristics:

● The couple's areas of common preference are based upon salient, objective dimensions rather than more subtle, hard-to-define cues. For example, a couple may easily agree on the number of bedrooms they need in the new home, but will have more difficulty achieving a common view of how the home should look.

● The couple agrees on a system of *task specialization*, where each is responsible for certain duties or decision areas and does not interfere in the other's. For many couples, these assignments are likely to be influenced by their perceived sex roles. For example, the wife may seek out houses in advance that meet their requirements, while the husband determines whether the couple can obtain a mortgage.

● Concessions are based on the intensity of each spouse's preferences. One spouse will yield to the influence of the other in many cases simply because his or her level of preference for a certain attribute is not particularly intense, where in other situations he or she will be willing to exert effort to obtain a favourable decision.[59] In cases where intense preferences for different attributes exist, rather than attempt to influence each other, spouses will 'trade off' a less-intense preference for a more strongly felt one. For example, a husband who is indifferent to kitchen design may yield to his wife, but expect that in turn he will be allowed to design his own garage workshop. It is interesting to note that many men apparently want to be very involved in making some decorating decisions and setting budgets – more than women want them to be. According to one survey, 70 per cent of male respondents felt the husband should be involved in decorating the family room, while only 51 per cent of wives wanted them to be.[60]

Children as decision-makers: consumers-in-training

Anyone who has had the 'delightful' experience of supermarket shopping with one or more children knows that children often have a say in what their parents buy, especially for products like breakfast cereal.[61] In addition, children are increasingly being recognized as a potential market for traditionally adult products. For example, Kodak is putting a lot of promotional effort into encouraging children to become photographers. Currently, only 20 per cent of children aged 5–12 own a camera, and they shoot an average of just one roll of film a year. In a new effort called 'Big Shots', ads portray photography as a cool pursuit and as a form of rebellion. Cameras are packaged with an envelope to mail the film directly back so parents can't see the photos.[62]

Parental yielding occurs when a parental decision-maker is influenced by a child's request and 'surrenders'. The likelihood of this occurring is partly dependent on the dynamics within a particular family – as we all know, parental styles range from permissive to strict, and they also vary in terms of the amount of responsibility children are given to make decisions.[63] The strategies children use to request purchases have been documented in a study. While most children simply asked for things, other common tactics included saying they had seen it on television, saying that a sibling or friend has it, or bargaining by offering to do chores. Other actions were less innocuous; they included directly placing the object in the trolley and continuous whining – often a 'persuasive' behaviour![64]

As shown in Figure 11.5 on page 363, children begin making selections and purchases of products at an early age. By the time they reach their teens, the process of socialization and peer influence is well under way. Teenage girls and their horses are a clear example of this socialization process with respect to lifestyle choices and consumption behaviours.

Children often play important roles in family consumer decision-making, and they are gaining responsibility as consumers in their own right. They continue to support the toy and sweet industries, of course, but now they also buy and/or influence the purchase of many other products as well. For better or for worse, the new generation is, as the bumper sticker proclaims, 'Born to Shop'. Shopping now ranks among the top seven interests and activities of America's children.[65] Over 80 per cent of young respondents in one survey said their primary wish was to have more money to buy things.[66] In the next section, we'll consider how children learn to make these choices.

Consumer socialization

Children do not spring from the womb with consumer skills already in memory. **Consumer socialization** has been defined as the process 'by which young people acquire skills, knowledge, and attitudes relevant to their functioning in the market-place'.[67] Where does this knowledge come from? Friends and teachers certainly participate in this process. For instance, children talk to one another about consumer products, and this tendency increases with age.[68] Especially for young children, though, the two primary socialization sources are the family and the media.

Influence of parents

Parents' influences in consumer socialization are both direct and indirect. They deliberately try to instill their own values about consumption in their children ('you're going to learn the value of the kroner/guilder/pound . . . euro'). Parents also determine the degree to which their children will be exposed to other information sources, such as television, salespeople and peers.[69] Grown-ups serve as significant models for observational learning (see Chapter 3). Children learn about consumption by watching their parents' behaviour and imitating it. This modelling is facilitated by marketers who package adult products in child versions.

The process of consumer socialization begins with infants, who accompany their parents to shops where they are initially exposed to marketing stimuli. Within the first two years of life, children begin to make requests for desired objects. As children learn to walk, they also begin to make their own selections when they are in shops. By the age of 5, most children are making purchases with the help of parents and grandparents, and by 8 most are making independent purchases and have become fully fledged consumers.[70] The sequence of steps involved in turning children into consumers is summarized in Figure 11.5.

MARKETING PITFALL

Three dimensions combine to produce different 'segments' of parental styles. Parents characterized by certain styles have been found to socialize their children differently.[71] 'Authoritarian parents', who are hostile, restrictive and emotionally uninvolved, do not have warm relationships with their children, are active in filtering the types of media to which their children are exposed, and tend to have negative views about advertising. 'Neglecting parents' also do not have warm relationships, but they are more detached from their children and exercise little control over what their children do. In contrast, 'indulgent parents' communicate more with their children about consumption-related matters and are less restrictive. They believe that children should be allowed to learn about the marketplace without much interference.

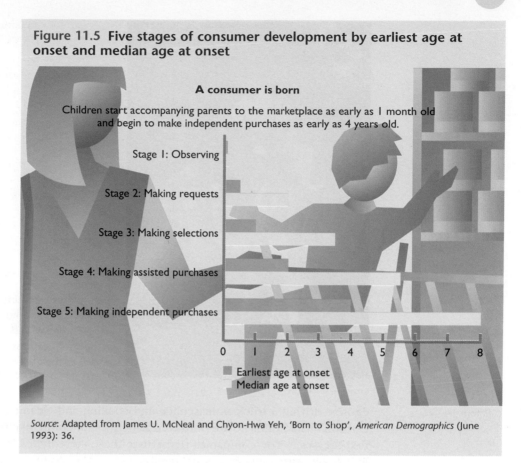

Figure 11.5 Five stages of consumer development by earliest age at onset and median age at onset

A consumer is born

Children start accompanying parents to the marketplace as early as 1 month old and begin to make independent purchases as early as 4 years old.

Stage 1: Observing

Stage 2: Making requests

Stage 3: Making selections

Stage 4: Making assisted purchases

Stage 5: Making independent purchases

0   1   2   3   4   5   6   7   8

■ Earliest age at onset
Median age at onset

Source: Adapted from James U. McNeal and Chyon-Hwa Yeh, 'Born to Shop', *American Demographics* (June 1993): 36.

Influence of television: 'the electric babysitter'

It's no secret that kids watch a lot of television. As a result, they are constantly bombarded with messages about consumption, both contained in commercials and in the shows themselves. The media teach people about a culture's values and myths. The more a child is exposed to television, whether the show is *Tweenies* or *Third Rock from the Sun,* the more he or she will accept the images depicted there as real.[72] A British TV show called *Teletubbies* targets viewers from three months to two years old. In 2000 the show became a national obsession, attracting viewers from more than 20 countries every weekday morning – despite accusations by a major US religious leader who questioned the sexuality of one of the characters because he's purple and carries a red handbag. A Teletubbie record even sold enough copies to make it to the number one spot on the British charts.[73]

In addition to the large volume of programming targeted directly at children, children are also exposed to idealized images of what it is like to be an adult. Since children over the age of 6 spend about a quarter of their television viewing during prime time, they are affected by programmes and commercials targeted at adults. For example, young girls exposed to adult lipstick commercials learn to associate lipstick with beauty.[74]

Sex-role socialization

Children pick up on the concept of gender identity at an earlier age than was previously believed – perhaps as young as age 1 or 2. By the age of 3, most children cat-

Champion sweatshirts, Oilily and Mexx overalls, Keds and Adidas shoes, Levi's jeans. European and global brands are part of the social expression of young children, as well as their parents!

egorize driving a truck as masculine and cooking and cleaning as feminine.[75] Even cartoon characters who are portrayed as helpless are more likely to wear frilly or ruffled dresses.[76] Toy companies perpetuate these stereotypes by promoting gender-linked toys with commercials that reinforce sex-role expectations through their casting, emotional tone and copy.[77]

One function of child's play is to rehearse for adulthood. Children 'act out' different roles they might assume later in life and learn about the expectations others have of them. The toy industry provides the props children use to perform these roles.[78] Depending on which side of the debate you're on, these toys either reflect or teach children about what society expects of males vs. females. While pre-school boys and girls do not exhibit many differences in toy preferences, after the age of 5 they part company: girls tend to stick with dolls, while boys gravitate towards 'action figures' and high-tech diversions. Industry critics charge that this is because the toy industry is dominated by males, while toy company executives counter that they are simply responding to children's natural preferences.[79]

Often 'traditional' sex roles are stressed in children's products: the same item may be designed and positioned differently for boys and girls. Huffy, for example, manufactures bicycles for both boys and girls. The boys' versions have names such as 'Sigma' and 'Vortex', and they are described as having 'maxed-out features that'll pump your pulse'. The girls' version is more demure. It is called 'Sweet Style', and comes in pink or purple. As a company executive described it in contrast to the boys' bikes, the girls' model 'is a fashion bike. It's not built for racing or jumping – just the look.'[80]

Cognitive development

The ability of children to make mature, 'adult' consumer decisions obviously increases with age (not that grown-ups always make mature decisions). Children can

Girls playing with Lego.
Photo by Søren Askegaard.

▶ be segmented by age in terms of their **stage of cognitive development**, or ability to comprehend concepts of increasing complexity. Some recent evidence indicates that young children are able to learn consumption-related information surprisingly well, depending on the format in which the information is presented (e.g. learning is enhanced if a videotaped vignette is presented to small children repeatedly).[81]

The foremost proponent of the idea that children pass through distinct stages of cognitive development was the Swiss psychologist Jean Piaget, who believed that each stage is characterized by a certain cognitive structure the child uses to handle information.[82] In one classic demonstration of cognitive development, Piaget poured the contents of a short, squat glass of lemonade into a taller, thinner glass. Five-year-olds, who still believed that the shape of the glass determined its contents, thought this glass held more liquid than the first glass. They were in what Piaget termed a *preoperational stage of development*. In contrast, six-year-olds tended to be unsure, but seven-year olds knew the amount of lemonade had not changed.

Many developmental specialists no longer believe that children necessarily pass through these fixed stages at the same time. An alternative approach regards children as differing in information-processing capability, or the ability to store and retrieve information from memory (see Chapter 3). The following three segments have been identified by this approach:[83]

1 *Limited*. Below the age of 6, children do not employ storage and retrieval strategies.

2 *Cued*. Children between the ages of 6 and 12 employ these strategies, but only when prompted.

3 *Strategic*. Children aged 12 and older spontaneously employ storage and retrieval strategies.

This sequence of development underscores the notion that children do not think like adults, and they cannot be expected to use information in the same way. It also reminds us that they do not necessarily form the same conclusions as adults do when presented with product information. For example, children are not as likely to realize that something they see on television is not 'real', and as a result they are more vulnerable to persuasive messages.

**MARKETING
PITFALL**

Hooper's Hooch, a lemon-flavoured alcoholic beverage made by Bass PLC, is one of a dozen different brands launched in the UK that is specifically targeted at children (other popular brands include Lemonhead and Mrs Pucker's). The drink's slogan: 'One taste and you're Hooched'. These drinks, known as 'alcopops', are now being test-marketed in the US in lemonade, cola and orange flavours and contain 4–5.5 per cent alcohol in order to appeal to teenagers. Alcohol laws are less restrictive in Britain than in the US – children under 18 can't purchase alcohol, but they can drink it in their homes. Critics argue that this marketing strategy helps those who don't have a taste for alcohol develop one, since children who grow up drinking Coke or Orangina will accept alcopops more readily than wine coolers.[84] What do you think?

Marketing research and children

Despite their buying power, relatively little real data on children's preferences or influences on spending patterns are available. Compared to adults, children are difficult subjects for market researchers. They tend to be unreliable reporters of their own behaviour, they have poor recall, and they often do not understand abstract questions.[85] This problem is compounded in Europe, where some countries restrict marketers' ability to interview children.

Still, market research can pay off, and many companies, as well as a number of specialized firms, have been successful in researching some aspects of this segment.[86] After interviewing elementary school pupils, Campbell's Soup discovered that children like soup, but don't like to admit it, because they associate it with 'nerds'. The company decided to reintroduce the Campbell kids in its advertising after a prolonged absence, but they are now slimmed down and more athletic to reflect an updated, 'un-nerdy' image.[87]

Product testing

A particularly helpful type of research with children is product testing. Young subjects can provide a valuable perspective on which products will succeed. One confectionery company has a Candy Tasters Club, composed of 1200 children aged 6 to 16, who evaluate its product ideas. For example, the group vetoed the idea of a Batman lollipop, claiming that the superhero was too macho to be sucked.[88] The Fisher-Price Company maintains a nursery known as the Playlab. Children are chosen from a waiting list of 4000 to play with new toys, while staff members watch from behind a one-way mirror.[89] H. J. Heinz recently held a contest for children to create new ketchup bottle labels and received about 60,000 entries. Binney & Smith is asking children to rename its Crayola crayons after personal heroes.[90]

Other techniques include ethnographic research, where researchers spend time with children or videotape them as they shop. The most successful interviewers are those who try not to be 'adultcentric' (i.e. like an adult authority figure who assumes that children's beliefs are just unreal fantasies): they act as a friend to the children and are willing to use a variety of projective techniques and props to get children to express themselves in their own terms.[91]

Message comprehension

Since children differ in their ability to process product-related information, many serious ethical issues are raised when advertisers try to appeal directly to them.[92] Children tend to accept what they see on television as real, and they do not necessarily understand the persuasive intent of commercials – that they are paid advertisements. Pre-school children may not have the ability to make any distinctions between programming and commercials.

Children's cognitive defences are not yet sufficiently developed to filter out commercial appeals, so in a sense altering their brand preferences may be likened to 'shooting fish in a barrel', as one critic put it.[93] Although some ads include a disclaimer, which is a disclosure intended to clarify a potentially misleading or deceptive statement, the evidence suggests that young children do not understand these either.[94] The Children's Advertising Review Unit (CARU) recently unveiled guidelines for child-oriented websites after receiving complaints that children had difficulty distinguishing ads from content. These include clear identification of the sponsor and the right to cancel purchases made online.[95]

Children's level of understanding is especially hard to assess, since pre-schoolers are not very articulate. One way round this problem is to show pictures of children in different scenarios, and ask the subjects to point to the sketch that corresponds to what a commercial is trying to get them to do. The problem with children's processing of commercials has been exacerbated by television programming that essentially promotes toys ('Transformers, for example). This format has been the target of a lot of criticism because it blurs the line between programming and commercials (much like 'infomercials' for adults, as described in Chapter 8).[96] Parents' groups object to such shows because, as one mother put it, the 'whole show is one big commercial'.[97]

Chapter summary

- Many purchasing decisions are made by more than one person. Collective decision-making occurs whenever two or more people are involved in evaluating, selecting or using a product or service.

- Demographics are statistics that measure a population's characteristics. Some of the most important of these relate to family structure, e.g. the birth rate, the marriage rate and the divorce rate. In Europe, collecting reliable and comparable data regarding the family unit has not always been a straightforward process.

- A household is an occupied housing unit. The number and type of European households is changing in many ways: through delays in getting married and having children, and in the composition of family households, which increasingly are headed by a single parent. New perspectives on the family life cycle, which focuses on how people's needs change as they move through different stages in their lives, are forcing marketers to consider more seriously such consumer segments as homosexuals, divorcees and childless couples when they develop targeting strategies.

- Families must be understood in terms of their decision-making dynamics. Spouses in particular have different priorities and exert varying amounts of influence in terms of effort and power. Children are also increasingly influential during a widening range of purchase decisions.

- Children undergo a process of socialization, whereby they learn how to be consumers. Some of this knowledge is instilled by parents and friends, but a lot of it comes from exposure to mass media and advertising. Since children are in some cases so easily persuaded, the ethical aspects of marketing to them are hotly debated among consumers, academics and marketing practitioners.

KEY TERMS

Accommodative purchase decision
  (p. 357)
Autocratic decision (p. 358)
Consensual purchase decision (p. 357)
Consumer socialization (p. 362)
Extended family (p. 350)
Family financial officer (FFO) (p. 358)
Family household (p. 350)

Family life cycle (FLC) (p. 355)
Fertility rate (p. 252)
Kin network system (p. 360)
Nuclear family (p. 350)
Parental yielding (p. 361)
Stage of cognitive development
  (p. 365)
Syncratic decisions (p. 358)

For additional material see the companion website at:
www.booksites.net/solomon_euro

Consumer behaviour challenge

1. Review a number of popular media which are published in countries in southern Europe as well as media targeted for northern European countries. How do the ads' depictions of *family* seem to differ by region? In what sorts of consumption situations do they seem highly similar? Why?

2. Do you think market research should be performed on children? Give the reasons for your answer. What do you think about the practice of companies and survey firms collecting public data (e.g. from marriage licences, birth records or even death announcements) to compile targeted mailing lists? State your opinion from both a consumer's and marketer's perspective.

3. Marketers have been criticized for donating products and services to educational institutions in exchange for free promotion. Is this a fair exchange, in your opinion, or should corporations be prohibited from attempting to influence youngsters in school?

4. For each of the following five product categories – groceries, cars, holidays, furniture and appliances – describe the ways in which you believe a married couple's choices would be affected if they had children.

5. In identifying and targeting newly divorced couples, do you think marketers are exploiting these couples' situations? Are there instances where you think marketers may actually be helpful to them? Support your answers with examples.

6. Arrange to interview two married couples, one younger and one older. Prepare a response form listing five product categories – groceries, furniture, appliances, holidays and cars – and ask each spouse to indicate, without consulting the other, whether purchases in each category are made by joint or unilateral decisions and to indicate whether the unilateral decisions are made by the husband or the wife. Compare each couple's responses for agreement between husbands and wives relative to who makes the decisions and compare both couples' overall responses for differences relative to the number of joint vs. unilateral decisions. Report your findings and conclusions.

7. Collect ads for three different product categories in which the family is targeted. Find another set of ads for different brands of the same items in which the family is not featured. Prepare a report on the effectiveness of the approaches.

8. Observe the interactions between parents and children in the cereal section of a local grocery shop. Prepare a report on the number of children who expressed preferences, how they expressed their preferences and how parents responded, including the number who purchased the child's choice.

9. Watch three hours of children's programming on commercial television stations and evaluate the marketing techniques used in the commercials in terms of the ethical issues raised in the final section of this chapter. Report your findings and conclusions.

10. Select a product category, and using the life cycle stages given in the chapter, list the variables that will affect a purchase decision for the product by consumers in each stage of the cycle.

11. Consider three important changes in modern European family structure. For each, find an example of a marketer who has attempted to be conscious of this change as reflected in product communications, retailing innovations, or other aspects of the marketing mix. If possible, also try to find examples of marketers who have failed to keep up with these developments.

Notes

1. Nancy Marx Better, 'Green Teens', *New York Times Magazine* (8 March 1992) 3: 44; Howard Schlossberg, 'Kids Teach Parents How to Change Their Buying Habits', *Marketing News* (1992): 8.

2. T. Eggerickx and F. Bégeot, 'Les recensements en Europe dans les années 1990. De la diversité des pratiques nationales à la comparabilité internationales des résultats', *Population* 41(2) (1993): 327–48.

3. F. Simoes-Casimiro and M. G. Calado-Lopes, 'Concepts and Typologies of Household and Family in the 1981 and 1991 Population Censuses in the Twelve Community Countries', unpublished report for Eurostat (Lisbon: Instituto Superior de Estatistica e Gescao de Informação, 1995); 'Gezinsleven binner de EU onder druk', *Nederlandse Dagblad* (7 July 1995); 'Statistics in Focus: Population and Social Conditions', Eurostat (Luxembourg: Office for Official Publications of the European Communities, 1996); 'Living Conditions in Europe: Statistical Pocketbook', Eurostat (Luxembourg: Office for Official Publications of the European Communities, 2000). A great deal of information on the European Union is available on the internet at: *http://europa.eu.int*. See also 'The Social Situation in the European Union 2000', European Commission, Statistics in Focus (Populations and Social Conditions).

4. 'Statistics in Focus: Population and Social Conditions', Eurostat (Luxembourg: Office for Official Publications of the European Communities, 2000).

5. Robert Boutilier, 'Diversity in Family Structures', *American Demographics Marketing Tools* (1993): 4–6; W. Bradford Fay, 'Families in the 1990s: Universal Values, Uncommon Experiences', *Marketing Research: A Magazine of Management & Applications* 5 (Winter 1993) 1: 47.

6. Ellen Graham, 'Craving Closer Ties, Strangers Come Together as Family', *Wall Street Journal* (4 March 1996): B1 (2).

7. 'Women and Men in the European Union: A Statistical Portrait', Eurostat (Luxembourg: Office for Official Publications of the European Communities, 1996); 'Families Come First', *Psychology Today* (September 1988): 11.

8. Christy Fisher, 'Kidding Around Making Sense', *Advertising Age* (27 June 1994): 34.

9. Alan R. Andreasen, 'Life Status Changes and Changes in Consumer Preferences and Satisfaction', *Journal of Consumer Research* 11 (December 1984): 784–94; James H. McAlexander, John W. Schouten and Scott D. Roberts, 'Consumer Behavior and Divorce', *Research in Consumer Behavior* 6 (1993): 153–84.

10. 'Men and Women in the European Union: A Statistical Portrait', Eurostat; 'The Population of the EU on 1 January, 1995', *Statistics in Focus. Population and Social Conditions* 8 (Luxembourg: Office for Official Publications of the European Communities, 1995); 'Living Conditions in Europe: Statistical Pocketbook', Eurostat (Luxembourg: Office for Official Publications of the European Communities, 2000): 22.

11. 'Men and Women in the European Union: A Statistical Portrait', Eurostat; 'Living Conditions in Europe: Statistical Pocketbook', Eurostat; 'The Big Picture', *American Demographics* (March 1989): 22–7; Thomas G. Exter, 'Middle-Aging Households', *American Demographics* (July 1992): 63.

12. Cyndee Miller, "Til Death Do They Part', *Marketing News* (27 March 1995): 1–2.

13. 'The Population of the EU on 1 January, 1995', *Statistics in Focus*; Nicholas Timmins, 'One in Five Women to Remain Childless', *The Independent* (4 October 1995).

14. 'Living Conditions in Europe: Statistical Pocketbook', Eurostat: 24.

15. 'Men and Women in the European Union: A Statistical Portrait', Eurostat: 72.

16. 'Living Conditions in Europe: Statistical Pocketbook', Eurostat: 22.

17. Peg Masterson, 'Agency Notes Rise of Singles Market', *Advertising Age* (9 August 1993): 17.

18. Christy Fisher, 'Census Data May Make Ads More Single Minded', *Advertising Age* (20 July 1992): 2.

19. Calmetta Y. Coleman, 'The Unseemly Secrets of Eating Alone', *Wall Street Journal* (6 July 1995): B1 (2).

20. Stephanie Shipp, 'How Singles Spend', *American Demographics* (April 1988): 22-7; Patricia Braus, 'Sex and the Single Spender', *American Demographics* (November 1993): 28-34.

21. 'Mothers Bearing a Second Burden', *New York Times* (14 May 1989): 26; 'Living Conditions in Europe: Statistical Pocketbook', Eurostat: 21.

22. Seth Mydans, 'A Tribunal to Get Neglected Parents Smiling Again', *New York Times* (27 December 1996): A4.

23. 'Men and Women in the European Union: A Statistical Portrait', Eurostat: 76.

24. 'Census Paints a New Picture of Family Life', *New York Times* (30 August 1994): 22.

25. For a review, see Russell W. Belk, 'Metaphoric Relationships with Pets', *Society and Animals* 4 (1996) 2: 121-46.

26. Diane Crispell, 'Pet Projections', *American Demographics* (September 1994): 59.

27. Howard G. Chua-Eoan, 'Reigning Cats and Dogs', *Time* (16 August 1993): 50 (2); Patricia Braus, 'Cat Beats Dog, Wins Spot in House', *American Demographics* (September 1993): 24 (2).

28. Quoted in Youssef M. Ibrahim, 'French Love for Animals: Too Fervent?', *New York Times* (2 February 1990): A5.

29. Woody Hochswender, 'The Cat's Meow', *New York Times* (16 May 1989): B7; Judann Dagnoli, 'Toothcare for Terriers', *Advertising Age* (20 November 1989): 8; 'For Fido, Broccoli and Yogurt', *New York Times* (16 April 1989); Howard G. Chua-Eoan, 'Reigning Cats and Dogs', *Time* (16 August 1993): 50 (2); William E. Schmidt, 'Right, Then: Your Policy Covers Fido for Therapy', *New York Times* (15 May 1994): 4.

30. Gary Younge, 'Parents Face a £66,000 Bill', *The Guardian* (27 May 1996); Liz Hunt, 'The Cost of Growing: Schoolchildren Need Huge Sums', *The Independent* (19 August 1996).

31. 'Key Figures: Bulletin of Economic Trends in Europe and Summaries, 7/97', Eurostat (Luxembourg: Office for Official Publications of the European Communities, 1997); 'Living Conditions in Europe: Statistical Pocketbook', Eurostat: 117.

32. Mary C. Gilly and Ben M. Enis, 'Recycling the Family Life Cycle: A Proposal for Redefinition', in Andrew A. Mitchell, ed., *Advances in Consumer Research* 9 (Ann Arbor, MI: ACR, 1982): 271-6.

33. Charles M. Schaninger and William D. Danko, 'A Conceptual and Empirical Comparison of Alternative Household Life Cycle Models', *Journal of Consumer Research* 19 (March 1993): 580-94; Robert E. Wilkes, 'Household Life-Cycle Stages, Transitions, and Product Expenditures', *Journal of Consumer Research* 22(1) (June 1995): 27-42.

34. These categories are an adapted version of an FLC model proposed by Gilly and Enis. Based on a recent empirical comparison of several competing models, Schaninger and Danko found that this framework outperformed others, especially in terms of its treatment of non-conventional households, though they recommend several improvements to this model as well. See Gilly and Enis, 'Recycling the Family Life Cycle': 271-6; Schaninger and Danko, 'A Conceptual and Empirical Comparison of Alternate Household Life Cycle Markets'; Scott D. Roberts, Patricia K. Voli and KerenAmi Johnson, 'Beyond the Family Life Cycle: An Inventory of Variables for Defining the Family as a Consumption Unit', in Victoria L. Crittenden, ed., *Developments in Marketing Science* 15 (Coral Gables, FL: Academy of Marketing Science, 1992): 71-5.

35. James H. McAlexander, John W. Schouten and Scott D. Roberts, 'Consumer Behavior and Divorce', in *Research in Consumer Behavior* (Greenwich, CT: JAI Press, 1992); Michael R. Solomon, 'The Role of Products as Social Stimuli: A Symbolic Interactionism Perspective', *Journal of Consumer Research* 10 (December 1983): 319-29; Melissa Martin Young, 'Disposition of Possession During Role Transitions', in Rebecca H. Holman and Michael R. Solomon, eds, *Advances in Consumer Research* 18 (Provo, UT: Association for Consumer Research, 1991): 33-9.

36. Harry L. Davis, 'Decision Making Within the Household', *Journal of Consumer Research* 2 (March 1972): 241-60; Michael B. Menasco and David J. Curry, 'Utility and Choice: An Empirical Study of Wife/Husband Decision Making', *Journal of Consumer Research* 16 (June 1989): 87-97; for a recent review, see Conway Lackman and John M. Lanasa, 'Family Decision-Making Theory: An Overview and Assessment', *Psychology & Marketing* 10 (March/April 1993) 2: 81-94.

37. Shannon Dortch, 'Money and Marital Discord', *American Demographics* (October 1994): 11 (3).

38. Daniel Seymour and Greg Lessne, 'Spousal Conflict Arousal: Scale Development', *Journal of Consumer Research* 11 (December 1984): 810-21.

39. For recent research on factors influencing how much influence adolescents exert in family decision-making, see Ellen Foxman, Patriya Tansuhaj and Karin M. Ekstrom, 'Family Members' Perceptions of Adolescents' Influence in Family Decision Making', *Journal of Consumer Research* 15 (March 1989) 4:

482–91; Sharon E. Beatty and Salil Talpade, 'Adolescent Influence in Family Decision Making: A Replication with Extension', *Journal of Consumer Research* 21 (September 1994) 2: 332–41.

40. Diane Crispell, 'Dual-Earner Diversity', *American Demographics* (July 1995): 32–7.

41. Thomas Hine, *Populuxe* (New York: Alfred A. Knopf, 1986).

42. Robert Boutilier, 'Targeting Families: Marketing To and Through the New Family', *American Demographics*, (1993).

43. Darach Turley, 'Dialogue with the Departed', *European Advances in Consumer Research* 2 (1995): 10–13.

44. Dennis L. Rosen and Donald H. Granbois, 'Determinants of Role Structure in Family Financial Management', *Journal of Consumer Research* 10 (September 1983): 253–8.

45. Robert F. Bales, *Interaction Process Analysis: A Method for the Study of Small Groups* (Reading, MA: Addison-Wesley, 1950); for a cross-gender comparison of food shopping strategies, see Rosemary Polegato and Judith L. Zaichkowsky, 'Family Food Shopping: Strategies Used by Husbands and Wives', *Journal of Consumer Affairs* 28 (1994): 2.

46. Alma S. Baron, 'Working Parents: Shifting Traditional Roles', *Business* 37 (January/March 1987): 36; William J. Qualls, 'Household Decision Behavior: The Impact of Husbands' and Wives' Sex Role Orientation', *Journal of Consumer Research* 14 (September 1987): 264–79; Charles M. Schaninger and W. Christian Buss, 'The Relationship of Sex Role Norms to Household Task Allocation', *Psychology & Marketing* 2 (Summer 1985): 93–104.

47. Cynthia Webster, 'Effects of Hispanic Ethnic Identification on Marital Roles in the Purchase Decision Process', *Journal of Consumer Research* 21 (September 1994) 2: 319–31; for a recent study that examined the effects of family depictions in advertising among Hispanic consumers, cf. Gary D. Gregory and James M. Munch, 'Cultural Values in International Advertising: An Examination of Familial Norms and Roles in Mexico', *Psychology & Marketing* 14(2) (March 1997): 99–120.

48. John B. Ford, Michael S. LaTour and Tony L. Henthorne, 'Perception of Marital Roles in Purchase Decision Processes: A Cross-Cultural Study', *Journal of the Academy of Marketing Science* 23(2) (Spring 1995): 120–31; for a recent study of husband–wife dyad decision-making for home purchase decisions, cf. Chankon Kim and Hanjoon Lee, 'A Taxonomy of Couples Based on Influence Strategies: The Case of Home Purchase', *Journal of Business Research* 36(2) (June 1996): 157–68.

49. Gary L. Sullivan and P. J. O'Connor, 'The Family Purchase Decision Process: A Cross-Cultural Review and Framework for Research', *Southwest Journal of Business & Economics* (Fall 1988): 43; Marilyn Lavin,

'Husband-Dominant, Wife-Dominant, Joint', *Journal of Consumer Marketing* 10 (1993) 3: 33–42; Nicholas Timmins, 'New Man Fails to Survive into the Nineties', *The Independent* (25 January 1996). See also Roger J. Baran, 'Patterns of Decision Making Influence for Selected Products and Services Among Husbands and Wives Living in the Czech Republic', in F. Hansen, ed., *European Advances in Consumer Research* 2 (Provo, UT: Association for Consumer Research, 1995); Jan Pahl, 'His Money, Her Money: Recent Research on Financial Organization in Marriage', *Journal of Economic Psychology* 16 (1995): 361–76; Carole B. Burgoyne, 'Financial Organization and Decision-making within Western "households"', *Journal of Economic Psychology* 16 (1995): 421–30; Erich Kirchler, 'Spouses' Joint Purchase Decisions: Determinants of Influence Tactics for Muddling Through the Process', *Journal of Economic Psychology* 14 (1993): 405–38.

50. Cynthia Webster, 'Effects of Hispanic Ethnic Identification on Marital Roles in the Purchase Decision Process', *Journal of Consumer Research* 21 (September 1994) 2: 319–31; for a recent study that examined the effects of family depictions in advertising among Hispanic consumers, see Gary D. Gregory and James M. Munch, 'Cultural Values in International Advertising: An Examination of Familial Norms and Roles in Mexico', *Psychology & Marketing* 14 (March 1997) 2: 99–120.

51. John Steere, 'How Asian-Americans Make Purchase Decisions', *Marketing News* (13 March 1995): 9.

52. Ford, LaTour and Henthorne, 'Perception of Marital Roles in Purchase Decision Processes'; for a recent study of husband–wife dyad decision-making for home purchase decisions, see Kim and Lee, 'A Taxonomy of Couples Based on Influence Strategies'.

53. Claudia Penteado, 'Coke Taps Maternal Instinct with New Latin American Ads', *Advertising Age International* (January 1997): 15.

54. Quoted in Miriam Jordan, 'India's Medicine Men Market an Array of Contraceptives', *Wall Street Journal Interactive Edition* (21 September 1999).

55. Louise Lee, 'Ad Agencies in Asia Hit a Nerve, Showing Men Doing Housework', *Wall Street Journal Interactive Edition* (14 August 1998).

56. Micaela DiLeonardo, 'The Female World of Cards and Holidays: Women, Families, and the Work of Kinship', *Signs* 12 (Spring 1942): 440–53.

57. Tony Bizjak, 'Chore Wars Rage On – Even When Wife Earns the Most', *Sacramento Bee* (1 April 1993): A1 (3).

58. C. Whan Park, 'Joint Decisions in Home Purchasing: A Muddling Through Process', *Journal of Consumer Research* 9 (September 1982): 151–62; see also William J. Qualls and Françoise Jaffe, 'Measuring Conflict in Household Decision Behavior: Read My Lips and Read My Mind', in *Advances in Consumer Research* 19, ed. John F. Sherry, Jr and Brian Sternthal

(Provo, UT: Association for Consumer Research, 1992).

59. Kim P. Corfman and Donald R. Lehmann, 'Models of Cooperative Group Decision-Making and Relative Influence: An Experimental Investigation of Family Purchase Decisions', *Journal of Consumer Research* 14 (June 1987).

60. Alison M. Torrillo, 'Dens are Men's Territory', *American Demographics* (January 1995): 11 (2).

61. Charles Atkin, 'Observation of Parent–Child Interaction in Supermarket Decision-Making', *Journal of Marketing* 42 (October 1978).

62. Emily Nelson, 'Kodak Aims to Put Kids Behind its Cameras', *Wall Street Journal Interactive Edition* (6 May 1997).

63. Les Carlson, Ann Walsh, Russell N. Laczniak and Sanford Grossbart, 'Family Communication Patterns and Marketplace Motivations, Attitudes, and Behaviors of Children and Mothers', *Journal of Consumer Affairs* 28(1) (Summer 1994): 25–53; cf. also Roy L. Moore and George P. Moschis, 'The Role of Family Communication in Consumer Learning', *Journal of Communication* 31 (Autumn 1981): 42–51.

64. Leslie Isler, Edward T. Popper and Scott Ward, 'Children's Purchase Requests and Parental Responses: Results From a Diary Study', *Journal of Advertising Research* 27 (October/November 1987).

65. Horst H. Stipp, 'Children as Consumers', *American Demographics* (February 1988): 27.

66. Melissa Turner, 'Kids' Marketing Clout Man-Sized', *Atlanta Journal* (18 February 1988): E10.

67. Scott Ward, 'Consumer Socialization', in *Perspectives in Consumer Behavior*, ed. Harold H. Kassarjian and Thomas S. Robertson (Glenville, IL: Scott, Foresman, 1980): 380.

68. Thomas Lipscomb, 'Indicators of Materialism in Children's Free Speech: Age and Gender Comparisons', *Journal of Consumer Marketing* (Fall 1988): 41–6.

69. George P. Moschis, 'The Role of Family Communication in Consumer Socialization of Children and Adolescents', *Journal of Consumer Research* 11 (March 1985): 898–913.

70. James U. McNeal and Chyon-Hwa Yeh, 'Born to Shop', *American Demographics* (June 1993): 34–9.

71. See Les Carlson, Sanford Grossbart and J. Kathleen Stuenkel, 'The Role of Parental Socialization Types on Differential Family Communication Patterns Regarding Consumption', *Journal of Consumer Psychology* 1 (1992) 1: 31–52.

72. See Patricia M. Greenfield, Emily Yut, Mabel Chung, Deborah Land, Holly Kreider, Maurice Pantoja and Kris Horsley, 'The Program-Length Commercial: A Study of the Effects of Television/Toy Tie-Ins on Imaginative Play', *Psychology & Marketing* 7 (Winter 1990): 237–56, for a study on the effects of commercial programming on creative play.

73. Marina Baker, 'Teletubbies say "Eh oh . . . It's war!"' *The Independent* (6 March 2000): 7; 'A Trojan Horse for Advertisers', *Business Week* (3 April 2000): 10.

74. Gerald J. Gorn and Renee Florsheim, 'The Effects of Commercials for Adult Products on Children', *Journal of Consumer Research* 11 (March 1985): 9, 62–7; for a recent study that assessed the impact of violent commercials on children, see V. Kanti Prasad and Lois J. Smith, 'Television Commercials in Violent Programming: An Experimental Evaluation of Their Effects on Children', *Journal of the Academy of Marketing Science* 22 (1994) 4: 340–51.

75. Glenn Collins, 'New Studies on "Girl Toys" and "Boy Toys"', *New York Times* (13 February 1984): D1.

76. Susan B. Kaiser, 'Clothing and the Social Organization of Gender Perception: A Developmental Approach', *Clothing and Textiles Research Journal* 7 (Winter 1989): 46–56.

77. D. W. Rajecki, Jill Ann Dame, Kelly Jo Creek, P. J. Barrickman, Catherine A. Reid and Drew C. Appleby, 'Gender Casting in Television Toy Advertisements: Distributions, Message Content Analysis, and Evaluations', *Journal of Consumer Psychology* 2 (1993) 3: 307–27.

78. Lori Schwartz and William Markham, 'Sex Stereotyping in Children's Toy Advertisements', *Sex Roles* 12 (January 1985): 157–70.

79. Joseph Pereira, 'Oh Boy! In Toyland, You Get More if You're Male', *Wall Street Journal* (23 September 1994): B1 (2); Joseph Pereira, 'Girls' Favorite Playthings: Dolls, Dolls, and Dolls', *Wall Street Journal* (23 September 1994): B1 (2).

80. Brad Edmondson, 'Snakes, Snails, and Puppy Dogs' Tails', *American Demographics* (October 1987): 18.

81. Laura A. Peracchio, 'How Do Young Children Learn to be Consumers? A Script-Processing Approach', *Journal of Consumer Research* 18 (March 1992): 4, 25–40; Laura A. Peracchio, 'Young Children's Processing of a Televised Narrative: Is a Picture Really Worth a Thousand Words?', *Journal of Consumer Research* 20 (September 1993) 2: 281–93; see also M. Carole Macklin, 'The Effects of an Advertising Retrieval Cue on Young Children's Memory and Brand Evaluations', *Psychology & Marketing* 11 (May/June 1994) 3: 291–311.

82. Jean Piaget, 'The Child and Modern Physics', *Scientific American* 196 (1957) 3: 46–51; see also Kenneth D. Bahn, 'How and When Do Brand Perceptions and Preferences First Form? A Cognitive Developmental Investigation', *Journal of Consumer Research* 13 (December 1986): 382–93.

83. Deborah L. Roedder, 'Age Differences in Children's Responses to Television Advertising: An Information Processing Approach', *Journal of Consumer Research* 8 (September 1981): 1, 44–53; see also Deborah Roedder John and Ramnath Lakshmi-Ratan, 'Age Differences in Children's Choice Behavior: The Impact of Available Alternatives', *Journal of*

Marketing Research 29 (May 1992): 216–26; Jennifer Gregan-Paxton and Deborah Roedder John, 'Are Young Children Adaptive Decision Makers? A Study of Age Differences in Information Search Behavior', *Journal of Consumer Research* (1995).

84. Tara Parker-Pope, 'Spiked Sodas, an Illicit Hit with Kids In U.K., Head for U.S.', *Wall Street Journal* (12 February 1996): B1.

85. Janet Simons, 'Youth Marketing: Children's Clothes Follow the Latest Fashion', *Advertising Age* (14 February 1985): 16.

86. Stipp, 'Children as Consumers'; see Laura A. Peracchio, 'Designing Research to Reveal the Young Child's Emerging Competence', *Psychology & Marketing* 7 (Winter 1990): 257–76, for details regarding the design of research on children.

87. 'Kid Power', *Forbes* (30 March 1987): 9–10.

88. Dena Kleiman, 'Candy to Frighten Your Parents With', *New York Times* (23 August 1989): C1.

89. Laura Shapiro, 'Where Little Boys Can Play with Nail Polish', *Newsweek* (28 May 1990): 62.

90. Matt Murray, 'Marketers Want Kids' Help and Their Parents' Loyalty', *Wall Street Journal Interactive Edition* (6 May 1997).

91. Cindy Clark, 'Putting Aside Adultcentrism: Child-Centered Ethnographic Research', unpublished manuscript (C. D. Clark Limited, 1991); Cindy Clark, 'Some Practical In's and Out's of Studying Children as Consumers', paper presented at the AMA Research Roundtable, March 1986.

92. Gary Armstrong and Merrie Brucks, 'Dealing with Children's Advertising: Public Policy Issues and Alternatives', *Journal of Public Policy and Marketing* 7 (1988): 98–113.

93. Bonnie Reece, 'Children and Shopping: Some Public Policy Questions', *Journal of Public Policy and Marketing* (1986): 185–94.

94. Mary Ann Stutts and Garland G. Hunnicutt, 'Can Young Children Understand Disclaimers in Television Commercials?', *Journal of Advertising* 16 (Winter 1987): 41–6.

95. Ira Teinowitz, 'CARU to Unveil Guidelines for Kid-Focused Web Sites', *Ad Age* (21 April 1997): 8.

96. Steve Weinstein, 'Fight Heats Up Against Kids' TV "Commershows"', *Marketing News* (9 October 1989): 2.

97. Alan Bunce, 'Are TV Ads Turning Kids Into Consumers?', *Christian Science Monitor* (11 August 1988): 1.

Chapter 12

Income and social class

Finally, the big day has come! David is going home with Julia to meet her parents. David had been doing some contracting work at the publishing company where Julia works, and it was love at first sight. Even though David had attended the 'School of Hard Knocks' on the streets of Liverpool, while Julia studied Classics at Trinity College, Oxford, somehow they knew they could work things out despite their vastly different social backgrounds. Julia's been hinting that the Caldwells have money from *several* generations back, but David doesn't feel intimidated. After all, he knows plenty of guys from both Liverpool and London who have wheeled-and-dealed their way into six figures; he thinks he can handle one more big shot in a silk suit, flashing a roll of bills and showing off his expensive modern furniture with mirrors and gadgets everywhere you look.

When they arrive at the family estate 90 minutes outside London, David looks for a Rolls-Royce parked at the end of the long, tree-lined driveway, but he sees only a Jeep Cherokee – which, he decides, must belong to one of the servants. Once inside, David is surprised by how simply the house is decorated and by how understated everything seems. The hall floor is covered with a faded Oriental rug, and all the furniture looks really old – in fact, there doesn't seem to be a stick of new furniture anywhere, just a lot of antiques.

David is even more surprised when he meets Mr Caldwell. He had half-expected Julia's father to be wearing a tuxedo and holding a large glass of cognac like the people on *Lifestyles of the Rich and Famous*. In fact, David had put on his best Italian silk suit in anticipation and was wearing his large cubic zirconium ring so Mr Caldwell would know that he had money too. When Julia's father emerges from his study wearing an old rumpled cardigan and plimsolls, David realizes he's definitely not in the same world . . .

Consumer spending and economic behaviour

As David's eye-opening experience at the Caldwells' suggests, there are many ways to spend money, and a wide gulf exists between those who have it and those who don't. Perhaps an equally wide one exists between those who have had it for a long time and those who 'made it the hard way – by earning it!' This chapter begins by considering briefly how general economic conditions affect the way consumers allocate their money. Then, reflecting the adage 'The rich are different', it will explore how people who occupy different positions in society consume in very different ways. Whether a person is a skilled worker like David or a child of privilege like Julia, his or her social class has a profound impact on what he or she does with money and on how consumption choices reflect the person's 'place' in society.

As this chapter illustrates, these choices play another purpose as well. The specific products and services we buy are often intended to make sure *other* people know what our social standing is – or what we would like it to be. Products are frequently bought and displayed as markers of social class: they are valued as **status symbols**. Indeed, it is quite common for a product to be positioned on the basis of its (presumed) place in the social hierarchy. The chapter concludes with an assessment of the evolving natures of such status symbols, and it considers some reasons why status-driven products are not always accurate indicators of a consumer's true social standing.

The field of **behavioural economics**, or economic psychology, is concerned with the 'human' side of economic decisions. Beginning with the pioneering work of the psychologist George Katona, this discipline studies how consumers' motives and their expectations about the future affect their current spending, and how these individual decisions add up to affect a society's economic well-being.[1]

Income patterns

Many Europeans would probably say that while they are comfortable, they don't earn enough money. In reality, the average European's standard of living continues to improve. Gross Domestic Product more than doubled and in some EU countries quadrupled between 1980 and 1995, although this boom was by no means shared equally among all consumer groups.[2] Individual income shifts were linked to two key factors: a shift in women's roles and increases in educational attainment.[3]

Woman's work

One reason for this increase in income is that there has also been a larger proportion of people of working age participating in the labour force. While men are more likely to have paid employment than women are, the greatest increases in paid employment in EU countries over the past decade have been among women. This steady increase in the numbers of working women is a primary cause of the increase in household incomes. Still, throughout the Union, women's average full-time earnings are less than men's. In 1995, the average gross monthly wage of women working on a full-time basis was 76 per cent of the earnings of a man. In Belgium,

Figure 12.1 Gap between the sexes is narrowing but remains substantial: female employment rates (15–64 years), 1989 and 1999

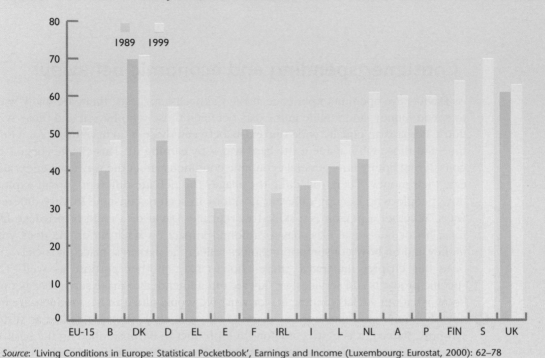

Source: 'Living Conditions in Europe: Statistical Pocketbook', Earnings and Income (Luxembourg: Eurostat, 2000): 62–78

Denmark, Luxembourg and Sweden, the average wages of women are equivalent to 84–85 per cent of men's. In Ireland, the Netherlands, and the UK, on the other hand, women's wages represent only 69–70 per cent of men's.[4] Figure 12.1 shows female employment rates (ages 15–64) for 1989 and 1999. Yet in spite of these increases in household income, women are more likely to be in part-time work, a situation which reflects the more traditional activities of caring for the household and children living at home – activities that are still seen as primarily their responsibility. Figure 12.2 shows the percentages of men and women part-time workers in a number of European countries. As discussed in the previous chapter, family situation, the number and age of children living at home and the educational level of women heavily influence their employment activities.

Yes, it pays to go to school!

Another factor that determines who gets a bigger slice of the pie is education. Although the expense of going to college often entails great sacrifice, it still pays in the long run. University and higher professional study graduates earn about 50 per cent more than those who have gone through secondary school only during the course of their lives. Close to half of the increase in consumer spending power during the 1990s came from these more highly educated groups. Figure 12.3 provides an overview of European Union earnings by level of education in 1995. Full-time employees with a tertiary education qualification earn on average considerably more than those who have completed upper secondary school (A-levels, Baccalaureate, Abitur, HBO or equivalent).

Figure 12.2 Part-time work: largely a phenomenon among women in northern Europe. Those working part-time (% of total employment), by sex, 1999

Source: Eurostat, European Labour Force Survey, 2000

Figure 12.3 Gross monthly earnings by level of education, 1995

Note: D(1) = former West Germany; D(2) = Newlander
Source: 'Social Portrait of Europe' (1998): 'The Distribution of Earnings in the European Union', No. 8/1998

To spend or not to spend, that is the question

A basic assumption of economic psychology is that consumer demand for goods and services depends on ability to buy *and* willingness to buy. While demand for necessities tends to be stable over time, other expenditures can be postponed or eliminated if people don't feel that now is a good time to spend.[5] For example, a person may decide to 'make do' with his current car for another year rather than buy a new car now.

Discretionary spending

▶ **Discretionary income** is the money available to a household over and above that required for a comfortable standard of living. European consumers are estimated to have discretionary spending power in billions of euros per year, and it is consumers aged 35–55 whose incomes are at a peak who account for the greatest amounts. As might be expected, discretionary income increases as overall income goes up. However, income distributions vary over different EU countries, with households earning more than 100,000 euros accounting for less than 5 per cent of all families. Still, they have more than a quarter of the EU's discretionary income at their disposal.[6] Within the EU, the bottom (poorest) 20 per cent of the population received only 7.6 per cent of total income in 1996, while the top (richest) 20 per cent received 39.3 per cent of total income (i.e. 5.2 times more). This gap between the most and least well-off persons (known as the *share ratio S80/S20*) is smallest in Denmark (2.9) and Austria (4.0). It is widest in the four southern member states, with Portugal recording the highest ratio (6.8). Figure 12.4 gives a graphic overview of inequity in the income distribution for all member states in 1996. While discretionary income is a powerful tool for predicting certain types of consumer behaviour, it is not always a measure for which straightforward comparisons between

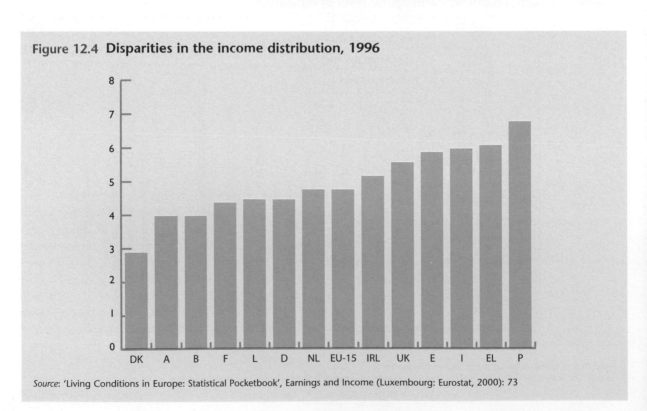

Figure 12.4 Disparities in the income distribution, 1996

Source: 'Living Conditions in Europe: Statistical Pocketbook', Earnings and Income (Luxembourg: Eurostat, 2000): 73

countries can be easily made. Factors such as different levels of sales tax (VAT) or varying levels of direct family benefits for children under 19 years living at home in various EU countries account for differences in what constitutes true discretionary income.

Individual attitudes towards money

Many consumers are entertaining doubts about their individual and collective futures, and are anxious about holding on to what they have. A consumer's anxieties about money are not necessarily related to how much he or she actually has: acquiring and managing money is more a state of mind than of wallet. Money can have a variety of complex psychological meanings: it can be equated with success or failure, social acceptability, security, love or freedom.[7] Some clinical psychologists even specialize in treating money-related disorders, and report that people feel guilty about their success and deliberately make bad investments to ease this feeling! Other clinical conditions include atephobia (fear of being ruined), harpaxophobia (fear of becoming a victim of robbers), peniaphobia (fear of poverty) and aurophobia (fear of gold).[8] The Roper/Starch survey found that security was the attribute most closely linked to the meaning of money. Other significant associations included comfort, being able to help one's children, freedom and pleasure.[9]

Consumer confidence

A consumer's beliefs about what the future holds is an indicator of **consumer confidence**, which reflects the extent to which people are optimistic or pessimistic about the future health of the economy and how they will fare in the future. These beliefs influence how much money he or she will pump into the economy when making discretionary purchases.

Many businesses take forecasts about anticipated spending very seriously, and periodic surveys attempt to 'take the pulse' of the European consumer. The Henley Centre conducts a survey of consumer confidence, as does Eurostat and the EuroMonitor. The following are the types of questions posed to consumers in these surveys:[10]

'My standard of living will change for the better over the next year.'

'My quality of life will improve over the next year.'

'I will have a lack of money when I retire.'

'I spend too much of my income, and intend to spend less next year.'

'I am concerned about the amount of free time I have.'

When people are pessimistic about their prospects and about the state of the economy, they tend to cut back their spending and take on less debt. On the other hand, when they are optimistic about the future, they tend to reduce the amount they save, take on more debt and buy discretionary items. The overall **savings rate** thus is influenced by individual consumers' pessimism or optimism about their personal circumstances (e.g. fear of being laid off vs. a sudden increase in personal wealth due to an inheritance), as well as by world events (e.g. the election of a new government or an international crisis such as the Gulf War) and cultural differences in attitudes towards saving (e.g. the Japanese have a much higher savings rate than do Europeans or Americans).[11]

Seeking value vs. quality

In an era of diminished resources, Europeans are redefining traditional relationships

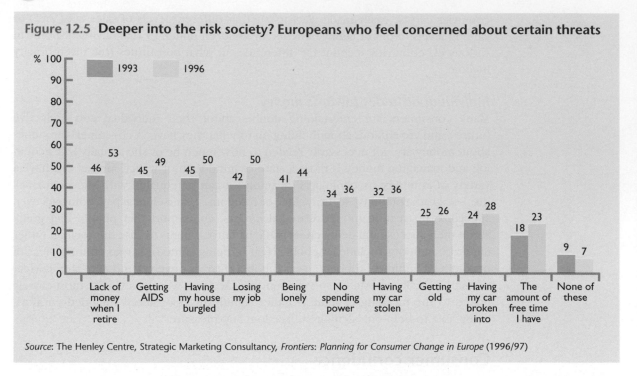

Figure 12.5 Deeper into the risk society? Europeans who feel concerned about certain threats

Source: The Henley Centre, Strategic Marketing Consultancy, *Frontiers: Planning for Consumer Change in Europe* (1996/97)

among price, value and quality. In the past (most notably in the 1980s), people seemed to be willing to pay almost anything for products and services. Consumers still claim to want quality – but at the right price. In surveys, most people report that they regret the conspicuous consumption of the 1980s and feel the need to live with less. The attitude of the 1990s was more practical and reflected a 'back to basics' orientation. People now want more hard news instead of 'hype' from advertising, and they appreciate ads that feature problem-solving tips or that save money or time. European youth (age range 12–24) in particular are more sceptical of advertising messages, relative to the total population.

Reflecting this new, more sober, state of mind, consider the findings of a large-scale survey of European households conducted by the Henley Centre to determine their priorities and concerns. Some of the findings are shown in Figure 12.5.[12]

Social class

All societies can be roughly divided into the haves and the have-nots (though sometimes 'having' is a question of degree). While social equality is a widely held value throughout Europe, the fact remains that some people seem to be more equal than others. As David's encounter with the Caldwells suggests, a consumer's standing in society, or **social class**, is determined by a complex set of variables, including income, family background and occupation.

The place one occupies in the social structure is not just an important determinant of *how much* money is spent. It also influences *how* it is spent. David was surprised that the Caldwells, who clearly had a lot of money, did not seem to flaunt it. This understated way of living is a hallmark of so-called 'old money'. People who have had it for a long time don't need to prove they've got it. In contrast, consumers who are relative newcomers to affluence might allocate the same amount of money very differently.

MARKETING OPPORTUNITY

Winston Churchill preferred his with starched linen collars and loops on the shoulders to hold up his braces. Prince Charles has his fitted in the privacy of his palace, while fashion mogul Ralph Lauren – who, you'd imagine, could get them for free at his own shop – sometimes orders dozens at a time. And then there's the rather eccentric customer who wants his to resemble Australian prisoner uniforms – but made of cream-coloured silk.

What all these people have in common – the politicians and powerbrokers, royals and the slightly offbeat – is a desire for the simple luxury of a custom-made shirt. And not just any old made-to-measure shirt: these garments must be from the famous craftsmen of Jermyn Street, whose shops in London's SW1 district cater to connoisseurs with a passion for fine tailoring and a perfect fit. At prices from £100 to £155 per shirt, depending on the cloth, and with a minimum order of between four and six, you probably can't afford to wear anything else.

Jermyn Street tailors have been practising the art of fine service and attention to detail for over a century – it's what their customers expect from the place acknowledged as the world's capital of made-to-measure shirts. 'We have created a unique market, and have attracted the top customers, who feel quite comfortable here', notes Paul Cuss, chief patternmaker at Turnbull and Asser, the holder of the coveted Royal Warrant for shirtmaking, and the shop that supplies Prince Charles and former President Ronald Reagan, among others. According to Mr Cuss, 'It's very establishment, very clubby.' With its heavy wooden furniture, stuffed hunting trophies and velvet Hapsburgian smoking jackets for sale, along with ties, bathrobes and boxer shorts and a framed picture of Winston Churchill, Turnbull and Asser's cosy emporium is a gentlemen's world straight out of *Country Life* magazine.

One can imagine the Jermyn Street of old, when landed gentry and Etonian schoolboys travelled there to buy their shirts in a rite of passage for the aristocracy, and in the process established the street's reputation. While Jermyn Street thrives on tradition, their clients come from all over the world. The French and fashion-conscious Italians come for the 'tailored English look', but the shirtmakers admit to following fashion trends: among the serious solid whites and blues are a few shocking pink, lilac and dayglow orange samples.

Precise construction of the shirt also means that it takes time to have the garment finished. After measuring, there's a wait of around two weeks for a sample to be made. Then there's a trial period of washing and wearing, to see if the fit is right. Finally, the hand-cutters and sewers get to work, and in six to eight weeks the masterpiece is ready – and you can walk proudly down the street, knowing you've joined an exclusive club whose members say price doesn't matter when it comes to style.[13]

A universal pecking order

In many animal species, a social organization develops whereby the most assertive or aggressive animals exert control over the others and have the first pick of food, living space and even mating partners. Chickens, for example, develop a clearly defined dominance–submission hierarchy. Within this hierarchy, each hen has a position in which she is submissive to all of the hens above her and dominates all of the ones below her (hence the origin of the term *pecking order*).[14]

People are no different. They also develop a pecking order where they are ranked in terms of their relative standing in society. This standing determines their access to such resources as education, housing and consumer goods. And people try to improve their ranking by moving up the social order whenever possible. This desire to improve one's lot, and often to let others know that one has done so, is at the core of many marketing strategies.

▶ While every culture has its **social hierarchies**, variations in terms of how explicit these distinctions are can be observed. Stratification of one sort or another is universal, even in societies that officially disdain such a process. For example, in China, a supposedly classless society, the children of top party officials, who are called *gaoganzidi*, irritate many Chinese. These offspring have a reputation for laziness, enjoying material pleasures and getting the best jobs by virtue of their family connections. They are thus a privileged class in a classless society.[15]

Multicultural dimensions

As the old saying goes, 'The rich get richer, and the poor get poorer.' Both the top and bottom ends of American income levels are swelling. Since 1980 the wealthiest fifth of the population has increased its income by 21 per cent, while wages for the bottom 60 per cent have stagnated or dipped. America's most powerful brands, from Levi's jeans to Ivory soap, were built on a mass marketing premise, but now that's changing. Stores such as Wal-Mart and Tiffany are reporting big earnings, whereas middle-class outlets like J. C. Penney have weak sales. Target Stores have been successful in providing upmarket brands at discount prices. Their positioning strategy as 'chic discount' is very successful. Referred to as 'tar-jay' by its many fans, Target is a Kmart for yuppies. Its bright red bull's eye logo has become a fashion statement for affordable chic.[16] This trend has led some companies to try to have their cake and eat it too by developing a two-tiered marketing strategy, in which separate plans are crafted for upmarket and downmarket consumers. For example, Walt Disney's Winnie the Pooh can be purchased as an original line-drawn figure on fine china or on pewter spoons in upmarket specialty and department stores, while a plump, cartoonlike Pooh is available on plastic key chains and polyester bed sheets at Wal-Mart. The Gap is remodelling its Banana Republic stores to make them more upmarket, and simultaneously developing its Old Navy stores for the low end.[17]

Social class affects access to resources

Just as marketers try to carve society into groups for segmentation purposes, sociologists have developed ways to describe meaningful divisions of society in terms of people's relative social and economic resources. Some of these divisions involve political power, while others revolve around purely economic distinctions. Karl Marx felt that position in a society was determined by one's relationship to the *means of production*. Some people (the haves) control resources, and they use the labour of others to preserve their privileged positions. The have-nots lack control and depend on their own labour for survival, so these people have the most to gain by changing the system. Distinctions among people that entitle some to more than others are perpetuated by those who will benefit by doing so.[18]

The sociologist Max Weber showed that the rankings people develop are not one-dimensional. Some involve prestige or 'social honour' (he called these *status groups*), some rankings focus on power (or *party*), and some revolve around wealth and property (*class*).[19]

Social class affects taste and lifestyles

The term 'social class' is now used more generally to describe the overall rank of people in a society. People who are grouped within the same social class are approximately equal in terms of their social standing in the community. They work in roughly similar occupations, and they tend to have similar lifestyles by virtue of their income levels and common tastes. These people tend to socialize with one another and share many ideas and values regarding the way life should be lived.[20]

MARKETING PITFALL

Stemar gazes over the expansive new verandah of his summer cottage on a tranquil island off Norway's south-eastern coast, chatting on his cell phone. The 50-year-old Oslo accountant recently added a host of amenities such as hot running water to his *hytte*, as Norwegians call their rustic summer cabins. Now he plans to put in a paved road to his front door and a swimming pool in the garden. 'There's nothing wrong with a little comfort', says Stemar. Well, maybe not in other summer playgrounds such as France's Côte d'Azur, but here in austere Norway, the words 'comfort' and 'vacation' are not synonymous. Thanks to the recent oil boom, many Norwegians are spending their new-found wealth upgrading spartan summer chalets with tennis courts, jacuzzis and even helipads. But in a country where simplicity and frugality are cherished virtues, and egalitarianism is strong, the display of wealth and money is suspect. Some politicians have suggested bulldozing the houses of the wealthy if they block access to the sea, and trade union leaders have blasted a new breed of Norwegians who favour showy yachts and life in the fast lane, and who build fences around private property.

'The rich can be quite vulgar', grumbles Stemar's neighbour Brit, who demanded that he trim a metre or so off his verandah because she and her husband, Gustav, could see it from their cabin lower down the hill. Both teachers, Brit and Gustav are nearing retirement, and have a more traditional Norwegian view of how to spend their summer, and how to spend their money. At stake, many say, are Norwegian ideals of equality and social democracy. These dictate that all Norwegians should have the same quality of life and share the national wealth equally. Norwegians champion austerity because they haven't always been prosperous. Before oil was discovered about 20 years ago, only a few families were considered wealthy. This frugality is obvious even in the capital, Oslo. For all the new oil money, plus low inflation, the city isn't a brash 'Kuwait of the North'.

Summer chalets should reflect the spartan mood, diehards say, and vacation activities must be limited. Scraping down paint is popular, as is hammering down loose floorboards. So is swimming in lakes, fishing for supper and chopping wood. But not much else. As another neighbour, Aase, puts it: 'We like to, uh, sit here. I'd like the rich to stay away from here. They would ruin the neighbourhood.'[21]

Social class is as much a state of being as it is of having: as David saw, class is also a question of what one *does* with one's money and how one defines one's role in society. Although people may not like the idea that some members of society are better off or 'different' from others, most consumers do acknowledge the existence of different classes and the effect of class membership on consumption. As one wealthy woman observed when asked to define social class: 'I would suppose social class means where you went to school and how far. Your intelligence. Where you live ... Where you send your children to school. The hobbies you have. Skiing, for example, is higher than the snowmobile ... It can't be [just] money, because nobody ever knows that about you for sure.'[22]

Social stratification

In college, some students always seem to be more popular than others. They have access to many resources, such as special privileges, expensive cars, generous allowances or dates with other equally popular classmates. At work, some people are put on the fast track and are promoted to prestige jobs, given higher salaries and perhaps such perks as a parking space, a large office or the keys to the executive bathroom.

In virtually every context, some people seem to be ranked higher than others. Patterns of social arrangements evolve whereby some members get more resources than others by virtue of their relative standing, power and/or control in the group.[23] The phenomenon of **social stratification** refers to this creation of artificial divisions in a society: 'those processes in a social system by which scarce and valuable resources are distributed unequally to status positions that become more or less permanently ranked in terms of the share of valuable resources each receives'.[24]

Achieved vs. ascribed status

If you recall groups you've belonged to, both large and small, you'll probably agree that in many instances some members seem to get more than their fair share while others are not so lucky. Some of these resources may have gone to people who earned them through hard work or diligence. This allocation is due to *achieved status*. Other rewards may have been obtained because the person was lucky enough to be born rich or beautiful. Such good fortune reflects *ascribed status*.

Whether rewards go to the 'best and the brightest' or to someone who happens to be related to the boss, allocations are rarely equal within a social group. Most groups exhibit a structure, or status hierarchy, in which some members are somehow better off than others. They may have more authority or power, or they are simply more liked or respected.

Class structure around the world

Every society has some type of hierarchical class structure, where people's access to products and services is determined by their resources and social standing. Of course, the specific 'markers' of success depend on what is valued in each culture. For the Chinese, who are just beginning to experience the bounties of capitalism, one marker of success is hiring a bodyguard to protect oneself and one's newly acquired possessions![25]

Japan is a highly status-conscious society, where upmarket, designer labels are popular and new forms of status are always being sought. To the Japanese, owning a traditional rock garden, formerly a vehicle for leisure and tranquillity, has become a coveted item. Possession of a rock garden implies inherited wealth, since aristocrats traditionally were patrons of the arts. In addition, considerable assets are required to afford the necessary land in a country where property is extraordinarily expensive. The scarcity of land also helps to explain why the Japanese are fanatic golfers: since a golf course takes up so much space, membership of a golf club is extremely valuable.[26]

On the other side of the world from Japan, there is always England: England is also a class-conscious country, and at least until recently, consumption patterns were preordained in terms of one's inherited position and family background. Members of the upper class were educated at public schools such as Eton and Harrow, and had a distinctive accent. Remnants of this rigid class structure can still be found. 'Hooray Henrys' (wealthy young men) play polo at Windsor and hereditary peers still sit in the House of Lords.

The dominance of inherited wealth appears to be fading in Britain's traditionally aristocratic society. According to a survey, 86 of the 200 wealthiest people in England made their money the old-fashioned way: they earned it. Even the sanctity of the Royal Family, which epitomizes the aristocracy, has been diluted because of tabloid exposure and the antics of younger family members who have been transformed into celebrities more like rock stars than royalty.[27]

Social mobility

To what degree do people tend to change their social class? In some traditional societies social class is very difficult to change, but in Europe, any man or woman can become prime minister. **Social mobility** refers to the 'passage of individuals from one social class to another'.[28]

This passage can be upward, downward or even horizontal. *Horizontal mobility* refers to movement from one position to another roughly equivalent in social status, like becoming a nurse instead of a junior school teacher. *Downward mobility* is, of course, not very desirable, but this pattern is unfortunately quite evident in recent years as redundant workers have been forced to join the dole queue or have joined the ranks of the homeless. In the United States, a conservative estimate is that 600,000 Americans are homeless on a given day.[29]

Despite that discouraging trend, demographics decree that there must be *upward mobility* in European society. The middle and upper classes reproduce less than the lower classes (an effect known as *differential fertility*), and they tend to restrict family size below replacement level. Therefore, so the reasoning goes, positions of higher status over time must be filled by those of lower status.[30] Overall, though, the offspring of blue-collar consumers tend also to be blue-collar while the offspring of white-collar consumers tend also to be white-collar.[31] People tend to improve their positions over time, but these increases are not usually dramatic enough to catapult them from one social class to another.

Components of social class

When we think about a person's social class, there are a number of pieces of information we can consider. Two major ones are occupation and income. A third important factor is educational attainment, which is strongly related to income and occupation.

Occupational prestige

In a system where (like it or not) a consumer is defined to a great extent by what he or she does for a living, *occupational prestige* is one way to evaluate the 'worth' of people. Hierarchies of occupational prestige tend to be quite stable over time, and they also tend to be similar in different societies. Similarities in occupational prestige have been found in countries as diverse as Brazil, Ghana, Guam, Japan and Turkey.[32]

A typical ranking includes a variety of professional and business occupations at the top (e.g. director of a large corporation, doctor or college lecturer), while those jobs hovering near the bottom include shoe shiner, unskilled labourer and dustman. Because a person's occupation tends to be strongly linked to his or her use of leisure time, allocation of family resources, political orientation, and so on, this variable is often considered to be the single best indicator of social class.

Income

The distribution of wealth is of great interest to social scientists and to marketers, since it determines which groups have the greatest buying power and market potential. Wealth is by no means distributed evenly across the classes. While there is a more equitable distribution of wealth across European countries relative to Latin America, Asia and America (the top fifth of the population in the US controls about 75 per cent of all assets),[33] there is still a disportionate share of wealth controlled by a small segment of the European population. As we have seen, income *per se* is often not a very good indicator of social class, since the way money is spent is more telling. Still, people need money to allow them to obtain the goods and services that they need to express their tastes, so obviously income is still very important.

The relationship between income and social class

Although consumers tend to equate money with class, the precise relationship between other aspects of social class and income is not clear and has been the subject of debate among social scientists.[34] The two are by no means synonymous, which is why many people with a lot of money try to use it to improve their social class.

One problem is that even if a family increases household income by adding wage-earners, each additional job is likely to be of lower status. For example, a housewife who gets a part-time job is not as likely to get one that is of equal or greater status than the primary wage-earner's. In addition, the extra money earned may not be pooled for the common good of the family. Instead it may be used by the individual for his or her own personal spending. More money does not then result in increased status or changes in consumption patterns, since it tends to be devoted to buying more of the same rather than upgrading to higher-status products.[35]

The following general conclusions can be made regarding the relative value of social class (i.e. place of residence, occupation, cultural interests, etc.) vs. income in predicting consumer behaviour:

● Social class appears to be a better predictor of purchases that have symbolic aspects, but low-to-moderate prices (e.g. cosmetics, alcohol).

● Income is a better predictor of major expenditures that do not have status or symbolic aspects (e.g. major appliances).

● Social class and income data together are better predictors of purchases of expensive, symbolic products (e.g. cars, homes, luxury goods).[36]

Measurement of social class

Because social class is a complex concept which depends on a number of factors, not surprisingly it has proved difficult to measure. Early measures included the Index of Status Characteristics developed in the 1940s and the Index of Social Position developed by Hollingshead in the 1950s.[37] These indices used various combinations of individual characteristics (e.g. income, type of housing) to arrive at a label of class standing. The accuracy of these composites is still a subject of debate among researchers; one recent study claimed that for segmentation purposes, raw education and income measures work as well as composite status measures.[38]

Blue-collar workers with relatively high-income jobs still tend to view themselves as working-class, even though their income levels may be equivalent to many white-collar workers.[39] This fact reinforces the idea that the labels 'working-class' or 'middle-class' are very subjective. Their meanings say at least as much about self-identity as they do about economic well-being.

Problems with measures of social class

Market researchers were among the first to propose that people from different social classes can be distinguished from each other in important ways. While some of these dimensions still exist, others have changed.[40] Unfortunately, many of these measures are badly dated and are not as valid today for a variety of reasons, four of which are discussed here.[41]

Most measures of social class were designed to accommodate the traditional nuclear family, with a male wage-earner in the middle of his career and a female full-time homemaker. Such measures have trouble accounting for two-income families, young singles living alone, or households headed by women which are so prevalent in today's society (see Chapter 11).

Another problem with measuring social class is attributable to the increasing anonymity of our society. Earlier studies relied on the *reputational method*, where extensive interviewing was done within a community to determine the reputations and backgrounds of individuals. This information, coupled with the tracing of interaction patterns among people, provided a very comprehensive view of social standing within a community.

This approach is virtually impossible to implement in most communities today. One compromise is to interview individuals to obtain demographic data and to combine these data with the subjective impressions of the interviewer regarding the person's possessions and standard of living. An example of this approach appears in Figure 12.6. Note that the accuracy of this questionnaire relies largely on the interviewer's judgement, especially regarding the quality of the respondent's neighbourhood. These impressions are in danger of being biased by the interviewer's own circumstances, which may affect his or her standard of comparison. This potential problem highlights the need for adequate training of interviewers, as well as for some attempt to cross-validate such data, possibly by employing multiple judges to rate the same area.

One problem with assigning people to a social class is that they may not be equal in their standing on all of the relevant dimensions. A person might come from a low-status ethnic group but have a high-status job, while another may live in a fashionable part of town but did not complete secondary school. The concept of **status crystallization** was developed to assess the impact of inconsistency on the self and social behaviour.[42] It was thought that since the rewards from each part of such an 'unbalanced' person's life would be variable and unpredictable, stress would result. People who exhibit such inconsistencies tend to be more receptive to social change than are those whose identities are more firmly rooted.

A related problem occurs when a person's social class standing creates expectations that are not met. Some people find themselves in the not unhappy position of making more money than is expected of those in their social class. This situation is known as an *overprivileged condition* and is usually defined as an income that is at least 25–30 per cent over the median for one's class.[43] In contrast, *underprivileged* consumers, who earn at least 15 per cent less than the median, must often devote their consumption priorities to sacrificing in order to maintain the appearance of living up to class expectations.

Lottery winners are examples of consumers who become overprivileged overnight. As attractive as winning is to many people, it has its problems. Consumers with a certain standard of living and level of expectations may have trouble adapting to sudden affluence and engage in flamboyant and irresponsible displays of wealth. Ironically, it is not unusual for lottery winners to report feelings of depression in the months after the win. They may have trouble adjusting to an unfa-

Figure 12.6 Living room clusters and social class

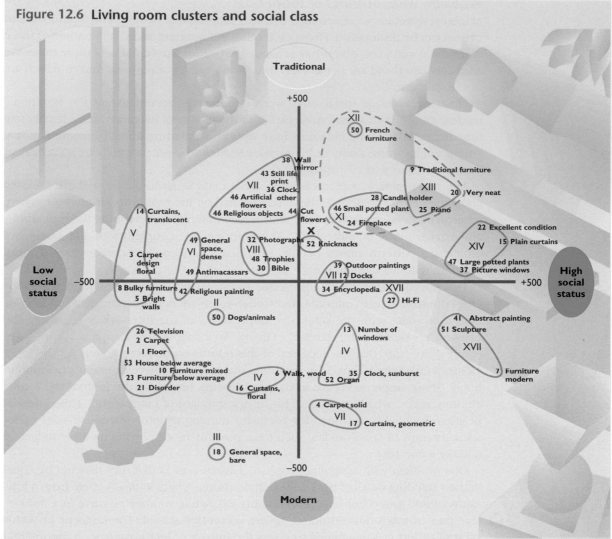

Source: Edward O. Laumann and James S. House, 'Living Room Styles and Social Attributes: The Patterning of Material Artifacts in a Modern Urban Community', *Sociology and Social Research* 54 (April 1970): 321–42.

miliar world, and they frequently experience pressure from friends, relatives and business people to 'share the wealth'.

One New York winner who was featured prominently in the media is a case in point. He was employed as a mail porter until he won $5 million. After winning the lottery, he divorced his wife and married his girlfriend. She wore a $12,000 gown to the ceremony and the couple arrived in a horse-drawn carriage. Other purchases included a Cadillac with a Rolls-Royce grill and a $5000 car phone. He later denied rumours that he was heavily in debt due to his extravagant spending.[44]

The traditional assumption is that husbands define a family's social class, while wives must live it. Women borrow their social status from their husbands.[45] Indeed, the evidence indicates that physically attractive women tend to 'marry up' to a greater extent than attractive men. Women trade the resource of sexual appeal, which historically has been one of the few assets they were allowed to possess, for the economic resources of men.[46] The accuracy of this assumption in today's world must be questioned. Many women now contribute equally to the family's well-being and work in positions of comparable or even greater status than their spouses. *Cosmopolitan* magazine offered this revelation: 'Women who've become liberated enough to marry any man they please, regardless of his social position, report how much more fun and spontaneous their relationships with men have become now that they no longer view men only in terms of their power symbols.'[47]

Employed women tend to average both their own and their husband's respective positions when estimating their own subjective status.[48] Nevertheless, a prospective spouse's social class is often an important 'product attribute' when evaluating alternatives in the interpersonal marketplace (as David and Julia were to find out). *Cosmopolitan* also discussed this dilemma, implying that social class differences are still an issue in the mating game: 'You've met the (almost) perfect man. You both adore Dashiell Hammett thrillers, Mozart, and tennis. He taught you to jet ski; you taught him the virtues of tofu . . . The problem? You're an executive earning ninety-thousand dollars a year. He's a taxi driver . . .'[49]

Problems with social class segmentation: a summary

Social class remains an important way to categorize consumers. Many marketing strategies do target different social classes. However, marketers have failed to use social class information as effectively as they could for the following reasons:

- They have ignored status inconsistency.
- They have ignored intergenerational mobility.
- They have ignored subjective social class (i.e. the class a consumer identifies with rather than the one he or she objectively belongs to).
- They have ignored consumers' aspirations to change their class standing.
- They have ignored the social status of working wives.

How social class affects purchase decisions

Different products and stores are perceived by consumers to be appropriate for certain social classes.[50] Working-class consumers tend to evaluate products in more utilitarian terms such as sturdiness or comfort rather than style or fashionability. They are less likely to experiment with new products or styles, such as modern furniture or coloured appliances.[51] In contrast, more affluent people tend to be concerned about appearance and body image, so they are more avid consumers of diet foods and drinks compared to people in small, working-class towns. These differences mean that the cola market, for example, can be segmented by social class.[52]

Class differences in worldview

A major social class difference involves the *worldview* of consumers. The world of the working class (including the lower-middle class) is more intimate and constricted. For example, working-class men are likely to name local sports figures as heroes and are less likely to take long holidays in out-of-the way places.[53] Immediate needs, such as a new refrigerator or TV, tend to dictate buying behaviour for these consumers, while the higher classes tend to focus on more long-term goals, such as saving for college fees or retirement.[54]

Working-class consumers depend heavily on relatives for emotional support and tend to orient themselves in terms of the community rather than the world at large. They are more likely to be conservative and family-oriented. Maintaining the appearance of one's home and property is a priority, regardless of the size of the house.

While they would like to have more in the way of material goods, working-class people do not necessarily envy those who rank above them in social standing.[55] The maintenance of a high-status lifestyle is sometimes not seen as worth the effort. As one blue-collar consumer commented: 'Life is very hectic for those people. There are more breakdowns and alcoholism. It must be very hard to sustain the status, the clothes, the parties that are expected. I don't think I'd want to take their place.'[56] Figure 12.7 shows the influences that income levels and age have on our concerns about 'the hectic life'.[57]

The blue-collar consumer quoted here may be right. While good things appear to go hand in hand with higher status and wealth, the picture is not that clear. The social scientist Emile Durkheim observed that suicide rates are much higher among the wealthy. He wrote in 1897, 'the possessors of most comfort suffer most'.[58] The quest for riches has the potential to result in depression, deviant behaviour and ruin. In fact, a recent survey of affluent American consumers (they made an average of $176,000 a year) supports this notion. Although these people are in the top 2.5 per cent income bracket in America, only 14 per cent said they are very well off.[59]

The concept of a **taste culture**, which differentiates people in terms of their aesthetic and intellectual preferences, is helpful in understanding the important yet subtle distinctions in consumption choices among the social classes. Taste cultures largely reflect education (and are also income-related).[60] A distinction is often made between low-culture and high-culture groups (this is discussed in more detail in Chapter 16).

While such perspectives have met with criticism due to the implicit value judge-

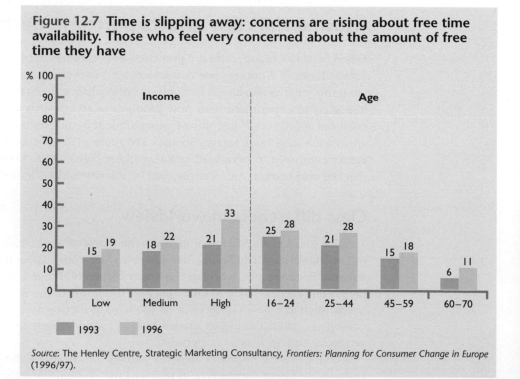

Figure 12.7 Time is slipping away: concerns are rising about free time availability. Those who feel very concerned about the amount of free time they have

Source: The Henley Centre, Strategic Marketing Consultancy, *Frontiers: Planning for Consumer Change in Europe* (1996/97).

ments involved, they are valuable because they recognize the existence of groupings based on shared tastes in literature, art, home decoration, and so on. In one of the classic studies of social differences in taste, researchers catalogued homeowners' possessions while asking more typical questions about income and occupation. Clusters of furnishings and decorative items which seemed to appear together with some regularity were identified, and different clusters were found depending on the consumer's social status. For example, religious objects, artificial flowers and still-life portraits tended to be found together in relatively lower-status living rooms, while a cluster containing abstract paintings, sculptures and modern furniture was more likely to appear in a higher-status home (see Figure 12.6).[61]

Another approach to social class focuses on differences in the types of *codes* (the ways meanings are expressed and interpreted by consumers) used within different social strata. Discovery of these codes is valuable to marketers, since this knowledge allows them to communicate to markets using concepts and terms most likely to be understood and appreciated by specific consumers.

The nature of these codes varies among social classes. **Restricted codes** are dominant among the working class, while elaborated codes tend to be used by the middle and upper classes. Restricted codes focus on the content of objects, not on relationships among objects. **Elaborated codes**, in contrast, are more complex and depend upon a more sophisticated worldview. Some differences between these two general types of codes are provided in Table 12.1. As this table indicates, these code differ-

Table 12.1 Effects of restricted versus elaborated codes

	Restricted codes	*Elaborated codes*
General characteristics	Emphasize description and contents of objects Have implicit meanings (context dependent)	Emphasize analysis and interrelationships between objects; i.e. hierarchical organization and instrumental connections Have explicit meanings
Language	Use few qualifiers, i.e. few adjectives or adverbs Use concrete, descriptive, tangible symbolism	Have language rich in personal, individual qualifiers Use large vocabulary, complex conceptual hierarchy
Social relationships	Stress attributes of individuals over formal roles	Stress formal role structure, instrumental relationships
Time	Focus on present; have only general notion of future	Focus on instrumental relationship between present activities and future rewards
Physical space	Locate rooms, spaces in context of other rooms and places: e.g. 'front room', 'corner shop'	Identify rooms, spaces in terms of usage; formal ordering of spaces: e.g. 'dining room', 'financial district'
Implications for marketers	Stress inherent product quality, contents (or trustworthiness, goodness of 'real-type'), spokesperson Stress implicit fit of product with total lifestyle Use simple adjectives, descriptors	Stress differences, advantages *vis-à-vis* other products in terms of some autonomous evaluation criteria Stress product's instrumental ties to distant benefits Use complex adjectives, descriptors

Source: Adapted from Jeffrey F. Durgee, 'How Consumer Sub-Cultures Code Reality: A Look at Some Code Types', in Richard J. Lutz, ed., *Advances in Consumer Research* 13 (Provo, UT: Association for Consumer Research, 1986): 332.

ences extend to the way consumers approach such basic concepts as time, social relationships and objects.

Marketing appeals that are constructed with these differences in mind will result in quite different messages. For example, a life insurance ad targeted at a lower-class person might depict in simple, straightforward terms a hard-working family man who feels good immediately after purchasing a policy. An upmarket appeal might depict a more affluent older couple surrounded by photos of their children and grandchildren and contain extensive copy emphasizing the satisfaction that comes from planning for the future and highlighting the benefits of a whole-life insurance policy.

Targeting the poor

While poor people obviously have less to spend than rich ones, they have the same basic needs as everyone else. Low-income families purchase such staples as milk, bread and tea at the same rates as average-income families. And minimum wage level households spend a greater than average share on out-of-pocket health care costs, rent, and food consumed at home.

The unemployed do feel alienated in a consumer society, since they are unable to obtain many of the items that our culture tells us we 'need' to be successful. However, idealized advertising portrayals don't seem to appeal to low-end consumers who have been interviewed by researchers. Apparently, one way to preserve self-esteem is by placing oneself outside the culture of consumption and emphasizing the value of a simple way of life with less emphasis on materialism. In some cases, they enjoy the advertising as entertainment without actually yearning for the products; a comment by one 32-year-old British woman is typical: 'They're not aimed at me, definitely not. It's fine to look at them, but they're not aimed at me so in the main I just pass over them.'[62]

Some marketers are developing products and services for low-income consumers. These strategies may be obvious in some cases (or even boarding on the insulting), as when S. C. Johnson & Son, manufacturers of Raid insect spray, regularly hosts 'cockroach evictions' at inner-city housing developments. Other strategies raise important ethical issues, especially when marketers of so-called 'sin products' such as alcohol and tobacco single out what many feel is a vulnerable audience. For example, manufacturers of malt liquors and fortified wines concentrate their efforts in poor areas where they know their products sell best.

Targeting the rich

We live in an age where elite department stores sell Donna Karan and Calvin Klein Barbies, and Mattel's Pink Splendor Barbie comes complete with crystal jewellery and a bouffant gown sewn with 24-carat threads.[63] To dress that 'living doll', Victoria's Secret offers its Million Dollar Miracle Bra, with over 100 carats of real diamonds.[64] *Somebody* must be buying this stuff . . .

Many marketers try to target affluent markets. This practice often makes sense, since these consumers obviously have the resources to expend on costly products (often with higher profit margins). *The Robb Report*, a magazine targeted to the affluent (average reader income is $755,000), in 1996 estimated that 4.8 million American households had a net worth of at least $1 million, up 118 per cent from 1992. The magazine segments the wealthy into three markets: the marginally rich (household income $70,000–$99,999), the comfortably rich (income of $100,000–$249,000), and the super rich ($250,000+).[65]

However, it is a mistake to assume that everyone with a high income should be placed in the same market segment. As noted earlier, social class involves more than absolute income: it is also a way of life, and affluent consumers' interests and spending priorities are significantly affected by such factors as where they got their money, how they got it, and how long they have had it.[66] For example, the marginally rich tend to prefer sporting events to cultural activities, and are only half as likely as the super rich to frequent art galleries or the opera.[67]

The rich *are* different. But they are different from one another as well. Income alone is not a good predictor of consumer behaviour, which reminds us that the wealthy can be further segmented in terms of attitudes, values and preferences. For example, according to industry experts drivers in the luxury car market can be segmented as follows:

● Cadillac owners want to be chauffeured. They are not very attentive to styling details or the car's colour. Their primary interests are in comfort and the impression they make on others.

● Porsche owners prefer to drive themselves. They are more interested in performance than luxury. The colour red is a favourite.

● Jaguar owners are more austere. They are interested in elegance and prefer darker colours.

● Mercedes owners like to feel they are in control. They tend to prefer muted shades of tan, grey and silver.

Multicultural dimensions

In a land where one-child families are the rule, Chinese parents spare few expenses when bringing up baby. They want to show off their pampered child and are eager to surround their 'little emperors' with status goods. To meet this need, foreign companies are rushing in, hawking the staples of Western baby care from disposable nappies to Disney cot sheets. These items are expensive luxuries in China, and plenty of families are splurging. Chinese families spend one-third to one-half of their disposable income on their children, according to industry estimates. The Disney Babies line of T-shirts, rattles and cot linens – all emblazoned with likenesses of baby Mickey Mouse and other familiar characters – are available in department stores in a dozen or so Chinese cities. These products are true extravagances: a Disney cotton T-shirt, for example, sells for the local equivalent of about $7.25–$8.45, compared to $1.20 for a Chinese-made shirt. But as a Disney spokesman observed, 'New parents are willing to pay the extra. Mickey is portrayed as fun and intelligent in China – characteristics parents want for their children.'[68]

Old money

When people have enough money for all intents and purposes to buy just about anything they want, ironically social distinctions no longer revolve around the amount of money one has. Instead, it appears to be important to consider *where* the money came from and *how* it is spent. The 'top out-of-sight class' (such as Julia's parents) live primarily on inherited money. People who have made vast amounts of money from their own labour do not tend to be included in this select group, though their flamboyant consumption patterns may represent an attempt to prove their wealth.[69] The mere presence of wealth is thus not sufficient to achieve social prominence. It must be accompanied by a family history of public service and philanthropy, which is often manifested in tangible markers that enable these donors to achieve a kind of immortality (e.g. Rockefeller University or the Whitney Museum).[70] 'Old money' consumers tend to make distinctions among themselves in terms of ancestry and lineage rather than wealth.[71] Old money people (like the Caldwells) are secure in their status. In a sense, they have been trained their whole lives to be rich.

The nouveaux riches

Other wealthy people do not know how to be rich. The Horatio Alger myth, where a person goes from 'rags to riches' through hard work and a bit of luck, is still a powerful force in Western society and, more recently, in Asian societies as well. Although many people do in fact become 'self-made millionaires', they often encounter a problem (although not the worst problem one could think of!) after they have become wealthy and have changed their social status: consumers who have achieved extreme wealth and have relatively recently become members of upper social classes are known as the *nouveaux riches*, a term that is sometimes used in a derogatory manner to describe newcomers to the world of wealth.

The *nouveau riche* phenomenon is also widespread in Russia and other eastern European countries, where the transition to capitalism has paved the way for a new class of wealthy consumers who are spending lavishly on luxury items. One study of wealthy Russians identified a group of 'super-spenders', who earn about $1000 a month and spend as much on discretionary items as they do on rent. They would like to spend more money, but are frustrated by the lack of quality products and services available to them![72]

MARKETING OPPORTUNITY

In a sixteenth-century fortress in Florence, the semi-annual Florence children's fashion show is on, and retail buyers from around the world are moving from one designer's booth to another, putting together their Spring 2001 lines. However, down in the basement, in an isolated booth, only buyers who have RSVP'd are allowed inside, and then only after entering a security code into a computer. Once in, they are served drinks in gold-rimmed goblets, and seated in gold chairs as they view video screens showing children playing and lounging in clothes that are elegant, understated, exquisitely detailed – and priced at hundreds of euros apiece. There are no actual clothes on display in the booth, nor order forms, nor any price lists. Such commercial touches are deemed *déclassé* by the creators of I Pinco Pallino.

'Definitely to my heart, our clothes are art,' says Stefano Cavalleri, the firm's 49-year-old founder. 'Extending our image is the key point, not selling more clothes.' But Pinco is indeed selling clothes. In a market where people have more money than ever and are always looking for new ways to spend it, Pinco is suddenly hot. These aren't children's clothes for everyone, not even among the rich. The target market: mothers who, in the words of the buyers thronging the Pinco booth, regard their children as 'fashion accessories'. The fashion house turns out some of the most expensive children's clothes available anywhere. A pale green organza dress embellished with hand-embroidered silk goes for 700 euros. Dressing a child in a complete Pinco ensemble – featuring jacket, handbag, shoes and hat in signature silks and laces with detailed embroidery and sequins – will run into well over 1100 euros. Already selling his creations at only the most fashionable of department stores and boutiques in Europe and America, Mr Cavalleri is working on a plan to open a Pinco boutique on Manhattan's Upper East Side in 2002, where he vows to introduce New Yorkers to his 'fairy-tale world'.[73]

Alas, many *nouveaux riches* are plagued by *status anxiety*. They monitor the cultural environment to ensure that they are doing the 'right' thing, wearing the 'right' clothes', being seen in the 'right places', using the 'right' caterer, and so on.[74]

Flamboyant consumption can thus be viewed as a form of symbolic self-completion, where the excessive display of symbols thought to denote 'class' is used to make up for an internal lack of assurance about the 'correct' way to behave.[75]

The 'Get Set'

While the possession of wealth is clearly an important dimension of affluence, this quality may be as much determined by attitudes towards consumption as it is by level of income. Some marketers have identified a consumer segment composed of well-off, but not rich, people who desire the best products and services, even though they may have to be more selective about those items they are able to buy. These consumers are realistic about what they can afford and prefer to sacrifice in some areas so that they can have the best in others. Various advertising and marketing research agencies have given this segment such labels as the *Influentials*, the *New Grown-Ups* and the *Get Set*.

While many upper-class brands tried in the past to downmarket themselves to attract the mass market, there are some indications that this strategy is reversing. Because of the Get Set's emphasis on quality, one scenario is that marketers will encourage the masses to 'buy up' into products associated with the upper classes, even if they are forced to buy less. A print campaign for Waterford Crystal exemplifies this approach. The theme line, 'Steadfast in a world of wavering standards', is calculated to appeal to consumers who desire authenticity and lasting value.[76]

Status symbols

People have a deep-seated tendency to evaluate themselves, their professional accomplishments, their material well-being, and so on, in relation to others. The popular phrase 'keeping up with the Joneses' (in Japan it's 'keeping up with the Satos') refers to the comparison between one's standard of living and that of one's neighbours.

Satisfaction is a relative concept, however. We hold ourselves to a standard defined by others that is constantly changing. Unfortunately, a major motivation for the purchase and display of products is not to enjoy them, but rather to let others know that we can afford them. In other words, these products function as status symbols. The desire to accumulate these 'badges of achievement' is summarized by the slogan 'He who dies with the most toys, wins'. Status-seeking is a significant source of motivation to procure appropriate products and services that the user hopes will let others know that he or she has 'made it'.

Conspicuous consumption

The motivation to consume for the sake of consuming was first discussed by the social analyst Thorstein Veblen at the turn of the century. Veblen felt that a major role of products was for **invidious distinction** – they are used to inspire envy in others through display of wealth or power. Veblen coined the term **conspicuous consumption** to refer to people's desire to provide prominent visible evidence of their ability to afford luxury goods. Veblen's work was motivated by the excesses of his time. He wrote in the era of the robber barons, where the likes of J. P. Morgan, Henry Clay Frick, William Vanderbilt and others were building massive financial empires and flaunting their wealth by throwing lavish parties. Some of these events of excess became legendary, as described in this account:

there were tales, repeated in the newspapers, of dinners on horseback; of banquets for pet dogs; of hundred-dollar bills folded into guests' dinner napkins; of a hostess who attracted attention by seating a chimpanzee at her table; of centerpieces in which lightly clad living maidens swam in glass tanks, or emerged from huge pies; of parties at which cigars were ceremoniously lighted with flaming banknotes of large denominations.[77]

The trophy wife

This flaunting of one's possessions even extended to wives: Veblen criticized the 'decorative' role women were often forced to play as they were bestowed with expensive clothes, pretentious homes and a life of leisure as a way to advertise the wealth of their husbands – a sort of 'walking advertisement'. Such fashions as high-heeled shoes, tight corsets, billowing trains on dresses and elaborate hairstyles all conspired to ensure that wealthy women could barely move without assistance, much less perform manual labour. Similarly, the Chinese practice of foot-binding turned women into cripples, who had to be carried from place to place.

The modern potlatch

Veblen was inspired by anthropological studies of the Kwakiutl Indians, who lived in the American Pacific North-west. These Indians had a ceremony called a **potlatch**, a feast where the host showed off his wealth and gave extravagant presents to the guests. The more one gave away, the better one looked to the others. Sometimes, the host would use an even more radical strategy to flaunt his wealth. He would publicly destroy some of his property to demonstrate how much he had.

This ritual was also used as a social weapon: since guests were expected to reciprocate, a poorer rival could be humiliated by being invited to a lavish potlatch. The need to give away as much as the host, even though he could not afford it, would essentially force the hapless guest into bankruptcy. If this practice sounds 'primitive', think for a moment about many modern weddings. Parents commonly invest huge sums of money to throw a lavish party and compete with others for the distinction of giving their daughter the 'best' or most extravagant wedding, even if they have to save for 20 years to do so.

The leisure class

This process of conspicuous consumption was, for Veblen, most evident among what he termed the *leisure class*, people for whom productive work is taboo. In Marxist terms, this reflects a desire to link oneself to ownership or control of the means of production, rather than to the production itself. Any evidence that one actually has to work for a living is to be shunned, as suggested by the term the 'idle rich'.

Like the potlatch ritual, the desire to convince others that one has a surplus of resources creates the need for evidence of this abundance. Accordingly, priority is given to consumption activities that use up as many resources as possible in non-constructive pursuits. This *conspicuous waste* in turn shows others that one has the assets to spare. Veblen noted that 'we are told of certain Polynesian chiefs, who, under the stress of good form, preferred to starve rather than carry their food to their mouths with their own hands'.[78]

The death – and rebirth – of status symbols

While ostentatious products fell out of favour in the early part of the 1990s, later in the decade there was a resurgence of interest in luxury goods. European companies such as Hermes International, LVMH Hennesey Louis Vuitton and Baccarat enjoyed

The tanning salon industry may be said to owe its success to consumers' desire to pay for the illusion that they have idle time to soak up the sun.

© Tim Barnwell/Stock Boston.

MARKETING OPPORTUNITY

Consolidating for luxury

The luxury goods sector in Europe is in the midst of an important consolidation, as smaller groups find it increasingly difficult to compete with bigger rivals in terms of advertising spending, retail networks and production capacity. As a result, groups such as French luxury goods giant LVMH, Moet Hennessy and Gucci have been buying up smaller names over the past years. Perhaps the biggest 'fashion family' is LMVH, with its stable of fashion brands including Louis Vuitton, Christian Dior, Givenchy, Christian Lacroix, Celine, Loewe, Kenzo, Fendi and Emilio Pucci.

In an effort to take full control of production in order to maintain high standards of quality and to meet rigorous delivery schedules demanded by global retail customers, Giorgio Armani SpA recently established a joint venture with Italian menswear group Ermenegildo Zagna SpA to produce one of its menswear lines. As the wealthy become more attracted to yachting, the yachtmaker Swan has been bought by fashion house Leonardo Ferragamo to close the gap between high fashion and the high seas.[79]

sales gains of between 13 and 16 per cent, as affluent consumers once again indulged their desires for the finer things in life. One market researcher termed this trend 'the pleasure revenge' – people were tired of buying moderately, eating low-fat foods, and so on, and as a result sales boomed for self-indulgent products from fur coats to premium ice creams and caviar. As the Chairman of LVMH put it, 'The appetite for luxury is as strong as ever. The only difference is that in the 1980s, people would put a luxury trademark on anything. Today only the best sells.'[80]

Parody display

As the competition to accumulate status symbols escalates, sometimes the best tactic is to switch gears and go into reverse. One way to do this is to deliberately *avoid* status symbols – that is, to seek status by mocking it. This sophisticated form of conspicuous consumption has been termed **parody display**.[81] A good example of parody display is the home-furnishing style known as High Tech, which was in vogue in America a few years ago. This motif incorporated the use of industrial equipment (e.g. floors were covered with plates used on the decks of destroyers), and pipes and support beams were deliberately exposed.[82] This decorating strategy was intended to show that one is so witty and 'in the know' that status symbols aren't necessary. Hence, the popularity of old, torn blue jeans and 'utility' vehicles such as jeeps among the upper classes. 'True' status is thus shown by the adoption of product symbolism that is deliberately not fashionable.

Chapter summary

- The field of behavioural economics considers how consumers decide what to do with their money. In particular, *discretionary expenditures* are made only when people are able and willing to spend money on items above and beyond their basic needs. *Consumer confidence* – the state of mind consumers have about their own personal situation, as well as their feelings about their overall economic prospects – helps to determine whether they will purchase goods and services, take on debt or save their money.

- In the past ten years, consumers overall have been relatively pessimistic about their future prospects. A lower level of resources has caused a shift towards an emphasis on quality products that are reasonably priced. Consumers are less tolerant of exaggerated or vague product claims, and they are more sceptical about marketing activities. Consumers in their twenties are particularly sceptical about the economy and marketing targeted at their age group.

- A consumer's *social class* refers to his or her standing in society. It is determined by a number of factors, including education, occupation and income.

- Virtually all groups make distinctions among members in terms of relative superiority, power and access to valued resources. This *social stratification* creates a status hierarchy, where some goods are preferred over others and are used to categorize their owners' social class.

- While income is an important indicator of social class, the relationship is far from perfect since social class is also determined by such factors as place of residence, cultural interests and worldview.

- Purchase decisions are sometimes influenced by the desire to 'buy up' to a higher social class or to engage in the process of *conspicuous consumption*, where one's status is flaunted by the deliberate and non-constructive use of valuable resources. This spending pattern is a characteristic of the *nouveaux riches*, whose relatively recent acquisition of income, rather than ancestry or breeding, is responsible for their increased *social mobility*.

- Products are used as status symbols to communicate real or desired social class. *Parody display* occurs when consumers seek status by deliberately avoiding fashionable products.

For additional material see the companion website at:
www.booksites.net/solomon_euro

KEY TERMS

Behavioural economics (*p. 375*)
Conspicuous consumption (*p. 395*)
Consumer confidence (*p. 379*)
Discretionary income (*p. 378*)
Elaborated codes (*p. 391*)
Invidious distinction (*p. 395*)
Parody display (*p. 397*)
Potlatch (*p. 396*)
Restricted codes (*p. 391*)

Savings rate (*p. 379*)
Social class (*p. 380*)
Social hierarchies (*p. 382*)
Social mobility (*p. 385*)
Social stratification (*p. 384*)
Status crystallization (*p. 388*)
Status symbols (*p. 375*)
Taste culture (*p. 390*)

Consumer behaviour challenge

1 The concepts *income* and *wealth* are measured in different ways throughout Europe, in spite of the standardization of currency that took place in 1999. Look through several recent issues of *Review of Income and Wealth* to get an idea of how these concepts differ across countries. For marketers, do you have any suggestions as to how to segment income groups for a European-wide strategy?

2 What are some of the obstacles to measuring social class in European society? Discuss some ways to get around these obstacles.

3 What consumption differences might you expect to observe between a family characterized as underprivileged vs. one whose income is average for its social class?

4 When is social class likely to be a better predictor of consumer behaviour than mere knowledge of a person's income?

5 How do you assign people to social classes, or do you at all? What consumption cues do you use (e.g. clothing, speech, cars, etc.) to determine social standing?

6 Thorstein Veblen argued that women were often used as a vehicle to display their husbands' wealth. Is this argument still valid today?

7 Given present environmental conditions and dwindling resources, what is the future of 'conspicuous waste'? Can the desire to impress others with affluence ever be eliminated? If not, can it take on a less dangerous form?

8 Some people argue that status symbols are dead. Do you agree?

9 Compile a list of occupations, and ask a sample of students who are studying a variety of subjects (both business and non-business) to rank the prestige of these jobs. Can you detect any differences in these rankings as a function of students' subjects?

10 Compile ads that depict consumers of different social classes. What generalizations can you make about the reality of these ads and about the media in which they appear?

11 Identify a current set of fraudulent status symbols, and construct profiles of consumers who are wearing or using these products. Are these profiles consistent with the images portrayed in each product's promotional messages?

12 The chapter observes that some marketers are finding 'greener pastures' by targeting low-income people. How ethical is it to single out consumers who cannot afford to waste their precious resources on discretionary items? Under what circumstances should this segmentation strategy be encouraged or discouraged?

Notes

1. Fred van Raaij, 'Economic Psychology', *Journal of Economic Psychology* 1 (1981): 1–24.
2. Peter S. H. Leeflang and W. Fred van Raaij, 'The Changing Consumer in the European Union: A Meta-analysis', *International Journal of Research in Marketing* 12 (1995): 373–87.
3. Data in this section are adapted from Fabian Linden, *Consumer Affluence: The Next Wave* (New York: The Conference Board, Inc., 1994); 'Women and Men in the European Union: A Statistical Portrait', Eurostat (Luxembourg: Office for Official Publications of the European Communities, 1995). See also 'Living Conditions in Europe: Statistical Pocketbook, Earnings and Income', Eurostat (Luxembourg: Office for Official Publications of the European Communities, 2000): 62–78.
4. 'Living Conditions in Europe: Statistical Pocketbook': 65.
5. Christopher D. Carroll, 'How Does Future Income Affect Current Consumption?', *Quarterly Journal of Economics* 109 (February 1994) 1: 111–47.
6. 'Demographic Statistics, 1997: Population and Social Conditions Series', Eurostat (Luxembourg: Office for Official Publications of the European Communities, 1997). See also the Europa Server at: *http://europa.eu.int*.
7. Jose J. F. Medina, Joel Saegert and Alicia Gresham, 'Comparison of Mexican-American and Anglo-American Attitudes Toward Money', *Journal of Consumer Affairs* 30(1) (1996): 124–45.
8. Kirk Johnson, 'Sit Down. Breathe Deeply. This is *Really* Scary Stuff', *New York Times* (16 April 1995): F5. For a scale that measures consumer frugality, see John L. Lastovicka, Lance A. Bettencourt, Renee Shaw Hughner and Ronald J. Kuntze, 'Lifestyle of the Tight and Frugal: Theory and Measurement', *Journal of Consumer Research* 26 (June 1999): 85–98.
9. Robert Sullivan, 'Americans and Their Money', *Worth* (June 1994): 60 (12).
10. 'Frontiers: Planning or Consumer Change in Europe 96/97', vol. 2 (London: The Henley Centre, 1996).
11. George Katona, 'Consumer Saving Patterns', *Journal of Consumer Research* 1 (June 1974): 1–12.
12. 'Frontiers: Planning or Consumer Change in Europe 96/97', vol. 2: 4.
13. Ernest Beck, 'Why Custom-Made Shirts Are a Cut Above', *Wall Street Journal Europe* (4–5 April 1997): 8.
14. Floyd L. Ruch and Davidip G. Zimbardo, *Psychology and Life*, 8th edn (Glenview, IL: Scott Foresman, 1971).
15. Louise Do Rosario, 'Privilege in China's Classless Society', *World Press Review* 33 (December 1986): 58.
16. Keith Naughton, 'Hitting the Bull's-Eye', *Newsweek* (11 October 1999): 64.
17. David Leonhardt, 'Two-Tier Marketing', *Business Week* (17 March 1997): 82 (7 pp.).
18. Jonathan H. Turner, *Sociology: Studying the Human System*, 2nd edn (Santa Monica, CA: Goodyear, 1981).
19. Ibid.
20. Richard P. Coleman, 'The Continuing Significance of Social Class to Marketing', *Journal of Consumer Research* 10 (December 1983): 265–80; Turner, *Sociology*.
21. Ernest Beck, 'Cabin Fever Swirls Around Posh Cottages on Norwegian Coast', *Wall Street Journal Europe* (6 August 1997): 1.
22. Quoted by Richard P. Coleman and Lee Rainwater, *Standing in America: New Dimensions of Class* (New York: Basic Books, 1978): 89.
23. Ibid.
24. Turner, *Sociology*.
25. Nicholas D. Kristof, 'Women as Bodyguards: In China, It's All the Rage', *New York Times* (1 July 1993): A4.
26. James Sterngold, 'How Do You Define Status? A New BMW in the Drive. An Old Rock in the Garden', *New York Times* (28 December 1989): C1.
27. Robin Knight, 'Just You Move Over, 'Enry 'Iggins: A New Regard for Profits and Talent Cracks Britain's Old Class System', *U.S. News & World Report* 106 (24 April 1989): 40.
28. Turner, *Sociology*: 260.
29. See Ronald Paul Hill and Mark Stamey, 'The Homeless in America: An Examination of Possessions and Consumption Behaviors', *Journal of Consumer Research* 17 (December 1990): 303–21.
30. Joseph Kahl, *The American Class Structure* (New York: Holt, Rinehart and Winston, 1961).
31. Leonard Beeghley, *The Structure of Social Stratification in The United States*, 3rd edn (Allyn and Bacon, 2000).
32. Coleman and Rainwater, *Standing in America*: 220.
33. Turner, *Sociology*.
34. See Coleman, 'The Continuing Significance of Social Class to Marketing'; Charles M. Schaninger, 'Social Class Versus Income Revisited: An Empirical Investigation', *Journal of Marketing Research* 18 (May 1981): 192–208.
35. Coleman, 'The Continuing Significance of Social Class to Marketing'.
36. Bernard Dubois and Gilles Laurent, 'Is There a Euroconsumer for Luxury Goods?', in W. Fred van Raaij and Gary J. Bamossy, eds, *European Advances in Consumer Research* 1 (Provo, UT: Association for Consumer Research, 1993): 59–69; Bernard Dubois and Gilles Laurent, 'Luxury Possessions and Practices: An Empirical Scale', in F. Hansen, ed., *European Advances in Consumer Research* 2 (Provo, UT: Association for Consumer Research, 1995): 69–77; Bernard Dubois and Patrick Duquesne, 'The Market

for Luxury Goods: Income versus Culture', *European Journal of Marketing* 27(1) (1993): 35–44.

37. August B, Hollingshead and Fredrick C. Redlich, *Social Class and Mental Illness: A Community Study* (New York: John Wiley, 1958).

38. John Mager and Lynn R. Kahle, 'Is the Whole More than the Sum of the Parts? Re-evaluating Social Status in Marketing', *Journal of Business Psychology*, in press.

39. R. Vanneman and F. C. Pampel, 'The American Perception of Class and Status', *American Sociological Review* 42 (June 1977): 422–37.

40. Donald W. Hendon, Emelda L. Williams and Douglas E. Huffman, 'Social Class System Revisited', *Journal of Business Research* 17 (November 1988): 259.

41. Coleman, 'The Continuing Significance of Social Class to Marketing'.

42. Gerhard E. Lenski, 'Status Crystallization: A Non-Vertical Dimension of Social Status', *American Sociological Review* 19 (August 1954): 405–12.

43. Richard P. Coleman, 'The Significance of Social Stratification in Selling', in *Marketing: A Maturing Discipline, Proceedings of the American Marketing Association 43rd National Conference*, ed. Martin L. Bell (Chicago: American Marketing Association, 1960): 171–84.

44. Melinda Beck and Richard Sandza, 'The Lottery Craze: Multimillion Dollar Prizes Raise New Concerns That the Games Prey on the Poor', *Newsweek* (2 September 1985): 16; Rhoda E. McKinney, 'Has Money Spoiled the Lottery Millionaires?', *Ebony* (December 1988): 150.

45. E. Barth and W. Watson, 'Questionable Assumptions in the Theory of Social Stratification', *Pacific Sociological Review* 7 (Spring 1964): 10–16.

46. Zick Rubin, 'Do American Women Marry Up?', *American Sociological Review* 33 (1968): 750–60.

47. Sue Browder, 'Don't be Afraid to Marry Down', *Cosmopolitan* (June 1987): 236.

48. K. U. Ritter and L. L. Hargens, 'Occupational Positions and Class Identifications of Married Working Women: A Test of the Asymmetry Hypothesis', *American Journal of Sociology* 80 (January 1975): 934–48.

49. Browder, 'Don't Be Afraid to Marry Down': 236.

50. J. Michael Munson and W. Austin Spivey, 'Product and Brand-User Stereotypes Among Social Classes: Implications for Advertising Strategy', *Journal of Advertising Research* 21 (August 1981): 37–45.

51. Stuart U. Rich and Subhash C. Jain, 'Social Class and Life Cycle as Predictors of Shopping Behavior', *Journal of Marketing Research* 5 (February 1968): 41–9.

52. Thomas W. Osborn, 'Analytic Techniques for Opportunity Marketing', *Marketing Communications* (September 1987): 49–63.

53. Coleman, 'The Continuing Significance of Social Class to Marketing'.

54. Jeffrey F. Durgee, 'How Consumer Sub-Cultures Code Reality: A Look at Some Code Types', in Richard J. Lutz, ed., *Advances in Consumer Research* 13 (Provo, UT: Association for Consumer Research, 1986): 332–7.

55. David Halle, *America's Working Man: Work, Home, and Politics Among Blue-Collar Owners* (Chicago: University of Chicago Press, 1984); David Montgomery, 'America's Working Man', *Monthly Review* (1985): 1.

56. Quoted in Coleman and Rainwater, *Standing in America*: 139.

57. 'Frontiers: Planning for Consumer Change in Europe 96/97' vol. 2: 14.

58. Durkheim (1958), quoted in Roger Brown, *Social Psychology* (New York: The Free Press, 1965).

59. Lenore Skenazy, 'Affluent, Like Masses, Are Flush with Worries', *Advertising Age* (10 July 1989): 55.

60. Herbert J. Gans, 'Popular Culture in America: Social Problem in a Mass Society or Social Asset in a Pluralist Society?', in, Howard S. Becker, ed., *Social Problems: A Modern Approach* (New York: Wiley, 1966); Helga Dittmar, 'Material Possessions as Stereotypes: Material Images of Different Socio-economic Groups', *Journal of Economic Psychology* 15 (1994): 561–85; Helga Dittmar and Lucy Pepper, 'To Have Is to Be: Materialism and Person Perception in Working Class and Middle Class British Adolescents', *Journal of Economic Psychology* 15 (1994): 233–5.

61. Edward O. Laumann and James S. House, 'Living Room Styles and Social Attributes: The Patterning of Material Artifacts in a Modern Urban Community', *Sociology and Social Research* 54 (April 1970): 321–42; see also Stephen S. Bell, Morris B. Holbrook and Michael R. Solomon, 'Combining Esthetic and Social Value to Explain Preferences for Product Styles with the Incorporation of Personality and Ensemble Effects', *Journal of Social Behavior and Personality* (1991) 6: 243–74.

62. Quoted in Richard Elliott, 'How Do the Unemployed Maintain Their Identity in a Culture of Consumption?', *European Advances in Consumer Research* 2 (1995): 1–4, at 3.

63. Cyndee Miller, 'New Line of Barbie Dolls Targets Big, Rich Kids', *Marketing News* (17 June 1996): 6.

64. Cyndee Miller, 'Baubles are Back', *Marketing News* (14 April 1997): 1 (2).

65. Anita Sharpe, 'Magazines for the Rich Rake in Readers', *Wall Street Journal* (16 February 1996): B1 (2).

66. 'Reading the Buyer's Mind', *U.S. News & World Report* (16 March 1987): 59.

67. Rebecca Piirto Heath, 'Life on Easy Street', *American Demographics* (April 1997): 33–8.

68. Quoted in 'Western Companies Compete to Win Business of Chinese Babies', *Wall Street Journal Interactive Edition* (15 May 1998).

69. Paul Fussell, *Class: A Guide Through the American Status System* (New York: Summit Books, 1983): 29.

70. Elizabeth C. Hirschman, 'Secular Immortality and the American Ideology of Affluence', *Journal of Consumer Research* 17 (June 1990): 31–42.

71. Coleman and Rainwater, *Standing in America*: 150.

72. M. H. Moore, 'Homing in on Russian "Super Spenders"', *Adweek* (28 February 1994): 14–16.

73. Monica Langley, 'Italian Firm Fashions a Look Tailor-Made for Indulgent Parents', *Wall Street Journal* (24 August 2000): A1.

74. Jason DeParle, 'Spy Anxiety: The Smart Magazine That Makes Smart People Nervous About Their Standing', *Washingtonian Monthly* (February 1989): 10.

75. For a recent examination of retailing issues related to the need for status, see Jacqueline Kilsheimer Eastman, Leisa Reinecke Flynn and Ronald E. Goldsmith, 'Shopping for Status: The Retail Managerial Implications', *Association of Marketing Theory and Practice* (Spring 1994): 125–30.

76. Dennis Rodkin, 'Wealthy Attitude Wins Over Healthy Wallet: Consumers Prove Affluence is a State of Mind', *Advertising Age* (9 July 1990): S4.

77. John Brooks, *Showing off in America* (Boston: Little, Brown, 1981): 13.

78. Thorstein Veblen, *The Theory of the Leisure Class* (1899; reprint, New York: New American Library, 1953): 45.

79. Teri Agins, 'Luxury Match? LVMH Targets Donna Karan', *Wall Street Journal* (19 December 2000): B1; Deborah Ball, 'High Style on the High Seas', *Wall Street Journal* (14 September 2000): B1; Ball, 'Italy's Finpart to Acquire Cerruti': B16.

80. Quoted in Miller, 'Baubles are Back': 1 (2). Elaine Underwood, 'Luxury's Tide Turns', *Brandweek* (7 March 1994): 18–22. See also Deborah Ball, 'Italy's Finpart to Acquire Cerruti; Gucci Set to Buy Zamasport Unit', *Wall Street Journal* (9 October 2000): B16.

81. Brooks, *Showing off in America*.

82. Ibid.: 31–2.

Chapter 13

Age subcultures

It's just a few months before winter weather really sets in, and Joost is lying on his bed 'channel surfing' on the TV and daydreaming about trying out his new ice-hockey skates on the frozen lakes near the flat where he and his father live in the suburbs of Amsterdam. His father tried to convince him to buy the classic 'hoge Noren' – black high-top touring skates with a long blade that have been 'classics' in Holland for decades, but Joost insisted on ice-hockey skates. His response was: 'Your skates are for middle-aged, old-fashioned skaters who are too serious about the whole thing. I want skates I can mess about in. Besides, these skates go well with my new Fila winter jacket.'

While Joost is switching from one channel to another, an advertisement for a skiing holiday comes on the screen and catches his limited attention. Images of 'extreme skiing' are mixed with scenes of young people sitting around a well-stocked breakfast table. Text appears at the bottom of the screen, instructing the viewer to go to the teletext page for more information. The entire advertisement lasts 15 seconds. Joost uses the remote control to switch to the teletext page, and scans the ski package offerings. Great! Ten days in Austria for just 415 euros. It includes round-trip bus transportation, twin rooms, half-board and nine days of ski passes. Before moving on to the next channel, he notes down the travel agent's website address. With the TV still on, he logs on to his computer and checks the website. He can book the trip on the Web. First, he needs to ask a few friends to see if they want to go during the Christmas break. Then he just needs his Dad's permission . . . and his credit card number.

Age and consumer identity

The era in which a consumer grows up creates for that person a cultural bond with the millions of others born during the same time period. As we grow older, our needs and preferences change, often in unison with others who are close to our own age. For this reason, a consumer's age exerts a significant influence on his or her identity. All things being equal, we are more likely than not to have things in common with others of our own age. In this chapter, we'll explore some of the important characteristics of some key age groups, and consider how marketing strategies must be modified to appeal to diverse age subcultures.

Age cohorts: 'my generation'

▶ An **age cohort** consists of people of similar ages who have undergone similar experiences. They share many common memories about cultural heroes (e.g. Clint Eastwood vs. Brad Pitt, or Frank Sinatra vs. Kurt Cobain), important historical events (e.g. the 1968 student demonstrations in Paris vs. the fall of the Berlin Wall in 1989), and so on. Although there is no universally accepted way to divide people into age cohorts, each of us seems to have a pretty good idea of what we mean when we refer to 'my generation'.

Marketers often target products and services to one or more specific age cohorts. They recognize that the same offering will probably not appeal to people of different ages, nor will the language and images they use to reach them. In some cases separate campaigns are developed to attract consumers of different ages. For example, travel agencies throughout Europe target youth markets during the months of May and June for low-cost summer holidays to Mallorca, and then target middle-aged, more affluent consumers for the same destination during September and October. What differ in the two campaigns are the media used, the images portrayed and the prices offered.

Choosing for 'hockey'-style ice skates goes well beyond just product and price considerations. Review this chapter's opening consumer vignette for the more complete picture of the complex choice processes of teens.

Documenting their time together at World Cup '98, this group of young adult fans from Belgium and Holland create their own 'Paris souvenir'.

The appeal of nostalgia

Because consumers within an age group confront crucial life changes at roughly the same time, the values and symbolism used to appeal to them can evoke powerful feelings of nostalgia (see Chapter 3). Adults aged 30+ are particularly susceptible to this phenomenon.[1] However, young people as well as old are influenced by references to their past. In fact, research indicates that some people are more disposed to be nostalgic than others, regardless of age. A scale that has been used to measure the impact of nostalgia on individual consumers appears in Table 13.1.

Chapter 3 noted that product sales can be dramatically affected by linking a brand to vivid memories and experiences, especially for items that are associated with childhood or adolescence. Vespa scooters, Hornby electric trains and the coupon

---

Table 13.1 The nostalgia scale

Scale items

- They don't make 'em like they used to.
- Things used to be better in the good old days.
- Products are getting shoddier and shoddier.
- Technological change will ensure a brighter future (reverse coded).
- History involves a steady improvement in human welfare (reverse coded).
- We are experiencing a decline in the quality of life.
- Steady growth in GNP has brought increased human happiness (reverse coded).
- Modern business constantly builds a better tomorrow (reverse coded).

Note: Items are presented on a nine-point scale ranging from strong disagreement (1) to strong agreement (9), and responses are summed.

Source: Morris B. Holbrook and Robert M. Schindler, 'Age, Sex, and Attitude Toward the Past as Predicters of Consumers' Aesthetic Tastes for Cultural Products', *Journal of Marketing Research* 31 (August 1994): 416.

'saving-points' from Douwe Egberts coffee are all examples of products that have managed to span two or more generations of loyal consumers, giving the brand a strong equity position in competitive and crowded markets.

Many advertising campaigns have played on the collective memories of consumers by using older celebrities to endorse their products, such as American Express's campaign which featured Eric Clapton and Lou Reed. In Japan, Ringo Starr (the Beatles's drummer) is used to help promote demand for apples. The target market is middle-aged consumers, and it doesn't hurt that, phonetically, 'Ringo' means *apple* in Japanese. To assess just how pervasive nostalgia is, pay attention to television commercials, and notice how often they are produced against a background of 'classic songs'. *Memories* magazine, which was founded to exploit the nostalgia boom, even offers advertisers a discount if they run old ads next to their current ones.

The teen market: it totally rules

In 1956, the label 'teenage' first entered the (American) vocabulary, as Frankie Lymon and the Teenagers became the first pop group to identify themselves with this new subculture. The concept of teenager is a fairly new cultural construction; throughout most of history a person simply made the transition from child to adult (often accompanied by some sort of ritual or ceremony, as we'll see in a later chapter). The magazine *Seventeen*, launched in 1944, was based on the revelation that young women didn't want to look just like their mothers. In the early 1960s, the teenage drama between rebellion and conformity began to unfold, pitting Elvis Presley with his greased hair and suggestive hip-swivels against more 'parentally approved' types such as Cliff Richard. Now, this rebellion is played out by being detached from the adult world, as exemplified by teen idols like hip-hop star Eminen or the confused, sullen teenagers appearing daily on Ricki Lake, Gerry Springer and other daytime talk shows which are broadcast on European satellite networks.[2]

Teen values and conflicts

As anyone who has been there knows, puberty and adolescence can be both the best of times and the worst of times. Many exciting changes happen as individuals leave the role of child and prepare to assume the role of adult. These changes create a lot of uncertainty about the self, and the need to belong and to find one's unique identity as a person becomes extremely important. At this age, choices of activities, friends and 'looks' are crucial to social acceptance. Teenagers actively search for cues from their peers and from advertising for the 'right' way to look and behave. Advertising geared to teenagers is typically action-oriented and depicts a group of 'in' teenagers using the product. Teenagers use products to express their identities, to explore the world and their new-found freedom in it, and also to rebel against the authority of their parents and other socializing agents. Joost's rejection of his father's suggestion to buy 'classic' skates, and his choice of ice-hockey skates which fashionably matched his Fila jacket, are mild expressions of these sorts of expressive consumption behaviours. Marketers often do their best to assist in this process. The range of consumer products targeted at teenagers (and particularly young ones) is greater than ever. Then again, so is teenagers' disposable income from part-time jobs and weekly pocket money.[3]

Teenagers in every culture grapple with fundamental developmental issues as they make the transition from childhood to adult. According to research by Saatchi & Saatchi, there are four themes of conflict common to all teens:

1 *Autonomy vs. belonging*. Teenagers need to acquire independence so they try to break away from their families. On the other hand, they need to attach themselves to a support structure, such as peers, to avoid being alone. A thriving internet sub-culture has developed to serve this purpose. The net (World Wide Web) is becoming the preferred method of communication for many young people, since its anonymity makes it easier to talk to people of the opposite sex, or of different ethnic and racial groups.[4]

2 *Rebellion vs. conformity*. Teenagers need to rebel against social standards of appearance and behaviour, yet they still need to fit in and be accepted by others. Cult products that cultivate a rebellious image are prized for this reason. Skeleteens, a line of natural soft drinks in flavours like Brain Wash, Black Lemonade and DOA, is developing such a following thanks to its 'dangerous' mystique. This underground product was first discovered by California bikers in America, who were drawn to the images of skulls and crossbones on the labels.[5]

3 *Idealism vs. pragmatism*. Teenagers tend to view adults as hypocrites, while they see themselves as being sincere. They have to struggle to reconcile their view of how the world should be with the realities they perceive around them.

4 *Narcissism vs. intimacy*. Teenagers can be obsessed with their appearance and needs. On the other hand, they also feel the desire to connect with others on a meaningful level.[6]

Teenagers throughout history have had to cope with insecurity, parental authority and peer pressure. At the start of the new millennium, however, these issues are compounded by concerns about the environment, racism, AIDS, and other pressing social problems. Today's teenagers often have to cope with additional family responsibilities as well, especially if they live in non-traditional families where they must take significant responsibility for shopping, cooking and housework. Marketers have a difficult time 'defining' the values of today's European teens, perhaps because they are living in such socially dynamic and demanding times. A recent study among 500 young opinion leaders aged 14–20 across 16 European countries suggests that this age group's credo should be: 'don't define us – we'll define ourselves'. Respondents

Teenagers in every culture grapple with personal and social issues as they make the transition from childhood to adulthood. What better way to work through issues than together, at the snack bar!

were asked their opinions on a wide range of subjects, from new technology to family relationships, divorce, drugs, alcohol, politics, fashion, entertainment, sex and advertising. Some of the highlights of this study[7] are:

● Living life to the 'fullest' is mandatory; ambition drives them, as does the fear of failure. Young eastern europeans strongly believe that hard work will give them a high standard of living and education is their passport to this better life.

● They perceive the 'digitized' future as one that lacks warmth – something Europe's teenagers, a divorce-experienced generation, is actively seeking.

● New technology which allows for '24-hour commerce' will lead to further stress for this generation, and a blurring of home/office means they will work longer and harder than any previous generation.

● The phone at home is still a central method for teens to talk to each other, although mobile phones are quickly penetrating this group's social network.

● This is a very visually literate generation, with clear understanding of a commercial's aims. Clichés will not be tolerated, and will lead to immediate rejection, particularly in the Nordic countries. Only eastern European teens have yet to achieve this level of 'advertising cynicism'.

● This generation is both brand-aware and brand-dismissive. It represents an opportunity, but not a homogeneous market. The successful marketer will be aware that for these consumers, an aspirational quality is essential, that heritage is an advantage, and that nothing is forever.

Multicultural dimensions

Teen rebellion is a new phenomenon in Japan, a country known for rigid conformity and constant pressure to succeed. Now more and more teenagers are questioning the rules. The dropout rate among students in junior and senior high school increased by 20 per cent in a two-year period. More than 50 per cent of girls have had intercourse by their senior year of high school.[8]

Japanese youth are very style-conscious, and currently there are several niches or 'tribes', each with very well-defined looks and rules.[9] A popular look for Japanese girls is called the 'Gals': they are easily recognized by their bleached yellow hair, salon-tanned skin, chalk-white lipstick and 7-inch platform heels. Other groups include the Sports Clique (low-heeled Air Mocs and Gap clothing) and the Back-Harajuku Group (baggy sweatshirts, colourful jeans, sneakers (trainers) and long scarves).

To try to win the loyalty of young consumers in Japan, five big companies including Toyota, Matsushita and Asahi Breweries formed a marketing alliance. They are introducing a range of products, from beer to refrigerators, all with the same brand name of 'Will' (yes, Will). Critics are not sure the plan will work because these companies as of now do not have very modern images, so only time will tell if this ambitious plan Will or won't.[10]

Appealing to the teen market

Consumers in this age subculture have a number of needs, including experimentation, belonging, independence, responsibility and approval from others. Product usage is a significant medium to express these needs. Because they are so interested in many different products and have the resources to obtain them, the teen market is avidly courted by many marketers. Much of this money goes towards 'feel-good' products – cosmetics, posters and fast food – with the occasional body piercing

Table 13.2 Affluent lifestyles leading children into temptation. 'During the last seven days, have you spent any of your own money on the following items?' (% saying yes)

| | 12–13-year-olds | | 14–15-year-olds | |
	boys	girls	boys	girls
Crisps	38	42	43	46
Biscuits	16	10	14	8
Fast food (hot)	34	25	42	32
Arcade games (for fun)	22	7	20	7
Arcade gambling	12	3	14	4
Computer games	18	4	13	2
Leisure/sports centre	24	15	23	13
National lottery (gambling)	16	10	24	16

Source: 'Affluent Lifestyle Leading Children into Temptation', *The Independent* (23 September 1996).

thrown in as well. Table 13.2 summarizes the sorts of activities which British teenagers experiment in, and pay for with their own money.

Because today's teenagers were raised on TV and they tend to be much more canny than older generations, marketers must tread lightly when they try to reach them. As Joost illustrated with his five minutes of information-gathering on the TV, teletext and internet, teenagers in Europe have increasingly complex media consumption habits, and are acknowledged as being more advertising-literate. In particular, the messages must be seen as authentic and not condescending. In spite of their more critical evaluation of television advertising, there is no doubt that TV adverts have a clear influence on youth purchases, as Figure 13.1 shows.

Marketers view teenagers as 'consumers-in-training', since brand loyalty is developed during this age. A teenager who is committed to a brand may continue to pur-

Figure 13.1 Percentage of 16–24-year-olds who have taken action as a direct result of watching a television programme or commercial

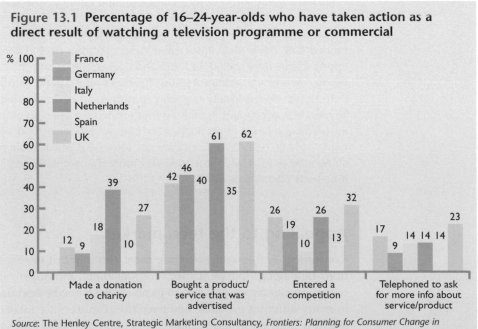

Source: The Henley Centre, Strategic Marketing Consultancy, *Frontiers: Planning for Consumer Change in Europe* (1996/7)

chase it for many years to come. Such loyalty creates a barrier-to-entry for other brands that were not chosen during these pivotal years. Thus, advertisers sometimes try to 'lock in' consumers to certain brands so that they will buy these brands in the future more or less automatically. As one teen magazine ad director observed, 'We . . . always say it's easier to start a habit than stop it.'[11]

MARKETING OPPORTUNITY

Pre-teen girls are a major market unto themselves. Marketers use the term *tweens* to describe the 20+ million children aged 8–14 who spend $14 billion euros a year on clothes, CDs, movies and other 'feel-good' products. Limited Too sells mostly to 10- and 11-year-old girls and now mails a catalogue directly to pre-teen girls rather than to their parents. Not surprising, since pre-teen girls buy over $4.5 billion of clothing a year. Limited Too is developing make-up products targeted at this age segment as well, featuring fragrances like Sugar Vanilla and Snow Musk.[12]

Tweens are 'between' childhood and adolescence and exhibit characteristics of both age groups. As one tween commented, 'When we're alone we get weird and crazy and still act like kids. But in public we act cool, like teenagers.' This age group drove the success of movies like *Titanic* and boy groups like 'N Sync – they account for about 9 per cent of all CD sales.[13] They like to talk on the phone and in chat rooms, they squeal and shout when the Backstreet Boys take the stage – and they've definitely got marketers' attention.

For example, Kodak made a $75 million, five-year commitment to convince tween girls to buy its single-use Kodak Max cameras. According to internal research, this segment is 50 per cent more likely than boys of the same age to own a camera. When girls were asked to name their most prized possession, 15 per cent said photographs, while only 4 per cent of their male counterparts put photos at the top of their lists. Kodak discovered that a majority of girls keep journals, collect quotes and maintain online bulletin boards, and the company is betting that this desire to share experiences with friends will turn into a picture-perfect marketing strategy.[14]

Teenagers also exert a strong influence on the purchase decisions of their parents (see Chapter 11).[15] In addition to providing 'helpful' advice to parents, teenagers are increasingly buying products on behalf of the family. As discussed in Chapter 11, mothers are most likely to return to the workforce (most often to part-time work) once the children in the household are at school and have become more independent.[16]

Researching the youth market

Research firms are coming up with innovative ways to tap the desires of teens, many of whom don't respond well to traditional survey techniques. Sometimes respondents are given a video camera and are asked to record a 'typical' day at school – along with play-by-play commentary to help interpret what's going on. Greenfield Consulting Group uses what it calls the 'teen-as-creative-director' technique. The firm gives teens camcorders and asks them to complete a two-part creative assignment that will be judged by their peers. A typical task is to create a video collage of the 'coolest/hippest/whateverest' things they can find and write a song/poem/story that describes what 'cool/hip' is all about. After the teens complete their assignments, they present their work to each other at a focus group facility, judge the work collectively, and award cash prizes to the creators of the best video and song/poem/story.

A recent study asked young people in the US and the Netherlands to write essays about what is 'cool' and 'uncool'.[17] The researchers found that being cool has several meanings, though there were a lot of similarities between the two cultures when kids use this term. Some of the common dimensions include having charisma, being in control and being a bit aloof. And many of the respondents agreed that being cool is a moving target: the harder you try to be cool, the more uncool you are! Some of their actual responses are listed here:

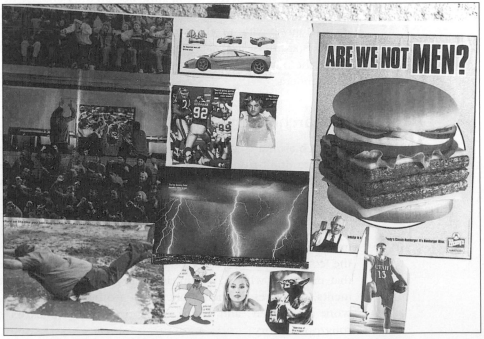

Shown here are two collages representing images of 'cool'. One collage was put together by a European and one by an American. Can you tell which is which? One person is male, the other female. Any predictions here?

- 'Cool means being relaxed, to nonchalantly be the boss of every situation, and to radiate that' (Dutch female).

- 'Cool is the perception from others that you've got "something" which is macho, trendy, hip, etc.' (Dutch male).

- 'Cool has something stand-offish, and at the same time, attractive' (Dutch male).

- 'Being different, but not too different. Doing your own thing, and standing out, without looking desperate while you're doing it' (American male).

- 'When you are sitting on a terrace in summer, you see those machos walk by, you know, with their mobile [phones] and their sunglasses. I always think, "Oh please, come back to earth!" These guys only want to impress. That is just so uncool' (Dutch female).

- 'When a person thinks he is cool, he is absolutely uncool' (Dutch female).

- 'To be cool we have to make sure we measure up to it. We have to create an identity for ourselves that mirrors what we see in magazines, on TV, and with what we hear on our stereos' (American male).

Baby busters: 'Generation X'

The cohort of consumers between the ages of 18 and 29 consists of over 30 million Europeans who will be a powerful force in years to come. This group, which has been labelled '**Generation X**', 'slackers' or 'busters', was profoundly affected by the economic downturn in the first part of the 1990s. So-called baby busters include many people, both in and out of higher education, whose tastes and priorities are beginning to be felt in fashion, popular culture, politics and marketing. While the percentage of Europeans aged 25–29 is high in terms of completing upper secondary education (71 per cent in 1999, compared to 50 per cent of persons aged 50–59), this group also has a large dropout rate, with one in five Europeans between the ages of 18 and 24 leaving the education system without completing a qualification beyond lower secondary schooling.[18] Even the World Bank is sensitive to targeting this group of future policy-makers in a vernacular they can relate to. Their Public Service Advertisement for World Hunger Day, which was broadcast by MTV in North America and Europe, is very 'Gen-X'. Images flash by of the globe, babies, food, war, fluorescent bananas and attractive young people gazing at the camera, backed by a beat with a jazz infusion and ending with words in distinctive type: 'The World Bank. Knowledge and resources for change'.[19]

Marketing to busters or marketing bust?

Although the income of this age cohort is below expectations, they still constitute a formidable market segment – partly because so many still live at home and have more discretionary income. Busters in their twenties are estimated to have an annual spending power of $125 billion, and their purchases are essential to the fortunes of such product categories as beer, fast food and cosmetics.

Because many busters have been doing the family shopping for a long time, marketers are finding that they are much more sophisticated about evaluating advertising and products. They are turned off by advertising that either contains a lot of hype or takes itself too seriously. They see advertising as a form of entertainment but are turned off by overcommercialization.[20] As the Vice-President of Marketing for MTV put it, 'You must let them know that you know who they are, that you understand their life experiences. You want them to feel you're talking directly to them.'[21]

Nike took a soft-sell approach to woo younger buyers of its athletic shoes. Its ads show little of the product, focusing instead on encouraging readers to improve themselves through exercise. Other ads make fun of advertising: an ad created for a Maybelline eye shadow depicts supermodel Christy Turlington coolly posing in a glamorous setting. She then suddenly appears on her living room couch, where she laughs and says 'Get over it'.

One of the more successful commercials created specifically for this group was from a bank! Midland Bank (now HSBC)'s qualitative market research showed that money was one of university students' major worries. Its series of TV ads featuring Sam, 'a new student', was humorous but avoided being patronizing. It also aimed to emphasize Midland's claim that it offered the best and cheapest deals. The message was reinforced by a no-nonsense PR campaign on student financing which received 25 editorial mentions in national publications. The success of the campaign took Midland to market leadership in this segment.[22]

Perhaps one reason why marketers' efforts to appeal to Xers with messages of alienation, cynicism and despair have not succeeded is that many people in their twenties aren't depressed after all! Generation Xers are quite a diverse group – they don't all wear reversed baseball caps and work in temporary, low-paid mindless jobs. Despite the birth of dozens of magazines catering to 'riot grrrls' and other angry Xers with names like *Axcess*, *Project X* and *KGB*, the most popular magazine for 20-something women is *Cosmopolitan*. What seems to make this age cohort the angriest is constantly being labelled as angry by the media![23]

The advertising agency Saatchi & Saatchi sent teams of psychologists and cultural anthropologists into the field to study the buster subculture. These researchers identified four key segments:

1 *Cynical disdainers*: The most pessimistic and sceptical about the world.

2 *Traditional materialists*: The most like baby boomers in their thirties and forties, these young people are upbeat, optimistic about the future, and actively striving for what they continue to view as the desire for material prosperity.

3 *Hippies revisited*: This group tends to espouse the non-materialistic values of the 1960s. Their priorities are expressed through music, retro fashion and a strong interest in spirituality.

4 *Fifties machos*: These consumers tend to be young conservatives. They believe in stereotyped gender roles, are politically conservative and are the least accepting of multiculturalism.[24]

MARKETING OPPORTUNITY

As part of their massive restructuring, British Telecommunications has hired a new ad agency to get some badly needed advice about how to make its brand more appealing to the youth market. St Luke's, the ad agency, is a creative hot shop in London's Soho district. They have targeted the 16–24-year-old market for BT through a website called *getoutthere.bt.com*. The site lets users upload their original music and short films onto a BT-branded site and share them online. *getoutthere.bt.com* has little relation to the products or services the telecom giant offers its customers. 'BT is in the communications business, and this is a relationship tool for them', says one of St Luke's managers. According to a BT manager involved with its marketing strategy, the company feels it is facing a 'youth time bomb'. BT doesn't have the contact with young people that other telecommunications companies have, and when those young people get older, BT fears its market share will shrink.[25]

Baby boomers

▶ The **baby boomers** are the source of many fundamental cultural and economic changes. The reason: power in numbers. As the Second World War ended, they began to establish families and careers at a record pace. Imagine a large python that has swallowed a mouse: the mouse moves down the length of the python, creating a moving bulge as it goes.

The cultural impact of boomers

So it is with baby boomers. Figures 13.2 and 13.3 show the projections of the European population for both youth and boomers for a 17-year period. This increase in the proportion of older citizens and decrease in the proportion of youth is often referred to as the 'greying and de-greening' of the European population, a structural trend which has major implications for the marketing of goods and services.

As teenagers in the 1960s and 1970s, this generation created a revolution in style, politics and consumer attitudes. As they have aged, their collective will has been behind cultural events as diverse as the Paris student demonstrations and hippies in the 1960s and Thatcherism and yuppies in the 1980s. Now that they are older, they continue to influence popular culture in important ways.

Economic power: he who pays the piper, calls the tune

Because of the size and buying power of the boomer group over the last 20 years, marketers focused most of their attention on the youth market. The popular slogan at the time, 'Don't trust anyone over thirty', also meant that people over 30 had trouble finding products appropriate to their age groups. Times have changed, and

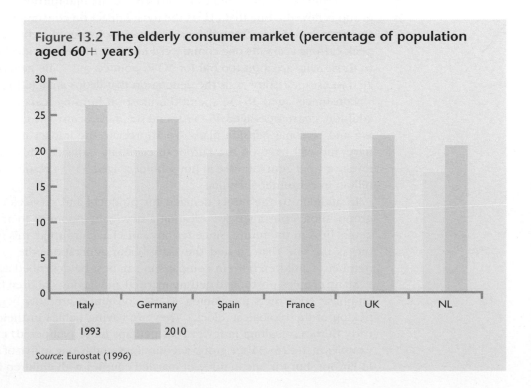

Figure 13.2 The elderly consumer market (percentage of population aged 60+ years)

1993   2010

Source: Eurostat (1996)

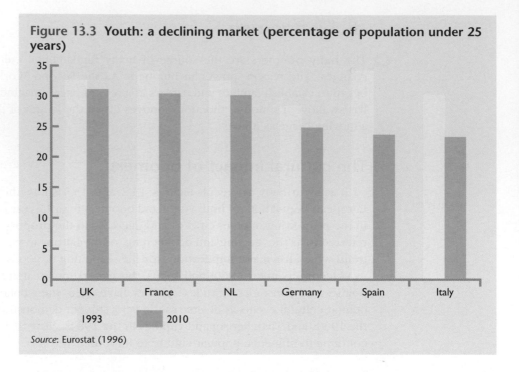

Figure 13.3 Youth: a declining market (percentage of population under 25 years)

1993   2010

Source: Eurostat (1996)

again it is the baby boomers who have changed them. For example, boomers tend to have different emotional and psychological needs from those who came before them. Domain, a high-fashion furniture chain, found that its core boomer clientele is as concerned about self-improvement as it is about home decor. The company launched a series of in-store seminars dealing with themes like women's issues and how to start a business, and found its repeat business doubled.[26]

This 'mouse in the python' has moved into its mid-thirties to fifties, and this age group is now the one that exerts the most impact on consumption patterns. Most of the growth in the market will be accounted for by people who are moving into their peak earning years. As one commercial for VH1, the music-video network that caters to those who are a bit too old for MTV, pointed out, 'The generation that dropped acid to escape reality . . . is the generation that drops antacid to cope with it'.

Consumers aged 35–44 spend the most on housing, cars and entertainment. In addition, consumers aged 45–54 spend the most of any age category on food, clothing and personal pension plans. To appreciate the impact middle-aged consumers have and will have on the European economy, consider this: at current spending levels, a 1 per cent increase in householders aged 35–54 results in an additional $8.9 billion in consumer spending.

In addition to the direct demand for products and services created by this age group, these consumers are creating a new baby boom of their own to keep marketers busy in the future. Since fertility rates have dropped, this new boom is not as big as the one that created the baby boom generation: the new upsurge in the number of children born in comparison can best be described as a *baby boomlet*.

Many couples postponed getting married and having children because of the new emphasis on careers for women. These consumers are now beginning to hear the ticking of the biological 'clock'. They are having babies in their late twenties and early thirties, resulting in fewer (but perhaps more pampered) children per family. Couples in the 25–34 age group account for roughly one in five of all married couples in Europe, but for one in three of married couples with children living at home.

**MARKETING
OPPORTUNITY**

Beer: a matter of taste, or age?

In one of his rare rhetorical flourishes, former Prime Minister John Major once proclaimed that Britain would remain a land of 'dog lovers, invincible green suburbs, and warm beer'. Today, the dogs still roam the leafy suburbs, but warm ales, long a symbol of British beer-drinking habits, are no longer 'cool'.

'Drink ice cold' instructs the new bottle for Worthington ale, a venerable British beer. T&R Theakston Ltd, renowned for such traditional tipples as Old Peculier, is rolling out an ale called Cool Cask, served at 50°F, compared with a typical 54°–56°F for traditional British ales. Far bolder, Guinness Ltd promotes an alternative version of its stout called Guinness Extra Cold, poured from the tap at 39°F, about the same as US-style lagers. Partisans of traditional ales are appalled. 'You might as well just serve water', says Mick Lewis, 49 years old, and chairman of the North London branch of the Campaign for Real Ale, whose members drown their sorrows the old-fashioned way.

Beer marketers, however, see more future in people like Alec Skelton. This 29-year-old British lawyer, dapper in rectangular glasses and a sleek charcoal-grey suit, glides to the bar at the Old Bell, a 330-year-old pub on Fleet Street. The offerings include Brakspear and Timothy Taylor Landlord, two revered English ales, hand pumped from the cellar. Mr Skelton doesn't hesitate: he calls for a cold bottle of Budweiser. 'I like the cool, crisp taste', he says. He also likes the image. In his mind, ale stands for a 'slightly older generation, family, countryside', while Bud is hip and urban. The clincher, perhaps, is that Mr Skelton's father drinks ale, and even brews it at home.

In the past, British beer seemed warm only to foreigners. Usually, it was served at least a few degrees below room temperature, a habit formed in the days before refrigeration, when beer was stored in cellars. But the average temperature of beer in the UK has been falling gradually for decades. Why this national cooling? The British have been steadily switching from ale to lager, the cold, golden style of beer that predominates in most parts of the world. In 1960 lager accounted for just 1 per cent of the British beer market. In 2000, lager's share was 62 per cent – a testament to decades of heavy advertising for foreign brands such as Budweiser, Stella Artois and Foster's. Once young drinkers get used to cold beer, they often find their fathers' ale too warm to be refreshing.[27]

The grey market

The old widowed woman sits alone in her clean but sparsely furnished apartment, while the television blares out a soap opera. Each day, she slowly and painfully makes her way out of the apartment and goes to the corner shop to buy essentials, bread, milk and vegetables, always being careful to pick the least expensive offering. Most of the time she sits in her rocking chair, thinking sadly of her dead husband and the good times she used to have.

Is this the image you have of a typical elderly consumer? Until recently, many marketers did. As a result, they largely neglected the elderly in their feverish pursuit of the baby boomer market. But as our population ages and people are living longer and healthier lives, the game is rapidly changing. A lot of businesses are beginning to replace the old stereotype of the poor recluse. The newer, more accurate image is of an elderly person who is active, interested in what life has to offer, and is an enthusiastic consumer with the means and willingness to buy many goods and services.

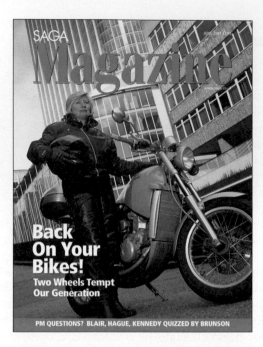

Saga Magazine is the UK's largest monthly magazine exclusively for people aged 50 and over.

Grey power: shattering stereotypes

By the year 2010, 20 per cent of Europeans will be 62 or older. This fastest-growing age segment can be explained by the aging of 'boomers', an increase in awareness of healthy lifestyles and nutrition, coupled with improved medical diagnoses and treatment. Over the past 50 years, life expectancy of men and women has risen steadily: by around 10 years for each sex. Throughout the European Union, women live longer than men. In 1998 the life expectancy of women in the EU-15 was 81 years, while that for men was 75. Estimates are that the life expectancy of women and men may reach 84 and 78 years respectively by the year 2020.[28] Not only is this segment growing and living longer, but older adults have large amounts of discretionary income, since they typically have paid off their mortgage, and no longer have the expense of raising and educating children.

Most elderly people lead more active, multidimensional lives than we assume. Many engage in voluntary work, continue to work and/or are involved in daily care of a grandchild. Still, outdated images of mature consumers persist. In one survey, one-third of consumers over age 55 reported that they deliberately did *not* buy a product because of the way an elderly person was stereotyped in the product's advertising.[29]

Seniors' economic clout

There is abundant evidence that the economic health of elderly consumers is good and getting better. Some of the important areas that stand to benefit from the surging **grey market** include holidays, cars, home improvements, cruises and tourism, cosmetic surgery and skin treatments, health, finance and legal matters, and 'how-to' books for learning to cope with retirement.

It is crucial to remember that income alone does not capture the spending power of this group. As mentioned above, elderly consumers are no longer burdened with the financial obligations that drain the income of younger consumers. Elderly consumers are much more likely to own their home, have no mortgage or have a (low-cost or subsidized) rented house or apartment. Across Europe, approximately 50 per cent of pensioners' income still comes from state pensions, yet it is clear that older consumers are time-rich, and have a significant amount of discretionary income to spend.[30] The relatively high living standards of future retirees (the baby boomers) and the stability of public finances in different European states has led to an active discussion of pension reform plans throughout the European Union. Nonetheless, pensions will continue to play an important role in the discretionary incomes of Europe's retired population. Table 13.3 shows the amounts paid out in pensions as a percentage of final salary.

Table 13.3 Amounts paid out in pensions as a percentage of final salary

Salary	20,000 euros	50,000 euros
Belgium	58%	45%
Finland	60%	59%
France	67%	51%
Germany	45%	43%
Greece	70%	48%
Ireland	53%	21%
Italy	78%	75%
The Netherlands	76%	31%
Portugal	74%	74%
Spain	94%	63%
UK	35%	14%
USA (for comparison)	71%	45%

Note: Different systems are not always directly comparable, as some base pensions on final salary, while others on average salary. Higher-income workers are treated differently, depending on country.
Sources: Fitch Investor Services; *Wall Street Journal* (30 October 2000): A21.

MARKETING OPPORTUNITY

A few marketers are beginning to recognize the vast potential of the senior market and are designing products and services to cater to the specific needs of the elderly. A growing number of magazines are also being targeted to meet the interests of the older consumer. *Active Life*, *Saga Magazine*, *Mature Tymes* and *Plus* are all targeted at the 'over 50' market, although you wouldn't necessarily know it by the magazines, photos, advertising or articles! Most covers show vital, active 50-plussers, and the advertising focuses on quality of service, value for money and straightforward communications. With the exception of a few older faces promoting incontinence products, you're more likely to see consumers on mountain bikes than tending the garden.

Even companies that have relatively many 65-plussers as a target market don't feel the need to associate 'old' with their products or services. Advertisements for river and ocean cruises (which have a high percentage of older clientele throughout Europe) show busy discos and swimming pools dominated by 30–40-year-old clients, with a few wrinkle-free elderly in the photo. The accent to the elderly market is on product benefits, and not whether the product is best suited for a particular age group.[31]

Researchers have identified a set of key values that are relevant to older consumers. For marketing strategies to succeed, they should be related to one or more of these factors:[32]

● *Autonomy*. Mature consumers want to lead active lives and to be self-sufficient. Financial services and financial planning are increasing markets for the elderly segment, who have a strong need to remain independent. While companies are the largest purchasers of cars in the UK, the majority of private buyers are 'greys' – a further sign of their financial muscle and desire for autonomy.[33]

● *Connectedness*. Mature consumers value the bonds they have with friends and family. While the 'grey' don't relate well to their own age group (most elderly report feeling on average ten years younger than they are, and feel that 'other' elderly behave 'older' than they do), they do value information which communicates clear benefits to cohorts in their age group. Advertisements which avoid patronizing stereotypes are well received.

● *Altruism*. Mature consumers want to give something back to the world. Thrifty Car Rental found in a survey that over 40 per cent of older consumers would select a rental car company if it sponsored a programme that gives discounts to senior citizens' centres. Based on this research, the company launched its highly successful 'Give a Friend a Lift' programme.

● *Personal growth*. Mature consumers are very interested in trying new experiences and developing their potential. By installing user-friendly interactive touch-screen computer stations in European stores, older consumers have become better educated about health issues, and are loyal to the GNC brand.[34]

Perceived age: you're only as old as you feel

The 'grey' market does not consist of a uniform segment of vigorous, happy, ready-to-spend consumers – nor is it a group of senile, economically marginalized, immobile people. In fact, research confirms the popular wisdom that age is more a state of mind than of body. A person's mental outlook and activity level has a lot more to do with his or her longevity and quality of life than does *chronological age*, or the actual number of years lived. In addition to these psychological dimensions of age, there are also cultural influences on what constitutes aging, and perceptions of what is 'elderly' across different European markets.[35]

A better yardstick to categorize the elderly is **perceived age**, or how old a person feels. Perceived age can be measured on several dimensions, including 'feel-age' (i.e. how old a person feels) and 'look-age' (i.e. how old a person looks).[36] The older con-

MARKETING PITFALL

Some marketing efforts targeted at the elderly have backfired because they reminded people of their age or presented their age group in an unflattering way. One of the more infamous blunders was committed by Heinz. A company analyst found that many elderly people were buying baby food because of the small portions and easy chewing consistency, so Heinz introduced a line of 'Senior Foods' made especially for denture wearers. Needless to say, the product failed. Consumers did not want to admit that they required strained foods (even to the supermarket cashier). They preferred to purchase baby foods, which they could pretend they were buying for a grandchild.

In Holland, a country where bicycles are an important mode of personal transportation, a specially designed 'elderly bicycle' was a resounding failure in spite of its competitive product benefits. While conventional marketing wisdom would suggest that a firm communicate its unique functional benefits to a target market, this wisdom backfired for the Dutch 'greys'. Positioning the bicycle as an easy-to-pedal 'senior bicycle' was met with a negative response, as the Dutch elderly who still ride a bicycle (a common sight in Holland!) feel too young to be riding a 'senior' bike.[38]

sumers get, the younger they feel relative to actual age. For this reason, many marketers emphasize product benefits rather than age appropriateness in marketing campaigns, since many consumers will not relate to products targeted to their chronological age.[37]

Segmenting seniors

The senior subculture represents an extremely large market: the number of Europeans aged 62 and over exceeds the entire population of Canada.[39] Because this group is so large, it is helpful to think of the mature market as consisting of four subsegments: an 'older' group (aged 55–64), an 'elderly' group (aged 65–74), an 'aged' group (aged 75–84) and finally a 'very old' group (85+).[40]

The elderly market is well suited for segmentation. Older consumers are easy to identify by age and stage in the family life cycle. Most receive Social Security benefits so they can be located without much effort, and many subscribe to one of the magazines targeted to the elderly, discussed earlier in this section. *Saga Magazine* in the UK has the largest circulation of any European magazine, with over 750,000 monthly readers. Selling holidays and insurance to the over-50s, the parent company also makes use of a database with over 4 million over-50s.

Several segmentation approaches begin with the premise that a major determinant of elderly marketplace behaviour is the way a person deals with being old.[41] *Social aging theories* try to understand how society assigns people to different roles across the lifespan. For example, when someone retires he/she may reflect society's expectations for someone at this life stage – this is a major transition point when people exit from many relationships.[42] Some people become depressed, withdrawn and apathetic as they age, some are angry and resist the thought of ageing, and some appear to accept the new challenges and opportunities this period of life has to offer.

Table 13.4 summarizes some selected findings from one current segmentation approach, called **gerontographics**, which divides the mature market into groups

Table 13.4 Gerontographics

Segment	55-plus	Profile	Marketing implications
Healthy indulgers	18%	Have experienced the fewest events related to aging, such as retirement or widowhood, and are most likely to behave like younger consumers. Main focus is on enjoying life.	Looking for independent living and are good customers for discretionary services like home-cleaning and answering machines.
Healthy hermits	36%	React to life events like the death of a spouse by becoming withdrawn. Resent that they are expected to behave like old people.	Emphasize conformity. They want to know their appearance is socially acceptable, and tend to be comfortable with well-known brands.
Ailing outgoers	29%	Maintain positive self-esteem despite adverse life events. They accept limitations but are still determined to get the most out of life.	Have health problems that may require a special diet. Special menus and promotions will bring these people into restaurants seen as catering to their needs.
Frail recluses	17%	Have adjusted their lifestyles to accept old age, but have chosen to cope with negative events by becoming spiritually stronger.	Like to stay put in the same house where they raised their families. Good candidates for redecorating, also for emergency response systems.

Source: Adapted from George P. Moschis, 'Life Stages of the Mature Market', *American Demographics* (September 1996): 44–50.

based on both level of physical well-being and social conditions, such as becoming a grandparent or losing a spouse.

MARKETING PITFALL

Many consumer products will encounter a more sympathetic reception from the elderly if products and the packages they come in are redesigned to be sensitive to physical limitations. While aesthetically appealing, packages are often awkward and difficult to manage, especially for those who are frail or arthritic. Also, many serving sizes are not geared to smaller families, widows or widowers and other people living alone, and coupons tend to be for family-sized products, rather than for single servings.

Older people may have difficulty with ring-pull cans and push-open milk cartons. Ziploc packages (self-sealing plastic bags) and clear plastic wrap are also difficult to handle. Packages need to be easy to read and should be made lighter and smaller. Finally, designers need to pay attention to contrasting colours. A slight yellowing of the eye's lens as one ages makes it harder to see background colours on packages. Discerning between blues, greens and violets becomes especially difficult. The closer identifying type colours are to the package's or advertisement's background colour, the less visibility and attention they will command.

In general, the elderly have been shown to respond positively to ads that provide an abundance of information. Unlike other age groups, these consumers are not usually amused, or persuaded, by imagery-oriented advertising. A more successful strategy involves the construction of advertising that depicts the aged as well-integrated, contributing members of society, with emphasis on them expanding their horizons rather than clinging precariously to life.

Some basic guidelines have been suggested for effective advertising to the elderly. These include the following:[43]

- Keep language simple.
- Use clear, bright pictures.
- Use action to attract attention.
- Speak clearly, and keep the word count low.
- Use a single sales message, and emphasize brand extensions to tap consumers' familiarity.
- Avoid extraneous stimuli (i.e. excessive pictures and graphics can detract from the message).

Chapter summary

- Europeans have many things in common with others merely because they are about the same age or live in the same country, or same part of the country. Consumers who grew up at the same time share many cultural memories, so they may respond to marketers' *nostalgia* appeals that remind them of these experiences.

- Important age cohorts include teenagers, 18–29-year-olds, baby boomers and the elderly. *Teenagers* are making a transition from childhood to adulthood, and their self-concepts tend to be unstable. They are receptive to products that help them to be accepted and enable them to assert their independence. Because many teenagers receive allowances, and/or earn pocket money but have few financial obligations, they are a particularly important segment for many non-essential or expressive products, ranging from chewing gum to hair gel, to clothing fashions and music. Because of changes in family structure, many teenagers are taking more responsibility for their families' day-to-day shopping and routine purchase decisions.

● 'Gen-Xers', consumers aged 18–29, are a difficult group for marketers to 'get a clear picture of'. They will be a powerful force in the years to come, whose tastes and priorities will be felt in fashion, popular culture, politics and marketing.

● *Baby boomers* are the most powerful age segment because of their size and economic clout. As this group has aged, its interests have changed and marketing priorities have changed as well. The needs and desires of baby boomers have a strong influence on demands for housing, child care, cars, clothing, and so on. Only a small proportion of boomers fit into an affluent, materialistic category.

● As the population ages, the needs of *elderly* consumers will also become increasingly influential. Many marketers traditionally ignored the elderly because of the stereotype that they are inactive and spend too little. This stereotype is no longer accurate. Most of the elderly are healthy, vigorous and interested in new products and experiences – and they have the income to purchase them. Marketing appeals to this age subculture should focus on consumers' self-concepts and perceived ages, which tend to be more youthful than their chronological ages. Marketers should emphasize the concrete benefits of products, since this group tends to be sceptical of vague, image-related promotions. Personalized service is of particular importance to this segment.

KEY TERMS

Age cohort (*p. 405*)	Gerontographics (*p. 421*)
Baby boomers (*p. 415*)	Grey market (*p. 419*)
Generation X (*p. 413*)	Perceived age (*p. 420*)

For additional material see the companion website at:
www.booksites.net/solomon_euro

Consumer behaviour challenge

1. As Europe moves further into the process of creating a single market and single currency, citizens' attitudes regarding different aspects of this complex process are monitored in all countries. See the following website for the most recent survey findings: *http://europa.eu.int/en/comm/dg10/infcom/epo/eo.html*. What sorts of tentative conclusions can you make with respect to the influence that age has on attitudes towards single currency, and other 'pan-European' efforts? What are the possible implications for the marketing of goods and services using a pan-European strategy?

2 Over the past few years, the Vatican has been involved in a variety of events aimed at developing a closer and stronger relationship with Europe's youth. At the invitation of the Pope, Bob Dylan (who is 50-something) gave a concert in 1997. Other Vatican-sponsored projects, such as World Youth Day, have enlisted French fashion designers (see Amy Barrett, 'John Paul II to Share Stage with Marketers', *Wall Street Journal Europe*, 19 August 1997: 4). Do a literature and web search to document the Vatican's activities that are targeted at youth. What goals do they seem to have in mind? What are the key segments? (Think in terms of age group segments, as well as geographic and cultural segmentation variables.) How successful a 'marketer' is the Vatican, in your opinion?

3 Below are a number of European retail websites. After reviewing the sites, give an analysis of target market and age segmentation strategies used by these firms.

> *www.waf.it.mall* (A weekend of shopping in Florence?)
> *www.one4you.be* (Interested in beer from Belgium?)
> *www.bexley.fr* ('Trend-resistant' shoes – French classics)
> *www.demon.co.uk/mace/cacmall.html* (Desert plants, offered in a variety of languages)
> *www.creor.com* (High-value jewellery from Italy, priced in dollars)
> *www.classicengland.co.uk* (Anglophile heaven – historical newspapers, teapots, etc.)

4 Why did baby boomers have such an important impact on consumer culture in the second half of the twentieth century?

5 How has the baby boomlet changed attitudes towards child-rearing practices and created demand for different products and services?

6 Is it practical to assume that people aged 55 and older constitute one large consumer market? What are some approaches to further segmenting this age subculture?

7 What are some important variables to keep in mind when tailoring marketing strategies to the elderly?

8 Find good and bad examples of advertising targeted at elderly consumers. To what degree does advertising stereotype the elderly? What elements of ads or other promotions appear to determine their effectiveness in reaching and persuading this group?

Notes

1. Bickley Townsend, 'Où sont les neiges d'antan? [Where are the snows of yesteryear?]', *American Demographics* (October 1988): 2.
2. Stephen Holden, 'After the War the Time of the Teen-Ager', *New York Times* (7 May 1995): E4.
3. 'Same Kids, More Money', Marketing (29 June 1995): 37; see also the following websites for some overviews of allowances: *http://www.kiplinger.com/drt.drthome.html* and *http://pages.prodigy.com/kidsmoney/*.
4. 'Same Kids, More Money'; Scott McCartney, 'Society's Subcultures Meet by Modem', *Wall Street Journal* (8 December 1994): B1 (2).
5. Sara Olkon, 'Black Soda with Skulls on Label Isn't Aimed at the Pepsi Generation', *Wall Street Journal* (24 May 1995): B1.
6. Junu Bryan Kim, 'For Savvy Teens: Real Life, Real Solutions', *Advertising Age* (23 August 1993): S1 (3pp.).
7. 'Hopes and Fears: Young European Opinion Leaders', GfK, adapted from *Marketing Week* (25 June 1998) (study of 500 opinion leaders aged 14–20 from 16 western and eastern European countries).
8. Howard W. French, 'Vocation for Dropouts is Painting Tokyo Red', *New York Times on the Web* (5 March 2000).
9. Yumiko Ono, 'They Say that a Japanese Gal is an Individualist: Tall, Tan, Blond', *Wall Street Journal Interactive Edition* (19 November 1999).
10. Yumiko Ono, 'Meet a Beer, a Car, a Refrigerator, and a Fabric Deodorizer, All Named Will', *Wall Street Journal Interactive Edition* (8 October 1999).
11. Ellen Goodman, 'The Selling of Teenage Anxiety', *Washington Post* (24 November 1979).
12. Yumiko Ono, 'Limited Too Will Blitz Preteens with Catalogs of Their Very Own', *Wall Street Journal Interactive Edition* (15 August 1998).

13. Quoted in Karen Springen, Ana Figueroa and Nicole Joseph-Goteiner, 'The Truth About Tweens', *Newsweek* (18 October 1999): 62–72, at 64.

14. Matthew Grimm, 'Snap It, Girlfriend!', *American Demographics* (April 2000): 66–7.

15. Ellen R. Foxman, Patriya S. Tansuhaj and Karim M. Ekstrom, 'Family Members' Perceptions of Adolescents' Influence in Family Decision Making', *Journal of Consumer Research* 15 (March 1989): 482–91.

16. 'Men and Women in the European Union: A Statistical Portrait', Eurostat (Luxembourg: Office for Official Publications of the European Communities, 1995).

17. Gary J. Bamossy, Trinske Antonidies, Michael R. Solomon and Basil G. Englis, 'You're not Cool if You Have to Ask: Gender in the Social Construction of Coolness', paper presented at the Association for Consumer Research Gender Conference, Chicago, June 2000; Trinske Antonides, 'The Underlying Dimensions of Coolness', unpublished masters thesis, Vrije Universiteit, Amsterdam, 2000. See also this website on 'cool': *http://www.pbs.org/wgbh/pages/frontline/shows/cool/*.

18. 'Living Conditions in Europe: Statistical Handbook', Eurostat (Luxembourg, Office for Official Publications of the European Communities, 2000): 29.

19. Deborah Klosky, 'World Bank Ads Target Youths', *Wall Street Journal Europe* (7 October 1997): 4; Karen Ritchie, *Marketing to Generation X* (New York: Lexington Books, 1995); Rob Nelson, *Revolution X: Survival Guide for Our Generation* (New York: Penguin Books, 1994); for a 'Gen-X' website, see *http://www.acent.net/in-mtl/v04n03/generax.htm*; Laura Zinn, 'Move Over, Boomers', *Business Week* (14 December 1992): 7.

20. 'Generation Next', *Marketing* (16 January 1997): 25.

21. Quoted in T. L. Stanley, 'Age of Innocence ... Not', *PROMO* (February 1997): 28–33, at 30.

22. 'Generation Next', 26.

23. Scott Donaton, 'The Media Wakes Up to Generation X', *Advertising Age* (1 February 1993): 16 (2); Laura E. Keeton, 'New Magazines Aim to Reach (and Rechristen) Generation X', *Wall Street Journal* (17 October 1994): B1.

24. Faye Rice, 'Making Generational Marketing Come of Age', *Fortune* (26 June 1995): 110–14.

25. Sarah Ellison, 'BT Taps St. Luke to Woo Youth Market', *Wall Street Journal* (30 November 2000): B2.

26. Rice, 'Making Generational Marketing Come of Age'.

27. James Hagerty, 'Cooler Heads Prevail as Britain Loses Lust for Warm, Cloudy Ales', *Wall Street Journal* (29 August 2000): A1.

28. 'Living Conditions in Europe: Statistical Handbook', Eurostat: 101.

29. 'Shades of Grey', *Marketing* (24 April 1997); 'Baby boom generatie moet oud-zijn modieus maken' ['Baby boom generation has to make "old" in fashion'], *NRC Handelsblad* (2 May 1996): 7; Melinda Beck, 'Going for the Gold', *Newsweek* (23 April 1990): 74.

30. 'Shades of Grey'.

31. 'Shades of Grey'; 'Baby boom generatie moet oud-zijn modieus maken'.

32. David B. Wolfe, 'Targeting the Mature Mind', *American Demographics* (March 1994): 32–6.

33. 'Shades of Grey'.

34. Allyson Steward-Allen, 'Marketing in Europe to the Consumer Over Age Fifty', *Marketing News* 31(16) (4 August 1997): 18.

35. Gabriele Morello, 'Old is Gold, But What is Old?', ESOMAR seminar on 'The Untapped Gold Mine: The Growing Importance of the Over-50s' (Amsterdam: ESOMAR, 1989); Gabriele Morello, 'Sicilian Time', in *Time and Society* (London: Sage Publications, 1997): 6(1): 55–69. See also 'Living Conditions in Europe: Statistical Handbook', Eurostat: 9–21.

36. Benny Barak and Leon G. Schiffman, 'Cognitive Age: A Nonchronological Age Variable', in Kent B. Monroe ed., *Advances in Consumer Research* 8 (Provo, UT: Association for Consumer Research, 1981): 602–6.

37. David B. Wolfe, 'An Ageless Market', *American Demographics* (July 1987): 27–55.

38. 'Baby boom generatie moet oud-zijn modieus maken'.

39. 'Demographic Statistics 1997', Eurostat (Luxembourg: Office for Official Publications of the European Communities, 1997); see also *http://europa.eu.int*; Lenore Skenazy, 'These Days, It's Hip to be Old', *Advertising Age* (15 February 1988).

40. This segmentation approach is based on the US population and follows William Lazer and Eric H. Shaw, 'How Older Americans Spend Their Money', *American Demographics* (September 1987): 36. See also 'Shades of Grey' for a two-segment approach to the UK elderly market, and 'Living Conditions in Europe: Statistical Handbook', Eurostat: 9–21.

41. Ellen Day, Brian Davis, Rhonda Dove and Warren A. French, 'Reaching the Senior Citizen Market(s)', *Journal of Advertising Research* (December/January 1987/88): 23–30; Warren A. French and Richard Fox, 'Segmenting the Senior Citizen Market', *Journal of Consumer Marketing* 2 (1985): 61–74; Jeffrey G. Towle and Claude R. Martin, Jr, 'The Elderly Consumer: One Segment or Many?', in Beverlee B. Anderson, ed., *Advances in Consumer Research* 3 (Provo, UT: Association for Consumer Research, 1976): 463.

42. Catherine A. Cole and Nadine N. Castellano, 'Consumer Behavior', *Encyclopedia of Gerontology* vol. 1 (1996): 329–39.

43. J. Ward, 'Marketers Slow to Catch Age Wave', *Advertising Age* (22 May 1989): S-1.

CASE STUDY 7

Jolly Cola: Jack the Dullard marketing against the global powers[1]

SØREN ASKEGAARD and FABIAN F. CSABA

'Once upon a time there were three brothers', the narrator begins as we are shown a parchment map of Denmark. 'The two oldest considered themselves rather attractive.' Two brothers appear, one cruising in a convertible, another on a motorcycle, both wearing heavy make-up and Baroque attire, '. . . but of course they had been to America and now they wanted to marry . . .' (we see a princess on a screen) '. . . the lovely Princess Tina'. The camera zooms out and we discover that the screen is mounted on a traditional Danish mobile hot-dog stand (*pølsevogn*) where a ragged dork watching the screen is completely dazed by her beauty. The stiff squeezes a half-litre bottle of cola of the 'Jolly' brand down in his right front pocket and sets off. While we see him driving his moped against the background of the parchment map, the narrator explains: 'the youngest brother was called Prince Jolly . . . but no one really counted on him. Nevertheless he also headed for the castle where Princess Tina was inspecting all her suitors.' A camera suspended from the ceiling moves over the line-up of hopefuls including the fancy older brothers of Prince Jolly. The wooers appearing on her monitor clearly do not excite her. 'In the middle of the ceremony', the narrator goes on, 'Prince Jolly walks in and shouts "Hey, aren't you the one with the ripe fruits?" The princess looks down at him and then looks closer.' The camera moves down the body of the prince and stops at the bulge in his trousers. The princess is clearly intrigued and steps down from her throne and approaches him. Prince Jolly, now in courtly attire, is seen holding the hand of his bride in front of a castle, both smiling blissfully. This image of the happy couple then appears on a photo. Another picture next to it shows three children. Between the family portraits is a half-full bottle of Jolly Cola. The story ends: 'And then they lived happily ever after. And if you think that it was his big Jolly Cola she fell for, think again. But it was good for the thirst . . . afterwards . . .'

This pastiche of Hans Christian Andersen's fairy tale *Klods Hans* (in English *Jack the Dullard*[2]) is one example in a series of advertising efforts to reinvigorate the image of the Danish soft drink Jolly Cola, and reclaim the strong market position it enjoyed throughout the 1960s and 1970s. Something of an anomaly in Europe, Jolly had managed to defend its home turf against the American cola giants and remained the dominant cola until it began to lose its grip on the market in the early 1980s and plunged to a mere 6 per cent of the market share in the late 1990s. The advertising fairy tale is a thinly veiled allegory. In Hans Christian Andersen's story, Jack the Dullard succeeds through limited means, making good use of whatever he comes across (a billygoat for transportation, a dead crow, a wooden shoe and a pocketful of wet clay). The prepared speeches and rehearsed wit of the older two brothers let them down in the strange scenario staged by the fussy and demanding princess. Jack's improvised, bold and crazy repartee, however, paves the way for an absurd interplay that wins her over. The commercial appears to be a projection of management's dream of outwitting the forceful, fancied and fanciful American contenders and winning the Danish consumer . . . and, of course, living happily ever after.

The history of Jolly reflects the changing and ambiguous reception of American culture in Denmark as well as the country's economic and political relationship with the United States. Coca-Cola came to Denmark in 1938 but only for a brief spell because of the shortages and rationing of sugar during the Second World War. A high special tax on cola was imposed to protect the Danish market and this meant that Coke did not return until 1959. By the time the cola tax was removed, 16 Danish breweries and soft-drink bottlers had joined forces to produce a Danish version of the American soft drink and prevent an American invasion. The name 'Jolly', with its rhyme on then popular names such as Tommy or Johnny, seems to have been chosen as a reference to the still vivid images of the merry Anglo-Saxon 'Tommies' – the liberators of Denmark after the German occupation during the war. Furthermore, its meaning was a direct reference to the leisurely values of the rising consumer society, inspired by the American missionaries of new consumer values, but in the hope that a local carrier would be able to hold the intruding strangers at bay. With an efficient and strong distribution system already in place, Jolly Cola quickly established itself and was advertised heavily in cinemas and popular weekly magazines. In the early 1970s, Jolly Cola was still the dominant brand. Its advertising campaigns featured groups of male and female teenagers relaxing and having fun together in the Danish summer, rowing canoes, splashing together in the sea on an inflatable mattress or strolling down a country road. The images of Coca-Cola and Pepsi (which entered the market in 1971) seemed to suffer from identification with America and their mass commodities with imperialist capitalism. Anti-American feelings were also fuelled by the Vietnam War and years later Danish marketers would joke that it would take another Vietnam War or something of that order to help Jolly Cola rebound. From the late 1970s the cultural mood seems to have swung and the American colas quickly gained ground. Media development became an important factor in the 1980s. The monopoly of the Danish state television was broken in 1988 and a new national network, TV2, began airing TV commercials for the first time on Danish television. Satellite and cable channels followed quickly. Coca-Cola made the most of the new advertising opportunities and at one point bought a whole commercial break and showed a range of its international Christmas ads. Confronted with such an overwhelming marketing attack, the dwindling local brand had to mount some kind of 'symbolic' defence of its remaining market share.

The allegory in the Prince Jolly commercial in fashioning the brand personality after Numskull Jack suggests that Jolly was in a bad shape image-wise and that management had to come up with some way of regenerating the brand. Other Jolly advertisements reflected the challenges of the local company in facing up to the marketing muscle flexed by the American cola giants in Denmark. One advertisement depicts a young, blond, Danish woman being interrogated by a customs officer upon her arrival at a US airport. The customs officer chides the woman for attempting to bring a Jolly cola into 'the United States of America . . . the home of cola'. The young woman suggests that the customs officer tastes the cola, which he does. Liking it, he decides to keep it 'for further investigation'. The final frame of the advertisement reveals that the bottle ends up empty alongside several other empty Jolly Cola bottles in a US Customs storage facility. The issue of measuring up to American tastes and standing up to American authority emerged in another commercial, a spoof on the blind taste approach in the 'Pepsi Challenge' campaign, in which a blindfolded

Jolly representative conducts a mock blind-test. Unable to see what he is doing, he turns the glass the wrong way round and spills Jolly Cola on the table he is sitting at as he tries to pour from the bottle. He discovers the mistake and manages to fill his glass. After having tasted the drink he exclaims: 'mmm ... Yes ... it's now proven that Jolly tastes good. Even in the dark'. Another advertisement showed a laboratory test of prototypes for a new, improved Jolly bottle, one more phallic than the other. The test responses ranged from delight to outrage, and the advertisement concludes that despite the exciting reactions Jolly will introduce a new bottle that is neither interesting nor sexy, but light and practical.

It is very clear that the commercial explicitly parodied American methods of promotion and marketing research. In doing so Jolly Cola simultaneously acknowledged the indisputable fact that there is something 'magic' about marketing icons such as Coke's hobbleskirt bottle and logo or the irrefutability of American marketing research techniques. But on the other hand, it invited (Danish) consumers to turn their backs on the unabashed American marketing wizardry and slick professionalism and go for the (stereo)typically Danish practical, no-nonsense approach to marketing and unpretentious, tongue-in-cheek advertising.

But the advertising efforts of Jolly Cola also suggest the difficulties of mounting an effective defence against the American colas. It is clear that the field of significations on which the positioning battle of colas in Denmark is fought favours Coke and Pepsi. Jolly needs to define itself against the 'Americanness' of the two giants in the Danish market, their references to world culture, their wars against each other, and the whole mythology created and maintained in the interplay between Coca-Cola the product, and Coca-Cola the icon of consumer culture. This way, paradoxically, the local character of Jolly Cola has only one point of gravity: the globality of the competitors.

Although several of the Jolly Cola commercials attracted a great deal of attention and were popular, they failed to appeal to the national collective identity and accomplish a turnaround for the fledgling local brand. We might say that Jolly's resistance has for the past decade been symbolic in the double sense of the word. It has been played out in a register of symbolic images copying and countering the marketing imagery of the global competitors. The efforts have, however, been largely in vain, the marketing communication generating some sympathy, but constantly trailing the competitors in terms of number of exposures and having had no positive impact in raising the market share of the brand.

It is evident that Jolly was unable to play effectively on a sense of national identity and traditional prejudices against America. And the question is whether young Danes care about Americanization while they have a Coke with their burger at one of the many new McDonald's or Burger King franchises that have mushroomed in Denmark in the past decade. It is obvious that Danish youth has an appetite and taste for American mass culture, and in appropriating it they are increasingly asking for (or perhaps just being served) the real thing.

The question is whether there were other ways of reviving Jolly than the Numskull Jack approach. One alternative strategy proposed in an advertising pitch for the Jolly account suggested a radical change of the target market of Jolly. The agency believed that Jolly should forget about the heavy consumers of cola in their teens and twenties, considering this age group a 'lost generation' for Jolly Cola, and instead target the very young, 6–10-year-olds, and their parents in the age group 32–49 years. The idea was to address an age group not yet prejudiced against Jolly, and to present the Jolly brand as a 'backyard puma', a charming, streetwise survivor whose personality would appeal to the kids. At the same time, their parents would be reminded nostalgically of the brand of their own youth.[3] However, this strategy was not adopted, and the Jolly brand is still struggling to stay alive in the market it dominated for a quarter of a century.

Questions

1 Which developments in the marketing environment contributed to the decline of Jolly Cola?

2 Explain the communication strategy of Jolly. How did the Numskull Jack approach try to appeal to the Danish customer?

3 Why did it become increasingly difficult for Jolly to position itself against Coca-Cola and Pepsi?

4 Assess the proposed 'backyard puma' marketing strategy of abandoning the heavy users in their teens and twenties and instead targeting families by capturing the imagination of the children and appealing to the nostalgia of their parents. Would it work?

5 Can you think of other examples of local companies using parody and national identification in their communication to consumers to fight off global competition? Any success examples?

Notes

1. For a full-length article discussion of this theme, see Søren Askegaard and Fabian F. Csaba, 'The Good, the Bad, and the Jolly: Taste, Image and the Symbolic Resistance to the Coca-Colonization of Denmark', in S. Brown and A. Patterson, eds, *Imagining Marketing* (London: Routledge, 2001): 124–40.
2. In English, the fairy tale is also known under the titles: Clod Hans, Clumsy Hans, Numskull Jack and Simple Simon.
3. Cf. John Hird and Kirsten Poulsen, *Danske reklamekampagner – forførende underholdning?* (Copenhagen: Gyldendal, 2000).

KILROY Travels International

SUZANNE BECKMANN

KILROY Travels International is an international enterprise with subsidiary companies in seven countries: Finland, Denmark, Norway, Sweden, Holland, the Netherlands and Spain. The firm was founded in 1991 and is primarily owned by student organizations from Finland, Denmark, Sweden, Norway and Iceland. KILROY is a market leader in several countries with regard to its target group, which consists of people younger than 26 and students younger than 33 years.

The basis for all activities is expressed in KILROY's mission statement, which says that: 'The corporate mission of KILROY Travels is providing students and other young people aged 16–32 with affordable quality travel products through our integrated group of distribution companies. We want to supply the most demanded travel conditions, the most appreciated travel services, and the best and most efficient distribution of our travel products to meet the specific needs of our costumer group, "The Young Independent Traveller".'

The product

The travels KILROY sells are based on the 'KILROY ticket', which is an air ticket. The ticket is designed according to what KILROY anticipates the target group will expect from a travel product. The ticket is based on freedom and flexibility, as the travel plan can be changed at any time, even after the travel has begun. The KILROY ticket is valid for a year, and tickets that have not been used can be reimbursed for a minor fee.

KILROY operates from its own retail shops in all European markets except Spain, where it operates as a wholesaler connected to a large network of agents. Worldwide, 130 service centres are attached, all of which are independent travel agencies but with their focus on young people and students. This means that they know the target group's needs. Travellers can seek advice and guidance at the centres, change their ticket to other destinations, or alter the duration of their travel even when underway. This network is extremely important in order that the flexibilty of the KILROY tickets can be fully used.

The consultants meeting the customers in the sales offices are themselves part of the 'Young Independent Traveller' target group. They all have experience with this particular kind of travel that KILROY sells, and therefore know precisely what questions young travellers typically have before they leave. Therefore all employees are an important part of the product KILROY sells.

The target group

Although KILROY often speaks of its target group as the 'Young Independent Traveller', and sells its product exclusively to people younger than 26 and students younger than 33 years, the target group for its communication is narrower, and is divided into primary and secondary segments.

- The primary target group is the one which makes up the largest part of KILROY's market. This group consists of students in higher education, aged 19–26.
- The secondary target group primarily consists of first-time travellers aged 16–19 from senior high schools.

Communication for the target group

KILROY's target group is familiar with the mass media and therefore has high expectations of all kinds of communication. The most important features are:

- An intelligent target group demands ads which allow them to think for themselves.
- Mainstream communication is not paid much attention by the target group.
- The consumption of all types of brands signals which identity the individual has or wishes to have.
- Cinema ads are valued more positively by the target group than are TV spots.
- Excessive repetition is perceived as condescending.

The market

The travel industry in Denmark was for many years – and still is – characterized by hard competition and as a consequence of this the market is full of cheap travel offers and low profit for the travel agencies. The worst years were 1996 and 1997 when respectively 12 and 11 travel agencies went bankrupt.

For several years prices were due to an oversupply of travel, forcing the agencies to sell part of their deals without profit. As a consequence, a number of the larger companies had deficits for several years. In 1998 approximately 1.2 million charter travels were offered and the industry agreed that this was 200,000 travels too much. Competition was further intensified by the emergence of internet-based suppliers who are able to keep down costs by lower expenses for rooms, personnel and administration. The airlines here also got an opportunity to reach the consumers more directly and thereby act without the involvement of the travel agencies.

KILROY is not in direct competition with the large charter companies, but it has still been exposed to some of the effects of unstable price development on the market. Travellers have had the opportunity to buy a much cheaper product than KILROY's by benefitting from the large companies' price dumping. It is not the same type of travel, but there is a certain price elasticity on KILROY's products compared to more conventional products.

KILROY's brand

Until KILROY's change of agency at the end of 1997, all marketing was based on the 'KILROY declaration of independence', a campaign designed by Ogilvy & Mather in Copenhagen. The campaign was based on the value of independence and the right to move freely around the world: all people (and especially young people) are independent, and KILROY can help them in manifesting this.

But in 1997 KILROY was facing a number of problems which forced it to reconsider its marketing: stagnating or decreasing sales in KILROY's markets, stagnating or falling levels of acquaintance, and lack of concordance between the target group's perception of KILROY and the image it wanted to give the target group.

The problem with independence

The problem concerning the target group's perception of KILROY became apparent in a target group analysis commissioned by the enterprise. The analysis contained an examination of the target group and a test of the 'KILROY declaration of independence'. Through a number of qualitative interviews it was found that the target group did not think that the very concept of independence – or the way it was used – bore a clear relation to 'travel'.

They found that the concept of the campaign (declaration of independence) was confusing because independence was perceived as a concept bound to an individual. Whether a person was independent or not was seen to be determined by the way in which a person relates to his/her surroundings. They saw KILROY's campaign as an attempt to signal that when travelling one is independent. Their clear attitude was that a person's independence was not determined by whether he or she often changed place geographically or not.

The result was that the target group came to have a negative attitude towards KILROY because the campaign was perceived as a primitive trick. None of the respondents doubted that the overall aim of communication was to sell travel. Therefore they were offended by KILROY's seeking to manipulate them into believing that the aim of the communication was about something else – more altruistic – by attributing to the product the capacity of being able to create –independence.

New objective

KILROY's aims for its new campaign were to:

- Maintain and develop a level of acquaintance.
- Create a positive relation between the target group's perception of KILROY's brand and its products over the long term.
- Create sufficient interest and attention in KILROY to make people go to the shops.
- Communicate and thus help in selling travel.
- Contain great creativity and intend to be untraditional.
- Be able to function internationally (in Denmark, Norway, Sweden, Finland, Germany and the Netherlands).

In the outline KILROY stressed that its campaigns should still be dominated by a 'crazy edge' so that KILROY could still be positioned as an alternative to the traditional travel agencies.

Budget

This objective should be reached on the basis of a relatively small budget. This meant that beyond the demand of the concept itself there was also a demand for creativity or ingenuity when it came to choice of media.

Questions

1 Is the *country of origin* relevant in relation to companies in the travel industry? In what ways could the new agency relate to the demand for an international communication platform? Ought national conditions to be taken into consideration in order to maintain the impression of nearness (e.g. safety)?

2 *Brand differentation (stress a unique feature/attribute).* Which attributes/consequences ought communication to focus on and what effects should it give?

3 *Dual component model.* Traditional communication in the travel industry takes its point of departure from the combination of blue water, palms and beach with a special price attached. Consider how KILROY can use the interplay between verbal and visual elements in endeavours to achieve a positively loaded differentiation.

4 *Fear appeals* are chiefly used in social/health-oriented campaigns (speed limit, cancer, AIDS, etc.). Could a fear appeal be used in KILROY's communication? Has a fear appeal any relevance in relation to product or target group (social context)?

5 Argue in relation to the ELM model whether the strategy for the new campaign should aim towards a change of attitude through a central or a peripheral way, and state the reasons.

CASE STUDY 9

Commodification, appropriation and singularization: the imaginary case of 'a 1985 Château Léoville Las-Cases'[1]

PER ØSTERGAARD, JAMES A FITCHETT and CHRISTIAN JANTZEN

Although hundreds of thousands of pairs of Levi's jeans are produced each year, it is amazing that you can tell your own pair from any other pair in the world. We take for granted the fact that we can distinguish between our own wristwatch and someone else's wristwatch, even if they are a similar or even an identical model. We might say, 'it just doesn't *feel* right', or, 'it just doesn't *look* like mine'. My Nintendo Gameboy is, quite clearly, my own, as is my mobile phone, my pair of Nike training shoes, and perhaps even my copy of *Consumer Behaviour: A European Perspective*.

Mass consumer goods are by definition mass-produced, and relationships between producer, seller and buyer tend to be indirect and abstract. As consumers we do not (and probably cannot) find out anything about those involved with the production of the goods we consume. It would be unusual if someone were to say to you, 'My Nokia mobile phone is really special and unique to me. I know the guy at the factory and he made this particular 7110 model just for me.' When we buy a new pair of Levi 501's, we do not expect to know anything about the person who made the jeans, or even in which country they were manufactured. Equally, the factory worker making the jeans does not have any knowledge about your own specifications or requirements when producing the product. Under these conditions goods take on the characteristic of commodities, that is, on the market they do not retain the identity of those involved in their production, and they are not tailored to the requirements of individual consumers. Most products are, quite literally, '*mass-produced*' for an unspecified generic or broadly segmented consumer group.

Despite these impersonal and abstract commodity relations, people in consumer societies use goods and services to shape, define and communicate a personal and individual social identity. Paradoxically, we all use mass-produced commodities to construct individual statements about ourselves to others. But in order for us to be able to consume mass-produced products *en masse*, and still feel that this is an individual, even unique expression of our 'self', we need to be able to appropriate and singularize commodities into a context relevant to our own lives and circumstances. It must be possible for individual consumers to take mass-produced goods such as mobile phones, computer consoles, branded running shoes and denim jeans, and make them their own. Some consumer behaviours can thus be thought of as processes of 'de-commodification' whereby mass-produced goods take on personal, private and individual values which replace the public and shared values of commodified goods. These processes of de-commodification are as important as the processes of manufacture and production. To illustrate these processes, let us consider the following hypothetical example:

Can you remember (or imagine) that back in 1987 you bought, soon after its initial release, a case of 1985 Château Léoville Las-Cases which you added to your then modest wine cellar. If you remember back to 1987 when you acquired the wine, you can remember knowing then as you do now that 1985 was a good harvest and can recall anticipating that it would be a good wine in years to come. During the intervening years you have opened five or perhaps six bottles, and can remember each of the special occasions when you drank the wine. Your memories of the people who shared the wine with you accompany your thoughts about how the wine has changed in taste and flavour each time you have opened a bottle. It is likely that you will think carefully about when it would be appropriate to open the remaining bottles, and with whom you would like to share them. Maybe an old friend who was with you back then in '87 but who you haven't seen for many years might get back in touch and come over, and you will open a bottle for old times' sake. Exactly how you will feel about the last bottle is difficult to predict, because it will in part rely on when and where you drink the remaining bottles. But it will probably be an important occasion, shared with close friends and family . . .

Now, what if we had never purchased that case of Château Léoville Las-Cases back in 1987? Instead you have been invited by a colleague to dinner one evening and (as is customary) you decide to stop off along the way and pick up a couple of bottles of wine so you have something appropriate to present to your host as a gift on arrival. Perhaps wanting to impress your colleague, or maybe just feeling that it is important that you make a good impression, you look around the wine shop and decide on two bottles of Château Léoville Las-Cases, '87. This acquisition, you determine, will demonstrate a number of values to your host. It will perhaps indicate that you have a sophisticated knowledge of wine (what we might term cultural capital). Of course your host needs to know something of wine in order for this knowledge, and this bottle, to be appreciated. The cost may also show that you are honoured by the invitation, and that you hold your host in high regard. Of course it might also suggest to your host that you are reasonably wealthy. After all, not all of us are either knowledgeable or wealthy enough to present two bottles of vintage wine each time we receive a dinner invitation.

The wine bought for the cellar and the wine bought for the dinner invitation are of course the same product. In fact if one were to replace a bottle from the cellar with a bottle from the wine store it is plausible to assume that you would not be able to tell the difference unless obvious marks or cues had been applied to the label or bottle. Both the bottle in your cellar and the bottle purchased from the wine store were produced in the same way and share a common origin. But this short example demonstrates how consumer goods can become wrapped in a metaphysical context that is produced or created not by a manufacturer, but by the consumer immediately before, during and after acquisition. Both bottles of wine gain, or are endowed by the consumer with, what we might think of as an 'aura' or set of personalized, customized values and meanings. Although the bottle from the first scenario (the 'cellar' wine) has 'acquired' a whole set of personal values for its owner that seem deeper or more meaningful than the wine purchased from the store, this bottle also acquires some additional values as soon as it is purchased for the dinner party gift. Symbolic values associated with status, cultural knowledge and so on are simply elements of another 'aura'.

We can therefore conclude that once acquired, some commodities are *appropriated* by consumers and consequently these products continue to collect and retain additional meaning and values. The consumer may therefore purchase a commodity and then begin *producing* its meaning after acquisition. All kinds of mass-produced goods have the potential to become sacred and reified objects. Goods can come to represent all kinds of personal nostalgia, emotion and other individual values. This is the process of *de-commodification*, which occurs when a good that was initially valued in terms of shared public and market defined meanings is appropriated or *singularized* by a consumer and attributed with private, specific and personalized meanings and value. By being singularized a product is moulded and shaped to meet the requirements and expectations of an individual consumer. It becomes a container of personal meanings and a materialization of emotions and longings. The appropriation of commodities involves the transformation of an object into a *property*, that is, a transformation into a reflection of its owner. This process shows how consumers are able to participate in mass markets yet also retain and construct a personal and social identity beyond the market and commodity relations.

Questions

1 What types of mass-produced commodities can be appropriated and de-commodified? Are some product categories more easily appropriated, and if so, why?

2 Should commodification be thought of as a linear process or a cyclical process? Can de-commodified objects be 're-commodified', and if so, how might this be applied to the example given above?

3 How could the concepts of de-commodification, appropriation and singularization be used to help us understand and explain consumption behaviour relating to second-hand clothing? How might this contrast and compare with appropriation and singularization behaviours associated with mobile phones, or computer game consoles?

4 How might these issues support and relate to the concept of the 'extended self'?

Note

1. This case is adapted from Per Østergaard, James A. Fitchett and Christian Jantzen, 'On appropriation and singularisation: two consumption processes', in E. J. Arnould and L. M. Scott, eds, *Advances in Consumer Research* 26 (Provo, UT: Association for Consumer Research, 1999): 405–9.

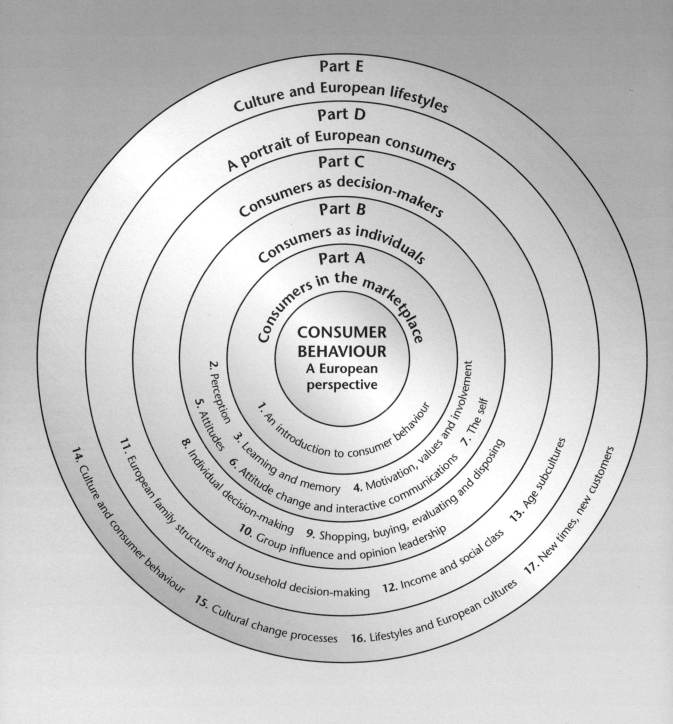

Part E
Culture and European lifestyles

Part D
A portrait of European consumers

Part C
Consumers as decision-makers

Part B
Consumers as individuals

Part A
Consumers in the marketplace

CONSUMER
BEHAVIOUR
A European
perspective

1. An introduction to consumer behaviour

2. Perception

3. Learning and memory

4. Motivation, values and involvement

5. Attitudes

6. Attitude change and interactive communications

7. The self

8. Individual decision-making

9. Shopping, buying, evaluating and disposing

10. Group influence and opinion leadership

11. European family structures and household decision-making

12. Income and social class

13. Age subcultures

14. Culture and consumer behaviour

15. Cultural change processes

16. Lifestyles and European cultures

17. New times, new customers

Part E

CULTURE AND EUROPEAN LIFESTYLES

The final part of this book considers consumers as members of a broad cultural system. Chapter 14 starts this part by examining some of the basic building blocks of culture and consumption, and shows how consumer behaviours and culture are constantly interacting with each other. Chapter 15 looks at the production of culture, and how the 'gatekeepers' of culture help shape our sense of fashion and consumer culture. Chapter 16 focuses on the importance of understanding consumers' lifestyles throughout Europe, and illustrates the lifestyle concept and its marketing applications with a discussion of food, drink and cars. Finally, in Chapter 17 we look at some new perspectives on consumers' behaviour, including environmentalism, postmodernism and globalization. We try to place our western European consumer behaviour into the larger context of the global marketplace. These reflections on social changes in consumption bring our study of consumer behaviour into the new millennium.

Chapter 14

Culture and consumer behaviour

It's Thursday night, 7.30. Sean puts down the phone after speaking with Colum, his study partner in his consumer behaviour class. The weekly night out for the Irish marketing students has begun! Sean has just spent the summer months travelling in Europe. He was always amazed, and delighted, to find a place claiming to be an Irish pub – regardless of how unauthentic the place was, an Irish pub always sold Guinness, a true symbol of Ireland, he reflected. Sean had begun to drink when he started university. Initially, bottled beers straight from the fridge had been his preference. However, now that he's in his third year and a more sophisticated, travelled and rounded person, he feels that those beers were just a little too – well, fashionable. He has thus recently begun to drink Guinness. His dad, uncle and grandad, in fact most of the older men he knows, drink Guinness. That day in consumer behaviour the lecturer had discussed the 'Guinness Time' TV commercial which had been run the previous year. It featured a young man doing a crazy dance around a settling pint of Guinness. The young man saved his most crazed expression for the point when he took his first sip. The lecturer had pointed out that the objectives of the ad were to associate Guinness with fun – an important reason why young people drink alcohol – and to encourage them to be patient with the stout, as a good pint takes a number of minutes to settle.

Sean has arranged to meet his friends in the local pub at 8.30. They will order 'three pints of the finest black stuff' and then have their own Guinness ritual. To begin, they watch it being poured and then look for the rising rings of the head – the best indication of a good pint. Once settled, a small top-up, and then ready for action. But they always wait and study their glasses before taking the first mouthful together – what a thing of beauty!

Damien McLoughlin, University College, Dublin, Ireland

Culture and consumption

Consumption choices cannot be understood without considering the cultural context in which they are made: culture is the 'prism' through which people view products and try to make sense of their own and other people's consumer behaviour.

Sean's beer-drinking reflects his desire to associate with and dissociate from (with help from the media and marketers) a certain style, attitude and trendiness. Being an Irishman, his attachment to Guinness has a very different meaning in his world than it would have in, for example, trendy circles in continental cities, where Guinness may be associated with the very fashionability that Sean tries to avoid.

Indeed, it is quite common for cultures to modify symbols identified with other cultures and present these to a new audience. As this occurs, these cultural products undergo a process of **cooptation**, where their original meanings are transformed and often trivialized by outsiders. In this case, an Irish beer was to a large extent divorced from its original connection with the Irish traditional working class or rurality and is now used as a trendy way of consuming 'Irishness' abroad (but without the rural or lower-class aspect).[1]

This chapter considers how the culture in which we live creates the meaning of everyday products and how these meanings move through a society to consumers. As Figure 14.1 shows, meaning transfer is largely accomplished by such marketing vehicles as the advertising and fashion industries, which associate products with symbolic qualities. These goods, in turn, impart their meanings to consumers through different forms of ritual and are used to create and sustain consumer identities.

This chapter deals mainly with the way cultural values and symbols are expressed

Figure 14.1 The movement of meaning

Source: Adapted from Grant McCracken, 'Culture and Consumption: A Theoretical Account of the Structure and Movement of the Cultural Meaning of Consumer Goods', *Journal of Consumer Research* 13 (June 1986): 72. Reprinted with permission of The University of Chicago Press.

in goods and how consumers appropriate these symbols through consumption rituals. The next chapter will then take a closer look at fashion and other change processes in consumer culture. The first part of this chapter reviews what is meant by culture and how cultural priorities are identified and expressed. These social guidelines often take the form of *values*, which have already been discussed in Chapter 4. The second part considers the role of myths and rituals in shaping the cultural meaning of consumer products and consumption activities. The chapter concludes by exploring the concepts of the sacred and the profane and their relevance for consumer behaviour.

Culture, a concept crucial to the understanding of consumer behaviour, may be thought of as the collective memory of a society. Culture is the accumulation of shared meanings, rituals, norms and traditions among the members of an organization or society. It is what defines a human community, its individuals, its social organizations, as well as its economic and political systems. It includes both abstract ideas, such as values and ethics, as well as the material objects and services, such as cars, clothing, food, art and sports, that are produced or valued by a group of people. Thus, individual consumers and groups of consumers are but part of culture, and culture is the overall system within which other systems are organized. This is a relatively new idea. Until recently, many researchers treated culture as a sort of variable that would explain differences in what they saw as the central dimension in society: economic behaviour. However, in our postindustrial society it has become increasingly evident that the principles of economy are themselves expressions of a specific kind of culture. Figure 14.2 provides an overview of this evolving approach to the relationship between culture and economy, indicating the all-encompassing influence that culture has on consumers.

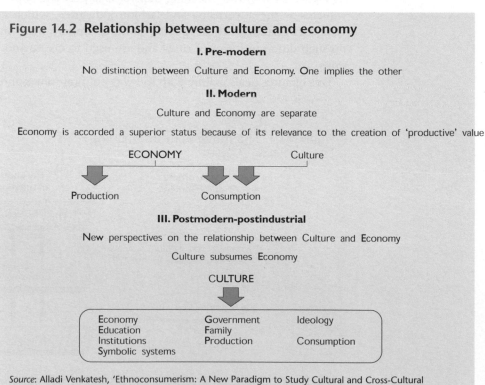

Figure 14.2 Relationship between culture and economy

I. Pre-modern

No distinction between Culture and Economy. One implies the other

II. Modern

Culture and Economy are separate

Economy is accorded a superior status because of its relevance to the creation of 'productive' value

ECONOMY   Culture

Production   Consumption

III. Postmodern-postindustrial

New perspectives on the relationship between Culture and Economy

Culture subsumes Economy

CULTURE

Economy	Government	Ideology
Education	Family	
Institutions	Production	Consumption
Symbolic systems		

Source: Alladi Venkatesh, 'Ethnoconsumerism: A New Paradigm to Study Cultural and Cross-Cultural Consumer Behavior', in J. A. Costa and G. Bamossy, eds, *Marketing in a Multicultural World* (Thousand Oaks, CA: Sage, 1995).

Ironically, the effects of culture on consumer behaviour are so powerful and far-reaching that this importance is sometimes difficult to grasp or appreciate. We are surrounded by a lot of practices, from seemingly insignificant behaviours like pressing the start button of our Walkman to larger movements like flying to an exotic honeymoon in Thailand. What is important is that these practices have meaning to us, that we know how to interpret them. Culture is basically this interpretation system which we use to understand all those daily or extraordinary **signifying practices**[2] around us. Culture as a concept is like a fish immersed in water – we do not always appreciate this power until we encounter a different environment, where suddenly many of the assumptions we had taken for granted about the clothes we wear, the food we eat, the way we address others, and so on no longer seem to apply. The effect of encountering such differences can be so great that the term 'culture shock' is not an exaggeration.

The importance of these cultural expectations is only discovered when they are violated. For example, while on tour in New Zealand, the Spice Girls created a stir among New Zealand's Maoris by performing a war dance only men are supposed to do. A tribal official indignantly stated, 'It is not acceptable in our culture, and especially by girlie pop stars from another culture.'[3] Sensitivity to cultural issues, whether by rock stars or by brand managers, can only come by understanding these underlying dimensions – and that is the goal of this chapter.

Consumer behaviour and culture: a two-way street

A consumer's culture determines the overall priorities he or she attaches to different activities and products. It also determines the success or failure of specific products and services. A product that provides benefits consistent with those desired by members of a culture at any point in time has a much better chance of attaining acceptance in the marketplace. It may be difficult to guess the success or failure of certain products. Some years ago, the American business magazine *Forbes* predicted the imminent bankruptcy of the Danish stereo manufacturer Bang & Olufsen, and advised everybody to sell off their stocks in the company. In addition, they mocked the company's new product as a ghettoblaster, with the difference that the price was $3000 and not $300. The product was the new 'on-the-wall' stereo with automatic sliding doors – the product was an instant success and the value of Bang & Olufsen stocks multiplied by 40![4] Here was a product that was launched when the time was right – something that *Forbes* overlooked.

The relationship between consumer behaviour and culture is a two-way street. On the one hand, products and services that resonate with the priorities of a culture at any given time have a much better chance of being accepted by consumers. On the other hand, the study of new products and innovations in product design successfully produced by a culture at any point in time provides a window on the dominant cultural ideals of that period. Consider, for example, some products that reflect underlying cultural processes at the time they were introduced:

● Convenience foods and ready-to-eat meals, hinting at changes in family structure and the decline of the full-time housewife.

● Cosmetics like those of The Body Shop, made of natural materials and not tested on animals, which reflected consumers' apprehensions about pollution, waste and animal rights.

● Unisex fragrances, indicating new views on sex roles and a blurring of gender boundaries, as exemplified by Calvin Klein.

Aspects of culture

Culture is not static. It is continually evolving, synthesizing old ideas with new ones. A cultural system can be said to consist of three functional areas:[5]

1 *Ecology* – the way in which a system is adapted to its habitat. This area is shaped by the technology used to obtain and distribute resources (e.g. industrialized societies vs. less affluent countries).

2 *Social structure* – the way in which orderly social life is maintained. This area includes the domestic and political groups that are dominant within the culture (e.g. the nuclear family vs. the extended family).

3 *Ideology* – the mental characteristics of a people and the way in which they relate to their environment and social groups. This area revolves around the belief that members of a society possess a common **worldview**. They share certain ideas about principles of order and fairness. They also share an **ethos**, or a set of moral and aesthetic principles.

How cultures vary

Although every culture is different, a lot of research has aimed at reducing the cultural variation to simpler principles. Cultures differ in their emphasis on individualism vs. collectivism. In **collectivist cultures**, people subordinate their personal goals to those of a stable in-group. By contrast, consumers in **individualist cultures** attach more importance to personal goals, and people are more likely to change memberships when the demands of the group (e.g. workplace, church, etc.) become too costly. A Dutch researcher on culture, Geert Hofstede, has proposed this and three other dimensions, the relation to differences in social power, handling of uncertainty and risk, and the degree of masculine and feminine values, to account for much of this variability.[6] However, Hofstede's and similar approaches have been much criticized. The four dimensions do not account for the differences in the meaning and the role of the concepts in each culture. That each culture has to cope with problems of power, risk and uncertainty, gender roles and the relationship

One world? The theme of blurring gender boundaries is evident in several contemporary campaigns, as in this Danish shoe ad.
Artwork by Greg Arhus. Courtesy of Bianco Danmark A/S.

between the individual and society is obvious. But that the solutions to these problems are reducible to different levels on one and the same scale is dubious, to say the least. For example, it is difficult to assume that concepts such as 'risk' or 'masculine' would mean the same in all cultures.

Although we must be able to compare behaviour across cultures by using general concepts, we must do so by initially understanding and analysing every culture, and hence every consumer culture, on the basis of its own premises, an approach known as **ethnoconsumerism**.[7] In Figure 14.3 the principles of an ethnoconsumerist methodology are depicted. Note how central the notions of cultural categories and cultural practices are to this approach to studying consumption. To illustrate the contribution of such an approach to the study of consumer behaviour, consider a classic study of the meanings and roles of the Italian scooter in the Italian and British market contexts. Whereas in Italy, the scooter was mainly positioned as a symbol of the new, modern and liberated Italian woman, epitomized in the Italian superstar actresses of the 1950s, the scooter in Britain became caught in a cultural clash between the more 'masculine' heavy industry and the blue-collar jobs expressed in subcultural terms among the 'rockers' and their motorcycles, and the more white-collar youth subculture of the mods, heavily engaged in conspicuous consumption activities. The latter adopted the scooter as their prime symbol and

Figure 14.3 Principles for an ethnoconsumerist approach to studying consumption

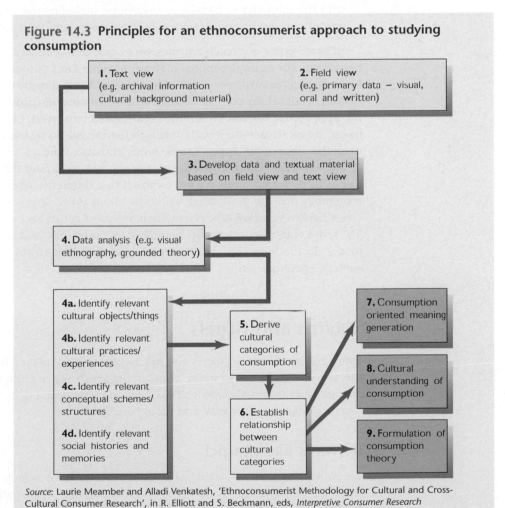

Source: Laurie Meamber and Alladi Venkatesh, 'Ethnoconsumerist Methodology for Cultural and Cross-Cultural Consumer Research', in R. Elliott and S. Beckmann, eds, *Interpretive Consumer Research* (Copenhagen: Copenhagen Business School Press, 2000): 87–108.

dominant mode of transportation.[8] Even a simple thing like drinking a cup of coffee does not hold the same meaning in different cultures.[9]

Rules for behaviour

Values, as we saw in Chapter 4, are very general principles for judging between good and bad goals, etc. They form the core principles of every culture. From these flow norms, or rules, dictating what is right or wrong, acceptable or unacceptable. Some norms, called *enacted norms*, are explicitly decided upon, such as the rule that a green traffic light means 'go' and a red one means 'stop'. Many norms, however, are much more subtle. These *crescive norms* are embedded in a culture and are only discovered through interaction with other members of that culture. Crescive norms include the following:[10]

▶ • A **custom** is a norm handed down from the past that controls basic behaviours, such as division of labour in a household or the practice of particular ceremonies.

▶ • **Mores** are customs with a strong moral overtone. Mores often involve a taboo, or forbidden behaviour, such as incest or cannibalism. Violation of mores often meets with strong censure from other members of a society.

▶ • **Conventions** are norms regarding the conduct of everyday life. These rules deal with the subtleties of consumer behaviour, including the 'correct' way to furnish one's house, wear one's clothes, host a dinner party, and so on.

All three types of crescive norms may operate to define a culturally appropriate behaviour. For example, mores may tell us what kind of food is permissible to eat. Note that mores vary across cultures, so eating a dog may be taboo in Europe, while Hindus would shun beef steak and Muslims avoid pork products. Custom dictates the appropriate hour at which the meal should be served. Conventions tell us how to eat the meal, including such details as the utensils to be used, table etiquette, and even the appropriate apparel to be worn at dinner time.

We often take these conventions for granted, assuming that they are the 'right' things to do (again, until we are exposed to a different culture!). And it is good to remember that much of what we know about these norms is learned *vicariously* (see Chapter 3), as we observe the behaviours of actors and actresses in movies and TV series, but also television commercials, print ads and other popular culture media. In the long run, marketers have an awful lot to do with influencing consumers' enculturation!

Myths and rituals

Every culture develops stories and practices that help its members to make sense of the world. When we examine these activities in other cultures, they often seem strange or even unfathomable. Yet our *own* cultural practices appear quite normal – even though a visitor may find them equally bizarre!

It works like magic!

To appreciate how so-called 'primitive' belief systems which some may consider irrational or superstitious continue to influence our supposedly 'modern', rational society, consider the avid interest of many Western consumers in magic. Marketers of health foods, anti-aging cosmetics, exercise programmes and gambling casinos often imply that their offerings have 'magical' properties that will ward off sickness, old age, poverty or just plain bad luck. People by the millions play their 'lucky numbers' in the lottery, carry lucky charms to ward off 'the evil eye', or have 'lucky' clothing or other products which they believe will bring them good fortune.

An interest in the occult tends to be popular, perhaps even more so when members of a society feel overwhelmed or powerless – magical remedies simplify our lives by giving us 'easy' answers. Marketing efforts are replete with more or less open references to magical practices.[11] And it is not just a matter of fooling consumers: magic is an active part also of our modern lives. Customers at river-rafting trips in America speak about the magical capacities of the river to transform their lives, heal psychological wounds and bring out the best in people.[12] Even a computer is regarded with awe by many consumers as a sort of 'electronic magician', with the ability to solve our problems (or in other cases to make data magically disappear!).[13] This section will discuss myths and rituals, two aspects of culture common to all societies, from the ancients to the modern world.

Myths

▶ Every society possesses a set of myths that define that culture. A **myth** is a story containing symbolic elements that expresses the shared emotions and ideals of a culture. The story may feature some kind of conflict between two opposing forces, and its outcome serves as a moral guide. In this way, a myth reduces anxiety because it provides consumers with guidelines about their world.

An understanding of cultural myths is important to marketers, who in some cases (most likely unconsciously) pattern their strategy along a mythic structure. Consider, for example, the way that a company like McDonald's takes on 'mythical' qualities.[14] The golden arches are a universally recognized symbol, one that is virtually synonymous with American culture. Not only do they signify the possibility for the whole world symbolically to consume a bite of Americana and modernity, but they also offer sanctuary to Americans around the world, who know exactly what to expect once they enter. Basic struggles involving good vs. evil are played out in the fantasy world created by McDonald's advertising, as when Ronald McDonald confounds the Hamburglar. McDonald's even has a 'seminary' (Hamburger University) where inductees go to learn appropriate behaviours and be initiated into the culture. But of course, one of the most fundamental myths of the Western world is the myth of the 'exotic Other' which is basically different from ourselves, expressed by Kipling in his 'East is East and West is West and never shall they meet'. This is reflected in consumer behaviour in the attraction to and collection of exotic goods such as Oriental carpets.[15]

The functions and structure of myths

Myths serve four interrelated functions in a culture:[16]

1 *Metaphysical* – they help to explain the origins of existence.

2 *Cosmological* – they emphasize that all components of the universe are part of a single picture.

3 *Sociological* – they maintain social order by authorizing a social code to be followed by members of a culture.

4 *Psychological* – they provide models for personal conduct.

Myths can be analysed by examining their underlying structures, a technique pioneered by the anthropologist Claude Lévi-Strauss. Lévi-Strauss noted that many stories involve *binary opposition*, where two opposing ends of some dimension are represented (e.g. good vs. evil, nature vs. technology). Characters and products often appear in advertisements to be defined by what they *are not* rather than by what they *are* (e.g. this is *not* a product for those who feel old, *not* an experience for the frightened, *not* music for the meek, etc.).

Recall from the discussion of Freudian theory in Chapter 4 that the ego functions as a kind of 'referee' between the opposing needs of the id and the superego. In a similar fashion, the conflict between mythical opposing forces is sometimes resolved by a *mediating figure*, who can link the opposites by sharing characteristics of each. For example, many myths contain animals that have human abilities (e.g. a talking snake) to bridge the gap between humanity and nature, just as cars (technology) are often given animal names (nature) like Jaguar or Mustang.

Myths are found everywhere in modern popular culture. While we generally equate myths with the ancient Greeks or Romans, modern myths are embodied in many aspects of popular culture, including comic books, movies, holidays and even commercials.

Comic book superheroes demonstrate how myths can be communicated to consumers of all ages. Indeed, some of these fictional figures represent a **monomyth**, a myth that is common to many cultures.[17] The most prevalent monomyth involves a hero who emerges from the everyday world with supernatural powers and wins a decisive victory over evil forces. He then returns with the power to bestow good things on his fellow men. This basic theme can be found in such classic heroes as Lancelot, Hercules and Ulysses. The success of the Disney movie *Hercules* reminds us that these stories are timeless and appeal to people through the ages.

Comic book heroes are familiar to most consumers, and they are viewed as more credible and effective than celebrity endorsers. Film spin-offs and licensing deals aside, comic books are a multi-million dollar industry. The American version of the monomyth is best epitomized by Superman, a Christ-like figure who renounces worldly temptations and restores harmony to his community. Heroes such as Superman are sometimes used to confer a product, store or service with desirable attributes. This imagery is sometimes borrowed by marketers – currently, PepsiCo is trying to enhance its position in the Japanese market by using a figure called 'Pepsiman', a muscle-bound caricature of an American superhero in a skin-tight uniform, to promote the drink. Pepsiman even appears in a Sega game called Fighting Vipers.[18]

But there are many other, less obvious, mythological figures surrounding us. For example, the role of Einstein as a mythological figure, and one that is used for giving meaning to and promoting certain consumable objects such as movies or posters, or in advertisements as a sort of indirect endorsement, has been studied by consumer researchers.[19]

Many blockbuster films and hit TV programmes draw directly on mythic themes. While dramatic special effects or attractive stars certainly don't hurt, a number of these films perhaps owe their success to their presentation of characters and plot structures that follow mythic patterns. Examples of these mythic blockbusters include:[20]

● *The Big Blue*. The sea is the offspring of many myths. Its inaccessibility and depth have always inspired humans to create imagery about this other world. The film depicts the search for a lost symbiosis between man and nature, where the only person with real access to this must give up his human life to become one with the purity and the graciousness of the sea, symbolized by the dolphins.

● *E.T.: The Extraterrestrial*. *E.T.* represents a familiar myth involving Messianic visitation. The gentle creature from another world visits Earth and performs miracles (e.g. reviving a dying flower). His 'disciples' are local children, who help him combat the forces of modern technology and an unbelieving secular society. The metaphysical function of myth is served by teaching that the humans chosen by God are pure and unselfish.

- *Easy Rider*. This 1969 cult movie can be seen as the forefather of the much-beloved road movie genre that has been among the most popular in recent decades, and which got its definitive feminist version with *Thelma and Louise*. These movies feature myths of freedom and rebelliousness against the banalities of daily life (as expressed in one of the theme songs from *Easy Rider*, Steppenwolf's 'Born to be Wild'), which are recycled in a lot of commercial contexts. For instance, in a recent commercial for Ford's new Cougar (another wild animal!) model, Dennis Hopper (anno 1998) driving a Cougar races with himself riding a motorbike in the original *Easy Rider* movie.[21]

- *Jaws*. This and films constructed around similar themes draw on myths of the beast, representing the wild, dangerous, untamed nature that is culture's (human being's) enemy. Such myths are known from Christianity and other religious mythologies, such as Norse mythology (the Midgaard Snake, the Fenris Wolf), and have played a central role in the way the Western world has regarded nature over the centuries.

Commercials as myths

Commercials can be analysed in terms of the underlying cultural themes they represent. For example, commercials for various food products ask consumers to 'remember' the mythical good old days when products were wholesome and natural. The mythical theme of the underdog prevailing over the stronger foe (i.e. David and Goliath) has been used by the car rental firm Avis in a now classic campaign where they stated 'We're only no. 2, we try harder'. Other figures from mythical narratives have been used by advertisers, such as the villain (a brand teasing its competitors), the hero (the brand in control) or the helper (the brand that helps you accomplish something).[22]

Rituals

▶ A **ritual** is a set of multiple, symbolic behaviours that occur in a fixed sequence and that tend to be repeated periodically.[23] Although bizarre tribal ceremonies, perhaps involving animal or virgin sacrifice, may come to mind when people think of rituals, in reality many contemporary consumer activities are ritualistic. Four major types of rituals are possession rituals, exchange rituals, grooming rituals and divestment rituals.[24] Below, we shall take a closer look at some of these.

Rituals can occur at a variety of levels, as noted in Table 14.1. Some of the rituals described are specifically American, but the US Super Bowl may be compared to the English FA Cup Final or the traditional ski jump competition in Austria on the first day of the new year. Some rituals affirm broad cultural or religious values, like the differences in the ritual of tea-drinking in Great Britain and France. Whereas tea seems a sensuous and mystical drink to the French, the drinking of coffee is regarded as having a more functional purpose. For the British, tea is a daily drink and coffee is seen more as a drink to express oneself.[25]

The ritual of going to a café with a selection of coffee opportunities was unknown outside the most metropolitan areas of the United States until recent times. No longer. The Starbucks Corporation has experienced phenomenal success by turning

The literal translation of the caption in this Dutch ad is 'With real butter, you can get them to the table'. Getting them to the table also infers in Dutch that you're getting two opponents to sit down and talk things out ... This ad makes a parody of the cultural clash of the Dutch 'Sinter Klaas', which is celebrated on 5 December, and 'Santa Claus', who is becoming more and more a part of Christmas celebrations on 25 December.

Photo by Gary Bamossy.

MET *Echte Boter* KRIJG JE ZE WEER AAN TAFEL.

the coffee break into a cultural event that for many has assumed almost cult-like status. The average Starbucks customer visits 18 times a month, and 10 per cent of the clientele stops by twice a day.[26] In the year 2000 Starbucks announced plans to add 450 stores to its existing base of over 2200 coffeehouses in the US, and eventually to add 100 locations in Asia and 50 in Britain to their already 300+ international stores.[27] Café culture Starbucks style is thus re-exported to the cultures of origin.

Table 14.1 Types of ritual experience

Primary behaviour source	Ritual type	Examples
Cosmology	Religious	Baptism, meditation, mass
Cultural values	Rites of passage	Graduation, marriage
	Cultural	Festivals, holidays (Valentine's Day), Super Bowl
Group learning	Civic	Parades, elections, trials
	Group	Business negotiations, office luncheons
	Family	Mealtimes, bedtimes, birthdays, Mother's Day, Christmas
Individual aims and emotions	Personal	Grooming, household rituals

Source: Dennis W. Rook, 'The Ritual Dimension of Consumer Behavior', *Journal of Consumer Research* 12 (December 1985): 251–64. Reprinted with permission of The University of Chicago Press.

Ritual artefacts

▶ Many businesses owe their livelihoods to their ability to supply **ritual artefacts**, or items used in the performance of rituals, to consumers. Birthday candles, diplomas, specialized foods and beverages (e.g. wedding cakes, ceremonial wine, or even sausages at the stadium), trophies and plaques, band costumes, greetings cards and retirement watches are all used in consumer rituals. In addition, consumers often employ a ritual script, which identifies the artefacts, the sequence in which they are used and who uses them. The proliferation of 'manners and style' books in recent years bears witness to the renewed interest in rituals after the belief of the beat generation that they could abolish ritual behaviour and just act 'normal' and be 'natural'. Of course, such behaviour required a whole new set of rituals . . .

But rituals are not restricted to the special occasions described above. Daily life is full of ritualized behaviour. Wearing a tie on certain occasions can be seen as a ritual, for example. The significance attached to rituals will vary across cultures ('Mother's Day' is slowly gaining popularity in several European countries), and will often be a mixture of private and public (generally shared) symbolism.[28]

Grooming rituals

Whether brushing one's hair 100 strokes a day or talking to oneself in the mirror, virtually all consumers undergo private grooming rituals. These are sequences of behaviours that aid in the transition from the private self to the public self or back again. These rituals serve various purposes, ranging from inspiring confidence before confronting the world to cleansing the body of dirt and other profane materials. Traditionally a female market, the grooming sector for men is a booming business. For example, Unilever is opening a new chain of barbershops in the UK that also offer facial treatments and manicures on top of the shaves and beard trims. The adaptation to the male market is almost perfect: the waiting rooms feature PlayStations and personal CD players instead of glossy magazines.[29]

When consumers talk about their grooming rituals, some of the dominant themes that emerge from these stories reflect the almost mystical qualities attributed to grooming products and behaviours. Many people emphasize a before-and-after phenomenon, where the person feels magically transformed after using certain products (similar to the Cinderella myth).[30]

Two sets of binary oppositions that are expressed in personal rituals are *private/public* and *work/leisure*. Many beauty rituals, for instance, reflect a transformation from a natural state to the social world (as when a woman 'puts on her face') or vice versa. In these daily rituals, women reaffirm the value placed by their culture on personal beauty and the quest for eternal youth.[31] This focus is obvious in ads for Oil of Olay beauty cleanser, which proclaim: 'And so your day begins. The Ritual of Oil of Olay'. Similarly, the bath is viewed as a sacred, cleansing time, a way to wash away the sins of the profane world.[32]

Gift-giving rituals

The promotion of appropriate gifts for every conceivable holiday and occasion provides an excellent example of the influence consumer rituals can exert on market-
▶ ing phenomena. In the **gift-giving ritual**, consumers procure the perfect object (artefact), meticulously remove the price tag (symbolically changing the item from a commodity to a unique good), carefully wrap it and deliver it to the recipient.[33]

Gift-giving used to be viewed by researchers primarily as a form of economic exchange, where the giver transfers an item of value to a recipient, who in turn is somehow obliged to reciprocate. However, gift-giving is interpreted more and more

Table 14.2 Effects of gift-giving on social relationships

Relational effect	Description	Example
Strengthening	Gift-giving improves the quality of a relationship	An unexpected gift such as one given in a romantic situation
Affirmation	Gift-giving validates the positive quality of a relationship	Usually occurs on ritualized occasions such as birthdays
Negligible effect	Gift-giving has a minimal effect on perceptions of relationship quality	Non-formal gift occasions and those where the gift may be perceived as charity or too good for the current state of the relationship
Negative confirmation	Gift-giving validates a negative quality of a relationship between the gift-giver and the receiver	The selection of gift is inappropriate, indicating a lack of knowledge of the receiver. Alternatively the gift is viewed as a method of controlling the receiver
Weakening	Gift-giving harms the quality of the relationship between giver and receiver	When there are 'strings attached' or the gift is perceived as a bribe, a sign of disrespect or offensive
Severing	Gift-giving harms the relationship between the giver and the receiver to the extent that the relationship is dissolved	When the gift forms part of a larger problem, such as a threatening relationship. Or when a relationship is severed through the receipt of a 'parting' gift

Source: Adapted from Julie A. Ruth, Cele C. Otnes and Frederic F. Brunel, 'Gift receipt and the reformulation of interpersonal relationships', *Journal of Consumer Research* 25 (March 1999): 385–402, Table 1, p. 389.

as a symbolic exchange, where the giver is motivated by acknowledging the social bonds between people. These might then be seen as more economic and reciprocal but may also be guided by unselfish factors, such as love or admiration, without expectations of anything in return. Some research indicates that gift-giving evolves as a form of social expression: it is more exchange-oriented (instrumental) in the early stages of a relationship, but becomes more altruistic as the relationship develops.[34] One set of researchers identified multiple ways in which giving a gift can affect a relationship. These are listed in Table 14.2.[35]

Every culture prescribes certain occasions and ceremonies for giving gifts, whether for personal or professional reasons. The giving of birthday presents alone is a major undertaking. Business gifts are an important component in defining professional relationships, and great care is often taken to ensure that the appropriate gifts are purchased.

Multicultural dimensions

The importance of gift-giving rituals is underscored by considering Japanese customs, where the wrapping of a gift is as important (if not more so) than the gift itself. The economic value of a gift is secondary to its symbolic meaning.[36] To the Japanese, gifts are viewed as an important aspect of one's duty to others in one's social group. Giving is a moral imperative (known as *giri*).

Highly ritualized gift-giving occurs during the giving of both household/personal gifts and company/professional gifts. Each Japanese has a well-defined set of relatives and friends with whom he or she shares reciprocal gift-giving obligations (*kosai*).[37]

Personal gifts are given on social occasions, such as at funerals, to people who are hospitalized, to mark movements from one stage of life to another (e.g. weddings, birthdays) and as greetings (e.g. when one is meeting a visitor). Company gifts are given to commemorate the anniversary of a corporation's founding or the opening of a new building, as well as being a routine part of doing business, as when rewards are given at trade meetings to announce new products.

Some of the items most desired by Japanese consumers to receive as gifts include gift coupons, beer and soap.[38] In keeping with the Japanese emphasis on saving face, presents are not opened in front of the giver, so that it will not be necessary to hide one's possible disappointment with the present.

The gift-giving ritual can be broken down into three distinct stages.[39] During *gestation*, the giver is motivated by an event to procure a gift. This event may be either *structural* (i.e. prescribed by the culture, as when people buy Christmas presents), or *emergent* (i.e. the decision is more personal and idiosyncratic). The second stage is *presentation*, or the process of gift exchange. The recipient responds to the gift (either appropriately or not), and the donor evaluates this response.

In the third stage, known as *reformulation*, the bonds between the giver and receiver are adjusted (either looser or tighter) to reflect the new relationship that emerges after the exchange is complete. Negativity can arise if the recipient feels the gift is inappropriate or of inferior quality. The donor may feel the response to the gift was inadequate or insincere or a violation of the reciprocity norm, which obliges people to return the gesture of a gift with one of equal value.[40] Both participants may feel resentful for being 'forced' to participate in the ritual.[41]

Self-gifts

People commonly find (or devise) reasons to give themselves something; they 'treat' themselves. Consumers purchase **self-gifts** as a way to regulate their behaviour. This ritual provides a socially acceptable way of rewarding themselves for good deeds, consoling themselves after negative events or motivating themselves to accomplish some goal.[42] Figure 14.4 is a projective stimulus similar to ones used in research on self-gifting. Consumers are asked to tell a story based on a picture such as this, and their responses are analysed to discover the reasons people view as legitimate for rewarding themselves with self-gifts. For example, one recurring story that might emerge is that the woman in the picture had a particularly gruelling day at work and needed a pick-me-up in the form of a new fragrance. This theme could then be incorporated into a promotional campaign for a perfume. With the growing evidence of hedonic motives for consumption in recent decades, self-gifts may represent an increasingly important part of the overall consumption pattern.

Holiday rituals

Holidays are important rituals in both senses of the word. Going on holiday was one of the most widespread rituals and tourism one of the biggest industries of the late twentieth century, and the trend looks set to continue.[43] On holidays consumers step back from their everyday lives and perform ritualistic behaviours unique to those times.[44] Holiday occasions are filled with ritual artefacts and scripts and are increasingly cast as a time for giving gifts by enterprising marketers. Holidays also often mean big business to hotels, restaurants, travel agents, and so on. For example, going to Disneyland in Paris may mean a ritualized return to the memories of our own dreams of a totally free (of obligations, duties and responsibilities) fantasy land of play.[45]

Figure 14.4 Projective drawing to study the motivations underlying the giving of self-gifts

Source: Based on David G. Mick, Michelle DeMoss and Ronald J. Faber, 'Latent Motivations and Meanings of Self-Gifts: Implications for Retail Management' (research report, Center for Retailing Education and Research, University of Florida, 1990).

For many businesses Christmas is the single most important season. Concerning the holidays of celebrations, most such holidays are based on a myth, and often a real (Guy Fawkes) or imaginary (Cupid on Valentine's Day) character is at the centre of the story. These holidays persist because their basic elements appeal to deep-seated patterns in the functioning of culture.[46]

The Christmas holiday is bursting with myths and rituals, from adventures at the North Pole to those that occur under the mistletoe. One of the most important holiday rituals involves Santa Claus, or an equivalent mythical figure, eagerly awaited by children the world over. Unlike Christ, this person is a champion of materialism. Perhaps it is no coincidence, then, that he appears in stores and shopping malls – secular temples of consumption. Whatever the origins of Santa Claus, the myth surrounding him serves the purpose of socializing children by teaching them to expect a reward when they are good and that members of society get what they deserve. Needless to say, Christmas, Santa Claus and other attached rituals and figures change when they enter into other cultural settings. Some of the transformations of Santa Claus in a Japanese context include a figure called 'Uncle Chimney', Santa Claus as a stand-in for the newborn Christ and Santa Claus crucified at the entrance of one department store with the words 'Happy Shopping' written above his head.[47] What does this tell us about the globalization process?

On Valentine's Day, standards regarding sex and love are relaxed or altered as people express feelings that may be hidden during the rest of the year. In addition to cards, a variety of gifts are exchanged, many of which are touted by marketers to represent aphrodisiacs or other sexually related symbols. It seems as if many people in consumer societies are always on the lookout for new rituals to fill their lives. This ritual was once virtually unknown in Scandinavia but is slowly becoming part of their consumption environment.[48] Also, the American ritual of celebrating Hallowe'en is now becoming fashionable in Europe, where the French in particular have adopted it as an occasion for festivities, dancing and the chance to show off new fashions.[49]

Rites of passage

What does a dance for recently divorced people have in common with 'college initiation ceremonies'? Both are examples of modern **rites of passage**, or special times marked by a change in social status. Every society, both primitive and modern, sets aside times where such changes occur. Some of these changes may occur as a natural part of consumers' life cycles (puberty or death), while others are more individual in nature (divorce and re-entering the dating market). As we saw with some of the other rituals, there seems to be a renewed interest in transition rites. They are increasingly becoming consumption objects in themselves as well as occasions for consumption. In order to satisfy the 'need' for rituals, not only do we import new ones from abroad, as we have seen, but in times of globalization many cultures also experience a renewed interest in the old rituals that have traditionally framed the cultural identity.[50]

Some marketers attempt to reach consumers on occasions in which their products can enhance a transition from one stage of life to another.[51] A series of Volkswagen ads underlined the role of the car in the freedom of women who were leaving their husbands or boyfriends.

Stages of role transition Much like the metamorphosis of a caterpillar into a butterfly, consumers' rites of passage consist of three phases.[52] The first stage, *separation*, occurs when the individual is detached from his or her original group or status (e.g. the first-year university student leaves home). *Liminality* is the middle stage, where the person is literally in between statuses (e.g. the new arrival on campus tries to work out what is happening during orientation week). The last stage, *aggregation*, takes place when the person re-enters society after the rite of passage is complete (the student returns home for the Christmas vacation as a 'real university student'). Rites of passage mark many consumer activities, as exemplified by confirmation or other rites of going from the world of the child to the world of the adult. A similar transitional state can be observed when people are prepared for certain occupational roles. For example, athletes and fashion models typically undergo a 'seasoning' process. They are removed from their normal surroundings (e.g. athletes are taken to training camps, while young models are often moved to Paris or Milan), indoctrinated into a new subculture and then returned to the real world in their new roles.

The final passage: marketing death The rites of passage associated with death support an entire industry. Death themes are replete in marketing.[53] Survivors must make expensive purchase decisions, often at short notice and driven by emotional and superstitious concerns. Funeral ceremonies help the living to organize their relationships with the deceased, and action tends to be tightly scripted down to the costumes (e.g. the ritual black attire, black ribbons for mourners, the body in its best suit) and specific behaviours (e.g. sending condolence cards or holding a wake). (However, more and more seem to emphasize a certain personal touch to commemorate the individuality of the deceased.) Mourners 'pay their last respects', and seating during the ceremony is usually dictated by mourners' closeness to the individual. Even the cortège is accorded special status by other motorists, who recognize its separate, sacred nature by not overtaking as it proceeds to the cemetery.[54]

Sacred and profane consumption

As we saw when considering the structure of myths, many types of consumer activity involve the demarcation, or binary opposition, of boundaries, such as good vs. bad, male vs. female – or even 'regular' vs. 'low-fat'. One of the most important of these sets of boundaries is the distinction between the sacred and the profane. ▶ **Sacred consumption** involves objects and events that are 'set apart' from normal activities, and are treated with some degree of respect or awe. They may or may not be associated with religion, but most religious items and events tend to be regarded ▶ as sacred. **Profane consumption** involves consumer objects and events that are ordinary, everyday objects and events that do not share the 'specialness' of sacred ones. (Note that profane does not mean vulgar or obscene in this context.)

Domains of sacred consumption

Sacred consumption events permeate many aspects of consumers' experiences. We find ways to 'set apart' a variety of places, people and events. In this section, we'll consider some examples of ways that 'ordinary' consumption is sometimes not so ordinary after all.

Sacred places

Sacred places have been 'set apart' by a society because they have religious or mystical significance (e.g. Bethlehem, Mecca, Stonehenge) or because they commemorate some aspect of a country's heritage (e.g. the Kremlin, Versailles, the Colosseum in Rome). Remember that in many cases the sacredness of these places is due to the property of contamination – that is, something sacred happened on that spot, so the place itself takes on sacred qualities. Tourism is one of the most common and rapidly spreading forms of consuming the sacred.[55]

Other places are created from the profane world and imbued with sacred quali-

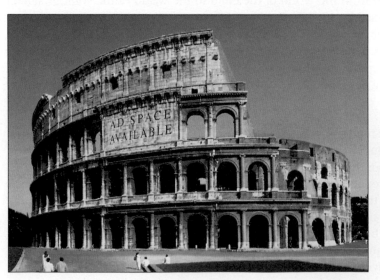

Sacred places are revered, not only in 'real life' but also in advertising, since they are immediately recognizable, highly visible and normally connote positive values. The present mythologies of the grandeur of antiquity and more generally myths attached to sacred places of world heritage are used here in a humorous (but also sacrilegious?) way for maximum attention and mind-provocation.
Used by permission.

ties. Graumann's Chinese Theater in Hollywood, where film stars leave their foot-prints in concrete for posterity, is one such place. When Ajax, the local football team of Amsterdam, moved from their old stadium, De Meern, to a larger, more modern stadium (De Arena), the turf from the old stadium was carefully lifted from the ground and sold to a local churchyard. The churchyard offers the turf to fans willing to pay a premium price to be buried under authentic Ajax turf!

Even the modern shopping mall can be regarded as a secular 'cathedral of con-sumption', a special place where community members come to practise shopping rituals. Theme parks are a form of mass-produced fantasy that take on aspects of sacredness. In particular, the various Disneylands are destinations for pilgrimages from consumers around the globe. Disneyland displays many characteristics of more traditional sacred places, especially for Americans, but Europeans too may consider these parks the quintessence of America. It is even regarded by some as the epitome of child(ish) happiness. A trip to the park is the most common 'last wish' for termi-nally ill children.[56]

In many cultures, the home is a particularly sacred place. It represents a crucial distinction between the harsh, external world and consumers' 'inner space'. In northern and western Europe the home is a place where you entertain guests (in southern Europe it is more common to go out), and fortunes are spent each year on interior decorators and home furnishings; the home is thus a central part of con-sumers' identities.[57] But even here there are vast differences between, e.g., the domi-nant traditionalist style of British homes and the modernist style of Danish homes.[58] Consumers all over the world go to great lengths to create a special environment that allows them to create the quality of homeliness. This effect is created by per-sonalizing the home as much as possible, using such devices as door wreaths, mantel arrangements and a 'memory wall' for family photos.[59] Even public places, like vari-ous types of cafés and bars, strive for a home-like atmosphere which shelters cus-tomers from the harshness of the outside world.

Sacred people

People themselves can be sacred, when they are idolized and set apart from the masses. Souvenirs, memorabilia and even mundane items touched or used by sacred people take on special meanings and acquire value in their own right. Indeed, many businesses thrive on consumers' desire for products associated with famous people. There is a thriving market for celebrity autographs, and objects once owned by celebrities, whether Princess Diana's gowns or John Lennon's guitars, are often sold at auction for astronomical prices. A store called 'A Star is Worn' sells items donated by celebrities – a black bra autographed by Cher sold for $575. As one observer commented about the store's patrons, 'They want something that belonged to the stars, as if the stars have gone into sainthood and the people want their shrouds.'[60]

MARKETING PITFALL

The sacredness of some celebrities has spawned a secondary industry – celebrity lookalikes and soundalikes. However, just as celebrity endorsements are risky businesses because of their dependence on the image of the celebrity, so too is the lookalike industry. When Diana, Princess of Wales, died suddenly it put 'her' lookalikes on the dole, according to one London-based booking agent. Having lookalikes perform as Diana following her death was deemed distasteful.[61] On the other hand, her death has brought profits to a lot of people, from biography authors and publishers, film-makers and TV companies to memorabilia industries and souvenir sellers.[62]

Sacred events

Many consumers' activities have taken on a special status. Public events in particular resemble sacred, religious ceremonies, as exemplified by the playing of the national anthems before a game or the reverential lighting of matches and lighters at the end of a rock concert.[63]

For many people, the world of sport is sacred and almost assumes the status of a religion. The roots of modern sports events can be found in ancient religious rites, such as fertility festivals (e.g. the original Olympics).[64] Indeed, it is not uncommon for teams to join in prayer prior to a game. The sports pages are like the Scriptures (and we describe ardent fans as reading them 'religiously'), the stadium is a house of worship, and the fans are members of the congregation. After the first Scottish victory in many years in a football match against England at Wembley Stadium, Scottish fans tore down the goals to bring pieces back home as sacred relics. Indeed, grass from stadiums of important matches, like World Cup finals, has been sold in small portions at large prices.

Devotees engage in group activities, such as tailgate parties and the 'Mexican Wave', where (resembling a revival meeting) participants on cue join the wave-like motion as it makes its way around the stadium. The athletes that fans come to see are godlike; they are reputed to have almost superhuman powers (especially football stars in southern Europe and Latin America). Athletes are central figures in a common cultural myth, the hero tale. As exemplified by mythologies of the barefoot Olympic marathon winner (Abebe Bikila from Ethiopia, 1960), or of boxing heroes (legally) fighting their way out of poverty and misery, often the person must prove him- or herself under strenuous circumstances. Victory is achieved only through sheer force of will. Of course, sports heroes are popular endorsers in commercials, but only a few of these sports personalities 'travel' very well, since sports heroes tend to be first and foremost national heroes. However, a few people are known worldwide, at least within the key target for the ads, so that they can be used in international campaigns.

If sport is one domain that is becoming increasingly sacred (cf. sacralization below), then the traditionally sacred realm of fine arts is considered by some in danger of desacralization. In a recent sale of a publishing company of classical music, various representatives voiced the fear that a takeover by one of the giants such as Sony, Polygram or EMI would mean the introduction of a market logic that would destroy its opportunities to continue to sponsor unknown artists and make long-term investments in them. It is argued that classical music is not a product that can be handled by any marketer, but requires special attention and a willingness to accept financial losses in order to secure artistic openness and creativity.[65] Such reactions (as justified as they may be) indicate that artists and managers conceive of themselves as dealing with sacred objects that cannot be subdued to what is conceived as the profane legitimacy of the market.[66] Indeed, art and marketing is the subject of study for more and more marketing and consumer researchers, for example in considering art as a kind of service.[67] Famous film directors make commercial campaigns and music videos (and music video-makers turn into great film directors), while commercial film-makers celebrate each other with their own sets of prizes for creativity. And consider 'art placement': one artist proposed a series of films featuring a mysterious 'Mr. Who' engaging in a lot of daily consumption activities and used clippings from commercials to portray Mr. Who's consumer universe.[68] Art and marketing, in short, are becoming increasingly blurred.[69]

Tourism is another example of a sacred, non-ordinary experience of extreme importance to marketers. When people travel on holiday, they occupy sacred time and space. The tourist is continually in search of 'authentic' experiences which differ from his or her normal world (think of Club Med's motto, 'The antidote to civilization').[70] This travelling experience involves binary oppositions between work and leisure and being 'at home' vs. 'away'. Norms regarding appropriate behaviour are modified as tourists scramble for illicit experiences they would not dream of engaging in at home.

The desire of travellers to capture these sacred experiences in objects forms the bedrock of the souvenir industry, which may be said to be in the business of selling sacred memories. Whether a personalized matchbook from a wedding or a little piece of the Berlin Wall, souvenirs represent a tangible piece of the consumer's sacred experience.[71]

In addition to personal mementoes, such as ticket stubs saved from a favourite concert, the following are other types of sacred souvenir icons:[72]

- Local products (e.g. goose liver from Périgord or Scotch whisky).
- Pictorial images (e.g. postcards).
- 'Piece of the rock' (e.g. seashells, pine cones). Sometimes this can be problematic, however. For example it is forbidden to bring home corals and seashells from a lot of diving places around the Earth, in order to prevent tourists from 'tearing down' the coral reef. But temptations are great. Even at Nobel Prize dinners approximately 100 of the noble guests each year cannot resist bringing home something, typically a coffee spoon, as a souvenir.[73]
- Symbolic shorthand in the form of literal representations of the site (e.g. a miniature Little Mermaid or Eiffel Tower).
- Markers (e.g. Hard Rock Café T-shirts).

From sacred to profane, and back again

Just to make life interesting, in recent times many consumer activities have moved from one sphere to the other. Some things that were formerly regarded as sacred have moved into the realm of the profane, while other, everyday phenomena are now regarded as sacred.[74] Both these processes are relevant to our understanding of contemporary consumer behaviour.

Desacralization

▶ **Desacralization** occurs when a sacred item or symbol is removed from its special place or is duplicated in mass quantities, becoming profane as a result. For example, souvenir reproductions of sacred monuments such as the leaning Tower of Pisa or the Eiffel Tower, 'pop' artworks of the Mona Lisa or adaptations of important symbols such as the Union Jack by clothing designers, tend to eliminate their special aspects by turning them into inauthentic commodities, produced mechanically and representing relatively little value.[75]

Religion itself has to some extent been desacralized. Religious symbols, such as stylized crosses or New Age crystals, have moved into the mainstream of fashion jewellery.[76] Religious holidays, particularly Christmas, are regarded by many (and criticized by some) as having been transformed into secular, materialistic occasions devoid of their original sacred significance. Benetton, the Italian clothing manufacturer, has been at the forefront in creating vivid (and often controversial) messages that expose us to our cultural categories and prejudices, but at times they have touched upon the issue of desacralization.[77]

Even the clergy are increasingly adopting secular marketing techniques. Especially

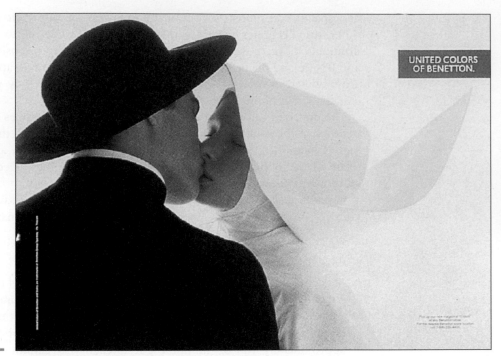

Desacralization? This controversial Benetton ad was rejected by some magazines because of what some perceived to be offensive religious symbolism.
Photo by Oliviero Toscani for Benetton.

in the United States, televangelists rely upon the power of television, a secular medium, to convey their messages. The Catholic Church generated a major controversy after it hired a prominent public relations firm to promote its anti-abortion campaign.[78] None the less, many religious groups have taken the secular route, and are now using marketing techniques to increase the number of believers. A Danish bishop addressed a number of major food producing companies for a joint venture in profiling Pentecost as an equally important holiday season as Christmas and Easter.[79] The question is whether the use of marketing changes the 'product' or 'service' of the churches?[80]

Multicultural dimensions

The American 'market for religious belief' with its televangelists and its heavy promotion of various churches and sects is a very exotic experience for many Europeans. The ad depicted opposite for a Minneapolis church to help recruit worshippers is typical of the American trend towards secular practices being observed by many organized religions. It even uses a pun (on the curing of a headache?) to pass on the message of salvation.

Sacralization

Sacralization occurs when objects, events and even people take on sacred meaning to a culture or to specific groups within a culture. For example, events like the Cannes Film Festival or Wimbledon and people like Elvis Presley or Princess Diana have become sacralized to some consumers.

Objectification occurs when sacred qualities are attributed to mundane items. One way that this process can occur is through *contamination*, where objects associated with sacred events or people become sacred in their own right. This explains the desire by many fans for items belonging to, or even touched by, famous people. One standard procedure through which objects become sacralized occurs when they become included in the collection of a museum.

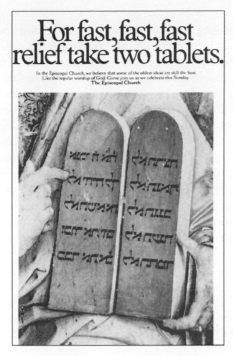

For fast, fast, fast relief take two tablets.

In the Episcopal Church, we believe that some of the oldest ideas are still the best. Like the regular worship of God. Come join us as we celebrate this Sunday.
The Episcopal Church

The ad for the Episcopal church discussed in the Multicultural dimensions block opposite.
Church Ad Project, 1021 Diffley, Eagan, MN 55123.

In addition to museum exhibits displaying rare objects, even mundane, inexpensive things may be set apart in private *collections*, where they are transformed from profane items to sacred ones. An item is sacralized as soon as it enters a collection, and it takes on special significance to the collector that, in some cases, may be hard to comprehend by the outsider. **Collecting** refers to the systematic acquisition of a particular object or set of objects, and this widespread activity can be distinguished from hoarding, which is merely unsystematic collecting.[81] Collecting typically involves both rational and emotional components, since collectors are fixed by their objects, but they also carefully organize and exhibit them.[82]

Name an item, and the odds are that a group of collectors are lusting after it. The contents of collections range from various popular culture memorabilia, rare books and autographs, to Barbie dolls, tea bags, lawnmowers and even junk mail.[83] The 1200 members of the American McDonald's Collectors' Club collect 'prizes' like sandwich wrappers and Happy Meal trinkets – rare ones like the 1987 Potato Head Kids Toys sell for $25.[84] Consumers are often ferociously attached to their collections; this passion is exemplified by the comment made in one study by a woman who collects teddy bears: 'If my house ever burns down, I won't cry over my furniture, I'll cry over the bears.'[85]

Some consumer researchers feel that collectors are motivated to acquire their 'prizes' in order to gratify a high level of materialism in a socially acceptable manner. By systematically amassing a collection, the collector is allowed to 'worship' material objects without feeling guilty or petty. Another perspective is that collecting is an aesthetic experience: for many collectors the pleasure emanates from being involved in creating the collection, rather than from passively admiring the items one has scavenged or bought. Whatever the motivation, hard-core collectors often devote a great deal of time and energy to maintaining and expanding their collections, so for many this activity becomes a central component of their extended selves (see Chapter 7).[86]

MARKETING OPPORTUNITY

Make your brand a collectible, and enhance your exposure and your brand loyalty. Certain products and brands become cult objects for devoted collectors. In the early 1990s, 'Swatch fever' infected many people. The company made more than 500 different models, some of which were special editions designed by artists. Collectors' interest made a formerly mundane product into a rare piece of art (e.g. a 'Jelly Fish' that originally sold for $30 was sold at auction for $17,000). Although thousands of people still collect the watches, the frenzy began to fade by around 1993.[87] Some collectors' items are more stable. One of the corporations exploiting this opportunity to its fullest is the Coca-Cola Company. With the plethora of Coca-Cola collectibles, a lot of devoted and often highly specialized collectors have been created all over the world. They appear as 'spokespersons' for the brand when they account for their sometimes fabulous collections in the media, and they create a lot of extra and extremely positive exposure for the brand. As one researcher noted: 'These are brand owners. Coca-Cola is theirs.'[88]

Consumer society – material culture

New books and art exhibitions witness the increasing importance of branding and advertising in our societies.[89] In 2000, it was announced that Huntington Beach, a Los Angeles suburb, has made Coca-Cola the official drink of the community. For $600,000 per year the company will exclude Pepsi and other soft drinks from official buildings and put up drink dispensers and advertisements all over the city. The city council initiated the deal, saying it was an alternative to higher taxes.[90]

Many people use the notion of the **consumer society** in order to describe the current type of social organization in the developed world. This is not only because we live in a world full of things, which we obviously do. Almost 24 hours a day we are surrounded by consumer objects, and lots of leisurely activities we engage in can also be characterized as consumption. But the most decisive step in the construction of consumer society is the new role of consumption activities. In most of the modern time period, it has been people's role in a production context that has been decisive for our social identity. The impact of our self-consciousness as workers, farmers, professors, artisans, etc. cannot be underestimated. But in recent decades we have seen a trend towards an increasing role for consumption patterns and style in people's identity formation. With the increase in consumption possibilities and the multiplication of styles and fashions, consumption has to some extent been cut off from its old connections to those production-defined roles. The plethora of goods and their varieties in range and styles has to a still higher degree made consumption choices statements about our personality, our values, aspirations, sympathies and antipathies, and our way of handling social relations.

Modern consumer culture is thus characterized by consumption-based identities, but other related features of a consumer society include many of the other topics discussed in this book: more and more aspects of human interaction available through the market, shopping as leisure activity combined with the variety of shopping possibilities including the new 'temples of consumption', the shopping malls, easier access to credit, the growing attention to brand images and the communicative aspects of product and packaging as well as the pervasiveness of promotion, the increasing political organization of consumers in groups with a variety of purposes and the sheer impossibility of not being a consumer and still participating in ordinary social life.[91] Things do matter.[92]

However, not all is well in consumer society. Many critics have attacked consumer society for a variety of reasons: that it erodes cultural differences, that it creates superficial and inauthentic forms of social interaction and that it inspires competition and individualism rather than solidarity and community. Whereas most of these assertions may not bear close scrutiny,[93] consumer society in general does represent some serious challenges for our future development, not least in terms of the pressure on the environment. While we will address environmental issues and consumption in the final chapter, the pressure of consumer society is not only felt on the environment but also on the individual consumer, sometimes with negative outcomes. **Consumer addiction** is a physiological and/or psychological dependency on products or services. While most people equate addiction with drugs, virtually any product or service can be seen as relieving some problem or satisfying some need to the point where reliance on it becomes extreme. In some cases, it is fairly safe to say that the consumer, not unlike a drug addict, has little or no control over consumption. The products, whether alcohol, cigarettes, chocolate or diet colas, control the consumer. Even the act of shopping itself is an addictive experience for some consumers.[94]

Chapter summary

- A society's *culture* includes its values, ethics and the material objects produced by its people. It is the accumulation of *shared meanings* and traditions among members of a society. A culture can be described in terms of ecology (the way people adapt to their habitat), its social structure and its ideology (including people's moral and aesthetic principles). This chapter describes some aspects of culture and focuses on how cultural meanings are created and transmitted across members of a society.

- Members of a culture share a system of *beliefs* and *practices*, including *values*. The process of learning the values of one's culture is called enculturation. Each culture can be described by a set of core values. Values can be identified by several methods, though it is often difficult to apply these results directly to marketing campaigns due to their generality.

- *Myths* are stories containing symbolic elements that express the shared ideals of a culture. Many myths involve some binary opposition, where values are defined in terms of what they are and what they are not (e.g. nature vs. technology). Modern myths are transmitted through advertising, films and other media.

- A *ritual* is a set of multiple, symbolic behaviours which occur in a fixed sequence and tend to be repeated periodically. Rituals are related to many consumption activities which occur in popular culture. These include holiday observances, gift-giving and grooming.

- A *rite of passage* is a special kind of ritual which involves the transition from one role to another. These passages typically entail the need to acquire products and services, called ritual artefacts, to facilitate the transition. Modern rites of passage include graduations, initiation ceremonies, weddings and funerals.

- Consumer activities can be divided into *sacred* and *profane* domains. Sacred phenomena are 'set apart' from everyday activities or products. People, events or objects can become sacralized. *Objectification* occurs when sacred qualities are ascribed to products or items owned by sacred people. *Sacralization* occurs when formerly sacred objects or activities become part of the everyday, as when 'one-of-a-kind' works of art are reproduced in large quantities. *Desacralization* occurs when objects that previously were considered sacred become commercialized and integrated into popular culture.

- *Collecting* is one of the most common ways of experiencing sacred consumption in daily life. It is simultaneously one of the domains where consumption and passions are most heavily intertwined.

- The importance of consumption for understanding social interactions is now so big that we have begun to talk about our own societies as *consumer societies*, indicating that consumption might well be the single most important social activity.

KEY TERMS

Collecting (*p. 461*)	**Monomyth** (*p. 448*)
Collectivist cultures (*p. 444*)	**Mores** (*p. 446*)
Consumer addiction (*p. 463*)	**Myth** (*p. 447*)
Consumer society (*p. 462*)	**Profane consumption** (*p. 456*)
Conventions (*p. 416*)	**Rites of passage** (*p. 455*)
Cooptation (*p. 441*)	**Ritual** (*p. 449*)
Culture (*p. 441*)	**Ritual artefacts** (*p. 451*)
Custom (*p. 446*)	**Sacralization** (*p. 460*)
Desacralization (*p. 459*)	**Sacred consumption** (*p. 456*)
Ethnoconsumerism (*p. 445*)	**Self-gifts** (*p. 453*)
Ethos (*p. 444*)	**Signifying practices** (*p. 443*)
Gift-giving ritual (*p. 451*)	**Worldview** (*p. 444*)
Individualist cultures (*p. 444*)	

For additional material see the companion website at:
www.booksites.net/solomon_euro

Consumer behaviour challenge

1. Culture can be thought of as a society's personality. If your culture were a person, could you describe its personality traits?

2. What is the difference between an enacted norm and a crescive norm? Identify the set of crescive norms operating when a man and woman in your culture go out for dinner on a first date. What products and services are affected by these norms?

3. How do the consumer decisions involved in gift-giving differ from other purchase decisions?

4. The chapter argues that not all gift-giving is positive. In what ways can this ritual be unpleasant or negative?

5. Construct a ritual script for a wedding in your culture. How many artefacts can you list that are contained in this script?

6. What are some of the major motivations for the purchase of self-gifts? Discuss some marketing implications of these.

7. Describe the three stages of the rite of passage associated with graduating from university.

8. Identify the ritualized aspects of various kinds of sports that are employed in advertising.

9. Some people have raised objections to the commercial exploitation of cultural figures. For example, in the US many consumers deplored the profits that film-makers and businesspeople made from films such as *Malcolm X* (e.g. by selling a 'Malcolm X' air freshener). Others argued that this commercialization merely helps to educate consumers about what such people stood for, and is inevitable in our society. What do you think?

10. Interview two or three of your fellow students about collecting, talking about either their own collections or a collection of somebody they know of. Use concepts about the sacred to analyse the responses.

Notes

1. See, e.g., A. Fuat Firat, 'Consumer Culture or Culture Consumed', in Janeen A. Costa and G. Bamossy, eds, *Marketing in a Multicultural World: Ethnicity, Nationalism, and Cultural Identity* (Thousand Oaks, CA: Sage, 1995): 105-25.

2. Paul du Gay, Stuart Hall, Linda Janes, Hugh MacKay and Keith Negus, *Doing Cultural Studies: The Story of the Sony Walkman* (London: Sage, 1997).

3. 'Spice Girls Dance into Culture Clash', *Montgomery Advertiser* (29 April 1997): 2A.

4. Personal communication with Jens Bernsen, 29 October 1997.

5. Clifford Geertz, *The Interpretation of Cultures* (New York: Basic Books, 1973); Marvin Harris, *Culture, People and Nature* (New York: Crowell, 1971); John F. Sherry, Jr, 'The Cultural Perspective in Consumer Research', in Richard J. Lutz, ed., *Advances in Consumer Research* 13 (Provo, UT: Association for Consumer Research, 1985): 573-5.

6. Geert Hofstede, *Culture's Consequences* (Beverly Hills, CA: Sage, 1980); see also Laura M. Milner, Dale Fodness and Mark W. Speece, 'Hofstede's Research on Cross-Cultural Work-Related Values: Implications for Consumer Behavior', in W. F. van Raaij and G. Bamossy, eds, *European Advances in Consumer Research* 1 (Provo, UT: Association for Consumer Research, 1993): 70-6.

7. Alladi Venkatesh, 'Ethnoconsumerism: A Proposal for a New Paradigm to Study Cross Cultural Consumer Behavior', in Costa and Bamossy, eds, *Marketing in a Multicultural World*: 26-67.

8. Dick Hebdige, 'Object as Image: The Italian Scooter Cycle', in J. B. Schor and D. B. Holt, eds, *The Consumer Society Reader* (New York: The New Press, 2000): 117-54.

9. Brad Weiss, 'Coffee Breaks and Coffee Connections: The Lived Experience of a Commodity in Tanzanian and European Worlds', in D. Howes, ed., *Cross-Cultural Consumption* (London: Routledge, 1996): 93-105.

10. George J. McCall and J. L. Simmons, *Social Psychology: A Sociological Approach* (New York: The Free Press, 1982).

11. Eric Arnould, Cele Otnes and Linda Price, 'Magic in the Marketing Age', in S. Brown, A. M. Doherty and B. Clarke, eds, *Proceedings of the Marketing Illuminations Spectacular* (Belfast: University of Ulster, 1997): 167-78.

12. Eric Arnould and Linda Price, 'River Magic: Extraordinary Experience and the Extended Service Encounter', *Journal of Consumer Research* 20 (June 1993): 24-45.

13. Molly O'Neill, 'As Life Gets More Complex, Magic Casts a Wider Spell', *New York Times* (13 June 1994): A1 (2).

14. Conrad Phillip Kottak, 'Anthropological Analysis of Mass Enculturation', in Conrad P. Kottak, ed., *Researching American Culture* (Ann Arbor, MI: University of Michigan Press, 1982): 40-74.

15. Güliz Ger and Fabian Csaba, 'Flying Carpets: The Production and Consumption of Tradition and Mystique', in S. Hoch and R. Meyer, eds, *Advances in Consumer Research* 27 (Provo, UT: Association for Consumer Research, 2000): 132–7.

16. Joseph Campbell, *Myths, Dreams, and Religion* (New York: E. P. Dutton, 1970).

17. Jeffrey S. Lang and Patrick Trimble, 'Whatever Happened to the Man of Tomorrow? An Examination of the American Monomyth and the Comic Book Superhero', *Journal of Popular Culture* 22 (Winter 1988): 157.

18. Yumiko Ono, 'PepsiCo's "American" Superhero in Japanese Ads is Alien to U.S.', *Wall Street Journal Interactive Edition* (23 May 1997).

19. James Fitchett, Douglas Brownlie and Michael Saren, 'On the Cultural Location of Consumption: The Case of Einstein as a Commodity', in *Marketing for an Expanding Europe*, ed. J. Berács, A. Bauer and J. Simon, Proceedings of the 25th EMAC Conference (Budapest: Budapest University of Economic Sciences, 1996): 435–53; James Fitchett and Michael Saren, 'Consuming Einstein: The Nine Billion Names of the Commodity', in Brown, Doherty and Clarke, eds, *Proceedings of the Marketing Illuminations Spectacular*: 252–63.

20. Elizabeth C. Hirschman, 'Movies as Myths: An Interpretation of Motion Picture Mythology', in Jean Umiker-Sebeok, ed., *Marketing and Semiotics: New Directions in the Study of Signs for Sale* (Berlin: Mouton de Guyter, 1987): 335–74.

21. *Markedsføring* 1 (1999): 18.

22. Benoît Heilbrunn, 'My Brand the Hero? A Semiotic Analysis of the Consumer-Brand Relationship', in M. Lambkin *et al.*, eds, *European Perspectives on Consumer Behaviour* (London: Prentice-Hall, 1998): 370–401.

23. See Dennis W. Rook, 'The Ritual Dimension of Consumer Behavior', *Journal of Consumer Research* 12 (December 1985): 251–64; Mary A. Stansfield Tetreault and Robert E. Kleine III, 'Ritual, Ritualized Behavior, and Habit: Refinements and Extensions of the Consumption Ritual Construct', in Marvin Goldberg, Gerald Gorn and Richard W. Pollay, eds, *Advances in Consumer Research* 17 (Provo, UT: Association for Consumer Research, 1990): 31–8.

24. Grant McCracken, *Consumption and Culture* (Bloomington, IN: Indiana University Press).

25. 'The Skill of the Chase', *Marketing Week* (30 April 1993): 38–40.

26. Bill McDowell, 'Starbucks is Ground Zero in Today's Coffee Culture', *Advertising Age* (9 December 1996): 1 (2 pp.). For a discussion of the act of coffee-drinking as ritual, see Susan Fournier and Julie L. Yao, 'Reviving Brand Loyalty: A Reconceptualization within the Framework of Consumer–Brand Relationships', working paper 96–039, Harvard Business School, 1996.

27. Louise Lee, 'Now, Starbucks Uses Its Bean', *Business Week* (14 February 2000): 92–4; Mark Gimein, 'Behind Starbucks' New Venture: Beans, Beatniks, and Booze', *Fortune* (15 May 2000): 80

28. Robert Grafton Small, 'Consumption and Significance: Everyday Life in a Brand-new Second-hand Bow Tie', *European Journal of Marketing* 27(8) (1993): 38–45.

29. 'Lynx to Create Chain of Male Grooming Stores', *Marketing* (24 August 2000): 5.

30. Dennis W. Rook and Sidney J. Levy, 'Psychosocial Themes in Consumer Grooming Rituals', in Richard P. Bagozzi and Alice M. Tybout, eds, *Advances in Consumer Research* 10 (Provo, UT: Association for Consumer Research, 1983): 329–33.

31. Diane Barthel, *Putting on Appearances: Gender and Attractiveness* (Philadelphia: Temple University Press, 1988).

32. Quoted in ibid.

33. Russell W. Belk, Melanie Wallendorf and John Sherry, Jr, 'The Sacred and the Profane in Consumer Behavior: Theodicy on the Odyssey', *Journal of Consumer Research* 16 (June 1989): 1–38.

34. Russell W. Belk and Gregory S. Coon, 'Gift Giving as Agapic Love: An Alternative to the Exchange Paradigm Based on Dating Experiences', *Journal of Consumer Research* 20 (December 1993) 3: 393–417.

35. Julie A. Ruth, Cele C. Otnes and Frederic F. Brunel, 'Gift Receipt and the Reformulation of Interpersonal Relationships', *Journal of Consumer Research* 25 (March 1999) 385–402.

36. Colin Camerer, 'Gifts as Economic Signals and Social Symbols', *American Journal of Sociology* 94 (Supplement 1988): 5180–214.

37. Robert T. Green and Dana L. Alden, 'Functional Equivalence in Cross-Cultural Consumer Behavior: Gift Giving in Japan and the United States', *Psychology & Marketing* 5 (Summer 1988): 155–68.

38. Hiroshi Tanaka and Miki Iwamura, 'Gift Selection Strategy of Japanese Seasonal Gift Purchasers: An Explorative Study', paper presented at the Association for Consumer Research, Boston, October 1994.

39. John F. Sherry, Jr, 'Gift Giving in Anthropological Perspective', *Journal of Consumer Research* 10 (September 1983): 157–68.

40. Daniel Goleman, 'What's Under the Tree? Clues to a Relationship', *New York Times* (19 December 1989): C1.

41. John F. Sherry, Jr, Mary Ann McGrath and Sidney J. Levy, 'The Dark Side of the Gift', *Journal of Business Research* 28(3) (1993): 225–45.

42. David Glen Mick and Michelle DeMoss, 'Self-Gifts: Phenomenological Insights from Four Contexts', *Journal of Consumer Research* 17 (December 1990): 327; John F. Sherry, Jr, Mary Ann McGrath and Sidney J. Levy, 'Egocentric Consumption: Anatomy of Gifts Given to the Self', in John F. Sherry, Jr, ed., *Contemporary Marketing and Consumer Behavior:*

An Anthropological Sourcebook (Thousand Oaks, CA: Sage, 1995).

43. On tourism as a central part of modern life, see John Urry, *The Tourist Gaze: Leisure and Travel in Contemporary Societies* (London: Sage, 1990), and John Urry, *Consuming Places* (London: Routledge, 1995). Scandinavians (or those who read Swedish!) may also consult Tom Odell, ed., *Nonstop! Turist i upplevelsesindustrialismen* (Lund: Historiska Media, 1999).

44. See, for example, Russell W. Belk, 'Halloween: An Evolving American Consumption Ritual', in Pollay, Gorn and Goldberg, eds, *Advances in Consumer Research* 17: 508–17; Melanie Wallendorf and Eric J. Arnould, 'We Gather Together: The Consumption Rituals of Thanksgiving Day', *Journal of Consumer Research* 18 (June 1991): 13–31.

45. Marc Augé, 'Un ethnologue à Euro Disneyland', *Le Monde Diplomatique* (September 1994).

46. Bruno Bettelheim, *The Uses of Enchantment: The Meaning and Importance of Fairy Tales* (New York: Alfred A. Knopf, 1976).

47. Brian Moeran and Lise Skov, 'Cinderella Christmas: Kitsch, Consumerism and Youth in Japan', in D. Miller, ed., *Unwrapping Christmas* (Oxford: Oxford University Press, 1993): 105–33.

48. *Markedsføring* 1 (1999): 4.

49. Anne Swardson, 'Trick or Treat? In Paris, It's Dress, Dance, Eat', *International Herald Tribune* (31 October 1996): 2.

50. Tuba Ustuner, Güliz Ger and Douglas B. Holt, 'Consuming Ritual: Reframing the Turkish Henna-Night Ceremony', in Hoch and Meyer, eds, *Advances in Consumer Research* 27: 209–14.

51. Michael R. Solomon and Punam Anand, 'Ritual Costumes and Status Transition: The Female Business Suit as Totemic Emblem', in Elizabeth C. Hirschman and Morris Holbrook, eds, *Advances in Consumer Research* 12 (Washington, D.C.: Association for Consumer Research, 1985): 315–18.

52. Arnold Van Gennep, *The Rites of Passage*, trans. Maika B. Vizedom and Gabrielle L. Caffee (London: Routledge and Kegan Paul, 1960; orig. published 1908); Solomon and Anand, 'Ritual Costumes and Status Transition'.

53. Stephanie O'Donohoe and Darach Turley, 'Dealing with Death: Art, Mortality and the Marketplace', in S. Brown and A. Patterson, eds, *Imagining Marketing, Art, Aesthetics, and the Avant-Garde* (London: Routledge, 2001): 86–106.

54. Walter W. Whitaker III, 'The Contemporary American Funeral Ritual', in Ray B. Browne, ed., *Rites and Ceremonies in Popular Culture* (Bowling Green, OH: Bowling Green University Popular Press, 1980): 316–25.

55. On sacredness in tourism, see, e.g., Urry, *The Tourist Gaze*, and Urry, *Consuming Places*.

56. Kottak, 'Anthropological Analysis of Mass Enculturation': 40–74.

57. Gerry Pratt, 'The House as an Expression of Social Worlds', in James S. Duncan, ed., *Housing and Identity: Cross-Cultural Perspectives* (London: Croom Helm, 1981): 135–79; Michael R. Solomon, 'The Role of the Surrogate Consumer in Service Delivery', *Service Industries Journal* 7 (July 1987): 292–307.

58. Malene Djursaa and Simon Ulrik Kragh, ' Syntax and Creolization in Cross-Cultural Readings of Rooms', in B. Dubois, T. Lowrey, L. J. Shrum and M. Vanhuele, eds, *European Advances in Consumer Research* 4 (Provo, UT: Association for Consumer Research, 1999): 293–303.

59. Grant McCracken, '"Homeyness": A Cultural Account of One Constellation of Goods and Meanings', in Elizabeth C. Hirschman, ed., *Interpretive Consumer Research* (Provo, UT: Association for Consumer Research, 1989): 168–84.

60. James Hirsch, 'Taking Celebrity Worship to New Depths', *New York Times* (9 November 1988): C1.

61. 'One Certain Legacy of Diana is Industry Exploiting Her Life', *Wall Street Journal Europe* (2 September 1997): 1–2.

62. 'Diana Factor Still Pulls Marketers', *Marketing* (August 27 1998): 18.

63. Emile Durkheim, *The Elementary Forms of the Religious Life* (New York: Free Press, 1915).

64. Susan Birrell, 'Sports as Ritual: Interpretations from Durkheim to Goffman', *Social Forces* 60 (1981) 2: 354–76; Daniel Q. Voigt, 'American Sporting Rituals', in Browne, ed., *Rites and Ceremonies in Popular Culture*: 125–40.

65. 'Sale of UK Publisher of Classical Music Strikes a Sour Note', *Wall Street Journal Europe* (9 September 1997): 1, 4.

66. Søren Askegaard, 'Marketing, the Performing Arts, and Social Change: Beyond the Legitimacy Crisis', *Consumption, Markets and Culture* 3(1) (1999): 1–25.

67. Simona Botti, 'What Role for Marketing in the Arts? An Analysis of Art Consumption and Artistic Value', in Y. Evrard, W. Hoyer and A. Strazzieri, eds, *Proceedings of the Third International Research Seminar on Marketing Communications and Consumer Behavior* (IAE Aix-en-Provence, 1999).

68. *Markedsføring* 2 (1999): 10.

69. Brown and Patterson, eds, *Imagining Marketing, Art, Aesthetics, and the Avant-Garde*.

70. Urry, *The Tourist Gaze*.

71. Belk *et al.*, 'The Sacred and the Profane in Consumer Behavior'.

72. Beverly Gordon, 'The Souvenir: Messenger of the Extraordinary', *Journal of Popular Culture* 20 (1986) 3: 135–46.

73. 'Even at the Dinner for the Nobel Prizes, They Steal the Spoons', *Wall Street Journal* (7 December 2000): A1, A16.

74. Belk *et al.*, 'The Sacred and the Profane in Consumer Behavior'.

75. Ibid.

76. Deborah Hofmann, 'In Jewelry, Choices Sacred and Profane, Ancient and New', *New York Times* (7 May 1989).

77. Roberto Grandi, 'Benetton's Advertising: A Case History of Postmodern Communication', unpublished manuscript, Center for Modern Culture and Media, University of Bologna, 1994; Shawn Tully, 'Teens: The Most Global Market of All', *Fortune* (16 May 1994): 90-7.

78. Quoted in 'Public Relations Firm to Present Anti-Abortion Effort to Bishops', *New York Times* (14 August 1990): A12.

79. *Markedsføring* 4 (1999): 8.

80. Per Østergaard, 'The Broadened Concept of Marketing as a Manifestation of the Postmodern Condition', in *Marketing Theory and Applications*, Proceedings of the AMA Winter Educators Conference 4, eds R. Varandarajan and B. Jaworski (Chicago: American Marketing Association, 1993): 234-9.

81. Dan L. Sherrell, Alvin C. Burns and Melodie R. Phillips, 'Fixed Consumption Behavior: The Case of Enduring Acquisition in a Product Category', in Robert L. King, ed., *Developments in Marketing Science* 14 (1991): 36-40.

82. Russell W. Belk, 'Acquiring, Possessing, and Collecting: Fundamental Processes in Consumer Behavior', in Ronald F. Bushard and Shelby D. Hunt, eds, *Marketing Theory: Philosophy of Science Perspectives* (Chicago: AMA, 1982): 185-90.

83. For an extensive bibliography on collecting, see Russell W. Belk, *Collecting in a Consumer Culture* (London: Routledge, 1995), or Russell W. Belk, Melanie Wallendorf, John F. Sherry, Jr and Morris B. Holbrook, 'Collecting in a Consumer Culture', in Russell W. Belk, ed., *Highways and Buyways* (Provo, UT: Association for Consumer Research, 1991): 178-215. See also Janine Romina Lovatt, 'The People's Show Festival 1994: A Survey', in S. Pearce, ed., *Experiencing Material Culture in the Western World* (London: Leicester University Press, 1997): 196-254; Werner Muensterberg, *Collecting: An Unruly Passion* (Princeton, NJ: Princeton University Press, 1994); Melanie Wallendorf and Eric J. Arnould, "My Favorite Things': A Cross-Cultural Inquiry into Object Attachment, Possessiveness, and Social Linkage', *Journal of Consumer Research* 14 (March 1988): 531-47.

84. Calmetta Y. Coleman, 'Just Any Old Thing from McDonald's Can be a Collectible', *Wall Street Journal* (29 March 1995): B1 (2).

85. Quoted in Ruth Ann Smith, 'Collecting as Consumption: A Grounded Theory of Collecting Behavior,' unpublished manuscript, Virginia Polytechnic Institute and State University, 1994: 14.

86. Cf. Belk, *Collecting in a Consumer Culture*.

87. 'A Feeding Frenzy for Swatches', *New York Times* (29 August 1991): C3; Patricia Leigh Brown, 'Fueling a Frenzy: Swatch', *New York Times* (10 May 1992): 1, 9; Mary M. Long and Leon G. Schiffman, 'Swatch Fever: An Allegory for Understanding the Paradox of Collecting', *Psychology & Marketing* 14 (August 1997) 5: 495-509.

88. Jan Slater, 'Collecting the Real Thing: A Case Study Exploration of Brand Loyalty Enhancement Among Coca-Cola Brand Collectors', in Hoch and Meyer, eds, *Advances in Consumer Research* 27: 202-8.

89. Jane Pavitt, 'The Art of Marketing', *Marketing* (19 October 2000).

90. *Markedsføring* 7 (1999): 12.

91. Celia Lury, *Consumer Culture* (New Brunswick, NJ: Rutgers University Press, 1996). Another excellent book on the rise of consumer culture is Don Slater, *Consumer Culture and Modernity* (Cambridge: Polity Press, 1997).

92. Daniel Miller, 'Why Some Things Matter', in D. Miller, ed., *Material Cultures: Why Some Things Matter* (London: UCL Books, 1998): 3-21.

93. Daniel Miller, 'Consumption as the Vanguard of History', in D. Miller, ed., *Acknowledging Consumption* (London: Routledge, 1995): 1-57; see also Cornelia Dröge, Roger Calantone, Madhu Agrawal and Robert Mackay, 'The Consumption Culture and Its Critiques: A Framework for Analysis', *Journal of Macromarketing* (Fall 1993): 32-45.

94. Richard Elliott, 'Addictive Consumption: Function and Fragmentation in Postmodernity', *Journal of Consumer Policy* 17 (1994): 159-79; Thomas C. O'Guinn and Ronald J. Faber, 'Compulsive Buying: A Phenomenological Exploration', *Journal of Consumer Research* 16 (1989): 147-57.

Chapter 15

Cultural change processes

Michael and Erik are riding in the suburban train, going downtown after having completed a meeting in their study group. Erik takes out a small electronic device from his bag. 'What's that?' Michael asks. 'It is the new Stephen King novel,' Erik answers. 'What?' Michael is surprised. 'Do you mean that this is a book?' 'Well, not exactly,' says Erik, 'it is an e-book. It has software that permits me to download novels and other things and read them much like I read a real book, I mean no scrolling the text and all that.' 'Argh!' Michael looks at Erik with signs of contempt, thinking to himself that this gadget will never be able to replace the feeling of taking out a real book, running your fingers over the pages so that you can almost feel the pleasure you had reading through it, and then finally settling on the page you had reached. 'Well,' Erik says, 'even though it is still in its early stages people expect e-books to cover 10 per cent of the book market in a few years' time. Of course, there is still the question of which standard will be the winning one, you know, much like it was with VHS and Betamax in the early days of videotaping.' 'There you have it,' Michael answers, 'nothing can compete with the good old paper standard', and he leans back thinking about how awful this machine looks compared to his parents' large bookshelves with the big encyclopedia and all the other gems of their collection.

Introduction

The Rolling Stones. Miniskirts. Kipper ties. Fast food. High-tech furniture. New architecture. James Bond. We inhabit a world brimming with different styles and possibilities. The food we eat, the cars we drive, the clothes we wear, the places we live and work, the music we listen to – all are influenced by the ebb and flow of popular culture and fashion. Consumers may at times feel overwhelmed by the sheer choice in the marketplace. A person trying to decide on something as routine as a tie has many hundreds of alternatives from which to choose. Despite this seeming abundance, however, the options available to consumers at any point in time actually represent only a *small fraction* of the total set of possibilities. In this chapter, we shall follow marketers' and cultural gatekeepers' attempts to set their marks on which possibilities get the most attention and which trends and tendencies become victorious in the battle for a place in our minds as consumers. We will take a closer look at the processes of change driving the ever-changing styles of consumption we are presented with. And, referring back to Figure 14.1, we will look at how fashions and consumption styles spread within and among societies.

Even though most of the consumers we have been dealing with in this book may live in Western middle-class areas, each with their national and local characteristics, they are often able to 'connect' symbolically with millions of other consumers by relating to styles that originated far away – even though the original meanings of those styles may have little relevance to them. The spread of fashions in consumption is just one example of what happens when the meanings created by some members of a culture are interpreted and produced for mass consumption.

Take the example of rap music. Baggy jeans and outfits featuring gold vinyl skirts, huge gold chains and bejewelled baseball caps which used to be seen only on the streets of impoverished urban areas are being adapted by haute couture fashion designers for the catwalks of Manhattan and Paris. In addition, a high proportion of people who buy recordings of rap music are white. How did rap music and fashions, which began as forms of expression in the black urban subculture, make it to mainstream America and the rest of the world? A brief chronology is given in Table 15.1.

Cultural selection

The selection of certain alternatives over others – whether cars, dresses, computers, recording artists, political candidates, religions or even scientific methodologies – is the culmination of a complex filtration process resembling a funnel, as depicted in Figure 15.1. Many possibilities initially compete for adoption, and these are steadily narrowed down as they make their way down the path from conception to consumption in a process of **cultural selection**.

The internet has made the spotting and selection of the various trends and changes in society, the *symbol pool*, easier. New trend-watching services can be paid to scour the world for new possibilities in colours, fabrics, designs or combinations. They can access pictures from the catwalks of great fashion shows, look at store decorations from H&M or Banana Republic, or look at photos of cool L.A. kids

Table 15.1 The mainstreaming of popular music and fashion

Date	Event
1968	Hip-hop is invented in the Bronx by DJ Kool Herc.
1973–8	Urban block parties feature break dancing and graffitti.
1979	A small record company named Sugar Hill becomes the first rap label.
1980	Graffitti artists are featured in Manhattan art galleries.
1981	Blondie's song 'Rapture' hits No. 1 on the charts.
1985	Columbia Records buys the Def Jam label.
1988	MTV begins *Yo! MTV Raps*, featuring Fab 5 Freddy.
1990	Hollywood gets into the act with the hip-hop film *House Party*; Ice-T's rap album is a hit on college radio stations; amid controversy, white rapper Vanilla Ice hits the big time; NBC launches a sitcom, *Fresh Prince of Bel Air*.
1991	Mattel introduces its Hammer doll (i.e. a doll in the likeness of the rap star Hammer, formerly known as M.C. Hammer); designer Karl Lagerfeld shows shiny vinyl raincoats and chain belts in his Chanel collection; designer Charlotte Neuville sells gold vinyl suits with matching baseball caps for $800; Isaac Mizrahi features wide-brimmed caps and take-offs on African medallions (including an oversized, gold Star of David); Bloomingdale's launches Anne Klein's rap-inspired clothing line by featuring a rap performance in its Manhattan store.
1992	Rappers start to abandon this look, turning to low-fitting baggy jeans, sometimes worn backwards; white rapper Marky Mark appears in a national campaign wearing Calvin Klein underwear exposed above his hip-hugging pants; composer Quincy Jones launches a new magazine for people who are into hip-hop, and it gains a significant white readership.[1]
1993	Hip-hop fashions and slang continue to cross over into mainstream consumer culture. An outdoor ad for Coca-Cola proclaims, 'Get Yours 24–7'. The company is confident that many viewers in its target market will know that the phrase is urban slang for 'always' (i.e. 24 hours a day, 7 days a week).
1994	Designers persevere in their adaptations of street fashion. The late Italian designer Versace, among others, pushes oversized overalls favoured by urban kids. In one ad he asks, 'Overalls with an oversize look, something like what rappers and homeboys wear. Why not a sophisticated version?'[2]
2000	*360hip-hop.com*, a web-based community dedicated to the hip-hop culture, is launched. In addition to promoting the hip-hop lifestyle consumers can purchase clothing and music online while watching video interviews with such artists as Will Smith and Busta Rymes.[3]

sporting the latest rebellious twist to the clothing companies' standard offerings. Even though the subscription to these services is pretty costly, many companies think they are well worth their price, because they save in business trips and other types of costly trend-spotting field work.[4]

Our tastes and product preferences are not formed in a vacuum. Choices are driven by the images presented to us in the media, by our observations of those around us, and even by our desires to live in the fantasy worlds created by marketers. These options are constantly evolving and changing. A clothing style or type of cuisine that is 'hot' one year may be 'out' the next.

Figure 15.1 The culture production process

Source: Adapted from Michael R. Solomon, 'Building Up and Breaking Down: The Impact of Cultural Sorting on Symbolic Consumption', in J. Sheth and E. C. Hirschman, eds, *Research in Consumer Behavior* (Greenwich, CT: JAI Press, 1988): 325–51.

Culture production systems

No single designer, company or advertising agency is solely responsible for creating popular culture. Every product, whether a hit record, a car or a new fashion, requires the input of many different participants. The set of individuals and organizations responsible for creating and marketing a cultural product is a **culture production system (CPS)**.[5]

The nature of these systems helps to determine the types of product that eventually emerge from them. Factors such as the number and diversity of competing systems and the amount of innovation vs. conformity that is encouraged are important. For example, an analysis of the Country & Western music industry has shown that the hit records it produces tend to be similar to one another during periods when it is dominated by a few large companies, whereas there is more diversity when a greater number of producers are competing within the same market.[6]

The different members of a culture production system may not necessarily be aware of or appreciate the roles played by other members, yet many diverse agents work together to create popular culture.[7] Each member does his or her best to anticipate which particular images will be most attractive to a consumer market. Of course, those who are able to forecast consumers' tastes consistently will be successful over time.

Components of a CPS

A culture production system has three major subsystems: (1) a *creative subsystem* responsible for generating new symbols and/or products; (2) a *managerial subsystem* responsible for selecting, making tangible, mass producing and managing the distribution of new symbols and/or products; and (3) a *communications subsystem* responsible for giving meaning to the new product and providing it with a symbolic set of attributes that are communicated to consumers.

An example of the three components of a culture production system for a record would be (1) a singer (e.g. Madonna, a creative subsystem); (2) a company (e.g. Sire Records, which manufactures and distributes Madonna's records, a managerial subsystem); and (3) the advertising and publicity agencies hired to promote the albums (a communications subsystem). Table 15.2 illustrates some of the many *cultural specialists*, who operate in different subsystems, who are required to create a hit CD.

Table 15.2 Cultural specialists in the music industry

Specialist	Functions
Songwriter(s)	Compose music and lyrics; must reconcile artistic preferences with estimates of what will succeed in the marketplace
Performer(s)	Interpret music and lyrics; may be formed spontaneously, or may be packaged by an agent to appeal to a predetermined market (e.g. New Kids on the Block and the Spice Girls)
Teachers and coaches	Develop and refine performers' talents
Agent	Represent performers to record companies
A&R (artist & repertoire) executive	Acquire artists for the record label
Publicists, image consultants, designers, stylists	Create an image for the group that is transmitted to the buying public
Recording technicians, producers	Create a recording to be sold
Marketing executives	Make strategic decisions regarding performers' appearances, ticket pricing, promotional strategies, and so on
Video director	Interpret the song visually to create a music video that will help to promote the record
Music reviewers	Evaluate the merits of a recording for listeners
Disc jockeys, radio programme directors	Decide which records will be given airplay and/or placed in the radio stations' regular rotations
Record shop owner	Decide which of the many records produced will be stocked and/or promoted heavily in the retail environment

Cultural gatekeepers

Many judges or 'tastemakers' influence the products that are eventually offered to consumers. These judges, or **cultural gatekeepers**, are responsible for filtering the overflow of information and materials intended for consumers. Gatekeepers include film, restaurant and car reviewers, interior designers, disc jockeys, retail buyers and magazine editors. Collectively, this set of agents is known as the *through-put sector*.[8]

Speaking the language of beauty

A recent study of cultural gatekeepers in the fashion and beauty industry illustrates how some cultural 'products' (in this case, fashion models) are selected and championed over other stylistic possibilities.[9] Editors at such women's magazines as *Cosmopolitan*, *Marie Claire*, *Depêche Mode* and *Elle* play an important role in selecting the specific variations of beauty that will appear in the pages of these 'bibles of fashion'. These images, in turn, will be relied on by millions of readers to decide what 'look' they would like to adopt – and, of course, which particular products and services (such as hairstyles, cosmetics, clothing styles, exercise programmes) they will need to attain these images.

In this study, decision-makers at a group of influential magazines identified a small set of 'looks' that characterize many of the diverse fashion models they evaluate on a daily basis. What is more, though each editor was studied independently, overall respondents exhibited a very high level of agreement among themselves regarding what the 'looks' are, what they arc called, which are more or less desirable *and* which they expect to be paired with specific product advertisements. This research suggests that cultural gatekeepers tend to rely on the same underlying cultural ideals and priorities when making the selections that in turn get passed down the channel of distribution for consideration by consumers.

High culture and popular culture

Do Beethoven and Björk have anything in common? While both the famous composer and the Icelandic singer are associated with music, many would argue that the similarity stops here. Culture production systems create many diverse kinds of products, but some basic distinctions can be offered regarding their characteristics.

Arts and crafts

One distinction can be made between arts and crafts.[10] An **art product** is viewed primarily as an object of aesthetic contemplation without any functional value. A **craft product**, in contrast, is admired because of the beauty with which it performs some function (e.g. a ceramic ashtray or hand-carved fishing lures). A piece of art is original, subtle and valuable, and is associated with the elite of society. A craft tends to follow a formula that permits rapid production. According to this framework, elite culture is produced in a purely aesthetic context and is judged by reference to recognized classics. It is high culture – 'serious art'.[11]

High art vs. low art

The distinction between high and low culture is not as clear as it may first appear. In addition to the possible class bias that drives such a distinction (i.e. we assume that the rich have culture while the poor do not), high and low culture are blending together in interesting ways. Popular culture reflects the world around us: these phenomena touch rich and poor. In many places in Europe, advertising is widely appreciated as an art form and TV/cinema commercials have their own Cannes festival. In France and Great Britain certain advertising executives are public figures in their respective countries. For over ten years, Europeans in different countries have paid relatively high entrance fees to watch an all-night programme in a cinema consisting of nothing but television commercials.[12]

The arts are big business. All cultural products that are transmitted by mass media become a part of popular culture.[13] Classical recordings are marketed in much the same way as Top 40 albums, and museums use mass-marketing techniques to sell their wares. The Parisian museums even run a satellite gift shop at the Charles de Gaulle airport.

Marketers often incorporate high art imagery to promote products. They may sponsor artistic events to build public goodwill or feature works of art on shopping bags.[14] When observers from Toyota watched customers in luxury car showrooms, the company found that these consumers tended to view a car as an art object. This theme was then used in an ad for the Lexus with the caption: 'Until now, the only fine arts we supported were sculpture, painting and music'.[15]

Cultural formulae

Mass culture, in contrast, churns out products specifically for a mass market. These products aim to please the average taste of an undifferentiated audience and are predictable because they follow certain patterns. As illustrated in Table 15.3, many popular art forms, such as detective stories or science fiction, generally follow a ▶ **cultural formula**, where certain roles and props often occur consistently.[16] Computer programs even allow users to 'write' their own romances by systematically varying certain set elements of the story. Romance novels are an extreme case of a cultural formula. The romance novel and other formulae reflect the consumer society by the way consumption events and different brands play a role in the story and in the construction of the different atmospheres described.[17]

Reliance on these formulae also leads to a *recycling* of images, as members of the creative subsystem reach back through time for inspiration. Thus, young people in Britain watch retro channels like Granada Plus and UK Gold broadcasting classic

Table 15.3 Cultural formulae in public art forms

Art form/genre	Classic western	Science fiction	Hard-boiled detective	Family sitcom
Time	1800s	Future	Present	Anytime
Location	Edge of civilization	Space	City	Suburbs
Protagonist	Cowboy (lone individual)	Astronaut	Detective	Father (figure)
Heroine	Schoolmistress	Spacegirl	Damsel in distress	Mother (figure)
Villain	Outlaws, killers	Aliens	Killer	Boss, neighbour
Secondary characters	Townsfolk, Indians	Technicians in spacecraft	Police, underworld	Children, dogs
Plot	Restore law and order	Repel aliens	Find killer	Solve problem
Theme	Justice	Triumph of humanity	Pursuit and discovery	Chaos and confusion
Costume	Cowboy hat, boots, etc.	High-tech uniforms	Raincoat	Normal clothes
Locomotion	Horse	Spaceship	Beat-up car	Family estate car
Weaponry	Six-gun, rifle	Rayguns	Pistol, fists	Insults

Source: Arthur A. Berger, *Signs in Contemporary Culture: An Introduction to Semiotics*, 2/E. Copyright © 1984, 1999 by Sheffield Publishing Company, Salem, WI. Reprinted with permission of the publisher.

This advertisement demonstrates the adaptation of famous paintings ('high art') to sell products ('low art').

Used with permission of Robson-Brown Ad Agency, Newcastle upon Tyne, England.

decade-old soaps, and old themes are recycled for new soap series. Designers modify styles from Victorian England or colonial Africa, DJs sample sound bites from old songs and combine them in new ways, and The Gap runs ads featuring deceased celebrities including Humphrey Bogart, Gene Kelly and Pablo Picasso dressed in khaki pants. With easy access to VCRs, CD burners, digital cameras and imaging software, virtually anyone can 'remix' the past.[18]

Artists and companies in the popular music or film industry may be more guided by ideas of what could make a 'hit' than by any wish for artistic expression. And creators of aesthetic products are increasingly adapting conventional marketing methods to fine-tune their mass-market offerings. In the United States, market

These Absolut ads featuring popular artists help to blur the boundaries between marketing activities and popular culture.

V&S Vin & Spirit AB.

1940. 'The Patriot' by the Emerson Radio Corporation.

1946. No longer manufactured.

1947. Out of date.

1953. Garaged.

1980. Garage Sale.

1981. Flea Market.

1983. Antique Show.

1984. Madison Avenue Gallery.

1989. The Metropolitan Museum of Art.

Nothing endures but change. HG HOUSE & GARDEN

This *House & Garden* ad illustrates the life cycle of an Emerson radio to show how ideas about a mass-produced cultural product can change over time and create a classic and valuable collector's item.
Condé Nast Publications Inc.

research is used, for example, to test audience reactions to film concepts. Although testing cannot account for such intangibles as acting quality or cinematography, it can determine if the basic themes of the movie strike a responsive chord in the target audience. This type of research is most appropriate for blockbuster movies, which usually follow one of the formulae described earlier. In some cases research is combined with publicity, as when the producers of the movie *Men in Black*, featuring Will Smith, showed the first 12 minutes of the film to an advance audience and then let them meet the stars to create a pre-release buzz.[19]

Even the content of films is sometimes influenced by this consumer research. Typically, free invitations to pre-screenings are handed out in malls and cinemas. Attendees are asked a few questions about the film, then some are selected to participate in focus groups. Although groups' reactions usually result in only minor editing changes, occasionally more drastic effects result. When initial reaction to the ending of the film *Fatal Attraction* was negative, Paramount Pictures spent an additional $1.3 million shooting a new one.[20] Of course, this feedback isn't always accurate – before the megahit *E.T.: The Extra-Terrestrial* was released, consumer research indicated that no one over the age of four would go to see the movie! [21] Whoever did that research project needs to phone home ...

Reality engineering

Let us take a short trip to a cosy corner of the United States. The village of Riverside, Georgia, has a colourful history. You can look at the sepia photographs showing the town in the nineteenth century, or read excerpts from period novels lauding the settlement's cosmopolitan flair. You'll also discover that the town was used as a Union garrison during the American Civil War. There's only one hitch: Riverside didn't exist until 1998. The account of nineteeth-century Riverside is a clever fabrication created to promote a new housing and commercial development. The story 'is a figment of our imagination', acknowledges the developer.[22]

Like Riverside, many of the environments in which we find ourselves, whether shopping centres, sports stadiums or theme parks, are composed at least partly of images and characters drawn from products, marketing campaigns or the mass media. **Reality engineering** occurs as elements of popular culture are appropriated by marketers and converted to vehicles for promotional strategies.[23] These elements include sensory and spatial aspects of everyday existence, whether in the form of products appearing in films, odours pumped into offices and shops, advertising hoardings, theme parks, video monitors attached to shopping trolleys, and so on.

The people of Disney Corporation are probably the best-known reality engineers worldwide, through their theme parks in California and Florida, and their newer parks in Japan and Europe. Disneyland-Paris got off to a problematic start when it opened in 1991. Fewer visitors and especially too few clients for the hotel and congress facilities created economic problems. But the conceptualization of the park was changed, made less American and more European, and now the park is drawing huge crowds. Other consumption facilities and housing areas have been created around it, including a giant shopping centre where one of the streets will be a recreation of a 'typical street' of one of the local villages.[24] But other themed environments like the Asterix park, future parks or artificially created tropical environments are becoming increasingly popular for shorter vacations throughout Europe. The British-owned chain Center Parcs now has 13 villages in Europe – five in the Netherlands, three in the UK, two each in Belgium and France, and one in Germany – all of them built on the concept of constructing a happy and safe environment for the confirmation of family values – a life 'in brackets' away from the risks and hassles of 'real society'.[25]

The Lost City, a new resort in South Africa, blurs the boundaries even further: it has created a 'fake' Africa for affluent guests. The complex is drought-proof and disease-proof, and it features a three-storey water slide, an 'ocean' with a panic button that will stop the wave motion on command, and a nightly volcanic eruption complete with 'non-allergenic' smoke.[26] The melding of marketing activity with popular culture is evident in other contexts as well. A British coffee ad recently borrowed the words from the Beatles' song 'A Day in the Life' and went so far as to include a shot of John Lennon's signature round-framed glasses sitting on a table. The British Boy Scouts announced that they would begin accepting corporate sponsorships for merit badges.

Multicultural dimensions

One of the most controversial intersections between marketing and society occurs when companies provide 'educational materials' to schools. In the United States, many firms, including such companies as Nike and Nintendo, provide free book covers covered with ads. Almost 40 per cent of secondary schools in the US start the day with a 'video feed' from Channel One, which exposes students to commercials in the classroom in exchange for educational programming. Similarly, an internet company called ZapMe! gives client schools free computers and internet connections as well as a network of 11,000 educational sites in exchange for a promise to use the computers at least four hours a day. Commercials run continuously on the lower left-hand quarter of the screen, and the company has permission to monitor the students' browsing

▶

habits, breaking down the data by age, sex and zip code. In a few cases companies are contracting with schools to run focus groups with their students during the school day in order to get reactions to new product ideas. Coca-Cola signed a ten-year, $8 million exclusive beverage contract with the Colorado Springs, Colorado, school system. In some schools nine-year-olds practise maths by counting Tootsie Rolls (a brand of sweets), and use reading software that sports logos from KMart, Coke, Pepsi and Cap'n Crunch cereal.

Corporate involvement with schools is hardly new – in the 1920s Ivory Soap sponsored soap-carving competitions for students. But the level of intrusion is increasing sharply as companies scramble to compensate for the decrease in children's viewership of television on Saturday mornings and weekday afternoons and find themselves competing with videos and computer games for their attention. Many educators argue that these materials are a godsend for resource-poor schools that otherwise would have hardly any other way to communicate with students. What do you think?[27]

Nor is this a purely American phenomenon any longer. The Danish consumer ombudsman attacked a new series of mathematics books for primary schools for including references to brand names. The publishers defended themselves with the argument that it was to provide more realistic cases for the schoolchildren.

Marketing sometimes seems to exert a self-fulfilling prophecy on popular culture. As commercial influences on popular culture increase, marketer-created symbols make their way into our daily lives to a greater degree. Historical analyses of plays, best-selling novels and the lyrics of hit songs, for example, clearly show large increases in the use of brand names over time.[28]

Reality engineering is accelerating due to the current popularity of product placements by marketers. It is quite common to see real brands prominently displayed or to hear them discussed in films and on television. In many cases, these 'plugs' are no accident. **Product placement** refers to the insertion of specific products and/or the use of brand names in film and TV scripts. Perhaps the greatest product placement success story was Reese's Pieces: sales jumped by 65 per cent in the American market after it appeared in the film *E.T.*[29]

Since that time, products are popping up everywhere: for example, an Apple PowerBook can clearly be seen in *Mission: Impossible* (in return, Apple underwrote a television advertising campaign for the film, and also created an online website for the release free of charge). Sometimes these placements even result in changes to the programme itself. The film *Flipper* showed a Coke can in one scene. When producers signed a marketing deal with Pizza Hut, which is owned by PepsiCo, they had to spend about $40,000 changing the drink label digitally to Pepsi.[30]

Even in China, product placement is emerging as a new way to get noticed. Most commercials on Chinese state-run TV play back-to-back in ten-minute segments, making it difficult for any one 30-second ad to attract attention. So, enterprising marketers are embedding product messages in the shows instead. A soap opera called *Love Talks* features such products as Maybelline lipstick, Motorola mobile phones and Ponds Vaseline Intensive Care lotion.[31]

Some critics argue that the practice of product placement has got out of hand: shows are created with the purpose of marketing products rather than for their entertainment value. Some children's shows have been berated for essentially being extended commercials for a toy. One major film company sent a letter to large consumer product companies to solicit product placements for forthcoming film production and even provided a fee scale: US$20,000 for the product to be seen in the film; US$40,000 for an actor to mention the product by name; and US$60,000 for the actor to use the product.[32] The director of strategic planning at Saatchi & Saatchi New York predicts: 'any space you can take in visually, anything you hear in the future will be branded, I believe. It's not going to be the Washington Monument. It's going to be the *Washington Post* Monument.'[33] From various countries (and the film *Fierce Creatures*!) it is known how companies sponsor zoo animals; often animals are attached to the company through the company logo or name. The live penguin in the Copenhagen zoo thus becomes a representation of the penguin logo of a Danish bank! The 'original' symbolizes the 'copy'!

Media images significantly influence consumers' perceptions of reality, affecting viewers' notions about such issues as dating behaviour, racial stereotypes and occupational status.[34] Studies of the **cultivation hypothesis**, which relates to the media's ability to shape consumers' perceptions of reality, have shown that heavy television viewers tend to overestimate the degree of affluence in the country, and these effects also extend to such areas as perceptions of the amount of violence in one's culture.[35] Also, the depiction of consumer environments in programmes and advertisements may lead to further marginalization of, e.g., unemployed people, who cannot afford to buy into the depicted lifestyle,[36] or to outright addicted consumers, who cannot refrain from constantly buying various goods, although they may not use these at all.

The diffusion of innovations

New products and styles termed innovations constantly enter the market. An **innovation** is any product or service that is perceived to be new by consumers. These new products or services occur in both consumer and industrial settings. Innovations may take the form of a clothing style (e.g. Jean-Paul Gaultier's skirts for men), a new manufacturing technique, or a novel way to deliver a service. If an innovation is successful (most are not), it spreads through the population. First it is bought and/or used by only a few people, and then more and more consumers decide to adopt it, until, in some cases, it seems that almost everyone has bought or tried the innovation. *Diffusion of innovations* refers to the process whereby a new product, service or idea spreads through a population. There is a tendency that especially technical goods diffuse more rapidly these days. Some 16 per cent of the Swedish population possessed a portable phone in 1994 – six years later, in 2000, the number was 80 per cent. Likewise, the number of Swedes with internet access was 55 per cent in 2000, up from a mere 1 per cent in 1995.[37]

Adopting innovations

A consumer's adoption of an innovation may resemble the decision-making sequence discussed in Chapter 8. The person moves through the stages of awareness, information search, evaluation, trial and adoption, although the relative importance of each stage may differ depending on how much is already known about a product,[38] as well as on cultural factors that may affect people's willingness to try new things.[39] A study of 11 European countries found that consumers in individualistic cultures are more innovative than consumers in collective cultures.[40]

However, even within the same culture, not all people adopt an innovation at the same rate. Some do so quite rapidly, and others never do at all. Consumers can be

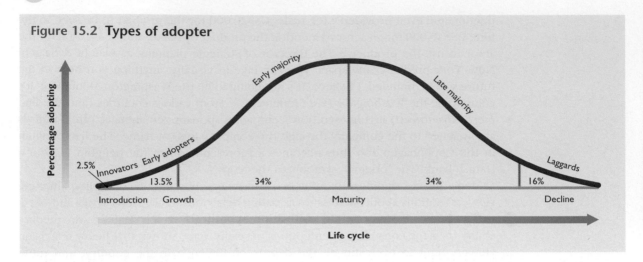

Figure 15.2 Types of adopter

placed into approximate categories based upon the likelihood of adopting an innovation. The categories of adopters, shown in Figure 15.2, can be related to phases of the product life cycle concept used widely by marketing strategists.

As can be seen in Figure 15.2, roughly one-sixth of the population (innovators and early adopters) are very quick to adopt new products, and one-sixth (laggards) are very slow. The other two-thirds are somewhere in the middle, and these majority adopters represent the mainstream public. In some cases people deliberately wait before adopting an innovation because they assume that its technological qualities will be improved or that its price will fall after it has been on the market.[41] Keep in mind that the proportion of consumers falling into each category is an estimate: the actual size of each depends upon such factors as the complexity of the product, its cost, and other product-related factors, but it possibly also varies from country to country.

Even though innovators represent only 2.5 per cent of the population, marketers are always interested in identifying them. According to standard theory, these are the brave souls who are always on the lookout for novel developments and will be the first to try a new offering. Just as generalized opinion leaders do not appear to exist, so innovators tend to be category-specific. A person who is an innovator in one area may even be a laggard in another. For example, someone who prides himself on being at the cutting edge of fashion may have no conception of new developments in recording technology and stereo equipment.

Despite this qualification, some generalizations can be offered regarding the profile of innovators.[42] Not surprisingly they tend to have more favourable attitudes towards taking risks. They are also, at least in an American context, likely to have higher educational and income levels and to be socially active. However, in a European study of the fashion and clothing market, the same correlation between socio-demographic variables and innovative or early adopting behaviour could not be found.[43] On the other hand, a Spanish study, perhaps not surprisingly, concluded that innovators tend to be younger and, more interestingly, that publicity and advertisement would have the biggest influence on product adoption in the early years of commercialization of a product, whereas word-of-mouth and other non-producer controlled information becomes more important later on.[44]

Early adopters share many of the same characteristics as innovators, but an important difference is their degree of concern for social acceptance, especially with regard to expressive products such as clothing, cosmetics, and so on. Generally

Table 15.4 Decision styles of market segments based on adoption, innovation and personal involvement

Adoption decision process stage	Less-involved adopters	Innovators	More-involved adopters
Problem recognition	Passive, reactive	Active	Proactive
Search	Minimal, confined to resolution of minor anomalies caused by current consumption patterns	Superficial but extensively based within and across product class boundaries	Extensive within relevant product category; assiduous exploration of all possible solutions within that framework
Evaluation	Meticulous, rational, slow and cautious; objective appraisal using tried and tested criteria	Quick, impulsive, based on currently accepted criteria; personal and subjective	Careful, confined to considerations raised by the relevant product category: but executed confidently and (for the adopter) briskly within that frame of reference
Decision	Conservative selection within known range of products, continuous innovations preferred	Radical: easily attracted to discontinuously new product class and able to choose quickly within it. Frequent trial, followed by abandonment	Careful selection within a product field that has become familiar through deliberation, vicarious trial, and sound and prudent pre-purchase comparative evaluation
Post-purchase evaluation	Meticulous, tendency to brand loyalty if item performs well	Less loyal; constantly seeking novel experiences through purchase and consumption innovations	Loyal if satisfied but willing to try innovations within the prescribed frame of reference; perhaps tends towards the dynamically continuous

Source: Gordon R. Foxall and Seema Bhate, 'Cognitive Style and Personal Involvement as Explicators of Innovative Purchasing of Health Food Brands', *European Journal of Marketing* 27(2) (1993): 5–16. Used with permission.

speaking, an early adopter is receptive to new styles because he or she is involved in the product category and also places high value on being in fashion. The universality of the dichotomy of innovators and adopters has been challenged by research pertaining to health foods, suggesting that (1) three groups can be distinguished, namely innovators, more-involved adopters and less-involved adopters, and (2) there is not a big difference between the purchase rate of new products between innovators and adopters; rather the difference lies in the kind of innovations tried and the approach to trying new products.[45] Table 15.4 gives a brief description of the different types of consumers and their approach to new product trials.

Types of innovations

Innovations can contain a technological level and involve some functional change (e.g. car air bags) or be of a more intangible kind, communicating a new social meaning (e.g. a new hairstyle). However, contrary to what much literature states,[46] both are symbolic in the sense that one refers to symbols of technical performance and safety and the other to less tangible symbols, such as courage and individuality. Both types refer to symbols of progress.[47] New products, services and ideas have characteristics that determine the degree to which they will probably diffuse. Innovations that are more novel may be less likely to diffuse, since they require bigger changes in people's lifestyles and thus more effort. On the other hand, most innovations are close to being of the 'me too' kind, and thus do not necessarily possess qualities that would persuade the consumer to shift from existing product types. In any case, it should be noted that in spite of all the good intentions of the marketing concept to ensure that there is a market before the product is developed, the failure rate of new products is as high as ever, if not higher.[48]

Behavioural demands of innovations

Innovations can be categorized in terms of the degree to which they demand changes in behaviour from adopters. Three major types of innovation have been identified, though these three categories are not absolutes. They refer, in a relative sense, to the amount of disruption or change they bring to people's lives.

▶ A **continuous innovation** refers to a modification of an existing product, as when a breakfast cereal is introduced in a sugar-coated version, or Levi's promoted 'shrink-to-fit' jeans. This type of change may be used to set one brand apart from its competitors. Most product innovations are evolutionary rather than revolutionary. Small changes are made to reposition the product, add line extensions or merely to alleviate consumer boredom.

Consumers may be lured to the new product, but adoption represents only minor changes in consumption habits, since innovation perhaps adds to the product's convenience or to the range of choices available. A typewriter company, for example, many years ago modified the shape of its product to make it more user-friendly. One simple change was the curving of the tops of the keys, a convention that was carried over on today's computer keyboards. One of the reasons for the change was that secretaries had complained about the difficulty of typing with long fingernails on the flat surfaces.

▶ A **dynamically continuous innovation** is a more pronounced change in an existing product, as represented by self-focusing cameras or touch-tone telephones. These innovations have a modest impact on the way people do things, creating some behavioural changes, although the touch-tone telephone is an expression of a larger innovation involving many discontinuous renewals of daily life: the digitalization of communication. When it was introduced, the IBM electric typewriter, which used a 'golf ball' rather than individual keys, enabled typists to change the typeface of manuscripts simply by replacing one ball with another.

▶ A **discontinuous innovation** creates major changes in the way we live. Major inventions, such as the aeroplane, the car, the computer and the television, have radically changed modern lifestyles, although, as can be seen from these examples, major changes normally take some time from the point of introduction. The personal computer has, in many cases, supplanted the typewriter, and it has created the phenomenon of 'telecommuters' by allowing many people to work from their homes. Of course, the cycle continues, as new innovations (e.g. new versions of software) are constantly being made; dynamically continuous innovations, such as the keyboard 'mouse', compete for adoption; and discontinuous innovations like wristwatch personal computers loom on the horizon.

MARKETING OPPORTUNITY

These days, the new interactive communication technologies provide a lot of opportunities for product innovations. Electrolux, the large Swedish appliance producer, is currently testing household reactions and changes in consumer lifestyles in 50 Danish homes following the installment of the world's first intelligent refrigerator, the Electrolux Screenfridge. In collaboration with an Ericsson subsidiary, the company has developed this new communication centre of the home, with built-in touch screen on the refrigerator door that provides perpetual access to broadband communication technology (including automated shopping lists), internet, TV and radio. Even more 'intelligent features' are being developed for the product. Says one young mother from one of the test households: 'I enjoy the online internet access in the kitchen, as it is the place we spend most of our time. I believe I'll use the Screenfridge for everyday information, like looking up phone numbers, finding bus schedules or getting dinner ideas. I know I'll also try internet food shopping; with two children it would be great to have the groceries delivered to the home.'[49]

Prerequisites for successful adoption

Regardless of how much behavioural change is demanded by an innovation, several factors are desirable for a new product to succeed:[50]

- *Compatibility*. The innovation should be compatible with consumers' lifestyles. As an illustration, a manufacturer of personal care products tried unsuccessfully several years ago to introduce a hair remover cream for men as a substitute for razors and shaving cream. This formulation was similar to that widely used by women to remove hair from their legs. Although the product was simple and convenient to use, it failed because men were not interested in a product they perceived to be too feminine and thus threatening to their masculine self-concepts.

- *Trialability*. Since an unknown is accompanied by high perceived risk, people are more likely to adopt an innovation if they can experiment with it prior to making a commitment. To reduce the perceived risk, companies often choose the expensive strategies of distributing free 'trial-size' samples of new products. For example, the Swedish coffee brand Gevalia has distributed free samples targeted especially at young people, because there is some evidence that fewer young people are drinking coffee, and that those that do, begin later in life.

- *Complexity*. The product should be low in complexity. A product that is easier to understand and use will often be preferred to a competitor. This strategy requires

A cultural emphasis on science in the late 1950s affected product designs, as seen in the design of cars with large tailfins (to resemble rockets).
R. Gates/Frederic Lewis.

less effort from the consumer, and it also lowers perceived risk. Manufacturers of videocassette recorders, for example, have put a lot of effort into simplifying VCR usage (such as on-screen programming) to encourage adoption.

● *Observability*. Innovations that are easily observable are more likely to spread, since this quality makes it more likely that other potential adopters will become aware of their existence. The rapid proliferation of 'bumbags' (pouches worn around the waist in lieu of wallets or purses) was due to their high visibility. It was easy for others to see the convenience offered.

● *Relative advantage*. Most importantly, the product should offer relative advantage over alternatives. The consumer must believe that its use will provide a benefit other products cannot offer. For example, the success of many environmentally friendly product alternatives may be due to the fact that, once consumers have been convinced about the environmental advantages of the product, it has a clear and easily understandable advantage compared to competing products.

The social context of innovations

One critical but relatively little researched aspect is the importance of the social context of product adoption behaviour.[51] This is linked to the importance of visibility of the product innovation as well as the influence of the reference group which is seen as related to the new product. For example, Western products are admired in many contexts in Asia and Africa, or the marketizing economies of eastern Europe, for the sole reason of being linked to the status of the Western world, which is seen as 'better', more 'developed' and generally of a higher status.[52] Likewise, in Europe the association of new products with the American way of life will have a significant impact on the adopting behaviour of various groups in society but will differ in different European countries.

Another aspect of the social dimension of innovation is the pitfall of being caught up in too many continuous innovations due to an ever finer market segmentation and customization approach. This may take resources away from more strategic considerations of changing 'the way things are done'.[53] For example, a British bank had created such a complex structure of financial services and accounts, as well as charges attached to these services, that customers began to complain about waiting time and lack of understanding of their own financial affairs. The bank simplified the structure to one account type and a much simpler charge system and successfully made this a unique selling proposition in a market dominated by more complex offerings.[54]

The fashion system

 The **fashion system** consists of all those people and organizations involved in creating symbolic meanings and transferring these meanings to cultural goods. Although people tend to equate fashion with clothing, be it haute couture or streetwear, it is important to keep in mind that fashion processes affect *all* types of cultural phenomena, from the more mundane (what do you think of high fashion diaper (nappy) bags in unisex style?[55]) to high art, including music, art, architecture and even science (i.e. certain research topics and scientists are 'hot' at any point in time). Even business practices are subject to the fashion process: they evolve and change depending on which management techniques are in vogue, such as total quality management or 'the learning organization'.

Fashion can be thought of as a *code*, or language, that helps us to decipher these meanings.[56] However, fashion seems to be *context-dependent* to a larger extent than language. That is, the same item can be interpreted differently by different consumers and in different situations.[57] The meaning of many products is *undercoded* – that is, there is no one precise meaning, but rather plenty of room for interpretation among perceivers.

At the outset, it may be helpful to distinguish between some confusing terms. ▶ **Fashion** is the process of social diffusion by which a new style is adopted by some group(s) of consumers. In contrast, *a fashion* (or style) refers to a particular combination of attributes. And to be *in fashion* means that this combination is currently positively evaluated by some reference group. Thus, the term *Danish Modern* refers to particular characteristics of furniture design (i.e. a fashion in interior design); it does not necessarily imply that Danish Modern is a fashion that is currently desired by consumers.[58]

Cultural categories

▶ The meaning that does get imparted to products reflects underlying **cultural categories**, which correspond to the basic ways we characterize the world.[59] Our culture makes distinctions between different times, between leisure and work, between genders, and so on. The fashion system provides us with products that signify these categories. For example, the clothing industry gives us clothing to denote certain times (e.g. evening wear, beach wear), it differentiates between leisure clothes and work clothes, and it promotes masculine, feminine or unisex styles.

Interdependence among product meanings

These cultural categories affect many different products and styles. As a result, it is common to find that dominant aspects of a culture at any point in time tend to be reflected in the design and marketing of very different products. This concept is hard to grasp, since on the surface a clothing style, say, has little in common with a piece of furniture or with a car. However, an overriding concern with a value such as achievement or environmentalism can determine the types of product likely to be accepted by consumers at any point in time. These underlying or latent themes then surface in various aspects of design. A few examples of this interdependence will help to demonstrate how a dominant fashion motif reverberates across industries.

- Costumes worn by political figures or film and rock stars can affect the fortunes of the apparel and accessory industries. The appearance of the actor Clark Gable in a film not wearing a waistcoat (unusual at that time) dealt a severe setback to the men's apparel industry, while Jackie Kennedy's famous 'pillbox' hat prompted a rush for hats by women in the 1960s. Other cross-category effects include the craze for ripped sweatshirts instigated by the movie *Flashdance* or the singer Madonna's legitimization of lingerie as an acceptable outerwear clothing style.

- Some years ago, the Louvre in Paris was remodelled to include a controversial glass pyramid at the entrance designed by the architect I. M. Pei. Shortly thereafter, several designers unveiled pyramid-shaped clothing at Paris fashion shows.[60]

- In the 1950s and 1960s, much of the Western world was preoccupied with science and technology. This concern with 'space-age' mastery was fuelled by the Russians' launching of the Sputnik satellite, which prompted fears that the West (and here, most importantly the US) was falling behind in the technology race.

The theme of technical mastery of nature and of futuristic design became a motif that cropped up in many aspects of popular culture – from car designs with prominent tailfins to high-tech kitchen styles.

Collective selection

Fashions tend to sweep through countries; it seems that all of a sudden 'everyone' is doing the same thing or wearing the same styles. Some sociologists view fashion as a form of *collective behaviour*, or a wave of social conformity. How do so many people get tuned in to the same phenomenon at once, as happened with hip-hop styles?

Remember that creative subsystems within a culture production system attempt to anticipate the tastes of the buying public. Despite their unique talents, members of this subsystem are also members of mass culture. Like the fashion magazine editors discussed earlier, cultural gatekeepers are drawing from a common set of ideas and symbols, and are influenced by the same cultural phenomena as the eventual consumers of their products.

The process by which certain symbolic alternatives are chosen over others has been termed **collective selection**.[61] As with the creative subsystem, members of the managerial and communications subsystems also seem to develop a common frame of mind. Although products within each category must compete for acceptance in the marketplace, they can usually be characterized by their adherence to a dominant theme or motif – be it the Grunge look, sixties nostalgia, Danish Modern or nouvelle cuisine.

Behavioural science perspectives on fashion

Fashion is a very complex process which operates on many levels. At one extreme, it is a macro, societal phenomenon affecting many people simultaneously. At the other, it exerts a very personal effect on individual behaviour. A consumer's pur-

This ad for Maidenform illustrates that fashions have accentuated different parts of the female anatomy throughout history.

Copyright © 1994 by Maidenform, Inc.

chase decisions are often motivated by his or her desire to be in fashion. Fashion products are aesthetic objects, and their origins are rooted in art and history. For this reason, there are many perspectives on the origin and diffusion of fashion. Although these cannot be described in detail here, some major approaches can be briefly summarized.[62]

Psychological models of fashion

Many psychological factors help to explain why people are motivated to be in fashion. These include conformity, variety-seeking, personal creativity and sexual attraction. For example, many consumers seem to have a 'need for uniqueness': they want to be different, but not too different.[63] For this reason, people often conform to the basic outlines of a fashion, but try to improvise and make a personal statement within these guidelines.

One of the earliest theories of fashion proposed that 'shifting **erogenous zones**' (sexually arousing areas of the body) accounted for fashion changes. Different parts of the female body are the focus of sexual interest, and clothing styles change to highlight or hide these parts. For example, people in the Victorian era found shoulders exciting, a 'well-turned ankle' was important at the beginning of the twentieth century, while the back was the centre of attention in the 1930s.

While these shifts may be due to boredom, some have speculated that there are deeper reasons for changes in focus: body areas symbolically reflect social values. In medieval times, for example, a rounded belly was desirable. This preference was most likely a reflection of the fact that multiple pregnancies were necessary to maintain population growth in an age when infant mortality was high. Interest in the female leg in the 1920s and 1930s coincided with women's new mobility and independence, while the exposure of breasts in the 1970s signalled a renewed interest in breastfeeding.[64] Breasts were de-emphasized in the 1980s as women concentrated on careers, but some analysts have theorized that a larger bust size is now more popular as women try to combine professional activity with child-rearing. Now, some suggest that the current prevalence of the exposed midriff reflects the premium our society places on fitness.[65] It's important to note that until very recently the study of fashion focused almost exclusively on its impact on women. Hopefully, this concentration will broaden as scholars and practitioners begin to appreciate that men are affected by many of the same fashion influences.

Psychological research suggests that it is possible to distinguish between two different personality types, respectively more or less sensitive to the opinion of their social surroundings (also called high and low self-monitors). The high self-monitors have been demonstrated to stress the brand of a consumer good (specifically clothing) more than low self-monitors, who are, on the other hand, more positive in their attitudes towards functional product attributes.[66]

Economic models of fashion

Economists approach fashion in terms of the model of supply and demand. Items that are in limited supply have high value, while those readily available are less desirable. Rare items command respect and prestige.

Veblen's notion of **conspicuous consumption** proposed that the wealthy consume to display their prosperity, for example by wearing expensive (and at times impractical) clothing. The functioning of conspicuous consumption seems more complex in today's society, since wealthy consumers often engage in *parody display*, where they deliberately adopt formerly low-status or inexpensive products, such as jeeps or jeans. On the other hand, new hierarchies develop between generic

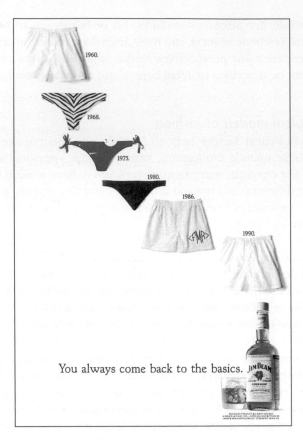

You always come back to the basics.

This Jim Beam ad illustrates the cyclical nature of fashion.
Courtesy of Jim Beam Brand, Inc.

jeans signalling a traditional, work-oriented, classless or lower-class environment and designer jeans expressing an urban, upmarket, class-distinctive and more contemporary lifestyle.[67] Other factors also influence the demand curve for fashion-related products. These include a *prestige-exclusivity effect*, where high prices still create high demand, and a *snob effect*, where lower prices actually reduce demand ('only a cheapskate would pay so little for that!').[68]

Sociological models of fashion

The collective selection model discussed previously is an example of a sociological approach to fashion. In addition, much attention has been focused on the relationship between product adoption and class structure.

The **trickle-down theory**, first proposed in 1904 by Georg Simmel, has been one of the most influential approaches to understanding fashion. It states that there are two conflicting forces that drive fashion change. First, subordinate groups try to adopt the status symbols of the groups above them as they attempt to climb up the ladder of social mobility. Dominant styles thus originate with the upper classes and *trickle down* to those below. However, this is where the second force comes into play: those people in the superordinate groups are constantly looking below them on the ladder to ensure that they are not imitated. They respond to the attempts of lower classes to 'impersonate' them by adopting even *newer* fashions. These two processes create a self-perpetuating cycle of change – the engine that drives fashion.[69]

The trickle-down theory was quite useful for understanding the process of fashion changes when applied to a society with a stable class structure, which permitted the easy identification of lower- vs. upper-class consumers. This task is not so easy in modern times. In contemporary Western society, then, this approach must be modified to account for new developments in mass culture.[70]

- A perspective based on class structure cannot account for the wide range of styles that are simultaneously made available in our society. Modern consumers have a much greater degree of individualized choice than in the past because of advances in technology and distribution. Just as an adolescent is almost instantly aware of the latest style trends by watching MTV, *elite fashion* has been largely replaced by *mass fashion*, since media exposure permits many groups to become aware of a style at the same time.

- Consumers tend to be more influenced by opinion leaders who are similar to them. As a result each social group has its own fashion innovators who determine fashion trends. It is often more accurate to speak of a *trickle-across effect*, where fashions diffuse horizontally among members of the same social group.[71]

- Anybody who has been on a skiing holiday will have noticed the *subcultural fashions* demonstrated among the skiers. In fact, more and more consumption-based subcultures, like sailing enthusiasts, for instance, adopt their own fashions in order to reinforce their community feeling and distinguish themselves from outsiders.[72]

- Finally, current fashions often originate with the lower classes and *trickle up*. Grass-roots innovators typically are people who lack prestige in the dominant culture (like urban youth). Since they are less concerned with maintaining the status quo, they are more free to innovate and take risks.[73] Whatever the direction of the trickling, one thing is sure: that fashion is always a complex process of variation, of imitation and differentiation, of adoptions and rejections in relation to one's social surroundings.[74]

This blurring of the origins of fashion has been attributed to the condition of postmodernity, where there is no fashion, only fashions, and no rules, only choices,[75] and where the norms and rules can no longer be dictated solely by the haute couture or other cultural gatekeepers but where the individual allows him- or herself more freedom in creating a personal look by mixing elements from different styles.[76] This obviously has as a consequence that the relatively linear models of fashion cycles discussed below become less able to predict actual fashion developments.[77]

A French researcher followed the development in the editorial content of a French fashion magazine since 1945. It turned out that the content became more global and less 'French' over the years, but also that the magazine gradually shifted away from a dictate of one certain fashion style at each point in time to an approach in the 1990s where several styles were promoted in each issue and consumers were invited to mix and match and create their own personal style independently of high fashion.[78] A similar blurring of high and low fashion was demonstrated by a prize-winning campaign where a charity organization used former international top model Renee Toft Simonsen to promote clothes from their second-hand shops.[79] Neither she nor the agency got any payment for their participation . . .

The fashion system, then, is becoming increasingly complex. Brands may be very significant to consumers and they may be less ashamed to admit that than previously but they are less committed to any one brand over a longer period. The fashion industry is trying to compensate for this by over-exposing their brands, putting the brand name very conspicuously all over clothing, bags, accessories, etc. in order to get a maximum of exposure out of each 'catch'.[80] The fashion industry is also exploring the individual styles for new market opportunities and new meanings of fashion goods for wider distribution.[81] Even those trying to rebel against fashion dictates by turning to ugliness as a motif for their choice of 'look' cannot escape. Ugliness in a variety of forms is becoming increasingly fashionable; as one consumer said: 'these shoes were so ugly I just had to have them'.[82] The ugly and disgusting seems to form a specific trend in certain companies' marketing strategies.[83]

**MARKETING
PITFALL**

A *knockoff* is a style that has been deliberately copied and modified, often with the intention of selling to a larger or different market. Haute couture clothing styles presented by top designers in Paris and elsewhere are commonly 'knocked off' by other designers and sold to the mass market. The Web is making it easier than ever for firms to copy these designs – in some cases so quickly that their pirated styles show up in stores at the same time as the originals. Wildcatters such as First View have set up websites to show designers' latest creations, sometimes revealing everything from a new collection. Things have got so bad that the House of Chanel requires photographers to sign contracts promising their shots will not be distributed on the internet.[84] But isn't imitation the sincerest form of flattery?

Cycles of fashion adoption

In 1997, a little digital animal swept across the planet. After enjoying considerable success in Japan in 1996 with about 3 million units sold, it spread throughout the world during 1997 so that by the summer the population had increased to a total of 7 million, with approximately twice that number in back orders. The Tamagochi, as it was known, was an electronic pet that had to be nurtured, played with and taken care of just like a living being. Failure to do so meant that it would weaken and show signs of maltreatment until it eventually died. That is, in the Japanese version it died. This unhappy ending did not appeal to Americans who therefore created their own version where it flew off to another planet if not treated well. Needless to say, the Japanese 'authentic' versions quickly became collector's items (cf. the discussion of collections in the previous chapter). Today, many consumers might not know what a Tamagochi is, but anybody with children will know what a Pokémon is.

Figure 15.3 A normal fashion cycle

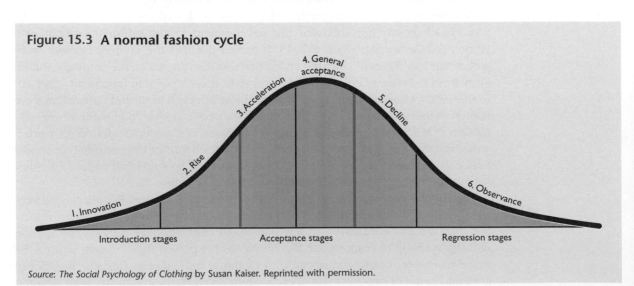

Source: *The Social Psychology of Clothing* by Susan Kaiser. Reprinted with permission.

The stories of the Tamagochi or the Pokémon show how quickly a consumer craze can catch on globally. Although the longevity of a particular style can range from a month to a century, fashions tend to flow in a predictable sequence. The ▶ **fashion life cycle** is quite similar to the more familiar product life cycle. An item or idea progresses through basic stages from birth to death, as shown in Figure 15.3.

Variations in fashion life cycles

The diffusion process discussed earlier in this chapter is intimately related to the popularity of fashion-related items. To illustrate how this process works, consider ▶ how the **fashion acceptance cycle** works in the popular music business. In the *introduction stage*, a song is listened to by a small number of music innovators. It may be played in clubs or on 'cutting-edge' radio stations, which is exactly how 'grunge rock' groups such as Nirvana got their start. During the *acceptance stage*, the song enjoys increased social visibility and acceptance by large segments of the population. A record may get wide airplay on 'Top 40' stations, steadily rising up the charts 'like a bullet'. This process may of course be supported or even generated by marketing efforts from the record company.

In the *regression stage*, the item reaches a state of social saturation as it becomes overused, and eventually it sinks into decline and obsolescence as new songs rise to take its place. A hit record may be played once an hour on a Top 40 station for several weeks. At some point, though, people tend to get sick of it and focus their attention on newer releases. The former hit record eventually winds up in the discount rack at the local record store.

Not everybody shares the same musical tastes. Nor, as we discussed above, is everybody necessarily influenced by the same fashion in clothing any more. As society may become more characterized by lifestyles than by generalizable consumption patterns spreading through social classes, as in the class-based fashion models, so the social groups in question may consist more of a particular lifestyle than of actual social classes. For example, one may distinguish generally between the more risk-prone and the more prudent fashion consumers, and each of these two groups have their own independent fashion cycles that do not necessarily influence the other groups.[85]

Figure 15.4 illustrates that fashions are characterized by slow acceptance at the beginning, which (if the fashion is to 'make it') rapidly accelerates and then tapers off. Different classes of fashion can be identified by considering the relative length of the fashion acceptance cycle. While many fashions exhibit a moderate cycle, taking several years to work their way through the stages of acceptance and decline, others are extremely long-lived or short-lived.

▶ A **classic** is a fashion with an extremely long acceptance cycle. It is in a sense 'anti-fashion', since it guarantees stability and low risk to the purchaser for a long period of time. Keds sneakers, classical so-called 'tennis shoes' introduced in the US in 1917, have been successful because they appeal to those who are turned off by the high-fashion, trendy appeal of L.A. Gear, Reebok and others. When consumers in focus groups were asked to project what kind of building Keds would be, a common response was a country house with a white picket fence. In other words, the shoes are seen as a stable, classic product. In contrast, Nikes were often described as steel-and-glass skyscrapers, reflecting their more modernistic image.[86]

▶ A **fad** is a very short-lived fashion. Fads are usually adopted by relatively few people. Adopters may all belong to a common subculture, and the fad 'trickles across' members but rarely breaks out of that specific group.[87] Some key characteristics of fads include:

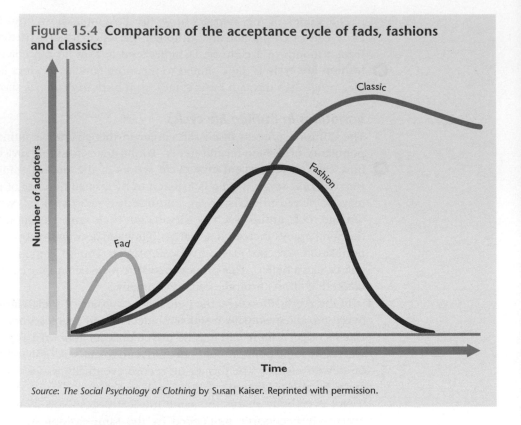

Figure 15.4 Comparison of the acceptance cycle of fads, fashions and classics

Source: *The Social Psychology of Clothing* by Susan Kaiser. Reprinted with permission.

● The fad is non-utilitarian – that is, it does not perform any explicit purpose function.

● The fad is often adopted on impulse; people do not undergo stages of rational decision-making before joining in.

● The fad diffuses rapidly, gains quick acceptance, and is short-lived.

Some successful fad products include 'this summer's toy' kinds of things like hula hoops, yo-yos and the like. However, with the more unpredictable nature of the fashion system, fads seem to spread in different way (cf. the discussion of memes below). Put simply, it is more problematic to foresee what the toy of the season will be. Consumers flock around obscure toys and toy store managers have greater difficulties than ever stocking the right items, leading to customer dissatisfaction when they are told that the delivery time for a specific toy may be several months.[88]

Distinguishing beforehand between fads or more lasting tendencies of change is not easy, and many consulting agencies make a living out of being trend-spotters. However, here are a few points that may be helpful in distinguishing short-lived fads from longer-lasting innovations:[89]

● Does it fit with basic lifestyle changes? If a new hairstyle is hard to care for, this innovation will not be consistent with women's increasing time demands. On the other hand, the movement to shorter-term vacations is more likely to last because this innovation makes trip-planning easier for harried consumers.

● What are the benefits? The switch to leaner meats and cuts came about because these meats were perceived as healthier, so a real benefit was evident.

● Can it be personalized? Enduring trends tend to accommodate a desire for individuality, whereas styles such as mohawk haircuts or the grunge look are inflexible and don't allow people to express themselves.

● Is it a trend or a side-effect? An increased interest in exercise is part of a basic trend towards health consciousness, although the specific form of exercise that is 'in' at any given time will vary (e.g. low-impact aerobics vs. in-line skating).

● What other changes have occurred in the market? Sometimes the popularity of products is influenced by *carryover effects*. The miniskirt fad in the 1960s brought about a major change in the hosiery market, as sales of pantyhose and tights grew from 10 per cent of this product category to more than 80 per cent in two years. Now, sales of these items are declining due to the casual emphasis in dressing.

● Who has adopted the change? If the innovation is not adopted by working mothers, baby boomers, or some other important market segment, it is not likely to become a trend.

A 'medical' model of fashion

For years and years, the lowly Hush Puppy was a shoe for nerds. Suddenly – almost overnight – the shoe became a chic fashion statement even though the company did nothing to promote this image. Why did this style diffuse through the population so quickly? **Meme theory** has been proposed to explain this process using a medical metaphor. A *meme* is an idea or product that enters the consciousness of people over time – examples include tunes, catch-phrases ('Is that your final answer?') or styles like the Hush Puppy. In this view, memes spread among consumers in a geometric progression just as a virus starts off small and steadily infects increasing numbers of people until it becomes an epidemic. Memes 'leap' from brain to brain via a process of imitation.

The meme idea is itself catching on. A website called *memepool.com* is a pool for ideas that attracts 7000 users a day who post random thoughts that others may adopt.[90] More generally, the diffusion of many products in addition to Hush Puppies seems to follow the same basic path. The product initially is used by a few people, but change happens in a hurry when the process reaches the moment of critical mass – which one author has called the *tipping point*. For example, Sharp introduced the first low-price fax in 1984 and sold about 80,000 in that year. There was a slow climb in the number of users over the next three years. Then suddenly, in 1987, enough people had faxes that it made sense for everyone to have one – Sharp sold a million units that year. Cell phones followed the same trajectory.[91]

Chapter summary

● The styles prevalent in a culture at any point in time often reflect underlying political and social conditions. The set of agents responsible for creating stylistic alternatives is termed a *culture production system*. Factors such as the types of people involved in this system and the amount of competition by alternative product forms influence the choices that eventually make their way to the marketplace for consideration by end consumers.

● Culture is often described in terms of high (or elite) forms and low (or popular) forms. Products of popular culture tend to follow a cultural formula and contain predictable components. On the other hand, these distinctions are blurring in modern society as imagery from 'high art' is increasingly being incorporated into marketing efforts and marketed products (or even marketing products like advertisements) are treated and evaluated as high art.

- The *diffusion of innovations* refers to the process whereby a new product, service or idea spreads through a population. A consumer's decision to adopt a new item depends on his or her personal characteristics (i.e. if he or she is inclined to try new things) and on the characteristics of the item. Products sometimes stand a better chance of being adopted if they demand relatively little change in behaviour from consumers and are compatible with current practices. They are also more likely to diffuse if they can be tested prior to purchase, if they are not complex, if their use is visible to others and, most importantly, if they provide a relative advantage *vis-à-vis* existing products.

- The fashion system includes everyone involved in the creation and transference of symbolic meanings. Meanings that express common cultural categories (e.g. gender distinctions) are conveyed by many different products. New styles tend to be adopted by many people simultaneously in a process known as *collective selection*. Perspectives on motivations for adopting new styles include psychological, economic and sociological models of fashion.

- Fashions tend to follow cycles that resemble the product life cycle. The two extremes of fashion adoption, classics and fads, can be distinguished in terms of the length of this cycle.

KEY TERMS

Art product (*p. 475*)
Classic (*p. 493*)
Collective selection (*p. 488*)
Conspicuous consumption (*p. 489*)
Continuous innovation (*p. 484*)
Craft product (*p. 475*)
Cultivation hypothesis (*p. 481*)
Cultural categories (*p. 487*)
Cultural formula (*p. 476*)
Cultural gatekeepers (*p. 475*)
Culture production system (CPS)
  (*p. 473*)
Cultural selection (*p. 471*)
Discontinuous innovation (*p. 484*)

Dynamically continuous innovation
  (*p. 484*)
Early adopters (*p. 482*)
Erogenous zones (*p. 489*)
Fad (*p. 493*)
Fashion (*p. 487*)
Fashion acceptance cycle (*p. 493*)
Fashion life cycle (*p. 493*)
Fashion system (*p. 486*)
Innovation (*p. 481*)
Meme theory (*p. 495*)
Product placement (*p. 480*)
Reality engineering (*p. 479*)
Trickle-down theory (*p. 490*)

For additional material see the companion website at:
www.booksites.net/solomon_euro

Consumer behaviour challenge

1 Construct a 'biography' of a product, tracing its progress from the time it was introduced. How long did it take to diffuse to the mass market? Do the same consumers use the product now as did those who first adopted it? What are its future prospects – is it destined for obsolescence? Would you characterize the product as either a classic or a fad?

2 Some consumers complain that they are 'at the mercy' of designers: they are forced to buy whatever styles are in fashion, because nothing else is available. Do you agree that there is such a thing as a 'designer conspiracy'?

3 What is the basic difference between a fad, a fashion and a classic? Provide examples of each.

4 What is the difference between an art and a craft? Where would you characterize advertising within this framework?

5 Think about some innovative products that you can remember, but which disappeared. Try to reflect on the reasons why these innovations failed.

6 Then try to remember some successful innovations. What characteristics made them successful? Do the successes and failures fit with the criteria mentioned in this chapter?

7 The chapter mentions some instances where market research findings influenced artistic decisions, as when a film ending was reshot to accommodate consumers' preferences. Many people would oppose this use of consumer research, claiming that books, films, records or other artistic endeavours should not be designed merely to conform to what people want to read, see or hear. What do you think?

8 Many are claiming a more individualistic style of fashion these years. Discuss whether individualism in style and fashion has actually increased or whether we are being conformist in new ways.

Notes

1. Nina Darnton, 'Where the Homegirls Are', *Newsweek* (17 June 1991): 60; 'The Idea Chain', *Newsweek* (5 October 1992): 32.

2. Cyndee Miller, 'X Marks the Lucrative Spot, But Some Advertisers Can't Hit Target', *Marketing News* (2 August 1993): 1.

3. Eryn Brown, 'From Rap to Retail. Wiring the Hip-Hop Nation', *Fortune*, (17 April 2000): 530.

4. Teri Agins, 'To Track Fickle Fashion, Apparel Firms Go Online', *Wall Street Journal* (11 May 2000): B1.

5. Richard A. Peterson, 'The Production of Culture: A Prolegomenon', in Richard A. Peterson, ed., *The Production of Culture*, Sage Contemporary Social Science Issues 33 (Beverly Hills, CA: Sage, 1976): 7–22.

6. Richard A. Peterson and D. G. Berger, 'Entrepreneurship in Organizations: Evidence from the Popular Music Industry', *Administrative Science Quarterly* 16 (1971): 97–107.

7. Elizabeth C. Hirschman, 'Resource Exchange in the Production and Distribution of a Motion Picture', *Empirical Studies of the Arts* 8 (1990) 1: 31–51; Michael R. Solomon, 'Building Up and Breaking Down: The Impact of Cultural Sorting on Symbolic Consumption', in J. Sheth and E. C. Hirschman, eds, *Research in Consumer Behavior* (Greenwich, CT: JAI Press, 1988): 325–51.

8. See Paul M. Hirsch, 'Processing Fads and Fashions: An Organizational Set Analysis of Cultural Industry Systems', *American Journal of Sociology* 77 (1972) 4: 639–59; Russell Lynes, *The Tastemakers* (New York: Harper and Brothers, 1954); Michael R. Solomon, 'The Missing Link: Surrogate Consumers in the Marketing Chain', *Journal of Marketing* 50 (October 1986): 208–19.

9. Michael R. Solomon, Richard Ashmore and Laura Longo, 'The Beauty Match-Up Hypothesis: Congruence Between Types of Beauty and Product Images in Advertising', *Journal of Advertising* 21 (December 1992): 23–34.

10. Howard S. Becker, 'Arts and Crafts', *American Journal of Sociology* 83 (January 1987): 862–89.

11. Herbert J. Gans, 'Popular Culture in America: Social Problem in a Mass Society or Social Asset in a Pluralist Society?', in Howard S. Becker, ed., *Social Problems: A Modern Approach* (New York: Wiley, 1966).

12. Peter S. Green, 'Moviegoers Devour Ads', *Advertising Age* (26 June 1989): 36.

13. Michael R. Real, *Mass-Mediated Culture* (Englewood Cliffs, NJ: Prentice-Hall, 1977).

14. Annetta Miller, 'Shopping Bags Imitate Art: Seen the Sacks? Now Visit the Museum Exhibit', *Newsweek* (23 January 1989): 44.

15. Kim Foltz, 'New Species for Study: Consumers in Action', *New York Times* (18 December 1989): A1.

16. Arthur A. Berger, *Signs in Contemporary Culture: An Introduction to Semiotics* (New York: Longman, 1984).

17. Stephen Brown, 'Psycho Shopper: A Comparative Literary Analysis of "the Dark Side"', in Flemming Hansen, ed., *European Advances in Consumer Research* 2 (Provo, UT: Association for Consumer Research, 1995): 96–103; Stephen Brown, 'Consumption Behaviour in the Sex'n'Shopping Novels of Judith Krantz: A Post-structuralist Perspective', in J. Lynch and K. Corfman, eds, *Advances in Consumer Research* 23 (Provo, UT: Association for Consumer Research, 1996): 96–103.

18. Michiko Kakutani, 'Art is Easier the 2nd Time Around', *The New York Times* (30 October 1994): E4. See also Stephen Brown, *Retro-Marketing* (London: Routledge, 2001).

19. Nigel Andrews, 'Filming a Blockbuster is One Thing; Striking Gold is Another', *Financial Times*, accessed via Simon & Schuster College Newslink (20 January 1998).

20. Helene Diamond, 'Lights, Camera ... Research!', *Marketing News* (11 September 1989): 10.

21. Andrews, 'Filming a Blockbuster is One Thing; Striking Gold is Another'.

22. 'A Brand-New Development Creates a Colorful History', *Wall Street Journal Interactive Edition* (18 February 1998).

23. Michael R. Solomon and Basil G. Englis, 'Reality Engineering: Blurring the Boundaries Between Marketing and Popular Culture', *Journal of Current Issues and Research in Advertising* 16 (Fall 1994) 2: 1–17.

24. 'Hollywood-sur-Brie', *Le nouvel observateur* (14 November 1996): 18–19.

25. 'Les "mondes artificiels" attirent toujours plus de vacanciers', *Le Monde* (22–23 December 1996); cf. also John Urry, 'Cultural Change and Contemporary Holiday Making', *Theory, Culture, and Society* 5(1) (1988).

26. Bill Keller, 'For Rich Tourists (and Not Too African)', *New York Times* (3 December 1992) 2: A1.

27. Suzanne Alexander Ryan, 'Companies Teach All Sorts of Lessons with Educational Tools They Give Away', *Wall Street Journal* (19 April 1994): B1 (2); Cyndee Miller, 'Marketers Find a Seat in the Classroom', *Marketing News* (20 June 1994): 2.

28. T. Bettina Cornwell and Bruce Keillor, 'Contemporary Literature and the Embedded Consumer Culture: The Case of Updike's Rabbit', in Roger J. Kruez and Mary Sue MacNealy, eds, *Empirical Approaches to Literature and Aesthetics: Advances in Discourse Processes* 52 (Norwood, NJ: Ablex Publishing Corporation, 1996): 559–72; Monroe Friedman, 'The Changing Language of a Consumer Society: Brand Name Usage in Popular American Novels in the Postwar Era', *Journal of Consumer Research* 11 (March 1985): 927–37; Monroe Friedman, 'Commercial Influences in the Lyrics of Popular American Music of the Postwar Era', *Journal of Consumer Affairs* 20 (Winter 1986): 193.

29. Benjamin M. Cole, 'Products That Want to Be In Pictures', *Los Angeles Herald Examiner* (5 March 1985): 36; see also Stacy M. Vollmers and Richard W. Mizerski, 'A Review and Investigation into the Effectivenss of Product Placements in Films', in Karen Whitehill King, ed., *Proceedings of the 1994 Conference of the American Academy of Advertising*: 97–102; Solomon and Englis, 'Reality Engineering': 2: 1–17.

30. David Leonhardt, 'Cue the Soda Can', *Business Week* (24 June 1996): 64 (2).

31. Peter Wonacott, 'Chinese TV is an Eager Medium for (Lots of) Product Placement', *Wall Street Journal Interactive Edition* (26 January 2000).

32. Randall Rothenberg, 'Is it a Film? Is it an Ad? Harder to Tell?', *New York Times* (13 March 1990): D23.

33. Quoted in Mary Kuntz and Joseph Weber, 'The New Hucksterism', *Business Week* (1 July 1996): 75 (7), 78.

34. George Gerbner, Larry Gross, Nancy Signorielli and Michael Morgan, 'Aging with Television: Images on Television Drama and Conceptions of Social Reality', *Journal of Communication* 30 (1980): 37–47.

35. Stephen Fox and William Philber, 'Television Viewing and the Perception of Affluence', *Sociological Quarterly* 19 (1978): 103–12; W. James Potter, 'Three Strategies for Elaborating the Cultivation Hypothesis', *Journalism Quarterly* 65 (Winter 1988): 930–9; Gabriel Weimann, 'Images of Life in America: The Impact of American T.V. in Israel', *International Journal of Intercultural Relations* 8 (1984): 185–97.

36. Stephanie O'Donohue, 'On the Outside Looking In: Advertising Experiences Among Young Unemployed Adults', in Hansen, ed., *European Advances in Consumer Research* 2: 264–72; Richard Elliott, 'How Do the Unemployed Maintain Their Identity in a Culture of Consumption?', in ibid.: 273–6.

37. 'Mobilen har blivit en vardagspryl', *Info* 9 (2000): 52–4.

38. Susan B. Kaiser, *The Social Psychology of Clothing* (New York: Macmillan, 1985); Thomas S. Robertson,

Innovative Behavior and Communication (New York: Holt, Rhinehart and Winston, 1971).

39. Eric J. Arnould, 'Toward a Broadened Theory of Preference Formation and the Diffusion of Innovations: Cases from Zinder Province, Niger Republic', *Journal of Consumer Research* 16 (September 1989): 239-67.

40. Jan-Benedict E. M. Steenkamp, Frenkel ter Hofstede and Michel Wedel, 'A Cross-national Investigation into the Individual and National Cultural Antecedents of Consumer Innovativeness', *Journal of Marketing* 63 (2) (1999): 55-69.

41. Susan L. Holak, Donald R. Lehmann and Farena Sultan, 'The Role of Expectations in the Adoption of Innovative Consumer Durables: Some Preliminary Evidence', *Journal of Retailing* 63 (Fall 1987): 243-59.

42. Hubert Gatignon and Thomas S. Robertson, 'A Propositional Inventory for New Diffusion Research', *Journal of Consumer Research* 11 (March 1985): 849-67.

43. Frank Huber, 'Ein Konzept zur Ermittlung und Bearbeitung des Frühkaufersegments im Bekleidungsmarkt', *Marketing ZFP* 2 (2nd Quarter 1995): 110-121.

44. Eva Martinez, Yolanda Polo and Carlos Flavián, 'The Acceptance and Diffusion of New Consumer Durables: Differences Between First and Last Adopters', *Journal of Consumer Marketing* 15(4) (1998): 323-42.

45. Gordon R. Foxall and Seema Bhate, 'Cognitive Style and Personal Involvement as Explicators of Innovative Purchasing of Health Food Brands', *European Journal of Marketing* 27(2) (1993): 5-16.

46. Elisabeth C. Hirschman, 'Symbolism and Technology as Sources of the Generation of Innovations', in Andrew Mitchell, ed., *Advances in Consumer Research* 9 (Provo, UT: Association for Consumer Research, 1981): 537-41.

47. Søren Askegaard and A. Fuat Firat, 'Towards a Critique of Material Culture, Consumption and Markets', in Susan M. Pearce, ed., *Experiencing Material Culture in the Western World* (London: Leicester University Press, 1997): 114-39.

48. Stephen Brown, *Postmodern Marketing* (London: Routledge, 1995).

49. Erik Kruse, 'New Product Development and Design: The Kitchen of the Future, the Refrigerator with the Internet Screen and Household-Consumer Contexts', paper presented at the Association for Consumer Research Conference, Salt Lake City, Utah, 16-19 October 2000. See also ***www.kitchengate.dk***.

50. Everett M. Rogers, *Diffusion of Innovations*, 3rd edn (New York: Free Press, 1983).

51. Robert J. Fisher and Linda L. Price, 'An Investigation into the Social Context of Early Adoption Behavior', *Journal of Consumer Research* 19 (December 1992): 477-86.

52. Güliz Ger and Russell W. Belk, 'I'd Like to Buy the World a Coke: Consumptionscapes of the "Less Affluent World"', *Journal of Consumer Policy* 19 (1996): 271-304.

53. W. Chan Kim and Renée Mauborgne, 'Value Innovation: The Strategic Logic of High Growth', *Harvard Business Review* (January-February 1997): 103-12.

54. 'Dare to be Different', *Marketing* (13 February 1997): 22-3.

55. 'Diaper Bag Double Take', *Discount Merchandiser* (March 2000).

56. Umberto Eco, *A Theory of Semiotics* (Bloomington, IN: Indiana University Press, 1979).

57. Fred Davis, 'Clothing and Fashion as Communication', in Michael R. Solomon, ed., *The Psychology of Fashion* (Lexington, MA: Lexington Books, 1985): 15-28.

58. Melanie Wallendorf, 'The Formation of Aesthetic Criteria Through Social Structures and Social Institutions', in Jerry C. Olson, ed., *Advances in Consumer Research* 7 (Ann Arbor, MI: Association for Consumer Research, 1980): 3-6.

59. Grant McCracken, 'Culture and Consumption: A Theoretical Account of the Structure and Movement of the Cultural Meaning of Consumer Goods', *Journal of Consumer Research* 13 (June 1986): 71-84.

60. 'The Eternal Triangle', *Art in America* (February 1989): 23.

61. Herbert Blumer, *Symbolic Interactionism: Perspective and Method* (Englewood Cliffs, NJ: Prentice-Hall, 1969); Howard S. Becker, 'Art as Collective Action', *American Sociological Review* 39 (December 1973); Richard A. Peterson, 'Revitalizing the Culture Concept', *Annual Review of Sociology* 5 (1979): 137-66.

62. For more details, see Susan Kaiser, *The Social Psychology of Clothing*; George B. Sproles, 'Behavioral Science Theories of Fashion', in Solomon, ed., *The Psychology of Fashion*: 55-70.

63. C. R. Snyder and Howard L. Fromkin, *Uniqueness: The Human Pursuit of Difference* (New York: Plenum Press, 1980).

64. Alison Lurie, *The Language of Clothes* (New York: Random House, 1981).

65. Linda Dyett, 'Desperately Seeking Skin', *Psychology Today* (May/June 1996): 14.

66. Susan Auty and Richard Elliott, 'Social Identity and the Meaning of Fashion Brands', in B. Englis and A. Olofsson, eds, *European Advances in Consumer Research* 3 (Provo, UT: Association for Consumer Research, 1998): 1-10.

67. John Fiske, *Understanding Popular Culture* (Boston: Unwin Hyman, 1989): esp. 1-21.

68. Harvey Leibenstein, *Beyond Economic Man: A New Foundation for Microeconomics* (Cambridge, MA: Harvard University Press, 1976).

69. Georg Simmel, 'Fashion', *International Quarterly* 10 (1904): 130-55.

70. Grant D. McCracken, 'The Trickle-Down Theory Rehabilitated', in Solomon, ed., *The Psychology of Fashion*: 39–54.

71. Charles W. King, 'Fashion Adoption: A Rebuttal to the 'Trickle-Down' Theory', in Stephen A. Greyser, ed., *Toward Scientific Marketing* (Chicago: American Marketing Association, 1963): 108–25.

72. Gillian Hogg, Suzanne Horne and David Carmichael, 'Fun, Fashion, or Just Plain Sailing? The Consumption of Clothing in the Sailing Community', in B. Dubois, T. Lowrey, L. J. Shrum and M. Vanhuele, eds, *European Advances in Consumer Research* 4 (Provo, UT: Association for Consumer Research, 1999): 336–40.

73. Alf H. Walle, 'Grassroots Innovation', *Marketing Insights* (Summer 1990): 44–51.

74. Patrick Hetzel, 'The Role of Fashion and Design in a Postmodern Society: What Challenges for Firms?', in M. J. Baker, ed., *Perspectives on Marketing Management* 4 (London: John Wiley & Sons Ltd, 1994): 97–118.

75. Stuart and Elizabeth Ewen, cited in Mike Featherstone, *Consumer Culture and Postmodernism* (London: Sage, 1993): 83.

76. Hetzel, 'The Role of Fashion and Design in a Postmodern Society: What Challenges for Firms?'

77. Anne F. Jensen, 'Acknowledging and Consuming Fashion in the Era after "Good Taste" – From the Beautiful to the Hideous', doctoral dissertations from the Faculty of Social Science 40 University of Southern Denmark, Odense, 1999.

78. Patrick Hetzel, 'A Socio-Semiotic Analysis of the Media/Consumer Relationships in the Production of Fashion Systems: The Case of the "Elle-France" Magazine', in Englis and Olofsson, eds, *European Advances in Consumer Research* 3: 104–107.

79. 'Topmodel i genbrugstøj', *Fyens Stiftstidende, Erhverv* (1 November 2000): 1.

80. 'Panik i mode-fabrikken', Intervju med Alladi Venkatesh, *Dagens Nyheter* (27 June 2000): B1.

81. Don Slater, *Consumer Culture and Modernity* (Cambridge: Polity Press, 1997).

82. Anne F. Jensen and Søren Askegaard, 'In Pursuit of Ugliness: Searching for a Fashion Concept in the Era After Good Taste', Working Paper in Marketing 17 (Odense: Odense University, 1998).

83. Anonymous, 'FCUK Consumer Research: On Disgust, Revulsion and Other Forms of Offensive Advertising', paper submitted to the 2001 Association for Consumer Research European Conference, Berlin, 20–23 June.

84. Robin Givhan, 'Designers Caught in a Tangled Web', *Washington Post* (5 April 1997): C1 (2 pp.).

85. Anne F. Jensen and Per Østergaard, 'Dressing for Security or Risk? An Exploratory Study of Two Different Ways of Consuming Fashion', in Englis and Olofsson, eds, *European Advances in Consumer Research* 3: 98–103.

86. Anthony Ramirez, 'The Pedestrian Sneaker Makes a Comeback', *New York Times* (14 October 1990): F17.

87. B. E. Aguirre, E. L. Quarantelli and Jorge L. Mendoza, 'The Collective Behavior of Fads: The Characteristics, Effects, and Career of Streaking', *American Sociological Review* (August 1989): 569.

88. 'Suddenly, Toys 'R' Hard to Find', *Wall Street Journal* (7 December 2000): B1.

89. Martin G. Letscher, 'How to Tell Fads from Trends', *American Demographics* (December 1994): 38–45.

90. Janet Kornblum, 'Everybody into the Memepool for Links to Some Very Odd Sites', *USA Today* (4 May 2000): 3D.

91. Malcolm Gladwell, *The Tipping Point* (New York: Little, Brown and Co., 2000).

Chapter 16

Lifestyles and European cultures

Tina and Caroline are both executives in an advertising agency. After a particularly gruelling week, they are looking forward to a well-deserved weekend off. Tina is enthusiastically telling Caroline about her plans. Since she won't have to get up early in the morning, she's going to sleep late in her new apartment. Then she's planning to go window shopping and maybe meet some friends for lunch in one of the cafés where she knows that some of them will be. Then she'll go back and rest in the afternoon until it's time to join her friend Anna to go to the new techno and rave place, which she heard about the other day. There, they'll dance their hearts out all night.

Caroline just chuckles to herself: while Tina's wasting her time in bed in the city, *she's* going to get up early to join a tour to a nearby bird sanctuary organized by the environmental group of which she's a member. She has heard that it will also be possible to see some rare orchids. By four o'clock, she plans to be comfortably planted in front of the computer in order to write an open letter to the municipal authorities concerning the current debate on whether to stop using pesticides in public parks and along the roadsides. Then she'll just sit back and relax, perhaps watch a rented video of one of the good films she missed due to lack of time . . .

Caroline is sometimes amazed at how different she is from Tina, though both think of themselves as sophisticated and in touch with the times. They also earn the same salary and do almost the same things at work all week long. How can their tastes be so different at the weekend? Oh well, Caroline sighs to herself, that's why they make chocolate and vanilla.

Lifestyles and consumption choices

Caroline and Tina strongly resemble one another demographically. They were both raised in middle-class households, have similar educational backgrounds, are about the same age and they share the same occupation and income. However, as their leisure choices show, it would be a mistake to assume that their consumption choices are similar as well. Caroline and Tina each choose products, services and activities that help them define a unique *lifestyle*. This chapter first explores how marketers approach the issue of lifestyle and then how they use information about these consumption choices to tailor products and communications to individual lifestyle segments. It then considers how lifestyle choices are affected by where people live, and it considers some issues that occur when firms attempt to market their products in unfamiliar cultures.

Lifestyle: who we are, what we do

In traditional societies, which place a high value on a collective mentality, consumption options arc largely dictated by class, caste, village or family. In a modern consumer society, however, people are freer to select the products, services and activities that define themselves and, in turn, create a social identity that is communicated to others. One's choice of goods and services makes a statement about who one is and about the types of people with whom one wishes to identify – as well as those from whom we wish to maintain some distance!

Lifestyle refers to a pattern of consumption reflecting a person's choices of how he or she spends time and money, but in many cases it also refers to the attitudes and values attached to these behavioural patterns. Many of the factors discussed in this book, such as a person's self-concept, reference group and social class, are used as 'raw ingredients' to fashion a unique lifestyle. In an economic sense, one's lifestyle represents the way one has elected to allocate income, both in terms of relative allocations to different products and services and to specific alternatives within these categories.[1] Other distinctions describe consumers in terms of their broad patterns of consumption, such as those that differentiate between consumers in terms of how proportions of their income are allocated to various sectors of consumption. Often, these allocations create a new kind of status system based less on income than on accessibility to information about goods and how these goods function as social markers.[2]

Lifestyles may be considered as group identities. Marketers use demographic and economic approaches in tracking changes in broad societal priorities, but these approaches do not begin to embrace the symbolic nuances that separate lifestyle groups. Lifestyle is more than the allocation of discretionary income. It is a statement about who one is in society and who one is not. Group identities, whether of hobbyists, athletes, or drug users, take their form based on acts of expressive symbolism. The self-definitions of group members are derived from the common symbol system to which the group is dedicated. Such self-definitions have been described by a number of terms, including *lifestyle, public taste, consumer group, symbolic community* and *status culture*.[3]

Each lifestyle is (somewhat) unique. Patterns of consumption based on lifestyles are often composed of many ingredients that are shared by others in similar social and economic circumstances. Still, each person provides a unique 'twist' to this pattern which allows him or her to inject some individuality into a chosen lifestyle. For example, a 'typical' student (if there is such a thing) may dress much like his or her friends, go to the same places and like the same foods, yet still indulge a passion for running marathons, stamp collecting or community service, activities which make him or her unique.

Lifestyles don't last forever, and are not set in stone; unlike deep-seated values, people's tastes and preferences evolve over time, so that consumption patterns that were viewed favourably at one point in time may be laughed or sneered at a few years later. If you don't believe that, simply think back to what you, your friends and your family were wearing, doing and eating five or ten years ago: where *did* you find those clothes? Because people's attitudes regarding physical fitness, social activism, sex roles for men and women, the importance of home life and family, and many other things, do change, it is vital for marketers to monitor the social landscape continually to try to anticipate where these changes will lead.

Lifestyle marketing

The lifestyle concept is one of the most widely used in modern marketing activities. It provides a way to understand consumers' everyday needs and wants, and a mechanism to allow a product or service to be positioned in terms of how it will allow a person to pursue a desired lifestyle. A **lifestyle marketing perspective** recognizes that people are increasingly conscious about the fact that we all sort ourselves and each other into groups on the basis of the things we/they like to do, how we/they like to spend their leisure time and how we/they choose to spend disposable income.[4] These choices in turn create opportunities for market segmentation strategies that recognize the potency of a consumer's chosen lifestyle in determining both the types of products purchased and the specific brands more likely to appeal to a designated lifestyle segment.

Products are the building blocks of lifestyles

To study lifestyles is to appreciate the profoundness of the superficial, as one lifestyle analyst has put it.[5] Consumers often choose products, services and activities over others because they are associated with a certain lifestyle. For this reason, lifestyle marketing strategies attempt to position a product by fitting it into an existing pattern of consumption. According to a German survey of 291 of the biggest marketing research and advertising agencies, 68 per cent of them used lifestyle research of some kind, mostly for the sectors of food, cosmetics, cars, drinks and fashion and clothing.[6]

Because a goal of lifestyle marketing is to provide consumers with opportunities to pursue their chosen ways to enjoy their lives and express their social identities, a key aspect of this strategy is to focus on product usage in desirable social settings (see Chapter 10). The goal of associating a product with a social situation is a long-standing one for advertisers, whether the product is included in a round of golf, a family barbecue or a night at a glamorous disco surrounded by 'jetsetters'.[7] Thus

Figure 16.1 Linking products to lifestyle

people, products and settings are combined to express a certain consumption style, as shown in Figure 16.1.

Product complementarity

The adoption of a lifestyle marketing perspective implies that we must look at *patterns* of behaviour to understand consumers. We can get a clearer picture of how people use products to define lifestyles by examining how they make choices in a variety of product categories. Indeed, many products and services do seem to 'go together', usually because they tend to be selected by the same types of people. In many cases, products do not seem to 'make sense' if unaccompanied by companion products (e.g. fast food and paper plates, or a suit and tie) or are incongruous in the presence of others (e.g. a big, upholstered chair in a high-tech office or Chivas Regal whisky at the local café, as illustrated in the French ad overleaf). Therefore, an important part of lifestyle marketing is to identify the *set* of products and services that seems to be linked in consumers' minds to a specific lifestyle. As one study noted, 'all goods carry meaning, but none by itself. ... The meaning is in the relations between all the goods, just as music is in the relations marked out by the sounds and not in any one note.'[8]

Product complementarity occurs when the symbolic meanings of different products are related to each other.[9] Bacardi rum and Coca-Cola have for some time advertised their products together. Some marketers have gone as far as putting their brands on the same product, a phenomenon known as *co-branding*. For example, in various European countries one product variant of Häagen-Dazs ice cream was co-branded with Bailey's Irish Cream liqueur. Most often, though, consumers themselves, inspired by opinion leaders and other parts of the culture production system (cf. Chapters 10, 14 and 15), will construct the product complementarities themselves.

These sets of products, termed **consumption constellations**, are used by consumers to define, communicate and perform social roles.[10] For example, the (American) 'yuppie' of the 1980s was defined by such products as a Rolex watch, BMW car, Gucci briefcase, a squash racket, fresh pesto, white wine and brie. The yuppie culture eventually spread to Europe and somewhat similar constellations could be found for what were called 'Sloane Rangers' in the United Kingdom and 'Bon Chic Bon Genre' in France. While people today take pains to avoid being classified as yuppies, this social role had a major influence on defining cultural values and consumption priorities in the 1980s.[11] Sometimes these constellations do actually take the form of anti-constellations from the very beginning, at least for some consumer segments. That is, people define their own style more in terms of what they

On trouve Chivas Regal au Café de la Jatte·

Mais pas chez Robert·

This ad illustrates how the product is complementary to a certain environment and not to another, as exemplified by two actually existing Parisian restaurants.
Chivas Regal.

are not, through a set of non-choices (due to lack of affordability, accessibility or availability) or anti-choices (due to abandonment, avoidance or aversion) of products and/or brands.[12] What positive and/or negative consumption constellations might characterize you and your friends today?

Psychographics

As Tina and Caroline's lifestyle choices demonstrated, consumers can share the same demographic characteristics and still be very different people. For this reason, marketers need a way to 'breathe life' into demographic data to identify, understand and target consumer segments that will share a set of preferences for their products and services. Chapter 7 discussed some of the important differences in consumers' self-concepts and personalities that play a big role in determining product choices. When personality variables are combined with knowledge of lifestyle preferences, marketers have a tool with which to view consumer segments. This tool is known as **psychographics**, which involves the description of consumers based mainly on such psychological and social psychological factors as values, beliefs and attitudes, and is used to explain why these consumers have a propensity to consume certain products or brands, use certain services, devote time to certain activities and use certain media.[13]

Psychographic research was first developed in the 1960s and 1970s to address the shortcomings of two other types of consumer research: motivational research and quantitative survey research. *Motivational research*, which involves intensive personal interviews and projective tests, yields a lot of information about individual consumers. The information gathered, however, was often idiosyncratic and deemed not very useful or reliable.[14] At the other extreme, *quantitative survey research*, or large-scale demographic surveys, yields only a little information about a lot of people. As some researchers observed, 'The marketing manager who wanted to know why people ate the competitor's corn flakes was told "32 per cent of the respondents said *taste*, 21 per cent said *flavour*, 15 per cent said *texture*, 10 per cent said *price*, and 22 per cent said *don't know* or *no answer*".'[15]

In many applications, the term 'psychographics' is used interchangeably with 'lifestyle' to denote the separation of consumers into categories based on differences in choices of consumption activities and product usage. While there are many psychographic variables that can be used to segment consumers, they all share the underlying principle of going beyond surface characteristics to understand consumers' motivations for purchasing and using products.

Conducting a psychographic analysis

Some early attempts at lifestyle segmentation 'borrowed' standard psychological scales (often used to measure pathology or personality disturbances) and tried to relate scores on these tests to product usage. As might be expected, such efforts were largely disappointing (see Chapter 7). These tests were never intended to be related to everyday consumption activities and yielded little in the way of explanation for purchase behaviours. The technique is more effective when the variables included are more closely related to actual consumer behaviours. If you want to understand purchases of household cleaning products, you are better off asking people about their attitudes towards household cleanliness than testing for personality disorders.

Most contemporary psychographic research attempts to group consumers according to some combination of three categories of variables – Activities, Interests and Opinions – which are known as **AIOs**. Using data from large samples, marketers create profiles of customers who resemble each other in terms of their activities and patterns of product usage.[16] The dimensions used to assess lifestyle are listed in Table 16.1.

To group consumers into common AIO categories, respondents are given a long list of statements and are asked to indicate how much they agree with each one. Lifestyle is thus teased out by discovering how people spend their time, what they find interesting and important and how they view themselves and the world around them, as well as demographic information.

Typically, the first step in conducting a psychographic analysis is to determine which lifestyle segments are producing the bulk of customers for a particular product. Researchers attempt to determine who uses the brand and try to isolate heavy, moderate and light users. They also look for patterns of usage and attitudes towards

Table 16.1 Lifestyle dimensions

Activities	Interests	Opinions	Demographics
Work	Family	Themselves	Age
Hobbies	Home	Social issues	Education
Social events	Job	Politics	Income
Holiday	Community	Business	Occupation
Entertainment	Recreation	Economics	Family size
Club membership	Fashion	Education	Dwelling
Community	Food	Products	Geography
Shopping	Media	Future	City size
Sports	Achievements	Culture	Stage in life cycle

Source: William D. Wells and Douglas J. Tigert, 'Activities, Interests and Opinions', *Journal of Advertising Research* 11 (August 1971): 27–35.

the product. In some cases, just a few lifestyle segments account for the majority of brand users.[17]

After the heavy users are identified and understood, the brand's relationship to them is considered. Heavy users may have quite different reasons for using the product; they can be further subdivided in terms of the *benefits* they derive from using the product or service. For instance, marketers at the beginning of the walking shoe craze assumed that purchasers were basically burned-out joggers. Subsequent psychographic research showed that there were actually several different groups of 'walkers', ranging from those who walk to get to work to those who walk for fun. This realization resulted in shoes aimed at different segments.

Psychographic segmentation can be used in a variety of ways.

- *To define the target market*. This information allows the marketer to go beyond simple demographic or product usage descriptions (e.g. middle-aged men or frequent users).

- *To create a new view of the market*. Sometimes marketers create their strategies with a 'typical' customer in mind. This stereotype may not be correct because the actual customer may not match these assumptions. For example, marketers of a facial cream for women were surprised to find their key market was composed of older, widowed women rather than the younger, more sociable women to whom they were pitching their appeals.

- *To position the product*. Psychographic information can allow the marketer to emphasize features of the product that fit in with a person's lifestyle. Products targeted at people whose lifestyle profiles show a high need to be around other people might focus on the product's ability to help meet this social need.

- *To communicate product attributes better*. Psychographic information can offer very useful input to advertising creatives who must communicate something about the product. The artist or writer obtains a much richer mental image of the target consumer than that obtained through dry statistics, and this insight improves his or her ability to 'talk' to that consumer. For example, an American study conducted for one beer brand found that heavy beer-drinkers tended to feel that life's pleasures were few and far between. Commercials were developed using the theme that told these drinkers: 'You only go around once, so reach for all the gusto you can'.[18]

- *To develop overall strategy*. Understanding how a product fits, or does not fit, into consumers' lifestyles allows the marketer to identify new product opportunities, chart media strategies and create environments most consistent and harmonious with these consumption patterns.

- *To market social and political issues*. Psychographic segmentation can be an important tool in political campaigns and can also be employed to find similarities among types of consumers who engage in destructive behaviours, such as drug use or excessive gambling.

Lifestyle segmentation typologies

Marketers are constantly on the lookout for new insights that will allow them to identify and reach groups of consumers that are united by a common lifestyle. To meet this need, many research companies and advertising agencies have developed their own *segmentation typologies* which divide people into segments. Respondents answer a battery of questions that allow the researchers to cluster them into a set of distinct lifestyle groups. The questions usually include a mixture of AIOs, plus other items relating to their perceptions of specific brands, favourite celebrities, media preferences, and so on. These systems are usually sold to companies wanting to learn more about their customers and potential customers.

At least at a superficial level, many of these typologies are fairly similar to one another, in that a typical typology breaks up the population into roughly 5–10 segments. Each cluster is given a descriptive name, and a profile of the 'typical' member is provided to the client. Lifestyle categories in this system include such segments as 'avant guardians' (interested in change), 'pontificators' (traditionalists, very British), 'chameleons' (follow the crowd) and 'sleepwalkers' (contented underachievers). Unfortunately, it is often difficult to compare or evaluate different typologies, since the methods and data used to devise these systems are frequently *proprietary* – this means that the information is developed and owned by the company, and the company feels that it would not be desirable to release this information to outsiders.

Lifestyle analyses are widely used in Europe. For example, one British company recently unveiled ConsumerBank, a database with 240 pieces of information on each of 40 million consumers.[19] Increasingly sophisticated efforts are being made to develop lifestyle typologies that transcend national borders. Many of these systems have been developed to understand European buying habits, and in particular to determine if it is possible to identify 'Euroconsumers', who share the same lifestyle orientations despite living in, say, France vs. Italy. These studies have had mixed success, with most researchers reporting that people in each nation still have a lot of idiosyncrasies that make it difficult to group them together.[20] Below we will provide some examples of such international lifestyle segmentation efforts.

RISC

Since 1978, the Research Institute on Social Change (RISC) has conducted international measurements of lifestyles and socio-cultural change in more than 40 countries, including most European countries. The long-term measurement of the social climate across many countries makes it possible to give more qualified guesses and anticipations of future change. It makes it possible to see signs of change in one country before it eventually spreads to other countries. For example, concern for the environment appeared in Sweden in the early 1970s, then in Germany in the late 1970s, in France at the beginning of the 1980s and in Spain in the early 1990s.[21]

The values and attitudes questions are the foundation of the measurement of 'trends', defined as the degree of agreement or disagreement with a set of attitudes that have been selected to define this trend. Based on statistical analysis of the respondents' scores on each trend, each individual is located in a virtual space described by three axes, representing the three most discriminating dimensions in the data material. The vertical axis (Exploration/Stability) separates people motivated by change, creativity, volatility and openness from people motivated by stability, familiarity, tradition and structure. The horizontal axis (Social/Individual) distinguishes people oriented towards collective needs from people oriented more towards satisfaction of individual needs. The third axis (Global/Local) indicates a distance between people who are comfortable with broad and unfamiliar environments, multiple loose connections and large-scale networking from people preferring close-knit relationships and a desire for the elements of life to be connected in a predictable manner. The population is then divided into ten segments referring to their position in this virtual space. Figure 16.2 illustrates the ten segments (G for global, L for Local (behind)) and their main life aspirations.

Each of the 40 trends can also be located in the space according to the gravity

Figure 16.2 The ten RISC segments

Source: 'RISC Methodology' (Paris: RISC International, 1997): 14.

point of the people who scored highest on the particular trend. Trends that are related to exploration will thus be located near the top of the map, individualism trends to the right, locality trends are smaller because they are at the back, and so on. While the position of the trends tends not to vary greatly, the percentage of various populations (countries, age groups, heavy users of a brand) supporting each trend will differ greatly. In the example in Figure 16.3, the indices are for the United Kingdom as compared to the European total. Darker colours indicate the trends that are more important in Britain as compared to the European average: cultural mobility, expanding vitality, narrow bounds, law and leaders, social recognition, well-being and epicurism (a quality-of-life orientation towards 'the finer things' in life).

The use of RISC typically involves identifying users of a brand and understanding those users better; it is also used to monitor changes in the profiles of users over time. Furthermore, potential target groups, the product benefits and the kind of communication that would attract and reach them can be indicated by systems such as RISC. In the example in Figure 16.4 we see the lifestyle profiling of German car brand B (approximately 21 per cent of the population) and car brand M (approximately 19 per cent) as their first, second or third choice if they were going to buy a new car. Car brand B has a strong profile, individual and experimental, with both global and local orientations. Car brand M, in contrast, has a more uniform profile, with evidence of popularity across all segments of the population. However, there is a very strong presence in cell 1, the group that is most interested in new designs, technologies and functions.

CCA socio-styles

A Paris-based agency, the CCA (Centre de Communication Avancé), introduced a European lifestyle typology in the early 1990s. Although the mapping principle of this lifestyle typology is similar to that of most other typologies, they use a somewhat different methodological approach since their questionnaires are not attitude-based,

Figure 16.3 **Trend map of the UK**

EXPLORATION
Human potentials•

Resilience•

Integrity• Well-being•
Collective goals• Epicurism• Strategic opportunism•
Ecosystem• •Social participation •Cultural mobility Emotions•
Environment• Self-conditioning• •Achievement
  •Networking
Social fairness• •Expanding vitality Polysensuality•
Intraception•
Cellulization• •Social recognition Risks•
New roots• Uncertainty•
Spirituality• Pleasure•
Blurring of sexes• •Interacting

Expression• Flexibility•
Law and Leaders• Appearance•
[Consumption]• •Hypernatural

[Fears]•

•[Aimlessness]
G [Status]•

[Security]•
Narrow bounds•
Unquestioned system•
STABILITY

S O C I A L (left axis) I N D I V I D U A L (right axis)

Source: RISC International, Paris, 1997.

Figure 16.4 **Choice of brand for the next new car, Germany, brand B/brand M, 1995**

152
89 90 151 114
87 82 131 121
56

21.3%
Car B

159
111 102 95 90
91 97 110 92
86

18.7%
Car M

Source: RISC International, Paris, 1997.

Figure 16.5 CCA Eurostyles, 16 lifestyles in 6 mentalities

Source: CCA, Paris, 1990.

but use a variety of question formats and also projective techniques, like for instance various scenario descriptions of future social forms or consumption types that the respondent must relate to, or suggestive drawings and vignettes.[22]

The CCA study divided the European population into 16 lifestyles, regrouped into 6 so-called 'mentalities'. The resulting lifestyle map, presented in the usual suggestive vignette format, is seen in Figure 16.5. One of the advantages of this system was that the 16 individual lifestyles could be gathered in other larger groups than just the mentalities to form marketing segments specifically adapted to a specific product sector. So some lifestyles would be grouped to form food segments, others to form car segments. In terms of innovative approaches used for lifestyle segmentation, this is probably one of the more interesting ones.[23]

Towards a theoretically based lifestyle approach?

One leading French sociologist, Pierre Bourdieu, has proposed a lifestyle concept that is closely linked to social class. In a major empirical study, he tried to demonstrate how people's tastes and lifestyles in French society are dependent on what he named **habitus** (systems of classification of phenomena adopted from our socialization processes) and our economic and cultural capital.[24] He distinguished between various forms of capital that the individual can use as assets to construct his or her lifestyle, tastes and consumption patterns. This approach has been applied within American consumer research to distinguish between consumer tastes among various social groupings.[25] More recently, an attempt has been made to translate Bourdieu's terms into a relatively simple lifestyle categorization scheme. Based on Bourdieu's notions of economic capital (income and wealth) and cultural capital (education plus the ability to distinguish between cultural styles and categories) combined with Mary Douglas's grid-group theory,[26] four different but fundamental consumer types are proposed. This model, depicted in Figure 16.6, has so far only been applied in Denmark, but since it has a strong theoretical base, it is likely to function in other countries as well.

The distinction between grid and group refers to an individual's relation to his or her own social group and to the general social system (or grid). So the model distinguishes between people with high and low group identification and a more or less affirmative (high and low) relation to the organization of society (the grid). The model ends up with the following segments:

- *1st quadrant*: Professional, career-oriented people, with higher education and income, and with a rather individualistic attitude and an unproblematic relation to the social organization (they are responsible for much of it anyway). Their search for meaning is characterized by ambition for power and wealth.

- *2nd quadrant*: Well-educated intellectuals with less well-paid career opportunities (many university professors here), with a high degree of identification with their professional group, but with a critical attitude towards society. Their search for meaning lies in the realization of their own intellectual ideals.

- *3rd quadrant*: Relatively wealthy people, with low education or not so culturally interested (the stereotypical self-made (wo)man). They do not show any particular interest, neither on a group level nor on a social level, and they may even tend to consider the rest of society (and everything strange) as relatively hostile.

- *4th quadrant*: Low on both types of capital, money and education, but with strong group affiliation and a relatively affirmative attitude towards society, these people tend to be locally oriented. The search for meaning is rooted in their daily activities and daily lives.[27]

Figure 16.6 A theoretically based lifestyle model

High cultural capital High economic capital Low group High grid	High cultural capital Low economic capital High group Low grid
Low cultural capital High economic capital Low group Low grid	Low cultural capital Low economic capital High group High grid

Source: Adapted from Henrik Dahl, *Hvis din nabo var en bil* (Copenhagen: Akademisk forlag, 1997).

Lifestyles outside western Europe

VALS

The most well-known and widely used segmentation system in America is **VALS**, developed at SRI International and now operated out of SRI Consulting Business Intelligence in California. Originally, VALS combined two perspectives to create lifestyle clusters. One was based on the Maslow hierarchy of needs (discussed in Chapter 4). Maslow's hierarchy stipulates that people's needs must be satisfied sequentially – that is, companionship is not a priority until physical needs are met, and so on. The second perspective was based on the distinction made by the sociologist David Riesman between *inner-directed* people, who value personal expression and individual taste, and *outer-directed* people, who tend to be swayed by the behaviour and reactions of others.

Responding to criticisms of the VALS model, as well as to changing social values, the developers decided to update the system.

Increasing social diversity made social values less effective as predictors of consumer behaviour. The current VALS system measures consumer behaviour on the basis of psychological dimensions, which are more resilient in periods of social change, and key demographics.

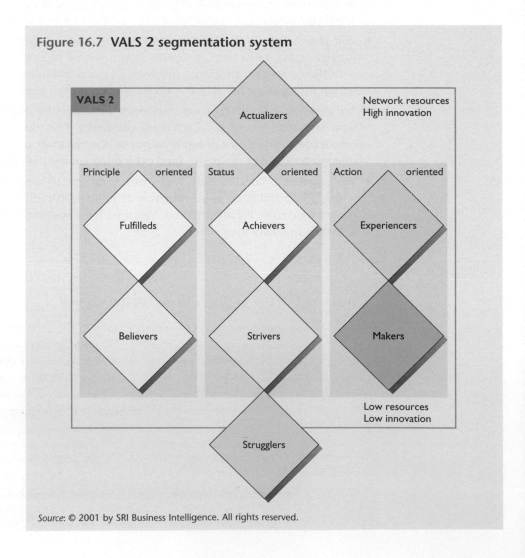

Figure 16.7 VALS 2 segmentation system

Source: © 2001 by SRI Business Intelligence. All rights reserved.

The current VALS system divides U.S. adults into eight groups determined both by psychological characteristics and 'resources', which include such factors as income, education, energy levels and eagerness to buy. In the VALS structure, groups are arrayed vertically by resources and horizontally by self-orientation, as shown in Figure 16.7. Actualizers are at the top of the figure because they have the highest level of resources. Actualizers are successful, sophisticated, take-charge people. They are open to change and enjoy self-discovery. The next three groups also have sufficient resources but differ in their self-orientations:[28]

- *Fulfilleds* are satisfied, reflective and comfortable. They tend to be practical and value functionality.

- *Achievers* are career-oriented and prefer predictability over risk or self-discovery.

- *Experiencers* are impulsive, young and enjoy offbeat or risky experiences.

The next three groups have fewer resources but also differ in their self-orientation:

- *Believers* have strong principles and favour proven brands.

- *Strivers* are trendy, approval-seeking and resource-constrained, favour stylish products and emulate the purchases of people with greater material wealth.

- *Makers* are action-oriented and tend to focus their energies on self-sufficiency. They are more likely than other groups to work on their cars, can their own vegetables, or build their own houses.

Strugglers are at the bottom of the resource ladder. They are most concerned with meeting the needs of the moment.

Other international lifestyle segmentations

Japanese culture values conformity; one way to refer to the desire to fit in is *hiton-ami consciousness*, which translates as 'aligning oneself with other people'. Despite this overall emphasis, there is a growing segment of Japanese consumers who are swimming against the tide. These people have been called 'life designers' to reflect their interest in crafting their own lifestyle patterns. One Japanese segmentation scheme divides consumers into 'tribes' and includes among others the 'crystal tribe' (which prefers well-known brands), 'my home tribe' (family-oriented) and 'impulse buyer tribe'.[29]

As countries in *eastern Europe* convert to free market economies, many marketers are exploring ways to segment these increasingly consumption-oriented societies. Some Western products such as Marlboro cigarettes and McDonald's are already firmly entrenched in Russia. The D'Arcy Masius Benton & Bowles Advertising Agency, which has offices in Moscow and St Petersburg, conducted a psychographic study of Russian consumers, and has proclaimed that the country's 150 million consumers can be divided into five segments, including 'Cossacks' (status-seeking nationalists who drive BMWs, smoke Dunhill cigarettes and drink Rémy Martin cognac), *Kuptsi* (merchants who value practical products and tend to drive Volkswagens, smoke Chesterfields and drink Stolichnaya vodka) and 'Russian Souls' (passive consumers who drive Lada cars, smoke Marlboros and drink Smirnoff).[30]

The value of lifestyle typologies

Generally, lifestyle analyses of consumers are exciting because they seek to provide a sort of complete sociological view of the market and its segments and trends, but their general character is their biggest weakness, since the underlying assumption – that these general segments have relatively homogeneous patterns of consumer behaviour – is far from proven.[31] One needs only to consider the index numbers in

Figure 16.4 to realize that the predictive power of this typology is not extraordinary. Add to this the generally weak theoretical foundation and the problems of reliability and validity linked to the large-scale questionnaires and to the operationalization of complex social process in simple variables, and it is understandable why some marketers see lifestyles more as a way of 'thinking the market' and as an input to creative strategies than as descriptions of segments defined by their consumer behaviour.[32]

One attempt to overcome the problem of generally defined segments is the introduction of sectorial lifestyles, an idea proposed by the CCA in the 1980s. The principle behind sectorial lifestyles is that only variables (attitudes, behaviour, etc.) that are considered relevant to a specific domain of consumption are included in the survey. The lifestyles defined on the basis of such an approach thus pertain to this specific sector of consumption only. Later in this chapter, we shall discuss an example of such a sectorial lifestyle system: food-related lifestyles.

MARKETING OPPORTUNITY

Maybe the age of the grand segmentation systems is over anyway. With the help of information technology more and more marketers are pursuing the potential of one-to-one marketing. Obviously the internet has great potential for tailor-made marketing, but new printing technology will probably also make possible a relatively targeted print-media advertising. The general TV stations, however, will have increasing problems in documenting their reach, since viewers will increasingly be able to shop around for an individual programme profile selected for the offers of digital TV.[33] However, the opportunities presented by the internet encounter their own cross-cultural difficulties. The different laws regulating marketing efforts in the countries of the EU make it problematic for companies to construct e-commerce strategies that are acceptable in all contexts, especially since EU legislation seems to point in the direction that complaints shall be handled at courts in the customer's home country, not in the company's.[34]

Geographic influences on lifestyles

The consumption patterns of different countries' regions have been shaped by unique climates, cultural influences and resources. These national and regional differences can exert a major impact on consumers' lifestyles, since many of our preferences in foods, entertainment, and so on are dictated by local customs and the availability of some diversions rather than others. The lifestyles of people in each country and each region differ in a variety of ways, some quite subtle and some quite noticeable, some easy to explain and some not so obvious. Needless to say, between northern and southern Italy, northen and southern Germany, Paris and Provence, London and Scotland there may be large differences in terms of consumption patterns and lifestyles and, consequently, in marketing and marketing research practices.[35]

Regional consumption differences: the macro-level

In some cases, it may make sense to distinguish between larger regions comprising several countries. For example, many companies operating in Europe consider Scandinavia (Denmark, Norway and Sweden) or the Benelux (Belgium, the Netherlands and Luxembourg) to be more or less one market due to the perceived similarities between the countries. That there are relative similarities between these countries is a matter of fact, but marketers should beware of over-estimating the homogeneity of such macro-regions. Portraits of macro-regions can be drawn with rough strokes only with a very big brush. In the following section we will look at a couple of examples of such macro-regions in Europe.

Such regions are taken increasingly seriously by marketers. In the wake of the construction of the bridge over the strait of Øresund linking Copenhagen in Denmark with Malmö in the southern part of Sweden, the potential for a whole new region of education, research, shopping and other kinds of interaction has been created.[36] As a consequence, a regional dairy producer introduced what may well be the first-ever deliberately transnational regional product – a fermented yogurt-type product specifically designed and tested to span the variations in taste found in the Swedish and Danish markets. The product, named after the strait, comes with complete text in Swedish and Danish and features a person bathing in the water that separates but now (re)connects the two regions.

Since food consumption is traditionally linked to geographical conditions such as climate, or distance from the sea or mountains, another study hypothesized the importance of local or regional patterns of consumption across national borders compared to national consumption patterns.[37] The results of an analysis of 138 food-related variables from 15 countries, however, showed that national or linguistic borders seem more significant in defining patterns of food consumption. Figure 16.8 illustrates the 12 general food cultures in Europe suggested by this study. To list a few of the defining characteristics of some of the food cultures, the French/French–Swiss, Wallonian and Italian clusters are characterized by, among other things, the importance of sensory pleasure and the high consumption of red wine; the Germanic cluster of countries by a high degree of health consciousness; the Portuguese and Greek food cultures by relatively traditional eating patterns with a

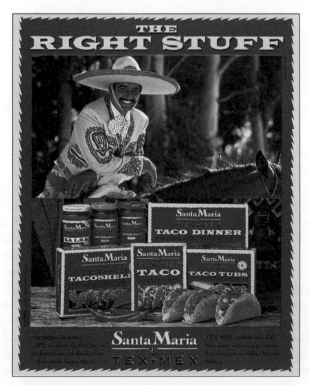

Mexican cuisine is popular in Scandinavia. This ad appeared in a Swedish magazine.
Courtesy of Nordfalks AB.

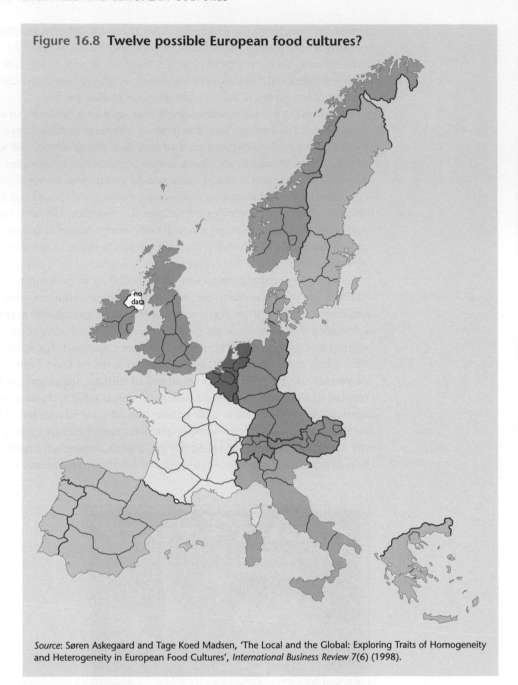

Figure 16.8 Twelve possible European food cultures?

Source: Søren Askegaard and Tage Koed Madsen, 'The Local and the Global: Exploring Traits of Homogeneity and Heterogeneity in European Food Cultures', *International Business Review* 7(6) (1998).

fascination for new 'global' food; the Norwegian and Danish food cultures by their openness to convenience products (and, for the Danes, also the love of beer); and the British and Irish for their extraordinary desire for sweets and tea.

Interestingly, it is predominantly in the centre of Europe that food cultures exhibit overlapping national borders (France–Switzerland; Germany–Switzerland–Austria; the Netherlands–Flanders), the only exception being the British–Irish food culture. The more geographically peripheral countries (Scandinavia, Iberia, Italy and Greece) show 'national food cultures'. Is this due to more exchange and interrelationship historically among the people in the 'crossroads of Europe'? Or is it language that decides basic cultural patterns? If so, this would confirm the famous Whorf–Sapir hypothesis that language is not only a means for expressing culture but actually creates it by instituting certain schemes of classification of events, things and people. The fact that the food cultures defined in this study exactly follow linguistic lines of division (with the exception of there being two French-speaking clusters) could point in that direction. Or it could reflect the simple fact that the language of the questionnaire is very decisive for the response pattern. If the latter is the case, then it would be a strong criticism of the way in which marketers use surveys as a cross-national research instrument.[38] The truth probably lies somewhere in between the two.

We have seen the fact that grand traits of differences can be located between certain regions in Europe, for instance a distinction between Teutonic, Gallic and Anglo-Saxon styles of communicating,[39] stressing the logical strictness of the argument, its rhetorical qualities and its empirical validity respectively. Such grand traits of similarities do not necessarily permit us to conclude that there are broad similarities in the food consumption or other consumption areas as well. Obviously it is a matter of scope. Certain parts of Europe tend to have consumption patterns similar to each other compared to China, for example. But whether these similarities are detailed enough to be useful to marketers other than in a very broad sense is another question.

National consumption differences

A series of articles recently discussed 'the changing consumer' in various European countries. The focus in these articles was predominantly macro-oriented changes in demography and economy, aggregate family expenditures or size of distribution outlets and similar information.[40] However relevant such information is, it does not provide a very vivid 'flesh-and-blood' portrait of European consumers in various countries. Needless to say, such portraits are extremely difficult to draw unless one wants to fall back on the most simple use of stereotypes: the French with baguette, cheese and Renault; the Spanish with paella, tapas and Seat; the British with tea, biscuits and Rover; the German with sauerkraut, sausage and Volkswagen.

We will try to refrain from such portraits here, and instead provide a set of examples that should illustrate some similarities and differences among European countries. We will do that by referring to research results pertaining to consumer behaviour from four different market sectors.

Food

Food is one of the most important fields of consumption when it comes to the impact on the structure of people's daily lives. The wealth of symbolic meanings attached to various kinds of food and hence food's capacity as a 'marker' of certain roles, status, situations, rituals, etc. is well documented.[41] How is the meal prepared and eaten? How often do we eat and at what times during the day? What do we drink with the meals? What is the social function of eating? These are questions for which the answers vary from country to country and from segment to segment.

Western European households spend typically between 14 and 17 per cent of their income on food, although the UK (10.1 per cent) and the Netherlands (11.0 per cent) are exceptions to this rule.[42] How this sum is spent varies greatly from country to country, depending on local production and local culinary patterns. The per capita consumption of different food products in European countries varies several hundred per cent in all categories. For example, the consumption of fresh fish in Spain and Portugal is about ten times that of Austria or the UK, and the consumption of pork in Denmark about ten times that of France. The consumption of potatoes is high in Ireland, but it is actually higher in Greece, and by far the lowest in Italy, which consumes approximately four times more pasta per inhabitant than the number two in the European market (Switzerland)![43]

A group of researchers developed a food-related lifestyle instrument based on means–end theory (cf. Chapter 4).[44] The instrument includes attitude statements concerning five different domains: quality aspects, ways of shopping, cooking methods, consumption situations and purchasing motives. Tests of its cross-cultural validity showed reasonable results, at least within north-western Europe.[45] An application of the food-related lifestyle model in four European countries between 1993 and 1995 suggested that certain segments are found in all countries, some are found in three countries and some only in one country. The size of the segments, however, varies significantly, as seen in Table 16.2 These differences may shed some light on the differences between the national food cultures in question.

The 'uninvolved' segment (predominantly in Germany and France) have little interest in food, do not attach importance to quality, tend to nibble and graze rather than eat 'real meals' and use convenience products and fast food more than the average. Single males with a low education level are over-represented in this segment. The 'careless' segment (predominantly in the UK and Denmark) are spontaneous food shoppers, tempted by new products. They are attracted by convenience foods, are younger, single and have relatively high incomes. The 'rational consumers' segment (predominantly in France and the UK) are very interested in food and are careful planners of both dinner and shopping. They try to maximize the quality/price ratio of their purchases, and get self-fulfilment from cooking. They tend to be female, with families, working part-time. The 'conservative' segment (predominantly the UK and Germany) consider cooking a woman's task. They plan their meals and shopping, eat at fixed hours and seek security in their eating behaviour by sticking to traditions. They are older, rural and with lower income and education. The 'adventurous' segment (predominantly Denmark and Germany) like to try new (exotic) recipes and products, they go for quality products and often shop in specialized stores. The whole family takes part in the cooking, and the social aspects of eating are considered very important. They are generally well-educated families with double income and children.

Apart from the relative distributions of the segments, two of the segments found may tell us something specific about the national consumption environments. In Denmark the 'ecologically moderate' (moderately involved in food, highly involved in environmentally friendly produce) indicate the strength of the market share of ecological produce (35 per cent increase in sales volume in 1996). The hedonists in France are a little less adventurous than their 'sister segments' of that name in other countries, but they are more focused on the sensory pleasure of eating, indicating a gastronomic sophistication. For example, it has been suggested that French consumers have more sophisticated purchasing behaviour for beef than consumers in Germany, the UK and Spain.[46]

Research such as this food-related lifestyle study may be taken as evidence that it is easier to define segments across countries and cultures based on psychological rather than behavioural variables. This would seem to be the case, since similar motivations may result in very different kinds of behaviour, which are influenced by Europe's varying cultural norms and habits.

Drink

Drinking, like eating, is an activity full of symbolic dimensions linked to gender, class, lifestyle, situations and rituals.[47] The drinking cultures in Europe differ highly

Table 16.2 Food-related lifestyle segments in four countries

	France	Germany	UK	Denmark
Uninvolved	18%	21%	9%	11%
Careless		11%	27%	23%
Rational	35%	26%	33%	11%
Moderate	16%			
Ecological moderate				20%
Conservative	13%	18%	19%	11%
Adventurous		24%	12%	25%
Hedonistic	18%			

Source: Adapted from Karen Brunsø, Klaus G. Grunert and Lone Bredahl, 'An Analysis of National and Cross-National Consumer Segments Using the Food-Related Lifestyle Instrument in Denmark, France, Germany and Great Britain', MAPP Working Paper no. 35 (The Aarhus School of Business, January 1996).

in terms of what is drunk, how and when. One of the most obvious differences in the European drinking pattern is the distinction between beer cultures and wine cultures. Countries such as Germany, Belgium, Austria, Denmark and Ireland have the highest per capita consumption of beer, whereas Italy, France, Portugal and Luxembourg lead the way in wine consumption.[48] To explain such huge differences, it has been argued that in some of these countries, such as Germany, France and Italy, consumption of beer and wine is so interwoven in daily lifestyles and the cultural fabric that it is hard to imagine those cultures without them. Economic and public policy factors are also important, and reflect attitudes towards alcohol in governmental institutions. In countries such as Finland, Norway and Sweden, alcoholic beverages stronger than 'light beer' (around 2 per cent alcohol) are sold only in state monopolies and are heavily taxed. Hence, the figures in Table 16.3 may be understated by up to 30 per cent due to legal and illegal duty-free imports and home production.[49]

It has been suggested that we should distinguish between two kinds of drinking traditions in Europe. Multidimensional drinking patterns characterize drinking that occurs in connection with other social activities. Examples would be wine with meals in southern Europe, beer and wine festivals in Germany, or drinking while socializing in pubs in the UK and Ireland. Drinking in these countries is traditionally not related to excess or to special occasions only. On the other hand, unidimensional drinking patterns occur in countries where moderate continuous drinking linked to daily social activities is replaced by occasional drinking (weekends or holidays only) but is characterized by people drinking excessively.[50]

Other major variations in drink consumption patterns are revealed by statistics. Carbonated drinks are most popular in Great Britain, Ireland and Denmark, whereas mineral water consumption is especially high in France, Belgium and Italy. The Germans, Dutch, Finns and Greeks consume most spirits among western Europeans, while Italians have the lowest consumption level of such drinks.[51] Obviously, statistics of this kind do not reveal much about the types of product consumed, nor about the consumption situations. For example, schnapps may account for the spirits consumption in Germany, ouzo in Greece, genever in the Netherlands and vodka in Finland. Furthermore, the commonness of various consumption situations for such drinks varies across countries and among lifestyles. Wine may be used at religious

Table 16.3 Beer and wine consumption per capita in 19 countries

Ranked in order of per capita consumption in 1991 (wine in litres)			Ranked in order of per capita consumption in 1991 (beer in litres)		
Rank	Country	1991	Rank	Country	1991
1	France	66.8	1	Germany	142.7
2	Portugal	62.0	2	Denmark	125.9
3	Luxembourg	60.3	3	Austria	123.7
4	Italy	56.8	4	Ireland	123.0
5	Switzerland	48.7	5	Luxembourg	116.1
6	Spain	34.3	6	Belgium	111.3
7	Austria	33.7	7	United Kingdom	106.2
8	Greece	32.4	8	Netherlands	88.5
9	Germany	24.9	9	USA	87.4
10	Belgium	23.9	10	Finland	85.3
11	Denmark	22.0	11	Spain	70.9
12	Netherlands	15.3	12	Switzerland	70.1
13	Sweden	12.3	13	Portugal	67.4
14	United Kingdom	11.5	14	Sweden	59.3
15	Finland	7.4	15	Norway	52.8
16	USA	7.2	16	France	40.5
17	Norway	6.9	17	Greece	40.0
18	Ireland	4.6	18	Iceland	24.2
19	Iceland	4.4	19	Italy	22.5

Source: Adapted from David Smith and J. Robert Skalnik, 'Changing Patterns in the Consumption of Alcoholic Beverages in Europe and the United States', in Flemming Hansen, ed., European Advances in Consumer Research 2 (Provo, UT: Association for Consumer Research, 1995): 343–55. Used with permission.

ceremonies or at dinner each evening, beer on the beach or in a bar after working hours, carbonated drinks after sports or for children's birthday parties, and so on. What kinds of various rituals involving drinking can you think of in your country?

Trends in European drinking patterns seem to indicate that increasing health consciousness leads to a trend in drinking lower alcohol content beverages. This may also be due to increasingly blurred borders between multidimensional and unidimensional drinking patterns. In general, drinking patterns are becoming more similar across Europe. Traditional wine-drinking countries show the largest increase in beer consumption over time, while an increase in wine-drinking is occurring in traditional beer countries.[52]

Cars

The car is a third highly symbolic good with a great deal of cultural significance attached to it. Again, consumption differs among European countries for various reasons, such as local infrastructure, local production facilities, taxation or traditions. For instance, the percentage of families owning two cars is highest in Italy (41 per cent), France (30 per cent), the UK (29 per cent) and (West) Germany (26 per cent). The numbers reflect, among many other factors, the power and importance of local car industries to shape conditions so that car ownership is feasible. But industry efforts to facilitate car ownership only help explain a general 'car culture' in these countries. The reasons for a low number of families having two cars may vary from relative poverty (Greece, Portugal, Spain) to small distances (the Netherlands) and high taxation (Denmark).[53]

In the car market, as in many other markets, the discussion continues as to whether it makes sense to segment consumers across countries. One argument for segmentation which cuts across countries is that the benefits of private car owner-ship are strongly felt, regardless of the differing driving habits and transportation cir-cumstances in different countries. Thus, in principle, all car consumers should be found in one of the basic proposed categories: pleasure seekers, image seekers and functionality seekers.

The German car manufacturer BMW has argued that although their customers' demographic and economic profiles are quite similar, they do not operate with a standard European consumer market and standardized marketing activities.[54] This is due to two reasons: first, they argue that the differences in size of the various seg-ments are so great that it makes no sense to target the same segment in various coun-tries; but more importantly, they also argue that they have discovered variations between the *benefits ultimately sought* by car drivers in different countries.

As a consequence of a study conducted in Italy, France, the Netherlands, Switzerland and Austria, BMW can break purchase criteria down into three levels: criteria that are important in *all* countries, criteria that are important to all motorists in *one* country, and criteria that are important to *some consumers in all* countries. On the pan-European level the following criteria were detected: reliability, safety, quality and advanced technology. These are thus necessary minimum requirements to be considered as a potential supplier. On the national level, the following set of differences was detected. In the Netherlands, much importance is attached to the car's overall integrity rather than to qualities such as interior design. Furthermore, the reputation of the brand turned out to be very important for the Dutch. In France, special importance was attached to the self-confidence provided by the car and to its road-holding abilities. Both Austrian and Swiss customers were very demanding, but, unlike the Austrians, the Swiss wanted a car to be discreet while Austrians placed importance on a car as a prestigious status symbol. Finally, the Italians looked for a car in accordance with their personal style and with dynamic driving capaci-ties. In general, the study's conclusions were that BMW drivers are more demanding in terms of styling, exclusiveness, driving dynamics and advanced technology than average European drivers, but that, within this segment, special importance was attached to different dimensions across different countries. In the five countries studied, BMW discovered a total of seven common segments whose names speak more or less for themselves: the unpretentious car fan (18 per cent); the prestige-oriented sporty driver (25 per cent); the hedonist (9 per cent); the utilitarian thinker (13 per cent); the traditionalist (17 per cent); the prestige-oriented achiever (10 per cent); and the understatement buyer (9 per cent). However, as shown in Figure 16.9, the size of each of the segments varies considerably in each country. The country-specific results indicate that different models appeal to different segments in different countries. For example, it could be types 6 and 2 in Austria whereas it could be types 1 and 4 in Switzerland. The case of BMW is a good combination of pan-European and country-specific approaches to analysing consumer behaviour.

European advertising preferences and regulations

Consumers in different countries are accustomed to different forms of advertising. In many cases, advertising content is regulated by the government. For example, tobacco advertising in Denmark is not allowed to depict young people, and Swedish tobacco advertising targeted at end-users must not show any people at all. The

Figure 16.9 Distribution of car segments in five European countries

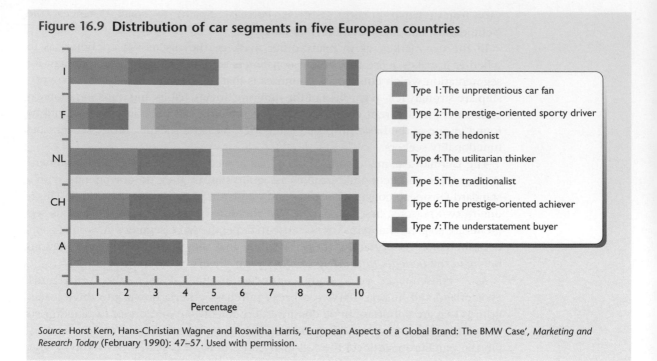

Source: Horst Kern, Hans-Christian Wagner and Roswitha Harris, 'European Aspects of a Global Brand: The BMW Case', *Marketing and Research Today* (February 1990): 47–57. Used with permission.

European Commission in Brussels has taken initiatives to impose even stricter controls on advertising, introducing among other things a total ban on tobacco advertising in Europe.

In Germany, pricing is controlled, and special sales can be held only for a particular reason, such as going out of business or the end of the season. Advertising also focuses more on the provision of factual information rather than on the aggressive hard sell. Indeed, it is illegal to mention the names of competitors.[55] Unlike the Anglo-Saxon advertising culture, comparative advertising is banned in most Latin and Germanic countries in Europe.

But the differences among European countries are not restricted to the legal area. There are also differences concerning which type of television advertising spots and print ads will work best in various European countries. A comparative study of French and German TV spots revealed a distinct profile of the ads in these two countries. French TV ads tended to have less product information, to have a less direct way of communicating about socially sensitive topics, to rely more on non-verbal and implicit communication types and to present women in a more seductive and sexually alluring manner.[56] The same differences concerning the general image of French communication as seductive and imaginative vs. a more factual and sober German style were confirmed when looking at other types of communication such as television news programmes and news magazines. Another study of all ads sent out on a couple of TV channels in each country confirmed this difference, stressing the more frequent use of puns and the more rapid and personalized rhythm of the French ads, although no difference in information level was found.[57] Surprisingly, in the latter study not one single common ad was sampled in Germany and France. Seems like the use of pan-European advertising is still limted . . .

One possible explanation for this difference may be due to the distinction between **low-context** and **high-context cultures**.[58] In a high-context culture, messages tend to be more implicit, and built into the communication context, whereas communication in low-context cultures tends to be more explicit, specific and direct. France, according to this perspective of classifying culture, is relatively high-context compared to Germany, which belongs among the most low-context cultures in the world.

In comparison, the British have a more favourable attitude to advertising than either the French or the Germans. They tend to think of advertising as a humorous and entertaining part of daily life, and have less concerns about its manipulative capacities.[59] Indeed, the British ads may be funnier. One study found a relatively big difference between the degree to which humour is used in televised advertising. Humour was used in 88.8 per cent of British ads compared to 74.5 per cent in France and only 61 per cent in Germany. And in a sample of internationally used ads, the share of humorous ads dropped to 32.2 per cent.[60] Seems like humour is still a very national thing. Or may there be other explanations? These findings are supported by another source which concluded that, relative to Americans, the British tended to regard advertising as a form of entertainment. Compared to the United States, British television commercials also contained less information.[61] One advertising executive stated outright that from watching a sample reel of German and British car ads respectively, it would be evident that the German ones would be much more rational and the British ones much more emotional.[62]

Not only do attitudes about ads vary across Europe, the same can be said for preferences of media. For example, in France outdoor posters are a highly developed and popular medium for creative campaigns. Cinema advertising is also enjoyable to the French. In the UK, adverts in daily newspapers are more important compared to other European countries, and in Germany the radio medium is more important than elsewhere.[63] But the use of various media is difficult to compare among countries due to variations in the regulation of media use. For example, interrupting programmes with advertising is not permitted in Scandinavian countries, and is not practised on German public TV channels.

Cultural differences may influence actual reader comprehension of a certain advertisement. Most of these studies have concluded that ads, like other pictures or communications, are understood culturally, and that readership is so different that a standardized execution of the ad becomes problematic.[64] When two different TV spots (called 'Hitchhiker' and 'Quackers') for the chocolate bar KitKat were tested in six different countries, the consumers (all younger people) showed significant differences in what they retained as the main idea of the ad and the main product characteristic (see Table 16.4).[65]

The variations could be explained by different factors such as relative familiarity with the product concept (in Italy), the small size of the product in relation to local competitors (the Netherlands), popularity of English-style humour (Germany) and the prevailing advertising style in the country (France). Another study comparing Danish and American readings of international ads has detected similar variations in readership due to cultural backgrounds. For example, an ad for a lemon-flavoured soft drink featuring young people enjoying themselves on a beach was interpreted by the Danes as showing the strength of the community and by Americans as showing individual freedom.[66] It is probably safe to conclude that, although there are often certain similarities in the way ads are understood across cultures, the readership tends to focus on different themes in different countries.[67]

Table 16.4 Differences in message decoding of two ads in six European countries

Main idea

	Hitchhiker	Quackers
Belgium	Product for young people	You can share it
England	A break with KitKat	
Holland	Product for young people	A break with KitKat
Italy	Product quality	
Germany	To relax	A break with KitKat
France	'Magic effect'	To relax

© Copyright GfK
Source: ESOMAR, Madrid, 1992.

Main product characteristics

	Hitchhiker	Quackers
Belgium	Good product	Crispy bar
England	Chocolate bar with wafer	A snack
Holland	Little	
Italy	Good product	
Germany	Relax with KitKat	Chocolate bar
France	Crispy bar	Good product

© Copyright GfK
Source: ESOMAR, Madrid, 1992.

Source: J. Andrew Davison and Erik Grab, 'The Contributions of Advertising Testing to the Development of Effective International Advertising: The KitKat Case Study', *Marketing and Research Today* (February 1993): 15–24. Used with permission.

Multicultural dimensions

The internet is bringing new cultural differences to the marketplace. The Scandinavians are those who have the highest home-internet linkage frequency in Europe, but the sales leaders by far in terms of turnover are Germany and the UK. These two countries alone account for about 55 per cent of the e-commerce turnover in Europe (Germany 30 per cent and the UK 25 per cent). It takes France, Italy, the Netherlands and Sweden combined just to reach the turnover level of the UK.[68] Also, there are big differences in user profiles. The UK is heavily overrepresented among the group of 12–17-year-old Europeans who surf the net, whereas the Germans are very underrepresented. On the other hand, relatively more French (21–34 years) and Germans (age group 25–34 only) surf the internet compared to the British.[69]

Regional consumption differences: the micro-level

Geodemography

▶ The term **geodemography** refers to analytical techniques that combine data on consumer expenditures and other socio-economic factors with geographic information about the areas in which people live in order to identify consumers who share common consumption patterns.

Geodemography is based on the assumption that 'birds of a feather flock together' – that people who have similar needs and tastes tend to live near one another. Given this, it should be possible to locate 'pockets' of like-minded people who can then be reached more economically by direct mail and other methods. Important dimensions in differentiating between neighbourhoods or townships are factors such as income level, ethnic background and demographics (most notably age). Geographic information is increasingly being combined with other data to paint an even more complete picture of the consumer. Several marketing research ventures now employ **single-source data** where information about a person's actual purchasing history is combined with geodemographic data, thus allowing marketers to learn even more about the types of marketing strategies that motivate some people to respond.

Ethnic and religious subcultures

Sevgi, waking up early on Saturday morning, braces herself for a long day of errands and chores. As usual, her mother expects her to do the shopping while she is at work, and then help prepare the food for the big family get-together tonight. Of course, her older brother would never be asked to do the shopping or help out in the kitchen – these are women's jobs.

Family gatherings make a lot of work, and Sevgi wishes that her mother would use prepared foods once in a while, especially on a Saturday when Sevgi has an errand or two of her own to do. But no, her mother insists on preparing most of her food from scratch; she rarely uses any convenience products, to ensure that the meals she serves are of the highest quality.

Resigned, Sevgi watches TRTint on the family's cable-TV while she's getting dressed, and then she heads down to the local newsagent in 'De Pijp' to buy a magazine – there are dozens of Turkish magazines and newspapers for sale, and she likes to pick up new ones occasionally. Then Sevgi buys the grocery items her mother wants; the Islamic Halal butcher is a long-time family friend and already has the cuts of lamb prepared for her. The vendors at the open air stalls on the Albert Cuyp Market where she and her mother shop all the time know her, and provide her with choice quality olives and vegetables. One quick stop at the local sweet shop to pick up the family's favourite drop (licorice) and she's almost done. With any luck, she'll have a few minutes to stop at the music store and pick up Jennifer Lopez's newest CD. She'll listen to it in the kitchen while she chops, peels and stirs. Sevgi smiles to herself: despite a busy day preparing the house and meal for the family party, she feels that Amsterdam is a great place to live.

Subcultures and consumer identity

Yes, Sevgi lives in Amsterdam, not Ankara. However, this consumer vignette could just as easily have taken place in London, Berlin, Stockholm, Marseilles or thousands of other cities throughout Europe. There are well over 25 million Europeans who belong to an ethnic sub-group, and in several European countries such as France, Belgium and Germany, they collectively account for around 10 per cent of the total population. In the UK, the ethnic communities represented are forecast to double in population to over 6 million within the next 30 years.[70]

Turkish consumers have much in common with members of other racial and ethnic groups who live in Europe. These groups of consumers observe the same national holidays, their expenditures are affected by the country's economic health

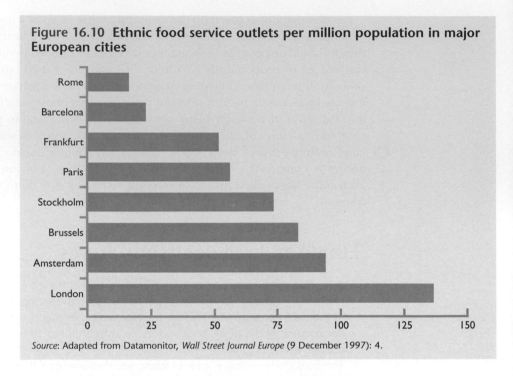

Figure 16.10 Ethnic food service outlets per million population in major European cities

Source: Adapted from Datamonitor, *Wall Street Journal Europe* (9 December 1997): 4.

and they may join together in rooting for their host country's national team in the football World Cup. None the less, while European residency (and in most cases European citizenship) provides the raw material for some consumption decisions, others profoundly affect (see Figure 16.10) and are profoundly affected by the enormous variations in the social fabric of the country where they live.

Consumers' lifestyles are affected by group memberships *within* the society at large. These groups are known as **subcultures**, whose members share beliefs and common experiences that set them apart from others. While subcultural group memberships often have a significant impact on consumer behaviour, some subcultural identifications are more powerful than others. Major subcultural consumer groups based on age have already been discussed in Chapter 13.

Ethnic and racial subcultures

Ethnic and religious identity is a significant component of a consumer's self-concept. An **ethnic** or **racial subculture** consists of a self-perpetuating group of consumers who are held together by common cultural and/or genetic ties, and is identified both by its members and by others as being a distinguishable category.[71]

In some countries, such as Japan, ethnicity is almost synonymous with the dominant culture, since most citizens claims the same homogeneous cultural ties (although Japan has sizeable minority populations, most notably people of Korean ancestry). In heterogeneous societies like those found in Europe, many different cultures are represented, and consumers may expend great effort to keep their subcultural identification from being submerged into the mainstream of the dominant society.

Ethnicity and marketing strategies

Although some companies may feel uncomfortable at the notion that people's racial and ethnic differences should be explicitly taken into account when formulating marketing strategies, the reality is that these subcultural memberships are frequently paramount in shaping people's needs and wants. Membership in these groups is often predictive of such consumer variables as level and type of media exposure, food preferences, the wearing of distinctive apparel, political behaviour, leisure activities and even willingness to try new products.

Furthermore, research evidence indicates that members of minority groups are more likely to find an advertising spokesperson from their own group to be more trustworthy, and this enhanced credibility in turn translates into more positive brand attitudes.[72] In addition, the way marketing messages should be structured depends on subcultural differences in how meanings are communicated. As discussed earlier in this chapter, sociologists make a distinction between *high-context cultures* and *low-context cultures*. In a high-context culture, group members tend to be tightly knit, and they are likely to infer meanings that go beyond the spoken word. Symbols and gestures, rather than words, carry much of the weight of the message. Many minority cultures are high-context and have strong oral traditions, so perceivers will be more sensitive to nuances in advertisements that go beyond the message copy.[73]

'To be or not to be: that is the answer'

One important way to distinguish between members of a subculture is to consider the extent to which they retain a sense of identification with their country of origin vs. their host country. **Acculturation** refers to the process of movement and adaptation to one country's cultural environment by a person from another country.[74] The nature of this transition process is affected by many factors. Individual differences, such as whether the person speaks the host country language, influence how difficult the adjustment will be.

The person's contact with **acculturation agents** – people and institutions that teach the ways of a culture – are also crucial. Some of these agents are aligned with the *culture of origin* (in Sevgi's case, Turkey). These include family, friends, the mosque, local businesses and Turkish-language media that keep the consumer in touch with his or her country of origin. Other agents are associated with the *culture of immigration* (in this case, the Netherlands), and help the consumer to learn how to navigate in the new environment. These include state schools and Dutch-language media.

As immigrants adapt to their new surroundings, several processes come into play. *Movement* refers to the factors motivating people to uproot themselves physically from one location and go to another. Although many ethnic members throughout Europe are second-generation (born in the country where they live), their parents are more likely to have been the first to arrive in the new country. On arrival, immigrants encounter a need for *translation*. This means attempting to master a set of rules for operating in the new environment, whether learning how to decipher a different currency or understanding the social meanings of unfamiliar clothing styles. This cultural learning leads to a process of *adaptation*, where new consumption patterns are formed.

As consumers undergo acculturation, several things happen. Many immigrants undergo (at least to some extent) *assimilation*, where they adopt products that are identified with the mainstream culture. At the same time, there is an attempt at *maintenance* of practices associated with the culture of origin. Immigrants stay in touch with people in their country, and many continue to eat ethnic foods and read ethnic newspapers. Their continued identification with their home culture may cause *resistance*, as they resent the pressure to submerge their identities and take

Figure 16.11 A model of consumer acculturation

Source: Adapted from Lisa Peñalosa, '*Atravesando Fronteras*/Border Crossings: A Critical Ethnographic Exploration of the Consumer Acculturation of Mexican Immigrants', *Journal of Consumer Research* 21 (June 1994): 32–54.

on new roles. Figure 16.11 provides an overview of the processes involved in consumer acculturation.

These processes illustrate that ethnicity is a fluid concept, and that the boundaries of a subculture are constantly being recreated. An *ethnic pluralism* perspective argues that ethnic groups differ from the mainstream in varying degrees, and that adaptation to the larger society occurs selectively. Research evidence argues against the notion that assimilation necessarily involves losing identification with the person's original ethnic group. For example, Sevgi feels comfortable in expressing her 'Turkishness' in a variety of consumption-related ways: the magazines she buys, the TV programmes on the Turkish network she chooses to watch, her choice of ethnically appropriate gifts for events such as weddings and holidays. Alternatively, she has no problems at all in expressing consumption behaviours of the mainstream culture – she loves eating *drop* (Dutch licorice), buys 'Western' music and has her favourite outfits for going out to the cinema and clubs. The best indicator of ethnic assimilation, these researchers argue, is the extent to which members of an ethnic group have social interactions with members of other groups in comparison to their own.[75]

The impact of religion on consumption

Religion *per se* has not been studied extensively in marketing, possibly because it is seen as a taboo subject. The very low-key or non-existent approach by large multinational or pan-European companies reflects the same sort of caution that these companies have in targeting ethnic groups – companies are having to decide whether religiously or ethnic-tailored programmes foster greater brand loyalty or whether any advantage is outweighed by the risks of misreading the target market and causing offence. Without question, the most successful companies targeting and serving both ethnic and religious segments are small businesses, whose managers and owners are often members of the group.[76] However, the little evidence that has been accumulated indicates that religious affiliation has the *potential* to be a valuable predictor of consumer behaviour.[77] Religious subcultures have been shown to exert an impact on such consumer variables as personality, attitudes towards sexuality, birth rates and household formation, income and political attitudes.

Putting together descriptive demographic profiles of Europe's major religious groups is not an exact science. For example, French law prohibits any question on religion in national censuses, although with an estimated 4–5 million Muslim inhabitants France undoubtedly has the biggest Islamic community in western Europe. As a faith, Islam is now second only to Roman Catholicism in France.[78] Similar problems with taking a census are found in the UK. Britain's one million-strong Muslim population is small, but has the fastest growth rate of all religions in the country. The thousand or so existing mosques are likely to be converted warehouses, churches or community halls. The hundreds of new mosques being built feature traditional Islamic domes and minarets – a trend which signals the growing economic vitality of British Muslims, as well as local authorities' growing acceptance of mosques.[79] While Islam is the fastest-growing religion in Europe, it is difficult to generalize about Muslims beyond belief in the teachings of the Koran, identifying holidays and periods of fasting such as Ramadan, and certain dietary restrictions. Coming from more than 120 countries and a variety of ethnic groups (Blacks, Asians, Arabs, Europeans), they are like many groups of consumers in Europe – diverse in their celebrations of consumption habits!

Christianity has dominated the history and cultural development of Europe, and has played an important role in the shaping of the European continent. While the many denominations of Christians make it the largest religious grouping in Europe, active membership is on the decline, with fewer and fewer adults attending services on any given Sunday.[80] In response to this trend, the Vatican has been involved in a variety of events aimed at developing closer and more active relationships with Europe's youth. Enlisting French fashion designers for World Youth Day, having Bob Dylan perform at a Vatican-sponsored rock concert, and having Easter Mass and information about the Vatican on a website are recent attempts to get youth involved with the church.[81] Divided roughly into the more Protestant North and the predominantly Catholic South, Christianity still makes up the majority religion in Europe in terms of claimed membership. Its major holidays of Easter and Christmas and celebrations such as 'Carnival' (*Faschung* in Germany) are celebrated or observed to such an extent that large industries such as travel and retailing rely on these seasons as the times of the year when they earn the most revenues.

MARKETING PITFALL

There are mixed feelings in the Catholic community about the spread of religious imagery in popular culture. On the one hand, the Vatican museum recently opened its first boutique outside Vatican walls, and is now selling silk ties and scarves designed for the Vatican by Salvatore Ferragamo.[82] On the other hand, an ad in a Danish campaign for the French car manufacturer Renault had to be withdrawn after protests from the Catholic community. The ad described a dialogue during confession between a Catholic priest and a repenting man. The man's sins can be atoned for by reciting Ave Marias until he confesses to having scratched the paint of the priest's new Renault – at which point the priest shouts 'heathen' and orders the man to pay a substantial penalty to the church.[83]

Euro-consumers: do they exist?

A number of trends seem to be valid for all western European markets.[84] These include:

- a tendency to more unevenly distributed income
- an increasing number of older people
- a decrease in household size
- a growing proportion of immigrants
- increase in environmental concern and consumption of 'green' products
- relatively increasing consumption of services compared to durable goods.

In spite of these common trends, there are, as we have seen, big differences in the local contexts in which these trends are found as well as differences in the degree to which the trend is significant in each individual country.

Many European managers expect an increase in the importance of Euro-brands and Euro-consumers.[85] However, *why* and *when* companies should or could adopt pan-European strategies or not remains a complex matter. One study suggested 21 influencing factors on pan-European marketing standardization, including management characteristics, firm characteristics, industry characteristics and government characteristics, but not market characteristics![86]

We believe that consumer behaviour analysis must play an important role in the decision to standardize or adapt marketing strategies. All consumers will differ to some extent in what they buy, why they buy, who makes the purchase decision, how they buy, when they buy and where they buy.[87] Some of these differences may be explained at the lifestyle level and less so on the national level, and some are very obviously related to national or regional differences. It is also obvious that some differences are disappearing, due to the increasingly international supply of goods and the increasing internationalization of the retailing system in Europe.[88] However, not even the fact that similar goods are bought in similar stores across European countries permits us to confirm the existence of the Euro-consumer. Product usage and knowledge, and to a certain extent imagery, may be relatively shared among Europeans, but as soon as one takes the contexts of acquisition, consumption and disposal into account, the actual role and meaning of the product in daily life becomes coloured by the local culture. No lifestyle survey has yet demonstrated a truly European profile in any of the lifestyles; European segments continue to be defined in rather abstract common denominators.

It is often asserted that segments such as international businesspeople, or younger people mainly influenced by trends from MTV and other 'global youth culture' phenomena, are especially prone to standardized marketing. European managers are people who tend to be prime consumers of pan-European media, like business magazines or CNN (in hotel rooms).[89] So there may be a tendency to a higher degree of internationalization among younger, wealthier and more educated people. The question is how deep the similarity really is. A study of consumption of luxury goods in five major European markets concluded that the pan-European consumer of luxury brands is between 35 and 49 years old, lives in a major city, has a high income and a university education, and occupies a managerial job. On the other hand, there were big differences between the various countries in the level of brand awareness and purchase level, and the degree of significance of socio-economic factors for purchase of luxury brands. For example, Spain and Italy are strongly segmented due to socio-economic differences, while France, the UK and Germany are less useful in explaining luxury consumption. The level of purchase and awareness was found to be high in France, the UK and Italy, and low in Germany and Spain. The most 'mature' market for luxury brands was France, the UK and a narrow Italian segment, whereas the rest of the Italians lacked the money, the Germans lacked the motivation and the Spanish lacked both.[90]

In general, the absence of the Euro-consumer does not mean that Svensson of Sweden, Smith of the UK, Smit of Holland, Simón of Spain and Schultz of Germany cannot have more in common in certain aspects than they have with their compatriots. But it means that these similarities can be analysed and understood only with methods that are also able to take the differences into consideration. Hence the call for an understanding of the new cultural units that make up today's marketplace of international lifestyles, global issues, national rituals and local habits.[91]

Chapter summary

- A consumer's *lifestyle* refers to the ways he or she chooses to spend time and money and how his or her values, attitudes and tastes are reflected by consumption choices. Lifestyle research is useful to track societal consumption preferences and also to position specific products and services to different segments.

- Marketers segment by lifestyle differences, often by grouping consumers in terms of their *AIOs* (activities, interests and opinions).

- *Psychographic techniques* attempt to classify consumers in terms of psychological, subjective variables in addition to observable characteristics (demographics). A variety of systems, such as RISC, have been developed to identify consumer 'types' and to differentiate them in terms of their brand or product preferences, media usage, leisure time activities, and attitudes towards such broad issues as politics and religion.

- Interrelated sets of products and activities are associated with social roles to form *consumption constellations*. People often purchase a product or service because it is associated with a constellation which, in turn, is linked to a lifestyle they find desirable.

- Where one comes from is often a significant determinant of lifestyle. Many marketers recognize national or regional differences in product preferences, and develop different versions of their products for different markets.

- Because a consumer's culture exerts such a big influence on his or her lifestyle choices, marketers must learn as much as possible about differences in cultural norms and preferences when marketing in more than one country. One important issue is the extent to which marketing strategies must be tailored to each culture, vs. standardized across cultures.

- Consumers identify with many groups that share common characteristics and identities. These large groups that exist within a society are called *subcultures*, and membership in them often gives marketers a valuable clue about individuals' consumption decisions. A large component of a person's identity is determined by his or her ethnic origins, racial identity and religious background. The growing numbers of people who claim multi-ethnic backgrounds are beginning to blur the traditional distinctions drawn among these subcultures.

- Recently, several minority groups have caught the attention of marketers as their economic power has grown. Segmenting consumers by their *ethnicity* can be effective, but care must be taken not to rely on inaccurate (and sometimes offensive) ethnic stereotypes.

● Because a consumer's culture exerts such a major influence on his or her lifestyle choices, marketers must learn as much as possible about differences in cultural norms and preferences when marketing in more than one country.

● Given that we, as consumers, must take part in many activities that reflect our local cultures, Euro-consumers as an overall segment do not exist. The existence of a Euro-consumer is at best limited to certain segments of the population, the young and the (international) managerial class, and to certain situations.

KEY TERMS

Acculturation (*p. 529*)
Acculturation agents (*p. 529*)
AIOs (*p. 507*)
Consumption constellations (*p. 505*)
Ethnic subculture (*p. 528*)
Geodemography (*p. 526*)
Habitus (*p. 512*)
High-context culture (*p. 524*)
Lifestyle (*p. 503*)

Lifestyle marketing perspective (*p. 504*)
Low-context culture (*p. 524*)
Product complementarity (*p. 505*)
Psychographics (*p. 506*)
Racial subculture (*p. 528*)
Single-source data (*p. 527*)
Subcultures (*p. 528*)
VALS (*p. 514*)

For additional material see the companion website at:
www.booksites.net/solomon_euro

Consumer behaviour challenge

1   Compare and contrast the concepts of lifestyle and social class.

2   In what situations is demographic information likely to be more useful than psychographic data, and vice versa?

3   Discuss some concrete situations in which international similarities in lifestyles may be more relevant than national cultural differences for market segmentation and for the understanding of consumer behaviour.

4   Compile a set of recent ads that attempt to link consumption of a product with a specific lifestyle. How is this goal usually accomplished?

5   The chapter mentions that psychographic analyses can be used to market politicians. Conduct research on the marketing strategies used in a recent, major election. How were voters segmented in terms of values? Can you find evidence that communications strategies were guided by this information?

6   Using media targeted to the group, construct a consumption constellation for the social role of university students. What set of products, activities and interests tend to appear in advertisements depicting 'typical' university students? How realistic is this constellation?

7 If you were segmenting European consumers in terms of their relative level of materialism, how might your advertising and promotional strategy take this difference into account? Construct two versions of an ad for a suntan lotion, one to appeal to a high materialism country and one to appeal to a low materialism country (under the untenable assumption of all other things being equal).

8 There are, of course, people of most lifestyle types in all European countries, but their numbers vary. Try to determine which lifestyles are the most common in some European countries that you know.

9 If you have access to foreign TV channels, try to compare the advertising in the ones from your own country with the foreign ones. Are the styles different? Are the predominant products different? Is the use of a certain style of advertisement for a certain type of product similar or dissimilar?

10 Locate one or more consumers (perhaps family members) who have immigrated from another country. Interview them about how they adapted to their host culture. In particular, what changes did they make in their consumption practices over time?

Notes

1. Pierre Valette-Florence, *Les styles de vie* (Paris: Nathan, 1994); Benjamin Zablocki and Rosabeth Moss Kanter, 'The Differentiation of Life-Styles', *Annual Review of Sociology* (1976): 269-97.
2. Mary T. Douglas and Baron C. Isherwood, *The World of Goods* (New York: Basic Books, 1979).
3. Richard A. Peterson, 'Revitalizing the Culture Concept', *Annual Review of Sociology* 5 (1979): 137-66.
4. Søren Askegaard, 'Livsstilsundersøgelser: Henimod et teoretisk fundament', doctoral dissertation, School of Business and Economics: Odense University, 1993.
5. Henrik Dahl, *Hvis din nabo var en bil* (Copenhagen: Akademisk Forlag, 1997).
6. Thomas Drieseberg, 'Lebensstile in der Marktforschung - eine empirische Bestandsaufnahme', *Soziologie - Planung und Analyse* 5 (1992): 18-26.
7. William Leiss, Stephen Kline and Sut Jhally, *Social Communication in Advertising* (Toronto: Methuen, 1986).
8. Douglas and Isherwood, *The World of Goods*: 72-3.
9. Michael R. Solomon, 'The Role of Products as Social Stimuli: A Symbolic Interactionism Perspective', *Journal of Consumer Research* 10 (December 1983): 319-29.
10. Michael R. Solomon and Henry Assael, 'The Forest or the Trees?: A Gestalt Approach to Symbolic Consumption', in Jean Umiker-Sebeok, ed., *Marketing and Semiotics: New Directions in the Study of Signs for Sale* (Berlin: Mouton de Gruyter, 1988): 189-218; Michael R. Solomon, 'Mapping Product Constellations: A Social Categorization Approach to Symbolic Consumption', *Psychology & Marketing* 5 (1988) 3: 233-58; see also Stephen C. Cosmas, 'Life Styles and Consumption Patterns', *Journal of Consumer Research* 8 (March 1982) 4: 453-5.
11. Russell W. Belk, 'Yuppies as Arbiters of the Emerging Consumption Style', in Richard J. Lutz, ed., *Advances in Consumer Research* 13 (Provo, UT: Association for Consumer Research, 1986): 514-19.
12. Margaret Hogg, 'Anti-Constellations: Conceptualization and Content', in B. Englis and A. Olofsson, eds, *European Advances in Consumer Research* 3 (Provo, UT: Association for Consumer Research, 1999): 44-9.
13. Askegaard, 'Livsstilsundersøgelser: Henimod et teoretisk fundament': 103-5.
14. Bill Schlackman, 'An Historical Perspective', in S. Robson and A. Foster, eds, *Qualitative Research in Action* (London: Edward Arnold, 1989): 15-23.
15. William D. Wells and Douglas J. Tigert, 'Activities, Interests, and Opinions', *Journal of Advertising Research* 11 (August 1971): 27.
16. Alfred S. Boote, 'Psychographics: Mind Over Matter', *American Demographics* (April 1980): 26-9; William D. Wells, 'Psychographics: A Critical Review', *Journal of Marketing Research* 12 (May 1975): 196-213.
17. Joseph T. Plummer, 'The Concept and Application of Life Style Segmentation', *Journal of Marketing* 38 (January 1974): 33-7.
18. Berkeley Rice, 'The Selling of Lifestyles', *Psychology Today* (March 1988): 46.
19. 'CMT 'Lifestyle' Launch', *Marketing* (3 February 1994): 4.
20. Valerie Latham, 'Do Euroconsumers Exist?', *Marketing* (24 June 1993): 3.
21. Document, RISC.
22. Bernard Cathelat, *Socio-Styles-Système* (Paris: Editions d'organisation, 1990).

23. Askegaard, 'Livsstilsundersøgelser: Henimod et teo-retisk fundament': 67-77.

24. Pierre Bourdieu, *La distinction: critique social du jugement* (Paris: Editions de Minuit, 1979; Eng. trans. 1984).

25. Douglas B. Holt, 'Does Cultural Capital Structure American Consumption?', *Journal of Consumer Research* 25 (June 1998): 1-25.

26. Mary Douglas, *Natural Symbols* (New York: Random House, 1973).

27. Dahl, *Hvis din nabo var en bil*: 55-81.

28. Martha Farnsworth Riche, 'VALS 2', *American Demographics* (July 1989): 25.

29. Leiss *et al.*, *Social Communication in Advertising*.

30. Stuart Elliott, 'Sampling Tastes of a Changing Russia', *New York Times* (1 April 1992) 2: D1.

31. Valette-Florence, *Les styles de vie*.

32. Askegaard, 'Livsstilsundersøgelser: Henimod et teo-retisk fundament'.

33. *Markedsføring* 14 (1999): 16.

34. 'Marketers Fear EU Regs Will Hinder E-commerce', *Advertising Age* (2 October 2000): 16.

35. 'Going it Alone', *Marketing News* (11 September 2000).

36. Per Olof Berg, Anders Linde-Laursen and Orvar Löfgren, eds, *Invoking a Transnational Metropolis* (Lund: Studentlitteratur, 2000).

37. Søren Askegaard and Tage Koed Madsen, 'The Local and the Global: Patterns of Homogeneity and Heterogeneity in European Food Cultures', *International Business Review* 7(6) (1998): 549-68.

38. Cf. discussions in the following: Alladi Venkatesh, 'Ethnoconsumerism: A New Paradigm to Study Cultural and Cross-Cultural Consumer Behaviour', in Janeen A. Costa and G. Bamossy, eds, *Marketing in a Multicultural World* (Thousand Oaks: Sage, 1995): 26-67; Jean-Claude Usunier, *Marketing Across Cultures*, 3rd edn (London: Prentice-Hall, 2000); Askegaard and Madsen, 'The Local and the Global: Patterns of Homogeneity and Heterogeneity in European Food Cultures'; Klaus Grunert, Suzanne Grunert and Sharon Beatty, 'Cross-Cultural Research on Consumer Values', *Marketing and Research Today* 17 (1989): 30-9.

39. Usunier, *Marketing Across Cultures*.

40. Peter S. H. Leeflang and W. Fred van Raaij, 'The Changing Consumer in the European Union: A "Meta-Analysis"', *International Journal of Research in Marketing* 12(5) (1996): 373-87.

41. Cf. among many sources M. Douglas, 'Food as a System of Classification', in *In the Active Voice* (London: Routledge & Kegan Paul, 1982): 82-124; P. Farb and G. Armelagos, *Consuming Passions: The Anthropology of Eating* (Boston: Houghton Mifflin, 1980); P. Fieldhouse, *Food and Nutrition: Customs and Culture* (London: Croom Helm, 1986); C. Fischler, *L'Homnivore* (Paris: Ed. Odile Jacob, 1990); A. Warde, *Consumption, Food, and Taste* (London: Sage, 1997).

42. Euromonitor, *European Marketing Data and Statistics* (1997): 6, 254.

43. Ibid.: 328-31.

44. Klaus G. Grunert, Karen Brunsø and Søren Bisp, 'Food-Related Lifestyle: Development of a Cross-Culturally Valid Instrument for Market Surveillance', in L. Kahle and L. Chiagouris, eds, *Values, Lifestyles and Psychographics* (Mahwah, NJ: Lawrence Erlbaum Associates, 1997): 337-54.

45. See, however, Søren Askegaard and Karen Brunsø, 'Food-Related Lifestyle in Singapore: Preliminary Testing of a Western European Research Instrument in Southeast Asia', *Journal of Euromarketing* 7(4) (1999): 65-86.

46. Klaus G. Grunert, 'What's in a Steak? A Cross-Cultural Study on the Quality Perception of Beef', MAPP Working Paper 39 (Aarhus: The Aarhus School of Business, 1996).

47. Mary Douglas, ed., *Constructive Drinking: Perspectives on Drink from Anthropology* (Cambridge: Cambridge University Press, 1987).

48. David Smith and J. Robert Skalnik, 'Changing Patterns in the Consumption of Alcoholic Beverages in Europe and the United States', in Flemming Hansen, ed., *European Advances in Consumer Research* 2 (Provo, UT: Association for Consumer Research, 1995): 343-55.

49. Ibid.

50. Pekka Sulkunen, 'Drinking Patterns and the Level of Alcohol consumption: An International Overview', in R. J. Gibbins *et al.*, eds, *Research Advances in Alcohol and Drug Problems* 3 (New York: John Wiley).

51. Euromonitor, *European Marketing Data and Statistics*: 334.

52. Smith and Skalnik, 'Changing Patterns in the Consumption of Alcoholic Beverages in Europe and the United States'.

53. Yves Marbeau, 'Eurodemographics? Nearly There!', *Marketing and Research Today* (March 1992): 47-57.

54. Horst Kern, Hans-Christian Wagner and Roswitha Harris, 'European Aspects of a Global Brand: The BMW Case', *Marketing and Research Today* (February 1990): 47-57.

55. Matthias D. Kindler, Ellen Day and Mary R. Zimmer, 'A Cross-Cultural Comparison of Magazine Advertising in West Germany and the U.S.', unpublished manuscript, University of Georgia, Athens, 1990.

56. Michael Schroeder, 'Germany–France: Different Advertising Styles – Different Communication Concepts', in W. F. van Raaij and G. Bamossy, eds, *European Advances in Consumer Research* 1 (Provo, UT: Association for Consumer Research, 1993): 77-83.

57. Björn Walliser and Fabienne Moreau, 'Comparaison du style français et allemand de la publicité télévisée', *Cahiers du CESAG* 98 11 1/11 (1998).

58. Edward T. Hall, *Beyond Culture* (New York: Doubleday, 1976).

59. Hans Heyder, Karl Georg Musiol and Klaus Peters, 'Advertising in Europe – Attitudes Towards Advertising in Certain Key East and West European Countries', *Marketing and Research Today* (March 1992): 58–68.

60. Ullrich Appelbaum and Chris Halliburton, 'How to Develop International Advertising Campaigns that Work: The Example of the European Food and Beverage Sector', *International Journal of Advertising* 12(3) (1993): 223–41.

61. Marc G. Weinberger and Harlan E. Spotts, 'A Situational View of Information Content in TV Advertising in the U.S. and U.K.', *Journal of Marketing* 53 (January 1989): 89–94; see also Abhilasha Mehta, 'Global Markets and Standardized Advertising: Is It Happening? An Analysis of Common Brands in USA and UK', in *Proceedings of the 1992 Conference of the American Academy of Advertising* (1992): 170.

62. 'Abroadminded', *Marketing* (24 April 1997): 20–1.

63. Heyder, Musiol and Peters, 'Advertising in Europe'.

64. Wendelin G. Müller, 'Die Standardisierbarkeit internationaler Werbung: Kulturen verlangen Adaptionen', *Marketing ZFP* 3 (3rd Quarter 1996): 179–90.

65. J. Andrew Davison and Erik Grab, 'The Contributions of Advertising Testing to the Development of Effective International Advertising: The KitKat Case Study', *Marketing and Research Today* (February 1993): 15–24.

66. Douglas B. Holt, Søren Askegaard and Torsten Ringberg, '7Ups and Downs: Cross Cultural Differences in the Reading Profile of Advertising' (in press).

67. Eduardo Camargo, 'The Measurement of Meaning: Sherlock Holmes in Pursuit of the Marlboro Man', in Sebeok, ed., *Marketing and Semiotics*: 463–83.

68. 'Marketers Fear EU Regs Will Hinder E-commerce'.

69. Source: mmxi Europe, *www.mmxieurope.com/data/metrixcentral*.

70. Demographic Statistics 1997: Population and Social Conditions Series, (Luxembourg: Office for Official Publications of the European Communities, 1997); 'Colour Blind', *Marketing Week* (21 June 1996): 38–40.

71. See Frederik Barth, *Ethnic Groups and Boundaries: The Social Organization of Culture Difference* (London: Allen and Unwin, 1969); D. Bell, 'Ethnicity and Social Change', in N. Glazer and D. P. Moynihan, eds, *Ethnicity: Theory and Experience* (Cambridge, MA: Harvard University Press, 1975): 141–74; D. L. Horowitz, 'Ethnic Identity', in ibid.: 109–40; J. Kotkin, *Tribes* (New York: Random House, 1993); Venkatesh, 'Ethnoconsumerism'; Michel Laroche, Annamma Joy, Michael Hui and Chankon Kim, 'An Examination of Ethnicity Measures: Convergent Validity and Cross-Cultural Equivalence', in Rebecca H. Holman and Michael R. Solomon, eds, *Advances in Consumer Research* 18 (Provo, UT: Association for Consumer Research, 1991): 150–7; Melanie Wallendorf and Michael Reilly, 'Ethnic Migration, Assimilation, and Consumption', *Journal of Consumer Research* 10 (December 1983): 292–302; Milton J. Yinger, 'Ethnicity', *Annual Review of Sociology* 11 (1985): 151–80.

72. Rohit Desphandé and Douglas M. Stayman, 'A Tale of Two Cities: Distinctiveness Theory and Advertising Effectiveness', *Journal of Marketing Research* 31 (February 1994): 57–64; Stephen Riggins, 'The Media Imperative: Ethnic Minority Survival in the Age of Mass Communication', in S. H. Riggins, ed., *Ethnic Minority Media: An International Perspective* (London: Sage, 1992): 1–22.

73. Steve Rabin, 'How to Sell Across Cultures', *American Demographics* (March 1994): 56–7.

74. Cf. Lisa Peñaloza, '*Atravesando Fronteras*/Border Crossings: A Critical Ethnographic Exploration of the Consumer Acculturation of Mexican Immigrants', *Journal of Consumer Research* 21 (June 1994) 1: 32–54.

75. A. Fuat Firat, 'Consumer Culture or Culture Consumed?', in Costa and Bamossy, eds, *Marketing in a Multicultural World*: 105–25; Michael Laroche, Chankon Kim, Michael K. Hui and Annamma Joy, 'An Empirical Study of Multidimensional Ethnic Change: The Case of the French Canadians in Quebec', *Journal of Cross-Cultural Psychology* 27(1) (January 1996): 114–31.

76. Elizabeth C. Hirschman, 'Religious Affiliation and Consumption Processes: An Initial Paradigm', *Research in Marketing* (Greenwich, CT: JAI Press, 1983): 131–70.

77. See, for example, Nejet Delener, 'The Effects of Religious Factors on Perceived Risk in Durable Goods Purchase Decisions', *Journal of Consumer Marketing* 7 (Summer 1990): 27–38.

78. 'The Muslims in France: Rejecting their Ancestors the Gauls', *The Economist* (16 November 1996): 113–14.

79. Clare Garner, 'Builders Answer Islam's Growing Call to Prayer', *The Independent* (4 February 1997): 7.

80. Madeline Bunting, 'Churchgoing Bottoms Out', *The Guardian* (10 August 1996): 2; 'Catholic Church Loses Mass Appeal', *The Guardian* (30 January 1996): 4; 'België is niet langer katholiek ([Belgium is no longer Catholic]',) *Trouw* (19 September 1996); Madeline Bunting, 'Revolving Door Throws Doubt on Evangelical Churches' Revival', *The Guardian* (28 August 1996).

81. Amy Barrett, 'John Paul II to Share Stage with Marketers', *Wall Street Journal Europe* (19 August 1997): 4; see also *www.mix.it/rai/papa*.

82. 'Vatican Opens Boutique Outside Walls', *Montgomery Advertiser* (10 June 1996): 4A.

83. *Markedsføring* 10 (1996): 22.

84. Leeflang and van Raaij, 'The Changing Consumer in the European Union: A "Meta-Analysis"'.

85. Massoud Saghafi and Donald Sciglimpaglia, 'Marketing in an Integrated Europe', in M. Bergadaà, ed., *Marketing Today and for the 21st Century* 1 (ESSEC:

Proceedings of the 24th EMAC Conference, 1995): 1069–76.

86. Fred van Eenennaam, 'Standardization of International Marketing Processes in a pan-European Context: Some Research Hypotheses', in Bergadaà, ed., *Marketing Today and for the 21st Century* 2: 1221–41.

87. Vern Terpstra and Kenneth David, *The Cultural Environment of International Business*, 2nd edn (Cincinnati: Southwestern, 1985).

88. André Tordjman, 'European Retailing: Convergences, Differences, and Perspectives', in P. J. McGoldrick and G. Davies, eds, *International Retailing: Trends and Strategies* (London: Pitman, 1995): 17–50.

89. 'Abroadminded'.

90. Bernard Dubois and Gilles Laurent, 'Is There a Euroconsumer for Luxury Goods?', in van Raaij and Bamossy, eds, *European Advances in Consumer Research* 1: 58–69.

91. Susan P. Douglas and C. Samuel Craig, 'The Changing Dynamic of Consumer Behavior: Implications for Cross-Cultural Research', *International Journal of Research in Marketing* 14 (1997): 379–95.

Chapter 17

New times, new consumers

Six weeks before St Valentine's Day, called Lovers' Day in Turkey, Ayşe starts planning for that special romantic evening. She remembers that last year she and her husband could not find a table in any restaurant in Ankara, all hotels and restaurants had been fully booked and florists had run out of red roses. So she acts early and makes a reservation for two at a good restaurant. She starts window shopping for a gift that she would like to receive. She sees a St Valentine's Day Swatch that she really likes. Two weeks before Lovers' Day she starts asking her husband what he is thinking of getting her. She takes him to the shopping mall and shows him the St Valentine's Day Swatch and tells him that she'd like that *very* much. On Lovers' Day Ayşe's husband remembers that he has not yet bought anything, goes to get the St Valentine's Day Swatch – only to discover that the shop has run out of them. Instead he buys a much more expensive Swatch. When he comes home, he finds his wife, dressed up ready to go out for dinner. Excited, she closes her eyes and puts her arm forward, confident that he will put a watch around her wrist. And he does. But when she opens her eyes and sees that it is not the St Valentine's Day Swatch, she is upset – and furious. She bursts into tears; they have an argument; and Ayşe goes to the bedroom and takes off her nice clothes. They spend the evening at home, in separate rooms, not talking to each other. Some Lovers' Day, she thinks.

Later, Ayşe tells the story to her friends, some of whom think it's very funny . . .

Güliz Ger, Bilkent University, Ankara

Introduction

The opening vignette illustrates one of the processes related to changes in consumer societies that are discussed in this chapter, globalization. Lovers' Day started to be celebrated in Turkey about a decade ago, first by exchanging cards among school-friends. It has become more widespread in the last few years, mostly among the urban middle class who now exchange gifts and make a special evening of it. St Valentine's Day, appropriated as Lovers' Day, is taking root among married and unmarried couples in this Muslim country where traditional norms of respectability did not allow dating – dating is not what 'nice' girls were supposed to do, and many from conservative or lower-middle-class families still frown on it. As well as globalization, we will take a closer look at two other tendencies that may profoundly be changing the way we consume and behave in the marketplace, namely environmentalism and political consumption on the one hand and postmodernism on the other.

Environmentalism: saving the planet with a shopping basket

The environmental issue has gained a lot of momentum in recent years. The environmental concerns of the general public endure in spite of a certain backlash and disbelief in the flourishing 'green marketing' strategies in the 1990s.[1] There is a growing awareness that rather short-sighted lifestyles in all parts of the world lead to the depletion of energy sources, pollution, deterioration of soil fertility, reductions in biodiversity and climate change. And there is also an awareness that consumption patterns play a direct or an indirect role in all of these problems.[2] Furthermore, there is a growing awareness that a 'greener consumer society' need not be one of joylessness and abstention and need not be in total opposition to the current system of production and marketing.[3] But it all started some decades ago with the encouragement to recycle . . .

Recycling

The issue of product disposition and **recycling** is doubly vital because of its enormous public policy implications. We live in a throw-away society, which creates problems for the environment and also results in a great deal of unfortunate waste. Training consumers to recycle has become a priority in many countries. Japan recycles about 40 per cent of its waste, and this relatively high rate of compliance is partly due to the social value the Japanese place on recycling: citizens are encouraged by waste disposal lorries which periodically rumble through the streets playing classical music or children's songs.[4] Companies continue to search for ways to use resources more efficiently, often at the prompting of activist consumer groups. For example, McDonald's restaurants bowed to pressure by eliminating the use of styrofoam packages, and its outlets in Europe are experimenting with edible breakfast platters made of maize.[5] Even in China, the waste problem is taken more seriously, as hundreds of restaurants have started washing and recycling chopsticks, and the government is planning to put a tax on disposable chopsticks.[6]

Several studies have examined the relevant goals consumers have to recycle. One used a means–end chain analysis of the type described in Chapter 4 to identify how specific instrumental goals are linked to more abstract terminal values. The most important lower-order goals identified were: 'avoid filling up landfills', 'reduce waste', 're-use materials' and 'save the environment'. These were linked to the terminal values of: 'promote health/avoid sickness', 'achieve life-sustaining ends' and 'provide for future generations'. Another study reported that the perceived effort involved in recycling was the best predictor of whether people would go to the trouble – this pragmatic dimension outweighed general attitudes towards recycling and the environment in predicting intention to recycle.[7] Yet another (European) study concluded, among other things, that one major motivating factor for recycling was a high perceived effectiveness of the action, that is, whether the consumer thinks it makes a difference if he or she recycles.[8] By applying such techniques to the study of recycling and other product disposal behaviours, it will be easier for social marketers to design advertising copy and other messages that tap into the underlying values that will motivate people to increase environmentally responsible behaviour.[9]

Even taking into account the difficulties in measurement, statistics reveal that the production of waste differs enormously among the countries of Europe. In the late 1980s, the yearly municipal solid waste per capita in western European countries ranged from 231 kg in Portugal to 608 kg in Finland. As a comparison, the corresponding figure in the US was 864 kg. The different levels of waste generation are due to differences in general income level and to differences in consumption styles.[10]

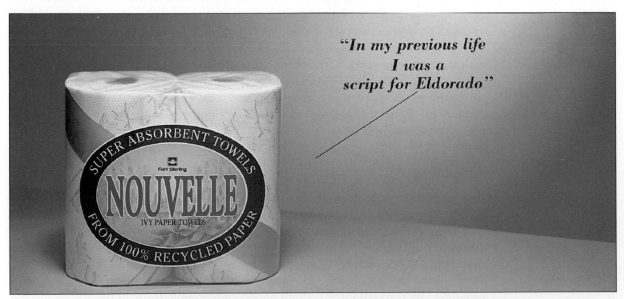

This British ad for paper towels takes a humorous route to emphasize that the paper towels are made from recycled paper.

Lurzer's Archiv, 1994, 91. Photo courtesy of BDH, Manchester, UK. Creative team: Wayne Hanson, Graham Daldry.

En als u erop uitgekeken bent,
ruimen we hem weer netjes op.

Volkswagen. Wie anders?

This Dutch Volkswagen ad focuses on recycling.
The copy says, 'And when you've had enough of it,
we'll clear it away nicely'.
Lurzer's Archiv, 1994. Photo courtesy of Volkswagen and DDB
Needham Worldwide BV Amsterdam.

Waste management also differs among countries. Different types of recycling programmes in Denmark encourage people to cut down on household waste and recycle as much as possible, as the municipal waste management systems charge consumers according to weight or volume of the household waste.[11] The Danish model of waste management, which stresses local responsibility for source separation programmes, is now marketed globally through on-site visits and video cassettes.[12] In Germany, producers are required by law to be responsible for the redistribution and recycling of used products.[13] In addition to recycling, other disposal programmes have caught the authorities' interest. In several European countries, including Spain, Italy, France and Denmark, economic incentives have been offered by the state to encourage car owners to replace their old car with a newer one, in order to reduce air pollution and increase road safety.[14]

Recycling has proved to be only the beginning of a more profound process, taking into consideration not only recyclability but also environmental issues connected to the production process. Concern for the environment, or **environmentalism**, is no longer confined to recycling but applies to all aspects of the production and consumption processes and is affecting marketing strategies for products ranging from nappies to fast food. For example, Ecover, a highly environmentally conscious Belgian producer of detergents and cleaning products, appealed to consumers' environmental concerns in a tongue-in-cheek way by recycling its competitors' old TV commercials. The company used five black-and-white commercials from the 1950s and superimposed a colour picture of its brand over the competing brand while a voice-over explained that the old commercial had been recycled.[15] It has been argued that environmental concern is gradually becoming a new universal value, not in its militant form but as a more tacit precondition for the degree of acceptability of products.[16] One commentator expressed it in a paradox: 'Environmentalism means that we will no longer have ecological milk. We will have milk and industrial milk.' This might also lead to more sensitivity towards various kinds of natural products and products from smaller, independent producers. Different consumer groups are thus increasing pressure on producers to demonstrate that they are producing in such a way as to preserve nature and resources rather than exploit them.

Certain retail chains in Europe have been pioneering environmentally friendly policies. Migros, the largest Swiss retail chain, has cut down on packaging material, increased its use of train transportation, and introduced various forms of non-toxic, well-insulated stores to cut energy consumption, etc. Tengelmann of Germany (chlorine-free products, milk-dispensing machines for recyclable milk containers), Otto, the world's largest mail-order company (environmental friendliness as corporate culture, collaborations with the World Wildlife Fund), Sainsbury (recycled plastic bags, a 'Penny Back Scheme' donating refunded pennies to charity) and Tesco (comprehensive labelling, healthy eating programme and organically grown produce) of the UK are among the pioneering retailers for environmental issues.[17]

There are obvious differences among various European countries concerning the role of environmentalism. It is a politically more important issue in such countries as Germany, Denmark and Sweden. A study of the relative importance of environmental concern in car purchases ranked Germany first, followed by the UK, France and Spain.[18]

Environmentalist attitudes and behaviours have proved hard to predict. Some have argued that the trend is waning since an organization such as Greenpeace has experienced a decline in membership. Others have concluded that while attitudes are 'green', actual behaviour is less likely to change. This was the conclusion of one 1991 study of Danish consumers.[19] Since then, the demand for ecological produce in the dairy, egg and vegetable sectors has exploded, in Denmark as in many other countries. One major indication that environmentalism is becoming a (more or less) global value and is not just a passing fad is the role that concern for the environment plays in youth-oriented media such as MTV and, not least, in school curricula.[20]

Many consumer studies have tried to establish a distinct value profile for environmentally oriented consumers,[21] discussing, for example, whether they are more individually or socially oriented.[22] Values such as 'close relationships to others' and 'social justice' have been identified as being associated with a higher degree of environmentally conscious attitudes and behaviour.[23]

An environmentally related issue such as the use of growth hormones in milk and beef is a major problem in trade negotiations between Europe and the US. Some argue by references to scientific data stating that there is no risk,[24] but others maintain that it is a matter of production and consumption ethics more than of actual risks to consumers.

Lately, the debate over the risks concerning hormone-growth beef has been overshadowed by the problems relating to the spreading of BSE (or Mad Cow's Disease) which created a general distrust of British beef when the disease was first detected in 1996, both in Britain and abroad.[25] Since then, the disease has spread to other European countries, creating a virtual consumer flight from beef in certain countries, notably Germany and Italy (where sales dropped 30 per cent nationwide).[26] Even in Sweden, where no cases of BSE have been detected, 41 per cent of consumers have become doubtful whether they should eat beef and 11 per cent have begun to eat less. Two per cent stopped eating beef altogether.[27]

Such food scares have led to a growing distrust in modern industrial production methods, especially within the food industry, following the logic expressed by many consumers that 'when you make the poor cows into cannibals just for profitability, things are bound to go wrong'. It has been suggested that we live in a **risk society**, where our ways of producing goods are increasingly producing just as many and even more 'bads' or risks,[28] risks that the consumer will have to take into account in his or her decision-making. Another field where such unknown risks have made consumers sceptical about the benefits suggested to them by the industry is that of gen-

The labels on the ketchup bottles say 'Heinz organically produced ketchup from free-range tomatoes'. This ad plays on the search for more environmentally sound production and consumption by referring to the product as organic produce and simultaneously making a joking reference to the debate on animal welfare and the tendency to have more and more free-range animal production. Note the several layers of cultural meaning also inherent in the ad. The stall is a typical roadside outlet at small farms in the Danish countryside, where the farmer will sell home-produced fruit and vegetables. The little moneybox (note that it does not have a lock on it) often contains a little change in case the customer does not have the exact amount. Thus, the ad refers both to the 'small is beautiful' ideology, to historical and nostalgic feelings about what (all) farming used to be like, and to the trust that is believed to exist between (small and local) producers and consumers.

Used by permission from Leo Burnett, Denmark.

etically manipulated organisms (GMO). One fear expressed by consumers in one study of acceptance or rejection of GMO foods in Sweden and Denmark was exactly that of a too large concentration of power at a few giant corporations dominating both research and industry.[29] Thus, what is at stake on the consumer level, disregarding the international economic interests involved, seems to be the confrontation of an economic vs. a moral logic.

Similar results were found for several European countries in a cross-national study. Testing consumer attitudes and purchase intentions to GMO foods, it was concluded that an overall rejection of the technology as such was found in Denmark, Germany, Great Britain and Italy, although a slightly less negative attitude was found in Italy (mainly because consumers said that they knew less about GMO).[30] In connection with this study, various types of information material were also tested, some more informational, some more emotional, in order to estimate the potential of informational campaigns in changing negative attitudes. But whatever information was given to the consumers, it only made their attitude *more* negative. Thus, any cue that reminded the consumers about the fact that the product contained or had used GMO in the production process immediately turned the consumers against the product even if the cues were positive, something which points to the deep-seated nature of this scepticism among European consumers.[31]

The political consumer

The discussion above points to an increasing awareness of the political and moral consequences of consumption choices among many consumers. This means that the green consumer is gradually being followed by, or maybe is turning into, the **political consumer**.[32] The political consumer uses his or her buying pattern as a weapon against companies he or she doesn't like and in support of the companies that reflect values similar to the consumer's own. This consumer type selects products according to the company's ethical behaviour, which includes respect for human rights, animal protection, environmental friendliness and support for various benevolent causes. The political consumer is supported by such agencies as the Vancouver-based Adbusters, which engages in twisting campaigns from major companies that, for some reason, have come into their spotlight for immoral or harmful behaviour. For example, they made a spoof on the well-known Coca-Cola polar bear campaign by depicting a family of bears on a tiny ice floe, with the sign 'Enjoy Climate Change' written in that well-known type from the Coca-Cola logo, thereby protesting against the company's use of ozone-harming gases in its vending machines.[33] This kind of 'peaceful' rebelliousness against what is seen as major companies' control over our minds and imagination is called *culture jamming*.[34]

Not all companies are on the defensive, though. Companies such as The Body Shop are founded on the idea of natural and non-animal-tested products and a maximum of environmental concern. But their concerns are becoming directed towards a broader array of social values. They recently took up the debate over beauty ideals by introducing 'Ruby', a Barbie lookalike doll but one with considerably rounder forms, in order to fight the tyranny of thinness and the impossible body ideal of the supermodels which are also endorsed by Barbie's shape. The reaction was predictable: Mattel Inc., the producers of Barbie, took out an injunction against The Body Shop because Ruby's face was too like Barbie's.

Many other companies are now working proactively to avoid the sort of trouble Shell ran into in Denmark, the Netherlands and Germany with the Brent Spar case (see below), or the difficulties French exporters experienced in the wake of nuclear testing in 1996. Just to mention a few cases, the mineral water company Ramlösa is

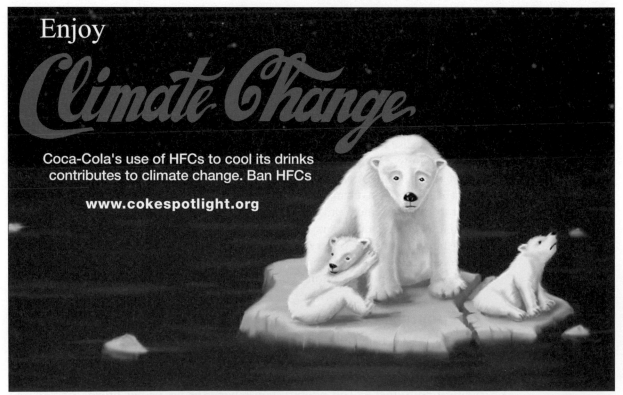

The Adbusters's comment on Coca-Cola's use of HFC gases. And it worked. In a press release from August 2000, Adbusters congratulates the Coca-Cola Company on its decision to abolish the use of HFC gases by the 2004 Athens Olympic Games at the latest.

Source: *www.cokespotlight.org*. Used by permission.

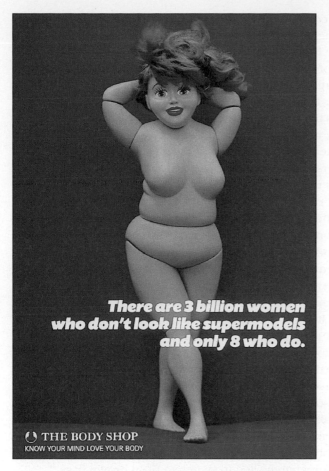

There are 3 billion women who don't look like supermodels and only 8 who do.

THE BODY SHOP
KNOW YOUR MIND LOVE YOUR BODY

The Body Shop's Ruby, a Barbie lookalike doll but with considerably rounder forms, introduced in order to fight the tyranny of thinness and impossible body ideal of the supermodels which are reinforced by Barbie's shape.
The Body Shop International Arts PLC.

campaigning for clean water acts in the Third World together with the Red Cross in Scandinavia under the slogan 'Water for Life',[35] and British Telecom has run a campaign underlining its work for elderly and disabled people.[36] The two brewery giants Heineken and Carlsberg both withdrew plans for large-scale investments in Myanmar (Burma) after consumers' protests against what was seen as direct support for the repressive military government there.

There is a risk that the political consumer may become an even more moralizing, politically correct consumer, as has occurred in the US's political and cultural climate. In fact, some British consumer groups have taken action against the companies that screened commercials during the TV broadcast of the controversial film *The Last Temptation of Christ*.[37] The question is: where is the dividing line between morality and moralizing?

Consumer boycotts

As we have seen, we live in a period when many consumers are becoming increasingly aware that their consumption pattern is part of a global political and economic system, to the extent that they become political consumers. Sometimes a negative experience can trigger an organized and devastating response, as when a consumer group organizes a *boycott* of a company's products. These efforts can include protests against everything from investing in a politically undesirable country (as when Carlsberg withdrew their investments from Myanmar, as mentioned above, or when Shell was accused of tolerating pollution and political repression of the people of the Ogoni region of Nigeria) to efforts to discourage consumption of products from certain companies or countries (as during the boycott of French wines and other products during the nuclear testing in the Pacific in 1996, an action which was especially strongly felt in the Netherlands and in the Scandinavian countries). In the United States, the inclusion of obscene or inflammatory lyrics led to boycott threats, as when law enforcement organizations threatened to boycott Time Warner after it distributed a rap song by Ice-T entitled 'Cop Killer'.

One well-known case was the boycott of Shell following its plans to dump an old drilling platform, Brent Spar, in the North Sea. In Germany, the company's revenue fell by almost 30 per cent; the boycott was felt in Denmark and the Netherlands too. Ironically, Shell's quick reversal of the decision to dump the platform only seemed to confirm to consumers that they were indeed guilty, in spite of evidence that deep-water disposal was the most environmentally friendly solution to the problem.[38]

Boycotts are not always effective – studies show that normally only a limited percentage of a country's consumers participate in them. However, those who do are disproportionately vocal and well educated, so they are a group companies especially don't want to alienate. The negative PR that arises from media coverage of the boycott may be problematic for the company in the long run, since competitors may gain relative advantages. After the boycott of French wines in Denmark had calmed down, French wines had lost 20 per cent of the market share. However, that was not seen as the biggest problem, since the general impression was that consumers could be persuaded to switch back to French wines. But many supermarket shelves had been reorganized in order to give more space to Italian and Spanish wines, and this was considered a more serious problem.[39]

One increasingly popular solution used by marketers is to set up a joint task force with the boycotting organization to try to iron out the problem. In the US, McDonald's used this approach with the Environmental Defence Fund, which was concerned about its use of polystyrene containers and bleached paper. The company agreed to test a composting programme and to switch to plain brown bags.[40]

Lately, much of consumers' political resistance to the behaviour of companies and marketers has been related to the processes of globalization. The global marketplace has been accused of being based on unfair trade principles and of eroding cultural and social patterns around the world, favouring the rich countries and cultures of the western world at the expense of the rest of the world's populations and cultures. Demonstrations at the gatherings of the World Trade Organization have attracted much media attention, as has the action led by a French cheese-producer against the construction of a McDonald's restaurant in his home town in southern France. The target was not so much McDonald's *per se* as the processes it represents, sometimes called *McDonaldization*,[41] the cultural erosion and the withering of quality standards for cheap, large-scale production. Consequently, the activists behind this formed an organization whose name translates into something like 'farmers against lousy food'.[42] This and other organizations, like ATTAC, questioning the benefits of what they perceive as an uncontrolled global market, have enjoyed considerable success recently. Hence, we will take a closer look at some aspects of globalization, consumption and marketing.

Global marketing and culture

Learning about the practices of other cultures is more than just interesting – it is an essential task for any company that wishes to expand its horizons and become part of the international or global marketplace at the beginning of the new millennium.

In this section, we'll consider some of the issues confronting marketers who seek to use a global marketing approach. We'll also consider the consequences of the 'Americanization' or 'Westernization' of global culture, as marketers continue to export Western popular culture to a globe of increasingly affluent consumers, many of whom are eagerly waiting to replace their traditional products and practices with the offerings of Benetton, Levi's, McDonald's, Nestlé and Unilever.

Think globally, act locally

As corporations increasingly find themselves competing in many markets around the world, the debate has intensified regarding the necessity of developing separate marketing plans for each culture. A lively debate has ensued regarding the need to 'fit in' to the local culture. Let's briefly consider each viewpoint.

Adopting a standardized strategy

Proponents of a standardized marketing strategy argue that many cultures, especially those of relatively industrialized countries, have become so homogenized that the same approach will work throughout the world. By developing one approach for multiple markets, a company can benefit from economies of scale, since it does not have to incur the substantial time and expense of developing a separate strategy for each culture.[43] This viewpoint represents an **etic perspective**, which focuses on commonalities across cultures. An etic approach to a culture is objective and analytical: it reflects impressions of a culture as viewed by outsiders, which assume that there are common, general categories and measurements which are valid for all cultures under consideration.

Adopting a localized strategy

On the other hand, many marketers choose to study and analyse a culture using an **emic perspective**, which focuses on variations within a culture. This approach assumes that each culture is unique, with its own value system, conventions and

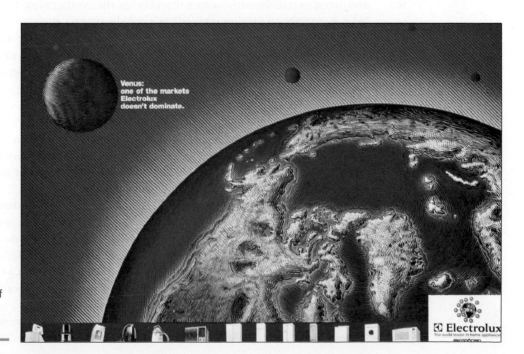

This Brazilian ad for Electrolux points to the global strength of this company and its products.

▶ regulations. This perspective argues that each country has a **national character**, a distinctive set of behaviour and personality characteristics.[44] An effective strategy must be tailored to the sensibilities and needs of each specific culture. An emic approach to a culture is subjective and experiential: it attempts to explain a culture as it is experienced by insiders.

Multicultural dimensions

The etic approach has been chosen by many companies who have adopted a standardized strategy for marketing products in Europe. Although the unification of the European Community (into the European Union) has not happened as smoothly as some predicted, the prospect of many separate economies eventually being massed into one market of 325 million consumers has led many companies to begin to standardize their prices, brand names and advertising.[45]

Many companies are responding to this dramatic change by consolidating the different brands sold in individual countries into common *Eurobrands*. In the United Kingdom and France, for example, the Marathon chocolate bar sold by Mars, Inc., is now called Snickers (a somewhat risky move, considering that the British refer to women's underwear as 'knickers').[46]

Major pan-European or global campaigns were launched in 1996 and 1997 by such companies, brands and organizations as American Express, Ciba-Geigy, Dockers, Eurotunnel, Hewlett-Packard, Lee Jeans, Mazda, Pepsi, TDK, Visa International, Volvo and WorldWide Fund for Nature.[47]

Given the sizeable variations in tastes within a relatively homogeneous country like the US, it is hardly surprising that people around the world have developed their own preferences. Unlike Americans, for example, Europeans favour plain chocolate over milk chocolate, which they regard as suitable only for children. Whisky is considered a 'classy' drink in France and Italy, but not in England. Crocodile bags are popular in Asia and Europe, but not in the US. Americans' favourite tie colours are red and blue, while the Japanese prefer olive, brown and bronze. Even global brands are perceived differently across markets. In the Netherlands and the UK, Heineken beer is positioned (and perceived) as a middle-priced, mainstream beer, while in the US and the rest of Europe it is perceived (and priced) as a premium beer. Alternatively, Budweiser beer (the American brand, not the original Czech brand) has a very middle-price and mainstream position in the US, yet is a premium-priced beer in Europe and South America.[48]

Superstitions and cultural sensitivities

Marketers must be aware of a culture's norms regarding such sensitive topics as taboos and sexuality. For example, the Japanese are superstitious about the number four. *Shi*, the Japanese word for four, also means death. For this reason, in Japan Tiffany sells glassware and china in sets of five.

The consequences of ignoring these issues became evident during the 1994 soccer World Cup, when both McDonald's and Coca-Cola made the mistake of reprinting the Saudi Arabian flag, which includes sacred words from the Koran, on disposable packaging used in promotions. Despite their delight at having a Saudi team in contention for the cup, and the satisfaction with Coca-Cola sponsoring the team, Muslims around the world protested at this borrowing of sacred imagery, and both companies had to scramble to rectify the situation.[49]

Cultures vary sharply in the degree to which references to sex and bodily functions are permitted. Many American consumers would blush at much European advertising, where sexuality is much more explicit. This dimension is particularly interesting in Japan, which is a culture of contradictions. On the one hand, the Japanese are publicly shy and polite. On the other hand, sexuality plays a significant role in this society. *Manga*, the extremely popular Japanese comic books which comprise a billion-dollar industry, stress themes of sex and violence. Nudity is quite commonplace in Japanese advertising and general media.[50]

In contrast, a recent controversy in India illustrates problems that can arise in a more conservative culture. The government-run television network rejected a spot for KamaSutra condoms which showed a couple sitting on a bed playing chess. As the woman sweeps the pieces off the board, she mouths the word 'Check' while he mouths the word 'Mate'. The tagline reads, 'For the pleasure of making love'.[51]

Multicultural dimensions

Strongly held values can make life very difficult for marketers, especially when they are selling sensitive products. This is the case with tampons: while 70 per cent of American women use them, only 100 million out of a potential market of 1.7 billion eligible women around the world use this product. Resistance to the product posed a major problem for *Tambrands*, which does not make other products and must expand its customer base to remain viable.

The company has found it difficult to sell its feminine hygiene products in some cultures such as Brazil, where many young women fear they will lose their virginity if they use a tampon. A commercial developed for this market included an actress who says in a reassuring voice, 'Of course, you're not going to lose your virginity', while a second woman adds, 'That will happen in a much more romantic way'.

To counteract this problem prior to launching a new global advertising campaign for Tampax in 26 countries, the firm's advertising agency conducted research and divided the world into three clusters based on residents' resistance to using tampons (resistance was so intense in Muslim countries that the agency didn't even attempt to reach women in these markets).

In Cluster One (including the US, the UK and Australia), women felt comfortable with the idea and offered little resistance. A teaser ad was developed to encourage more frequency of use: 'Should I sleep with it, or not?'

In Cluster Two (including France, Israel and South Africa), about 50 per cent of women use the product, but some concerns about virginity remain. To counteract these objections, the marketing strategy focused on obtaining the endorsements of gynaecologists within each country.

In Cluster Three (including Brazil, China and Russia), the greatest resistance was encountered. To try to make inroads in these countries, the researchers found that the first priority is simply to explain how to use the product without making women feel squeamish – a challenge they are still trying to puzzle out.[52]

Does global marketing work?

So, after briefly considering some of the many differences one encounters across cultures globally, the often voiced question still remains: does global marketing work? Given the growth of global brands and global marketing strategies over the past few decades, the practical answer has to be 'yes'. But this doesn't add much in terms of insights for managers. Perhaps the more appropriate question is, *when* and *why* does it work?

Although the argument for a homogeneous world culture is appealing in principle, in practice it has met with mixed results. We have discussed how one reason for the difficulties of using a global marketing approach is that consumers in different countries have different conventions and customs, which may mean that they simply do not use products in the same way. Kellogg, for example, discovered that in Brazil big breakfasts are not traditional – cereal is more commonly eaten as a dry snack.

Some large corporations, such as Coca-Cola, have been successful in crafting a single, international image. Still, even Coca-Cola must make minor modifications to the way it presents itself in each culture. Although Coke commercials are largely standardized, local agencies are permitted to edit them to highlight close-ups of local faces.[53] Says one executive: 'Coca-Cola is a *multi-local* company'.[54]

As the world's borders seem to shrink due to advances in communications, many companies continue to develop global advertising campaigns. In some cases they are encountering obstacles to acceptance, especially in less-developed countries or in those areas, such as central and eastern Europe, that are only just beginning to embrace Western-style materialism as a way of life.[55]

To maximize the chances of success for these multicultural efforts, marketers must locate consumers in different countries who none the less share a common worldview. This is more likely to be the case among people whose frame of reference is relatively more international or cosmopolitan, and/or who receive much of their information about the world from sources that incorporate a worldwide perspective.

Who is likely to fall into this category? The same two segments that were candidates for pan-European marketing: (1) affluent people who are 'global citizens' and who are exposed to ideas from around the world through their travels, business contacts and media experiences, and as a result share common tastes. For example, one study found that with the exceptions of musical taste and food consumption, the new elite in Zimbabwe to a high degree emulated the consumption tastes and styles of the UK and the USA;[56] (2) young people whose tastes in music and fashion are strongly influenced by international pop culture broadcasting many of the same images and sounds to multiple countries.[57]

MARKETING PITFALL

The language barrier is one problem confronting marketers who wish to break into foreign markets. One technique that is used to avoid this problem is where a translated ad is retranslated into the original language by a different interpreter to catch errors. Some specific translation obstacles that have been encountered around the world include the following:[58]

● Wrigley's Spearmint Gum reads as 'Shark's sperm' in some east European countries.
● When Vauxhall launched its Nova model in Spain, it realized that the name meant 'doesn't go' in Spanish.
● Also in Spain, Mitsubishi discovered that its four-wheel-drive model Pajero would be known as 'Wanker'.
● When Rolls-Royce introduced its Silver Mist model in Germany, it found that the word 'mist' is translated as 'excrement'. Similarly, Sunbeam's hair curling iron, called the Mist-Stick, translated as 'manure wand'. To add insult to injury, Vicks is German slang for sexual intercourse, so that company's name had to be changed to Wicks in this market.

The Coca-Cola invasion: exporting Western lifestyles

The allure of Western consumer culture has spread throughout the world, as people in other societies slowly but surely fall under the spell of far-reaching advertising campaigns, contact with tourists and the desire to form attachments with other parts of the world. This attraction sometimes results in bizarre permutations of products and services, as they are modified to be compatible with local customs. Consider these events:[59]

- In Peru, Indian boys can be found carrying rocks painted to look like transistor radios.
- In Papua New Guinea, some tribesmen put Chivas Regal wrappers on their drums · and wear Pentel pens through their noses, instead of traditional nose bones.
- Bana tribesmen in the remote highlands of Kako, Ethiopia, pay to watch 'Pluto the Circus Dog' on a Viewmaster.
- When a Swazi princess marries a Zulu king, she wears red touraco wing feathers around her forehead and a cape of windowbird feathers and oxtails. He is wrapped in a leopard skin. All is recorded on a Kodak movie camera while the band plays 'The Sound of Music'.
- In addition to traditional gifts of cloth, food and cosmetics, Nigerian Hausa brides receive cheap quartz watches although they cannot tell the time.

'I'd like to buy the world a Coke'

As indicated by these examples, many formerly isolated cultures now incorporate Western objects into their traditional practices. In the process, the meanings of these objects are transformed and adapted to local tastes (at times in seemingly bizarre ways). Sometimes the process enriches local cultures, sometimes it produces painful stresses and strains the local fabric.

The West (and especially the US) is a *net exporter* of popular culture. Western symbols in the form of images, words and products have diffused throughout the world. This influence is eagerly sought by many consumers, who have learned to equate Western lifestyles in general and the English language in particular with

As this Swedish ad for Wrangler jeans shows, products associated with the 'authentic' American West are in demand around the world.

modernization and sophistication. As a result, people around the world are being exposed to a blizzard of Western products that are attempting to become part of local lifestyles.

For example, American-inspired TV game shows are popular around the world: *Geh Aufs Ganze* (Let's Make a Deal) is one of Germany's top shows. Although *The Dating Game* went off the air in the US in 1989, it is now seen in ten foreign countries and is top in its time slot in Poland, Finland and England, where it's called *Blind Date*. In Singapore a cult has formed around locally produced broadcasts of *The $25,000 Pyramid*, while in France *Le Juste Prix* (The Price is Right) attracts almost half the country's viewers. Not everyone in these countries is happy with the Western influence – producers of *The Dating Game* in Turkey received death threats from Muslim fundamentalists.[60]

The American appeal is so strong that some non-US companies go out of their way to create an American image. A British ad for Blistex lip cream, for example, includes a fictional woman named 'Miss Idaho Lovely Lips' who claims Blistex is 'America's best-selling lip cream'.[61] Recent attempts by American marketers to 'invade' other countries include:

● Kellogg is trying to carve out a market for breakfast cereal in India, even though currently only about 3 per cent of Indian households eat such products. Most middle-class Indians eat a traditional hot breakfast which includes such dishes as chapatis (unleavened bread) and *dosas* (a fried pancake), but the company is confident that it can entice them to make the switch to Corn Flakes, Froot Loops and other American delicacies.[62] However, India has proved quite a difficult market to change, even for powerful multinational companies.[63]

● The National Basketball Association is fast becoming the first truly global sports league. Nearly $500 million of licensed merchandise was sold *outside* the US in 1996. A survey of 28,000 teenagers in 45 countries conducted by the DMB&B advertising agency found that Michael Jordan is by far the world's favourite athlete. In China, his Chicago Bulls team (translated as 'The Red Oxen') is virtually everyone's favourite.[64]

● The British are avid tea-drinkers, but how will they react to American-style iced tea? US companies like Snapple are hoping they can convince the British that iced tea is more than hot tea that's gone cold. These firms may have some way to go, based on the reactions of one British construction worker who tried a canned iced tea for the first time: 'It was bloody awful'.[65]

● Pizza Hut is invading, of all places, Italy. The country that invented pizza will be exposed to the American mass-produced version, quite a different dish from the local pizza, which is often served on porcelain dishes and eaten with a knife and fork. On the other hand, one of Pizza Hut's top performing restaurants is now located in Paris, a centre of fine cuisine, so only time will tell if Italians will embrace pizza 'American-style'.[66]

The West invades Asia

Although a third of the world's countries have a per capita GNP of less than $500, people around the world now have access to Western media, where they can watch reruns of shows like *Lifestyles of the Rich and Famous* and *Dallas*, idealized tributes to the opulence of Western lifestyles. To illustrate the impact of this imagery around the world, it is interesting to compare its impact in two very different Asian countries.

Consider how the material expectations of consumers in the People's Republic of China have escalated. Twenty years ago, the Chinese strove to attain what they called the 'three bigs': bikes, sewing machines and wristwatches. This wish list was later modified to become the 'new big six', adding refrigerators, washing machines and televisions. At the last count, the ideal is now the 'eight new things'. The list now includes *colour* televisions, cameras and video recorders.[67] Chinese women are starting to demand Western cosmetics costing up to a quarter of their salaries, ignoring domestically produced competitors. As one Chinese executive noted, 'Some women even buy a cosmetic just because it has foreign words on the package.'[68]

In contrast to China, the Japanese have already become accustomed to a bounty of consumer goods. Still, the Japanese are particularly enthusiastic borrowers of Western culture. American music and films are especially popular, perhaps because they are the best way to experience US lifestyles and popular culture. They have even recreated an entire Dutch village (complete with real Dutch people who 'perform' daily), which is one of Japan's top honeymoon destinations.

The Japanese often use Western words as a shorthand for anything new and exciting, even if they do not understand their meaning. The resulting phenomenon is known as 'Japlish', where new Western-sounding words are merged with Japanese. Cars are given names like Fairlady, Gloria and Bongo Wagon. Consumers buy *deodoranto* (deodorant) and *appuru pai* (apple pie). Ads urge shoppers to *stoppu rukku* (stop and look), and products are claimed to be *yuniku* (unique).[69] Coca-Cola cans say 'I feel Coke & sound special', and a company called Cream Soda sells products with the slogan 'Too old to die, too young to be happy'.[70] Other Japanese products with English names include Mouth Pet (breath freshener), Pocari Sweat ('refreshment water'), Armpit (electric razor), Brown Gross Foam (hair-colouring mousse), Virgin Pink Special (skin cream), Cow Brand (beauty soap) and Mymorning Water (canned water).[71]

Emerging consumer cultures in transitional economies

In the early 1980s the American TV show *Dallas* was broadcast by the Romanian communist government to show the decadence of Western capitalism. The strategy backfired, and instead the devious (but rich!) J.R. became a revered icon in parts of eastern Europe and the Middle East – to the extent that a tourist attraction outside Bucharest includes a big white log gate that announces (in English) the name: 'South Fork Ranch'.[72] Western 'decadence' appears to be infectious.[73]

Mainland China is one of the newest markets opening up to Western business and culture. When McDonald's opened in Beijing in the early 1990s, this new restaurant became their largest outlet in the world with more than 700 seats and 1000 employees. Many competed for these highly valued positions that are perceived to offer prestige and upward mobility.

This poster promotes the Tom Cruise film *Far and Away* to the Japanese, who are huge fans of American popular culture.
© Jeffrey Aaronson/Aspen Network.

After the collapse of communism, eastern Europeans emerged from a long winter of deprivation into a springtime of abundance. The picture is not all rosy, however, since attaining consumer goods is not easy for many in **transitional economies**, where the economic system is still 'neither fish nor fowl', and governments ranging from China to Portugal struggle with the difficult adaptation from a controlled, centralized economy to a free market system. These problems stem from such factors as the unequal distribution of income among citizens, as well as striking rural–urban differences in expectations and values. The key aspect of a transitional economy is the rapid change required on social, political and economic dimensions as the populace is suddenly exposed to global communications and external market pressures.[74]

Some of the consequences of the transition to capitalism include a loss of confidence and pride in the local culture, as well as alienation, frustration and an increase in stress as leisure time is sacrificed to work ever harder to buy consumer goods. The yearning for the trappings of Western material culture is perhaps most evident in parts of eastern Europe, where citizens who threw off the shackles of communism now have direct access to coveted consumer goods from the US and western Europe – if they can afford them. One analyst observed, 'as former subjects of the Soviet empire dream it, the American dream has very little to do with liberty and justice for all and a great deal to do with soap operas and the Sears Catalogue'.[75] But consumers regularly have found themselves in situations where their real income and their employment security have gone down. Typically, the share of income used on basics such as food has risen, so for a large part of the population the question is how much wealth and happiness consumer society has brought, at least in the short term.[76] This frustrating situation, and the lack of experience with 'real capitalism', has made too many consumers an easy prey for hustlers, who persuade them to invest their money in pyramid games and dubious investment companies. This does not just happen in small side streets. One Russian investment company paid free metro tickets to all Muscovites and advertised heavily on TV. For those who knew what advertising was about, this was a sign of economic potency, while those who did not took it as some kind of officially approved encouragement from the state. Both resulted in a lot of confidence in the firm. Unfortunately, the whole thing ended in political scandal and enormous losses for the consumers-turned-investors.[77] In 1990 more than 60 countries had a GNP of *less* than $10 billion. In contrast, more than 135 transnational companies had revenues greater than that figure. The dominance of these marketing powerhouses has helped to create a *globalized consumption ethic*. As people the world over are increasingly surrounded by goods and tempting images of them, a material lifestyle becomes more important to attain. Shopping evolves from being a weary, task-oriented struggle to locate even basic necessities to being a leisure activity, where possessing consumer goods becomes a mechanism to display one's status – often at great personal sacrifice. In Turkey one researcher met a rural consumer, a mother who deprived her child of nutritious milk from the family's cow and instead sold it in order to be able to buy sweets for her child because 'what is good for city kids is also good for my child'.[78] As the global consumption ethic spreads, the products wished for in different cultures become homogenized – Christmas is now celebrated among some urbanites in Muslim Turkey, even though gift-giving (even on birthdays) is not customary in many parts of that country.

In some cases, the meanings of these desired products are adapted to local customs and needs. In Turkey some urban women use ovens to dry clothes and dishwashers to wash muddy spinach. The process of **creolization** occurs when foreign influences are absorbed and integrated with local meanings – just as modern Christianity incorporated the pagan Christmas tree into its own rituals. Thus, a traditional clothing style such as a *bilum* worn in Papua New Guinea may be combined with Western items like Mickey Mouse shirts or baseball caps.[79] These processes make it unlikely that global homogenization will overwhelm local

Consumption of global products and symbols: Japanese motorcyclists with 'chopped' bikes, jackets, jeans and that 'rebel' look.

Harley Davidson Inc.

cultures, but rather that there will be multiple consumer cultures, each blending global icons such as Nike's pervasive 'swoosh', with indigenous products and meanings.

Consumer resistance: back to the roots?

Despite the proliferation of Western culture around the world, there are signs that this invasion is slowing. Japanese consumers are beginning to show signs of waning interest in foreign products as the health of their country's economy declines. Some of the latest 'hot' products in Japan now include green tea and *yukata*, traditional printed cotton robes donned after the evening bath.[80] Several locally made products are catching on in parts of eastern Europe due to their lower prices and improved quality, combined with the perceptions that sometimes the imported products are inferior versions. Some Muslims are rejecting Western symbols as they adhere to a green Islamic philosophy which includes using natural, traditional products.[81]

Some critics in other countries deplore the creeping Americanization of their cultures. Debates continue in many countries on the imposition of quotas that limit American television programming.[82] The conflict created by exporting American culture was brought to a head in recent trade negotiations on WTO (the global trade agreement), which deadlocked over the export of American films to Europe (the US share of the European cinema market is about 75 per cent). As one French official put it, 'French films are the cinema of creation. American films are products of marketing.'[83]

In Europe the French have been the most outspoken opponents of creeping Americanization. They have even tried to ban the use of such 'Franglish' terms as *le drugstore*, *le fast food* and even *le marketing*, though this effort was recently ruled unconstitutional.[84] The French debate over cultural contamination was brought to a head by the 1991 opening of EuroDisney in a Paris suburb. In addition to the usual attractions, hotels with names like The Hotel New York, The Newport Bay Club and The Hotel Cheyenne attempt to recreate regions of America. The park seems to have rebounded after a shaky start, including renaming it Disneyland Paris since EuroDisney somehow seemed incompatible. But some Europeans have been less than enthusiastic about the cultural messages being sent by the Disney organization. One French critic described the theme park as 'a horror made of cardboard, plastic and appalling colours – a construction of hardened chewing gum and idiotic folklore taken straight out of a comic book written for obese Americans'.[85]

Globalization: not a one-way street

Based on these discussions, we are now able to reflect a little more on the notion of **globalization**. An anthropological study of developments in the British food culture revealed four different types of consumption practices that are currently shaping the way local and foreign products and practices enter into the British way of creating a self-identity through food.[86] The *global food* culture, represented mainly by American fast food, indicates a willingness either to buy into the particular context of Americana, or quite the opposite, to join a wave of globally uniform consumption patterns that are found everywhere and therefore belong nowhere in particular. *Expatriate food* refers to the search for authentic meals and products from other cultures – a 'real Tuscany evening for you and your partner'. Thus it also depends on global knowledge of food cultures, but focuses on the differences between local food cultures. Thirdly, *nostalgia food* represents a search for local authenticity –

Stilton cheese, toffee puddings – from the cultural heritage, which is threatened by the internationalization of British cooking patterns. The study quotes the *Sunday Times*: 'Having shamefully neglected our own traditional dishes for 40 years, we now have a flashy, meretricious cuisine based, for the most part, on ersatz imitations of Mediterranean food'.[87] Finally, *creolization* of food involves blending various traditions into new ones, such as Chinese dishes omitting ingredients considered unappetizing in Western culture, Mexican food with less chilli, or Indianized versions of sandwiches. This creolization, or 'localizing' of foods, is found in many European countries. In the Netherlands, Indonesian food has been adapted to fit the tastes of the mainstream culture, just as Turkish sandwiches have been modified in Germany.[88] These trends probably exist in all European countries but vary in importance and in their influence and outcomes in terms of eating behaviour.

It is interesting to note that all four are related to globalization trends, but only global food leads to a tendency to standardize consumption patterns. The typology is also interesting because in a fairly comprehensible way, it illuminates that globalization is much more than McDonaldized homogenization. And we may see these tendencies as relevant for all types of consumption, not just for consumption of food. So whether we look at retailing, interior decoration, tourism or musical tastes, we may find at least these four tendencies, taking the notion of globalization beyond the interpretation of it as homogenization. It also includes the increasing awareness of other styles and tastes, and the search for 'exotic authenticity', as well as the incorporation of this 'exoticism' into local habits and consumption styles. And finally, the exposure to all this 'otherness' often makes consumers more aware of their own cultural roots, and the tastes and consumption styles that they would define as 'our own'. All these offers of old and new, strange and familiar, authentic and creolized, tend to coexist in the marketplace. Therefore, it is not so strange that some authors discuss globalization more in terms of fragmentation than in terms of homogenization.[89] Fragmentation is also a key aspect of the postmodern view on consumers and consumption, to which we shall now turn.

MARKETING PITFALL

Cigarettes are among the most successful of Western exports. Asian consumers alone spend $90 billion a year on cigarettes, and Western tobacco manufacturers continue to push relentlessly into these markets. Cigarette advertising, often depicting glamorous Western models and settings, is found just about everywhere, on hoardings, buses, shopfronts and clothing, and many major sports and cultural events are sponsored by tobacco companies. Some companies even hand out cigarettes and gifts in amusement areas, often to pre-teens.

A few countries have taken steps to counteract this form of Westernization. Singapore bans all promotions that mention a product's name. Hong Kong has prohibited cigarette ads from appearing on radio and TV. Japan and South Korea do not allow ads to appear in women's magazines. Industry executives argue that they are simply competing in markets that do little to discourage smoking (e.g. Japan issues health warnings like 'Please don't smoke too much'), often against heavily subsidized local brands with names like Long Life (Taiwan). The warnings and restrictions are likely to increase, however: smoking-related deaths have now overtaken communicable diseases for the 'honour' of being Asia's No. 1 killer.[90]

Postmodernism?

Many of the themes mentioned earlier in this section, such as the globalization process, reality engineering or the blurring of the fashion picture, have been linked to larger social processes dominating the last part of the twentieth century. One proposed summary term for these processes is **postmodernism** – one of the most widely discussed and disputed terms in consumer research in the past five years.[91]

Postmodernists argue that we live in a modern era where we share beliefs in certain central values of modernism and industrialism. Examples of these values include the benefits of economic growth and industrial production, and the infallibility of science. In opposition, postmodernism questions the search for universal truths and values, and the existence of objective knowledge.[92] Thus a keyword is **pluralism**, indicating the coexistence of various truths, styles and fashions. Consumers (and producers) are relatively free to combine elements from different styles and domains to create their own personal expression.

There have been several attempts to sum up features of postmodernism and their implications for marketing and consumer behaviour.[93] Together with pluralism, one European researcher has suggested that postmodernism can be described by six key features:[94]

- **Fragmentation**. The splitting up of what used to be simpler and more mass-oriented, exemplified by the ever-growing product ranges and brand extensions in more and more specialized variations. Even within the retailing environment we experience the proliferation of outlets within the concentration of bigger outlets (shopping malls). Such specialized and stylized outlets often carry an in-depth assortment of a very narrow product range, such as teas or ties. The advertising media have also become fragmented, with more and more specialized TV channels, magazines, radio stations and websites for placing one's advertising.

- **De-differentiation**. Postmodernists are interested in the blurring of distinctions between hierarchies such as 'high and low culture', or 'politics and show business'. Examples would be the use of artistic works in advertising and the celebration of advertising as artistic works. Companies such as Coca-Cola, Nike and Guinness have their own museums. Another clear example is the blurring of advertisements and TV programmes, wherein more and more TV programmes feature advertising for themselves (in order to increase viewer ratings) and TV commercials look like 'real' programming, as in the ongoing soap opera with a couple spun around the coffee brand Gold Blend. The blurring of gender categories also refers to this aspect of postmodernism.

- **Hyperreality**. The spreading of simulations and the loss of the sense of the 'real' and the 'authentic', as in the cases of re-engineered environments discussed earlier in this chapter, or in shopping centres simulating ancient Rome (The Forum in Las Vegas) or a Parisian street (West Edmonton Mall, Canada). Finally, products can be hyperreal to the extent that they simulate something else: for instance, sugarless sugar, fat-free fat (olestra) or the butter replacement brand I Can't Believe It's Not Butter! In fact, it has been argued that marketing may be the most important contributor to the creation of hyperreality, since the essence of marketing and particularly advertising is to create a simulated reality by resignifying words, situations and brands.[95]

- **Chronology**. This refers to the consumer's search for the authentic and a preoccupation with the past – like real or authentic Chinese or Italian foods or the

MARKETING PITFALL

Sometimes companies may fall victim to their own hyperreality. It is the dream of many producers to create a strong brand with a solid position in cultural life. But as they do so, their brand images are incorporated into the general cultural sign system, and the company loses control over the signs attached to the brand name. For example, the name 'Barbie' today is much more than a brand name – it has almost become a name for a personality type. When a Danish pop group, Aqua, enjoyed a huge success with the song 'Barbie', which contained lyrics alluding to the sex life of this hyperreal personality (e.g. 'you can dress my hair, undress me everywhere'), the Mattel Inc. Company was not amused. They sued the pop group for abuse of the Barbie name and for destroying the pure and positive image of Barbie's world created through a long range of expensive campaigns. This is yet another example of the blurring of marketing and popular culture, and the question is: can you patent culture?[96]

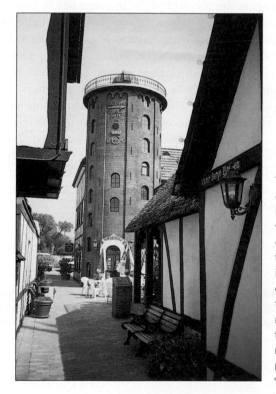

The seventeenth-century Danish landmark of the 'round tower' of Copenhagen has been recreated (in a slightly smaller version) in the simulated Danish environment of Solvang, California, founded as a 'little Denmark' by Danish immigrants in the nineteenth century, but gradually becoming more of a hyperreal theme park under the influence of marketing in the postwar period. The tower in Solvang houses a local pizza restaurant: Tower Pizza, of course!
Photo: Søren Askegaard.

search for one's nostalgic roots in foods (or other consumer goods) as we 'used to know it'.[97] Likewise, the increase in the 'no-nonsense' formats of various advertising campaigns may be seen as a return to a simpler, less contrived period of the past. What appeals to consumers here is that in a period of accelerating change, the stability of the good old days remains comforting.

● **Pastiche**. The playful and ironic mixing of existing categories and styles is typical of pastiche. An example would be one advertisement doing a parody of another or making references to slogans or other elements borrowed from other campaigns. Pastiche also involves self-referentiality (i.e. the advertisement recognizes itself as being an ad, by showing (mock) scenes from its own creative process). Table 17.1 provides a set of examples of such parodies and self-referentialities from British advertising. Self-referentiality may create hyperreality, as when a

British ad for the Yellow Pages featuring an author searching for a retail store where he could find a copy of his own old book about fly fishing actually led to the writing of such a book. Needless to say, when the book was launched, the advertisement was re-run![98]

Other pastiches flourish, as when we see deliberate blurring of styles such as advertisements borrowing from films, or films and TV programmes borrowing from the advertisement style, all of it done 'tongue-in-cheek'. A British ad for cream depicted a Mona Lisa looking first to one side, then to the other, then she would draw out an éclair (cake with cream) and munch it, followed by the pay-off line: 'Naughty but nice'.[99] Indeed, one discussion of postmodernism and its impact on marketing was in itself a pastiche using a lot of cinematic metaphors and changed film titles to structure its chapters.[100]

● • **Anti-foundationalism**. This last feature of postmodern marketing efforts refers not to parody but to an outright 'anti-campaign campaign' – for example campaigns encouraging the receiver of the message *not* to take notice of the message since somebody is trying to seduce and take advantage of him or her. Other examples include anti-product products like 'death brand cigarettes', Jolt Cola ('with all the caffeine and twice the sugar'[101]) or the Icelandic Aquavit brand's appropriation of its own nickname 'black death', complete with new labels including skulls. Finally, there's 'anti-fashion' – consumers' claims that they search for certain types of ugliness when buying shoes and clothing in order to construct a very personal and ostentatious style (sound like anyone you know?).[102] The green movement and the political consumer discussed above, as well as groups involved in movements of voluntary simplicity (particularly active in the United States) or the like, can be seen as anti-foundational in their rejection of standard products in favour of alternative choices which they perceive as less harmful to the natural and human environments.

Postmodernism has also been attached to such themes as the ability of readers to see through the hype of advertising.[103] This may suggest that we are becoming more

Table 17.1 A few examples of pastiche in British advertising

Category	Content	Examples
Parody		
Direct	One advertisement parodies another	Carling Black Label (lager) spoof of Levi's (jeans) celebrated 'laundrette' sequence
Indirect	Advert 'appropriates' byline/icon etc. of another	Do It All (DIY superstores) advertised 'the united colors of Do It All' (Benetton)
Self-referentiality		
Direct	Adverts about advertising (set in advertising agency; adverts for forthcoming ads, etc.)	Next 'instalment' of advertising soap operas (Renault 21 family; Gold Blend couple, etc.) advertised beforehand
Indirect	Retransmission of old adverts that have acquired new meanings in the interim, or stylistic evocation of old ads	Repeat showings of 'I'm going well, I'm going Shell' series featuring Bing Crosby, etc. Once innovative, now quaint

skilled consumers and readers/interpreters of advertising, recognizing ads as hyper-real persuasion or seduction attempts which do not intend to reflect our own daily experiences. This skilled readership may have sparked various of the tendencies to anti-ads or pastiches discussed above. Younger consumers especially may be prone to detect and enjoy the self-referentiality or intertextuality of advertising.[104]

Another process attached to postmodernism is the greater significance of the aesthetics of everyday life, referring to the tendency to focus more and more on the design and appearance of goods or objects. According to this view, the style and imagery attached to consumer objects becomes of primary importance when judging your purchase. Indeed, some may argue that the consumer lifestyle in itself becomes a kind of work of art. More and more people act as if they are the main character in the film about their own life, and their activities and styles have to be selected carefully in order to meet the quality and excitement criteria of this personally staged biography.[105]

Certain postmodernists stress the liberatory aspects of postmodernism – that consumers are free to play with symbols and create their own constellations of products and lifestyles from available elements while being less concerned with norms and standards. Since there is an inherent scepticism in postmodernism, a postmodernist attitude is also a critical attitude.[106] Others point to the fact that the refusal to accept, indeed to *care* about, values, may lead to passivity and political degeneration of societies[107] and to the inherent contradictions within the positions taken by postmodernists.[108] Whether one sees the 'postmodern consumer' as a critical and creative person, or as a passive, entertainment-seeking 'couch potato', the changes in marketing and consumption referred to in the postmodern framework are fundamental for understanding changes in our European markets as we move into the twenty-first century.

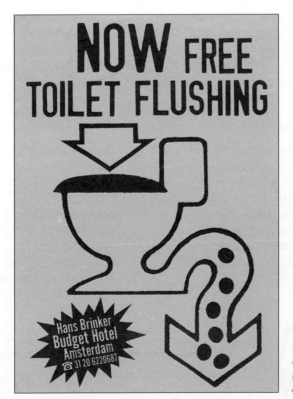

Self-parody is one approach to communication in our postmodern era.
Used with permission.

Chapter summary

- The *green movement* is a common denominator in the trend towards increased attention to the environmental impact of human activities. In terms of consumption, this has broadened the scope of enviromental judgement from recycling of scarce resources to attention to the whole production and distribution process.

- The green movement may be an indication of an even broader trend towards more conscious reflection on the ethical aspects of consumption. The *political consumer* 'votes with his/her shopping basket' in an attempt to influence companies to care for the natural as well as the human environment, adding issues such as human rights to the set of dimensions that influence purchases.

- Followers of an *etic perspective* believe that the same universal messages will be appreciated by people in many cultures. Believers in an *emic perspective* argue that individual cultures are too unique to permit such standardization: marketers instead must adapt their approaches to be consistent with local values and practices. Attempts at global marketing have met with mixed success: in many cases this approach is more likely to work if the messages appeal to basic values and/or if the target markets consist of consumers who are more internationally rather than locally oriented.

- The Western world is a net exporter of popular culture. Consumers around the world have eagerly adopted Western products, especially entertainment vehicles and items that are linked symbolically to a uniquely Western lifestyle (e.g. Marlboro, Levi's, BMW, Nestlé). Despite or because of the continuing 'Americanization' or 'Westernization' of cultures in the world, some consumers are alarmed by this influence, and are instead emphasizing a return to local products and customs.

- Postmodernism involves processes of social change in an era, where the 'grand truths' of modernism such as scientific knowledge or the progressiveness of economic growth are no longer taken for granted. Postmodernism includes social processes such as fragmentation, de-differentiation, hyperreality, chronology, pastiche and anti-foundationalism.

KEY TERMS

Anti-foundationalism (*p. 562*)
Chronology (*p. 560*)
Creolization (*p. 557*)
De-differentiation (*p. 560*)
Emic perspective (*p. 549*)
Environmentalism (*p. 543*)
Etic perspective (*p. 549*)
Fragmentation (*p. 560*)
Globalization (*p. 558*)

Hyperreality (*p. 560*)
National character (*p. 550*)
Pastiche (*p. 561*)
Pluralism (*p. 560*)
Political consumer (*p. 545*)
Postmodernism (*p. 560*)
Recycling (*p. 541*)
Risk society (*p. 544*)
Transitional economies (*p. 556*)

For additional material see the companion website at:
www.booksites.net/solomon_euro

Consumer behaviour challenge

1. In your opinion, in which areas have environmental issues had the biggest impact on consumer behaviour? Why do you think that is the case?

2. Is the 'political consumer' a fad or a new and growing challenge for marketers and producers? Discuss.

3. Go to your local supermarket to check the selection of ecological products. How are they presented in the store? What does that say about the way these products are regarded?

4. Try to provide an estimate about how often environmental issues are mentioned in advertising. Are these messages credible? Why or why not?

5. What do you think about boycotts as consumers' response to what is perceived as companies' unethical behaviour?

6. What role does the globalization process play in your personal consumption profile? After reflecting on that, take a walk in your nearest shopping area and look for signs of the global and the local. What is from 'somewhere else'? What is distinctively local? Are there mixtures, or are these two domains separate?

7. Try to collect advertisements that reflect the postmodern features of fragmentation, de-differentiation, hyperreality, chronology, pastiche and anti-foundationalism.

8. Reflect on your and your friends' consumption patterns in the same light. What do you see?

Notes

1. Andrew Crane, 'Facing the Backlash: Green Marketing and Strategic Reorientation in the 1990s', *Journal of Strategic Marketing* 8 (2000): 277–96.

2. John Thøgersen, 'Making Ends Meet: A Synthesis of Research on Consumer Behaviour and the Environment', Working Paper 99-1 (The Aarhus School of Business: Dept of Marketing, 1999).

3. James Fitchett and Andrea Prothero, 'Contradictions and Opportunities for a Green Commodity', in E. Arnould and L. Scott, eds, *Advances in Consumer Research* 26 (Provo, UT: Association for Consumer Research, 1999): 272–5.

4. Mike Tharp, 'Tchaikovsky and Toilet Paper', *U.S. News and World Report* (December 1987): 62; B. Van Voorst, 'The Recycling Bottleneck', *Time* (14 September 1992): 52–4; Richard P. Bagozzi and Pratibha A. Dabholkar, 'Consumer Recycling Goals and Their Effect on Decisions to Recycle: A Means–End Chain Analysis', *Psychology & Marketing* 11 (July/August1994) 4: 313–40.

5. 'Finally, Something at McDonald's You Can Actually Eat', *Utne Reader* (May–June 1997): 12.

6. Philip Pan, 'Chop Shoo-ey', *Washington Post* (30 January 2001).

7. Debra J. Dahab, James W. Gentry and Wanru Su, 'New Ways to Reach Non-Recyclers: An Extension of the Model of Reasoned Action to Recycling Behaviors', in Frank Kardes and Mita Sujan, eds, *Advances in Consumer Research* 22 (Provo, UT: Association for Consumer Research, 1994): 251–6.

8. Rik G. M. Pieters, 'Changing Garbage Disposal Patterns of Consumers: Motivation, Ability, and Performance', *Journal of Public Policy and Marketing* 10(2) (1991): 59–76.

9. Richard P. Bagozzi and Pratibha A. Dabholkar, 'Consumer Recycling Goals and Their Effect on Decisions to Recycle: A Means–End Chain Analysis', *Psychology & Marketing* 11 (July/August 1994): 5; see also L. J. Shrum, Tina M. Lowrey and John A. McCarty, 'Recycling as a Marketing Problem: A Framework for Strategy Development', *Psychology & Marketing* 11 (July/August 1994) 4: 393–416.

10. John Thøgersen, 'Wasteful Food Consumption: Trends in Food and Packaging Waste', in W. F. van Raaij and G. Bamossy, eds, *European Advances in Consumer Research* 1 (Provo, UT: Association for Consumer Research, 1993): 434–9.

11. Suzanne C. Grunert, 'Antecedents of Source Separation Behaviour: A Comparison of Two Danish Municipalities', in *Marketing for an Expanding Europe*, Proceedings of the 25th EMAC Conference, ed. J. Berács, A. Bauer and J. Simon (Budapest: Budapest University of Economic Sciences, 1996): 525–37.

12. 'Global markedsføring af danske miljøløsninger', *Markedsføring* 8 (1995): 12.

13. Manfred Kirchgeorg, 'Kreislaufwirtschaft – Neue Herausforderungen für das Marketing', *Marketing ZFP* 4 (4th Quarter 1995): 232–48.

14. Timothy Aeppel, 'From License Plates to Fashion Plates', *Wall Street Journal* (21 September 1994): B1 (2).

15. *Advertising Age* (2 May 1992).

16. Giampaolo Fabris, 'Consumer Studies: New Perspectives', *Marketing and Research Today* (June 1990): 67–73.

17. Walter Hopfenbeck, *The Green Management Revolution: Lessons in Environmental Excellence* (Englewood Cliffs, NJ: Prentice-Hall, 1993).

18. Armin Herker, 'Eine Erklärung des Umweltbewußten Konsumentenverhaltens', *Marketing ZFP* 3 (3rd Quarter, 1995): 149–61.

19. Suzanne C. Grunert, 'Everybody Seems Concerned About the Environment: But is This Concern Reflected in (Danish) Consumers' Food Choice?', in van Raaij and Bamossy, eds, *European Advances in Consumer Research* 1: 428–33.

20. Carolyn Strong, 'A Preliminary Investigation: A Step Towards an Understanding of Children as Environmentally Conscious Consumers', in *Marketing for an Expanding Europe*: 2139–49.

21. Paul M. W. Hackett, 'Consumers' Environmental Concern Values: Understanding the Structure of Contemporary Green Worldviews', in van Raaij and Bamossy, eds, *European Advances in Consumer Research* 1 (Provo, UT: Association for Consumer Research): 416–27.

22. Jean-Luc Gianneloni, 'The Combined Effect of Age, Level of Education and Personal Values on the Attitude Towards the Protection of the Environment', *Marketing Today and for the 21st Century*, Proceedings of the 24th EMAC Conference, ed. Michelle Bergadaà (Cergy-Pontoise: ESSEC, 1995): 373–89.

23. Suzanne C. Grunert and Kai Kristensen, 'The Green Consumer: Some Danish Evidence', *Marketing for Europe – Marketing for the Future*, Proceedings of the 21st EMAC Conference, ed. K. G. Grunert and D. Fuglede (Aarhus: The Aarhus School of Business, 1992): 525–39.

24. J. Robert Skalnik, Patricia Skalnik and David Smith, 'Growth Hormones in Milk-Producing Cows: For the Consumer, Much Ado About Nothing ... Perhaps', in Flemming Hansen, ed., *European Advances in Consumer Research* 2 (Provo, UT: Association for Consumer Research): 201–3.

25. Andrew P. Smith, James A. Young and Jan Gibson, 'How Now, Mad-Cow? Consumer Confidence and Source Credibility During the 1996 BSE Scare', *European Journal of Marketing* 33(11/12) (1999): 1107–22.

26. 'Mad-Cow Scare Pulls Italy's Head From the Sand' *Wall Street Journal* (17 January 2001): A21.

27. SIFO survey, reported in *Aftonbladet* (5 February 2001): 8–9.

28. Ulrich Beck, *Risk Society* (London: Sage Publications, 1992).

29. Karin Ekström and Søren Askegaard, 'Daily Consumption in Risk Society: The Case of Genetically Modified Foods', in S. Hoch and R. Meyer, eds, *Advances in Consumer Research* 27 (Provo, UT: Association for Consumer Research, 2000): 237–43.

30. Lone Bredahl, 'Determinants of Consumer Attitudes and Purchase Intentions with Regard to Genetically Modified Foods – Results from a Cross-National Survey', MAPP Working Paper no. 69 (Aarhus: The Aarhus School of Business, 2000).

31. Klaus Grunert, 'Consumers' Attitudes to Genetically Modified Foods', research presentation, Lund University, 8 March 2001.

32. Bente Halkier, 'Consequences of the Politicization of Consumption: The Example of Environmentally Friendly Consumption Practices', *Journal of Environmental Policy & Planning* 1 (1999): 25–41.

33. *www.cokespotlight.org*; see also *www.adbusters.org* and *www.corpspotlight.org*.

34. Kalle Lasn, 'Culture Jamming', in J. B. Schor and D. B. Holt, eds, *The Consumer Society Reader* (New York: The New Press, 2000): 414–32.

35. 'Vand for livet – et unikt kampagnesamarbejde', *Markedsføring* 5 (1996): 2.

36. 'BT Pushes Community Role', *Marketing* (12 December 1996): 9.

37. 'Crossing the Moral Minefield', *Marketing* (22 June 1995): 11.

38. 'Oil and Troubled Waters', *Marketing* (29 June 1995): 13.

39. 'Bordeaux vil generobre den tabte hyldeplads', *Markedsføring* 12 (1996): 6.

40. Marcus Mabry, 'Do Boycotts Work?', *Newsweek* (6 July 1992) 3: 35.

41. George Ritzer, *The McDonaldization of Society* (Thousand Oaks: Pine Forge Press, 1993); George Ritzer, *The McDonaldization Thesis* (Thousand Oaks: Pine Forge Press, 1998).

42. José Bové & François Dufour, *Le monde n'est pas une marchandise. Des paysans contre la malbouffe* (Paris: La Découverte, 2000).

43. Theodore Levitt, *The Marketing Imagination* (New York: The Free Press, 1983).

44. Terry Clark, 'International Marketing and National Character: A Review and Proposal for an Integrative Theory', *Journal of Marketing* 54 (October 1990): 66–79.

45. Kevin Cote, 'The New Shape of Europe', *Advertising Age* (9 November 1988): 98.

46. Steven Prokesch, 'Selling in Europe: Borders Fade', *New York Times* (31 May 1990): D1.

47. 'Abroadminded', *Marketing* (24 April 1997): 20–1.

48. Julie Skur Hill and Joseph M. Winski, 'Goodbye Global Ads: Global Village is Fantasy Land for Marketers', *Advertising Age* (16 November 1987): 22; Margaret K. Hogg and Maria H. Savolainen, 'Symbolic Consumption and the Situational Self', in Basil Englis and Anna Olofsson, eds, *European Advances in Consumer Research* 3 (Provo, UT: Association for Consumer Research, 1998).

49. 'Packaging Draws Protest', *Marketing News* (4 July 1994): 1.

50. Laurel Anderson Hudson and Marsha Wadkins, 'Japanese Popular Art as Text: Advertising's Clues to Understanding the Consumer', *International Journal of Research in Marketing* 4 (1988): 259–72.

51. David Alexander, 'Condom Controversy: Suggestive KamaSutra Ads Arouse India', *Advertising Age International* (27 April 1992): I-12.

52. Yumiko Ono, 'Tambrands Ads Try to Scale Cultural, Religious Obstacles', *Wall Street Journal Interactive Edition* (17 March 1997), *http://interactive4.wsj.com/archive*.

53. Hill and Winski, 'Goodbye Global Ads'.

54. Søren Askegaard and Fabian Csaba, 'The Good, the Bad and the Jolly: Taste, Image and the Symbolic Resistance to the Coca-Colonization of Denmark', in S. Brown and A. Patterson, eds, *Imagining Marketing* (London: Routledge, 2001): 124–240.

55. See, for example, Russell W. Belk and Güliz Ger, 'Problems of Marketization in Romania and Turkey', *Research in Consumer Behavior* 7 (Greenwich, CT: JAI Press, 1994): 123–55.

56. Russell W. Belk, 'Consumption Patterns of the New Elite in Zmbabwe', paper presented at the Association for Consumer Research Conference, Salt Lake City, 16–19 October 2000.

57. See also Ulf Hannerz, 'Cosmopolitans and Locals in World Culture', in Mike Featherstone, ed., *Global Culture* (London: Sage, 1990): 237–52.

58. 'Abroadminded'.

59. Eric J. Arnould and Richard R. Wilk, 'Why Do the Natives Wear Adidas?: Anthropological Approaches to Consumer Research', in Elisabeth C. Hirschman and Morris B Holbrook, eds, *Advances in Consumer Research* 12 (Provo, UT: Association for Consumer Research, 1985): 748–52.

60. Robert LaFranco, 'Long-Lived Kitsch', *Forbes* (26 February 1996): 68.

61. Dana Milbank, 'Made in America Becomes a Boast in Europe', *Wall Street Journal* (19 January 1994): B1 (2).

62. Suman Dubey, 'Kellogg Invites India's Middle Class to Breakfast of Ready-to-Eat Cereal', *Wall Street Journal* (29 August 1994): B3B.

63. Giana Eckhardt and Humaira Mahi, 'Globalization and the Consumer in Emerging Markets: India Will Survive', paper presented at the Association for Consumer Research Conference, Salt Lake City, 16–19 October 2000.

64. 'They All Want to be Like Mike', *Fortune* (21 July 1997): 51–3.

65. Tara Parker-Pope, 'Will the British Warm up to Iced Tea? Some Big Marketers are Counting on It', *Wall Street Journal* (22 August 1994): B1 (2).

66. John Tagliabue, 'Proud Palaces of Italian Cusine Await Pizza Hut', *New York Times* (1 September 1994): A4.

67. David K. Tse, Russell W. Belk and Nan Zhou, 'Becoming a Consumer Society: A Longitudinal and Cross-Cultural Content Analysis of Print Ads from Hong Kong, the People's Republic of China, and Taiwan', *Journal of Consumer Research* 15 (March 1989): 457–72; see also Annamma Joy, 'Marketing in Modern China: An Evolutionary Perspective', *CJAS* (June 1990): 55–67, for a review of changes in Chinese marketing practices since the economic reforms of 1978.

68. Quoted in Sheryl WuDunn, 'Cosmetics from the West Help to Change the Face of China', *New York Times* (6 May 1990): 16.

69. John F. Sherry, Jr and Eduardo G. Camargo, '"May Your Life be Marvelous": English Language Labeling and the Semiotics of Japanese Promotion', *Journal of Consumer Research* 14 (September 1987): 174–88.

70. Bill Bryson, 'A Taste for Scrambled English', *New York Times* (22 July 1990): 10; Rose A. Horowitz, 'California Beach Culture Rides Wave of Popularity in Japan', *Journal of Commerce* (3 August 1989): 17; Elaine Lafferty, 'American Casual Seizes Japan: Teenagers Go for N.F.L. Hats, Batman and the California Look', *Time* (13 November 1989): 106.

71. Lucy Howard and Gregory Cerio, 'Goofy Goods', *Newsweek* (15 August 1994): 8.

72. Prof. Russell Belk, University of Utah, personal communication, 25 July 1997.

73. Material in this section adapted from Ger and Belk, 'I'd Like to Buy the World a Coke: Consumptionscapes of the "Less Affluent World"', *Journal of Consumer Policy* 19(3) (1996): 271–304; Russell W. Belk, 'Romanian Consumer Desires and Feelings of Deservingness', in Lavinia Stan, ed., *Romania in Transition* (Hanover, NH: Dartmouth Press, 1997): 191–208; cf. also Güliz Ger, 'Human Development and Humane Consumption: Well Being Beyond the Good Life', *Journal of Public Policy and Marketing* 16(1) (1997): 110–25.

74. Prof. Güliz Ger, Bilkent University, Turkey, personal communication, 25 July 1997.

75. Erazim Kohák, 'Ashes, Ashes ... Central Europe After Forty Years', *Daedalus* 121 (Spring 1992): 197–215, at 219, quoted in Belk, 'Romanian Consumer Desires and Feelings of Deservingness'.

76. Elena Milanova, 'Consumer Behavior in an Economy

of Distress', in Arnould and Scott, eds, *Advances in Consumer Research* 26: 424-30.

77. Natasha Tolstikova, 'MMM as a Phenomenon of the Russian Consumer Culture', in B. Dubois, T. Lowrey, L. J. Shrum and M. Vanhuele, eds, *European Advances in Consumer Research* 4 (Provo, UT: Association for Consumer Research, 1999): 208-15.

78. Güliz Ger, 'The Positive and Negative Effects of Marketing on Socioeconomic Development: The Turkish Case', *Journal of Consumer Policy* 15 (1992): 229-54.

79. This example courtesy of Prof. Russell Belk, University of Utah, personal communication, 25 July 1997.

80. Jennifer Cody, 'Now Marketers in Japan Stress the Local Angle', *Wall Street Journal* (23 February 1994): B1 (2).

81. Ger and Belk, 'I'd Like to Buy the World a Coke: Consumptionscapes of the "Less Affluent World"'.

82. Steven Greenhouse, 'The Television Europeans Love, and Love to Hate', *New York Times* (13 August 1989): 24.

83. Charles Goldsmith and Charles Fleming, 'Film Industry in Europe Seeks Wider Audience', *Wall Street Journal* (6 December 1993): B1 (2).

84. Sherry and Camargo, '"May Your Life Be Marvelous"; 'French Council Eases Language Ban', *New York Times* (31 July 1994): 12.

85. Quoted in Alan Riding, 'Only the French Elite Scorn Mickey's Debut', *New York Times* (1992) 2: A1.

86. Allison James, 'Cooking the Books: Global or Local Identities in Contemporary British Food Cultures?', in David Howes, ed., *Cross-Cultural Consumption* (London: Routledge, 1996): 77-92.

87. Ibid.: 89.

88. Ayse S. Caglar, 'McDöner Kebap and the Social Positioning Struggle of German Turks', in J. A. Arnold and G. J. Bamossy, eds, *Marketing in a Multicultural World: Ethnicity, Nationalism, and Cultural Identity* (London: Sage, 1995): 209-30.

89. A. Fuat Firat, 'Globalization of Fragmentation - A Framework for Understanding Contemporary Global Markets', *Journal of International Marketing* 5(2) (1997): 77-86.

90. Mike Levin, 'U.S. Tobacco Firms Push Eagerly into Asian Market', *Marketing News* (21 January 1991) 2: 2.

91. Two special issues of *International Journal of Research in Marketing* 10(3) (1993) and 11(4) (1994), both edited by A. Fuat Firat, John F. Sherry, Jr and Alladi Venkatesh, have been decisive for the introduction of themes of postmodernism in marketing and consumer research.

92. Craig J. Thompson, 'Modern Truth and Postmodern Incredulity: A Hermeneutic Deconstruction of the Metanarrative of "Scientific Truth" in Marketing

Research', *International Journal of Research in Marketing* 10(3) (1993): 325-38.

93. See, for example, A. Fuat Firat and Alladi Venkatesh, 'Postmodernity: The Age of Marketing', *International Journal of Research in Marketing* 10(3) (1993): 227-49; James Ogilvy, 'This Postmodern Business', *Marketing and Research Today* (February 1990): 4-22; W. Fred van Raaij, 'Postmodern Consumption', *Journal of Economic Psychology* 14 (1993): 541-63.

94. Stephen Brown, *Postmodern Marketing* (London: Routledge, 1995): 106ff.

95. Fuat Firat and Venkatesh, 'Postmodernity: The Age of Marketing'.

96. Eric Arnould and Søren Askegaard, 'HyperCulture: The Next Stage in the Globalization of Consumption', paper presented at the 1997 Annual Association for Consumer Research Conference in Denver, Colorado, 16-19 October.

97. Cf. James, 'Cooking the Books'.

98. Brown, *Postmodern Marketing*.

99. Judith Williamson, *Consuming Passions: The Dynamics of Popular Culture* (London: Marion Boyars, 1988).

100. Stephen Brown, 'Marketing as Multiplex: Screening Postmodernism', *European Journal of Marketing* 28(8/9) (1994): 27-51.

101. Brown, *Postmodern Marketing*.

102. Anne F. Jensen and Søren Askegaard, *In Pursuit of Ugliness: On the Complexity of the Fashion Concept After the Era of Good Taste*, Working Paper in Marketing no. 14 (Odense University: School of Business and Economics, 1997).

103. Richard Elliott, Susan Eccles and Michelle Hodgson, 'Re-coding Gender Representations: Women, Cleaning Products, and Advertising's "New Man"', *International Journal of Research in Marketing* 10(3) (1993): 311-24.

104. Stephanie O'Donohoe, 'Raiding the Postmodern Pantry: Advertising Intertextuality and the Young Adult Audience', *European Journal of Marketing* 31(3/4) (1997): 234-53.

105. Mike Featherstone, *Consumer Culture and Postmodernisn* (London: Sage, 1991).

106. A. Fuat Firat and Alladi Venkatesh, 'Liberatory Postmodernism and the Reenchantment of Consumption', *Journal of Consumer Research* 22 (December 1995): 239-67.

107. Dominique Bouchet, 'Rails Without Ties: The Social Imaginary and Postmodern Culture. Can Postmodern Consumption replace Modern Questioning?', *International Journal of Research in Marketing* 11(4) (1993): 405-22.

108. Brown, 'Marketing as Multiplex: Screening Postmodernism'.

CASE STUDY 10

Alessi: Italian design and the re-enchantment of everyday objects

BENOÎT HEILBRUNN, E.M. Lyon

One of the main characteristics of consumer society is the serialization of objects and their subsequent loss of uniqueness, distinctness and authenticity due to their ever increasing reproduction and diffusion. The fact that objects are repeatedly produced leads to a fade-out of meaning of most of these everyday objects, which in turn become mere commodities and thus lose their substance. This loss of meaning of most consumer objects is partly due to a societal shift from craftsmanship to industrialization which leads to serialization of objects, and partly due to a marketing approach based on the design of objects which respond most closely to consumer needs and therefore exclude a surprise effect. This phenomenon inevitably leads to an impoverishment of sensory experience and a loss of a relationship with objects. Consider the fact that at the beginning of the nineteenth century, a four-person, average-income family was surrounded by only 150 to 200 objects at the most (including crockery and clothes), and that nowadays, a similar family owns between 2500 and 3000 objects, including electrical appliances and decorative objects. Today, a person is said to come into daily contact with approximately 20,000 products. Consumers thus often seem to be immersed in an uncontrolled number of signs and confronted with the well-known phenomenon of semiotic pollution.

Therefore, designers have to invent products and design signs which can survive in a consumption and societal environment saturated with a tremendous and ever-increasing number of product and signs. Design thus has an essential role in giving meaning to objects through shapes, colours and materials. Also, the penetration of science and technology into our daily environment has eliminated most technical barriers to the production of objects. New forms and functions can now be used, thus enlarging the field of possibilities and the creative abilities of designers.

One of the most remarkable examples of this will to poetize life through object design is the Italian company Alessi, which was founded in 1921 by Giovanni Alessi. The first articles produced were coffee pots and trays, which were soon followed by a large series of accessories for table service. The company, now in its fourth generation, is headed by Alberto Alessi who has recruited renowned industrial designers and architects to create signature products for the company. This venture has been extremely successful with many objects becoming cult objects such as Aldo Rossi's conical kettle, Philippe Starck's juicer and Michael Graves's bird kettle. At present production is grouped under the trademarks Alessi (mass production, mainly of steel and plastic), Officina Alessi (small or medium series production in different metals: silver, nickel silver, titanium, brass, stainless steel, iron, tin-plate), Tendentse (porcelain) and Twergi (wood).

Officina Alessi is extremely representative of a design tradition which focuses more on existential values than on the mere utilitarian approach to objects. This new Alessi trademark was introduced in 1983 to identify an aspect of the company's activity which in the past had remained in books of blueprints or at the prototype state. Their objective is to research and experiment with innovative forms, styles, functions and methods of manufacture, free from the limits usually imposed by industrial mass production. The company wants to offer a wide range of products which combine both sophisticated industrial technology and traditional handicraft processes to a keen and culturally curious public. In particular the use of 'historical' metals such as nickel silver, brass, copper silver and tin are chosen not only for their intrinsic value, but also to match the characteristics of each design (Presentation catalogue of Officina Alessi, 1994). According to the circumstances, the results take the form of standard production, or a limited series or even unique pieces. For instance, Officina Alessi launched a series of Tea and Coffee Piazzas which were commissioned from 11 internationally recognized architects. The 11 sets were each produced in limited editions of 99, priced individually at about £12,000, and in 1983 galleries in Milan and New York simultaneously hosted their launch, thus reinforcing the cultural status and economic exclusivity of the objects.

What this example of design innovation illustrates is that, even though the shape of an object more or less follows its function, the shape of an object may by far overlap its function. There is always a degree of freedom which gives the designer the opportunity to disconnect (sometimes quite radically) form from function. If the shape of the object always more or less indicates its use, it also adds an inescapable aesthetic dimension which may contribute to a real redefinition of the object. Therefore design really means 'to illuminate, to clarify, to modify, to dignify, to dramatize, to persuade, and perhaps even to amuse' (Rand 1993:3). This definition, given by an American designer, points out two approaches to design which refer to two distinct traditions in Europe. The first approach considers design as a way to clarify and to persuade. This approach may be said to be characteristic of German and Nordic design of which companies like Braun and Bang & Olufsen may be considered very representative. In these countries, design appears to be more functional in the sense that it aims at expressing the mere function of the object. The approach to the object is essentially seen as utilitarian because the object design has to persuade the user that it serves particular functions. The role of design is to convey an impression of effectiveness, solidity, through appropriate features, colours and materials.

The second approach, which is usually more representative of southern European countries (Italy, Spain, partly France), tends to develop objects with stronger existential connotations, such as emotional values (the object design has to arouse feeling and affective state), ludic values (the object is considered as a potential game) and epistemic values (the ability of the product to arouse curiosity and to provide novelty). This approach to design refers to the necessity of consumers to live new experiences through the use of products which provide innovative combinations of shape, materials, colours, etc. The importance of these existential values in the choice of products and brands, and therefore in the way consumers perceive the design of products, is also related to hedonistic consumption which is a very important paradigm of consumption in these countries.

The design philosophy promoted by Alberto Alessi is highly representative of this second approach in the sense that it aims at overcoming both technological and marketing constraints which dominate the actual production of consumer goods and result in a world of anonymous and impassive objects. The company's mission is hence seen as a way to literally poetize everyday objects. At the same time, the company is also preoccupied with the functional dimension of objects, as illustrated by this quote from Alessandro Mendini (who designed the Falstaff pots for Alessi):

> with their simple elegance the Falstaff pots seek to present a group of utensils, that harmonise with the kitchen surroundings and at the same time enhance the practise of that supreme domestic culinary art of gastronomy . . . They arc model pots of the latest generation, a design intended as a multiple art form, a kitchen landscape with pots . . . At work and at rest, they form a bouquet of reflectively polished, convex objects, discreetly present; sometimes slightly invisible; sometimes brilliantly present perhaps poetic kitchen sculptures. Actors perhaps, that tell us mysterious tales while they cook . . . Stressing the idea of play, of magic, invention and ritual, present today in the pleasure of performing numerous ancient actions that are no longer a chore but actually fun – for example, the act of cooking itself. (Presentation catalogue of the Falstaff collection)

The implicit objective is to transform everyday consumer objects into objects of aesthetic contemplation through the application of colour, pattern and additional elements. It also means there is no single meaning assigned to an object, but on the contrary, a plurality of meanings. An object is different from a tool in the sense that it does not necessarily boil down to a mere utilitarian function. The objective of a brand like Alessi is to break the conventional codes of representation of the object to transform an apparently boring practice (cooking) into a joy and a pleasing activity.

This leads to a real exploration of the communicative boundaries of design illustrated by the juicer designed by Philippe Starck, which looks like a rocket, or the

Alessi's rocket-style juicer, designed by Philippe Starck, 1990–1

Conical kettle designed by Michael Graves. These objects propose totally new approaches to familiar objects. By breaking the usual codes of representation, the designer opens the object to a multitude of meanings, which contribute to re-semantizing the objects beyond their functional purpose. Thus the design of any object implies two dimensions: (1) an *endophoric* dimension which guarantees that the object belongs to a certain class and organizes the invariable elements, and (2) an *exophoric* dimension which allows for radical formal innovation in the object category. On the one hand, the endophoric axis limits, crystallizes and adjusts; it is more or less related to utilitarian values. On the other hand, the exophoric axis invents, diffuses and disorientates. The first axis makes the object recognizable and has a reassurance function, whereas the second axis destructures the object, which responds to new expectations. Consider, for instance, the kettle designed by Michael Graves for Alessi: this object is very strongly exophoric because of its very cone shape which destabilizes the idea of a kettle, but also because of the little bird sitting on the spout which conveys the idea of lightness and defies the geometric rigidity of the object. Looking at the kettle for the first time, one is disorientated by the object whose identity as a kettle is seriously questioned and searches for a new identity outside the functional aspect. Playing with the exophoric dimension, the designer does nothing less than break the endophoric codes in order to open the object to new interpretations. One could even say that such objects may be considered as postmodern objects, in the way that Robert Venturi defines them:

> elements which are hybrid rather than 'pure', compromising rather than 'clear', distorted rather than 'straightforward', ambiguous rather than 'articulated', perverse as well as 'impersonal', conventional rather than 'designed', accommodating rather than 'excluding', redundant rather than simple, vestigial as well as innovating, inconsistent rather than direct and clear. (Venturi 1966, quoted in Woodham 1997:191)

The other interesting phenomenon is that despite the fact that Alessi's objects seem at first glance to be very much culturally bound, they met a wide success in

Alessi's bird kettle and related items, designed by Michael Graves, 1985–8

most European countries. Furthermore, the growing success of such objects led to the notion of a 'New International Style', which initially emerged in the 1980s due to the influence of such designers as Ettore Sottsass and Andrea Branzi from Italy, Hans Hollein from Austria, Michael Graves from the United States, Xavier Mariscal from Spain, Philippe Starck from France. During the 1980s, shows of the group's work were held in the major museums in capital cities around the world and its products marketed under the banner of the 'New International Style'. This notion indicated the commodification of particular concepts within a global concept (Woodham 1997:161). This notion of 'design as art' was generally collected for its visual identity and implicit cultural values rather than any premium on function or practicality. Specializing on what has been termed the 'tabletop industry' or 'micro-architecture', companies like Alessi focused on the commissioning of small-scale piece of decorative arts by well-known architects and designers. Most products were exposed in museums all around the world which also means a collapse of the boundaries between art and everyday life. This phenomenon has been said to be very representative of the postmodern condition, as Mike Featherstone emphasizes it as 'the effacement of the boundary between art and everyday life ... a general stylistic promiscuity, and playful mixing codes' (Featherstone 1991:65).

Questions

1 How would you explain the fact that despite their focus on intangible and aesthetic product features, Alessi's objects are successful in nearly all European countries? Can you identify key target markets based on gender, age, income or lifestyle?

2 To what extent would you agree with the idea that objects represent communication devices?

3 Do you think that consumers from each European country would be willing to pay a price premium to get a product from one of Alessi's collections? Why or why not?

4 Alessi's objects are said to be very postmodern. To what extent would you agree with this assertion?

Sources

Alessi, various promotional material

Cova, Bernard and Sventfelt, Christian (1993), 'Societal innovations and the postmodern aestheticization of everyday life', *International Journal of Research in Marketing* 10: 297–310.

Featherstone, Mike (1991), *Consumer Culture and Postmodernism* (London: Sage).

Heilbrunn, Benoît (1998), 'In search of the lost aura: the object in the age of marketing re-illumination', in Stephen Brown *et al.*, eds, *Romancing the Market* (London: Routledge).

Polinoro, Laura (1989), *L'officina Alessi* (F.A.O. spa, Crusinello).

Rand, Paul (1993), *Design, Form & Chaos* (New Haven & London: Yale University Press).

Venturi, Robert (1996), *Complexity and Contradiction in Architecture* (New York: Museum of Modern Art).

Woodham, Jonathan M (1997), *Twentieth-Century Design* (Oxford: Oxford University Press).

CASE STUDY 11

Tatlýses Lahmacun

TOYGUN OZDEN, Bilkent University, Ankara

People first became acquainted with the name Ýbrahim Tatlýses by listening to his folk songs, performed in an impressive voice and with a distinctive style of interpretation. He was making a kind of music called 'Arabesk', an Arabic-style music that told the stories of poor and deprived people and their loves and misfortunes. This style of music caught the attention of Turkish people and his cassettes were sold in large numbers. This probably came as something of a surprise to him, for he became famous while he was working as a plasterer in the construction industry. This sudden and successful jump in his life was a source of interest for the Turkish people.

Ýbrahim Tatlýses became more and more famous as one new song or cassette followed another. Meanwhile, he began to appear in films and worked as a film producer. Then he established his own public transportation company, the Tatlýses Bus Tourism Company. After that Tatlýses Radio Channel began to serve the public as a private channel. The most important of his enterprises, however, in terms of both profitability and expansion opportunities, was the establishment of a fast-food restaurant chain under the name of Tatlýses Lahmacun.

The success of the first Tatlýses Lahmacun fast-food restaurant led to the opening of others. A franchise system was implemented whereby the franchisees would pay $100,000 as brand equity (McDonald's charged $35,000) and would transfer certain percentages of their revenues to the parent company. The first restaurant was established in 1993; by 1998 the number of restaurants had increased to 21, with branches all over Turkey, 14 of them in Istanbul.

One of the secrets underlying the success of Tatlýses Lahmacun was probably the perception of Lahmacun in Turkish people's minds as a traditional,[1] very delicious[2] and popular[3] Turkish meal. It is seen as an ordinary and simple[4] food by the people, so it is generally preferred as a starter before the main meal at restaurants. This explains why it is mostly preferred as a fast-food meal. Lahmacun is prepared by laying a mixture of minced meat, onion, tomato and different types of spices (a mixture of 12 different types of ingredients altogether) on a thin, round-shaped dough. It is baked in a wood-burning oven. Although it is still traditional fare in rural areas, it has almost been forgotten by the people living in big cities. By establishing fast-food lahmacun restaurants, Tatlýses reminded people about lahmacun and made it popular again.

The accelerating trend of interest in local and regional foods and music must have played an important role in all this. The increase in sales and publication of new cookery books whose subjects are regional or local foods and new songs including local sounds show clear evidence of recent demand by Turkish people to acknowledge traditional local tastes. Lahmacun is a traditional food from Urfa, a city in the south-east of Turkey and Tatlýses' home town, so it probably received a significant boost from this trend.

Moreover, as in so many other parts of the world, the issue of ethnic origins has been gaining importance in Turkey. Turkish people are not afraid to question their origins in public. Their aim is not to deny their Turkish identity, but to acknowledge other elements besides. This creates a situation in which small cultural differences between ethnic groups are not hidden, but practised more and more enthusiatically. Thus lahmacun does not just represent a kind of food, but also the cultural values of its region.

Another factor in the success of Tatlýses Lahmacun could be Ýbrahim Tatlýses himself. He is well known by everybody and people generally tend to like him, although there are some who are not so keen. One of the sources of the negative feelings about him is the cultural values that 'Arabesk' music is associated with. If a cultural map of Turkey is drawn, a clear gap emerges between west and east. People in the west are more like Europeans, and more willing to adopt European lifestyles, possibly as a result of their early exposure to European technology and culture and the rich physical resources of the West. They perceive Western culture as modern and adopt Western patterns of behaviour. One of these is listening to foreign pop music, so 'Arabesk' music represents the values that they have been trying to distance themselves from, and so too does Ýbrahim Tatlýses. The second reason is his tough, macho, saucy behaviour; he talks with a distinctive accent and behaves as if he were an ignorant peasant. All this makes some people dislike him. However, the feeling of dislike is rarely very strong, and generally most people either do not care or really love him. This usually means that people prefer his lahmacun over other restaurants' imitations. The effect of Tatlýses' name is so strong that, although no advertisement campaigns about Tatlýses Lahmacun restaurants have been carried out up to now, almost everyone is aware of them.

At a typical Tatlýses Lahmacun restaurant, one can have lahmacun with lemon slices and parsley leaves, *künefe*,[5] *ayran*[6] and coke. But the menus may differ from place to place, depending on customer demand and the level of local competition. While some restaurants may serve *döner*,[7] soup and salad, others may serve only lahmacun. Although the management of Tatlýses Lahmacun fast-food restaurants has been trying to increase the varieties of product on offer by adding extra options such as döner, salad bar and soup to the menu, they have realized that offering these kinds of additional food may damage the image of Tatlýses Lahmacun restaurants and may cause people to perceive them as ordinary kebap[8] restaurants.

The management has also been trying to develop new types of lahmacun made with chicken meat or diet lahmacun (including soyabean, etc., without meat) or frozen lahmacun to be sold at department stores. *Çið köfte*[9] is another traditional meal that they would like to serve in the near future, but there is a problem with its preparation that has held this up. Çið köfte should be consumed within one or two hours of its preparation, and the technology required to keep it fresh all day is not yet available.

All Tatlýses Lahmacun restaurants feature modern decor and materials that create an impression of light and space. (The materials used are very close to those at McDonald's, the main differences being their forms, colours and placements.) The dominant colour for the furniture and walls is yellow and green, the colour of the football team of Tatlýses' home town. Some of the restaurants use flowers and small trees to create a lively atmosphere; there is also a playing area for the children and popular Turkish and foreign music. Although these are not features of every Tatlýses

Lahmacun restaurant, management hopes to make them so. Great attention is also paid to cleanliness: employees in uniform clean everywhere continuously using modern cleaning techniques. (Most customers seem to take great pleasure in watching someone continuously cleaning).

The kitchen is on full view to customers, who can see how lahmacun is made by hand and baked in the oven. The self-service nature of the restaurant means that food can be provided quickly without waiting at the table for service. According to some Turkish people who ate at both Tatlýses Lahmacun and McDonald's, two pieces of lahmacun are as satisfying as a BigMac, and at nearly half the price.

The company targets all people from all age and income segments who like lahmacun and are familiar with the notion of fast food. Consumers state that they feel at home in Tatlýses Lahmacun restaurants and like the atmosphere. Management believes that by offering top-quality food and service, their high prices compared to their competitors' can be justified.

The management has received pressing demands from some businessmen living in countries such as Germany, the UK, Israel and Japan for permission to operate new lahmacun restaurants under the franchising system. However, the top management do not feel ready for a rapid expansion, reasoning that they have not yet perfected the franchising system and have had some problems especially with monitoring standards. To tackle these, a factory was built in Istanbul where a standard mixture of lahmacun could be produced under very hygienic conditions. According to the management, this was the first big step in maintaining standardization and monitoring the chain's activities more effectively. On the other hand, the eagerness of tourists to try Turkish cuisine's different tastes (tourists seem to be very willing to try *gözleme*, which is also a very traditional Turkish food consisting of crumbled cheese pieces put in a thin layer of dough, prepared by hand and cooked on an iron plate over a wood fire) and the interest shown by businessmen in many different countries caused the management to consider expanding into the European market in 1998.

However, they have to find answers to some difficult questions first. For instance: What will be the criteria for deciding which countries to expand to? What should the menu include, how should the interiors look? Will Europeans find it unhygienic to see the cooks preparing lahmacun or çið köfte with their bare hands, or will they perceive this as a natural, unique and authentic style? Will their eating habits fit the native eating style (lahmacun is mostly eaten with bare hands in Turkey)? In addition, should they develop the technology necessary for serving some additional options like çið köfte in their fast-food restaurants? These are some of the problems they face as they try to carry a local food to the global marketplace.

A possible solution

Two possible strategies could be adopted: (1) a standardized strategy like McDonald's, or (2) a localized strategy. In other words, should all Tatlýses Lahmacun restaurants be the same in product variety, in store design and atmosphere? Or should some modifications be made according to Europeans' cultural preferences and tastes and to their perceptions of Turkish culture and cuisine?

If a standardized strategy is implemented, then establishing new factories that can prepare and distribute the standard mixture of lahmacun will be more meaningful. However, if a localized strategy is adopted, then an effective monitoring system will have to be used to to control the franchising system.

Some specific points that could be useful for both strategies are the following:

Positioning: Special food from Turkish culture.

Target market: People of all ages who enjoy different tastes and food from different cultures, look for alternative food and are time-conscious.

Integrated 4Ps:

Product

- Increased variety of products: döner, çið köfte, different kinds of lahmacun (diet, vegetarian, cheese, chicken, etc.), some kinds of kebaps that are suitable for serving as fast food.

- Special Turkish ice cream and desserts may be introduced. The level of sugar can be adjusted according to European preferences.

- If there is sufficient demand for products such as çið köfte, the necessary technology should be developed.

Place

- The modern atmosphere may be enhanced with the addition of some Turkish artefacts such as small carpets and china.

- Employees may wear special clothes representing Turkish culture.

Promotion

- Special advertising campaigns could be run emphasizing high quality, delicious and different foods from Turkish cuisine.

- In order to avoid problems arising from the difference in eating habits between European and Turkish people, videos showing 'How lahmacun is eaten' could be used as an entertainment.

- Lahmacun could be distributed to people in small portions in order to create awareness about the company and its products.

Price

- By analysing the environmental factors in the foreign market, a price level could be determined that would support the high quality and service image.

Questions

1 Discuss the various options Tatlýses Lahmacun has in order to develop a positive image among Europe's fast-food consumers.

2 On which cultural foundations could such an image be constructed?

3 How is consumer culture, notably myths and rituals, relevant for Tatlýses Lahmacun?

4 According to which of the following criteria should countries be selected for the expansion: geographic proximity? Buying power of segments? Pre-established fast-food culture? Food culture in general?

5 Should the menu be adapted to local conditions or kept 'Turkish'?

6 Should the interior design be kept global or 'Turkeyfied' in order to convey the message of exoticism?

Notes

1. Lahmacun is traditional, since it is known by almost everyone, has been eaten for years and is still preferred at some occasions (at wedding ceremonies in villages in eastern Turkey, it has always been included in the menu).

2. At the surveys and interviews, nearly all of the respondents stated that if it was properly done it would really be delicious.

3. It is well known and people tend to eat it if the right conditions exist (most of the respondents said that they would eat it if it was prepared and cooked properly. However, exactly what this meant varied from one person to another.)

4. Respondents stated that as it was easily prepared and cooked, and included ordinary items such as minced meat, tomato, onion and types of spices that were not expensive, they did not perceive it as a special meal.

5. *Künefe* is a baked dessert which has a soft cheese filling inside layers of dough filaments and is eaten hot. Originating from south-east Anatolia, it is not commonly available in other parts of Turkey and is hence a speciality item.

6. *Ayran* is a traditional drink formed by mixing yoghurt and water.

7. *Döner* is meat roasted on a revolving vertical split and served cut into thin slices with pilaff or inside bread.

8. At an ordinary kebap restaurant, it takes time to prepare the main meal, so different kinds of appetizers are served with special kinds of breads. Various salads are offered with the main meal. Turkish people go to these restaurants with their friends and chat while waiting for the meal. After the meal tea or Turkish coffee is served.

9. *Çið köfte* is made of uncooked meat, pounded wheat and various spices (mostly red pepper). All the ingredients are kneaded together with bare hands till the mixture gains a proper degree of consistency and density. It should be consumed within in one or two hours of preparation, otherwise it may lose its fresh taste.

CASE STUDY 12

When a fashion victim customer becomes a fashion designer

PATRICK HETZEL, Université Panthéon-Assas Paris, 2, France

Isabelle is a 35-year-young executive who works at a Parisian advertising agency located in the 'Triangle d'Or'[1] of Paris. She is single and lives in Le Marais.[2] Every morning, as she walks to her office, she passes the Christian Dior and Thierry Mugler boutiques. Very often, she has the same kind of thoughts about those brands: 'they are very conventional and much too easy to interpret'. Being a real 'Bobo'[3] type, she prefers more trendy brands, and her colleagues consider her a fashion victim in her own way. She is looking for brands that try to develop a sophisticated discourse, with a strong intellectual background, brands that are not known to everyone, with a strong image, but only within a small group of people.

Therefore, one of her favourite fashion designers is Issey Miyake. Born in 1935 in Hiroshima, he studied graphic design. He started his career in haute couture places like Guy Laroche and Hubert de Givenchy in Paris and rounded out his apprenticeship years in the employ of Geoffrey Beene in New York City. In 1970, he chose to return to Japan to found Miyake Design Studio. Though much of his work is undeniably linked to the silhouettes and materials of traditional Japanese clothing, Issey Miyake has sought to create a new style that is both multicultural and metacultural. He has attempted throughout his career to create design truths, and that is exactly why Isabelle likes his work so much. He is a real intellectual who tries to create a new kind of relationship between the consumers and his brand.

Issey Miyake is probably best known for 'Pleats Please', an ongoing line of clothing established in 1990s, and Isabelle's wardrobe is full of products coming from that specific branch of the designer. She has been collecting the products since the brand was launched and does not want to give away any piece. She is very proud to wear, from time to time, some clothes from the Issey Miyake 'Pleats Please' collection that are ten years old. A lot of people around her at work notice that she has a very unique style of dressing and make some very nice comment about her clothes. This is part of her identity. But what she probably appreciates the most is that only she knows how expensive the clothes are because only fashion insiders are able to realize that her clothes were created by Miyake. When people wear Chanel or Gucci, everyone is able to tell that those clothes are expensive, but the geometrically shaped garments which become the bases for tight furtuny pleats give a very unique appearance. In the Miyake collection, the fabrics are usually unpatterned, allowing the lights and darks created by the pleated surface to take precedence. While the overall effect may sound severe, it is in fact the opposite. Remarkably, clothing from the 'Pleats Please' collection is both relaxed and elegant, and this is exactly what Isabelle is looking for. In some cases, when the geometric base shape of a piece is more elaborate, the resulting form has an organic sort of complexity, but does not lose its approachability. Miyake is a brand for those who have a very strong fashion culture. The products are not easily accessible, and they convey a very specific semiological content.

More recently, Issey Miyake has created a new brand, 'A-POC' (A Piece of Cloth), which empowers the wearer to become the designer. This remarkable collection is based on yardages of cloth which have been woven in such a way that the complete articles of clothing, ready to be cut along, break in the weave in a yardage matrix.

At the autumn 1999 fashion show (being a very good customer, Isabelle was of course invited), Miyake presented the design process as theatre. Standing on the catwalk with a model in a long-sleeved, hooded, floor-length gown, he took a pair of scissors to the outfit before an astounded audience and proceeded to alter it into an entirely different ensemble. Models also presented the work uncut as long banners, glorifying the fabric itself. The show was a dramatic expression of the tenets of Miyake's design philosophy of individuality in the context of universality.

A few weeks later, in February 2000, Issey Miyake opened his first 'A-POC' show in Tokyo, and a second shop was opened in Paris in September 2000, in Le Marais, where Isabelle lives. This served to reinforce her identification with the brand. The location expresses the clear desire of the designer to attract an intellectual, avant-garde customer more capable of appreciating his work than the traditional French 'golden mile' of the Faubourg Saint Honoré.

Isabelle was also invited to the opening ceremony of the shop. Situated on a corner, the shop lies in a zone of heavily pedestrian traffic. On the day of the opening, the mobs of guests were so thick that visitors could not fit onto the pavement and had to walk down the middle of the street. Upon approaching the shop, Isabelle was immediately aware of the stark contrast between the bright white light of the interior and the relative darkness of the narrow street. The façade along the street is lined with milk-white windows, which allow not even a glimpse of the interior. This air of mystery intrigues, while the guests inside experience the wall as a gift of privacy and a testimony of their belonging to the 'happy few' of the Miyake tribe.

That evening, the store was full of Issey Miyake 'connoisseurs'. Isabelle already knows some of them, because they meet at least twice a year, when the company organizes fashion shows in Paris. She feels as though she belongs to a secret society with its specific codes of aesthetic and rituals of adoration. Isabelle knows everything about Issey Miyake's life, his collections, his philosophy. Such an event is a good opportunity to approach the designer and to experience something unique. In the middle of the store, Issey Miyake is introducing the Bouroullec Brothers to the guests of the evening. They are the architects who worked on the store and interior design of the place. Ronan Bouroullec says a few words to the audience: 'We were not given restricted specifications about the functioning, capacity or even the materials and the colour scheme of the boutique. Nevertheless we were to follow a concept: to recreate the atmosphere of a workshop, a tailor's atelier, as Issey Miyake considers that A-POC is in perpetual evolution. We therefore worked on the idea of flexibility in such a way as to be able to adapt the boutique to the evolving concept.' And Issey Miyake also adds a few words: 'My dear friends, all you need is a pair of scissors. With this new brand I wanted to create a new relationship between you and my work. When I was conceptualizing this new collection, I was thinking about your conjoint relationship. Who is the designer? You or me? Now you know, the answer is: you AND me. Hereby, I wanted to materialize the fact that we are all fashion designers and fashion wearers. I wish that this collection will allow you to desacralize my work. By using scissors, you are becoming tailors of a conjoint creation process. I hope that I will learn a lot from you and that I will see my product in forms that I did not even imagine myself or expect.'

Isabelle is very enthusiastic about what she hears and sees. She feels very proud, and her ten-year loyalty to the fashion designer enables her to be part of a small tribe of 'trendsetters'. When she returns home that evening, she has the following thought: 'I am so happy to have this secret garden, this very unique relationship with Issey Miyake. This brings some sunshine to my everyday life and it allows me to escape from the massification of our contemporary consumption.'

Questions for discussion

1 How would you describe the psychological profile of Isabelle?

2 How would you describe a 'fashion tribe'?

3 To what extent would you agree with the idea that clothes represent communication devices?

4 What makes the difference between Issey Miyake customers and purchasers of more 'conventional' fashion brands?

5 Why do you think that fashion consumption is so central in Isabelle's life?

6 Do you agree with Isabelle when she says: 'it allows me to escape from the massification of our contemporary consumption'?

7 What is so unique in the 'A-POC' concept?

8 'A-POC' clothes are said to be very postmodern. To what extent would you agree with this assertion?

Notes

1. The 'Triangle d'Or' is an area of Paris where most of the luxury shops and boutiques of haute couture are located. It is the most expensive shopping place in the city.
2. 'Le Marais' is a trendy, arty quarter of Paris.
3. Bobo stands for 'Bourgeois-Boheme'. For more details, see David Brooks, *Bobos in Paradise* (New York: Simon & Schuster, 2000).

Glossary

Absolute threshold the minimum amount of stimulation that can be detected on a sensory channel *(p. 44)*

Accommodative purchase decision the process to achieve agreement among a group whose members have different preferences or priorities *(p. 357)*

Acculturation the process of learning the beliefs and behaviours endorsed by another culture *(pp. 111, 529)*

Acculturation agents friends, family, local businesses and other reference groups which facilitate the learning of cultural norms *(p. 529)*

Activation models of memory approaches to memory stressing different levels of processing that occur and activate some aspects of memory rather than others, depending on the nature of the processing task *(p. 77)*

Actual self a person's realistic appraisal of his or her qualities *(p. 191)*

Adaptation the process that occurs when a sensation becomes so familiar that it is no longer the focus of attention *(p. 48)*

Affect the way a consumer feels about an attitude object *(p. 129)*

Age cohort a group of consumers of the same approximate age who have undergone similar experiences *(p. 405)*

Agentic goals goals that stress self-assertion and mastery and are associated with males *(p. 198)*

AIOs (Activities, Interests and Opinions) the psychographic variables used by researchers in grouping consumers *(p. 507)*

Androgyny the possession of both masculine and feminine traits *(p. 199)*

Anti-foundationalism an anti-campaign campaign encouraging the consumer not to take notice of a message *(p. 562)*

Art product a creation viewed primarily as an object of aesthetic contemplation without any functional value *(p. 475)*

Atmospherics the use of space and physical features in store design to evoke certain effects in buyers *(p. 286)*

Attention the assignment of cognitive capacity to selected stimuli *(p. 48)*

Attitude a lasting, general evaluation of people (including oneself), objects or issues *(p. 127)*

Attitude object (A₀) anything towards which one has an attitude *(p. 127)*

Attitude towards the act of buying (A_{act}) the perceived consequences of a purchase *(p. 145)*

Attitude towards the advertisement (A_{ad}) a predisposition to respond favourably to a particular advertising stimulus during an exposure situation *(p. 133)*

Autocratic decisions purchase decisions that are made exclusively by one spouse *(p. 358)*

Baby boomers a large cohort of people born between 1946 and 1964 who are the source of many important cultural and economic changes *(p. 415)*

Balance theory considers relations among elements a person might perceive as belonging together and people's tendency to change relations among elements in order to make them consistent or balanced *(p. 138)*

Behaviour a consumer's actions with regard to an attitude object *(p. 129)*

Behavioural economics the study of the behavioural determinants of economic decisions *(p. 375)*

Behavioural influence perspective the view that consumer decisions are learned responses to environmental cues *(p. 236)*

Behavioural learning theories the perspectives on learning that assume that learning takes place as the result of responses to external events *(p. 65)*

Binary opposition a defining structural characteristic where two opposing ends of a dimension are presented *(p. 448)*

Body cathexis a person's feelings about aspects of his or her body *(p. 206)*

Body image a consumer's subjective evaluation of his or her physical appearance *(p. 205)*

Brand equity a brand that has strong positive associations and consequently commands a lot of loyalty *(p. 71)*

Brand loyalty a pattern of repeat product purchases accompanied by an underlying positive attitude towards the brand *(p. 259)*

Chronology the consumer's search for the authentic and a preoccupation with the past *(p. 560)*

Classic a fashion with an extremely long acceptance cycle *(p. 493)*

Classical conditioning the learning that occurs when a stimulus eliciting a response is paired with another stimulus which initially does not elicit a response on its own but will cause a similar response over time because of its association with the first stimulus *(p. 65)*

Cognition the beliefs a consumer has about an attitude object *(p. 129)*

Cognitive development the ability to comprehend

concepts of increasing complexity as a person ages (*p. 364*)

Cognitive learning the learning that occurs as a result of internal mental processes (*p. 69*)

Cognitive structure the factual knowledge or set of beliefs about a product and the way these are organized (*p. 250*)

Collecting the accumulation of rare or mundane and inexpensive objects, which transforms profane items into sacred ones (*p. 461*)

Collective selection the process whereby certain symbolic alternatives tend to be chosen jointly in preference to others by members of a group (*p. 488*)

Collectivist culture a cultural orientation which encourages people to subordinate their personal goals to those of a stable in-group (*p. 444*)

Communal goals goals that stress affiliation and the fostering of harmonious relations and are associated with females (*p. 198*)

Communications model a framework specifying that a number of elements are necessary for communication to be achieved including a source, message, medium, receivers and feedback (*p. 157*)

Comparative influence the process whereby a reference group influences decisions about specific brands or activities (*p. 304*)

Compatibility a prerequisite for a product's adoption; the product should fit the consumer's lifestyle (*p. 485*)

Compensatory decision rules allow information about attributes of competing products to be averaged; poor standing on one attribute may be offset by good standing on another (*p. 261*)

Complexity ease of understanding and use of a product; greater ease lowers the effort and perceived risk in adoption (*p. 485*)

Conformity a change in beliefs or actions as a reaction to real or perceived group pressure (*p. 313*)

Consensual purchase decision a decision in which the group agrees on the desired purchase and differs only in terms of how it will be achieved (*p. 357*)

Conspicuous consumption the purchase and prominent display of luxury goods as evidence of the consumer's ability to afford them (*pp. 395, 489*)

Consumer addiction a physiological and/or psychological dependency on products or services (*p. 463*)

Consumer behaviour the processes involved when individuals or groups select, purchase, use or dispose of products, services, ideas or experiences to satisfy needs or desires (*p. 5*)

Consumer confidence the state of mind of consumers relative to their optimism or pessimism about economic decisions; people tend to make more discretionary purchases when their confidence in the economy is high (*p. 379*)

Consumer satisfaction/dissatisfaction (CS/D) the overall attitude a person has about a product after it has been purchased (*p. 289*)

Consumer socialization the process by which people acquire skills that enable them to function in the marketplace (*p. 362*)

Consumption constellations a set of products and activities used by consumers to define, communicate and perform social roles (*p. 505*)

Continuous innovation a product change or new product that requires relatively little adaptation in the consumer's behaviour (*p. 484*)

Convention norms regarding the conduct of everyday life (*p. 446*)

Cooptation a cultural process where the original meaning of a product or other symbol associated with a subculture is modified by members of mainstream culture (*p. 441*)

Craft product a creation valued because of the beauty with which it performs some function; this type of product tends to follow a formula that permits rapid production; it is easier to understand than an art product (*p. 475*)

Creolization the blending of various eating traditions with new ones to make national food tastes fit the tastes of mainstream culture (*pp. 557*)

Cultivation hypothesis a perspective emphasizing media's ability to distort consumers' perceptions of reality (*p. 481*)

Cultural categories the grouping of ideas and values that reflect the basic ways members of society characterize the world (*p. 487*)

Cultural formula where certain roles and props often occur consistently in many popular art forms, such as detective stories or science fiction (*p. 476*)

Cultural gatekeepers individuals who are responsible for determining the types of message and symbolism to which members of mass culture are exposed (*p. 475*)

Cultural selection the process where some alternatives are selected in preference to those selected by cultural gatekeepers (*p. 471*)

Culture the values, ethics, rituals, traditions, material objects and services produced or valued by members of society (*p. 441*)

Culture production system (CPS) the set of individuals or organizations responsible for creating and marketing a cultural product (*p. 473*)

Custom a norm that is derived from a traditional way of doing something (*p. 446*)

Database marketing involves tracking consumers' buying habits and crafting products and information tailored to people's wants and needs (*p. 13*)

De-differentiation the blurring of distinctions between

hierarchies such as high and low cultures or politics and show business (p. 560)

Deindividuation the process whereby individual identities are submerged within a group, reducing inhibitions against socially inappropriate behaviour (p. 316)

Demographics the observable measurements of a population's characteristics, such as birth rates, age distribution income (p. 9)

Desacralization the process that occurs when a sacred item or symbol is removed or is duplicated in mass quantities and as a result becomes profane (p. 459)

Desire to wish or long for consumer goods which contribute to the formation of consumers' self-image; also refers to the sociogenic nature of needs (p. 102)

Differential threshold the ability of a sensory system to detect changes or differences among stimuli (p. 44)

Discontinuous innovation a product change or new product that requires a significant amount of adaptation of behaviour by the adopter (p. 484)

Discretionary income the money available to an individual or household over and above that required for maintaining a standard of living (p. 378)

Drive theory focuses on the desire to satisfy a biological need in order to reduce physiological arousal (p. 95)

Dynamically continuous innovation a product change or new product that requires a moderate amount of adaptation of behaviour by the adopter (p. 484)

Early adopters people receptive to new styles because they are involved in the product category and place high value on being fashionable (p. 482)

Ego the system that mediates between the id and the superego (p. 101)

Ego involvement the importance of a product to a consumer's self-concept (p. 106)

Elaborated codes the ways of expressing and interpreting meanings that are complex and depend on a sophisticated worldview; they tend to be used by the middle and upper classes (p. 391)

Elaboration likelihood model (ELM) the approach that one of two routes to persuasion (central vs. peripheral) will be followed, depending on the personal relevance of a message; the route taken determines the relative importance of message contents vs. other characteristics, such as source attractiveness (p. 179)

Emic perspective an approach to studying cultures that stresses the unique aspects of each culture (p. 549)

Encoding the process in which information from short-term memory is entered into long-term memory in recognizable form (p. 75)

Enculturation the process of learning the beliefs and behaviours endorsed by one (p. 111)

Environmentalism a general concern for the environment as it is affected by all aspects of production and consumption processes (p. 543)

Erogenous zones areas of the body considered by members of a culture to be focuses of sexual attractiveness (p. 489)

Ethnic subculture a self-perpetuating group of consumers held together by common cultural ties (p. 528)

Ethnoconsumerism the understanding and analysis of each culture, including consumer culture, on the basis of its own premises (p. 445)

Ethos a set of moral, aesthetic and evaluative principles (p. 444)

Etic perspective an approach to studying culture that stresses the commonalities across cultures (p. 549)

Evaluative criteria the dimensions used by consumers to compare competing product alternatives (p. 253)

Evoked set those products already in memory plus those prominent in the retail environment that are actively considered during a consumer's choice process (pp. 78, 249)

Exchange the process whereby two or more organizations or people give and receive something of value (p. 6)

Exchange theory the perspective that every interaction involves an exchange of value (p. 289)

Expectancy disconfirmation model the perspective that consumers form beliefs about product performance based on prior experience with the product and/or communications about the product that imply a certain level of quality; their actual satisfaction depends on the degree to which performance is consistent with these expectations (p. 290)

Expectancy theory the perspective that behaviour is largely 'pulled' by expectations of achieving desirable 'outcomes' or positive incentives, rather than 'pushed' from within (p. 95)

Experiential perspective an approach stressing the gestalt or totality of the product or service experience, focusing on consumers' affective responses in the marketplace (p. 236)

Exposure an initial stage of perception where some sensations come within range of consumers' sensory receptors (p. 44)

Extended family traditional family structure where several generations and/or relatives such as aunts, uncles and cousins live together (p. 350)

Extended problem-solving an elaborate decision-making process often initiated by a motive that's fairly central to the self-concept and accompanied by perceived risk; the consumer tries to collect as much information as possible and carefully weighs product alternatives (p. 237)

Extended self the definition of self created by the external objects with which one surrounds oneself (p. 196)

Extinction the process whereby learned connections between a stimulus and response are eroded so that the response is no longer reinforced *(p. 66)*

Fad a short-lived fashion *(p. 493)*

Family financial officer (FFO) the family member who is in charge of making financial decisions *(p. 358)*

Family household a housing unit containing at least two people who are related by blood or marriage *(p. 350)*

Family life cycle (FLC) a classification scheme that segments consumers in terms of changes in income and family composition and the changes in demands placed on this income *(p. 355)*

Fantasy a self-induced shift in consciousness, often focusing on an unattainable or improbable goal; sometimes fantasy is a way of compensating for a lack of external stimulation or for dissatisfaction with the actual self *(p. 191)*

Fashion the process of social diffusion by which a new style is adopted by a group or groups of consumers *(p. 487)*

Fashion acceptance cycle the diffusion process of a style through three stages: introduction, acceptance and regression *(p. 493)*

Fashion life cycle the 'career' or stages in the life of a fashion as it progresses from launch to obsolescence *(p. 493)*

Fashion system those people or organizations involved in creating symbolic meanings and transferring these meanings to cultural goods *(p. 486)*

Fear appeal an attempt to change attitudes or behaviour through the use of threats or by the highlighting of negative consequences of non-compliance with the request *(p. 176)*

Fertility rate a rate determined by the number of births per year per 1000 women of child-bearing age *(p. 252)*

Figure-ground principle the gestalt principle whereby one part of a stimulus configuration dominates a situation while other aspects recede into the background *(p. 47)*

Foot-in-the-door technique based on the observation that a consumer is more likely to comply with a request if he or she has first agreed to comply with a smaller request *(p. 137)*

Fragmentation the splitting up of what used to be simple and mass-oriented, exemplified by ever-growing product ranges and brand extensions *(p. 560)*

Frequency marketing a marketing technique that reinforces regular purchasers by giving them prizes with values that increase along the amount purchased *(p. 74)*

Functional theory of attitudes a pragmatic approach that focuses on how attitudes facilitate social behav-iour; attitudes exist because they serve some function for the person *(p. 128)*

Generation X (Gen-Xers or baby busters) the cohort of consumers aged 18–29, who were profoundly affected by the economic recession of the early 1990s *(p. 413)*

Geodemography techniques that combine consumer demographic information with geographic consumption patterns to permit precise targeting of consumers with specific characteristics *(p. 526)*

Gerontographics a research tool which divides the mature market into groups based on level of physical well-being and social conditions *(p. 421)*

Gestalt psychology a school of thought that maintains people derive meaning from the totality of a set of stimuli rather than from an individual stimulus *(p. 46)*

Gift-giving ritual the events involved in the selection, presentation, acceptance and interpretation of a gift *(p. 451)*

Goal a consumer's desired end-state *(p. 93)*

Grey market term used to describe the phenomenon of a fast-growing segment of consumers aged 62 or older *(p. 419)*

Habitual decision-making the consumption choices that are made out of habit, without additional information search or deliberation among products *(p. 237)*

Habitus systems of classification of phenomena adopted from our socialization processes *(p. 512)*

Hedonic consumption the multisensory, fantasy and emotional aspects of consumers' interactions with products *(p. 37)*

Heuristics the mental rules of thumb that lead to a speedy decision *(p. 254)*

Hierarchy of effects a fixed sequence of steps that occurs during attitude formation; this sequence varies depending on such factors as the consumer's level of involvement with the attitude object *(p. 130)*

High-context culture group members tend to be tightly knit and messages and meanings are implicit and built into the communication context *(p. 524)*

Homeostasis the state of being where the body is in physiological balance; goal-oriented behaviour attempts to reduce or eliminate an unpleasant motivational state and returns to a balanced one *(p. 95)*

Hyperreality a phenomenon associated with modern advertising in which what is initially stimulation or hype becomes real *(p. 560)*

Icon a sign that resembles the product in some culturally meaningful way *(p. 52)*

Id the system oriented to immediate gratification *(p. 100)*

Ideal of beauty a model, or exemplar, of appearance valued by a culture *(p. 206)*

Ideal self a person's conception of how he or she would like to be *(p. 191)*

Impulse buying a process that occurs when the consumer experiences a sudden urge to purchase an item that he or she cannot resist *(p. 286)*

Individualist culture a cultural orientation that encourages people to attach more importance to personal goals than to group goals; values such as personal enjoyment and freedom are stressed *(p. 444)*

Inertia the process whereby purchase decisions are made out of habit because the consumer lacks the motivation to consider alternatives *(pp. 104, 259)*

Information power power given simply because one knows something others would like to know *(p. 311)*

Information search the process whereby a consumer searches for appropriate information to make a reasonable decision *(p. 240)*

Informational social influence the conformity that occurs because the group's behaviour is taken as evidence about reality *(p. 314)*

Innovative communicators opinion leaders who are also early purchasers *(p. 325)*

Instrumental values those goals that are endorsed because they are needed to achieve desired end-states or terminal values *(p. 113)*

Interactionist a perspective on human communication which relies on three basic premises about communication, i.e. the meaning of things, ideas and actions *(p. 159)*

Interference a process whereby additional learned information displaces earlier information resulting in memory loss for the item learned previously *(p. 81)*

Interpretant the meaning derived from a symbol *(p. 52)*

Interpretation the process whereby meanings are assigned to stimuli *(p. 50)*

Interpretivism a research perspective that produces a 'thick' description of a consumer's subjective experiences and stresses the importance of the individual's social construction of reality *(p. 26)*

Invidious distinction the display of wealth or power to inspire envy in others *(p. 395)*

Involvement the motivation to process product-related information *(p. 104)*

ISO standards a set of quality criteria developed in 1987 to regulate product quality by the International Standards Organization *(p. 290)*

JND (just noticeable difference) the minimum change in a stimulus that can be detected by a perceiver *(p. 44)*

Kin network system the rituals intended to maintain ties among family members, both immediate and extended *(p. 360)*

Knowledge structures organized systems of concepts relating to brands, stores and other concepts *(p. 78)*

Laddering a technique for uncovering consumers' associations between specific attributes and general consequences *(p. 115)*

Lateral cycling a process where already purchased objects are sold to others or exchanged for other items *(p. 292)*

Latitudes of acceptance and rejection formed around an attitude standard; ideas that fall within a latitude will be favourably received, while those falling outside this zone will not *(p. 138)*

Learning a relatively permanent change in a behaviour as a result of experience *(p. 65)*

Lifestyle a set of shared values or tastes exhibited by a group of consumers especially as these are reflected in consumption patterns *(p. 503)*

Lifestyle marketing perspective a perspective that recognizes that people are increasingly conscious that we sort ourselves and each other into groups on the basis of the things we/they like to do and how we/they spend our/their disposable income *(p. 504)*

Limited problem-solving a problem-solving process in which consumers are not motivated to search for information or evaluate rigorously each alternative; instead they use simple decision rules to arrive at a purchase decision *(p. 237)*

Long-term memory the system that allows us to retain information for a long period *(p. 77)*

Looking-glass self the process of imagining the reaction of others towards oneself *(p. 193)*

LOV (list of values) a scale developed to isolate values with more direct marketing applications *(p. 113)*

Low-context culture messages tend to be more explicit, specific and direct *(p. 524)*

Market beliefs the specific beliefs of decision rules pertaining to marketplace phenomena *(p. 254)*

Market maven a person who often serves as a source of information about marketplace activities *(p. 325)*

Match-up hypothesis in a celebrity ad campaign, the celebrity's image and that of the product he or she endorses should be similar for the campaign to be effective *(p. 165)*

Materialism the importance consumers attach to worldly possessions *(p. 116)*

Means–end chain a research approach that assumes that very specific product attributes are linked at levels of increasing abstraction to terminal values *(p. 115)*

MECCAs (Means–end Conceptualization of the Components of Advertising Strategy) a research approach in which researchers generate a map depicting relationships between functional product or service attributes and terminal values and then use this information to develop advertising strategy *(p. 115)*

Memory a process of acquiring information and storing it over time *(p. 75)*

Metaphor the use of an explicit comparison between a product and some other person, place or thing *(p. 178)*

Monomyth a myth with basic characteristics that are found in many cultures *(p. 448)*

Mores norms with strong moral overtones *(p. 446)*

Motivation an internal state that activates goal-oriented behaviour *(p. 93)*

Motivational research a qualitative research approach based on psychoanalytical (Freudian) interpretations with a heavy emphasis on unconscious motives for consumption *(p. 101)*

Multiattribute attitude models those models that assume that a consumer's attitude (evaluation) of an attitude object depends on the beliefs he or she has about several or many attributes of the object; the use of a multiattribute model implies that an attitude towards a product or brand can be predicted by identifying these specific beliefs and combining them to derive a measure of the consumer's overall attitude *(p.140)*

Myth a story containing symbolic elements which expresses the shared emotion and ideals of a culture *(p. 447)*

National character a distinctive set of behaviour and personality characteristics that describe a country's people or culture *(p. 550)*

Negative reinforcement the process whereby a negative reward weakens responses to stimuli so that inappropriate behaviour is avoided in the future *(p. 67)*

Non-compensatory decision rules a set of simple rules used to evaluate competing alternatives; a brand with a low standing on one relevant attribute is eliminated from the consumer's choice set *(p. 260)*

Normative influence the process in which a reference group helps to set and enforce basic standards of conduct *(p. 303)*

Normative social influence the conformity that occurs when a person alters his or her behaviour to meet the expectations of a person or group *(p. 314)*

Norms the informal rules that govern what is right and wrong *(p. 313)*

Nostalgia a bittersweet emotion when the past is viewed with sadness and longing; many 'classic' products appeal to consumers' memories of their younger days *(p. 82)*

Nuclear family a contemporary living arrangement composed of a married couple and their children *(p. 350)*

Object a semiotic term, the product that is the focus of the message *(p. 52)*

Observability the visibility of a product *(p. 486)*

Observational learning the process in which people learn by watching the actions of others and noting the reinforcements they receive for their behaviours *(p. 70)*

Operant conditioning the process by which the individual learns to perform behaviours that produce positive outcomes and to avoid those that yield negative outcomes *(p. 67)*

Opinion leaders those people who are knowledgeable about products and who are frequently able to influence others' attitudes or behaviours with regard to a product category *(p. 323)*

Opinion seekers usually opinion leaders who are also involved in a product category and actively search for information *(p. 325)*

Paradigm a widely accepted view or model of phenomena being studied. The perspective that regards people as *rational information processors* is currently the dominant paradigm, though this approach is now being challenged by a new wave of research that emphasizes the frequently subjective nature of consumer decision-making *(p. 25)*

Parental yielding the process that occurs when a parental decision-maker is influenced by a child's product request *(p. 361)*

Parody display the deliberate avoidance of widely used status symbols, whereby the person seeks status by mocking it *(p. 397)*

Pastiche the playful and ironic mixing of existing categories and styles *(p. 561)*

Perceived age how old a person feels rather than his or her chronological age *(p. 420)*

Perceived risk the belief that use of a product has potentially negative consequences, either physical or social *(p. 246)*

Perception the process by which stimuli are selected, organized or interpreted *(p. 36)*

Perceptual selectivity the process in which people attend to only a small portion of the stimuli to which they are exposed *(p. 46)*

Persuasion an active attempt to change attitudes *(p. 155)*

Pluralism the coexistence of various styles, truths and fashions *(p. 560)*

Point-of-purchase stimuli (POP) the promotional materials that are deployed in shops or other outlets to influence consumers; decisions at the time products are purchased *(p. 288)*

Political consumer the political consumer uses his or her buying pattern as a weapon against or support for companies which share the person's own values *(p. 545)*

Popular culture the music, films, sports, books, celebrities and other forms of entertainment consumed by the mass market *(p. 14)*

Positive reinforcement the process whereby rewards provided by the environment strengthen response to stimuli *(p. 67)*

Positivism a research perspective that relies on the principles of the 'scientific method' and assumes that a single reality exists; events in the world can be objectively measured; and the causes of behaviour can be identified, manipulated and predicted *(p. 26)*

Postmodernism a theory that questions the search for universal truths and values and the existence of objective knowledge *(p. 560)*

Potlatch a Kwakiutl Indian feast at which the host displays his wealth and gives extravagant gifts *(p. 396)*

Priming the process in which certain properties of a stimulus are more likely to evoke a schema than others *(p. 51)*

Principle of closure implies that consumers tend to perceive an incomplete picture as complete *(p. 47)*

Principle of cognitive consistency the belief that consumers value harmony among their thoughts, feelings and behaviours and that they are motivated to maintain uniformity among these elements *(p. 134)*

Principle of similarity the gestalt principle that describes how consumers tend to group objects that share similar physical characteristics *(p. 47)*

Problem recognition the process that occurs whenever the consumer sees a significant difference between his or her current state and some desired or ideal state; this recognition initiates to the decision-making process *(p. 238)*

Product complementarity the view that products in different functional categories have symbolic meanings that are related to one another *(p. 505)*

Product placement the process of obtaining exposure for a product by arranging for it to be inserted into a film, television programme or some other medium *(p. 480)*

Profane consumption the process of consuming objects and events that are ordinary or of the everyday world *(p. 456)*

Psychographics the use of psychological, sociological and anthropological factors to construct market segments *(pp. 9, 506)*

Punishment the process or outcome that occurs when a response is followed by unpleasant events *(p. 67)*

Racial subculture a self-perpetuating group held together by ties of common culture and/or genetics, identified by its members and others as a distinguishable category *(p. 528)*

Rational perspective a view of the consumer as a careful, analytical decision-maker who tries to maximize utility in purchase decisions *(p. 235)*

Reactance a boomerang effect that may occur when consumers are threatened with a loss of freedom of choice; they respond by doing the opposite of the behaviour advocated in a persuasive message *(p. 317)*

Reality engineering the process whereby elements of popular culture are appropriated by marketers and become integrated into marketing strategies (e.g. product placement) *(p. 479)*

Recycling the re-use of resources in order to protect the environment *(p. 541)*

Reference group an actual or imaginary individual or group which has a significant effect on an individual's evaluations, aspirations or behaviour *(p. 303)*

Referent power the power of prominent people to affect others' consumption behaviours by virtue of product endorsements, distinctive fashion statements or championing causes *(p. 311)*

Relationship marketing the strategic perspective that stresses the long-term, human side of buyer/seller interactions *(p. 13)*

Relative advantage the belief that a product's use will provide a benefit other products cannot offer *(p. 486)*

Resonance a literary device, frequently used in advertising, which uses a play on words to communicate a product benefit *(p. 178)*

Response bias a form of contamination in survey research where some factor, such as the desire to make a good impression on the experimenter, leads respondents to modify their true answers *(p. 86)*

Restricted codes the ways of expressing and interpreting meanings that focus on the content of objects and tend to be used by the working class *(p. 391)*

Retrieval the process whereby desired information is accessed from long-term memory *(p. 75)*

RISC (Research Institute on Social Change) an organization that conducts international measurements of socio-cultural change in more than 40 countries *(p. 509)*

Risky shift group members show a greater willingness to consider riskier alternatives following group discussions than they would if each member made his or her own decision without prior discussion *(p. 316)*

Rites of passage sacred times marked by a change in social status *(p. 455)*

Ritual a set of multiple, symbolic behaviours that occur in fixed sequence and that tend to be repeated periodically *(p. 449)*

Ritual artefacts items or consumer goods used in the performance of rituals *(p. 451)*

Role theory the perspective that much of consumer behaviour resembles action in a play *(p. 5)*

Rumour a word-of-mouth campaign to promote one product and criticize its competitors (p. 320)

Sacralization a process that occurs when ordinary objects, events or people take on sacred meaning to a culture or to specific groups within a culture (p. 460)

Sacred consumption the process of consuming objects and events that are set apart from normal life and treated with some degree of respect or awe (p. 456)

Savings rate the amount of money saved for later use influenced by consumers' pessimism or optimism about their personal circumstances and perceptions of the economy (p. 379)

Schema an organized collection of beliefs and feelings represented in a cognitive category (pp. 36, 79)

Self-concept the attitude a person holds to him- or herself (p. 190)

Self-gifts the products or services bought by consumers for their own use as a reward or consolation (p. 453)

Self-image congruence models the approaches based on the prediction that products will be chosen when their attributes match some aspect of the self (p. 195)

Self-perception theory an alternative explanation of dissonance effects; it assumes that people use observations of their own behaviour to infer their attitudes towards an object (p. 136)

Semiotics a field of study that examines the correspondence between a sign and the meaning(s) it conveys (p. 52)

Sensation the immediate response of sensory receptors to such basic stimuli as light, colour and sound (p. 36)

Sensory memory the temporary storage of information received from the senses (p. 76)

Sex-typed traits characteristics that are stereotypically associated with one sex or another (p. 198)

Shopping orientation a consumer's general attitudes and motivations regarding the act of shopping (p. 278)

Short-term memory the system that allows us to retain information for a short period (p. 76)

Sign the sensory imagery that represents the intended meanings of the object (p. 52)

Signifying practices practices that have meaning to individuals, who know how to interpret them, thanks to the understanding of culture as the interpreting system (p. 443)

Single-source data a compilation of information that includes different aspects of consumption and demographic data for a common consumer segment (p. 527)

Sleeper effect the process whereby differences in attitude change between positive and negative sources seem to diminish over time (p. 167)

Social class the overall rank of people in society; people who are grouped within the same social class are approximately equal in terms of their social standing, occupations and lifestyles (p. 380)

Social comparison theory the perspective that people compare their outcomes with others' as a way to increase the stability of their own self-evaluation, especially when physical evidence is unavailable (p. 315)

Social hierarchy a ranking of social desirability in terms of consumers' access to such resources as money, education and luxury goods (p. 382)

Social judgement theory the perspective that people assimilate new information about attitude objects in the light of what they already know or feel; the initial attitude as a frame of reference and new information are categorized in terms of this standard (p. 137)

Social marketing the promotion of causes and ideas (social products), such as energy conservation, charities and population control (p. 19)

Social mobility the movement of individuals from one social class to another (p. 385)

Social stratification the process in a social system by which scarce and valuable resources are distributed unequally to status positions which become more or less permanently ranked in terms of the share of valuable resources each receives (p. 384)

Sociometric methods the techniques for measuring group dynamics that involve tracing of communication patterns in and among groups (p. 327)

Source attractiveness the dimensions of a communicator which increase his or her persuasiveness; these include expertise and attractiveness (p. 163)

Source credibility a communication source's perceived expertise, objectivity or trustworthiness (p. 163)

Stage of cognitive development segmentation of children by age or their ability to comprehend concepts of increasing complexity (p. 365)

Status crystallization the extent to which different indicators of a person's status are consistent with one another (p. 388)

Status symbols products that are purchased and displayed to signal membership in a desirable social class (p. 375)

Stimulus discrimination the process that occurs when behaviour caused by two stimuli is different as when consumers learn to differentiate a brand from its competitors (p. 67)

Stimulus generalization the process that occurs when the behaviour caused by a reaction to one stimulus occurs in the presence of other, similar stimuli (p. 66)

Storage the process that occurs when knowledge entered in long-term memory is integrated with what is already in memory and 'warehoused' until needed (p. 75)

Store gestalt consumers' global evaluation of a store (p. 286)

Store image   the 'personality' of a shop composed of attributes such as location, merchandise suitability and the knowledge and congeniality of the sales staff (*p. 285*)

Subculture   a group whose members share beliefs and common experiences that set them apart from the members of the main culture (*p. 528*)

Superego   the system that internalizes society's rules which works to prevent the id from seeking selfish gratification (*p. 101*)

Surrogate consumer   a professional who is retained to evaluate and/or make purchases on behalf of a consumer (*p. 325*)

Symbolic interactionism   a sociological approach stressing that relationships with people play a large part in forming the self; people live in a symbolic environment and the meaning attached to any situation or object is determined by a person's interpretation of those symbols (*p. 193*)

Symbolic self-completion theory   the perspective that people who have an incomplete self-definition in some context will compensate by acquiring symbols associated with a desired social identity (*p. 194*)

Syncratic decisions   purchase decisions that are made jointly by spouses (*p. 358*)

Taste culture   a group of consumers who share aesthetic and intellectual preferences (*p. 390*)

Terminal values   end-states desired by members of a culture (*p. 113*)

Theory of cognitive dissonance   a theory based on the premise that people have a need for order and consistency in their lives and that a state of tension is created when beliefs or behaviours conflict with one another (*p. 97*)

Theory of reasoned action   a version of the Fishbein multi-attitude theory that considers such factors as social pressure and the attitude towards the act of buying a product rather than attitudes towards just the product itself (*p. 144*)

Time style   determined by an individual's priorities, it incorporates such dimensions as economic time, past or future orientation, time submissiveness and time anxiety (*p. 274*)

Transitional economies   countries that are in the process of transforming their economic system from a controlled, centralized system to a free market one (*p. 556*)

Trialability   the likelihood of experimenting with an innovation prior to making a commitment (*p. 485*)

Trickle-down theory   the perspective that fashions spread as a result of status symbols associated with the upper classes trickling down to the other social classes as these consumers try to emulate those with higher status (*p. 490*)

Two-factor theory   the perspective that two separate psychological processes are operating when a person is repeatedly exposed to an ad; repetition increases familiarity and thus reduces uncertainty about the product, but over time boredom increases with each exposure and at some point the level of boredom begins to exceed the amount of uncertainty reduced, resulting in wear-out (*p. 171*)

Uses and gratifications theory   argues that consumers are an active, goal-directed audience who draw on mass media as a resource to satisfy needs (*p. 158*)

Value   a belief that some condition is preferable to its opposite (*p. 109*)

Value system   a culture's ranking of the relative importance of values (*p. 110*)

Values and Lifestyles (VALS)   a psychographic segmentation system used to categorize consumers into clusters (*p. 514*)

Want   the particular form of consumption chosen to satisfy a need (*p. 94*)

Word-of-mouth communication (WOM)   the information transmitted by individual consumers on an informal basis (*p. 317*)

Worldview   the ideas shared by members of a culture about principles of order and fairness (*p. 444*)

Indexes

Author index

Product/company/name index

Subject Index

Note: **bold** page numbers indicate terms emboldened in text or defined in **glossary**.